Contents

Section A
Communities of Faith.

* Denotes Higher Level

Section B
Foundations of Religion: Christianity.

Section C
Foundations of Religion: Judaism.

Section C
Foundations of Religion: Islam.

Section C
Foundations of Religion: Hinduism.

Section C
Foundations of Religion: Buddhism.

Religion for Living

Second Edition

Connie Duffy

Alpha Press Ltd.

To our sons James and Kevin,
for their inestimable support.

Section D
The Question of Faith.

Section E
The Celebration of Faith.

Section F
The Moral Challenge.

Section A - Communities of Faith

The *Syllabus Aims* in this section are:

- To explore the nature and pattern of human communities.
- To identify the characteristics of Communities of Faith/ Churches.
- To examine these characteristics as they occur in Communities of Faith/ Churches in local, national and international examples.

Concept Checklist (Section A - Communities of Faith)

Page

- ❑ **Authority** - the power given to an individual or group to make important decisions. 78, 85
- ❑ **Church** - a community of Christian people. 44, 50, 53, 56, 59
- ❑ **Commitment** - the decision to spend time and energy doing something on behalf of others. . . . 20, 23, 27, 29
- ❑ **Community** - a group of people who share common interests. 3
- ❑ **Community breakdown** - disruption in a group due to poor communication, lack of co-operation and failure to carry out roles responsibly.. 17
- ❑ **Communication** - the exchange of information and ideas with other people... 10
- ❑ **Co-operation** - people's willingness to work together for the benefit of all. 8
  Lack of co-operation - a refusal to work with others for selfish reasons. 8
- ❑ **Denomination** - a group within Christianity that has its own leaders, beliefs and practices. 42
- ❑ **Ecumenism** - a movement to help the Christian Churches become more united.. 70
- ❑ **Faith/ Belief** - a set of religious truths that all members of a community of faith believe.. 42
- ❑ **Founder** - the person who establishes a community or an organisation for a special purpose. . . 35, 38, 40, 62
- ❑ **Gospel** - the 'Good News' of the life, death and resurrection of Jesus Christ in the New Testament.. 35
- ❑ **Identity** - the distinct characteristics by which a person or group is recognised. 47
- ❑ **Inter-faith dialogue** - open and honest discussions between the major world religions. 73
- ❑ **Inspiring vision** - a dream or idea so powerful it motivates people to act on it. . . . 35, 38, 40, 50, 56, 59, 62
- ❑ **Leadership** - the task of a leader in guiding a group or organisation. 23, 27, 29, 76, 78, 85
- ❑ **Ministry** - special duties performed by priests, ministers and lay people to serve God and the Church. 82
- ❑ **Mission** - the specific work carried out by members of a faith community. 62
- ❑ **Preaching** - to speak out and explain a religious truth and urge people to act on it. 50, 56, 59
- ❑ **Religions** - organisations that express belief in God or gods through prayer, worship and a way of life. 31
- ❑ **Religious commitment** - the decision to make a sincere effort to put one's religious belief into practice. 50, 53, 56, 59
- ❑ **Religious conflict** - a clash or struggle between different religious groups. 65
- ❑ **Revelation** - the way in which God chose to make himself known to human beings. 35, 38, 40
- ❑ **Roles** - tasks that people are expected to perform in a community. 13
- ❑ **Sacred text** - the book of holy or sacred writings of a community of faith. 35, 38, 40
- ❑ **Sectarianism** - hatred of people because they belong to a different religious group. 65
- ❑ **Service** - work carried out to meet the needs of a person or a community.. . . . . 20, 23, 27, 29, 82
- ❑ **Sharing** - people dividing what they have with others. 5
- ❑ **Tolerance** - allowing everyone to have their own religious beliefs and practices. 68
- ❑ **Vision** - a vivid dream or mental image of something important. 23, 27, 29
- ❑ **Vocation** - a feeling of being called by God to serve others. 62

Community

Key Concept

Community: a group of people who share common interests.

Objective

Name different types of communities.

Activity: *"All about us"*

TASK: TO DISCOVER WHAT CLASSMATES HAVE IN COMMON WITH EACH OTHER.

✦ Fill in your own details below.

About me....
❋ Name:
❋ Age:
❋ Religion:
❋ Primary school attended:
❋ Best subject:
❋ Favourite sport:
❋ Favourite TV programme:
❋ I am good at:

✧ Now select a partner.

✧ Share details about yourself.

✧ Swap over and repeat.

✧ When everyone is ready, introduce your partner to the class.

Discuss

- What do members of this class have in common with each other?
- Make a list of what you have discovered.

  This is what we have in common as a class...

Community

We share a number of things in common with other people in the class.

The word community stems from the Latin *communis* meaning 'common'. A community is people considered a unit because they share something in common. It might be that they live together in the same place, work together in the same job or pray together in the same church.

There are different types of communities.

❖ A family community.

❖ A school community.

❖ A parish community.

Other communities might include:
a football team, a group of friends, a choir, a drama group, a neighbourhood, a youth club, the Catholic Church, the E.U., a religious order.

✦ Name the different communities - A, B, C, D.

✦ What do the members of each community have in common with one another?

A.

B.

C.

D.

Belonging to different communities

When we are part of a community we have "a sense of belonging". This is because:

- we know we have a place there.
- we know the other people.
- we know what is going on.
- we know what to do.

Most people belong to a number of different communities.

Calling a friend.

Schoolfriends

"You weren't in today, how are you feeling?....." "Okay, I'll be around tomorrow after school, but first I've got to bring my little brother to the shops. We're going to buy some of those cards he's collecting. I promised Mam I'd take him.....

Did you know basketball practice is cancelled tonight?.... I think I'll go along to the youth club instead. Sharon and Caroline say they are going anyway. There was a notice about it in the Parish Newsletter last Sunday.... Yeah, it's on at 8 o'clock,.... pity you can't come, hope you feel better soon. Anyway, I'll be around tomorrow with all the news.... No problem, I'll bring that DVD as well.... Right. See ya!"

a. To what communities does this young person belong?

b. To what communities do you belong? Make a list.

c. Where do you feel you belong?

Questions

Knowledge

1. What is a community?
2. Name four different types of communities.
3. To what communities might teenagers belong?
4. To what communities might adults belong?
5. In what communities do you:
   a. have no choice about belonging?
   b. have a choice about belonging?
6. How would you know that a person belongs to a particular community?

Understanding

1. a. How is a family a community?
   b. How is a school a community?
   c. How is a parish a community?
2. What does it mean to belong to a community?

Research

- Interview an adult, perhaps a member of your family.
  - Find out to what communities he/she belongs.
  - Report interesting findings to the class.

Interview
Date:
Time:
An interview with:
Topic of interview: Communities
Name three communities to which you belong.
1. 2. 3.
✦Select one community from the list.
- What do the members of this community have in common with each other?
- Share one or two interesting facts about this community.
Thank you for helping with this assignment.

Sharing

Key Concept

Sharing: people dividing what they have with others.

Objective

Show that sharing is a characteristic of communities.

Activity: *"Everyone counts"*

TASK: TO ASSIST CLASSMATES IN GETTING TO KNOW EVERYONE'S NAME.

You will need: A4 paper and pens.

A. Make your own name slip.

- Fold a page in half, lengthways.
- Print your name in bold capital letters on one half.
- Colour and decorate.
- Prop the completed name slip on the desk in front of you.

B. Now draw the classroom seating plan in your copy. Enter everyone's name.

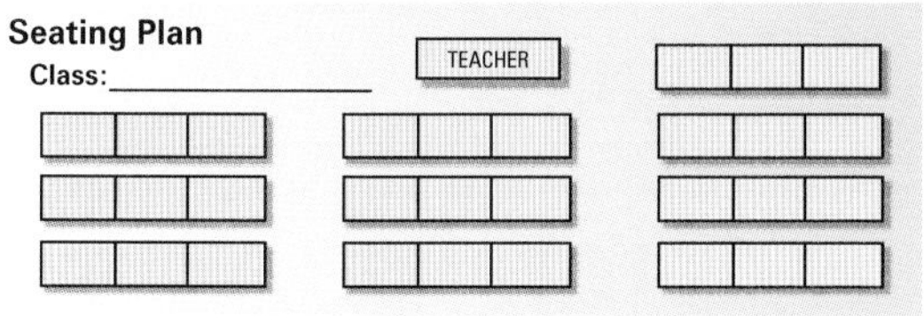
Seating Plan
Class:
TEACHER

Discuss

- Did you know everyone's name at the start of this class?
- How many names do you know now?
- Why is it important to know everyone's name in the class?

Sharing

The class is a new community.

Sharing is a characteristic of communities. People who belong to a community divide and share all kinds of things with one another. e.g.

- their time.
- their talents.
- their ideas.
- their possessions.

The class is made up of many different people. Each person is unique and has their own ideas and their own range of gifts and talents.

Everyone has talents that can be used for the benefit of others.

It is important to be aware of our own talents. It is equally important to know and appreciate the talents of other people. When we share what we have and what we are good at, the whole community benefits. Each one of us brings something special to the class and to the school. Everyone has something to offer.

- We are all good at something. What are you good at?

Obvious Talents

Quite a few people in the class might have obvious talents such as being good at music, sport, debating or excelling in a particular subject. Think about your obvious talents, the things you do really well. Are you good at....?

- ❖ singing.
- ❖ reading.
- ❖ swimming.
- ❖ telling jokes.
- ❖ first aid.
- ❖ ironing.
- ❖ drawing cartoons.
- ❖ babysitting.
- ❖ playing football.
- ❖ computer games.
- ❖ other...

Select one obvious talent.

A - List the skills needed to carry out this task.

B - Identify a community that benefits from this talent of yours.

Hidden Talents

Some of our talents are less obvious. They are on the inside and part of our personality. They can be hidden, not everyone will see them straight away. Think about your hidden talents, the kind of person you are. Are you...?

- ❖ friendly.
- ❖ hardworking.
- ❖ brave.
- ❖ a good listener.
- ❖ cheerful.
- ❖ honest.
- ❖ kind.
- ❖ reliable.
- ❖ generous.
- ❖ loyal.
- ❖ other...

Select one hidden talent.

A - Describe how you use this talent for the good of others.

B - Identify a community that recently benefited from this hidden talent.

Developing our talents

Everyone has gifts and talents that can be used for the good of others in the community. In the Christian Bible Jesus tells a story to explain that God expects everyone to develop their talents.

The Parable of The Three Servants

(Adapted from Matt 25:14-30)

Long ago there was a king who had three servants. One day he gave each of them a different gift.

The first servant was given five talents.

The second servant was given two.

The third servant received one talent.

They were told to go and develop their talents for the good of others. When the king left, they each used their gifts in a different way.

A long time later the king returned and sent for his servants.

"Well, how did you get on?" he asked. "Did you use all the gifts I gave you?"

The first servant spoke up. "Yes, I made good use of all the talents you gave me. I used them in different ways for the good of others."

"Well done!" said the king.

The next servant said: "I put both my talents to good use. I used them in different ways for the good of others."

"Well done!" said the king.

Then the third servant said in a quiet voice: "I had only one talent. I was afraid to use it so I put it away. No one knows I have it."

"What!" said the king. "You wasted the one talent I gave you? You didn't use it at all?" The king was very disappointed and gave out to the servant and then sent him away.

Christians believe that they will be held responsible for the way they use the gifts and talents that God has given to them. Whether it is one talent, three or five, each must be developed for the good of the person and the whole community.

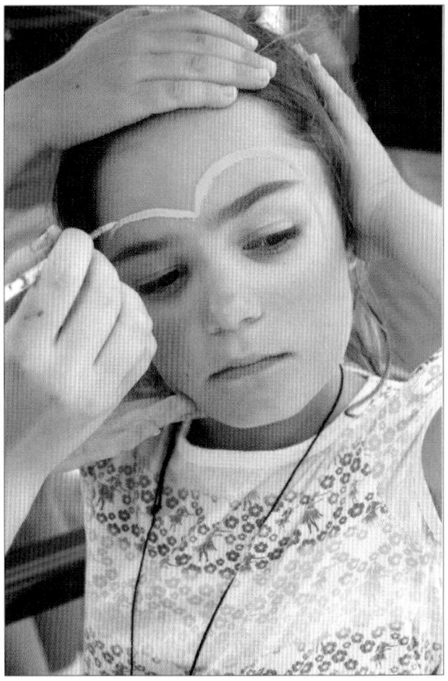

Offering to do face- painting at children's parties and fundraising events.

Questions

Knowledge

1. How many servants are in the story?
2. What were the servants asked to do with their talents?
3. Who made the best use of their talents?
4. What excuse did the third servant give for not using his talent?
5. Why was the king disappointed?
6. Compare the way each servant developed the potential of the talents they received.

Understanding

1. What do you think Jesus wants people to learn from the story of "The Three Servants"?
2. What excuses do we sometimes make for not using our gifts and talents?
3. Select someone you admire and describe how he/she has developed their abilities and talents.
4. How do communities benefit when people share their gifts and talents?

Research

- Identify the gifts or talents of members of your family.

  Think about each person separately.

  - What special gifts does each one bring to your family?
  - How does each person's gifts benefit the entire family?

Co-operation

Key Concepts

Co-operation: is people's willingness to work together for the benefit of all.

Lack of co-operation: is a refusal to work with others for selfish reasons.

Objectives

Show that co-operation is a characteristic of community life.

Distinguish between co-operation and lack of co-operation.

Activity: *"Teamwork"*

TASK: TO EXAMINE HOW CLASSMATES INTERACT DURING A TEAMWORK EXERCISE.

- You will need: five or six packs of playing cards.
  - Divide the class into teams.
  - Distribute packs of cards.
  - Each team works together to build one large pyramid of cards.
  - Use any number of cards - preferably on a non-slip surface.
  - Establish a time limit.
  - If the structure collapses it must be rebuilt.
  - Collect packs of cards.

Discuss

- How did your team get on? What happened?
- What kind of behaviour helped the most?
- What kind of behaviour got in the way of the task.
- What do you think teamwork is all about?

Co-operation

Working together to achieve a common goal.

Co-operation is a characteristic of communities. When people co-operate they are choosing to work togerther for everone's benefit. Lack of co-operation is a refusal to work with others, often for selfish reasons. When we work in a team,or as part of a group, we will notice that some people might want to do things differently to the way we do them; or they might work faster or slower than we do. This does not mean that what they are doing is wrong and that we are right. It means we are learning that our way is not the only way. We need to be patient, and we need to compromise. We still rely on everyone to play their part and do their best, and when that happens everyone benefits.

When people make an effort to get along with each other and help each other out, at home and at school, they are behaving in a co-operative way. Things get done when people are able to work together. Co-operation is at the heart of all communities including the family, the school and the parish.

A good team spirit.

Canada geese migrating.

Every single person has the ability to do something good for the communities to which they belong.

Helping each other out

Why do birds fly in a v-formation? Scientists studying the flight pattern of wild geese have recently found the answer. By flying in a v-formation the flying range of each bird is almost 70% greater than if it were flying alone.

Wild geese travel south on long journeys at the end of summer. The birds set off together in a group or a flock. As each bird flaps its wings it makes an uplift of air for the bird behind. If a bird falls out of formation it feels the wind resistence of trying to go it alone. It quickly gets back into line in order to benefit from the lifting power of the birds in front.

When the leader bird gets tired it drops back to let another bird take over. As the bird in front takes on the full force of the wind, the one behind gets its energy back on the uplift of air. The geese move around to help each other out. Those at the rear honk loudly to encourage those up front to keep going. Wild geese co-operate with each other to ensure they all arrive safely at their destination.

T
E
A
M

Questions

Knowledge

1. What is co-operation?
2. Explain the difference between co-operation and lack of co-operation.
3. Provide examples of co-operative behaviour in a family or a school community.
4. Why do birds fly in a v-formation?
5. How do wild geese support each other in their migration south?

Understanding

1. Why is co-operation important in a family and at school?
2. What are the effects of non-co-operation?
3. Is co-operation necessary in every community? Explain.
4. Does the account of the wild geese offer any insight into the need for co-operation in human communities?

Research

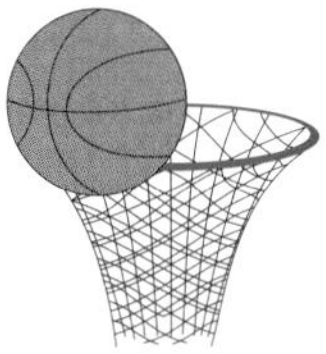

- Find out how co-operation and working together is vital in team sports.
  - Select a team sport (football, basketball, rugby etc.).
  - Draw a diagram of the pitch or court.
  - Mark in the different positions.
  - Make a presentation to the class explaining the importance of co-operation in this game. Use a brief film clip from a team sport to illustrate your point (optional).

Communication

Key Concept

Communication: the exchange of information and ideas with other people.

Objective

Show that good communication is characteristic of successful communities.

Activity: *"Body Sculpture"*

TASK: TO UNDERSTAND THE IMPACT OF BODY LANGUAGE IN COMMUNICATION.

- Divide into pairs and select a topic from the list below.

✧ I'm tired.	✧ I'm bored.
✧ I'm too warm.	✧ I'm nervous.
✧ I'm too cold.	✧ I'm angry.
✧ I'm in pain.	✧ I'm delighted.
✧ I'm in a hurry.	✧ I'm shocked.
✧ I'm shy.	✧ I'm embarrassed.
✧ I'm listening.	✧ Other: _________

- Discuss how to present the message to the class without the use of words - use body language instead.
- One partner acts as a sculptor who shapes the aspect and attitude of the other. Pay attention to facial expression, the shoulders, head, back, hands, arms and legs.
- Together display the message to the class.
- Invite the class to interpret the body language of each "sculpture".

Discuss

- Was this exercise easy or difficult to do?
- How good is the class at understanding body language?
- What has body language to do with communication?

Communication

Good communication is important in community life.

Communication is a characteristic of communities. Communication is the exchange of information and ideas that occurs when people talk, listen and pay attention to each other. During a conversation one person speaks, the other person listens. The speaker gives a message. The listener receives a message. Communication is always two-way.

Some people communicate very well. They are good at talking and are equally good at listening. It is important to be a good listener as it shows respect for other people when we listen carefully to what they have to say.

Good communication is essential in any community. When we communicate and share our ideas it helps us to get on better with people at home, at school and in the parish. We get on better with our friends too. Having good communication skills help us to respect and understand each other better. Everyone benefits.

Communication skills can be learned. In this lesson we will learn and practice three important communication skills:

Three communication skills

1. Good body language.
2. Good eye contact.
3. Active listening.

The teacher may invite volunteers from the class to demonstrate each of these skills.

Step 1 - Body Language

First, draw or write about "the most embarrassing thing that ever happened to you".

A - *Not listening*

Now divide into pairs: a speaker and a listener.

The speaker talks about "the most embarrassing thing that ever happened to me".

The listener shows through body language that he/she is not interested in the account.

TEACHER:

☆ Discuss the exercise.
Listener - what did you do that showed you were not listening?
Speaker - how does it feel when no one listens to you?

ES ST

B - *Listening*

Re-form into pairs. Adopt the same roles: speaker and listener.

The speaker again talks about "the most embarrassing thing that ever happened to me".

The listener shows through body language that now he/she is interested.

TEACHER:

☆ Discuss the exercise once more.
Listener - what did you do to show that you were listening?
Speaker - does it feel any different when someone listens to what you say?

Step 2 - Eye Contact

Next, draw or write about "something exciting that happened during the holidays".

A - *Not listening*

Now divide into pairs: a speaker and a listener.

The speaker talks about "something exciting that happened during the holidays".

The listener shows by eye movements that he/she is not interested in the account.

TEACHER:

☆ Discuss the exercise.
Listener - what did you do that showed you were not listening?
Speaker - how does it feel when no one listens to you?

NG

B - *Listening*

Re-form into pairs. Adopt the same roles: speaker and listener.

The speaker again talks about "something exciting that happened during the holidays".

The listener shows through eye movements that now he/she is interested.

TEACHER:

☆ Discuss the exercise once more.
Listener - what did you do to show that you were listening?
Speaker - how does it feel when you know someone is listening to you?

Step 3 - Active Listening

Finally, draw or list "four important facts about yourself".

A - ***Not really listening***

Now divide into pairs: speaker and listener.

The speaker talks about "four important facts about myself".

The listener pretends to listen to what is being said.

TEACHER:

✯ Discuss the exercise.

Listener - repeat what the speaker has just told you about him/her self.

Speaker - are all the facts correct? What is it like when someone does not give you their full attention?

B - ***Really listening***

Re-form into pairs. Adopt the same roles: speaker and listener.

The speaker again tells "four important facts about myself".

The listener really tries to pay attention to what is being said.

TEACHER:

✯ Discuss the exercise once more.

Listener - repeat what the speaker has just told you about him/her self.

Speaker - are all the facts correct? What is it like when someone gives you their full attention?

Questions

Knowledge

1. When you are talking to someone, how do you know by their ***body language***:
   a. that they are not listening to you?
   b. that they are listening to you?
2. When you are talking to someone, how do you know by their ***eye contact***:
   a. that they are not listening to you?
   b. that they are listening to you?
3. When you are talking to someone, how do you know by their ***reply*** afterwards:
   a. that they were not listening to you?
   b. that they were listening to you?
4. In a conversation between two people:
   - How can the ***speaker*** help communication?
   - How can the ***listener*** help communication?

Understanding

1. What does "communication" mean?
2. What do you think is the difference between good communication and poor communication between people?
3. How does listening to people with care and respect help build community either at home, at school, in church, or among friends?

Research

- Examine popular TV soaps for samples of good communication skills.
  - Select one brief example from a recorded episode.
  - Give the title of the programme.
  - Describe the scene.
  - Name the characters involved.
  - Identify the communication skills used.
  - Show the film clip (optional).
  - Discuss the benefits of good communication skills.

Roles and Responsibilities

Key Concept

Roles: tasks that people are expected to perform in a community.

Objective

Outline the different roles and responsibilities people have in a community.

Activity: *"At your service"*

TASK: TO BE AWARE OF THE DIFFERENT ROLES IN A SCHOOL COMMUNITY.

- Examine the list.
  In school to whom do you go if....?
  - You feel sick.
  - You want to talk about a family problem.
  - You need to get a locker.
  - You have an official form to get signed.
  - You arrive late.
  - You have to go to the dentist after break.
  - You want to change class.
  - You have a note for absence.
  - You have lost a jacket.
  - You want to go training or join a team.
  - You need a new journal.
  - You want to help with a charity event.
  - You want to pay for a trip.

Discuss

- Do you know all the answers?
- To whom do students go most often when they need help with something?
- What other people in the school assist students on a daily basis?

Roles

In school there are people who assist students in a variety of ways.

Roles are a characteristic of communities. A role is the task, or set of behaviours, that is expected of someone who has a position in the community.

We know what it is like to be part of different communities. We know that a family is a community, a school is a community and a parish is a community. In human communities no one person has all the gifts or talents necessary for an entire community to work effectively. Instead each member takes on a role. This means he/she carries out a special set of tasks for the rest of the community.

Everyone is expected to perform their role to the best of their ability. When that happens the whole community benefits.

The School Community

The school is an organisation for educating young people. Everyone in the school has a role. You have a role too. It is your role to be a good student.

France
France

A typical classroom.

As a student in the school it is your responsibility to learn and to develop all of your abilities.

Roles and Responsibilities in the School Community

Examine the list of roles that people have in a school.

The School Community

Role:	Name:	Responsibilities:
▶ Principal		
▶ Deputy Principal		
▶ Year Head		
▶ Tutor/Class Teacher		
▶ Chaplain		
▶ Counsellor		
▶ Secretary		
▶ Caretaker		
▶ Canteen staff		
▶ Cleaning staff		
▶ Bus driver		
▶ Traffic warden		
▶ Subject Teacher		
▶ Student		

✦ Name the people who have these roles in your school.

✦ State at least one thing each person is responsible for in their role in the school.

Each student has a role and certain responsibilities in the school community.

The Family Community

The family is a community of parents and children. It is a small community, yet it is the one that most of us know best. Families come in all shapes and sizes.

❖ In a nuclear family, children live at home with their parents.

A nuclear family.

❖ In an extended family, children live at home with parents and relatives.

❖ In a lone parent family children live at home with one parent.

❖ In a step family, children live in a new family with one of their biological parents, any brothers or sisters, a step-parent and any step-brothers or step-sisters.

People have different roles in a family. Being a parent is an important role in any family.

✦ List some of the tasks or responsibilities of a parent within a family community.

The Parish Community

A parish is a community of Christian people who gather together to pray and worship God. People take on various roles in their local parish. Some Roman Catholics for example will assist the priest in preparing for Sunday Mass. Even though the members of the group have different roles they all work together as a team. Everyone generously shares their talents in order to make Sunday Mass a special celebration for the parish community.

In the Catholic Church the Mass is special because Catholics believe Jesus is present under the appearance of bread and wine in the Eucharist.

Roles and Responsibilities at Sunday Mass

The choir.

The priest reads the Gospel.

Reading the prayers of the faithful.

Minister of the Word.

The offertory procession.

Role:	Responsibility:
✯ Priest:	the leader of the Christian community celebrates the Eucharist.
✯ Minister of the Eucharist:	a person who helps to give out Holy Communion.
✯ Minister of the Word:	a person who reads the Word of God from the Bible.
✯ Cleaners:	people who clean and polish the church every week.
✯ Flower arrangers:	people who decorate the church with fresh flowers.
✯ Altar society:	people who wash and iron the cloths used on the altar.
✯ Sacristan:	the person in charge of getting the church ready for Mass and the sacraments.
✯ Choir or folk group:	a group of people who sing hymns and play musical instruments at Mass.
✯ Usher:	a person who welcomes people and shows them to their seats.
✯ Readers of prayers of the faithful:	people who say prayers on behalf of the whole Church.
✯ Offertory procession:	people who bring up gifts of bread and wine to the altar at Mass.
✯ Altar servers:	boys and girls who help the priest at the altar during Mass.
✯ Collectors:	people who pass around baskets to collect money for the upkeep of the church.
✯ Booksellers:	people who sell religious books and magazines at the church bookstall.
✯ The Congregation:	people who attend Mass together to pray and worship God.

Minister of the Eucharist.

Altar servers.

Questions

Knowledge

1. What is a role?
2. Who has the role of leader in your school community?
3. Does someone have the role of chaplain in your school?
4. List two responsibilities of a school principal.
5. List three responsibilities of a school caretaker.
6. a. What is your role at school?
   b. What are your responsibilities?
7. Name a person who has the role of parent in your family?
8. List four responsibilities of a parent in a family community.
9. Who has the role of leader in a parish community?
10. At Mass what is the role and responsibility of:
    a. The Minister of the Word?
    b. The Minister of the Eucharist?

Understanding

1. What do we mean when we say someone has a particular role in a school?
2. What roles are essential for the celebration of Sunday Mass in a parish community?
3. a) Why do people have leadership roles in human communities?
   b) What would happen if everyone wanted to be the boss or the one in charge?
4. How important is co-operation, sharing and communication in a school, a family or parish community?

Research

- Invite a member of the school community to speak to the class about their role in the school. The school chaplain, the school secretary or the school caretaker for example, could be invited to describe his/her role in the school.

Checklist - Jobs for Everyone (✓)

Everyone in the class is given a role and is responsible for their part in making the visit a success.

Before the visit:

- ❑ Contact the invited guest to arrange a suitable day and time.
- ❑ Write a letter of invitation.
- ❑ Prepare a list of questions.

Room preparation:

- ❑ Tidy chairs, desks and bags.
- ❑ Remove litter.
- ❑ Open windows to ventilate the room.
- ❑ Write a welcome notice on the board.
- ❑ Arrange chairs for the visitor and teacher.
- ❑ Set out a jug of water and glasses.
- ❑ Check the room overall.

The visit:

- ❑ Bring the visitor to the classroom.
- ❑ Open the door, shake hands, show the visitor to his/her seat.
- ❑ Speech of welcome.
- ❑ Questions and answers.
- ❑ 'Thank you' speech.
- ❑ Escort visitor from the classroom.

After the visit:

- ❑ Write a 'thank you' letter.
- ❑ Write a summary on the role of the chaplain, secretary or caretaker in the school community.

Community Breakdown

Key Concept

Community breakdown: disruption in a group due to poor communication, lack of co-operation and failure to carry out roles responsibly.

Objective

Explain how tension can arise in human communities.

Activity: *"Family Survey"*

TASK: TO EXAMINE SIMILARITIES AND DIFFERENCES IN FAMILY LIFE.

✦ Find out if anyone's family corresponds with the descriptions of family life below. Indicate by a voluntary show of hands.

Family Survey

- A family who sometimes watch TV together.
- A family that has a pre-school child at home.
- A family where a parent has a part-time job.
- A family who sometimes have take-away meals.
- A family where someone has won a prize.
- A family that keeps pet animals or birds.
- A family that went on holiday together last summer.
- A family that has a nice garden.
- A family who attend church together.
- A family whose home has been burgled.
- A family who have lived in another country.
- A family who never have arguments.

Discuss

- Are any two families exactly alike?
- What does this survey tell you about family life in general?

Community Breakdown

All families have their ups and downs.

The family is an example of a community. Each family member has a role and certain responsibilities according to his/her age and level of maturity. When disagreements occur relationships within the family can sometimes break down. We know that communities have certain characteristics that enable them to function properly. All members try to communicate well, co-operate, share and carry out their roles responsibly.

If some people fail to do this it causes difficulties. There is tension. The atmosphere changes and members of the community become unhappy and dissatisfied. Relationships at home, at school, on a team or among friends can break down due to poor communication, lack of co-operation, a refusal to share and failure to carry out roles responsibly.

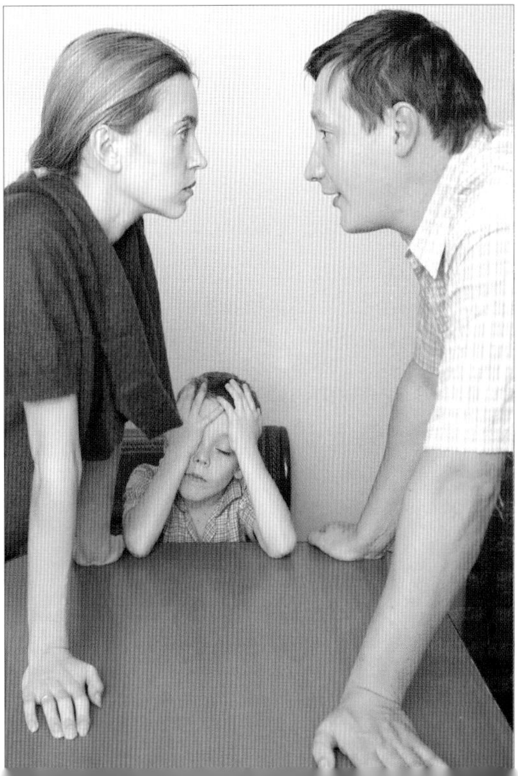

Disruption in a family community.

✦ Pick a community eg. a family, a group of friends, a class or a team. Describe how failure to communicate, share, and co-operate or to act responsibly, can lead to the breakdown of relationships in that community.

A dispute among friends.

Tension between an individual and the community

The family community

Teenagers are at an in-between stage in family life, no longer children but not yet adults. The young teenager is becoming a lot more independent. Teenagers are able to rely more on themselves. They have their own ideas. They want to do more, to have more freedom. Parents often feel this is happening too fast. Teenagers may feel it is not happening fast enough. Parents might want to protect their teenage children by not allowing them to do certain things. Teenagers may think they don't need that kind of protection any more. This difference of opinion can cause tension in the family. It can result in a temporary breakdown in relationships within the family.

Resolving disagreements

All families have their ups and downs. Disagreements can arise when parents and teenagers do not see eye-to-eye on certain matters. Generally there are two ways of dealing with disagreements, the mature way, and the immature way. The mature way is to communicate, to talk it out and listen to the other point of view.

The mature way

- Talk it out.
- Listen to the other point of view.
- Find a compromise.
- Forgive.

The immature way

- Be cheeky.
- Shout.
- Bang doors.
- Sulk.
- Hold a grudge.

Compromise

The family is where people first learn to share, to co-operate and to get on with others. The family teaches young children that they cannot get everything they want. It teaches teenagers that they cannot do everything they want. Boys and girls learn to understand this, and come to accept it.

Yet parents and their teenage children can also learn to meet each other half way. This is called compromise. A compromise is a way of settling disagreements. It is a "win-win" situation; both sides get something, no one gets everything. It is fair. Good communication is at the heart of compromise.

How to compromise

- ❖ Be calm.
- ❖ Talk it out.
- ❖ Listen to the other point of view.
- ❖ Give a little.
- ❖ Get a little.

Compromise means working together to find an answer to a problem, an answer which is fair to everyone. Solving problems is not easy, it takes time. It means talking and listening to each other. It means trying hard to understand the other person's point of view. This teaches people to be fair. If people learn to be fair at home they will be ready to treat people fairly outside the home.

Resolving conflict in the family.

"Ups and Downs"

What topics are the most common causes of arguments and disagreements in a family?

Arguments may be about: (✓)

❒ Homework.	❒ T.V.
❒ Money.	❒ Your room.
❒ Your friends.	❒ Phone.
❒ The internet.	❒ Alcohol.
❒ Clothes.	❒ Music.
❒ Hairstyle.	❒ A letter from the school.
❒ Housework.	❒ Staying out late.
❒ Smoking.	❒ Younger brothers and sisters.
OR__________	**OR**__________

Role Play

Write and act out a role play on how to resolve conflict in the family.

(i) *Group Work*
Choose one or more partners. Together think of all the things that can cause arguments at home between parents and teenagers. Pick one typical issue.

(ii) *Role Play*
Write a short true-to-life role play about the issue.
- Create two or three characters.
- Decide what they will say/do.
- Decide who causes the argument; who keeps the argument going; who tries to settle the argument.
- Decide how the characters agree a compromise.

Act it out.

(iii) *Discussion.*
a. What did the teenager want?
b. What was the parent concerned about?
c. How did it feel to be the teenager?
d. How did it feel being the parent?
e. Which role was harder to play? Why?
f. What was the compromise? Was it fair?

Conflict resolved.

Questions

Knowledge

1. What are the characteristics of a good community?
2. What leads to the breakdown of a community?
3. What might be a source or cause of tension:
   a. Within a family?
   b. Between friends?
   c. Among team mates?
4. What is a compromise?
5. How does a compromise work?

Understanding

1. Why do relationships within families or among friends break down from time to time?
2. How can communication reduce tension between the individual and the community when relationships break down?
3. What are the advantages and disadvantages of compromise as a way of settling disagreements?

Serving Others

Key Concepts

Service: work carried out to meet the needs of a person or a community.

Commitment: the decision to spend time and energy doing something on behalf of others.

Objective

Describe the role of communities and voluntary organisations in society.

Activity: *"Matching Exercise"*

TASK: TO BE AWARE OF THE RANGE OF VOLUNTARY ORGANISATIONS ACTIVE IN YOUR LOCALITY.

✦ On the noticeboard match the information to the correct organisation. (⟷)

What we do	Organisation
We help to tidy up our local area. ●	● Youth Club.
We help people in the developing world. ●	● Faith Friends.
We help families to prepare for the sacraments. ●	● SVP.
We help older people to enjoy themselves. ●	● Football Club.
We help people who are in despair. ●	● Christian Aid.
We help injured and unwanted animals. ●	● Amnesty International.
We help people with marriage problems. ●	● Residents Association.
We help people in need. ●	● Accord.
We help people to get their human rights. ●	● ISPCA.
We train people in team sports. ●	● The Samaritans.
We help people with savings and loans. ●	● Credit Union.
We help people who are out of home. ●	● Focus Ireland.
We help young people to enjoy organised activities in their free time. ●	● Active Agers Group.

Discuss

- How many organisations did you correctly identify?
- Are any of these organisations active in your area?
- Why do you think people get involved in organisations like these?
- Name organisations that serve the needs of people - locally (only in your area).
  - nationally (all over the country).
  - internationally (all over the world).

Service

People join groups that serve others locally, nationally and internationally.

Red Cross volunteers at a refugee reception centre.

A group of students in one school meet every Wednesday at lunch time, they call themselves ***The Justice Group***. They organise the meetings themselves with the help of the religion teacher. This group is in fact a small community because the members all share something in common. They volunteer to do practical things to be of service and to help people in need at home and abroad.

At Christmas they organise a sponsored fast for ***Concern*** and Christmas Hampers for ***St. Vincent de Paul***. Once a month they write letters and postcards to political prisoners for ***Amnesty International***. They even organised a poster campaign in the school to tell everyone what happens to street children in Brazil. They serve tea and biscuits after the annual **Remembrance service** for families whose babies died through cot death. They make and sell St. Brigid's Crosses for the ***Afri* Peace and Justice Campaign**. Now they are organising a non-uniform day for the ***Hospice*** in their area.

Commitment

The students show great commitment. They give up their free time, work hard and never miss a meeting. They get on well together, have fun and do a lot of useful work. The students think they are very lucky as they have everything they need. They know that many other people are not so lucky: their needs are not being met at all. The *Justice Group* try to do something about this by spending time and energy helping different local, national and international organisations.

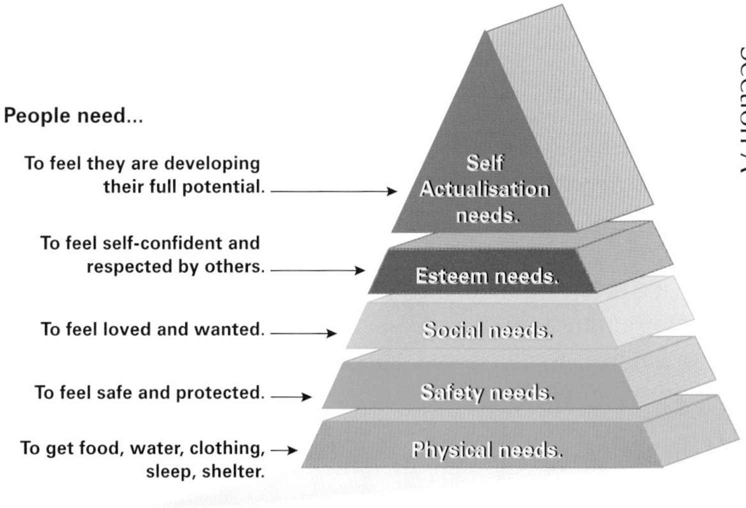
People need...
To feel they are developing their full potential.
Self Actualisation needs.
To feel self-confident and respected by others.
Esteem needs.
To feel loved and wanted.
Social needs.
To feel safe and protected.
Safety needs.
To get food, water, clothing, sleep, shelter.
Physical needs.

Maslow's Hierarchy of Needs

Human needs

A scientist named Abraham Maslow has shown that human beings everywhere have the same needs.

These needs can be listed in a certain order. He drew a diagram to illustrate his findings, it looks like a pyramid. The most basic human needs are at the base of the pyramid. A person's physical need for food, clothing and shelter must be taken care of first. Then his/her emotional needs for love and safety are focused on next, and so on.

Disaster relief

The challenge of meeting everyone's needs becomes very clear in situations where a disaster has occurred. In war torn countries for example, famine often develops and people crowd into refugee centres. These are set up by international aid agencies such as *GOAL* or *Concern*. The immediate response is to provide food, water and emergency shelter. Once people's basic physical needs are attended to, their need for health-care and safety are addressed next, followed by their more complex need for emotional care and personal development.

Food distribution at a refugee centre.

The Family

Parent and children.

Different communities address different human needs. The family community provides a unique service for its members. An important role of the family is to care for children and help them grow up to be responsible adults. Parents show great commitment in caring for their children. They spend time, money and effort meeting all their children's needs.

Physical needs: parents make sure their children have food, water, clean clothing and comfortable beds in their home.

Safety needs: parents protect their children and keep them safe.

Social needs: parents make sure their children feel loved and wanted.

Esteem needs: parents respect their children, praise them and help them to feel self-confident.

Self-actualisation needs: parents take their children to sports clubs, send them to school and take them to church. They do all these things to make sure that their children develop their full potential - in body, mind and spirit.

The family does a lot but it cannot do everything. Other communities such as the school, the neighbourhood, the Church and good friends support the role of the family in caring for its members. In this country when a family needs extra help, other organisations are there to provide a service when it is needed. For example:

- the *Health Service* will offer medical care.
- the *Gardai* will offer protection.
- *Social Welfare* will offer financial support.

Voluntary groups and organisations such as the *Credit Union, Childline, Neighbourhood Watch* and *Residents Associations* also provide useful services that may be needed from time to time. The *Society of St. Vincent De Paul, L'Arche* and the *Hospice* movement are other organisations that are committed to providing a service to individuals and families throughout Ireland.

Questions

Knowledge

1. Name four organisations that are supported by the school *Justice Group*.
2. Who was Abraham Maslow?
3. What are the basic physical needs of all human beings?
4. What kinds of emotional needs do human beings have?
5. What is the role of the family in society?
6. What does the family do to meet the needs of children?
7. How do parents show their commitment to their families?
8. What other communities and organisations assist the family to meet the needs of children?

Understanding

1. How do the members of the school *Justice Group* serve the needs of their local community?
2. a) Name one voluntary organisation that helps people in your area.
   b) How do local people benefit from the work of this organisation?
3. Identify one local, one national and one international charitable organisation. What services do these agencies provide for people at home or abroad?
4. Why do you think people belong to a range of different communities and voluntary organisations?

Research

- Find out about:
  a. the *Young Social Innovators Programme*, or
  b. a local organisation or community group that is active in your area.
  - What is the name of this group or organisation?
  - What service does it provide?
  - How do people benefit from its services?
  - What commitment is required of helpers and volunteers?
  - Why do people volunteer to work in this organisation?
  - Is it a local, national or international organisation?
  - Write a summary of the work of this group or organisation.

Society of St. Vincent de Paul

Key Concepts

Service: work carried out to meet the needs of a person or a community.

Vision: a vivid dream or mental image of something important.

Leadership: the task of a leader in guiding a group or organisation.

Commitment: the decision to spend time and energy doing something on behalf of others.

Objectives

Know the variety of roles within SVP, and the vision that inspires the work of SVP today.

Activity: *"Needs and Wants"*

TASK: TO DISTINGUISH BETWEEN NEEDS AND WANTS IN HUMAN LIFE.

✦ Complete each section of the form.

(✔) I need this - because as a human being I cannot live without it.

(✔) I want this - because some people I know already have it.

(*) I have this.

Item	NEED	WANT	*
Pocket money.			
Family car.			
Healthy food.			
Refrigerator.			
Own room.			
Colour TV.			
Mobile phone.			
Family holidays.			
Family home.			
Central heating.			
Good health care.			
Family bathroom.			
Hair styling.			
MP3 player.			
Secondary education.			
College education.			
Personal computer.			
Clean clothes.			
Fashionable clothes.			
Savings account.			
Garden.			
Clean water.			

Discuss

- What things do you need?
- What things could you do without?
- What would life be like if you had to do without some of the things you already have?

SVP *Society of St. Vincent de Paul* is an example of a community of faith. It is a Christian organisation that offers friendship and help to people in need.

Service

Some people do not have what everyone else takes for granted. Their only income is from social welfare, or from badly paid jobs. The SVP is an organisation that aims to help people in this situation.

"I have two children, and a baby of four months. Things were getting on top of me. I found it hard to make ends meet. It was coming up to Christmas and I was getting into debt. One evening Alice and Pat from the SVP came to visit me. They helped me to sort out my money problems. I got a loan from the Credit Union. Then two days before Christmas they turned up with a huge hamper. They even gave me a voucher for the turkey and ham!"

The work of SVP

The SVP in Ireland provides an essential service to help people in need in local communities through:

- ❖ Home visits.
- ❖ Money management.
- ❖ Hospital visits.
- ❖ Homework clubs.
- ❖ Prison visits.
- ❖ Meals on wheels.
- ❖ Hostels.

Hostels for homeless people.

- ❖ Thrift shops.

Vincents

Thrift Shop

- ❖ Holiday breaks.

Holiday breaks for children.

- ❖ Breakfast Clubs.
- ❖ Education Grants.
- ❖ Drugs Projects.
- ❖ Creches.

Vision

Blessed Frederic Ozanam 1813-1853
The founder of SVP as a young man.

The work of SVP is inspired by the teaching of Jesus in the Gospel.

SVP was started by a group of young people in France. The founder, Frederic Ozanam, was a student in the world famous university, the Sorbonne, in Paris. He was a Roman Catholic who firmly believed in Jesus' teaching to "love God and love your neighbour as yourself".

Frederic had a dream, a vision. He wanted to help people in need like Jesus did. He often talked to his friends about it. Eventually one evening he told them: "I'm tired of talking, let's act". They decided to set off to a poor part of the city. There Frederic and his friends visited the homes of people in need of help. Every week more and more students joined them. Very soon they all discovered that their contact with the poor made them more caring and more compassionate. By the end of the year over one hundred volunteers were working with the poor in the city. Frederic decided to call the group after a famous French saint who helped the poor - St. Vincent de Paul.

All that took place almost 180 years ago. Today SVP is an international organisation: it helps people in need in over 100 countries world-wide. In Ireland alone there are over 1,300 conferences or branches throughout the country.

Jesus said:
"When I was hungry - you gave me food.
When I was thirsty - you gave me something to drink.
When I was a stranger - you welcomed me.
When I was homeless - you gave me a place to stay.
When I was sick - you comforted me.
When I was in prison - you came to visit me."

The people asked in amazement:
"When Lord? When did we do these things for you? We never saw you."

Jesus replied:
"I say to you, what you did for one of them, you did for me."

(Adapted from Matt 25:35-40.)

The words of Jesus in the Gospel that inspired Frederic Ozanam to found the Society of St. Vincent de Paul.

Leadership

Leadership is a characteristic of communities. The role of a leader is to guide a community in following the vision of its founder. The SVP in Ireland elects a national leader or president and several regional leaders. All the local conferences throughout the country elect their own leaders.

The structure of the SVP

- National Council -

- Regional Councils -

- Area Councils -

- Local Conferences -

The leader of a conference meets the members to plan and organise what work needs to be done. SVP volunteers have different roles in the organisation. They help out in different ways according to their interests and talents. For example many do home visits and assist families to budget and manage their money, others organise after-school clubs. Some members prefer to work in thrift shops or in preparing meals for people who are housebound.

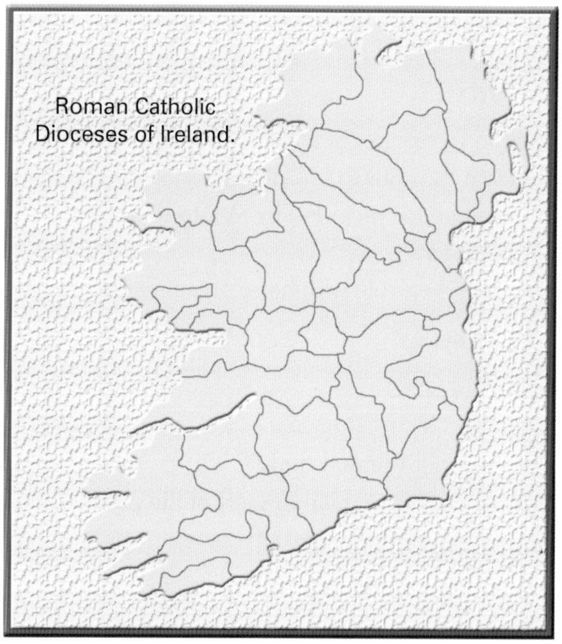
Roman Catholic
Dioceses of Ireland.

SVP is an international organisation with a strong national presence in this country. There is an active SVP Conference in most parishes of the Catholic Dioceses of Ireland.

Commitment

Adults and young people join SVP because they want to put their Christian belief into action. Members make a commitment to spend at least one afternoon or evening each week helping the less well off in their community.

Students from the SVP conference (UCD) on the *Big Sleepout*, an annual event to raise awareness about homelessness.

Activity

- Invite a member of a local SVP conference to visit the class to talk about:
  - The service provided by SVP to the local community.
  - Their own role within the organisation.

✦ **Checklist** (✓).

Before the visit:

- ❑ Contact SVP to arrange a suitable day and time.
- ❑ Prepare a list of questions.*
- ❑ Delegate roles to all members of the class.

Room preparation:

- ❑ Tidy chairs, desks and bags.
- ❑ Remove litter.
- ❑ Open windows to ventilate the room.
- ❑ Write a welcome notice on the board.
- ❑ Arrange chairs for visitor and teacher.
- ❑ Set out a jug of water and glasses.
- ❑ Check the room overall.

The visit:

- ❑ Bring the visitor to the classroom.
- ❑ Open the door, shake hands, show the visitor to his/her seat.
- ❑ Speech of welcome.
- ❑ Questions and answers.
- ❑ "Thank you" speech.
- ❑ Escort visitor from the classroom.

After the visit:

- ❑ Write a "thank you" letter.
- ❑ Write a paragraph on what you learned about SVP from conducting this research interview.

Sample Questions*

1. What does the SVP do for people?
2. How long have you been a member of SVP?
3. Why did you join SVP?
4. What is your role in SVP?
5. Do you like what you do? Is it hard?
6. Why do you stay in SVP?
7. How much of your free time do you give to SVP?
8. How is SVP run in the parish?
9. Does SVP have a local leader in the parish? What is his/her title?
10. Does SVP have a national leader for the entire country? What is his/her title?
11. What is the role of both a local and a national leader in SVP?
12. What role do young people have in SVP?

Questions

Knowledge

1. What does SVP stand for?
2. What is the work of SVP today?
3. Who was the founder of SVP?
4. What dream or vision inspired the founder of SVP?
5. How did the organisation get its name?
6. How is it that SVP is a local, national and international community, all at the same time?

Understanding

1. What service does SVP provide for the community?
2. How did the teaching of Jesus in the Gospel affect the life of Frederic Ozanam?
3. a) What roles, including leadership roles, do members have in the organisation?
   b) What skills and talents are required to carry out these roles?
4. What level of commitment do people make when they join SVP?
5. Why do you think people join SVP today?

Research

- Find out about one other lay organisation in the Catholic Church in addition to SVP, such as:
  - Trocaire.
  - Accord.
  - Pax Christi.
  - Catholic Girl Guides.
  - The Legion of Mary.
  - Catholic Youth Care (CYC).
  - The Knights of Columbanus.
  - The Pioneer Association.

  - ✸ What is the work of this organisation today?
  - ✸ In what way is the vision and work of this organisation based on the teaching of Jesus in the Gospels?
  - ✸ Discuss your findings with the class.

L'Arche

Key Concepts

Vision: a vivid dream or mental image of something important.

Leadership: the task of a leader in guiding a group or organisation.

Service: work carried out to meet the needs of a person or a community.

Commitment: the decision to spend time and energy doing something on behalf of others.

Objectives

Know the variety of roles within L'Arche, and the vision that inspires the work of L'Arche today.

Activity: *"Brainstorm"*

TASK: INTRODUCE THE CONCEPT OF DISABILITY AND EXPLORE IDEAS, PRECONCEPTIONS AND PREJUDICES ABOUT DISABILITY.

- Divide the blackboard in half by drawing a line from top to bottom.
- Write the word DISABILITY across the top of one half. Brainstorm any words/phrases associated with the word 'disability'.
- Write the word PERSON across the top of the other half. Brainstorm any words/phrases associated with the word 'person'.

Discuss

- Compare the two lists.
- What words are positive?
- What words are negative?
- What do you think this means?

The logo of the international L'Arche Comunity

Vision

Leadership

*L'Arche offers a happy home to men and women with an intellectual disability.**

L'Arche is an example of a community of faith. Jean Vanier, a Catholic layman, is the founder of L'Arche. He felt God was calling him to create a community where people with an intellectual disability and their assistants could live together in a spirit of friendship.

Jean Vanier and a friend from the L'Arche Community, Dublin.

Jean believed deeply in Jesus' teaching 'to love God and love one's neighbour as oneself.' He wanted to put the Gospel into action and build a community where people could live as Jesus did. Guided by the Holy Spirit, Jean Vanier founded the first L'Arche community in Trosly in France. L'Arche is a French word meaning *The Ark*. It is named after Noah's ark in the Bible. L'Arche means a place of safety and new life.

* Intellectual disability is a new term used for people with a mental handicap/learning disability.

The first L'Arche Community

In 1964 Jean rented a small house in the village of Trosly. He offered friendship and care to Raphael and Philippe, two local men with intellectual disabilities, and invited them to share his home. The three began to live as a family. They went shopping together and cooked their meals in the tiny kitchen. They cleaned the house, washed the clothes and worked in the garden and in the workshop. They prayed together at mealtimes and went to Mass on Sunday. They shared everything they had.

Raphael could barely speak and Philippe found it hard to concentrate, yet both men did their best and enjoyed helping out in their new home. Jean believes people with an intellectual disability are among the most rejected in society because of their special needs. He believes each person is unique and has their own gifts. Jean soon discovered that he had a lot to learn from Raphael and Philippe. This small group in Trosly became the first L'Arche community.

Service

Commitment

L'Arche is a community based on the life and teaching of Jesus. Its members try to follow his teaching to 'Love God and love your neighbour as yourself.' The members pray together every day, especially at mealtimes. They attend Mass on Sunday and celebrate Christmas and Easter together as a community.

Everyone lives together as equals as they work alongside each other in the house, in the garden, and in the workshops. L'Arche is a place where everyone values and respects one another and shares what they have.

People with intellectual disabilities are core members at the heart of each community. Assistants volunteer to live in L'Arche for a year, or maybe longer, helping in the house and in the workshops. Each community has its own leader. Jean Vanier has worked tirelessly establishing L'Arche. Today there are over one hundred communities in thirty countries throughout the world. There are already four communities in Ireland. L'Arche is home to everyone who lives there.

Questions

Knowledge

1. a. What is L'Arche?
   b. What does the word 'L'Arche' mean?

2. Who is the founder of L'Arche?

3. What inspired Jean Vanier to establish the L'Arche community?

4. a. Who lived in the first L'Arche community?
   b. What did the members of the community do together?

5. How many L'Arche communities are now established throughout the world?

Understanding

1. What is unique about L'Arche? What service does it provide?

2. How did the teaching of Jesus in the Gospel affect the life of Jean Vanier?

3. a. What roles, including leadership roles, do people have in L'Arche?
   b. What skills and talents are required to carry out these roles, in your opinion?

4. a. Why do you think young people volunteer to become assistants in L'Arche communities?
   b. What level of commitment is required of the assistants in L'Arche?

5. How are the characteristics of a good community, i.e. co-operation, sharing and communication, evident in a L'Arche community?

Research

- Find out more about life in L'Arche.
  - Contact L'Arche for information, by letter, phone or email.
  - Visit the L'Arche website.
  - Acquire leaflets or a printout on the L'Arche community.
  - Prepare an illustrated information file for the class. In it include:
    - The L'Arche symbol and its meaning.
    - A brief profile of Jean Vanier.
    - Life in a L'Arche community.
    - The role of core members, assistants and the leader.
    - A map locating L'Arche communities throughout the country.
  - Share the file with the class.

Hospice Care

Key Concepts

Service: work carried out to meet the needs of a person or a community.

Vision: a vivid dream or mental image of something important.

Leadership: the task of a leader in guiding a group or organisation.

Commitment: the decision to spend time and energy doing something on behalf of others.

Objectives

Know the variety of roles in hospice care, and the vision that inspires the work of the Hospice movement.

Activity: *"Desert Island"*

TASK: TO IDENTIFY ITEMS OF PERSONAL OR SENTIMENTAL VALUE.

- Imagine you are going to stay on a desert island and you want to create a "Home-from-Home" when you get there.

  Pack a few favourite items for the trip such as: some CD's, a poster, T-shirts, jacket, photograph, magazine, snack food, jewellery, soft toy. Make a list.

Discuss

- How does your list compare with that of others in the class?
- If you were allowed to take only one item of sentimental value, what would it be?
- Have you ever taken personal mementos with you when you have been away from home?
- Why do you think people might like to surround themselves with familiar things when they are in unfamiliar surroundings?

Service

A homely atmosphere is important in Hospice care.

A hospice is a community where care is given to people with a terminal illness. The doctors, nurses and other helpers have a special way of looking after people who are going to die. The first hospice was set up in Ireland in 1890. It was founded by the Sisters of Charity of St. Vincent de Paul in Harold's Cross, Dublin.

A hospice is run more like a home than a hospital. The walls are painted in bright colours, cheerful pictures decorate the walls, and colourful curtains hang by the windows. Fresh flowers and plants are in bloom everywhere. The patients make their rooms homely too, by putting up their photographs, pictures and mementos. They can use their own sheets, duvet covers, rugs and bedspreads. At meal times patients are given their favourite food and drink.

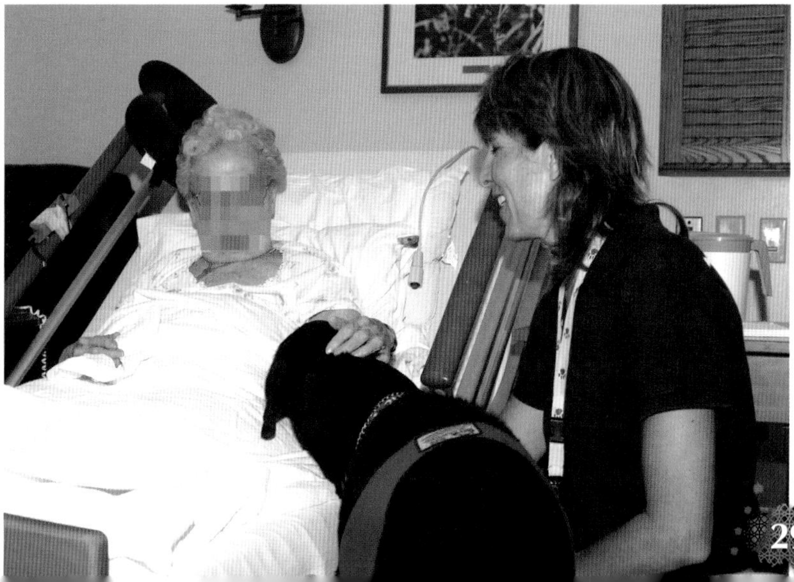

Visiting a patient in a hospice. (Patient's identity with-held.)

If people are able, they can take part in bingo, music, arts and crafts, or avail of aromatherapy, massage and hairdressing. When the weather is good there are wheelchair walks around the gardens. Visitors are always welcome. Families arrive with babies and small children. Favourite pets are sometimes brought along to visit their sick owners.

A person who comes to stay in a hospice knows that he/she is going to die. The staff are open and honest about death. Doctors and nurses spend a lot of time talking and listening to each patient. Drugs are given to ease and control the pain in the body. Counsellors are also available to help patients cope with their emotional pain. Chaplains visit too. They talk, listen and pray with each patient helping them to cope with the pain in their spirit. The staff and volunteers all work together to make each patient as comfortable as possible.

Vision

Dr. Cicely Saunders is the founder of the Modern Hospice Movement. In 1967 she founded St. Christopher's Hospice, London. Dr. Saunders is a Christian, a member of the Church of England. She believes God called her to care for the dying. It was her vision to help people to die with dignity. She wanted each person to be treated with love and kindness and to feel at peace near the end. When someone is very ill everyone is affected, family, friends and carers. Hospice care focuses on the welfare of each patient, and on his/her family as well.

Dr. Cicely Saunders

The care and respect shown to a dying person is also offered to the patient's family. This is often a sad and difficult time for relatives and friends. The hospice offers a counselling service to the families both before and after a bereavement. Today there are over 100 hospices throughout the UK, and a growing number in Ireland too. The Hospice Movement is developing internationally. Hospice care is now available in Europe and in the United States of America.

Leadership

Commitment

The Director is the leader of a hospice community. He or she ensures that the hospice is run according to the vision and ideas of the founder. The director must also ensure the hospice runs smoothly on a day to day basis. It is his/her task to co-ordinate the work of the doctors, nurses, counsellors, chaplains, volunteers, cleaning staff and catering staff.

Everything is done with the best interests of the patients in mind. Hospice staff work hard to provide a high level of patient care. They make a commitment to:

- ❖ Create a homely atmosphere in the Hospice.
- ❖ Provide pain relief and treat patients with love and respect.
- ❖ Help each person to die with dignity.

Questions

Knowledge

1. a. What is a hospice?
   b. What is a terminal illness?
2. What kind of service does the hospice provide for people with a terminal illness?
3. a. Who is the founder of the Modern Hospice Movement?
   b. What was the founder's vision for hospice care?

Understanding

1. a. Describe some of the roles for patient care in a hospice.
   b. What skills and gifts are required to carry out these roles effectively?
2. What is the level of commitment to patient care in a hospice?
3. Why might a family choose hospice care instead of hospital care for a dying relative.

Research

- Find out about hospice care in your area.
  a. Where is the hospice located?
  b. What is it like inside the building?
  c. What are the grounds like outside the building?
  d. What roles do full-time and volunteer staff have in the hospice?
  e. Describe the role of any one member of staff.
  f. Are fundraising events held for the hospice?
  - Compile the information on a fact sheet.

World Religions

Key Concept

Religions: organisations that express belief in God or gods through prayer, worship and a way of life.

Objective

Identify five major world religions or communities of faith found in Ireland today.

Activity: *"Settling in"*

TASK: DISCOVERING FACTS ABOUT MEMBERS OF THE CLASS COMMUNITY.

- Group together according to:
  - eye colour.
  - mode of transport to school.
  - participation in certain sports.
  - languages fluently spoken.
  - membersip of a church or religion.
  - sports clubs or teams supported.
  - preference for a particular type of music.

Discuss

- What new facts did you learn about other members of the class?
- Did everyone settle in and have a place among the groups?
- What religions are represented in this class, and in this school?
- Can you name the major world religions?

Religions

There are five major world religions.

A community of faith is a group of people who share the same set of religious beliefs. The majority of people living in this country are Christians and belong to the Christian community of faith. However people of other religions live here too.

St. Patricks Day
St. Patricks Day
People of many religions live here now.

Many families come to this country to find new jobs and a better way of life. Some even came here to escape war and violence in their own countries. When people settle in a new place, they bring their religious beliefs and way of life with them. So the religions of Judaism, Islam, Hinduism and Buddhism have become part of life here now. People who belong to these communities of faith now live in every country in the world.

World Religions

The five major world religions that express a belief in and worship God or gods are:

- Christianity.
- Judaism.
- Islam.
- Hinduism.
- Buddhism.

❖ Christianity, Judaism and Islam express a belief in one God.

❖ Hinduism expresses a belief in many gods.

❖ Belief in God or gods is not a feature of Buddhism.

❖ Each religion is referred to as a community of faith.

Christianity

❖ Christians believe in one God.

❖ Jesus Christ is the founder of Christianity.

❖ The Bible is the sacred text.

❖ A church is the place of worship.

❖ Christianity began about 2,000 years ago.

❖ The cross is the symbol of Christianity. The cross symbolises the crucifixion and resurrection of Jesus. Jesus was put to death on the cross. God raised him again to new life.

Judaism

❖ Jews believe in one God.

❖ Abraham and Moses are the founders of Judaism.

❖ The Tenakh is the sacred text.

❖ A synagogue is the place of worship.

❖ Judaism began about 4,000 years ago.

❖ The Star of David is the most widely used symbol of Judaism. David was one of the great kings of the Jewish people long ago.

Islam

❖ Muslims believe in one God.

❖ The prophet Muhammad is the founder of Islam.

❖ The Qur'an is the sacred text.

❖ A mosque is the place of worship.

❖ Islam began about 1,500 years ago.

❖ The five pointed star and crescent moon is the common symbol of Islam. The star represents the Five Pillars that are the basis of Muslim life.

Hinduism

❖ Hindus believe in many gods.

❖ This religion is so old that no one knows exactly who is the founder.

❖ The Vedas is the sacred text.

❖ A mandir is the place of worship.

❖ Hinduism began about 4,500 years ago.

❖ The symbol of Hinduism is the holy sound OM or AUM. This sound is used in a special type of prayer called meditation.

Buddhism

❖ Buddhists have no need for a belief in God or gods.

❖ Siddhartha Gautama, later known as the Buddha, is the founder of Buddhism.

❖ The Tipitaka is the sacred text.

❖ A temple is the place of worship.

❖ Buddhism began about 2,500 years ago.

❖ The symbol of Buddhism is an eight-spoked wheel. The wheel symbolises the eight steps for right living taught by the Buddha.

Basic facts about the major world religions

Religion	*Founder*	*Sacred text*	*Place of Worship*	*Founding Date*
Christianity	Jesus	The Bible	Church	2,000 years ago
Judaism	Abraham Moses	The Tenakh	Synagogue	4,000 years ago
Islam	Muhammad	The Qur'an	Mosque	1,500 years ago
Hinduism	Unknown	The Vedas	Mandir	4,500 years ago
Buddhism	Siddhartha Gautama-Buddha	The Tipitaka	Temple	2,500 years ago

Location of the major world religions today

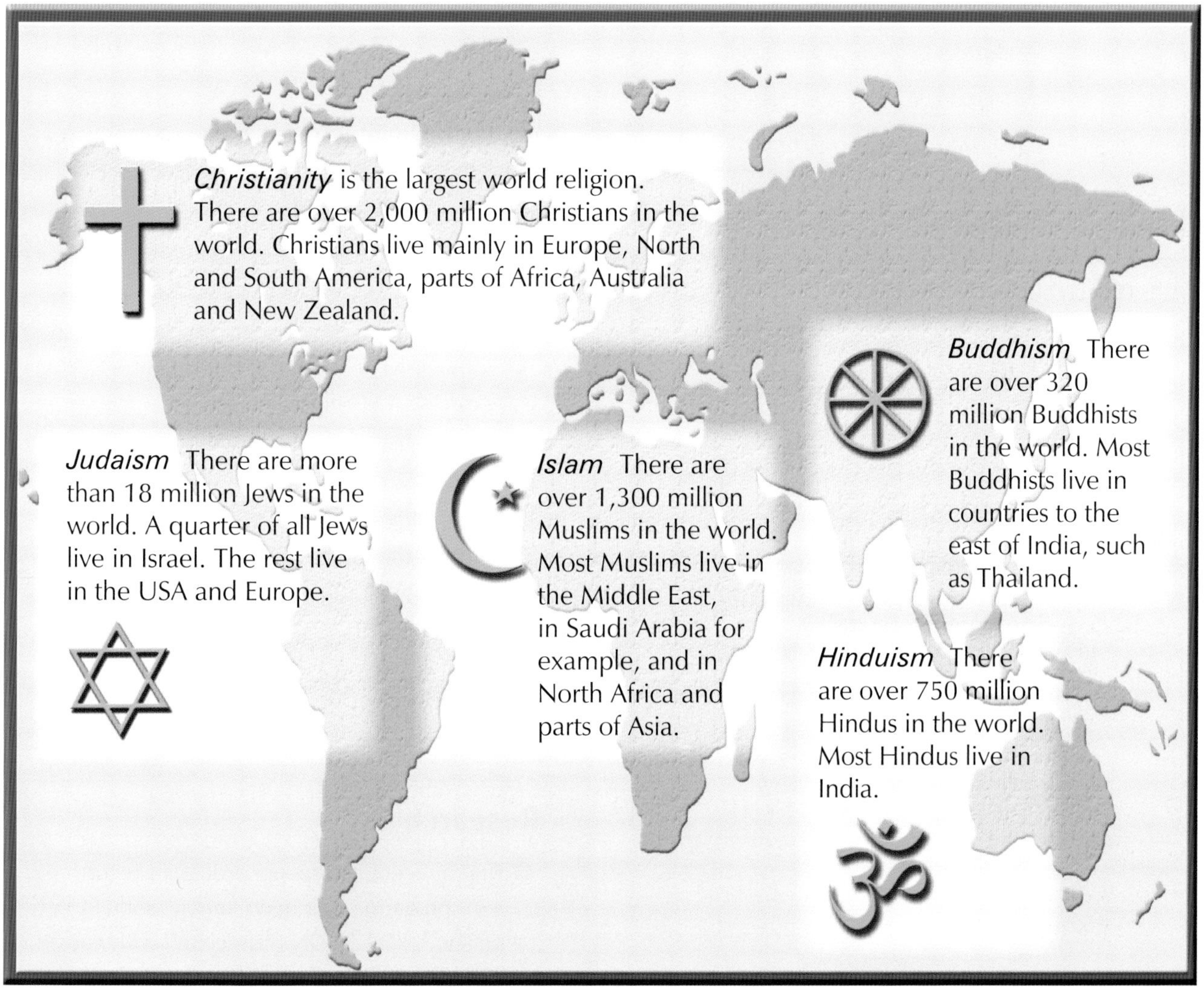
Christianity is the largest world religion. There are over 2,000 million Christians in the world. Christians live mainly in Europe, North and South America, parts of Africa, Australia and New Zealand.
Judaism There are more than 18 million Jews in the world. A quarter of all Jews live in Israel. The rest live in the USA and Europe.
Islam There are over 1,300 million Muslims in the world. Most Muslims live in the Middle East, in Saudi Arabia for example, and in North Africa and parts of Asia.
Buddhism There are over 320 million Buddhists in the world. Most Buddhists live in countries to the east of India, such as Thailand.
Hinduism There are over 750 million Hindus in the world. Most Hindus live in India.

Activity

Matching Exercise

1. Link the **founder** to the religion:

Jesus ❍	❍ Hinduism
Buddha ❍	❍ Judaism
Prophet Muhammad ❍	❍ Buddhism
Abraham and Moses ❍	❍ Christianity
Founder unknown ❍	❍ Islam

2. Link the **sacred text** to the religion:

The Tipitaka ❍	❍ Hinduism
The Bible ❍	❍ Judaism
The Qur'an ❍	❍ Buddhism
The Vedas ❍	❍ Christianity
The Tenakh ❍	❍ Islam

3. Link the **place of worship** to the religion:

Church ❍	❍ Hinduism
Synagogue ❍	❍ Judaism
Mandir ❍	❍ Buddhism
Mosque ❍	❍ Christianity
Temple ❍	❍ Islam

4. Link a **country** to a religion:

Ireland ❍	❍ Hinduism
Israel ❍	❍ Judaism
India ❍	❍ Buddhism
Thailand ❍	❍ Christianity
Saudi Arabia ❍	❍ Islam

5. Link the **founding date** to the religion:

1,500 years ago ❍	❍ Hinduism
2,000 years ago ❍	❍ Judaism
2,500 years ago ❍	❍ Buddhism
4,000 years ago ❍	❍ Christianity
4,500 years ago ❍	❍ Islam

Michael
Mathesie
David
Brian
Blake
Andy
Samantha
Kasten
David
Sheree
Alan
Slotnick
Harvey
Michael
Robert
Simon
Patrick
Cathy
Joy

Most people in the world today belong to a religion.

Questions

Knowledge

1. What is a community of faith?
2. Name five world religions or communities of faith found in Ireland today.
3. What three world religions express belief in one God?
4. Name the community of faith that expresses belief in many gods.
5. What is the oldest major world religion and where is it mainly found today?
6. Who is the founder of Buddhism?
7. What is the sacred text of Islam?
8. Where do Christians go to pray and worship God?
9. What is a synagogue?
10. Explain the symbol of Hinduism.

Research

- Find a recent newspaper article, or record a TV programme or news item about a person, place or event associated with any one of the five major world religions.
  - Present this information to the class.

Christianity

Key Concepts

Founder: the person who established a community or organisation for a special purpose.

Inspiring vision: a dream or idea so powerful it motivates people to act on it.

Sacred text: the book of holy or sacred writings of a community of faith.

Gospel: the 'Good News' of the life, death and resurrection of Jesus Christ in the New Testament.

Revelation: the way in which God chose to make himself known to human beings.

Objective

Retell the story of the founder and earliest followers of Christianity.

Activity: *"A class census"*

TASK: TO DISCUSS THE FUNCTION OF A CENSUS. (An official assessment of the population.)

✦ Carry out an informal census in the class and fill out the form below.

Class Census Date:_______	
Name of class:	
Name of religion teacher:	
Number of pupils present in class today:	
Number of pupils absent from class today:	
Number of pupils who normally go home for lunch:	
Number of pupils who stay in school for lunch:	
Number of pupils who walked to school today:	
Number of pupils who came to school by bus:	
Number of pupils who came to school by car:	
Number of pupils who cycled to school today:	
Name of student who filled in this census:______________	

Discuss

- What are the main findings in the class census?
- Explain how this information could be useful in school planning.
- A census was carried out by the Romans in Palestine at the time of Jesus. How would information from a census be of use to the Romans?

Founder

When Jesus was born the Romans were taking a census of the Jewish population in Palestine.

Jesus of Nazareth is the founder of Christianity. He lived about 2,000 years ago in Palestine, which is now called Israel.

The Birth of Jesus

Jesus' birth was a special event for many people. His mother was a young Jewish girl who lived in the village of Nazareth, her name was Mary. One day an angel spoke to Mary and told her she would have a baby. She would name him Jesus. Her child would be the Son of God.

Some time later, Mary and her fiancé Joseph travelled to Joseph's home town of Bethlehem to sign their name on a census for the Roman Emperor. The young couple found shelter in a stable. Mary's child was born there, and she laid him in a manger.

The rich and poor came to visit them. A group of shepherds left their flocks to look for a baby lying in a manger. "It is Christ the Lord," the angel told them.

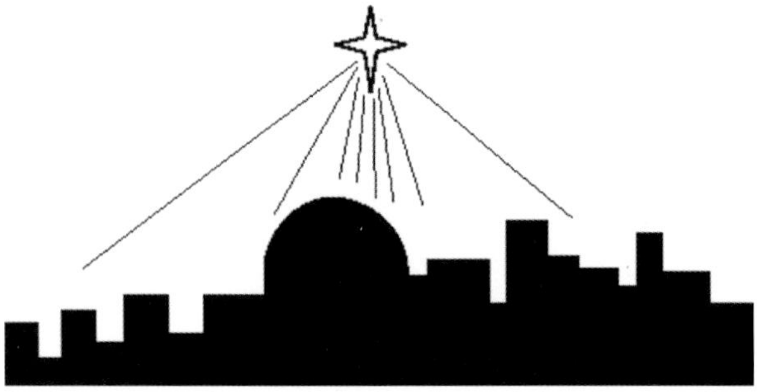

Wealthy astrologers arrived from the East following a new star in the night sky. They believed it was a sign that a new king was born.

The family later returned home to Nazareth where Jesus grew up with Mary, and Joseph his foster father. When he was old enough, Jesus learned a trade and became a carpenter and a builder in the village.

Inspiring Vision

The Baptism of Jesus

Jesus' adult life brought a change of direction. When he was thirty years old he went to John the Baptist at the River Jordan and asked to be baptised. There Jesus had a vision of God's great love for the world. He felt called to go and tell everyone about it. His vision of the love of God inspired him to become a travelling teacher.

The work of Jesus

Jesus went from town to town throughout Palestine, teaching and preaching about the love of God. He told parables to get his message across. He worked miracles and often healed people who were sick or disabled. He offered people God's forgiveness for their sins. Crowds followed him everywhere. They came to listen to his teaching and to be cured of their illnesses.

A small group joined Jesus and became his disciples. For almost three years they travelled together all over the country. When Jesus arrived in the city of Jerusalem, people lined the streets to welcome him. When he went up to the Temple, the Jewish place of worship, large crowds gathered around him to listen to his teaching.

The Crucifixion

INRI

Jesus' death and resurrection occurred a week later. The Jewish leaders in the city became worried. They were afraid the travelling teacher was getting too powerful. He was a danger, so they plotted to get rid of him.

On the Thursday evening Jesus had a special meal with his disciples. It was their last meal together, it is called the Last Supper.

Later that night Jesus was arrested and put on trial. He was sent to Pontius Pilate, the Roman Governor, who gave orders for Jesus to be put to death. On Friday Jesus was crucified and died on the cross. His body was placed in a tomb.

Easter Sunday

On Easter Sunday morning Jesus' friends went to visit the tomb, but found it was empty. Jesus later appeared to his followers. They were totally amazed. It was then they realised that Jesus was alive. God had raised him from the dead. Christians call this the Resurrection. Jesus appeared many times to his disciples before ascending body and soul to heaven.

At Pentecost, Jesus' followers realised he was alive and with them forever through the Holy Spirit of God. The apostles now had the confidence to travel far and wide teaching the Good News that Jesus Christ is the Son of God. This was the beginning of the religion of Christianity.

Sacred text

Gospel

Revelation

The Bible is the Word of God. It is the sacred text of Christianity. The story of Jesus is written in the first four books of the New Testament. This is the Gospel, it means "good news".

The Gospel tells the Good News of Jesus'
- Life,
  - Death,
    - Resurrection.

The Gospel is an account of Revelation, the special way in which Jesus himself reveals or shows to us what God is like.

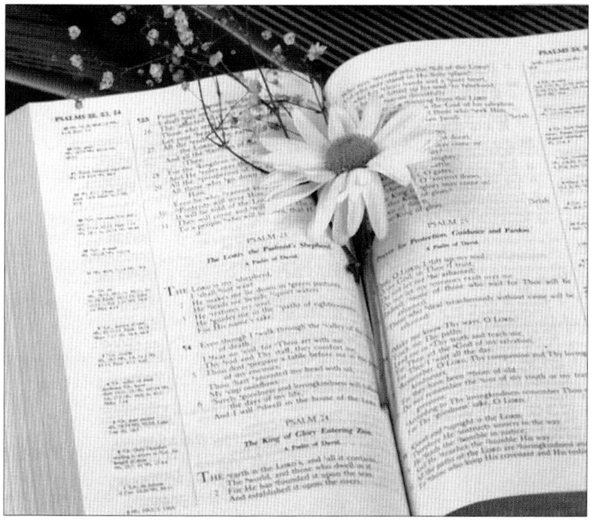

The Bible.

Questions

Knowledge

1. Name the community of faith founded by Jesus Christ.
2. Who is the founder of Christianity?
3. Who were the first followers of Jesus?
4. What religion was Jesus and his disciples born into?
5. Where did the religion of Christianity begin?
6. Where do Christians find most of their information about Jesus?
7. What is the Gospel?
8. What do Christians believe about Jesus Christ?

Understanding

1. How does the Gospel show that the birth of Jesus was an important event?
2. What inspired Jesus to become a travelling teacher?
3. What do Christians believe happened on the first Easter Sunday morning?
4. Why do you think Christians have such a high regard for their sacred text?

Research

- Jesus spent a large part of his life employed as a builder and a carpenter. Find out more about the work of a carpenter in Jesus' time.
  - What kind of buildings would Jesus have worked on?
  - What kind of woodwork skills would he have acquired?
  - In what way was it hard physical work?
  - Would his background as a tradesman have helped Jesus in any way as a travelling teacher spreading the Word of God?
  - Reflect on the information you uncover.
  - Discuss your ideas with the class.

Judaism

Key Concepts

Founder: the person who established a community or organisation for a special purpose.

Inspiring vision: a dream or idea so powerful it motivates people to act on it.

Sacred text: the book of holy or sacred writing of a community of faith.

Revelation: the way in which God chose to make himself known to human beings.

Objective

Retell the story of the founder/earliest followers of Judaism.

Activity: *"Trust Journey"*

TASK: TO UNDERSTAND THE CONCEPT OF TRUST.

You will need: two volunteers (A and B), and the use of a scarf.

✦ Select two students.
Demonstrate a trust journey to the class.
A = the guide. B = the traveller.

A. The guide must promise to lead the traveller safely on a journey around the classroom.

B. The traveller must agree to be guided around the classroom.

✦ The traveller is blindfolded. The guide takes the traveller's hand or arm.

✦ Both students set off slowly around the room. The guide assists the traveller to carefully negotiate such obstacles as desks, chairs, schoolbags etc.

Discuss

- Name the volunteers.
  - The guide was ________________.
  - The traveler was ________________.
- What did the guide promise to do?
- What did the traveler agree to do?
- Did the traveler trust the guide to lead him/her safely around the room? How do you know?
- What does it feel like to trust someone?

Founder
Inspiring Vision

Abraham trusted God to guide him on a long journey to the Promised Land.

Abraham, one of the founders of Judaism, lived about 4,000 years ago. He is sometimes given the title "Father of Judaism".

Abraham and his wife Sarah lived for many years in the city of Ur. They later moved to Haran. Although the couple were married a long time they had no children.

People at that time worshipped many different gods. It occured to Abraham that there is one God above all other gods. He began to worship the one God, it changed his life.

Abraham had a vision, an "inner call" from God. He believed God was asking him to leave everything and set out on a journey to another place. Abraham said "Yes" and agreed to go even though he did not know the way. He let God lead him because he trusted in God to take care of him. God promised Abraham land and many descendants and guided him safely to the Promised Land of Canaan.

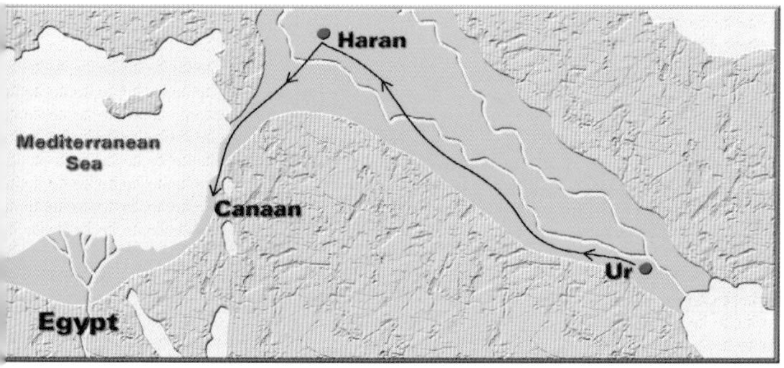
Haran
Mediterranean Sea
Canaan
Ur
Egypt

Abraham's journey to the Promised Land.

Sacred text

Revelation

God said, "This is the land that I promised you. I will give it to you and all your descendants". Abraham and Sarah set up their tents and lived peacefully in Canaan for many years.

One evening while Abraham was praying, God spoke to him again. He told him not to worry about not having any children: "You will have as many descendants as there are stars in the sky. Your descendants will be my special people". God then made a covenant with Abraham. This covenant was a sacred agreement. God promised to look after Abraham and his descendants forever. Abraham promised in return that his people would worship God, and obey God's laws.

In their old age Abraham and Sarah had a baby boy. They called their son Isaac.

The story of Abraham's journey of faith is told in a sacred text called the Torah which is part of the Tenakh, Judaism's sacred text. The Torah is written on scrolls in the Hebrew language. It contains an account of Revelation, the special way in which God revealed, or made himself known, to the Jewish people.

The Torah.

Questions

Knowledge

1. Name the community of faith first founded by Abraham and later Moses.
2. What title do Jews give to Abraham?
3. What vision changed the course of Abraham's life?
4. What is the Promised Land?
5. What is the name of the sacred agreement that God made with Abraham?
6. What did God promise Abraham?
7. What did Abraham promise God in return?
8. In what sacred text would you find the story of Abraham?

Understanding

1. Why is Abraham an important person in the history of Judaism? Give reasons for your answer.
2. What vision inspired Abraham to change the pattern of his life?
3. Where do we find the story of God's revelation to the Jewish people?
4. What do you think was so special about Isaac?

Research

- Find out more about the nomadic way of life.

Abraham and his family were nomads. Long ago they travelled across the deserts to the land of Canaan. The lifestyle of present day nomads, or Bedouin, in the Middle East has changed little since the time of Abraham.

- Find out about modern day nomadic life in the Middle East.
- Use the following headings: shelter; tents; clothing; food; travel; animals.
- Illustrate each section with drawings, pictures or diagrams.
- Share your findings with the class.

Islam

Key Concepts

Founder: the person who established a community or organisation for a special purpose.

Inspiring vision: a dream or idea so powerful it motivates people to act on it.

Sacred text: the book of holy or sacred writings of a community of faith.

Revelation: the way in which God chose to make himself known to human beings.

Objective

Retell the story of the founder and earliest followers of Islam.

Activity: *"Quick Quiz"*

TASK: FIND OUT WHAT EVERYONE ALREADY KNOWS ABOUT THE RELIGION OF ISLAM.

- Can you name....?
  - The founder of Islam.
  - The country where Islam began.
  - The God of Islam.
  - The sacred text of Islam.
  - The event that marked the start of Islam.
  - The holy city of Islam.
  - The location of Islam's holiest shrine.
  - The followers of the religion of Islam.

Discuss

- How many questions were you able to answer correctly?
- Apply a similar list of questions to another major world religion. Would you know most of those answers too?

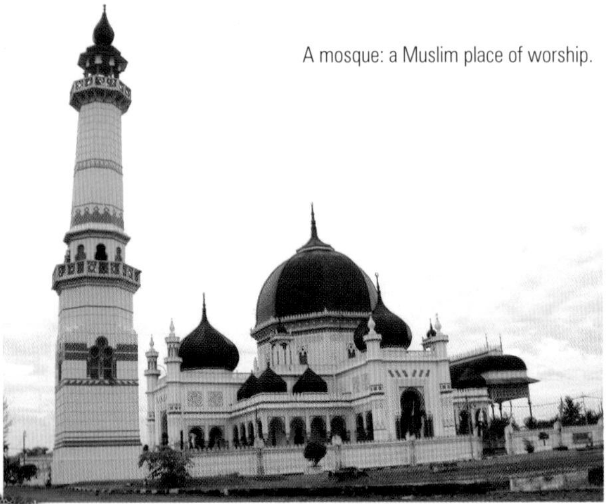

A mosque: a Muslim place of worship.

Founder

Inspiring Vision

Islam is one of the fastest growing religions in the world.

The religion of Islam was founded 1,500 years ago by the prophet Muhammad. Muhammad was born in Mecca in a country that today is called Saudi Arabia. His parents died when he was a child and he was raised by his uncle's family. Muhammad grew up to be a merchant in the city of Mecca where he bought and sold goods in the market. He got married in his mid-twenties and had a number of children.

Mecca in those days was a busy place. Traders came from far and wide to buy and sell goods in the market. Pilgrims came in large numbers to pray to statues of the gods at a shrine in the centre of the city. Local business people made a lot of money from both the traders and the pilgrims.

Muhammad became troubled by the level of corruption in Mecca. The people had a lot of bad habits - lying, cheating, gambling, fighting and drinking too much alcohol. Muhammad began to go off by himself to the hills outside the city. He needed to be alone to think and to pray.

One day when he was alone in a cave Muhammad had a vision. An angel spoke to him and told him that there is one God, Allah, and Muhammad was to be God's messenger. Muhammad rushed home to tell his wife what had happened. She was the first person to believe that Muhammad was a holy man, a prophet. The angel spoke to Muhammad many times. The angel's words to the prophet were later written down in a sacred text called the Qur'an.

Muhammad began to teach his message in the streets of Mecca. He told people about the one God, Allah and asked them to change their ways. Only a few listened. His message was bad for trade and business in the city. In the end he was forced to leave. Muhammad took his family and a small group of followers and travelled across the desert to Medina. The journey from Mecca to Medina is called the Hijra. This event marks the beginning of Islam.

Muhammad and his teachings were welcomed in Medina and he soon became ruler of the city. Muhammad later went back to Mecca with a large army. He removed all the statues of the gods from the shrine, and changed it into a shrine to the one God, Allah. Muhammad taught his followers to believe in Allah and live good lives. Mecca became the holy city of Islam. Muhammad died in Medina aged 62 years.

Sacred text
Revelation

The story of the prophet and the Word of Allah are contained in the Qur'an, the sacred text of Islam. The Qur'an is written in Arabic. Muslims believe the Word of Allah was revealed directly to Muhammad through the messages of the angel.

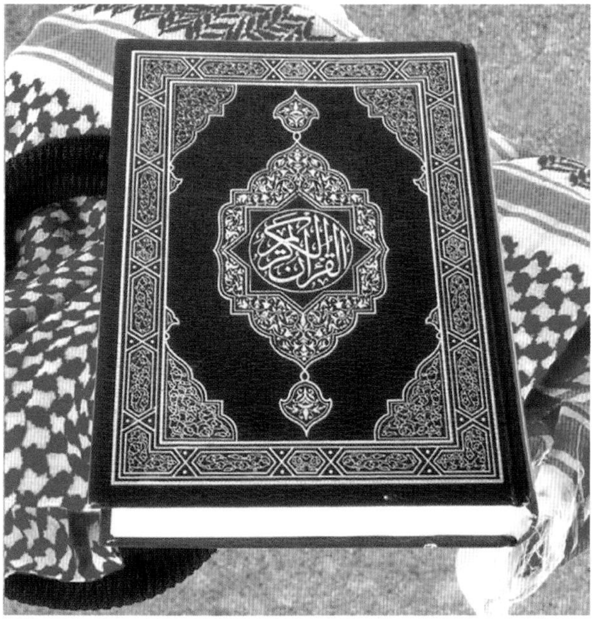

The Qur'an.

Questions

Knowledge

1. Name the community of faith founded by the prophet Muhammad.
2. In what country did Islam begin or originate?
3. Give two reasons why Mecca was a busy city long ago.
4. Where did Muhammad have his first vision or religious experience?
5. Who communicated God's revelation to Muhammad?
6. What message did the angel give to Muhammad?
7. Give two reasons why Muhammad and his followers left Mecca.
8. What is the sacred text of Islam?

Understanding

1. What vision inspired a successful businessman like Muhammad to give up everything and teach in the city of Mecca?
2. Why was Muhammad's teaching unpopular with certain people in Mecca?
3. What is the Hijra? Why is it an important event in the religion of Islam?
4. List all the reasons you can think of to explain why Mecca is important to Muslims.

Research

- Select one aspect of the life of the prophet Muhammad and research it in further detail.
  - Try to acquire more information from reference books and the internet. Assemble an account of this aspect of the prophet's life. Remember that, out of the tradition of respect, no image of the prophet may be painted or drawn, or represented in movement or drama.
  - Present an account of your research to the class.

Christian Communities of Faith

Key Concepts

Denomination: a group within Christianity that has its own leaders, beliefs and practices.

Faith/ belief: a set of religious truths that all members of a community of faith believe.

Objective

Name the main Christian Churches and religious groups found in Ireland today.

Activity:

"The Telephone Directory"

TASK: TO BECOME FAMILIAR WITH DIFFERENT CHURCHES AND RELIGIOUS GROUPS.

- ✦ The telephone directory lists all the Christian Churches and places of worship in your area.
- ✦ Notice that some Christian churches are Roman Catholic, some are Protestant and others are Orthodox.

▼ Churches *Golden Pages*

Apostolic Church
67 Pearse St 2 671549

Baptist Churches
Blanchardstown Baptist Church
PO Box 1641 Dublin 15 820533

Catholic
St Patrick's
Cambridge Rd 4 668412
Rivermount
Glenties Pk 11 834371
St Helena's Drive 834322
River Valley
2 river Valley Hts, Swords 840412
Rolestown 840151
Roundwood 281834
Rowlagh
30 Wheatfield Cl 22 623124
13 Glenfield ave 22 626312
Parish Officer 626010
Rush 842731
Rush 843109
Saggart 256920

Church of Ireland
Deanery, Werburgh St 8 278179
Director of Music 278869
St Patrick's Cathedral 375281
Office no 524947
Deanery 574533
Irish Church Missions
Bachelor's Walk 1 378082
If no reply ring 321216
Balbriggan 249224
Balgriffin 345477

Church of Jesus of Latter-Day Saints The (Mormon)
Chapels
48 Bushey Park Rd, Terenure Rd 6 290565
The Willows, Finglas Rd, Glasnevin 11 230995

Churches of Christ, Scientist
First Church of Christ, Scientist,
21 Herbert Pk, 4 268369
Christian Science Reading Room
15 Sth Gt George's St 2 479352

Congregational Church
Kilmainham, Inchicore Rd 8 293299

Coptic Orthodox Church
5 The Pines, Herbert Rd, Bray 286683

Elim Pentecostal Church
Ballyfermot 10 457246

Greek Orthodox Church
46 Arbour Hill 7 377901

Ireland Dublin Mission, The
The Willows, Finglas Rd 11 830681

Jehovah's Witnesses
Bray Congregation 368882
Also 381841
Swords Congregation 640394

Lutheran Church
Adelaide Rd 2 476651

Methodist Churches
Abbey St 1, Dublin Central Mission 674211
Blackrock 386674
Bray 487571
Clontarf 3 632311
Drimnagh 12 697405
Dundrum 14 498652
Dun Laoghaire 480433

Presbyterian Churches
Telephone 778024
Abbey Church 1 674280
Minister's Res 637866
18a Adelaide Rd, Donore 2 275284
Minister's Res 269471
Christ Church, Rathgar 6 497162
Minister's Res 290314

Religious Society of Friends
(Quakers)
Swanbrook Hse, Bloomfield Ave
Morehampton Rd 4 268366

Salvation Army
Public Relations Officer
114 Marlborough St 1 574092
Also evenings 633506
Headquarters Republic of Ireland
114 Marlborough St 1 374061

Unitarian Church
112 St Stephen's Gn West 2 2780638

Victory Christian Fellowship
35 Westland Row 2 331038

01 District

Discuss

- Name one Catholic church.
- Find one Church of Ireland church.
- Can you name one Methodist church?
- Where is the Baptist church?
- Is there a Presbyterian place of worship on this list?
- Can you find the Salvation Army?
- Is there an Orthodox church?
- What other Churches and religious groups are represented on the list?
- Now look up churches/places of worship in your own local telephone directory. Where are the main Christian churches in your area?

Christianity is one of the major world religions. It has over 2,000 million members worldwide. In Ireland, over 90% of the population regard themselves as belonging to a Christian community of faith. These communities are not all the same. There are many different denominations or communities of faith within Christianity.

Denomination

The religion of Christianity is divided. The three main parts within Christianity are:

- ✦ The Roman Catholic Church.
- ✦ The Protestant Churches.
- ✦ The Orthodox Churches.

There are many different Churches in the Protestant tradition. This is also the case, but to a lesser extent, in the Orthodox tradition. Each Church or denomination is a community of faith with its own leaders, and its own set of beliefs and practices.

Christianity

Roman Catholic Church | **Protestant Churches** | **Orthodox Churches**

Protestant Churches:
- Church of Ireland.*
- Methodist Church.
- Presbyterians.
- Baptists.
- Salvation Army.
- Society of Friends

Orthodox Churches:
- Greek.
- Russian.

*In England - Church of England.

Faith/ Belief

The religion of Christianity is based on the life, death and resurrection of Jesus Christ. All Christians share the same basic faith/ belief. They:

- Believe in God.
- Follow the teachings of Jesus.
- Accept the Bible as the Word of God.

However Roman Catholic, Protestant and Orthodox Christians have different beliefs about:

- The leadership of the Church.
- The number of sacraments.
- The meaning of the Eucharist.

Questions

Knowledge

1. To what religion do Catholics and Protestants belong?
2. What are the three main parts within Christianity?
3. a) Who is the founder of Christianity?
   b) Name the sacred text of Christianity?
4. Name six Protestant denominations or communities of faith found in Ireland today.
5. What religious beliefs do all Christians share in common?
6. On what aspects of religious belief do Roman Catholics, Protestants and Orthodox Christians differ?

Understanding

1. Explain how a Roman Catholic, a Protestant and an Orthodox Christian can all belong to the same religion.
2. Think of someone you know who belongs to a particular Christian denomination.
   - Name the community of faith to which he or she belongs.
   - Identify a religious belief that he or she holds.
   - List the ways in which he or she is a Christian just like all other Christians.
3. Why do you think Christians belong to different communities of faith?

Research

Find out about Christian Churches and Religious Groups in your area.

- Using the internet, telephone directory, local maps and the library, try to discover what Christian Churches and other religious groups are established in the area near your home, or near the school.
- In addition to the different Christian Churches, what other religions are represented in the local community?
- Do members of these Churches and religious groups: - live in your neighbourhood?
  - attend your school?
- With the aid of a map or diagram, show the location of different Christian churches and other religious buildings in your locality.

Divisions in Christianity

Key Concept

Church: a community of Christian people.

Objective

Explain the origin of the divisions within Christianity.

Activity: *"Disputes"*

TASK: TO EXPLORE INCIDENTS OF CONFLICT AND TENSION IN OUR LIVES.

- Number the following in order of seriousness.
  - Fight.
  - Difference of opinion.
  - Tiff.
  - Squabble.
  - Disagreement.
  - Schism.
  - Argument.
  - Dispute.
  - Feud.
  - Conflict.
  - Quarrel.
  - Misunderstanding.

Discuss

- What is at the top and bottom of the list?
- Think about an occasion recently where a row or dispute broke out among a group of friends.
  - What was it about?
  - Was it resolved?
- What is the best way to settle a dispute?
- What happens when a row or a dispute goes unresolved?

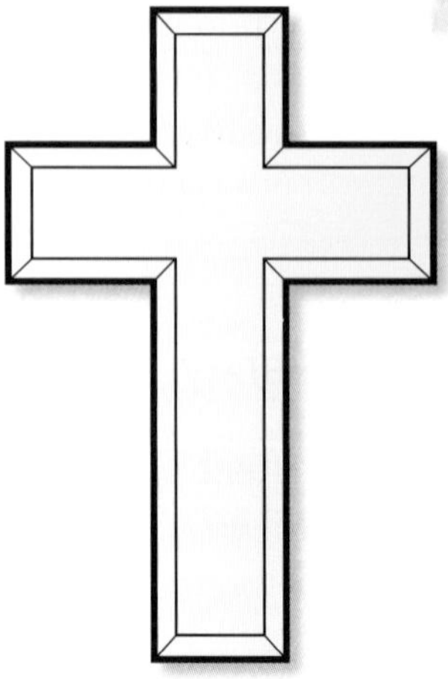

Church

Some disputes within Christianity went unresolved.

Christianity is divided into Roman Catholic, Orthodox and Protestant Churches. Have you ever wondered how these divisions came about?

After Jesus' death and resurrection, the apostles spread the Good News and the Christian Church grew and expanded for over 1,000 years. However as Christianity grew, certain problems began to develop. Disagreements arose about such issues as:

- Church leadership.
- Christian beliefs.

The dispute were not resolved. Things got worse and eventually caused two major divisions within Christianity.

The Great Schism in the 11th century, in which the Christian Church split into two parts: Catholic and Orthodox.

The Reformation in the 16th century, which gave rise to the Protestant Churches.

Christianity Timeline

1st century — **The beginning of Christianity**

11th century — **The Great Schism**
- Catholic Church.
- Orthodox Church.

16th century — **The Reformation**
- Protestant Churches.

21st century — **Christianity today**

Mostly Catholic.

Mostly Protestant.

Mostly Orthodox.

Black Sea
Rome
Constantinople.
Mediterranean Sea

Location of Roman Catholic, Protestant and Orthodox Churches in Europe today.

The Great Schism

For hundreds of years Christianity was the main religion in Europe. Then in the 11th century a dispute about Church leadership split Christianity in half. This division known as the Great Schism divided Eastern and Western Christianity.

Christians in the East wanted the Patriarch who lived in the city of Constantinople (now Istanbul) to be head of the Church. Christians in the West believed the head of the Church should continue to be the Pope who lived in Rome, in Italy. The disagreement was not resolved and in 1054CE the two sides separated. Christianity divided into Catholic and Orthodox, a division that continues to the present day.

It should be noted that:

- ❖ the word Catholic means universal, or everywhere in the the world.
- ❖ the word Orthodox means the correct or the right way.

In 1964 Pope Paul VI met Patriarch Athenagoras, the first time a Pope and a Patriarch met and spoke to one another since the Schism of 1054. This sculpture commemorates that occasion.

The Reformation

In the 16th century, almost 500 years later, Christianity divided again. Disagreements arose over issues of faith and belief including the best way to understand the Bible. There was also major concern over corrupt practices that had developed in the Church at the time.

Martin Luther published his "95 Theses" in the town of Wittenberg, Germany.

A German monk named Martin Luther protested strongly about all this and called for change and reform in the Catholic Church. His protest led to the Reformation, the second great split within Christianity. This gave rise to the division between Catholic and Protestant Churches. New Churches set up at that time were called Protestant because the people who formed them had made a protest.

Luther's ideas spread quickly. Other reformers such as John Calvin and John Knox added to the calls for change. Christians in Europe became divided between those who followed the reformers, and those who remained in the Catholic Church and sought to change it from within. In England for example people broke away from the Catholic Church and formed the Church of England. The English king became head of the Church.

By the end of the 16th century, Europe was divided into mainly Protestant and Catholic areas. This division continues to the present day. Over time different reformed, or Protestant, communities of faith were established such as Presbyterian and Baptist Churches, The Society of Friends (Quakers) and later the Methodist Church and The Salvation Army among others.

Questions

Knowledge

1. When did the first major division take place in Christianity?
2. What was the cause of the conflict between Christians in the East and West?
3. What happened as a result of the Great Schism?
4. Name some countries where Orthodox Churches exist today.
5. When did the second major split occur in the Christian religion?
6. Who was Martin Luther?
7. What was the source of the conflict between Christians at the time of the Reformation?
8. What happened as a result of the Reformation?
9. Why are certain Churches called Protestant Churches?
10. Name six Protestant Churches.

Understanding

1. Outline some key facts about:
   a. The Great Schism.
   b. The Reformation.
2. Describe the kind of person you think Martin Luther and the other reformers might have been. Give reasons for your answer.

Research

- Find out more about Martin Luther.
  - When and where was he born?
  - What early experience influenced his direction in life?
  - Where did he work?
  - What were some of the most challenging moments in his life?
  - Name some of the writings that he published.
  - When and where did he die?
  - Assemble a list of points and present them to the class.

Christian Identity

Key Concept

Identity: the distinct characteristics by which a person or group is recognised.

Objective

State how the main Christian Churches in this country express their unique identity.

Activity: *"Passports"*

TASK: TO EXPLORE INDIVIDUAL DIFFERENCE AMONG CLASS MEMBERS.

✦ You will need: a tape measure or ruler.

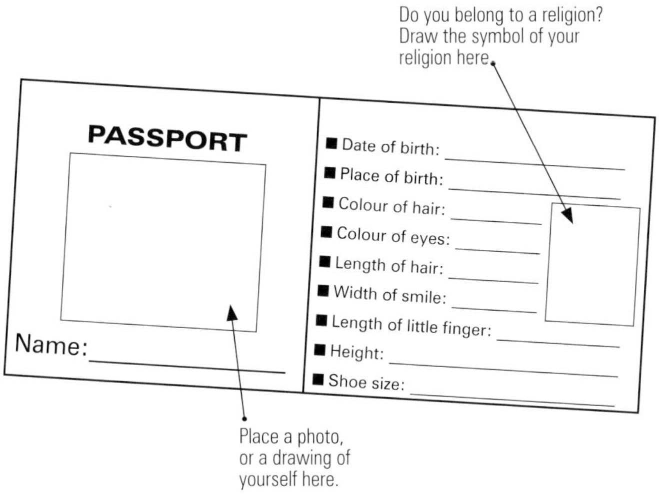

Do you belong to a religion? Draw the symbol of your religion here.
PASSPORT
Name:
Date of birth:
Place of birth:
Colour of hair:
Colour of eyes:
Length of hair:
Width of smile:
Length of little finger:
Height:
Shoe size:
Place a photo, or a drawing of yourself here.

A passport highlights a person's unique identity. Our identity is what makes us different from everybody else.

Discuss

- In what ways are members of the class different from one another?
- Can you think of any other ways in which people differ from each other?
- How should we treat people who are different from us?

Identity

One way in which people differ from each other is in their religious beliefs.

We all respect our own religious beliefs. We must also respect the beliefs and practices of people who belong to other religious traditions.

Christianity in the twenty first century is like a big family made up of different parts, the Roman Catholic Church, the Orthodox Churches and the Protestant Churches. These Churches are not different religions, they are different parts of one religion - Christianity.

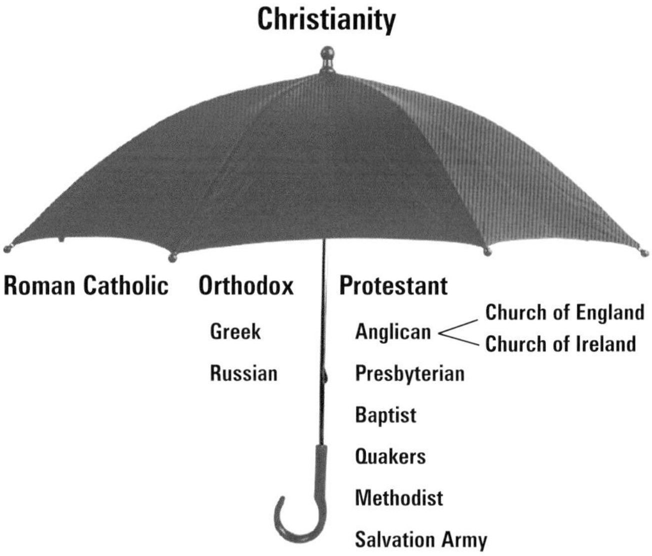

Christianity
Roman Catholic
Orthodox
Greek
Russian
Protestant
Anglican
Church of England
Church of Ireland
Presbyterian
Baptist
Quakers
Methodist
Salvation Army

The religion or community of faith to which a person belongs is an important part of who they are. All the Christian Churches have their own set of beliefs and practices. Each Church has its own identity, or distinct characteristics, by which it is recognised.

A Church's identity is expressed in:

- ❖ Its form of leadership.
- ❖ Its style of worship.

Roman Catholic

- The Pope is the leader of the Catholic Church and has authority over the Catholic Church throughout the world.

- The Archbishop, bishops and priests lead the Catholic community.
- The Eucharist is central in the Catholic Church, it is celebrated every day. Catholics attend Mass and receive Holy Communion on Sunday.
- Catholics have a special regard for Mary the Mother of God. They pray to Mary believing that she brings their prayers to God.

Orthodox

- The Patriarch of Constantinople is the most senior Bishop but does not have full authority over individual Orthodox Churches.
- A Patriarch, bishops and priests lead the Orthodox community.

- The priest celebrates Divine Liturgy in church on Sunday. Incense is widely used and a male voice choir sings hymns.
- People light candles and pray in front of icons (holy pictures).

Church of Ireland

- The Archbishop of Canterbury is the senior Bishop of the Anglican Communion worldwide, but he does not exercise overall authority.
- In Ireland the Archbishop, bishops, ministers and deacons lead the Church of Ireland community.

- Holy Communion is celebrated in most Anglican churches on Sunday.
- The Altar or Communion table is a central feature in an Anglican Church. A lectern in the shape of an eagle is a common feature in Anglican churches.

Presbyterian

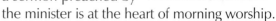

- There is no overall leader and there are no bishops in the Presbyterian tradition. The local church is governed by elders or presbyters.
- On Sunday the Bible, the Word of God, and a sermon preached by the minister is at the heart of morning worship.
- Presbyterians like their church buildings to be plain and simple, both inside and out. There are no stained glass windows, statues or pictures in a kirk, the Presbyterian place of worship.

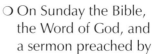

Baptist

- Each Baptist church governs itself. There is no overall leader, no bishops and no priests. A council of lay members makes decisions about church life.
- The pastor leads Sunday service at which there are prayers, hymn singing, Bible readings and a sermon preached from a pulpit.
- Adults, not babies, are baptised in Baptist churches. Adult baptism is by total immersion. It can take place in a baptismal pool in the church or outside in a river or lake.

Quakers

- The Society of Friends has no overall leader. There are no bishops, priests or ministers and there are no sacred buildings.

- An elder organises a meeting that Friends attend in a 'meeting house' on Sunday.
- The meeting is simple, there are no hymns, there is no sermon or communion service. Everyone sits together in silence until someone feels God wants them to speak.

Methodist

- There is no one individual leader and there are no bishops in the Methodist Church.
- Ministers and lay preachers lead Sunday worship. The readings from the Bible and the sermon preached from the pulpit is the focus of worship.

  Singing hymns together is an important part of worship in a Methodist chapel.

Salvation Army

- The structure of the Salvation Army is organised along military lines. Its leaders have military titles such as General, Major and Captain.
- The Minister is called an officer, the members are soldiers and wear uniform.
- The Salvation Army believes that Christians are like soldiers fighting evil in the world.
- Sunday meetings are held in the citadel, the place of worship. Members wear uniform and sing hymns accompanied by brass band music.

Questions

Knowledge

1. What does the word 'identity' mean?
2. What does the term 'religious identity' mean?
3. Select three different Christian Churches:
   a. What is the form of leadership in each Church?
   b. What is distinctive about Sunday worship in each Church?
4. List the main ways in which a person can show respect for:
   a. their own Christian Church.
   b. other Christian Churches.

Understanding

1. How do the Christian Churches express their religious identity?
2. All Christians believe the Good News that Jesus is God. Why then are there different Christian Churches with different forms of leadership and styles of worship?
3. Why is it important to respect the different beliefs and practices of other Christian Churches?

Research

- Discover more about the unique identity of one Protestant denomination through personal contacts, written material and web site exploration. The following headings may be useful in guiding your research.
  - Faith community.
  - Founder.
  - Religious beliefs.
  - Religious practices.
  - This faith community in our local area:
    - Church buildings.
    - Clergy.
    - Sunday services.
    - Church activities.
  - Organise the information you have assembled and present it to the class.

The Catholic Church

Key Concepts

Church: a community of Christian people.

Inspiring vision: a dream or idea so powerful it motivates people to act on it.

Religious Commitment: the decision to make a sincere effort to put one's religious beliefs into practice.

Preaching: to speak out and explain a religious truth and urge people to act on it.

Objectives

State the titles and names of leaders in the Roman Catholic Church.

Explain how Roman Catholics express their religious commitment.

Activity: *"Fact File"*

TASK: TO GATHER FACTUAL INFORMATION ABOUT A LOCAL CATHOLIC CHURCH.

✦ Select a Catholic church near your home or near your school.

1. Where is the church?
2. What is the name of the church?
3. When was the church built?
4. Is there a graveyard near the church?
5. Name a priest of this church.
6. What time is Mass in this church on Sunday?
7. Where is the altar located inside the church?
8. Is there a lectern in the church?
9. Where is the baptismal font?
10. Are there any stained glass windows in the church?

Discuss

- When did you last visit a Catholic church?
- Is the church open or locked during the day?
- Is there anything interesting about the outside of this particular Catholic church?
- What interesting things are there to notice inside the church?

Church

Inspiring vision

The word "church" has two meanings. The building where Catholics go to pray and worship God, and the people who belong to the Catholic Church worldwide.

Inside a Roman Catholic church.

- ❖ The Catholic Church is a community of Christian people who share the same faith in Jesus Christ. Catholics are inspired by the person and teaching of Jesus. They aim to follow his commandment to "love God and love one's neighbour as oneself". This is the inspiring vision behind the work of the Church today.
- ❖ The Church is led and guided by the Pope and by the bishops.
- ❖ The Word of God is found in the Bible and in the teaching of the Church.
- ❖ The Church celebrates seven sacraments.

Leadership roles in the Catholic Church.

People have a variety of leadership roles in the Catholic Church.

Pope
The Pope is the leader of the Catholic Church throughout the world. Catholics believe he is the representative of Jesus Christ on Earth. The Pope is the Bishop of Rome and lives in the Vatican.

Cardinal
Cardinals are chosen by the Pope. They give advice to the Pope on important Church matters.

Pope Francis

Cardinal Sean Brady
Archbishop of Armagh.

Archbishop
An archbishop is a very senior bishop. The Archbishop of Armagh is leader of the Roman Catholic Church in Ireland.

Bishop
The country is divided into large areas called dioceses. The bishop is the leader of the Catholic Church in a diocese. The role of the bishop is to preach and teach the Catholic faith to people in the diocese.

Priest
Within each diocese there are smaller areas called parishes. Priests are men ordained by the bishop to work in parishes. The parish priest is the leader of the Catholic community in a parish. The role of the priest is to celebrate Mass and the sacraments and to preach the message of Jesus.

Lay people
Lay people are baptised Catholics who are not ordained. Some Catholic men and women serve in their parish church on Sunday as Ministers of the Word or Ministers of the Eucharist. Other lay people help in the parish as members of parish organisations.

Religious Commitment

When people belong to a community or to an organisation they make certain commitments. A commitment is a decision to spend time and energy doing something on behalf of others. Being a member of the Catholic Church calls for religious commitment.

Catholics show their religious commitment and put their beliefs into practice by attending Mass on Sunday, celebrating the sacraments and living good Christian lives. Catholic clergy and lay people are called by God to follow Jesus and use their gifts in the service of God and their neighbour.

Sunday Worship

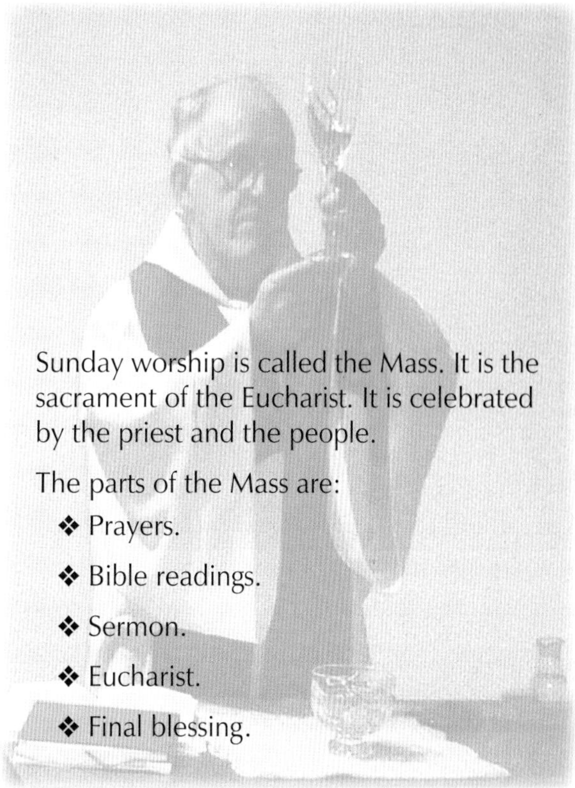

Sunday worship is called the Mass. It is the sacrament of the Eucharist. It is celebrated by the priest and the people.

The parts of the Mass are:

- Prayers.
- Bible readings.
- Sermon.
- Eucharist.
- Final blessing.

The Eucharist
The prayers of the Eucharist are a very important part of the Mass. At the Eucharist a change takes place in the gift of the bread and wine on the altar. Catholics believe it becomes the body and blood of Jesus Christ.

Catholics believe that Jesus is made present in the Eucharist under the appearance of bread and wine.

Sacraments

Seven sacraments are celebrated in the Catholic Church. These are: Baptism, Eucharist, Confirmation, Reconciliation, Marriage, Holy Orders and the Sacrament of the Sick.

Confirmation

Confirmation is a sacrament that is celebrated when a person is about twelve years of age. It is a big event for young people in their last year at primary school. At the ceremony a sponsor stands beside each boy and girl as they make their Confirmation promises. The bishop lays his hand on the young person's head and puts special oil, called chrism, on their forehead. Each candidate prays and welcomes the Holy Spirit of God into their lives.

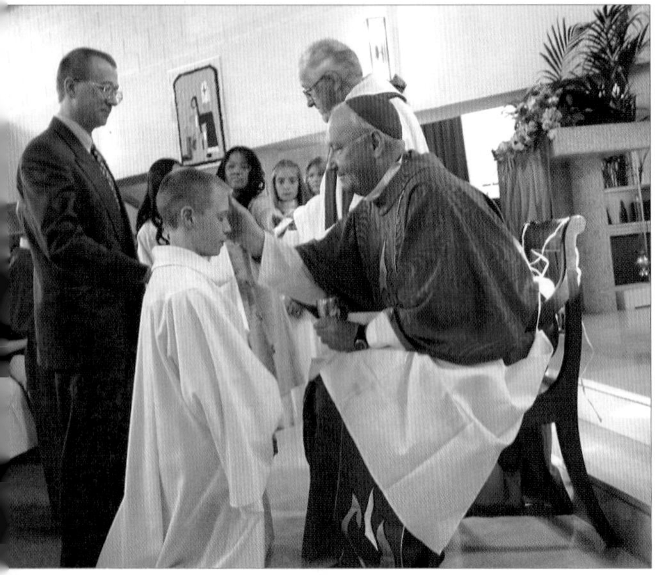

Confirmation in a Roman Catholic church.

Confirmation is a special day for all young people and their families. It is the day when Catholic boys and girls make a special religious commitment. They promise to make a sincere effort to put their faith into practice for the rest of their lives.

Preaching

An important part of the role of the bishop and the priest is to preach the Word of God to people in the diocese and the parish. Bishops and priests speak out and present:

- the teachings of Jesus,
- the teachings of the Church,

and urge Catholics to act on them.

Questions

Knowledge

1. What is the inspiring vision that motivates the work of the Catholic Church?
2. Who is the head of the Catholic Church throughout the world?
3. What is the title and the name of the leader of the Catholic Church in Ireland?
4. Who is the leader of a diocese in the Catholic Church?
5. Who is the leader of the Christian community in a parish?
6. What is the role of a Catholic bishop?
7. What is the role of a Catholic priest?
8. What is religious commitment?
9. State three ways in which Catholics show religious commitment to their faith.
10. Name the sacraments celebrated in the Catholic Church.
11. Who has the leadership role when the Catholic community gathers together at Mass?
12. What religious commitment do young Catholics undertake at the sacrament of Confirmation?

Understanding

1. How do bishops, priests and lay people show their religious commitment in the Catholic Church?
2. How do you think the work of the Catholic Church benefits:
   a. Members of the Church?
   b. Members of the wider community?
3. What do Catholics believe happens at the Prayers of the Eucharist during Mass?

Research

- Make enquiries and gather resources for a bulletin board display on the Catholic Church in your area.
  - Display a map of the local area outlining the extent of the school catchment.
  - Identify the Catholic diocese in which the school is situated. Name the bishop of the diocese and locate Catholic parishes where class members live. Find each parish church and name a priest in that parish.
  - Obtain and display a recent newsletter from each parish. Highlight any activities and events open to young people in these parishes.

The Orthodox Churches

Key Concepts

Church: a community of Christian people.

Religious commitment: the decision to make a sincere effort to put one's religious beliefs into practice.

Objective

State the titles of leaders, and show how religious commitment is expressed in the Orthodox Churches.

Activity: *"Map Work"*

TASK: KNOW THE LOCATION OF ORTHODOX CHURCHES.

Christians in the East who separated from Rome in the 11th century are called Orthodox. Today 90% of Orthodox Christians live in Greece, Russia, Cyprus, Romania, Bulgaria, and Serbia. The largest number live in Greece and Russia.

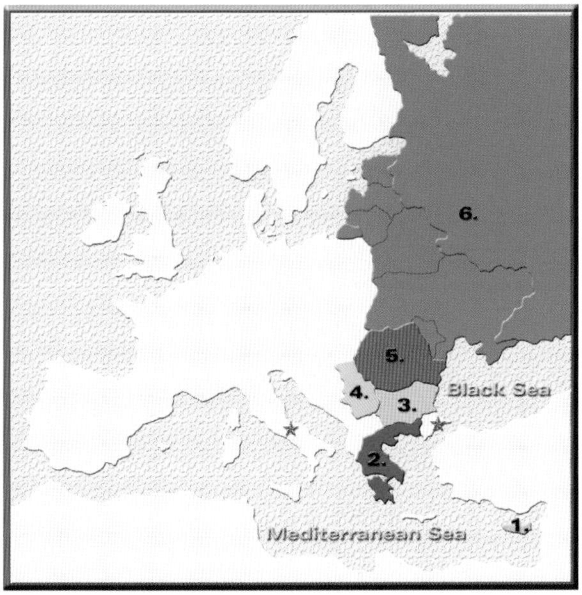
6.
5.
4.
3.
Black Sea
2.
1.
Mediterranean Sea

Countries where most Orthodox Christians live.

Discuss

Using your atlas:

- Name the city that is important for Orthodox Christians in the East.
- Name the city that is important for Roman Catholic Christians in the West.
- Name the countries in Eastern Europe (1-6) where Orthodox Christians live.
- Have you or your family ever visited one of these countries? What is it like there?

Church

Orthodox Christians live mainly in Eastern Europe, however a lot of families have emigrated to other countries in recent years. Many Orthodox families now live in this country where they continue to follow the beliefs and practices of their Church. In Ireland there are small communities of Christians belonging to the Greek and Russian Orthodox Churches.

The Orthodox Churches are a community of people who share the same faith in Jesus Christ. Orthodox Christians are inspired by the person and teaching of Jesus and aim to follow Jesus' commandment to "love God and ones neighbour as oneself".

- There is no overall leader. Each Church is led by a Patriarch and bishops.
- The Bible is important for Orthodox Christians. The Word of God is read and has a place of honour at Divine Liturgy on Sunday and in the celebration of the sacraments.
- Orthodox Churches celebrate seven sacraments.

Dome of an Orthodox Church in Greece.

Leadership roles in Orthodox Churches

Patriarchs
The leaders of the Orthodox Churches are called patriarchs. There is one for each country. The Patriarch of Constantinople is the most senior, yet he is not the overall leader. Instead he guides the other patriarchs in important matters.

Bishop
A bishop leads the Orthodox community in a diocese.

Monk
Monks are members of a community who live, work and worship together in a monastery.

An Orthodox priest.

Priest
Priests are ordained by the bishop to lead the Orthodox community in a parish. The role of a priest is to look after people's spiritual needs by celebrating the sacraments and preaching the message of Jesus.

Deacon
Deacons are men ordained to assist the priest in a parish. Many deacons are married and have families, some deacons become priests.

Religious Commitment

Religious commitment is the decision to make a sincere effort to put one religious beliefs into practice. Orthodox Christians show their religious commitment by:

- ❖ Attending Divine Liturgy on Sunday.
- ❖ Celebrating the sacraments.
- ❖ Living good Christian lives.

Clergy and lay people in the Orthodox Churches are called by God to follow the teaching of Jesus to love God and to love and serve others.

Inside an Orthodox church
In an Orthodox church the altar is behind a large screen decorated with icons. An icon is a picture of Jesus, Mary or the saints. Icons cover the walls and the pillars inside the church. People light candles and say a prayer in front of their favourite icons. There are usually no seats in the church as people stand during religious services. On Sunday the doors of the icon screen are opened and the priest celebrates the mystery of the Eucharist at the altar.

Sunday Worship

Sunday worship is called Divine Liturgy. The parts of Divine Liturgy are:

- ❖ Prayers.
- ❖ Bible reading.
- ❖ Sermon.
- ❖ Holy Eucharist.
- ❖ Final blessing.

Holy Eucharist is a very important part of the Divine Liturgy. Orthodox Christians believe the bread and wine offered to God becomes the body and blood of Jesus Christ. Like Catholics, Orthodox Christians believe in the real presence of Jesus in the Eucharist.

Incense is used a lot during the service. A male voice choir sings hymns; there is no organ music. The priests walk in a solemn procession among the people carrying the Bible and the bread and wine to the altar.

Inside an Orthodox church.

Orthodox priests and deacons leading a Church procession at Easter.

Sacraments

The Orthodox Church celebrates seven sacraments. They are called: Baptism, Chrismation (Confirmation), Holy Communion, Confession, Marriage, Ordination and Holy Unction (Anointing of the Sick).

Baptism

Every child in an Orthodox Church receives three sacraments when he/she is eight days old.

The family bring the baby to the church for the christening. During the ceremony the priest dips the baby three times into the water of the baptismal font. After the Baptism the parents dry the baby and put its clothes back on. Then the child is confirmed. In the Orthodox Church this sacrament is called Chrismation. The priest puts holy oil, called chrism, on the baby. After this, the baby receives Holy Eucharist. The priest gives the baby communion on a spoon.

Questions

Knowledge

1. Where in Europe do the majority of Orthodox Christians live?
2. Who is the most senior leader in an Orthodox Church?
3. What is a monk?
4. What is the role of an Orthodox priest?
5. In what ways do Orthodox Christians show religious commitment to their faith?
6. What happens at Divine Liturgy in church on Sunday?
7. Name the sacraments celebrated in the Orthodox Churches.
8. Which sacraments do Orthodox Christians receive in childhood?

Understanding

1. What titles do different religious leaders have in the Orthodox tradition?
2. How do clergy and lay people show their religious commitment in the Orthodox Churches?
3. What do Orthodox Christians believe happens at the prayers of Holy Eucharist during Sunday worship?

Research

- Find information about the celebration of Easter in the Orthodox Churches.
  - Examine a calendar - when does Easter occur?
  - What is distinctive about Easter ceremonies in the Orthodox tradition?
  - How does it compare with the celebration of Easter in one other Christian Church?
  - Prepare a report and present it to the class.

The Church of Ireland

Key Concepts

Church: a community of Christian people.

Inspiring vision: a dream or idea so powerful it motivates people to act on it.

Preaching: to speak out and explain a religious truth and urge people to act on it.

Religious commitment: the decision to make a sincere effort to put one's religious beliefs into practice.

Objectives

State the titles and names of leaders in the Church of Ireland.

Explain how its members express their religious commitment.

Activity: *"Fact File"*

TASK: TO GATHER FACTUAL INFORMATION ABOUT A LOCAL ANGLICAN CHURCH.

✦ Identify a Church of Ireland church near your home or near your school.

1. Where is the church?
2. What is the name of the church?
3. When was the church built?
4. Is there a graveyard near the church?
5. Name the priest or rector of this parish church.
6. What services are held in the church on Sunday?
7. Inside the church, where is the altar located?
8. Is there a pulpit in the church?
9. Where is the baptismal font?
10. Are there any stained glass windows in the church?

Discuss

- When did you last visit a Church of Ireland church?
- Is the church open or locked during the day?
- Is there anything interesting about the outside of a Church of Ireland church?
- What interesting things are there to notice inside the church?

Church

Inspiring vision

Inside a Church of Ireland church.

A Church is a community of Christian people. The Anglican Communion is the Church of England spread throughout the world. Anglicans in Ireland are members of the Church of Ireland. This is a community of people who share the same faith in Jesus Christ. The inspiration for the work of the Church is the life and teaching of Jesus Christ.

- An archbishop and bishops lead the Church of Ireland community.
- The Word of God in the Bible teaches everything that a person needs to know in order to have a relationship with God.
- The Church of Ireland celebrates two sacraments.

Leadership roles in the Church of Ireland

People have a variety of roles in the Church of Ireland.

Archbishop
The Archbishop of Canterbury is head of the Church of England and is based in England. He is a senior bishop in the Anglican Communion throughout the world, but does not have overall authority over it. In Ireland the Archbishop of Armagh is a leader of the Church of Ireland. He shares responsibility for guiding the Church throughout the whole of Ireland, North and South.

Justin Welby
Archbishop of Canterbury

Dr. Richard Clarke
Archbishop of Armagh
and Primate of All Ireland

Bishop
Bishops are in charge of large areas called diocese. A bishop is the religious leader of a diocese. Bishops preach the Word of God and look after the spiritual needs of the people of the diocese.

Priest Priests are in charge of smaller areas called parishes. A priest ordained in the Church of Ireland is called a rector. His/her role is to celebrate Holy Communion, preach from the Bible and look after the religious life of members of the parish.

Deacon A deacon is a person who is training to be a rector. He/she studies in college and helps in the parish.

Lay Reader A lay reader is a baptised lay person from the parish. He or she is trained to preach sermons and lead some religious services such as Morning and Evening Prayer.

Preaching

Religious Commitment

An important part of the role of the bishop and the rector is to preach the Word of God. Bishops and rectors speak out and explain the teaching of Jesus and urge people to act on it.

Being a member of the Church of Ireland calls for commitment. Members of the Church of Ireland show their religious commitment and put their beliefs into practice by:

- ❖ Attending church services.
- ❖ Celebrating the sacraments and special occasions.
- ❖ Living good Christian lives.

Sunday Worship

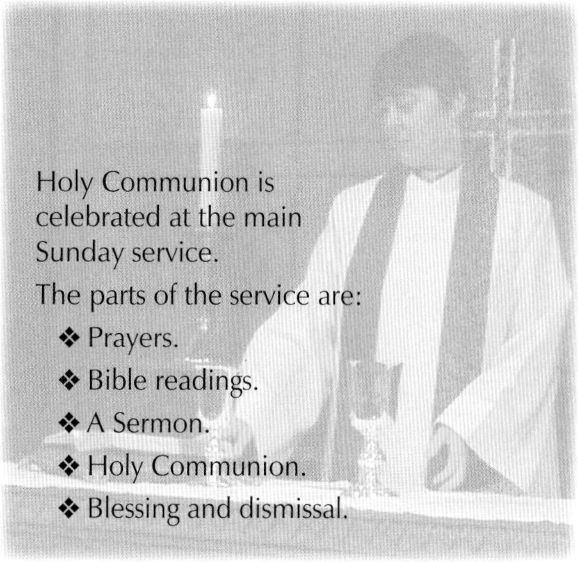

Holy Communion is celebrated at the main Sunday service.

The parts of the service are:

- ❖ Prayers.
- ❖ Bible readings.
- ❖ A Sermon.
- ❖ Holy Communion.
- ❖ Blessing and dismissal.

Holy Communion
The rector reads the Holy Communion Service and the people pray and sing hymns. Members of the Church of Ireland believe the bread and wine are special signs of God's presence at Holy Communion.

The Communion service can take place each week, while in some churches it occurs twice a month.

Sacraments

Two sacraments are celebrated in the Church of Ireland community:

- ❖ Baptism.
- ❖ Holy Communion.

Confirmation

Confirmation is not a sacrament, but it is a special occasion in the Church of Ireland. When children grow up and become teenagers they can be confirmed in the faith. At the ceremony their god-parents stand with them as Confirmation promises are made.

The Bishop lays a hand on the head of each boy and girl.

Confirmation in the Church of Ireland.

Confirmation is a day of special significance for young people and their families. It is the occasion when young teenagers express their commitment to the faith and become grown up members of their Church. They may now receive Holy Communion for the first time.

Questions

Knowledge

1. What is the inspiring vision that motivates the work of the Church of Ireland community?
2. What is the Anglican Communion called in Ireland?
3. a. What is the title of a senior leader of the Church of Ireland?
   b. Name a senior leader of the Church of Ireland.
4. Who is the leader of each diocese in the Church of Ireland?
5. Who is the leader of the Christian community in a parish?
6. What is the role of a lay preacher?
7. State three ways in which members of the Church of Ireland show religious commitment to their faith.
8. Name two sacraments celebrated in the Church of Ireland.
9. How often is the Holy Communion Service held in Church of Ireland churches?
10. Who has the leadership role at a Holy Communion Service?
11. What happens at a confirmation ceremony in the Church of Ireland?

Understanding

1. How do clergy and lay people show their religious commitment in the Church of Ireland.
2. How do you think the work of the Church of Ireland benefits:
   a. Members of the Church?
   b. Members of the wider community?
3. What do Anglicans believe happens at the Communion Service in their church?

Research

- Find out about the annual Harvest Festival in the Church of Ireland.
  - When does this event take place?
    - What does it celebrate?
    - How was it celebrated long ago?
  - How is it celebrated today?
    - Who gets involved in organising the church for the Harvest Festival?
    - What happens afterwards?
  - Present a detailed account with a supporting outline of the service. Include drawings/photos/artefacts (optional).

The Methodist Church

Key Concepts

Church: a community of Christian people.

Inspiring vision: a dream or idea so powerful it motivates people to act on it.

Preaching: to speak out and explain a religious truth and urge people to act on it.

Religious commitment: the decision to make a sincere effort to put one's religious beliefs into practice.

Objectives

State the titles of leaders in the Methodist Church in Ireland.

Explain how its members express their religious commitment.

Activity: *"Fact File"*

TASK: TO GATHER FACTUAL INFORMATION ABOUT A LOCAL METHODIST CHURCH.

✦ Identify a Methodist church near your home or near your school.

1. Where is the church?
2. What is the name of the church?
3. When was the church built?
4. Is there a graveyard near the church?
5. Name the minister of this church.
6. What service is held in the church on Sunday?
7. Inside the church, where is the pulpit located?
8. Is there an altar in the church?
9. Where is the baptismal font?
10. Are there any stained glass windows in the church?

Discuss

- When did you last visit a Methodist church?
- Is the church open or locked during the day?
- Is there anything interesting about the outside of a Methodist church?
- What interesting things are there to notice inside the church?

Church

Inspiring vision

The word "church" has two meanings. The building where Methodists go to pray and worship God, and the people who belong to the Methodist Church worldwide.

Inside a Methodist chapel.

A Church is a community of Christian people. The Methodist Church is a community of faith whose members all share the same faith in Jesus Christ. The inspiration for the work of the Church is the life and teaching of Jesus Christ.

- A new President elected every year at the annual Conference guides the Methodist community in this country.
- The Word of God in the Bible is very important for Methodists.
- The Methodist Church celebrates two sacraments.

Leadership roles in the Methodist Church

Methodism teaches that all people are equal - there is no single leader and there are no bishops in the Methodist Church.

President
Ministers and lay people meet at the Annual Conference to decide on important Church issues. Every year conference members elect a new president to guide the Methodist community in Ireland.

Ministers
Methodists ordain both men and women as ministers. A minister will look after a number of churches. He/she will preach, celebrate the sacraments and guide people in their faith.

Lay Preachers
Lay preachers are baptised men and women who are trained to preach and lead Sunday worship. They do not celebrate the sacraments.

John Wesley

The Methodist Church was founded in the 18th century by a Church of England clergyman named John Wesley. John felt the Church of England at the time had lost touch with ordinary people, and he wanted that to change. He devoted his life to preaching the Gospel at outdoor meetings throughout Britain and Ireland. He urged people to pray and study the Bible together and do good works among the poor.

John Wesley preaching a sermon.

John Wesley never intended to cause a split in the Church, but after his death in 1791 Methodism separated from the Church of England and became a new denomination.

Preaching

There is a strong emphasis on the Bible and preaching the Word of God in the Methodist Church. Ministers and lay preachers speak out and explain the teaching of Jesus and urge people to act on it. There is also great respect for the sermons and teachings of John Wesley, the founder of Methodism.

Religious Commitment

Being a Methodist involves devoting a considerable amount of time and energy to the practice of the faith. Members of the Methodist Church show their religious commitment by:

- Attending church services.
- Celebrating sacraments and special occasions.
- Living good Christian lives.

Sunday Worship

Methodists attend Morning Worship on Sunday. There is a simple free form of worship involving:

- Readings from the Bible.
- Prayers.
- Hymns.
- A sermon.

Once a month there is Holy Communion (or the Lord's Supper) at the service. The minister prepares bread and wine and says a prayer of thanksgiving. Methodists believe the bread and wine of Holy Communion are symbols of Jesus' body and blood and not the real presence of Jesus.

Individual cups of wine at Holy Communion.

Sacraments

Two sacraments are celebrated in the Methodist Church community.

- ❖ Baptism.
- ❖ Holy Communion (or the Lord's Supper).

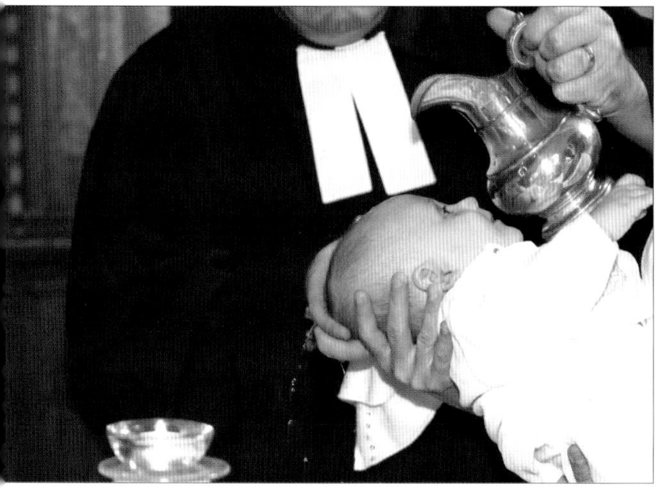

Baptism in a Methodist Church.

Confirmation

Confirmation is not a sacrament, but it is a special occasion in the Methodist Church. There is no fixed age for Methodists to be confirmed except that they need to be able to understand the promises they will be making.

At the confirmation service the minister lays his/her hands on the head of each person and welcomes them into membership of the Methodist Church.

At Confirmation Methodists publicly express their commitment to a Christian way of life. They promise to worship in their local church, study the Bible and be of service to their neighbour in the community.

Questions

Knowledge

1. What is the inspiring vision that motivates the work of the Methodist Church?
2. What is the title of the national leader of the Methodist Church?
3. Who are the leaders in the Methodist Church at local level?
4. What is the role of a minister in the Methodist Church?
5. What is the role of lay preachers in the Methodist Church?
6. Name the founder of the Methodist Church.
7. What prompted him to begin his work?
8. State three ways in which Methodists show religious commitment to their faith.
9. Name two sacraments celebrated in the Methodist Church.
10. What happens at a Confirmation service in the Methodist Church?

Understanding

1. How do clergy and lay people show their religious commitment in the Methodist Church?
2. What do you think is the impact of the work of the Methodist Church on:
   a. Members of the Church itself?
   b. Members of the wider community?
3. What do Methodists believe happens at Holy Communion during Morning Service.
4. In what way is the work of John Wesley an inspiration for Methodist Christians?

Research

- Find out how John Wesley inspires the Methodist community today.
  - Invite a member of the Methodist Church to visit the class to discuss one or all of the following topics.
    - Lay involvement and participation in the running of the Church.
    - Preaching Ministry: the roles of the lay preacher and the ordained minister.
    - Service to the poor in the community.
  - Write a report on the meeting and present it to the class.

Religious Orders

Key Concepts

Founder: the person who establishes a community or organisation for a special purpose.

Vocation: a feeling of being called by God to serve others.

Inspiring vision: a dream or idea so powerful it motivates people to act on it.

Mission: the specific work carried out by members of a faith community.

Objectives

Explain what a vocation is.

Identify the vision that inspires the life and work of one religious order.

Activity: *"A fundraising event"*

TASK: TO BE AWARE OF THE REALITY OF POVERTY IN THE WORLD.

You will need:

- Tickets - one for each person in the class. (One third white tickets, two thirds coloured tickets.)
- Two plates of biscuits - one fancy, the other plain. (Soft drinks, water and paper cups optional.)

✦ Students select a charity of their choice and agree a contribution of 50c, €1 or €2 each for a fund-raising event.

✦ On the appointed day distribute the tickets randomly.
  - The white ticket holders are directed toward a mouth-watering display on a table in the centre of the room.
  - The coloured-ticket holders are directed toward the uninspiring contents of a plate on a chair in a far corner of the room.

✦ Invite guests to tuck in and enjoy themselves!

> In the world today:
> - One third of the population have far more than they really need.
> - Two thirds of the population have almost nothing at all.

Discuss

- What colour was your ticket?
- What happened at the fund-raising event?
- Was the outcome fair or unfair?
- How do you feel about world poverty now?

Founder

The poor are at the heart of Jesus' teaching in the Bible.

The Missionaries of Charity is a Catholic religious order. It works among the poorest of the poor at a local, national and international level. It was founded in 1950 by Mother Teresa. Like other religious orders, the Missionaries of Charity is a community of faith.

Mother Teresa.

Vocation

As a young woman Mother Teresa felt she had a religious vocation. She felt God was calling her to serve others in a special way. At nineteen years of age she joined a religious order and trained to be a teacher. Later, when she went to live and work with the order in India, she saw the suffering of the poor at first hand. As a result she had what she described as "a call, within a call".

Inspiring Vision

Mother Teresa placed Jesus' teaching "to love God and love your neighbour as yourself" at centre of her life. She had a dream, a vision. She wanted to follow Jesus and his teaching by serving the poorest of the poor. In 1950 Mother Teresa became the founder of a religious order called the Missionaries of Charity.

The sisters live as a community and take vows of poverty, chastity and obedience. They own nothing themselves, they forfeit marriage and children, and will go and work where they are needed most. The sisters share everything. They live in the same house and have their meals together. They pray and attend daily Mass before going out to work among the poor.

Mission

Mother Teresa's mission began in India among homeless people in the city of Calcutta. The work of the Missionaries of Charity was to search the city streets to find people who were sick and destitute and care for them in their 'Home for the Dying'.

The sisters cared for men and women, for children and abandoned babies. Even when people had only a few hours to live, the sisters looked after them. They showed the love of God to each person, no matter how sick or neglected they were. The terminally ill benefit from the sisters' care by being able to die with dignity.

A mother waiting outside a health centre with her sick child.

In addition to the 'Home for the Dying', the Sisters have set up health centres on the streets, and have started classes for children and adults in the slums. For others, medical care and education raise standards and give people hope for a better future for themselves and their families.

Mother Teresa, known as "the saint of the gutters" died in 1997. In 2003 the Pope made her Blessed Mother Teresa. Today the Missionaries of Charity continue to work among the poorest of the poor in India and in one hundred and thirty five other countries throughout the world, including Ireland. Those who join the order are inspired by the life of Mother Teresa the founder, and the way she followed the example and teaching of Jesus.

A gathering of Missionaries of Charity at prayer.

Research

- The Missionaries of Charity founded by Mother Teresa is a religious order. Find out about the work of one other religious organisation, in any faith community.

  Some other religious orders in the Roman Catholic Church include:

  - Ursulines.
  - Franciscans.
  - De La Salle Brothers.
  - Marist Sisters.
  - Sisters of St. Louis.
  - Mercy Sisters.
  - Christian Brothers.
  - Dominicans.
  - Presentation Brothers.
  - Loreto.
  - Holy Faith.
  - Jesuits.
  - Salesians of Don Bosco.
  - Rosminians.

Create a profile of a religious order

- Give the title of the religious order.
- Name the founder.
- When and where was the order founded.
- What inspired the founder to start the order?
- What gifts and talents did the founder possess?
- What is the work or mission of the order today and its effect in local communities.
- What roles do people have in this religious order today?
- What kind of commitment is undertaken by members of this religious order?
- Write the story of this religious order and tell it to the class.

Reebok
adidas

Sisters of the Sacred Heart and friends.

Questions

Knowledge

1. Name a Catholic religious order founded in the twentieth century.
2. Who was the founder of the Missionaries of Charity?
3. When did Mother Teresa first realise she had a religious vocation?
4. What vision inspired Mother Teresa to found the Missionaries of Charity?
5. What is the work of the order in the city of Calcutta?
6. List the kind of commitments women make when they join a religious order such as the Missionaries of Charity.

Understanding

1. Could Mother Teresa be described as a person of faith? Explain.
2. How does the work of the Missionaries of Charity benefit local communities in the city of Calcutta?
3. What do you think inspires young women to join the Missionaries of Charity?
4. Outline the different skills and gifts that Mother Teresa and the Missionaries of Charity developed and utilised in the service of the poor.

Sectarianism

Key Concepts

Sectarianism: hatred of people because they belong to a different religious group.

Religious conflict: a clash or struggle between different religious groups.

Objective

Outline the implications of sectarianism in Ireland and elsewhere.

Activity: *"Bad Behaviour"*

TASK: TO EXPLORE UNFAIR TREATMENT AND ITS EFFECTS.

- You will need:
  - A packet of small self-adhesive stickers in different colours.
  - A page of instructions, cut into strips
- Assemble in an open space. Ask everyone to close their eyes.
- Explain that you are placing a coloured sticker on each person's forehead, and putting one instruction strip into each person's hand.
- Finally ask everyone to open their eyes and move around obeying the instruction.
- No physical contact permitted.
- Sample instructions:

- walk away from someone wearing a red sticker.
- glare at someone wearing a yellow sticker.
- circle, or walk around, someone wearing a blue sticker.
- shake a fist at someone wearing a ... sticker.
- turn your back on someone wearing a ... sticker.
- laugh at someone wearing a ... sticker.
- hiss at someone wearing a ... sticker.
- shout at someone wearing a ... sticker.

Discuss

- What happened during the exercise?
- What was it like to behave toward someone in this way?
- What is it like to be treated in this way?
- Are there situations where behaviour of this kind actually happens?

Sectarianism

Religious conflict

Sectarian behaviour causes pain and suffering.

In our society, people are treated unfairly for a lot of reasons. It can happen to some people because of their religion. They become a target for verbal and physical abuse because they are from a particular religious background. Things are deliberately said and done to cause them hurt and suffering. Sectarianism is hatred of people because they belong to a different religious group.

There are different world religions and many different Christian denominations. Difference can be very positive, but for some it is seen as negative and as a threat. Sectarianism is a hurtful and destructive way of dealing with difference.

Stop Sectarian Attacks!

Police say a recent incident in Co. Antrim has all the hallmarks of a sectarian attack.

Last week a pipe bomb was thrown through the front window of a house in Larne. It narrowly missed a mother and son sitting in their living room watching TV. The device only partly exploded. No one was hurt. The householder, who did not want to be identified, said "It was about 10.15 pm. I was in the kitchen and I heard glass breaking; then there was a loud bang. The house filled with smoke. We're still in shock. Nobody has slept since. We are all off school and off work."

Yesterday a local politician spoke about attitudes in the town. "One side says, 'Look, there are Catholics getting attacked', and the other side says 'There are more Protestants getting attacked', when really it's people that are being attacked. At the moment the problem is being caused by no more than a dozen individuals. More help is needed from the public to bring this violence to an end!"

Northern Ireland

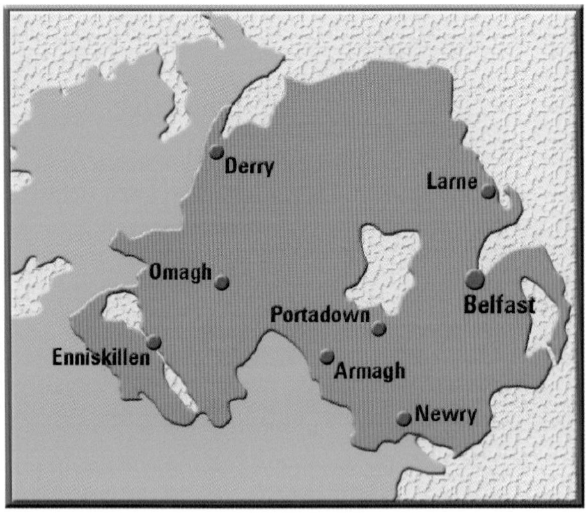
Derry
Larne
Omagh
Belfast
Portadown
Enniskillen
Armagh
Newry

Sectarianism has been a feature of life in Northern Ireland for a very long time. In the 1960's it erupted into violence causing injury and death to many people in Catholic and Protestant communities.

From May 1969 when "the Troubles" began, to the signing of the Good Friday Agreement in 1998, over three and a half thousand people were killed in the North.

Sectarianism and sectarian violence was the cause of great suffering in Northern Ireland.

Divided Communities

The causes of sectarianism in any country are deep and complex. However the effect of sectarianism is the same everywhere. There is hatred and tension, and communities become divided. People take sides; their world is divided into "us" and "them". People everywhere tend to form groups with others like themselves. However some groups can allow their differences to divide them from others in a destructive way.

In divided communities people keep to themselves and look down on others who are different. When people refuse to mix and fail to communicate they cannot get to know each other. Instead they become fearful and suspicious. They can end up disliking each other, even hating each other. This often results in tension and violence.

A community that becomes divided will stay divided if people continue to separate themselves into two opposing sides. It is essential to move beyond sectarianism in order to find a solution that will last and is sustainable.

"The Peace Wall" between Catholic and Protestant areas of West Belfast.

Religious Conflict

Sectarianism and religious conflict has occurred not only on this island but in other places throughout the world.

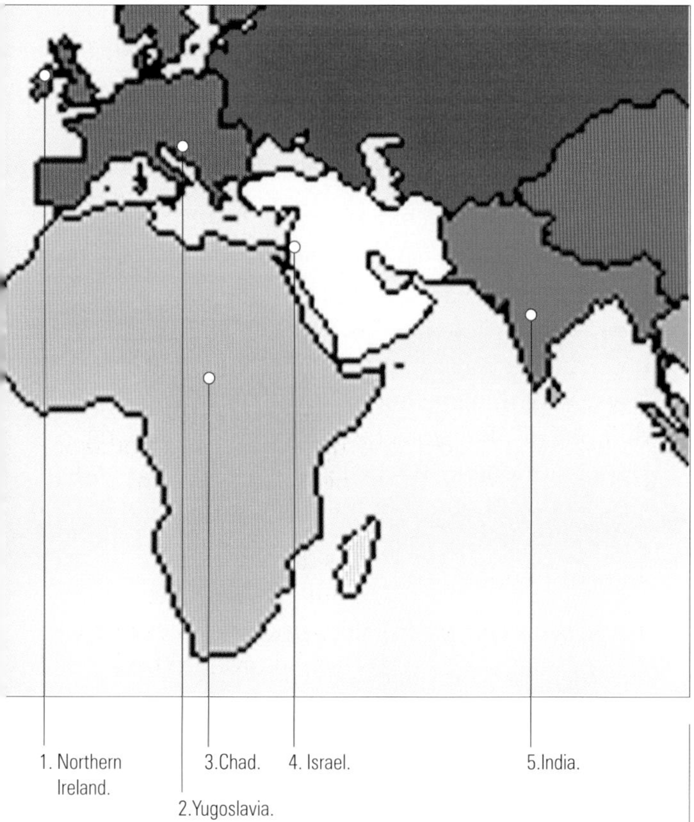
1. Northern Ireland.
2.Yugoslavia.
3.Chad.
4. Israel.
5.India.

A breakdown in the relationship between different communities of faith has led to religious conflict in many parts of the world. Such a clash or struggle has taken place in:

1. Northern Ireland
   - between Catholics and Protestants.
2. Former Yugoslavia
   - between Christians and Muslims.
3. Chad
   - between Muslims and Christians.
4. Israel
   - between Jews and Muslims.
5. India
   - between Hindus and Muslims.

Questions

Knowledge

1. What is sectarianism?
2. What are the signs that there is sectarianism in a particular place?
3. a. What happened in the sectarian attack on a house in Northern Ireland?
   b. Why was the family home attacked?
4. What are the causes of sectarianism?
5. What are the consequences of sectarianism?
6. Name two countries where conflict resulted from religious difference.

Understanding

1. What are the implications of sectarianism in Ireland and elsewhere?
2. Imagine a family is the victim of a sectarian attack. What effect might the attack have on:
   - their health and well-being?
   - their religious beliefs and practices?
   - their relationship with members of the other community?
3. Does religion have any part to play in sectarianism?

Research

- Examine newspapers, magazines or history books to find one example of sectarianism or religious conflict in another part of the world, past or present.
  - *In the past.*
    Where have people been hated, persecuted and killed because of their religious beliefs?
  - *At present.*
    In what parts of the world is religious conflict taking place?
  - Gather some facts and compile a report about one particular situation.

Tolerance

Key Concept

Tolerance: allowing everyone to have their own religious beliefs and practices.

Objective

Know the importance of respecting one's own religious beliefs and the beliefs of others.

Activity: *"Territories"*

TASK: TO KNOW AND APPRECIATE DIFFERENCE.

- Divide into groups and establish an imaginary community with its own territory, diet and social customs.
- Each group...
  a) Establishes a territory, marking it off with furniture, jackets, bags etc.
  b) Discusses the kinds of things the members might like to eat and drink.
  c) Identifies three customs which make their group different from all others. Members might for example:
  - leave shoelaces undone.
  - wear collars up.
  - say 'yes' when they mean 'no'.
  - sit sideways in chairs.
  - look away when spoken to.
- A representative from each group visits another group and tries to work out their customs while asking them what they like to eat and drink. (The rep. must however obey the customs of their own group while on this mission.)
- Each representative returns to his/her own group to report what they have learned about the customs and preferences of others.
- Repeat.

Discuss

- Which customs were a bit difficult to figure out.
- Did anything surprise you?
- Are there any real-life situations similar to this one?

Tolerance

Individual difference is to be respected.

Tolerance is key to solving sectarianism. To be tolerant is to accept that as people, we are different. Tolerance is a positive and constructive way of responding to difference. It is a way of thinking and acting that says 'respect difference!'. Religious tolerance is about having respect for one's own beliefs and the beliefs and convictions of others. It means allowing people to have their own religious beliefs and customs without interference.

Tolerance versus Intolerance

Sectarianism is intolerant and without respect for the religious beliefs and practices of other denominations. The problem of sectarianism needs to be addressed not by violence but through:

❖ Communication. ❖ Education. ❖ Government.

Meeting and accepting members of other communities.

Communication: The first step is to try and get people to meet and talk and really listen to each other. The way forward is to try and respect the other person's point of view.

Education: Finding out about other people's beliefs and way of life can help different groups to understand each other better.

Government: The government of a country can make laws to stop unequal treatment of different groups.

A response to sectarianism

In Ireland, the Glencree Centre for Reconciliation in Co. Wicklow was set up to build bridges between the Protestant and Catholic communities in Ireland, North and South.

In Northern Ireland the Corrymeela community in Co. Antrim was set up to promote tolerance between the different faith communities in the North.

The Corrymeela Community

The Corrymeela Community promotes tolerance between Catholic and Protestant communities in Northern Ireland. The Centre is situated on a hilltop overlooking the sea at Ballycastle, about sixty miles from Belfast. Corrymeela is a Christian community founded in the early 1960's by Rev. Ray Davey, a Presbyterian minister. It is a place where Catholics and Protestants can meet and get to know each other, and heal the divisions that exist between them. People of all ages visit the centre. Everyone is welcome.

Corrymeela is neutral territory. Catholics and Protestants go there to communicate freely with one another. For some, it is the first time they have had a chat with a person from "the other side".

Adults and young people from all parts of Ireland, North and South, can go for a week or a week-end. Young and old spend time talking and listening to each other in a relaxed way. They discuss their different backgrounds and way of life. This helps everyone to understand and respect one another a bit better. They try to keep this up when they return home to their own communities.

Meeting in small groups in the garden.

Questions

Knowledge

1. What is the key to solving the problem of sectarianism?
2. What is the meaning of tolerance?
3. How can people learn to be tolerant?
4. What can happen when people communicate in a positive way with one another?
5. Name two centres set up to curb sectarianism and promote tolerance in Ireland.
6. What happens in Corrymeela?

Understanding

1. What do you think:
   a. Builds up barriers between different communities?
   b. Breaks down barriers between communities?
2. What is the difference between a tolerant and an intolerant outlook?
3. Does good communication have any part to play in dealing with sectarianism?

Research

- Find out about another community that wants to move beyond sectarianism and promote tolerance in Northern Ireland, eg. - The Curragh Community.
  - The Cornerstone Community.
  - Where is the community located?
  - Who is the founder?
  - Who are its members?
  - What work does the community do?
  - What inspires people to undertake this kind of work?
  - What is the effect of this work in the local community?
  - Prepare a file and discuss its contents with the class.

Ecumenism

Key Concept

Ecumenism: a movement to help the Christian Churches become more united.

Objective

Explain what the Ecumenical Movement is, and outline its activities in the community.

Activity: *"Handle with care!"*

TASK: TO UNDERSTAND THAT RESPECT INVOLVES CARE AND THOUGHTFULNESS.

- You will need either:
  A hand bell, a tambourine, a maracas, a bunch of keys or a cup and saucer.
- Students form two parallel lines.
  Slowly and carefully pass one selected item along the length of each line.
  Try not to make a sound.

Discuss

- Was the item handled carefully? How do you know?
- Are people just as careful in the way they treat each other?
- Whom do you normally treat with care and respect?

Ecumenism

Christians are learning to respect each other's religious beliefs and religious practices.

All Roman Catholic, Protestant and Orthodox Christians have faith in God, follow the teaching of Jesus, and believe the Bible is the Word of God. Yet they have different beliefs about Church leadership, the sacraments, and the meaning of the Eucharist.

For centuries the Christian Churches were totally opposed to each other. Their differences prevented them from even talking to one another. They were completely divided. All that began to change in the twentieth century with the start of the Ecumenical Movement. Christians began to communicate and show greater respect for each others' religious beliefs and religious practices.

Catholic, Protestant and Orthodox clergy praying together at an ecumenical service.

The logo of the World Council of Churches.

The World Council of Churches

In 1948 the World Council of Churches (WCC) was set up to encourage the different Christian denominations to work together in an ecumenical way. The word ecumenical comes from the Greek OIKOUMENE which means "the whole household" or "everybody".

In 1964 a meeting of Catholic bishops in Rome, known as the Second Vatican Council, issued an important document on ecumenism. It supported the movement for unity among Christians. Today representatives of the Catholic Church and the World Council of Churches work together to foster ecumenism.

The Ecumenical Movement is not trying to make all Christians exactly the same, instead it is asking them to work together and understand and respect each other's differences.

Christian Unity Week

Christians from all Churches have started to meet and pray together. This happens especially during the Week of Prayer for Christian Unity. At the moment this event takes place each year in the month of January. Every parish tries to organise an ecumenical prayer service. An ecumenical service is a joint act of worship that Catholics, Protestants and Orthodox Christians attend together. It is organised by clergy and lay people from all the Churches involved.

At an ecumenical service there are:

- ❖ Prayers.
- ❖ Music and hymns.
- ❖ Bible readings.
- ❖ A homily or sermon.

Neighbours and friends from the different Churches are invited to attend. The service allows Catholic, Protestant and Orthodox Christians to stand side by side and pray for themselves and for each other.

Activities that promote Christian unity

Christians from all Churches now co-operate more with each other. They:

- ❖ Pray together, eg. at Ecumenical services during the Week of Prayer for Christian Unity.
- ❖ Join together to raise awareness about justice issues, eg. during Lent.
- ❖ Fundraise together for charity.
- ❖ Share each other's church buildings when the need arises.

Places that promote Christian unity

Examples of the Ecumenical movement in action in today's world include:

Corrymeela - an ecumenical community in Northern Ireland founded by Rev. Ray Davey to help members of the Protestant and Catholic communities to meet and understand each other's beliefs and practices.

Taize - an ecumenical community in France founded by Brother Roger Schultz as a place for Christians of all traditions to meet and pray together. An important aim of the community is to work for Christian unity.

Taize

Every summer thousands of young people interested in Christian unity visit Taize. The religious brothers who live and work in the community belong to different Christian Churches: some are Catholic, some are Orthodox, many are Protestant.

Those who visit Taize also belong to different Churches. They all make an effort to get on together, even though they come from very different backgrounds. Many arrive with backpacks and sleeping bags eager to spend a week or so in this ecumenical community. Young people like to visit Taize. It is a place where they can think and pray about their lives and the kind of world in which they want to live.

Arriving at Taize.

A day in Taize

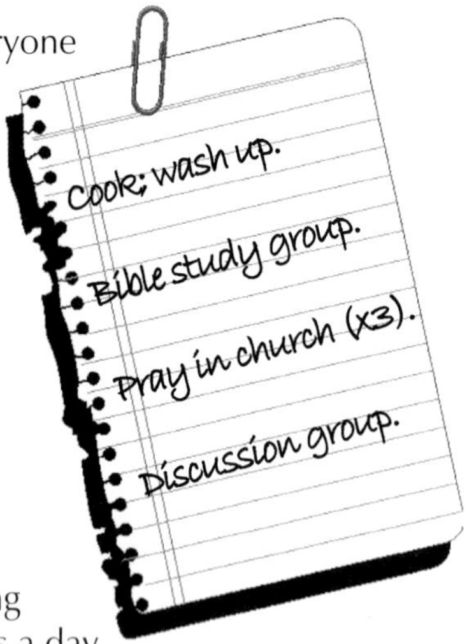
Cook; wash up.
Bible study group.
Pray in church (x3).
Discussion group.

During the day everyone helps with the cooking and the cleaning.

Then they gather in study groups to learn about the Christian faith.

Later they pray together in the church. Prayer is important in Taize, people pray and sing together three times a day.

Discussion groups are another feature of the community. At discussion time young men and women sit around in small groups talking about their life and what they believe. They all listen to each other with respect. It is no surprise that everyone makes new friends here. After a visit to Taize people promise to be just as prayerful and thoughtful when they return home to their own communities.

Taize Prayer

Taize prayer and Taize chants have now been adapted for Ecumenical gatherings world wide.

Evening prayer.

Examine the picture. What do you notice about:

- ❖ The size of the gathering.
- ❖ The seating arrangements.
- ❖ The lighting.
- ❖ The people.
- ❖ The atmosphere.

Questions

Knowledge

1. What beliefs unite all Christians?
2. How did the Christian Churches behave toward each other in the past?
3. How are the Christian Churches behaving toward each other now?
4. What is Ecumenism?
5. What occurs during Christian Unity Week?
6. What is an ecumenical service?
7. What can be done to promote Christian unity in local communities?
8. a. Where is Taize?
   b. What happens in Taize?

Understanding

1. Why is it important to work for better understanding between the different Christian Churches?
2. How is Taize an example of an ecumenical community?
3. Is Christian unity a good idea? Explain your answer.
4. Describe what you think is a good example of ecumenism in action.

Research

- Find out what is happening in your school or in the local community to promote unity among the Christian Churches.

  For example:

  a. Do the local Christian Churches mark the Week of Prayer for Christian Unity?

  b. Has an ecumenical service taken place in the school or in the parish at any time during the past year?

  c. In addition to joint acts of worship, is there any other type of joint venture among Christians in the community?

  - Write a report entitled *"Churches Together in our Community"*.

Inter-Faith Dialogue

Key Concept

Inter-faith dialogue: open and honest discussions between the major world religions.

Objective

Explain the meaning of inter-faith dialogue.

Activity: *"Airport"*

TASK: TO BE AWARE OF THE EFFECTS OF DIFFERENT FORMS OF COMMUNICATION.

- You will need: space to move about; paper and pens (at the end).
- Everyone spread out around the room.
- Imagine this is a busy airport. You are travelling on your own. You have a plane to catch, you are late and in a hurry.

1. Walk around. Try to get through the crowd as quickly as possible. Look straight ahead. Ignore everyone; just mind your own business. Do not bump into anyone. Stop.

2. Walk around. This time, notice people as you pass by. Make eye-contact, but don't stare at anyone. Stop.

3. Walk around. This time, as you pass someone do something to acknowledge their presence: say hello, nod, shake hands, smile etc. Try to make contact with as many people as possible. Stop.

4. Sit down. Ask the last person you met to sit down beside you. Do this word-puzzle together. Fit the names of five major world religions and two Christian denominations into the space provided.

Discuss

- In what ways did people ignore each other at the start?
- What is it like to be ignored?
- How was it different when you made eye-contact and greeted each other?
- Does anything change when people sit down and talk together?

D
I
A
L
O
RELIGIONS
U
E

Word puzzle.

Inter-faith dialogue

Most people in the world belong to a religion.

The five major world religions are:

- Christianity
- Judaism
- Islam
- Hinduism
- Buddhism

Each religion is a community of faith. There was a time when every religion was based in its own part of the world. All that has changed as people move around more now. As they travel from country to country people bring their religious beliefs and practices with them. Today, Christians, Jews, Muslims, Hindus and Buddhists often live in the same area and attend the same schools.

At a local level, people of different religions are interacting and getting to know about each others' beliefs and way of life. In addition, the influence of travel and the mass media helps us to become more aware of people and nations with outlooks different from our own.

The major world religions, Christianity, Judaism, Islam, Hinduism and Buddhism have different religious beliefs and practices.

The Major World Religions

Religion:	Deity	Founder	Sacred Text	Place of Worship	Leadership	Moral Code
Christianity:	God.	Jesus.	The Bible.	Church.	Bishops, Priests, Ministers, Elders.	2 Great Commandments.
Judaism:	Yahweh.	Abraham & Moses.	The Tenakh.	Synagogue.	Rabbi.	10 Commandments.
Islam:	Allah.	Muhammad.	The Qur'an.	Mosque.	Imam.	5 Pillars.
Hinduism:	Many gods.	Unknown.	The Vedas.	Mandir.	Priests.	Do good.
Buddhism:	No God or gods.	Siddhartha Gautama - Buddha.	The Tipitaka.	Temple.	Monks.	4 Noble Truths. 8-Fold Path.

Inter-faith dialogue is open and honest discussion between the major world religions. It involves representatives of the different world religions meeting and talking about their religion. Inter-faith dialogue is different from Ecumenism. Ecumenism is about contact between different Christian Churches. Inter-faith dialogue is about contact between different world religions. Good communication is at the heart of both.

Communication

When people communicate, they talk and listen to each other, and are willing to hear about each other's beliefs and way of life. They are prepared to learn from each other's experience. That rarely happened in the past. It is beginning to take place now.

In the Catholic Church the turning point came in 1965 when a document about inter-faith relations was issued at the Second Vatican Council. In it the bishops encouraged Catholics to meet and have discussions with people of other religions. Partners must respect their own beliefs and learn to understand and respect the beliefs of others.

Dialogue between different religions is not about people trying to convert each other. It is about people meeting and working together to build trust and understanding. Failure to communicate and a lack of understanding has, in the past, led to violence and religious conflict between people of different faiths. It is hoped that inter-faith dialogue will bring peace and an end to conflict based on religion.

Inter-faith dialogue aims to:
- Promote contact between the major world religions.
- Build trust between people of different faiths.
- Develop respect and tolerance for different points of view.
- Prevent religious conflict.

Religious leaders at a day of prayer for world peace.

МИР שלום PACE 平和 PEACE
和平 PAX FRIEDE ΕΙΡΗΝΗ VREDE

Activities that promote inter-faith dialogue

World Day of Peace

In 1986, 1993 and 2002 Pope John Paul II invited religious leaders from all over the world to go to the town of Assisi in Italy. Representatives of Christianity, Judaism, Islam, Buddhism and Hinduism met together for a day to work and pray for world peace. Side by side they each prayed in their own way for peace and understanding in the world.

Inter-faith services

Inter-faith dialogue has encouraged the development of inter-faith services in schools and local communities. On special occasions Christians, Muslims, Jews, Hindus and Buddhists gather together to pray, each in their own way. After the tragic events of September 11, 2001, when almost 3,000 people died as result of terrorist attacks on the World Trade Centre in New York, inter-faith services were held throughout the world.

In Dublin, members of the Christian, Muslim, Jewish, Hindu and Buddhist communities gathered together to pray for peace. There were prayers and readings from the sacred texts of the different religions. Those present offered one another a handshake as a sign of peace. Then soil was put around the roots of a young oak tree as a sign of new life. It was later planted out in the Phoenix Park in memory of the event.

At an inter-faith service there are:

- ❖ Prayers from the different religions.
- ❖ Music and hymns.
- ❖ Readings from the sacred texts of the different religions.
- ❖ A homily or sermon.

Organisations that promote inter-faith dialogue

The Council of Christians and Jews is an organisation set up in Britain and Ireland to promote good relations between Christians and Jews.

The Three Faiths Forum is an organisation set up to establish links between Christians, Jews and Muslims in Ireland. Dialogue is also being developed with the Hindu and Buddhist communities.

Questions

Knowledge

1. Name five major world religions.
2. State six features common to almost all religions.
3. What is inter-faith dialogue?
4. Name one Christian Church that encourages inter-faith dialogue.
5. What are the aims of inter-faith dialogue?
6. What activities promote good relations between the different faiths?
7. What is an inter-faith service?
8. What happened at the inter-faith service in Dublin after September 11, 2001?
9. Name two organisations that promote inter-faith dialogue in Ireland.
10. Have inter-faith services or events taken place in your local community?

Understanding

1. Why is it important to have dialogue and good relations between people of different faiths?
2. Why is it necessary for people to respect their own beliefs and the beliefs of others when they enter into inter-faith discussions?
3. Is inter-faith dialogue asking people to change their religion? Explain.
4. Inter-faith dialogue and ecumenism:
   - what is the difference between them?
   - what are the benefits of participating in each process?

Research

- Find out about inter-faith services or events that have taken place locally, nationally or internationally in recent times.
  a. What was the occasion?
  b. Where did it take place?
  c. Who was involved?
  d. What happened?
  e. What was the response/outcome?
  - ✸ Assemble the information. Collect pictures or photographs where possible.
  - ✸ Write a report and present it to the class.

Leadership

Key Concept

Leadership: the task of a leader in guiding a group or organisation.

Objective

Identify different styles of leadership and their impact on human communities.

Activity: *"Tough, soft or sound"*

TASK: TO IDENTIFY THREE STYLES OF PARENTAL LEADERSHIP IN THE HOME.

✦ Discuss each of the family scenarios (1-4).
In each case a parent has made a request. The request is challenged by a son or daughter. Your task is to write what the parent would say next.

1.
You're not going out in that!
I'll wear what I like!!
2.
Tidy your room. It's a mess.
But there's nothing wrong with it!!
3.
We want you home by 10.30 pm.
But it won't be over by then!!
4.
We're all going to visit Gran on Saturday.
But I'm meeting my friends in town on Saturday!

✦ What would you write if:
a. the parent was tough?
b. the parent was soft?
c. the parent was sound?

Discuss

- What style of leadership do parents usually use at home?
- What style of leadership is used in school?
- Which leadership style do you think brings out the best in people?

Leadership

There are three basic styles of leadership in human communities.

Leadership is a characteristic of communities. A leader is someone who guides a community and has the power to make things happen. There are different types of leaders, such as world leaders, national leaders and local leaders.

Rev. Peter Kennedy.
Parish priest, St. John's R.C. church.

Ban Ki-Moon.
Secretary General of the United Nations.

Michael D. Higgins.
President of Ireland.

Leadership roles also exist within the family and within the school. People have different styles of leadership and will lead their communities in different ways.

Styles of Leadership

There are three basic styles of leadership in human communities.

- ❖ Authoritarian leadership.
- ❖ Enabling leadership.
- ❖ Consultative/democratic leadership.

The different styles of leadership become apparent in the way decisions are made in a community.

Authoritarian
The leader decides everything and tells the group what to do, without seeking their opinion.

Enabling
The leader motivates and helps the group to make its own decisions.

Consultative/Democratic
The leader seeks the opinion of the group and allows their suggestions to influence his/her final decision.

However, different situations call for different styles of leadership. What style of leadership is best in the following situations?

a. A fire breaks out in a school. What to do?
b. The school tour. Where to go?
c. End of term party. What to bring?
d. Can you think of other situations where different styles of leadership might apply?

The 'Endurance' - a story of leadership

Early in the last century the London Times carried this small advertisement.

- WANTED -

Persons for dangerous journey. Small wages, bitter cold, long months of complete darkness, constant danger, safe return doubtful, honour and recognition if successful.

Sir Ernest Shackleton.

Over five thousand people responded. From these, Shackleton selected twenty eight volunteers to accompany him on an expedition to the Antarctic. In August 1914 they departed Plymouth harbour aboard the ship Endurance. As they approached Antarctica weather conditions worsened and Endurance became frozen in ice. Eventually the ice crushed the ship and Shackleton gave the order to abandon ship.

Shackleton discussed with his crew the possibility of leaving the ice floes and taking the life boats to a nearby island to await rescue. Once there he got a small boat ready and with a crew of four, sailed 1,300km (800 miles) to South Georgia for help. They navigated through the most treacherous seas in the world where waves of 16 metres (52 feet) were not uncommon. They reached South Georgia where Shackleton eventually got a ship and returned to the island and rescued all his men. Thomas Crean from Co. Kerry was a pivotal member of that expedition.

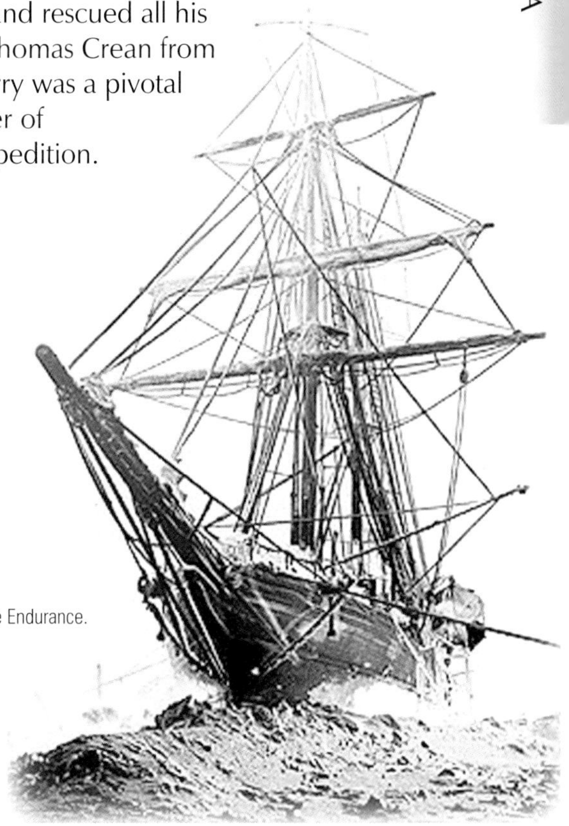

The Endurance.

Questions

Knowledge

1. What is a leader?
2. Name the different styles of leadership in human communities.
3. How does an authoritarian leader behave?
4. How does an enabling leader behave?
5. How does a democratic leader behave?
6. In what ways is the story of the *Endurance* an example of good leadership?

Understanding

1. What qualities do you consider essential in a good leader? Give reasons for your answer.
2. What style of leadership do you think might have been required at different stages of the Shackleton expedition?
3. Have you ever undertaken a leadership role? Select one instance and describe the leadership style you employed on that occasion.

Catholic Church Leadership

Key Concepts

Leadership: the task of a leader in guiding a group or organisation.

Authority: the power given to an individual or group to make important decisions.

Objective

Recognise the connection between leadership and authority in the Roman Catholic Church.

Activity: *"Who is the leader?"*

TASK: TO CONNECT A RELIGIOUS LEADER TO A RELIGION OR DENOMINATION.

✦ Identify the community of faith associated with the following religious leaders.

- Elder.
- Bishop.
- Dalai Lama.
- Patriarch.
- Guru.
- President.
- General.
- Imam.
- Rabbi.
- Minister.
- Archbishop.
- Pope.
- Pastor.
- Priest.

Discuss

- Did you correctly identify the religion or denomination associated with each leader.
- Do you know what style of leadership exists in any of the faith communities identified.
- What do you imagine is the impact of that style of leadership in that community of faith.

Leadership

Religious leaders guide those who belong to a community of faith.

Christianity is a world religion with over 2,000 million members. The Roman Catholic Church is the largest denomination within Christianity with 900 million members worldwide.

A Church is like a big organisation and like any organisation it needs leaders and people to run it. The Catholic Church is organised at several different levels:
- At local parish level.
- Nationally at diocesan level.
- At an international level by the Vatican in Rome.

The Roman Catholic Church

The Catholic Church is a worldwide community that shares a belief in Jesus Christ and follows his teaching. All its members form one community known as the People of God. All baptised Catholics are equal members in the Church. Each one is called by God to live a good Christian life in the service of God and their neighbour.

In the Catholic Church every person has a role and their gifts and talents are used to serve God in different ways. Lay people are important and have a special role in the Church. Church leaders meanwhile have the role and responsibility of guiding the Church at local, national and international level.

Down the ages the structure of leadership in the Catholic Church developed as a hierarchy. The Pope is head of the hierarchy as Bishop of Rome.

The Pope: The Pope serves God by giving leadership to the Roman Catholic Church

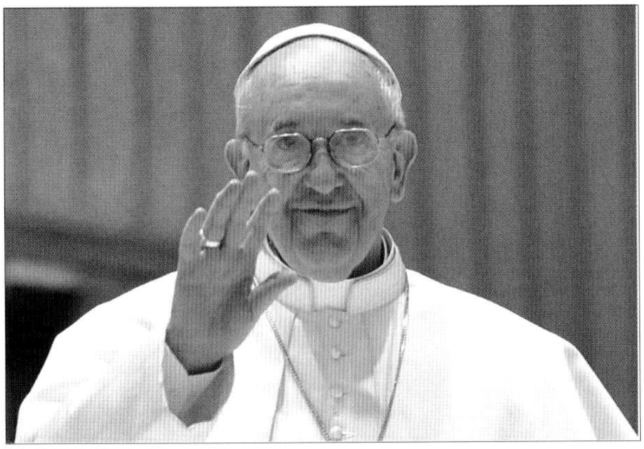

Pope Francis

throughout the world. Catholics believe that the Pope is the direct successor of St. Peter, the first leader of the Church. Jesus gave Peter the task of leading the Church when he said: "You are Peter and upon this rock I will build my Church" (Mt 16:18).

The Pope therefore has full authority over the Catholic Church. There have been more than 260 popes from Peter to the present time. The Pope lives in the Vatican in the city of Rome. Each new Pope is elected by a meeting of Cardinals.

Cardinals: Every country with a sizeable Catholic population has its own cardinal. Each Cardinal is selected by the Pope. Cardinals serve God by acting as chief advisers to the Pope on religious matters. There are 140 cardinals in the Catholic Church. When a Pope dies, cardinals from all over the world meet in the Sistine Chapel in Rome to elect the next Pope.

Bishops: There are many Catholic bishops and archbishops throughout the world. They serve God by looking after the needs of the Catholic Church in a particular country. Every country is divided into diocese. The bishop is the leader of the Catholic Church in each diocese. The senior bishop is called an archbishop. In Ireland the Archbishop of Armagh is the primate of all Ireland. Primate means senior bishop.

The role of the bishop is to spread the Catholic faith to all people in the diocese. He will confirm young people in the sacrament of Confirmation and ordain men to the priesthood.

There are twenty seven diocese in Ireland. Several times a year all the bishops attend an important meeting in Maynooth College, Co. Kildare. This meeting is called the Irish Bishops' Conference. It is usually chaired by the Archbishop of Armagh, the most senior bishop in Ireland. The bishops work together discussing issues of importance to the Church. Many people offer ideas and give advice to help the bishops in their work. The bishops listen to all the suggestions before making their decisions. Final decisions about certain Church teachings are made jointly between the Pope and the bishops.

Priests: A diocese is made up of a number of parishes. Each parish has at least one priest. Priests are ordained by a bishop to lead and serve the Catholic community in a parish. The priest looks after the religious welfare of Catholics in the parish for whom he celebrates the sacraments, especially the sacrament of the Eucharist. At Mass he will preach sermons on the Gospel and explain Church teachings.

In the parish, the priest and the people work together. The priest offers lay people the opportunity to serve God in the parish. Lay people can join different groups and committees according to their special gifts and talents. The priest will consult them for their ideas and will ask them for practical help and support in the running of the parish.

The Pope

Cardinals

Archbishops

Bishops

Priests

Lay people

Structure of leadership in the Roman Catholic Church.

Priests and lay people gather for the exposition of the Blessed Sacrament on the feast of Corpus Christi.

Lay people: Most Catholics are lay people. A lay person is an ordinary member of a parish who is not ordained like a priest. A lay person is someone who is baptised and is a full member of the Church. He or she may be young, old, single, married, a parent, widowed or separated and of any nationality.

Lay people serve God through prayer and by using their gifts and talents for the good of others. Each person will see what he or she can do to serve God at home, at school, at work and in the parish community.

In the parish lay people use their skills in different ways. They can:

- ❖ assist at Mass on Sundays.
- ❖ help in the parish during the week.
- ❖ be a member of the Parish Council, a group or a committee that offers the priest ideas and practical help in running the parish.

The priest and ministers of the Eucharist.

Organisation of the Catholic Church at National Level.

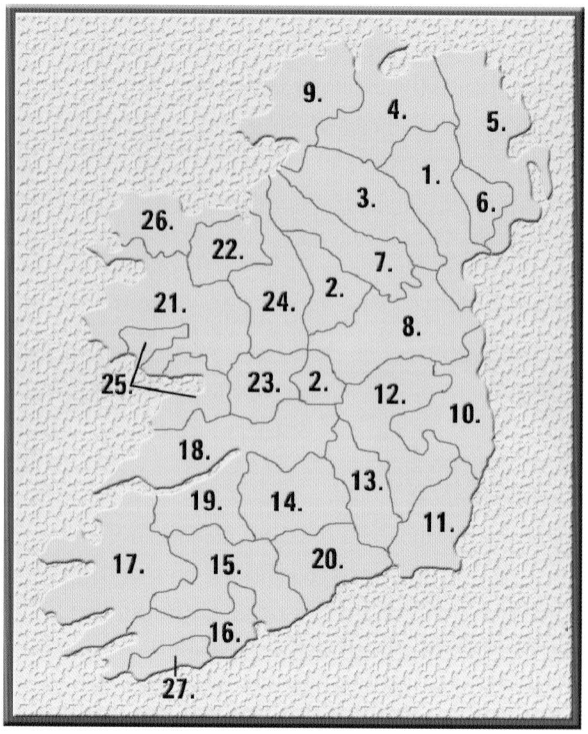
9.
4.
5.
1.
3.
6.
26.
22.
7.
2.
21.
24.
8.
25.
23.
2.
12.
10.
18.
13.
19.
14.
11.
17.
15.
20.
16.
27.

Roman Catholic Dioceses of Ireland.

1. Armagh
2. Ardagh & Clonmacnoise
3. Clogher
4. Derry
5. Down & Connor
6. Dromore
7. Kilmore
8. Meath
9. Raphoe
10. Dublin
11. Ferns
12. Kildare & Leighlin
13. Ossory
14. Cashel
15. Cloyne
16. Cork
17. Kerry
18. Killaloe
19. Limerick
20. Waterford & Lismore
21. Tuam
22. Achonry
23. Clonfert
24. Elphin
25. Galway
26. Killala
27. Ross

Authority

Authority is the power given to an individual or group to make important decisions that affect the lives of others. Jesus gave Peter and the apostles the authority to preach and teach the Good News. The apostles handed this authority on to other men by laying hands on their heads and calling on the Holy Spirit to help them. These men were called bishops. The bishops in turn laid hands on the heads of others to make new bishops. In this way the power to teach that Jesus gave to Peter and the apostles was passed down from one generation to the next to the present day. In the Catholic Church this is called apostolic succession.

The Magisterium is the teaching authority of the Church. It consists of the Pope and the bishops who have the authority to guide Catholics on matters of faith and how to live good moral lives. The teachings of the Catholic Church are found in:

- ❖ The Papal Encyclicals.
  (Documents issued by the Pope on certain topics.)
- ❖ The Catechism of the Catholic Church.
  (A book of questions and answers on Church teaching.)
- ❖ The Documents of Vatican II.
  (Teaching on many subjects prepared by the bishops at their last great meeting together in the Vatican.)

Leaders of the Catholic Church at St. Peter's in Rome.

Questions

Knowledge

1. How many members belong to the worldwide Catholic Church?
2. In what ways is a Church like a large organisation?
3. Give the titles of a local, national and international leader in the Roman Catholic Church.
4. How does the Pope serve God in the Catholic Church?
5. What happens at a meeting of the Irish Bishops' Conference?
6. Who is responsible for the day to day running of the Catholic Church at local level?
7. How do lay people assist priests in running a parish?
8. What is the source of authority in the Catholic Church?

Understanding

1. Explain the leadership structure of the Catholic Church.
2. What is meant by apostolic succession in the Catholic Church?
3. What is the Magisterium and its role in the Roman Catholic Church?
4. What style of leadership do you associate with the Catholic Church?

Research

- Find out the following points of information from a Roman Catholic diocesan and parish web site.
  - Name the diocese in which your home or school is located. Name the bishop of the diocese. Where is the Cathedral (the bishop's church) in the diocese?
  - Name the parish in which your home or your school is located. Name a priest in the parish? List ways in which lay people are involved in the life of the parish.
  - Are there photographs and articles showing the bishop, priests and lay people involved in an event or celebration at parish or diocesan level?
  - Assemble and print out an information bulletin.

The Parish Priest

Key Concepts

Ministry: special duties performed by priests, ministers and lay people to serve God and the Church.

Service: work carried out to meet the needs of a person or a community.

Objective

Show how a Catholic priest leads and serves a parish community.

Activity: *"Community Service"*

TASK: TO EXPLORE HOW INDIVIDUALS AND WELFARE ORGANISATIONS SERVE THE COMMUNITY.

- ✧ Butcher
- ✧ Baker
- ✧ Garda
- ✧ Postman
- ✧ Shopkeeper
- ✧ Busdriver
- ✧ Electrician
- ✧ Doctor
- ✧ Priest
- ✧ Traffic Warden
- ✧ Teacher
- ✧ Politician

Discuss

- In what ways do people in the above roles serve the community?
- Can you name any welfare organisations that serve the needs of people in your area?
- Some schools give people merit awards for their service to the school community. What kind of things might students do to deserve a merit award?

The priest serves the parish community by celebrating Mass and the sacraments.

Ministry
Service

A Catholic priest serves the people of the parish in a special way.

In the Catholic Church the priest is the leader of the Christian community in the parish. Priests try to follow the example of Jesus who showed that true leadership involves service to others. A priest is called by God to lead and serve people in the parish.

Jesus teaches the Disciples

Jesus washes the feet of his disciples to show what it means to serve others.
(Adapted from John 13:1-17)

It was the day before the Jewish Passover festival. Jesus and his disciples were at supper together. Jesus got up from the table and tied a towel around his waist. He poured water into a basin and began to wash the feet of his disciples. Then he dried them with a towel.

Peter, one of the disciples, would not allow Jesus to wash his feet. Jesus said, "If I do not wash your feet you will no longer be my disciple." Peter allowed Jesus to continue. Afterwards Jesus looked around at his disciples and asked did they understand what he had done. "I am your Lord and teacher," he said, "I have just acted like a servant and washed your feet. I have set an example of how I want you to serve each other. I want you all to put this into practice. Believe me it will make you happy if you do."

A Catholic priest celebrating the Eucharist.

The Priest in the Catholic Church

A Roman Catholic priest begins his ministry on the day of ordination when he recieves the sacrament of Holy Orders. A priest is to be like Jesus. He is ordained by the bishop to lead and serve the parish community and bring them to God. The priest serves the needs of the parish community in Jesus' name. It is his role to:

- Celebrate Mass.
  - Preach the message of God's love in the Gospel.
  - Celebrate the real presence of Jesus in the Eucharist.
- Celebrate the other sacraments.
  - Help people to see God's love at times of happiness and sadness in their lives.
- Give witness to the love of God.
  - Set good example.
  - Care for the sick, the distressed and people in need.
- Work with the parish council.
  - Encourage lay people to share their gifts and talents for the good of the parish community.

"Sharing the message of God's love."

"Celebrating the real presence of Jesus in the Eucharist."

Eucharist

"Helping people to see God's love in their lives in times of happiness and joy."

Baptism

Confirmation

Marriage

"Helping people to see God's love in their lives in times of pain and sorrow."

Sacrament of the Sick

Reconciliation

A Roman Catholic church.

A Priest's Diary

Diary - Sunday

8.00 am - Mass in the parish church.
10.30 am - Mass in the hospital: for patients, visitors and staff.
1.00 pm - Sunday lunch with the Anderson family.
5.00 pm - Rosary in the church.
6.00 pm - Tea.
7.30 pm - Visit the Pacelli family, help with arrangements for the funeral tomorrow.

Diary - Monday

8.00 am - Mass
9.00 am - Answer phone calls, write letters.
11.00 am - Funeral Mass for Luke Pacelli RIP.
12.30 pm - Lunch with teachers in the primary school. After lunch visit the First Communion Class.
2.00 pm - Parish Centre: call into the senior citizen's club.
3.00 pm - Parish office: see Kate about next Sunday's newsletter.
4.00 pm - Visit Amy Johnston (her child has a disability).
6.00 pm - Tea.
7.30 pm - Meeting with Leo and Carmel. Prepare for their wedding next month.

Rev. John Murray is parish priest of St. Mary's parish.

✦ Whom did he meet in the parish on those two days?

✦ How did he serve the needs of people in the parish?

Questions

Knowledge

1. Who is the leader of the Christian community in a parish?
2. How did Jesus' disciples learn that Christian leadership is about serving others?
3. What sacrament does a man receive at ordination?
4. Who ordains a Catholic priest?
5. Give practical examples of the ways in which a priest serves others.

Understanding

1. In the time of Jesus, washing feet was a task usually carried out by the lowest grade of servant. Do you think there was any difference in the way Jesus approached the task?
2. What is the role of the religious leader in a Roman Catholic parish?
3. How does the priest address the spiritual needs of people in a parish community?

Research

- Invite a Catholic priest to speak to the class.
  - Find out about the role of the priest as leader of the Christian community.
  - Prepare for the visit by involving the entire class.

Sample questions.

1. What is the name of the parish, and the parish church?
2. What is the size of the parish?
3. Is the number of people in the parish going up or going down?
4. What do you do on Sundays?
5. Tell us about some of the things you had to do during the past week.
6. Can you tell us why you became a priest.
7. What is it like being a priest?
8. Do you get a day off?

✱ Write a report on the visit.

Protestant Church*Leadership

Key Concepts

Leadership: the task of a leader in guiding a group or organisation.

Authority: the power given to an individual or group to make important decisions.

Objective

Recognise the connection between leadership and authority in two Churches.

Activity: *"Information Gathering"*

TASK: TO CHECK THE LEVEL OF KNOWLEDGE ABOUT TWO COMMUNITIES OF FAITH.

✦ How much do you know about:
- the Church of Ireland.
- the Methodist Church.

Discuss

- Does either Church have a congregation in this area? If so, where is its place of worship?
- What are the titles of the leaders of both Churches at local and national level?
- Can you name the leader of either Church at local and national level?
- What work do the clergy do for their respective communities?
- What is the inspiration behind their commitment to serve the community in this way?
- What do you think is the effect or impact of the clergy's work on either faith community?

The Church of Ireland

The Church of Ireland is part of the worldwide Anglican Communion which has 70 million members in 164 countries. The Church of Ireland is one Church covering Ireland, North and South. It has more than 370,000 members overall. The Church of Ireland traces its roots to the earliest days of Christianity in Ireland.

* The Church of Ireland.
The Methodist Church.

Leaders in the Anglican Communion.

Leadership

Archbishops

The Church of Ireland is divided into two provinces, Armagh and Dublin. Each province has an Archbishop. The Anglican Archbishops of Armagh and Dublin are the leaders of the provinces of the Church of Ireland.

Dr. Richard Clarke, Church of Ireland Primate and Archbishop of Armagh.

Most Rev. Dr. Michael Jackson, Archbishop of Dublin.

It is the role of the Archbishops to preside at an important meeting each year called the General Synod. This is the official law-making body of the Church of Ireland.

Bishops

The two provinces of the Church of Ireland are divided into twelve diocese. Each diocese is guided by a bishop who is elected by clergy and lay people of the diocese. A Diocesan Synod is held each year. It is a forum where elected representatives (clergy and lay people) meet to discuss serious issues affecting parish life in a diocese.

Priests

At parish level, the clergy are called ministers or rectors. Both men and women, single and married, are ordained for ministry in the Church of Ireland. A minister is appointed to a parish by a group of clergy and lay people representing the parish and the diocese. Ministers serve the spiritual needs of the parish community by preaching and leading Sunday worship, baptising new members and being present at significant moments in people's lives. Deacons assist in the parish as part of their training to be ordained ministers.

Lay People

Lay people have a central role in the Church assisting the minister to build community in the parish. Some are Sunday-school teachers. Others are appointed as 'lay-readers' and lead certain forms of worship such as Morning and Evening Prayer. Others are elected members of the select vestry, a committee responsible for the smooth running of the parish. Lay people are also elected to the Diocesan Synod which discusses Church matters at Diocesan level. The Diocesan Synod in turn elects clergy and lay people to represent the diocese at the annual General Synod.

In the Anglican Communion, of which the Church of Ireland is a part, no one person has complete authority. Instead, clergy and lay people are elected onto groups at:

- ❖ Parish level - Select Vestry.
- ❖ Diocesan level - Diocesan Synod.
- ❖ National level - General Synod.

Organised in this way men and women, lay and ordained, debate issues, make decisions, and lead the Church forward together.

Structure of leadership in the Church of Ireland.

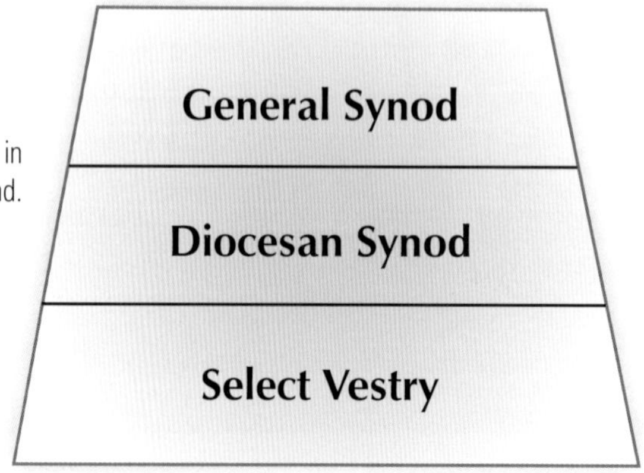
General Synod
Diocesan Synod
Select Vestry

'The General Synod of the Church of England.'
In the Anglican Communion decisions about major issues affecting the Church are made at the General Synod, an annual meeting of bishops, clergy and laity.

Authority

The General Synod is the ruling body of the Church of Ireland. It meets once a year to debate and make important decisions about issues of concern to the Church. Each diocese elects clergy and lay people to be their representatives at the Synod.

The Church of Ireland is a democratic Church. Its General Synod comprises 12 bishops, 216 clergy, and 432 lay people all working together for the benefit of the Church. The Archbishop of Armagh leads the proceedings at the General Synod of the Church of Ireland.

Questions

Knowledge

1. How many members belong to:
   a. The Anglican Communion worldwide?
   b. The Church of Ireland?
2. a. Give the title of a local and national leader in the Church of Ireland.
   b. Name one national leader of the Church.
3. a. How many diocese are in the Church of Ireland?
   b. What is a Diocesan Synod?
4. Who is responsible for the day to day running of the Church of Ireland at local level?
5. How does a rector and a bishop in the Church of Ireland get appointed to a parish and a diocese?
6. a. What does the term 'authority' mean?
   b. What is the General Synod of the Church of Ireland?

Understanding

1. Explain the leadership structure within the Church of Ireland.
2. What leadership style do you associate with the Church of Ireland: authoritarian, enabling, democratic? Explain your answer.
3. What is an important source of authority in the Church of Ireland? How does it operate?

The Methodist Church

The Methodist Church, founded by John Wesley and his brother Charles in the 18th century, has over fifty million members worldwide.

Leadership

There is a very democratic style of leadership in the Methodist Church. Church leadership relies on the contribution of clergy and lay people at every level. There are no bishops, decisions about the Church are made by a council of lay people and ministers at the Annual Conference.

Society

The local congregation is called a society. Members worship in church on Sunday, pray and study the Bible together and undertake good works in the community during the week. Local lay preachers are trained to preach and lead Morning Prayer on Sunday.

A society steward is a lay person who oversees the work of a society.

Circuit

Several societies link together in an area to form a circuit. An ordained minister may have to look after a number of churches in a circuit. He/she will preach the Gospel and celebrate Holy Communion in every church at least once a month.

A circuit superintendent is a senior minister who oversees the work of the circuit.

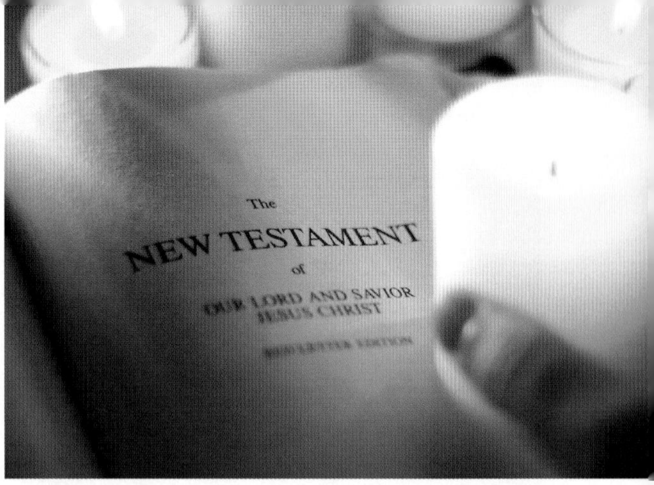
The
NEW TESTAMENT
of
OUR LORD AND SAVIOR
JESUS CHRIST

The Bible.

District

A district is a number of circuits joined together over a wider area. In Ireland there are eight districts.

A superintendent is elected by the district to oversee the work of the district and support the ministers who serve the congregations in their care.

Annual Conference

The Conference is the governing body of the Methodist Church in Ireland. The Annual Conference is attended by 250 ministers and lay people representing all the circuits in the country. Delegates meet to worship together, discuss new ideas, and make decisions about the best way to run the Church.

A new President is elected at the Annual Conference every year. He/she will lead the Methodist community and act as chief spokesperson of the Methodist Church in Ireland. The appointment is temporary, for one year only. The Methodist Church in Ireland is part of the Methodist Council, which is the worldwide association of Methodist Churches.

Structure of leadership in the Methodist Church.

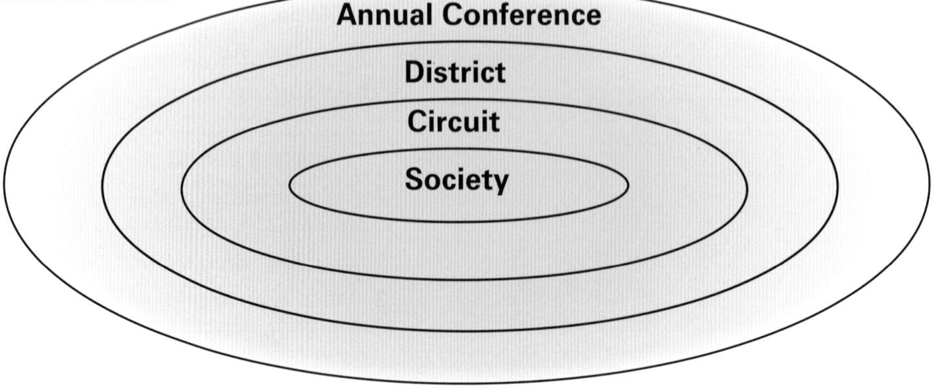
Annual Conference
District
Circuit
Society

Attending the Annual Conference
of the Methodist Church in Ireland.

Authority

The Methodist Church is a community of faith. The Bible is the only source of authority for the Methodist community. The Methodist Church is non-episcopal, meaning there are no bishops in authority, and no one person has overall authority. Decisions about Church matters are made by delegates at the annual Conference.

At the annual Conference ministers and lay people work together in partnership developing Church policy on a range of issues. A new president is elected at each Conference, it is his/her role to lead and guide the Methodist community for one year. The office of president is not a permanent appointment.

Questions

Knowledge

1. Name the founder of the Methodist Church.
2. How many members belong to the Methodist Church worldwide?
3. What is the unit of organisation in the Methodist Church at local level?
4. What is the title and role of one lay person in the Methodist Church at local level?
5. What is the title and role of an ordained person in a local Methodist church?
6. How often do Methodists elect a new national leader in their community?
7. What is the role of a national leader in the Methodist community?
8. What does it mean to say the Methodist Church is non-episcopal?

Understanding

1. Describe the structure of leadership in the Methodist community of faith.
2. What leadership style do you associate with the Methodist Church: authoritarian, enabling, democratic? Explain your answer.
3. What is the main source of authority in the Methodist Church?

Section B - Foundations of Religion: Christianity

The *Syllabus Aims* in this section are:

- To explore the context into which Jesus was born.
- To identify the Gospels as the main source of knowledge about Jesus.
- To examine the meaning of the life, death and resurrection of Jesus for his followers, then and now.

Concept Checklist (Section B - Foundations of Religion: Christianity)

Page

- ❑ **Ancient Judaism** - the history and culture of the Jewish people at the time of Jesus. 104, 107, 109
- ❑ **Christ/Messiah** - a title meaning 'anointed one'. Jesus is a spiritual leader sent by God. 197
- ❑ **Conflict with authority** - a clash or a struggle with people in power. 159, 161, 163, 169
- ❑ **Discipleship** - following Jesus and his teaching.. . . . . 152, 154, 157
- ❑ **Eucharist** - a Christian service of thanksgiving. In the Catholic Church the Eucharist is a sacrament. 166
- ❑ **Evangelist** - a Gospel writer (Mark, Matthew, Luke or John) who spread the 'Good News' of Jesus Christ. 113, 115
- ❑ **Evidence** - information about a religious tradition collected from different sources. 126, 128
- ❑ **Evidence from oral and written traditions** - the way information about Jesus passed from the spoken to the written word.. 120
- ❑ **Gospel** - the 'Good News' of Jesus Christ in the first four books of the New Testament. 113
- ❑ **Kingdom of God** - Jesus' vision of a way of life that loves God and does good to other people. 131, 133, 135, 137, 139, 141, 143, 145, 147, 149, 152, 154
- ❑ **Martyrdom** - a willingness to suffer and die for one's beliefs or a special cause.. 172
- ❑ **Memorial** - something done to honour and remember someone or something.. 166
- ❑ **Messianic expectation** - the hope of the Jewish people that a new leader, a Messiah, would bring them to freedom.. 111
- ❑ **Miracle** - an amazing cure or deed performed by Jesus to show the power and love of God. . . . 143, 145, 147
- ❑ **Mission** - the specific work carried out by members of a Christian community. 157
- ❑ **Missionary** - one who is sent on a journey to spread the Gospel by preaching, or by example.. 189
- ❑ **Parable** - a short story told by Jesus to teach people about the Kingdom of God. 133, 135, 137, 139, 141
- ❑ **Passover** - a Jewish festival to celebrate the Exodus. 166
- ❑ **Pentecost** - the day the apostles received the Holy Spirit and began spreading the message of Jesus.. 184
- ❑ **People of God** - Christian communities past and present who believe in God and follow the teaching of Jesus.. . . . . 186, 192
- ❑ **Presence** - the fact that Jesus exists and is truly present here and now.. . . . . 176, 179
- ❑ **Resurrection** - the central Christian belief that Jesus rose from the dead three days after he was crucified.. 176
- ❑ **Sacrifice** - something of value (one's life for example) offered to God for the sake of others. 166, 172
- ❑ **Son of God** - a title that shows the divine or holy relationship between Jesus and God the Father. 197
- ❑ **Son of Man** - a title that shows the human nature of Jesus, and the fact that his suffering and death is a sacrifice to benefit all humanity.. 197
- ❑ **Synoptic** - to be alike or be similar. The Gospels of Mark, Matthew and Luke are so alike they are known as the Synoptic Gospels.. 123
- ❑ **Table Fellowship** - the way Jesus shared meals with everyone to show the Kingdom of God is open to all. 149
- ❑ **The Holy Land** - a name for Palestine, the country where Jesus was born. 96, 100, 102
- ❑ **The Roman Empire** - the lands ruled by ancient Rome.. 98
- ❑ **Transformation** - a complete change in the appearance and nature of Jesus after the resurrection.. . . . 176, 179
- ❑ **Vocation** - a feeling of being called by God to serve others.. 157
- ❑ **Witness** - to proclaim or publicly announce one's religious faith.. 113

The Bible

Objective

To become familiar with the Bible and be able to look up Bible references.

Activity: *"Respect"*

TASK: TO BE AWARE THAT SACRED TEXTS ARE TO BE TREATED WITH RESPECT.

✡ **Religion:** Judaism
Sacred text: the Tenakh.
A copy of the Torah (part of the Tenakh) is placed on a reading stand in the centre of the synagogue. The reader will not touch the Torah, a small pointer is used instead.

✠ **Religion:** Christianity
Sacred text: the Bible.
In a church the Bible is placed in front of the congregation on a special stand called a lectern. This allows everyone to see how important it is.

Discuss

- How do people of different religions show respect for sacred texts in their place of worship?
- List ways in which copies of the Bible can be treated with respect in the classroom.

The Bible

Every religion has its own sacred text. The Bible is the sacred text of Christianity. The book is special and holy for all Christians because they believe it is the Word of God. The Christian Bible is divided into two sections. The first is called the Old Testament. The second part is called the New Testament.

The Old Testament

The Old Testament or Jewish Scripture was written before the time of Jesus. It tells the story of God's people, the Jews. This part of the Bible is special to the Jewish community.

The New Testament

The New Testament or Christian Scripture was written after the time of Jesus. It tells the story of Jesus and the first Christians. All Christians read both the Old and New Testaments. The Old Testament tells the story of how God prepared people for the coming of Jesus.

Discovering the Bible.

HOLY BIBLE

Bible References

The Christian Churches use different versions of the Bible. So when you want to look up a story or a prayer you do not use page numbers, you use Bible references.

Every book in the Bible:

- ❖ Has a name.
- ❖ Has chapters.
- ❖ Has verses.

Each page in the Bible has a series of numbers, big and small.

- ❖ The big numbers tell you the chapter.
- ❖ The small numbers tell you the verse.

A Bible reference helps you to find a sentence anywhere in the Bible. It tells you the book, the chapter and the verse to look for.

Mark 1:3 is an example of a Bible reference.

The name of the book is at the top of the page

Chapter

Verse

Mark

1 This is the Good News about Jesus Christ, the Son of God. [2]It began as the prophet Isaiah had written "God said 'I will send my messenger ahead of you to clear the way for you'.

[3]Someone is shouting in the desert, "Get the road ready for the Lord, make a straight path for him to travel!"

- ❖ Sometimes the name of the book is shortened, for example, **Mark** is shortened to **Mk**, **Genesis** is shortened to **Gen**.
- ❖ Sometimes more than one verse has to be read, for example **Mk 6:4-6**

The chapter.

The book. → **Mark 6:4-6**

All the verses from 4 to 6.

Reading the Bible.

Books in the Bible

The Bible itself is like a small library made up of many different books.

There are 72 books in the Jerusalem Bible
- 45 books in the Old Testament.
- 27 books in the New Testament.

Some books are quite long while others are short and have only a few pages. Every book in the Bible has its own name. Some have men's names, others have women's.

The books in the Old Testament were written over a thousand year period by many different authors. The books in the New Testament were written by only a few authors over a period of fifty years or so. When you open a copy of the Bible notice that the Old Testament is at the front of the book and the New Testament is at the back.

The Bible is like a small library.

The Christian Bible

In the Christian Bible there are twenty seven books in the New Testament alone. The first four books are the Gospels of Matthew, Mark, Luke and John.

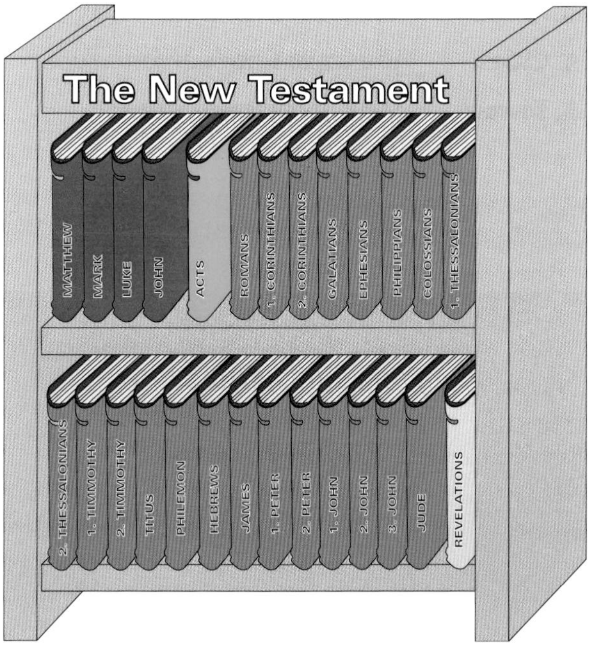

The New Testament
MATTHEW
MARK
LUKE
JOHN
ACTS
ROMANS
1. CORINTHIANS
2. CORINTHIANS
GALATIANS
EPHESIANS
PHILIPPIANS
COLOSSIANS
1. THESSALONIANS
2. THESSALONIANS
1. TIMMOTHY
2. TIMMOTHY
TITUS
PHILEMON
HEBREWS
JAMES
1. PETER
2. PETER
1. JOHN
2. JOHN
3. JOHN
JUDE
REVELATIONS

The twenty seven books in the New Testament in the Bible.

Questions

Knowledge

1. Name the sacred text of Christianity.
2. What do Christians believe about their sacred text?
3. Name the two parts of the Bible.
4. Which part of the Bible was written before the time of Jesus?
5. Which part of the Bible tells the story of Jesus and the early Christians?
6. Which part of the Bible tells the story of the Jewish people?
7. What is a Bible reference?
8. Why do people use Bible references and not page numbers when looking up something in the Bible?
9. Explain how to look up a Bible reference.
10. How many books are in the Old and New Testaments in the Jerusalem Bible?

Understanding

1. In what way is the Bible like a mini-library?
2. Closely examine a copy of the Bible. Explain how so many books can fit between the cover of one Bible. Give at least three reasons why this is possible.
3. Why do you think a sacred text should be treated with respect?

Research

- The different Christian Churches use different versions of the Bible.
  For example there is:
  - The Jerusalem Bible.
  - The Holy Bible (King James version).
  - RSV Bible.
  - Good News Bible.
  - Find out which version of the Bible is used in the Catholic Church.
  - What version of the Bible is used in some Protestant Churches?

The Holy Land

Key Concept

The Holy Land: a name for Palestine, the country where Jesus was born.

Objective

Describe the geography of Palestine, the country where Jesus lived.

Activity: *"Map Work"*

TASK: TO LOCATE PALESTINE ON A MAP.

- Examine the map.
  - Find the country where we live.
  - Identify two other countries in Europe.
  - Find Africa and Asia on the map.
  - Notice where Palestine is located.

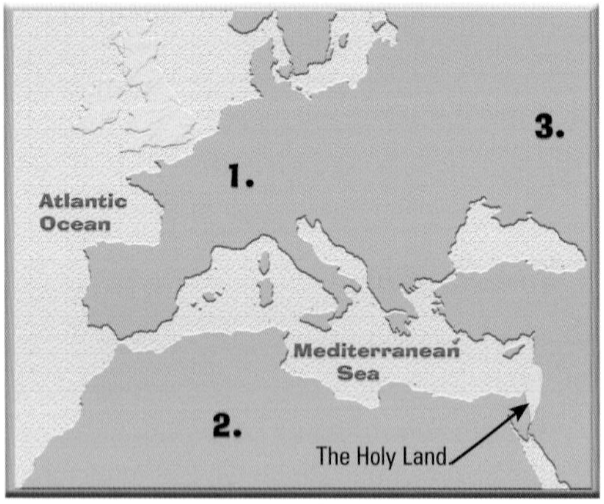
3.
1.
Atlantic Ocean
Mediterranean Sea
2.
The Holy Land

Jesus lived all his life in Palestine, a small country beside the Mediterranean Sea. It is surrounded by three continents: Europe, Africa and Asia. Today, the country where Jesus lived is called Israel. It is also known as the Holy Land.

Discuss

- In what country did Jesus live?
- What sea is located off the coast of Palestine?
- Name the continents 1, 2 and 3, that surround Palestine.
- What is Palestine called today?
- How many hours do you think it would take to travel there by airplane from here?

The Holy Land

Palestine is the country where Jesus lived all his life.

Palestine is a small country, it is about a quarter the size of Ireland. Despite its small size it is a land of many contrasts. There are snow capped mountains in the north, and a desert area in the south. In between, there are low hills and fertile valleys. Sheep graze on the hillsides, crops are grown in the good soil of the valleys. The weather in Palestine is usually very hot during the day (about 30-40°C), but it can get cold at night. Palestine was divided into three political districts or provinces. The country has two large lakes, one main river, one capital city, and many small towns.

▲ **Provinces**	The three provinces were Galilee, Samaria and Judaea.
▲ **Lakes**	The two lakes are the Sea of Galilee and the Dead Sea.
▲ **Rivers**	The main river is the Jordan.
▲ **Cities**	The capital city was Jerusalem.
▲ **Towns**	Some small towns were: - Nazareth, Cana and Capernaum in the north. - Bethlehem, Jericho and Bethany in the south.

Fishermen on Lake Galilee today.

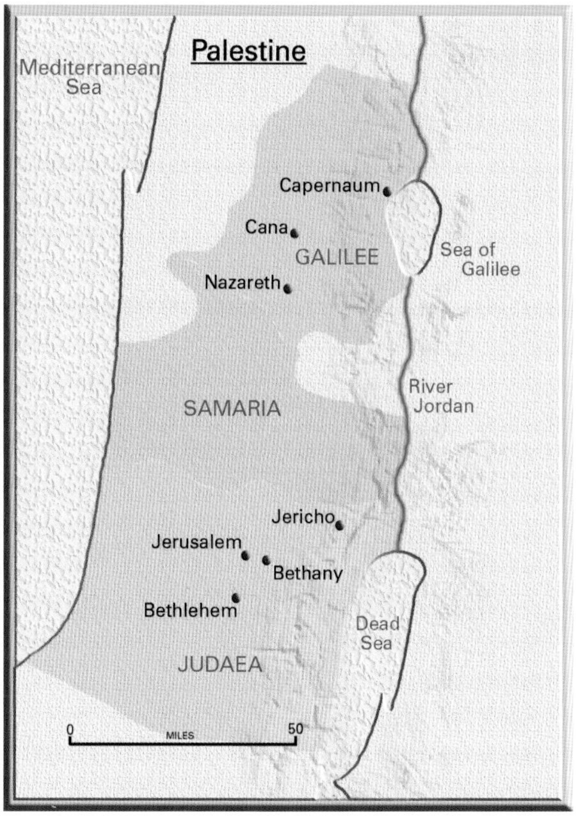
Palestine
Mediterranean Sea
Capernaum
Cana
GALILEE
Sea of Galilee
Nazareth
River Jordan
SAMARIA
Jericho
Jerusalem
Bethany
Bethlehem
Dead Sea
JUDAEA
0
MILES
50

Map of Palestine.

Palestine at the time of Jesus

Jesus grew up in Galilee in the north of Palestine. There he would have seen fishermen at work on the lake, shepherds on the hillsides minding sheep and farmers in the fields sowing crops and tending vines. Jesus began his public ministry after his baptism in the Jordan river. With his disciples to help him, he travelled all over the country teaching people about the love of God.

Key Events in the Life of Jesus

Jesus:	Bible References:
✠ Was born in Bethlehem.	Luke 2:5-7
✠ Grew up in Nazareth.	Luke 2:39-40
✠ Was baptised in the river Jordan.	Matt 3:13-17
✠ Performed his first miracle at Cana.	John 2:1-11
✠ Met his first disciples at the Sea of Galilee.	Matt 4:18-22
✠ Taught people in Capernaum.	Mark 2:1-2
✠ Healed people in Jericho.	Matt 20:29-34
✠ Visited friends in Bethany.	John 11:1-3
✠ Was crucified outside Jerusalem.	Luke 23:26-28

Questions

Knowledge

1. Where is the Holy Land?
2. a. What was the name of the Holy Land at the time of Jesus?
   b. What is it called today?
3. Name the three political regions or provinces in Palestine.
4. Name the following geographical features in Palestine:
   a. Two lakes.
   b. The river that flows between those two lakes.
   c. Three towns in Galilee.
   d. Three towns in Judaea.
5. Where in Palestine:
   a. was Jesus born?
   b. did Jesus grow up?
   c. was Jesus baptised?
   d. was Jesus put to death?

Understanding

1. Describe what you would notice about the physical features of Palestine (Israel) if you travelled by car today from the north to the south of the country - a distance of approximately 230 kms (145 miles).
2. Jesus and his disciples travelled on foot all over Palestine teaching people about the love of God. What arrangements would they have had to make at that time for a safe and comfortable journey?
3. Select one place in Palestine associated with the life of Jesus. State:
   - what occurred there.
   - what Jesus said or did.
   - how people responded to him.
   - why people responded to Jesus in this way.

Research

✪ Select a place in Palestine associated with the life of Jesus.
- ✸ Search internet websites for pictures and further information on that location as it exists today.
- ✸ Create a one-page brochure using drawings or pictures. Include at least four points of information about this location. State the importance of this place for Christians today.
- ✸ Present the finished work to the class.

The Roman Empire

Key Concept

The Roman Empire: the lands ruled by Ancient Rome.

Objective

Outline the political structure of Palestine at the time of Jesus.

Activity: *"Mapwork"*

TASK: TO KNOW THE EXTENT OF THE ROMAN EMPIRE IN THE FIRST CENTURY CE.

The heart of the Roman Empire was the city of Rome in Italy. Its leader was the Roman Emperor. The Roman Empire lasted more than 500 years. It was powerful for a long period because its soldiers had superior weapons and better fighting tactics than any other army. It also appointed members of the local population to help it administer and rule the occupied territories. The Romans took control of all the land bordering the Mediterranean Sea. The Roman Empire gradually spread throughout Europe, Western Asia and North Africa. When Jesus was born, Palestine was ruled by the Romans.

Discuss

- Who were the Romans?
- What area was eventually controlled by the Roman Empire?
- Who ruled Palestine at the time of Jesus?

The Roman Empire

At the time of Jesus Palestine was part of the Roman Empire.

Palestine was only a small country, yet it had an important strategic position. It was on the edge of the Roman Empire, at the cross-roads of three continents, Europe, Africa and Asia. Whoever had control of Palestine controlled the major trade routes in and out of these areas.

Roman Rule

In 63BCE, the Romans invaded Palestine. The Roman army marched into Jerusalem and took over the city. Very soon they took control of the entire country. The Romans put their own governors in charge to rule the people.

In 40BCE, Emperor Augustus appointed Herod as King of Palestine. He was a capable ruler and totally loyal to Rome. At the time of Jesus' birth Herod was King of Palestine. At the time of Jesus' death Galilee was ruled by Herod Antipas (a son of King Herod). Samaria and Judaea were both ruled by Pontius Pilate (a Roman governor).

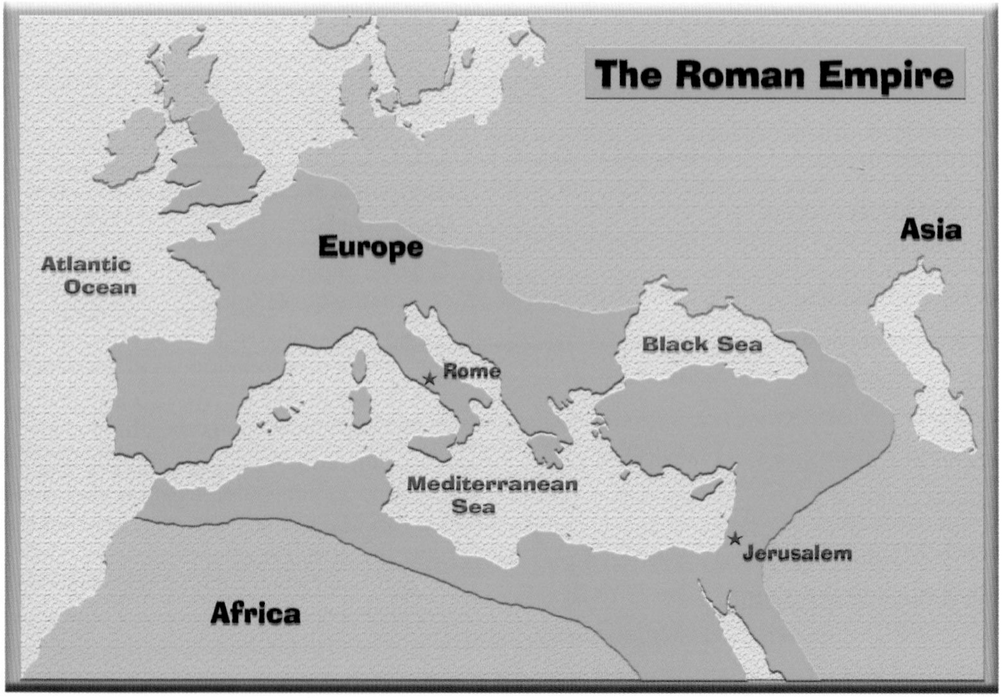
The Roman Empire
Europe
Asia
Atlantic Ocean
Black Sea
Rome
Mediterranean Sea
Jerusalem
Africa

The extent of the Roman Empire.

Roman soldiers.

A Roman governor had to make sure that the Jewish people of Palestine obeyed Roman laws and paid Roman taxes. In return the Jews were allowed to follow their own customs, and practice their own religion.

The Jews did not accept Roman rule and were unhappy with the Roman occupation. They believed Palestine was their land, given to them by God. They believed they were 'God's chosen people', to be ruled by God alone. It annoyed them that Roman soldiers were everywhere, marching throughout the country, patrolling towns and villages. Roman rule caused a lot of tension and political unrest in the land where Jesus lived.

Tax Collectors

At the the time of Jesus the ordinary people in Palestine lived very simple lives. They earned just enough money for food, clothes and a small house for their families. Following the occupation they had to pay extra taxes for the upkeep of the Roman army based in Palestine. The money was collected by local Jewish people called tax collectors.

Most Jews disliked tax collectors because they worked for the Romans. Tax collectors were regarded as traitors and cheats. They were allowed to keep a portion of the money they collected. Some, however, took more than their share and became very wealthy. At the time of Jesus tax collectors were shunned as social outcasts by the Jewish people of Palestine.

Questions

Knowledge

1. Where is Palestine on a map of the Roman Empire?
2. When did the Romans invade Palestine?
3. Who was King Herod?
4. Who was Pontius Pilate?
5. What was the role of Roman rulers in Palestine?
6. How did the Jews feel about Roman rule in Palestine?
7. What was the job of a tax collector at the time of Jesus?
8. How did people feel about the tax collectors?

Understanding

1. What was the political structure in Palestine at the time of Jesus?
2. Why did the Romans want control of Palestine?
3. How did the Roman occupation affect the lives of ordinary people living in Palestine?
4. Why did the Jews resent Roman rule in Palestine?

Research

The Roman Empire was an occupying power yet it brought many benefits to the countries it occupied. It had a building programme for towns and cities, public buildings were constructed, water systems installed and roadways were laid down.

- Find out about one aspect of Roman architecture or engineering that has survived to the present day in Israel, or elsewhere in what was formerly the Roman Empire.
- Write a report, include drawings, diagrams or pictures and present it to the class.

Homelife in Palestine

Key Concept

The Holy Land: a name for Palestine, the country where Jesus was born.

Objective

Describe home life in Palestine at the time of Jesus.

Activity: *"Houseplans"*

TASK: TO BE AWARE OF THE IMPACT OF SOCIAL AND ENVIRONMENTAL FACTORS ON HOUSE DESIGN.

✦ Think about your own family home, the homes of your friends and other houses in the neighbourhood.

Discuss

- How many rooms are in most houses today?
- What weather conditions and other environmental factors affect the way homes are built in this country?
- Does family lifestyle affect the way homes are designed today?
- Describe your own "dream home".

The Holy Land

Jesus lived with Mary and Joseph in a village house in Nazareth.

Jesus' family home would have been typical of the homes of ordinary people in first century Palestine. A village house was a small, one-roomed building with one window and one door. The walls of the house were built of clay bricks and stone and were white-washed to reflect the heat of the sun. The window was small to keep the house cool inside. The roof of the house was flat and thatched with reeds covered in clay. The surface was often strong enough to walk on. Steps at the side led up onto the roof. It was used as extra space to dry fruit and grain, hang out clothes to dry, and sit out for meals in the cool of the evening.

A mezuzah was fixed to the doorframe of all Jewish homes. It was a small wooden or leather box containing a tiny scroll on which the words of the Shema were written. The Shema was a prayer from a book of Jewish scripture (Deuteronomy 6:4). The mezuzah was touched prayerfully by Jews entering and leaving the home.

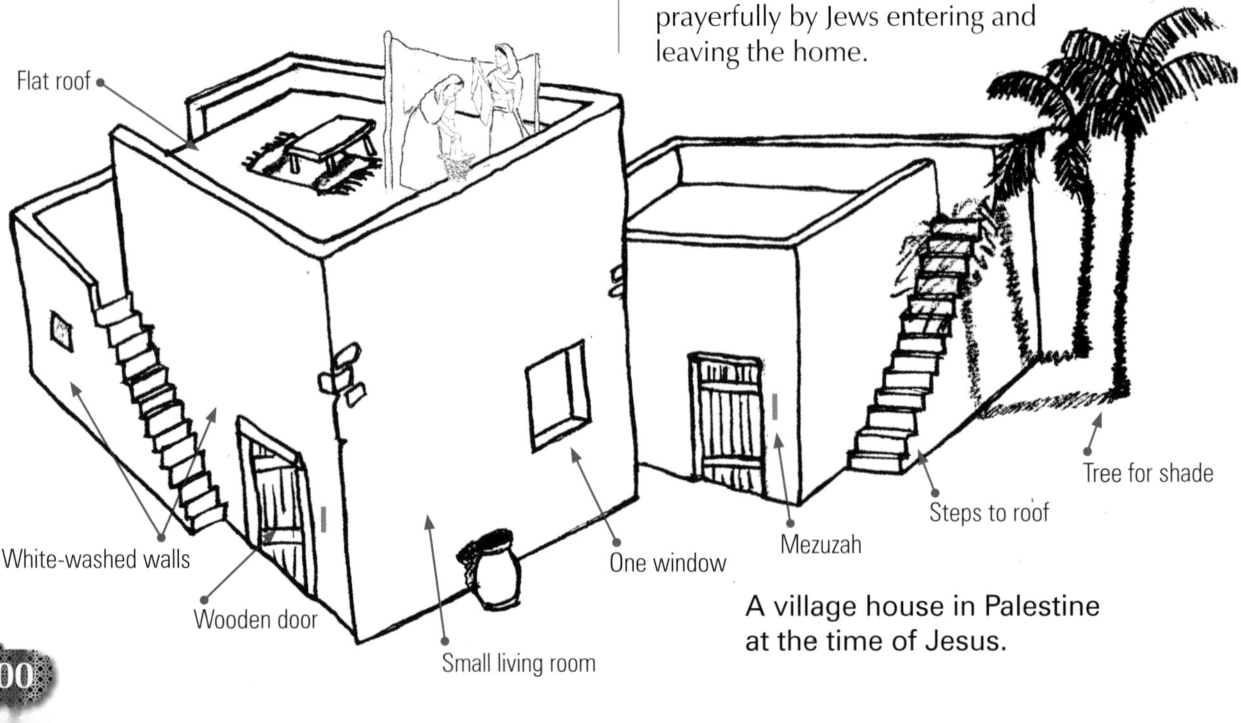
Flat roof
White-washed walls
Wooden door
Small living room
One window
Mezuzah
Steps to roof
Tree for shade

A village house in Palestine at the time of Jesus.

The interior of a village house in Palestine

The interior of village houses were cool, but dark and very crowded. Each one was divided into two levels:

- The family lived on the upper level.
- The lower level was used at night as a stable for animals.

There was an oil-lamp in the centre of each Jewish home. It was placed on a lamp stand and was always lit, day and night. Oil for the lamp was stored in a pottery jar, other jars held water and cooking oil. There were also some large jars for storing corn. At night the family slept on mats on the floor. In the morning, the mats were rolled up and stored in a corner. The floor of the house was bare earth covered with rushes and was swept each day with a broom. There was very little furniture. There were hooks on the wall to hang up clothes and wineskins, and most houses had a chest where families kept their scrolls and special belongings.

Ordinary families would have had a goat, a donkey and a few chickens. They were all brought in at night to keep them safe, and their feed put in a manger. In the morning, the animals were led outside again.

Mealtimes in a Jewish home

Traditional Eastern food.

All the family came together for the evening meal. After washing their hands, they sat around a mat on the floor. The meal began with a blessing, then everyone took food from a large dish. They dipped the fingers of their right hand into the dish to take out the food, no cutlery was used. Fresh bread was eaten with the meal. The bread was broken and divided amongst everyone. During the meal the father of a devout family would tell stories from Jewish scripture. The meal always ended with a blessing.

Questions

Knowledge

1. In what type of houses did ordinary people live at the time of Jesus?
2. How did families make use of the roof space on top of their houses?
3. What is a mezuzah?
4. Inside the house, how was the living space divided?
5. What item had a central place in every Jewish home?
6. How did people eat their food at mealtimes?
7. In what way was mealtime a holy occasion in Jewish homes?

Understanding

1. What factors influenced the type of houses built for ordinary people in Palestine at the time of Jesus?
2. Why did the inside of a house in Palestine seem dark and crowded?
3. What impact did religion have on the home life of ordinary people in Palestine?
4. Compare the home life of people in this country today with the home life of people in Palestine at the time of Jesus. What are the similarities and differences?

Research

- Read the following Bible references to find out what aspects of home life are referred to in the New Testament?

  - Luke 2:39 - Luke 2:5-7
  - Matt 5:15 - Mark 2:11-12
  - Luke 15:8 - Mark 2:2-4
  - Mark 14:20 - Luke 22:19

  - What image of home life in Palestine emerges from these passages in the New Testament?
  - Discuss your ideas with the class.

Worklife in Palestine

Key Concept

The Holy Land: a name for Palestine, the country where Jesus was born.

Objective

Describe the lifestyle and occupations of ordinary people in Palestine at the time of Jesus.

Section B

Activity: *"Shopping"*

TASK: TO BE AWARE OF THE VARIETY OF BUSINESSES AND SERVICES IN OUR TOWNS AND SHOPPING CENTRES TODAY.

- Just for a moment, think about your local town or shopping centre.
  - When do you go there? Is it at lunchtime, after school, or at the weekend?
  - What is it like?
  - Do you go mostly to look around, to meet friends, or to buy something?

Discuss

- Where is the best place in town to get a hair cut, buy new clothes, a CD, a DVD or a computer game?
- Name some of your favourite shops.
- Apart from clothes shops and music stores, what other shops and businesses are based in your local town or shopping centre?

Going to the well for water was a daily household task.

The Holy Land

At the time of Jesus, the marketplace in Nazareth was the centre of commercial activity.

Women went to the market every day to buy fresh food supplied by local farmers and fishermen. Occasionally they bought household goods from the workshops of local tradesmen. Daily life followed a familiar pattern.

"The morning is always a busy time in our house. We are awake at dawn. We roll up the sleeping mats and put them away, then the animals are attended to. Next we have breakfast of bread, cheese and fruit. After breakfast, the boys go off to school at the synagogue. The class sit around the rabbi who is a teacher in the synagogue. He teaches them Jewish scripture. The boys learn to read and write in Aramaic, our local language, and in Hebrew which is the ancient language of the Jewish people.

At school in the synagogue.

After school the boys work with their father for the rest of the day. Our oldest son will soon be thirteen, and will be leaving school to work full time at his father's trade. The girls stay at home with me. I teach them about home-making and childrearing and show them how to carry out religious duties in the home. Together we tidy the house, bake the bread and go to the well for water."

The market in Nazareth

"Later on we go to the market to do the shopping and walk through the narrow streets to the market square. We pass several small workshops where local tradesmen are busy at work. The carpenter is sawing and hammering wood; he sells chests, drawers and shelves. In another workshop, the potter is throwing clay on the potter's wheel. He sells jars, oil-lamps and food-dishes. Next door, the sandal-maker sells leather belts and sandals. The leather comes from the hide of sheep and goats.

The market square is in the centre of the village. It is always noisy and crowded. The merchants shout out their wares. They sell baskets, mats, cloth, oil and jewelery. Farmers come in from the country to sell fruit and vegetables and also grain for bread-making. Shepherds come down from the hills to sell wool and meat. Fishermen arrive from the lakes to sell their baskets of fish.

Nazareth is quite close to some important trade routes, so there are always traders from other countries passing through the village. They stop to buy and sell things in the market, and usually stay overnight at the village inn where the innkeeper always makes them welcome. They continue their journey again the next day. There are Roman soldiers around too. They keep law and order in the village. One or two soldiers stand guard beside the tax-collector's office. The locals don't like the Romans or the tax-collectors and tend to avoid them.

As we make our way home again we pass the synagogue. We usually give a coin to the beggar near the entrance, he is always there asking for help. Sometimes we see the rabbi going into the synagogue to teach scripture.

Back home we get the food ready for the evening meal. Everyone will arrive home soon, tired and hungry after their long day."

Questions

Knowledge

1. What was the morning routine in a typical family home in Palestine?
2. How were Jewish boys educated in first century Palestine?
3. What language:
   a. did children speak at home?
   b. did pupils learn at school?
4. Give a reason why you think boys and girls were taught separately at the time of Jesus.
5. How did ordinary people earn their living in Galilee when Jesus was growing up?
6. What kind of things did the women see and hear around them in the marketplace in Nazareth?

Understanding

1. Describe a typical day in the life of either a shepherd, an inn-keeper, a fisherman or a homemaker at the time of Jesus.
2. What impact did geographical features have on the way people earned their living in Palestine at the time of Jesus?
3. Do you think daily life was easy or difficult for ordinary men and women in Palestine 2,000 years ago? Explain your answer.

Research

- Look up each Bible reference.
  - What kind of people would Jesus have seen in the towns and villages of Palestine.

- Matt 13:47	- Luke 18:35
- Matt 9:9	- John 18:12
- Luke 8:5	- Luke 2:8
- John 3:2	- Mark 6:3

  - Check the results with the class.

Jewish History

Key Concept

Ancient Judaism: the history and culture of the Jewish people at the time of Jesus.

Objective

Give an account of significant people and events in Jewish history.

Section B

Activity: *"Ups and Downs"*

TASK: IDENTIFY HIGH POINTS AND LOW POINTS IN OUR PERSONAL HISTORY FROM BIRTH TO THE PRESENT TIME.

✦ Think about your life from the time you were born up to the present.
What ups (△) and downs (▼) have you experienced during that time?

✦ Can you plot some of these events on a life line?

Discuss

Have you ever:

- Moved house?
- Lived in another country?
- Had a disappointment?
- Succeeded at something?
- Made mistakes?
- Made a fresh start?
- Felt under pressure?
- Really looked forward to something?

Can you describe what happened on one of those occasions?

Ancient Judaism

There were many ups and downs in the history of the Jewish people long ago.

Jesus was a Jew. He grew up in a Jewish family in northern Palestine. We will take a brief look at the history of Judaism over a period of 2,000 years from the time of Abraham to the time of Jesus. There were many high points and low points in the history of the Jewish people throughout that time. The story unfolds in the part of the world located on the map below. Note that over the years the country where the Jews lived has been called The Promised Land, Canaan, Palestine and Israel. During this time the Jewish people have been known as God's Chosen People, Hebrews, Israelites and Jews.

Abraham's journey to Canaan.

Jacob's journey to Egypt.

Moses and the Exodus from Egypt.

Hebrew exile to, and return from, Babylon.

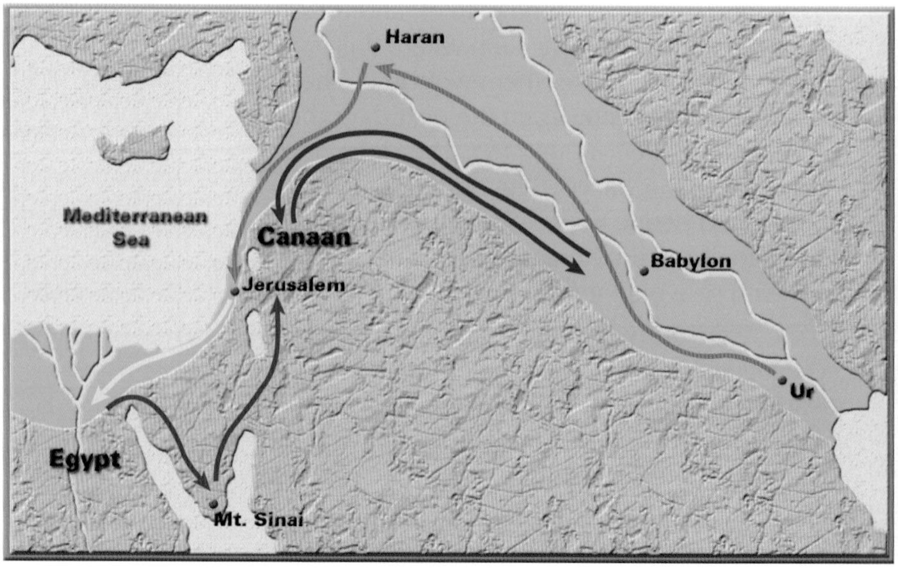
Haran
Mediterranean Sea
Canaan
Jerusalem
Babylon
Ur
Egypt
Mt. Sinai

The journeys of Abraham and his descendants through the Fertile Crescent. Today this territory is known as the Middle East.

Jewish History

The history of the Jews' special relationship with God begins 4,000 years ago in the Fertile Crescent (The Middle East). It involves a man called Abraham and his wife Sarah.

- Abraham
  God calls Abraham to lead his people from the city of Ur to the land of Canaan. God makes a covenant (a sacred agreement) with Abraham. His descendants, known as God's chosen people, all worship the one God.
- Slavery in Egypt
  A famine breaks out in Canaan and Abraham's grandson Jacob moves the family to Egypt. At first they are welcomed as guests but are later treated as slaves. They are enslaved for three hundred years.
- Moses
  God chooses Moses to lead the Jews out of slavery in Egypt. This is called the Exodus. At Mount Sinai, God gives Moses the Law and the Ten Commandments. The Jews promise to obey the Law of God.
- Return to Canaan
  Led by Joshua, the people return to Canaan. Life is hard and they struggle to survive. After many battles the kingdom of Israel is established.
- David
  Judges and prophets are sent to lead the Jews in the ways of God. Eventually the Jews establish a kingdom and David becomes king of all Israel. He is a great warrior and tries hard to keep his people faithful to the laws of God. He makes Jerusalem his capital city. His son Solomon builds the Temple in Jerusalem where everyone can worship God.
- The Prophets
  After Solomon's death the kingdom is divided. The Jews fall into wicked ways and fail to keep God's Law. God sends prophets, holy men such as Ezekiel and Jeremiah, to warn them of the danger of this. The Jews refuse to listen.
- Jerusalem Destroyed
  A crisis occurs and Jerusalem is invaded. The Temple is destroyed and the people are deported as slaves to Babylon.
- The Exile
  The Jews realise their mistake, they had deliberately turned away from God. In exile and far from home, they turn back to God once more. They write down their laws and beliefs about God. This will become the Torah, part of the sacred text of Judaism.

Jewish men meet to pray at the site of the ancient Temple in Jerusalem.

- Return from Exile
  The Jews are set free and return to Jerusalem where they rebuild the Temple. They make a fresh start. Rabbis begin to teach them how to practice their faith in a sincere way. The Jews pray in their local synagogues on the Sabbath and try their best to obey God's law.
- Foreign Rulers
  Over the next four hundred years one foreign power after another invades the country. The Romans invade Palestine in 63BCE and impose their laws on the Jewish people.
- The Messiah
  The Jews long for a leader, a Messiah to set them free. They want someone powerful like King David who will make their country a great Jewish Kingdom once more.

Ancient Judaism Time Line

BCE	2000	
	1900	Abraham
		Isaac
	1800	
		Jacob
	1700	
	1600	
	1500	
	1400	
	1300	Moses
	1200	Return to Canaan
	1100	
	1000	David
	900	
		Prophets
	800	
	700	
		The Temple destroyed
	600	
		The Exile
	500	Return from Exile
	400	
		Greek invasion
	300	
	200	
	100	Roman invasion
		Birth of Jesus
CE		

NOTE: No one is sure of the exact dates when many of these events took place.

Questions

1. Who was Abraham?
2. What is the Covenant?
3. How did God use Moses to help the "chosen people"?
4. What happened when the Jews returned to Canaan?
5. What was special about David?
6. Who were the prophets? What was their role?
7. What disaster took place in Jerusalem?
8. What important lesson did the people learn during the Exile?
9. What did the Jews do on their return from exile in Babylon?
10. How did the Jews practice their religion for the next 400 years?
11. Who ruled Palestine at the time Jesus was born?
12. Why were the Jews waiting for a Messiah?

Research

- Find out more about one of the key people in Jewish history.
  - Bible references are provided to help you locate certain aspects of each person's story.
  - Name the person.
  - Write a summary of their story.
  - Draw a picture(s) to go with the summary. (Optional.)
  - State why this person is so important in the history of the Jews.

Abraham	Genesis 12:1-9 & 21:1-3
Jacob	Genesis 28:1-4 & 46:1-7
Joseph	Genesis 37:1-36 & 47:1-12
Moses	Exodus 2:1-25 & 3:1-12 & 12:21-36 & 20:1-17
Joshua	Joshua 1:1-9
David	1 Samuel 16:1-13 & 2 Samuel 5:1-7
Ezekiel	Ezekiel 2:1-5 & 11:13-25
Jeremiah	Jeremiah 1:1-10 & 52:1-16
Ezra	Ezra 2:1 & 3:7-8 & 7:6-10
Daniel	Daniel 6:6-28

Jewish Religion

Key Concept

Ancient Judaism: the history and culture of the Jewish people at the time of Jesus.

Objective

Describe Jewish places of worship at the time of Jesus.

Activity: *"Amazing Places"*

TASK: TO BE AWARE OF THE AWESOME NATURE OF CERTAIN BUILDINGS.

✦ We are surrounded by buildings of all shapes and sizes. If we stop to think about it, some of them are quite impressive, even the older ones.

Discuss

- What is the most awesome place you have ever been in?
- What was it like?
- What happens there?

Ancient Judaism

Some religious buildings are amazing places.

At the time of Jesus, Jews had two kinds of religious buildings in which to worship God: the Temple in the city of Jerusalem, and the synagogues in each town and village in Palestine.

The Temple

The Temple in Jerusalem was a magnificent building. It was very large and could hold several thousand people. The Temple was probably the biggest building most people had ever seen. It was very ornate inside and out. The walls and pillars of pale stone were covered in gold.

The Temple was a sacred building. Jews believed it was the dwelling place of God. It was built originally to house the Ark of the Covenant, a chest containing the stone tablets on which the Ten Commandments were written. Jewish families went to the Temple once a year, on the feast of Passover, to pray and offer sacrifice to God.

The Temple in Jerusalem

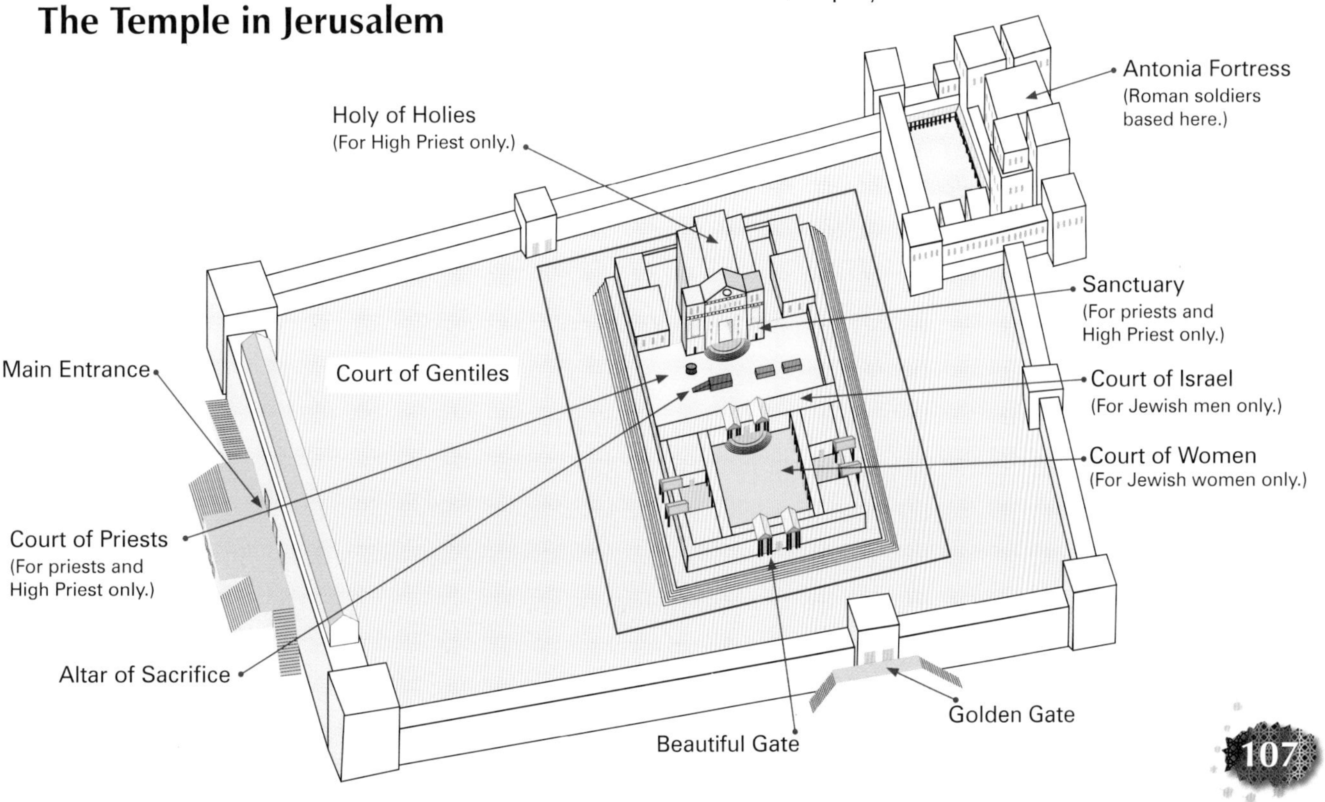
Antonia Fortress
(Roman soldiers based here.)
Holy of Holies
(For High Priest only.)
Sanctuary
(For priests and High Priest only.)
Main Entrance
Court of Gentiles
Court of Israel
(For Jewish men only.)
Court of Women
(For Jewish women only.)
Court of Priests
(For priests and High Priest only.)
Altar of Sacrifice
Golden Gate
Beautiful Gate

Section B

The Temple's outer courtyard was a marketplace called the Court of the Gentiles. It was here that Jewish pilgrims changed their Roman coins into Temple currency and bought birds and animals for sacrifice. The Temple priests took these offerings and sacrificed them on the altar in the Court of Priests.

The most important part of the Temple was the Sanctuary. Inside there was a special area called the Holy of Holies. A large curtain covered its entrance and no one, except the High Priest, was allowed to enter. He went inside once a year to offer sacrifice to God and to pray for forgiveness for all the people. The Temple in Jerusalem was destroyed by the Romans in 70CE. Part of one wall is all that remains. It is the holiest place in Judaism today.

The Synagogue

At the time of Jesus there was a synagogue in every town and village in Palestine. The synagogue was a meeting place for the Jewish community. Jews attended a weekly service in the synagogue on the Sabbath.

The synagogue was a plain, two-storey building. It was small, holding between fifty and one hundred people at a time. It had a porch in front with two doors. Women entered through one door and went upstairs to a gallery. Men and older boys went in another door and remained downstairs in the main part of the building.

At the Sabbath service a rabbi read from a scroll of sacred scripture and gave a talk about the readings. Scrolls were treated with great respect because this was the Word of God for Jewish people. The scrolls were kept in a special part of the synagogue called the Ark. A curtain was drawn in front of the Ark, and a light burned beside it. The light was never allowed to burn out. It reminded Jewish people that God was always with them. In front of the Ark, a special candle holder called a menorah held seven candles. The weekly Sabbath service usually lasted an hour and ended with a blessing.

Questions

Knowledge

1. Where was the Temple?
2. What did the Temple look like?
3. How often did Jewish people visit the Temple? Why did they visit?
4. What took place in the Court of Gentiles during Passover?
5. What was the most sacred part of the Temple? Who was allowed to enter?
6. How often did Jewish people attend a synagogue service?
7. What did a synagogue look like at the time of Jesus?
8. Where did people sit in the synagogue in Nazareth?
9. What was the purpose of the Ark in the synagogue?
10. What is a menorah?

Understanding

1. Why was the Temple so important to the Jews?
2. Describe what took place during a synagogue service at the time of Jesus.
3. How important was the local synagogue to Jewish life in Palestine?
4. The Temple was destroyed in the year 70CE. What effect do you think the destruction of the Temple had on the Jewish people?

Research

- Find out more about the Temple in Jerusalem.

Solomon's Temple	**Herod's Temple**
◆ When was it built?	◆ What was it like?
◆ What did it contain?	◆ Why was it built?
◆ How was it destroyed?	◆ How was it destroyed?
◆ The Second Temple:	
- When was it rebuilt?	
- Who rebuilt it?	

- Compare Herod's Temple with Solomon's Temple.
- Compile a report with supporting pictures and diagrams and present it to the class.

Religious Groups

Key Concept

Ancient Judaism: the history and culture of the Jewish people at the time of Jesus.

Objective

Describe the religious structure of Palestine at the time of Jesus.

Activity: *"Different Reactions"*

TASK: TO APPRECIATE THAT PEOPLE REACTED IN DIFFERENT WAYS TO THE ROMAN OCCUPATION OF PALESTINE.

The Jews were horrified when the Romans invaded Palestine, yet they just had to carry on with their day-to-day lives. Over time, different groups took a stand on the issue. Some Jews accepted the Romans as a fact of life. Other Jews rejected them. Each group had it's own followers.

The Sadducees accepted Roman rule. They adapted to the Romans, and tried to make the best of it.

The Pharisees rejected Roman rule. They ignored the Romans, and focused instead on practicing their religion.

The Zealots rejected Roman rule. They were angry with the Romans, and fought against them.

The Essenes rejected Roman rule. They were disgusted with the Romans and the Jewish leaders. They left Jerusalem and went off to live in the desert.

Discuss

- Which notice (A, B, C or D) represents the views of the Pharisees, the Sadducees, the Zealots and the Essenes.

B.
Romans Out! No Surrender!
C.
Roman rule best for all: new roads, more trade, law and order.
A.
God's Law, not Roman law.
D.
Roman Rule Never! We're out of here!

Ancient Judaism

The most significant political issue at the time of Jesus was the Roman occupation of Palestine.

Each religious group had its own outlook on Roman rule and its own view on the coming of the Messiah.

The Sadducees

The Sadducees accepted Roman rule and co-operated with the Romans. The Sadducees were Jews from wealthy families and many were priests. They were the religious leaders of the Temple in Jerusalem. The Temple was of great importance to them, they collected temple taxes and performed all the religious sacrifices. The High Priest in the Temple was always a Sadducee.

Even though the Romans ruled Palestine, they allowed the Jews to practice their religion. They also allowed the Jews to judge their own people if they broke Jewish religious laws.

The Sanhedrin

The Jewish court of law was called the Sanhedrin. It was based in the Temple in Jerusalem. The Sanhedrin had the power to punish Jews who broke religious laws but had no power to punish those who broke civil laws. This group had a lot of control over the lives of ordinary Jews.

The Sadducees co-operated with the Roman authorities because they wanted to safeguard their position in the Temple. They also valued the wealth and progress that the Romans had brought to Palestine.

The Sadducees did not expect a Messiah. They did not believe that they would ever be free from Roman rule. They therefore adapted to the situation and co-operated with the Romans in order to preserve their power and their wealth.

The Pharisees

The Pharisees rejected Roman rule. They ignored the Romans and focused instead on practising their religion. Pharisees were educated laymen from ordinary families, they were not priests. They were the religious leaders of the local synagogues.

The Law of God was important to the Pharisees. They studied God's Law and showed people how to keep it. They were very strict. They taught the Jews hundreds of small rules about the right way to live. The Pharisees carefully followed all these rules themselves and expected everyone else to do the same. In fact, they avoided anyone who did not follow the rules exactly as they did. The Pharisees called such people "sinners" and kept well away from them. The words and actions of the Pharisees had a great influence on the lives of ordinary people in Palestine. The Pharisees did not co-operate with the Romans, because the Romans did not follow God's Law. They looked forward to the day when the Jews would be free of Roman rule.

The Pharisees expected a Messiah. They believed the Messiah would be a king who would establish a peaceful kingdom in Palestine free from foreign rule.

The Zealots

The Zealots rejected Roman rule and refused to co-operate with the Romans. The Zealots were revolutionaries, the freedom of Palestine was very important to them. As religious Jews, they were very zealous, very keen about God's Law. They believed Palestine was God's gift to the Jewish people, so they wanted the Romans out of the country at all costs. They objected to paying taxes and used violence to try and force the Romans out of Palestine. They were ready to go to war if necessary. The Zealots caused a lot of unrest among ordinary Jewish people. Simon, one of the disciples, was a Zealot before he decided to follow Jesus.

The Zealots expected a Messiah. They believed the Messiah would be a military leader who would help them rebel and overthrow the Romans.

Questions

Knowledge

1. a. Who were the Sadducees?
   b. Did they co-operate with the Romans?
2. What was the Sanhedrin?
3. a. Who was the leader of the Sanhedrin?
   b. What crimes were judged in the court of the Sanhedrin?
4. a. Who were the Pharisees?
   b. Did they co-operate with the Romans?
5. About what matters were the Pharisees very strict?
6. a. Who did the Pharisees label as sinners?
   b. How did the Pharisees treat sinners?
7. a. Who were the Zealots?
   b. How did the Zealots cause unrest among ordinary people in Palestine?
8. What did the Sadducees, the Pharisees and the Zealots believe about the coming of the Messiah?

Understanding

1. What was the religious structure in Palestine at the time of Jesus?
2. What were the roles of the Sadducees and the Pharisees in Jewish life?
3. Compare the attitude of any two Jewish religious groups in first century Palestine to:
   a. Roman rule.
   b. The coming of the Messiah.

Research

- Find out about another group that probably had a lot of influence on the life of Jews in Palestine at the time of Jesus.

The Essenes

- Who were the Essenes? Why did they move to the desert areas of Palestine? Did they believe in the coming of the Messiah?
- Name one well-known site associated with the Essenes. What important discovery was made at this site over sixty years ago?
- Compile a summary to include a map, pictures and information.
- Present the summary to the class.

Awaiting the Messiah

Key Concept

Messianic expectation: the hope of the Jewish people that a new leader, a Messiah, would bring them to freedom.

Objective

Explain why the Jews, at the time of Jesus, expected a Messiah to come to their aid.

Activity: *"Great Expectations"*

TASK: TO APPRECIATE THE PLACE AND IMPORTANCE OF HOPE IN OUR LIVES.

- Just for a moment, close your eyes, or simply look down.
- Think about the things that you really look forward to, e.g.
  - Birthdays.
  - A special trip.
  - Some problem being solved.
  - Christmas.
  - New friendships.
  - Summer holidays.
- Think about the times when you waited for something to happen.

Discuss

- What kind of things do you look forward to.
- Identify at least one occasion when you waited for something important to happen.
- What kind of feelings do you associate with times of waiting?

Messianic Expectation

The Jews waited expectantly for the coming of the Messiah.

Palestine in the first century was part of the Roman Empire. The Roman occupation caused a lot of political unrest in the country. The Jewish population longed for a Messiah, a great leader who would restore their freedom.

The Prophets

The Jews believed God spoke to them through the prophets. Prophets were holy men and women who carried messages from God. The prophets told of God's promise to send a great leader to guide and rule the Jewish people. Prophets such as Jeremiah and Isaiah said a descendant of King David would rule over Israel at a future time.

The Jews had a troubled history, several times their land was invaded and their cities destroyed. They were ruled by the Persians, the Greeks, and then by the Romans. The Jews yearned for freedom. The one thing that kept them going was their belief that God would send them a great leader to set them free.

The Messiah

The Jewish people had a special name for a leader sent by God. He was called a Messiah. The word 'Messiah' means 'anointed one'. In Ancient Judaism all new leaders, such as kings and high priests, were anointed or blessed with oil. It was a sign that they were chosen by God for an important task. David, Israel's greatest king, was anointed with oil at the start of his reign. People looked back to David's time as a 'golden age' when they were a free and proud Jewish nation.

The young boy David is anointed. (1 Samuel 16:13)

Different viewpoints

Many Jews expected that the Messiah would be a king, someone wealthy and powerful, like King David of old. A great king who would secure their freedom and make them a powerful nation once more.

Others expected the Messiah to be a great warrior, someone brave and courageous who would, if necessary, use force to drive the Romans out of Palestine.

Whatever their viewpoint, all Jews lived in hope that one day the Messiah would arrive and there would be peace at last. By the first century, Jews in Palestine believed the Messiah:

- ❖ Would be a powerful king-like figure.
- ❖ Would free them from foreign rulers.
- ❖ Would bring God's peace and justice to all.

Today:

- ❖ Christians believe that Jesus is the Messiah.
- ❖ Jews believe that the Messiah has yet to come.

Questions

Knowledge

1. Name two prophets in the Old Testament.
2. What was the role of a prophet in Old Testament times?
3. Who invaded Palestine at different times before Jesus was born?
4. What title did the Jews give to the great leader they were expecting?
5. What does the title 'Messiah' mean?
6. Name one great Jewish leader who was anointed with holy oil long ago.
7. What did the Jews expect the Messiah to be like?
8. What did the Jews expect the Messiah to do for them?
9. Who do Christians believe is the Messiah?
10. What do Jews believe about the Messiah today?

Understanding

1. Why were the Jews looking forward to the arrival of a Messiah?
2. What were people's expectations of the Messiah at the time of Jesus?
3. Why do you think the memory of David was so important for the Jewish people?

Research

- Check with Amnesty International for information on the following:
  - Where in the world today are people forced to live under repressive governments?
  - Identify one such country.
  - Who rules that country?
  - What human rights are denied in that country?
  - Tell the story of one person who has suffered under this regime.
  - Has anyone emerged to lead and inspire the people of that country?
  - Check the details.
  - Tell the story to the class.

The New Testament

Key Concepts

Gospel: the 'Good News' of Jesus Christ in the first four books of the New Testament.

Evangelist: a Gospel writer (Mark, Matthew, Luke and John) who spread the 'Good News' of Jesus Christ.

Witness: to proclaim or publicly announce one's religious faith.

Objective

Explain the purpose of the four evangelists in writing the Gospels.

Activity: *"Good News"*

TASK: TO IDENTIFY SOME GOOD NEWS IN OUR OWN LIVES.

When a baby is born, it is good news for everyone in the family. Imagine a phone call that was made on the day you were born. Add your own words below....

"Hello ________. Great news! I'm here at the ________ hospital. The baby has arrived. It's a ________. It weighed ________ at birth. Yes, we've already picked a name. Our ________ will be called ________. Yes, mother is doing well too. She is just having a cup of tea at the moment. She was ________ hours in labour before your grandchild was born.

That's right, visiting hours are 2-4pm this afternoon. See you then. Must go now, I've got a few more calls to make - must spread the good news you know! See you soon. Bye."

Discuss

- Do you know all the details of your own birth?
- Why do you think parents are so eager to tell everyone about a new baby?
- What other kind of good news would get people excited?

Gospel

The Gospels in the New Testament are the principal source of evidence about Jesus.

The word Gospel means *good news*. For Christians the 'Good News' is that Jesus is the Son of God. This is the message of the first four books in the New Testament. There are four Gospels in the New Testament in the Bible.

- The Gospel of Mark.
- The Gospel of Matthew.
- The Gospel of Luke.
- The Gospel of John.

The Gospels explain the purpose of Jesus' life on Earth.

An image of Jesus in an Orthodox church.

Evangelist

The evangelists were the authors of the four Gospels. They were men of deep faith who wrote the Gospels to spread the Good News of Jesus Christ.

The four evangelists are:

- Mark.
- Matthew.
- Luke.
- John.

Their writings set out to show that Jesus is the Son of God, the Messiah, the Saviour of all. To achieve this aim they focused on the events in the final three years of Jesus adult life. The evangelists were not trying to write the complete life-story of Jesus. For instance, they barely mention the events surrounding his birth and write very little about his childhood or his teenage years. Jesus spent almost half his life working as a carpenter in Nazareth, this is hardly mentioned either.

Instead, the gospel writers concentrate on the last three years of Jesus' adult life. They focus in particular on his teaching, healing, death and resurrection. It is this final period of Jesus' life that is described in detail in the four Gospels.

Witness

The authors of the four Gospels firmly believed that Jesus is God. Mark, Matthew, Luke and John felt compelled to tell the Good News to other people. They were unable to keep it to themselves, they felt they had to tell others what they believed. The evangelists gave witness, or publicly proclaimed their faith, through their writings. They announced the Good News loud and clear for everyone's benefit.

The Gospels were written in the first century CE. The evangelists wrote the Gospels:

- To spread the Good News of Jesus.
- To enable others to have faith in Jesus too.

Their writings were for Christian communities in different parts of the Roman Empire. Their work would also be important for Christian communities in future times.

New
Testament

The Gospels in the New Testament were written by the four evangelists.

Questions

Knowledge

1. Where in the Bible are the Gospels located?
2. What does the word 'Gospel' mean?
3. What is the Good News of the Gospels?
4. What is an evangelist?
5. Name the evangelists who wrote the four Gospels.
6. What part of Jesus' life do the four evangelists focus on in the Gospels?
7. How did Matthew, Mark, Luke and John bear witness to their faith in Jesus Christ?
8. For whom were the Gospels written?

Understanding

1. What inspired the evangelists to write the Gospels?
2. What are the four Gospels all about?
3. How do we know the Gospel writers were people of faith?
4. How did the evangelists hope people would benefit from the Gospel message?

Research

- The first copies of the New Testament were written on papyrus and rolled up into scrolls. Later, single sheets of papyrus, or parchment, were cut and joined together to make a book. This early type of book was called a codex.

  Find out about the **Codex Sinaiticus**.

  - When was this copy of the New Testament written?
  - In what language was it written?
  - When was it found?
  - Where was it found?
  - Who discovered it?
  - Where was it later put for safe-keeping?
  - Compile a summary of the information and present it to the class.

The Evangelists

Key Concept

Evangelist: a Gospel writer (Mark, Matthew, Luke and John) who spread the 'Good News' of Jesus Christ.

Objective

Explain how the Gospels came to be written by the four evangelists.

Activity: *"Viewfinder"*

TASK: TO BE AWARE THAT THERE ARE DIFFERENT SIDES TO EVERYONE.

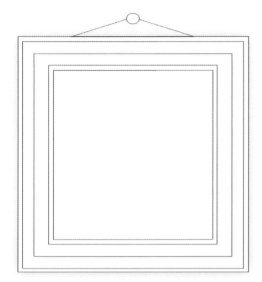

Discuss

- There is only one ________________ , but
  (YOUR NAME)
  people sometimes see different sides of you.
- How would you be described by your...
  - parent.
  - friend.
  - teacher.
  - coach/trainer.
- Why do you think people can describe you in different ways?
- Which description of you is true? Or is there some truth in everyone's point of view?

Four different authors
writing for people in four different contexts.

Evangelist

In the New Testament, the evangelists tell the story of Jesus from different points of view.

The Gospel is the Good News that Jesus is the Son of God. The Gospels were written for Christians in the Roman Empire in the first century CE. Each community had its own problems. The evangelists emphasised certain aspects of Jesus' life and teaching to meet the needs of each community.

It is important to remember that although there are four Gospels, there is only one Jesus. The evangelists show us different sides of Jesus:

- His suffering side...in Mark.
- His teaching side...in Matthew.
- His caring side...in Luke.
- His spiritual side...in John.

The evangelists tell the same story about Jesus, but in different ways.

The Four Evangelists

The evangelists wrote their Gospels at different times and for different people in the Roman Empire.

Mark

My name is Mark. I am a Christian now, I used to be a Jew. I knew Peter the disciple very well. He often came to our house and told us about Jesus. I listened carefully and wrote down everything Peter said about Jesus, especially all the miracles he performed.

My Gospel was written around 70CE. It was written for new Christians in the city of Rome. I was very worried about them, they were suffering a lot at the hands of the Romans. I wanted them to know that Jesus understands their suffering. Jesus is God and he suffered too. He was crucified and died on the cross.

Luke

I'm Luke. I am a Christian now, I used to be a Gentile (a non-Jew). I trained as a doctor. When I heard about Jesus, I was impressed by the way he healed people.

My Gospel was written around 85CE. It was written for new Christians in the city of Corinth. They had once been Gentiles like myself. I understood how they felt. I know what it is like to be an outsider, to be different from everyone else. That's what is great about Jesus. He is the saviour of all people: Jews and Gentiles, the rich and the poor. He is a friend to everyone. He is especially caring to the sick and disabled.

Matthew

I'm Matthew. I am a Christian now, I used to be a Jew. I worked as a teacher for a while, I was a rabbi and taught Jewish scripture in the synagogue.

My Gospel was written around 85CE. It was written for new Christians in the city of Antioch. They had been Jews until they learned that Jesus is the Messiah. At first it was hard for them to change their Jewish ways. They felt insecure and a bit confused. I did my best to show them that Jesus is indeed the Messiah promised by the prophets long ago. I think it helps to point out the links between Judaism and Christianity in this way.

John

My name is John. I am a Christian now, I used to be a Jew. My friend, who is also called John, was the youngest disciple. He taught me a lot about Jesus.

My Gospel was written around 95CE. It was written for Christians in the city of Ephesus. They were not new Christians, they had been followers of Jesus for many years. They all believed in Jesus, yet they needed to understand his words and actions a bit better. I try to explain it all and I hope this helps them to have a deeper faith in Jesus, and to believe he is the Messiah that was promised.

The Four Gospels

Gospel	Evangelist	Date	Written for.....	Main points
★ **Mark**	❑ Mark was a Jew before he became a Christian. ❑ He knew Peter, who was Jesus' closest disciple. Mark listened carefully to Peter and wrote down all the stories Peter told him about Jesus.	❑ Around 70CE. The first Gospel to be written.	❑ New Christians in the city of Rome. ❑ They were suffering terrible persecution at the hands of the Romans.	★ Jesus is the Son of God. ★ Jesus had feelings like everyone else. He suffered a lot. He was crucified and died on the cross.
✯ **Matthew**	❑ Matthew was a Jew before he became a Christian. ❑ He was a rabbi(a teacher) who taught Jewish scripture in the synagogue.	❑ Around 85CE. Written about fifteen years after Mark's Gospel.	❑ New Christians in the city of Antioch. ❑ They had been Jews until they realised that Jesus is the Messiah. This changed their lives.	✯ Jesus is the Messiah. ✯ Jesus knew a lot of Jewish scripture. He taught his followers a new way of living.
✪ **Luke**	❑ Luke was a Gentile (a non-Jew) before he became a Christian. ❑ He was a doctor. Luke was impressed by the healing work of Jesus.	❑ Around 85CE. Written about the same time as Matthew's Gospel.	❑ New Christians in the city of Corinth. ❑ They had been Gentiles (non-Jews) before they heard about Jesus. The Good News changed their lives.	✪ Jesus is the Saviour of all people. ✪ Jesus was a friend to everyone: he cared for rich and poor, Jew and Gentile, sinners and sick people…
☆ **John**	❑ John was a Jew before he became a Christian. ❑ He was a follower of the youngest disciple of Jesus, who was also called John.	❑ Around 95CE. The last Gospel to be written.	❑ Mature Christians in the city of Ephesus. ❑ They had been Christians for many years and needed help to deepen their faith.	☆ Jesus is the Messiah, the Son of God. ☆ Jesus had a spiritual nature and thought deeply about things. Follow him and have faith in him.

NOTE: No one is sure of the <u>exact</u> dates the Gospels were written.

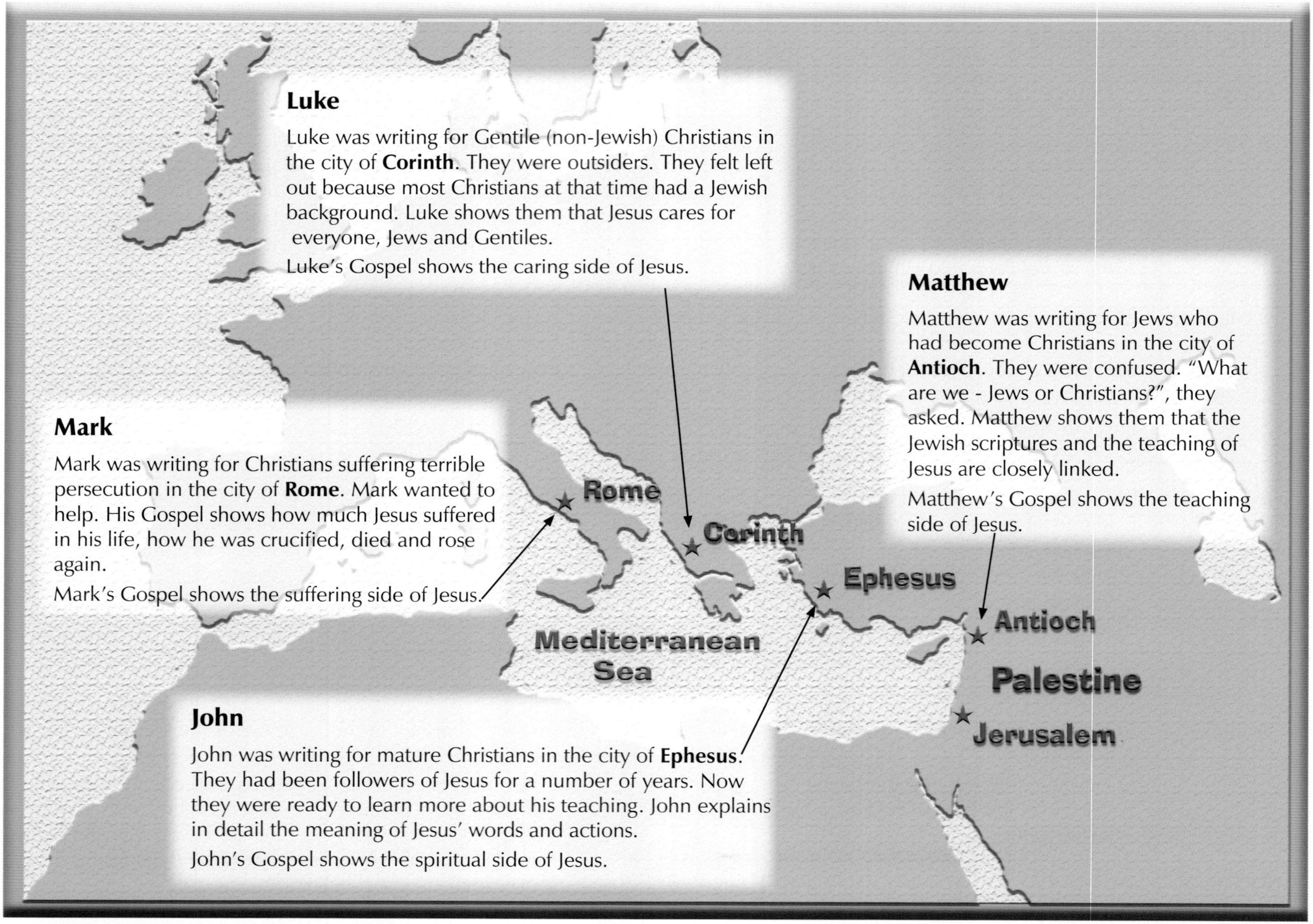
Rome
Corinth
Ephesus
Antioch
Palestine
Jerusalem
Mediterranean
Sea

Luke

Luke was writing for Gentile (non-Jewish) Christians in the city of **Corinth**. They were outsiders. They felt left out because most Christians at that time had a Jewish background. Luke shows them that Jesus cares for everyone, Jews and Gentiles.

Luke's Gospel shows the caring side of Jesus.

Matthew

Matthew was writing for Jews who had become Christians in the city of **Antioch**. They were confused. "What are we - Jews or Christians?", they asked. Matthew shows them that the Jewish scriptures and the teaching of Jesus are closely linked.

Matthew's Gospel shows the teaching side of Jesus.

Mark

Mark was writing for Christians suffering terrible persecution in the city of **Rome**. Mark wanted to help. His Gospel shows how much Jesus suffered in his life, how he was crucified, died and rose again.

Mark's Gospel shows the suffering side of Jesus.

John

John was writing for mature Christians in the city of **Ephesus**. They had been followers of Jesus for a number of years. Now they were ready to learn more about his teaching. John explains in detail the meaning of Jesus' words and actions.

John's Gospel shows the spiritual side of Jesus.

Symbols of the Evangelists

The Early Christian Church used four symbols to represent the four evangelists. Each symbol is based on a figure mentioned in the Book of Ezekiel 1:6-11 in the Old Testament.

A page from the Book of Kells showing symbols representing the four evangelists.

- Matthew is represented as a man, perhaps because his Gospel begins with the genealogy of Jesus (his family tree), emphasising the human nature of Jesus.
- Mark is represented as a lion, perhaps because of his courage in writing his Gospel for persecuted Christians in the city of Rome.
- Luke is represented as an ox, perhaps because his Gospel begins with the story of Zechariah, a priest whose duties involved the sacrificing of animals in the Temple. The Gospel ends with the sacrifice of Jesus' death on the cross.
- John is represented as an eagle, perhaps because this majestic bird soars higher in the sky than any other, its power emphasising the divine, heavenly nature of Jesus.

Questions

Knowledge

1. Name the evangelists who wrote the four Gospels.
2. What Gospels were written first and last.
3. What Gospels were most likely written by a doctor and a rabbi?
4. Which evangelists were friends of Jesus' disciples John and Peter?
5. When were the Gospels written?
6. For whom were each of the Gospels written?
7. What aspect of Jesus was highlighted most in each Gospel?
8. What are the symbols of the four evangelists?

Understanding

1. Select <u>one</u> of the evangelists and answer the following questions.
   - For whom did the evangelist write his Gospel?
   - What was the main problem in this community?
   - What did the evangelist tell the community about Jesus?
   - Why did the evangelist show the people this particular aspect of Jesus?
   - What difference would the Gospel have made to the people in that community do you think?
2. What picture of Jesus emerges from the four Gospels?
3. Does any one Gospel contain the full and complete account of Jesus' life and teaching? Explain.

Research

- Find out about the Lindisfarne Gospels.
  - Who was responsible for producing these handmade copies of the Gospels?
  - What images are used to represent the four evangelists in these manuscripts?
  - From what scriptural reference in the Old Testament are these images derived?
  - What could be the meaning of each image?
  - Show the results of your research to the class.

Three Gospel Stages

Key Concept

Evidence from oral and written traditions: the way information about Jesus passed from the spoken to the written word.

Objective

Trace the development of the Gospels from an oral tradition to the written word.

Activity: *"Storytelling"*

TASK: CLARIFY THE PROCESS OF RECORDING AN INCIDENT - FROM THE INITIAL EVENT TO THE ORAL STAGE, TO THE FINAL WRITTEN STAGE.

1. The Event

- Think about an event that happened in your life recently. Something....

❑ exciting. ❑ embarrassing. ❑ funny.
❑ nice. ❑ annoying. ❑ _______

(✓ select one experience)

2. Tell it

- Now choose a partner.
  TELL your partner what happened.
  "Something ________ happened to me recently."
  Say... When it happened.
  Where it happened.
  What happened.
  How different people reacted.
- Your partner listens carefully to your story.
- Swop over.

3. Write it

- WRITE down your partner's story. Describe what happened to him/her on that occasion.

Discuss

- How does your written account compare with your partner's oral account?
- Ask him/her to check and grade what you have written.
  (Grades: Excellent, Very good, Good, Fair or Poor.)

Evidence from oral and written traditions

The Gospels record certain key events in the life of Jesus.

The evangelists (Mark, Matthew, Luke and John) believed in Jesus and wrote about him in their Gospels. Yet none of these men actually met Jesus when he was alive. In fact, the evangelists wrote the Gospels more than forty years after Jesus' death and resurrection.

So where did the evangelists get their information about Jesus? What sources did they use? Why did they spend several years putting all the evidence together, and what did they hope to achieve?

To answer these questions we note that the Gospels came together in three separate stages.

1. The life stage.

2. The oral stage.

3. The written stage.

The Life Stage

The 'Life Stage' is about the actual life, death and resurrection of Jesus. After Jesus was baptised, he became a travelling teacher. He went all over Palestine with his disciples teaching about the love of God. Many were brought to him who were sick or disabled. Eye-witnesses who were there and saw Jesus' miracles and heard his teaching were greatly impressed. However when he arrived in Jerusalem he was arrested and put on trial. He was crucified and died on the cross. Three days later Jesus was raised from the dead.

After the resurrection, Jesus appeared to his disciples many times. The words, actions, death and resurrection of Jesus convinced the disciples that Jesus was the Messiah, the Son of God. This is called the life stage of the Gospels. The events of this stage occurred over a period of about three years.

The Oral Stage

The 'Oral Stage' is about the apostles telling others about Jesus. After Pentecost there was great excitement. Jesus' followers wanted to tell everyone that "Jesus is alive, Jesus is the Son of God!" Empowered by the Holy Spirit, the apostles travelled all over Palestine spreading the Good News. Some decided to go further, bringing the Good News to every part of the Roman Empire.

The apostles told the story of Jesus to everyone they met. They described what he did and what he said, and many people believed and became Christians. Jesus' story was memorised and retold again and again. It was passed from person to person by word of mouth.

This is called the oral stage of the Gospel. This stage lasted about forty years.

The Written Stage

The 'Written Stage' is about the evangelists writing about Jesus in the Gospels. As time passed the apostles, the main witnesses of all Jesus said and did, became older and some of them died. Soon there were very few eye-witnesses left who had seen or heard Jesus for themselves. It became important to write down Jesus' story accurately before it was too late. A written Gospel would help new Christians to get to know Jesus. It would also, in the future, help others to have faith in him and follow his teaching.

A big effort was made to collect everything known about Jesus. All Jesus' parables, key sayings and teachings were gathered together. Details of Jesus' healing miracles were taken from witnesses who were present at the time and saw them all happen. Others gave first-hand accounts of Jesus' crucifixion, death and resurrection. Everything was carefully recorded. After the evidence was collected from the apostles and other witnesses, it had to be sorted. The evangelists examined everything. They picked out what they wanted for the Christian communities for whom they were writing. Inspired by the Holy Spirit, the four evangelists eventually wrote the story of Jesus in the Gospels of Mark, Matthew, Luke and John. The written Gospel was now ready to be passed on to future generations.

This is called the written stage of the Gospel. This stage lasted about thirty years.

Stages in the making of the Gospels

Stage 1 - The Life Stage (30-33CE)

❖ The last three years of Jesus' life, when he teaches, performs miracles, is crucified and dies on the cross.

❖ After three days, Jesus is raised from the dead and appears to his disciples.

Stage 2 - The Oral Stage (33-70CE)

❖ A period when the apostles travel all over the Roman Empire to TELL the Good News that Jesus is the Messiah, the Son of God.

Stage 3 - The Written Stage (70-95CE)

❖ A period when the evangelists, Mark, Matthew, Luke and John, WRITE down the story of Jesus in the four Gospels.

The Gospel Timeline

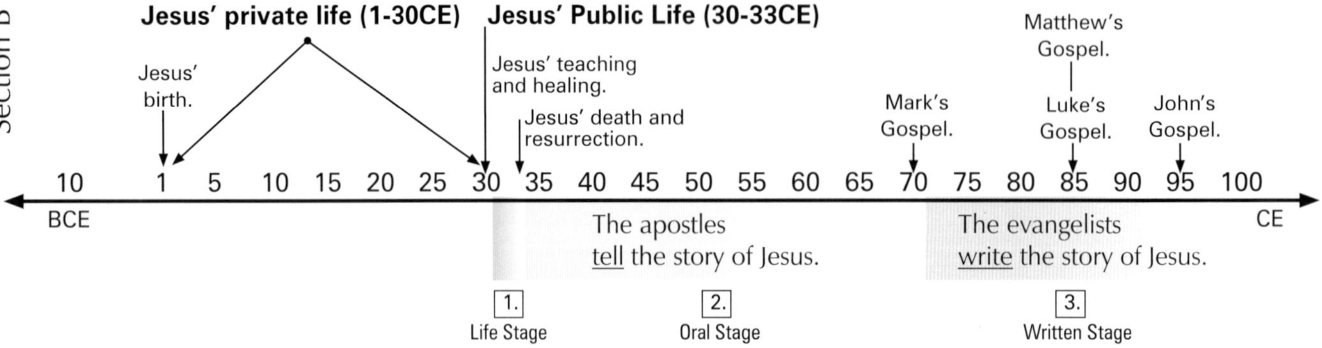
Jesus' private life (1-30CE)
Jesus' Public Life (30-33CE)
Jesus' birth.
Jesus' teaching and healing.
Jesus' death and resurrection.
Mark's Gospel.
Matthew's Gospel.
Luke's Gospel.
John's Gospel.
10 1 5 10 15 20 25 30 35 40 45 50 55 60 65 70 75 80 85 90 95 100
BCE
CE
The apostles tell the story of Jesus.
The evangelists write the story of Jesus.
1. Life Stage
2. Oral Stage
3. Written Stage

NOTE: The time before Jesus was born is called BCE = Before Common or Christian Era (formerly BC).

The time after Jesus was born is called CE = Common or Christian Era (formerly AD).

Exercise

- Examine the timeline and figure out the dates.
  - What letters stand for "Before Christian Era"?
  - What letters stand for "Christian Era"?
  - How old was Jesus when he began teaching and healing?
  - How old was Jesus at the time of his death?
  - How long did Jesus' private life last?
  - How long did Jesus' public life last?
  - When did the oral stage of the Gospel begin? How long did it last?
  - How many years after the resurrection was the first Gospel written?
  - When was the last Gospel written?
  - Over what period of time were the four Gospels written?

Questions

Knowledge

1. How many stages were involved in the making of the Gospels?
2. What happened in the first stage?
3. What happened in the second stage?
4. What happened in the third stage?
5. How long did each stage last?
6. What kind of evidence was collected from eye-witnesses before the Gospels were written?
7. Name the four Gospels written about Jesus.

Understanding

1. Explain what is meant by:
   a. The Oral Tradition.
   b. The Written Tradition.
2. Why did the evangelists decide to write down the story of Jesus?
3. Can you explain why the disciples first reaction was to go and tell the Good News, instead of writing it down straight away.
4. In the formation of the Gospel, what is the difference between the contribution of:
   a. The apostles?
   b. The evangelists?

The Synoptic Gospels

Key Concept

Synoptic: to be alike or similar. The Gospels of Mark, Matthew and Luke are so alike they are known as the Synoptic Gospels.

Objective

Identify the characteristics of the Synoptic Gospels.

Activity: *"Parables"*

TASK: TO COMPARE THREE PARABLES IN THE GOSPELS OF MARK, MATTHEW AND LUKE.

The Parable of the Mustard Seed

"What shall we say the Kingdom of God is like?" asked Jesus. "What story shall we use to explain it? It is like this. A man takes a mustard seed, the smallest seed in the world, and plants it in the ground. After a while it grows up and becomes the biggest of all plants. It puts out such large branches that the birds come and make their nests in the shade." *Mark 4:30-32*

The Parable of the Mustard Seed

Jesus told them another story. "The Kingdom of Heaven is like this. A man takes a mustard seed and sows it in his field. It is the smallest of all seeds, but when it grows up, it is the biggest of all plants. It becomes a tree, so that birds come and make their nests in its branches." *Matt 13:31-32*

The Parable of the Mustard Seed

Jesus asked "What is the Kingdom of God like? What shall I compare it with? It is like this. A man takes a mustard seed and sows it in his field. The plant grows and becomes a tree, and the birds make their nests in its branches."
Luke 13:18-19

Discuss

- Having read the three stories of the "Mustard Seed", underline all the words the stories have in common.
- What do you notice about the three stories now?
- Why do you think the stories are so alike?
- Can you explain why the same story appears in three different Gospels? (Remember: the Gospels were written by different authors at different times, for different people.

Synoptic

The first three Gospels are very alike. They are sometimes called the Synoptic Gospels.

The word *synoptic* means to be alike or similar. When the Gospels of Mark, Matthew and Luke are lined up, side by side, it is clear that they share a lot in common.

They agree on:

- The main events in Jesus' life.
- The order in which those events occurred.
- Jesus words on those occasions.

In some cases, the three Gospels are so alike that they could have been copied from one another. Indeed, that is probably what happened!

Similarities in the Synoptic Gospels

The similarities in the first three Gospels are due to:

- ❖ Mark's Gospel being written first.
- ❖ Matthew and Luke borrowing most of Mark's Gospel for their own work.

Mark wrote his Gospel first. His Gospel is based on the apostles' teaching about Jesus in the years following the resurrection. Mark's Gospel is the shortest and contains 661 verses.

The Gospels of Matthew and Luke were written twenty years later. They each used Mark's account of Jesus' life as the basis of their own work. Matthew borrowed 606 verses from Mark, while Luke used 320 verses.

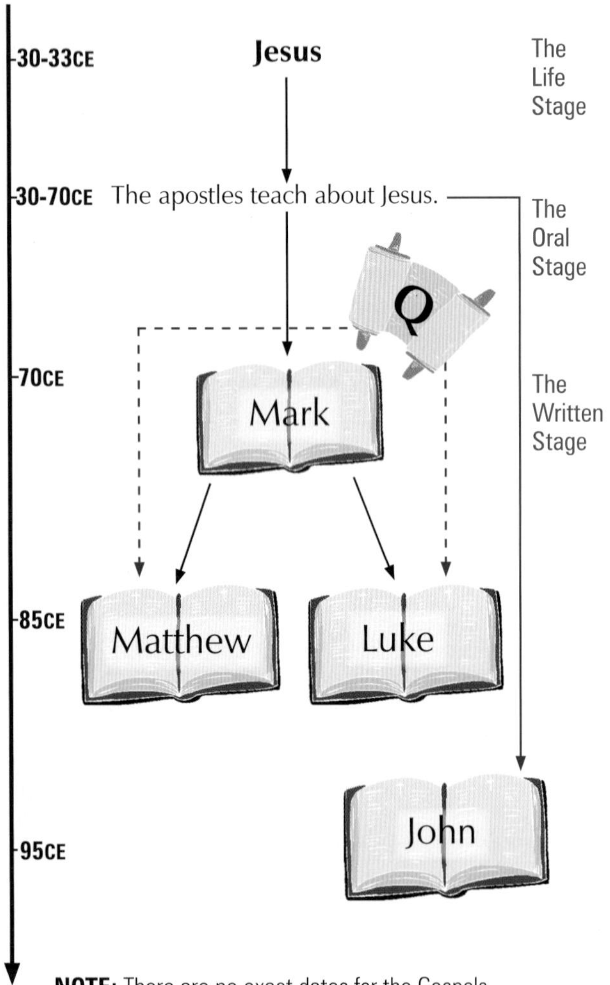

30-33CE
Jesus
The Life Stage
30-70CE
The apostles teach about Jesus.
The Oral Stage
Q
70CE
Mark
The Written Stage
85CE
Matthew
Luke
95CE
John

NOTE: There are no exact dates for the Gospels.

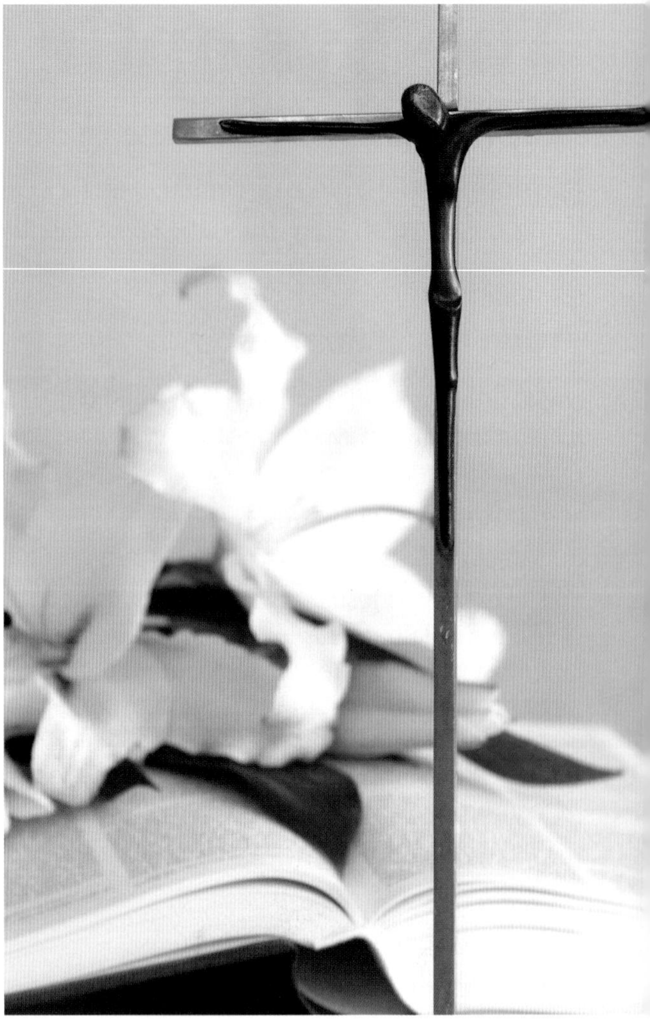

The evangelists wrote about the life, death and resurrection of Jesus in the Gospels.

Differences in the Synoptic Gospels

The differences in the first three Gospels are due to the fact that Matthew and Luke used other sources in addition to Mark's account. Notice that the Gospels of Matthew and Luke are much longer than the Gospel of Mark. It raises the question, "Where did the extra information come from?"

The 'Q' document

Bible experts think the additional information came from a document called 'Q', which is short for 'quelle' (meaning 'source' in German). This is a collection of Jesus' sayings written down at an earlier time. Only Matthew and Luke used 'Q'. Mark did not use it at all. For example, the Beatitudes and the Lord's Prayer are in the Gospels of Matthew and Luke, they are not in Mark's Gospel.

The Fourth Gospel

There are four Gospels in the New Testament. John's Gospel is not one of the Synoptic Gospels. The Gospel of John did not rely on Mark, nor did it use the 'Q' document. John's Gospel was written last and used other sources to tell the story of Jesus.

Distinctive features of John's Gospel

The writing style in John's Gospel is different to that of the Synoptic Gospels. It is more poetic and abstract, which can make it somewhat harder to understand. The content is different too. John's Gospel focuses more on explaining who Jesus is, rather than describing the things he says and does. In the fourth Gospel, for example, there are no references to Jesus' parables, and there are few references to Jesus' miracles.

IC
XC
O
N
A mosaic from St. Peter's basilica in Rome.

Questions

Knowledge

1. Name the Synoptic Gospels.
2. In what ways are the Synoptic Gospels similar to each other?
3. Which Gospel is the shortest, the simplest and the first to be written?
4. What source did Mark use in writing his Gospel?
5. Who used Mark's Gospel as the basis of their work?
6. What sources did Matthew and Luke use when writing their Gospels?
7. What are the differences between the Synoptic Gospels?
8. In what way is John's Gospel different from the Synoptic Gospels?

Understanding

1. Why are certain Gospels called Synoptic Gospels?
2. What features do the Gospels of Mark, Matthew and Luke share in common. Provide an example of a Gospel story in support of your answer.
3. Give reasons why there are certain differences in the synoptic accounts of Jesus' life and work.

Research

- Compare different Gospel accounts of the same event.
  - Listen carefully as three good readers read aloud the well known miracle story 'Jesus calms a storm' from the Gospels of:
    - Mark 4:35-41
    - Matt 8:23-27
    - Luke 8:22-25
  - What is the same in all three Gospel accounts?
  - Did you notice what is different?
  - Can you explain the similarities between the three accounts?
  - Can you explain why part of the Gospel accounts are different?
  - Which Gospel account appears to have more points in common with the other two?
  - Discuss the conclusions that could be drawn from this.

Documents of History

Key Concept

Evidence: information about a religious tradition collected from different sources.

Objective

Give an overview of the sources of information about Jesus that exist outside the New Testament.

Activity: *"Schoolbag Search"*

TASK: TO FOCUS ATTENTION ON HISTORY TEXTS AS A SOURCE OF FACTUAL INFORMATION ABOUT PEOPLE AND EVENTS.

✦ What subjects are you studying this year? (✓)

- ❑ English.
- ❑ Irish.
- ❑ Maths.
- ❑ Science.
- ❑ French.
- ❑ German.
- ❑ Religion.
- ❑ History.
- ❑ ________
- ❑ Home Economics.
- ❑ Business Studies.
- ❑ P.E.
- ❑ Geography.
- ❑ Technical Graphics.
- ❑ Woodwork.
- ❑ Metalwork.
- ❑ Art.
- ❑ ________

Discuss

- How many school books are in your bag today? (Excluding copies and school journal.)
- Name one book you have for English class.
- What is the title of your History book?
- What are you learning about in History class at the moment?
- How do you know that the people mentioned in history books are real, and did actually exist?

Some historical texts were written a long time ago. Two documents in particular were written almost 2,000 years ago, at the time of the Roman Empire.

Evidence

Most of what we know about Jesus comes from the New Testament in the Bible. Other information comes from historical documents written at the end of the 1st and the beginning of the 2nd centuries CE. One of these documents was written by a man called Josephus, a Jew. He was asked to write a book to explain the religion of Judaism to the Romans.

Fact File

Name:	◆ ***Josephus.***
Religion:	◆ Jew.
Occupation:	◆ Historian.
Document:	◆ "The Jewish Antiquities" written around 94CE
Type of document:	◆ An historical document to explain the religion of Judaism to the Romans.
Information about Jesus:	◆ He was a wise man.
	◆ He was a teacher.
	◆ He did wonderful works.
	◆ Many Jews and people of other religions became his disciples.
	◆ Pontius Pilate sentenced him to die on the cross.
	◆ His disciples claimed he was alive and appeared to them three days after his crucifixion.
	◆ His followers are called Christians.
Date:	◆ Josephus wrote this about 60 years after the death of Jesus.

Another document was written by a man called Tacitus, a Roman. He was asked to write a book about important people and events in the Roman Empire.

Fact File

Name:	◆ ***Tacitus.***
Religion:	◆ Roman religion.
Occupation:	◆ Historian.
Document:	◆ "The Annals" written around 115CE.
Type of document:	◆ An historical document about important people and events in the Roman Empire.
Information about Jesus:	◆ There was a group of people called Christians. ◆ They got their name from Jesus Christ. ◆ Jesus was the founder of this group. ◆ He was executed. ◆ He was sentenced to death by Pontius Pilate. ◆ Tiberius was the Roman Emperor at the time.
Date:	◆ Tacitus wrote this about 80 years after the death of Jesus.

Both Josephus and Tacitus were historians. They wrote the facts about people and events in the Roman Empire. They were non-Christian writers. They did not belong to the Christian religion, neither of them had any personal interest in Jesus or his teachings. However the two writers mention Jesus in their work.

Both historians report that Jesus lived in Palestine; a group of people known as Christians were his followers; and he was sentenced to death by Pontius Pilate, governor of Palestine.

The writings of Josephus and Tacitus state objectively that Jesus was a real person. He did exist. He did live in Palestine in the 1st century CE.

Sources of Information

There are two sources of information about Jesus.

❖ Christian sources.

❖ Non-Christian sources.

The Christian sources of information are the Gospels in the New Testament. The non-Christian sources are the historical documents written for the Romans in the 2nd century CE.

The documents of faith from Christian sources set out to show that Jesus is the Son of God. The historical documents from non-Christian sources independently confirm that Jesus was a historical person, he did exist. Jesus lived in Palestine in the 1st century CE and founded a new religion.

Questions

Knowledge

1. What first-century historians mention Jesus in their documents?
2. a. Who was Josephus?
   b. Who was Tacitus?
3. List three things Josephus said about Jesus.
4. How did Jesus die, according to Tacitus?
5. Name one Christian source of information about Jesus.
6. Name two non-Christian sources of information about Jesus.

Understanding

1. Summarise the points of information about Jesus provided by Josephus and Tacitus.
2. Did Jesus exist? What kind of evidence is provided by Josephus and Tacitus?
3. What is the difference between a document of faith and a document of history?

Research

✪ Find out about two other non-Christian writers who provide historical evidence about Jesus.

✷ *Pliny*
(a Roman governor in the 2nd century).
- To whom did Pliny write a letter in 110CE?
- What did he say about Jesus Christ and the Christians?

✷ *Suetonius*
(a Roman historian and lawyer in the 2nd century).
- What emperor was Suetonius writing about in 120CE?
- What did he say about Jesus Christ and the Christians?

Documents of Faith

Key Concept

Evidence: information about a religious tradition collected from different sources.

Objective

Be able to demonstrate that the Gospels are documents of faith rather than history.

Section B

Activity:

"Words, Words, Words."

TASK: TO IDENTIFY DIFFERENT TYPES OF WRITING.

- Letter.
- Scientific report.
- Fairy story.
- Historical account.
- Biography.
- Court evidence.
- Love letter.
- Novel.

Discuss

- Identify the different types of writing numbered 1-8 opposite.
- Select any three examples.
  For each one state:
  - the purpose of that type of writing.
  - the rules of that type of writing.
- Why do you think there are so many different types of writing?

1. *Once upon a time there lived a beautiful princess in a faraway kingdom....*

2. Your Honour, the defendant stated that at 9.00pm on the night in question he was at home at 23 Acorn Avenue watching TV in the company of his wife.

3. *In November 1773 the "Boston Tea Party" took place. Local people dressed as Indians and dumped tea chests from British ships into the harbour. It was a protest against the hated tea duty.*

4. *Sweetheart, I miss you already. How much longer? I'm counting the days and the hours...*

5. I was born in St. Mary's Hospital on a damp grey morning in 1962. My brother John, then aged 3½, was brought in to see me. "Look, she has no teeth and no hair." My mother remembers his comment to this very day.

6. Dear Grandma,
It's not so bad here after all. I've made a new friend already. How are Jack, Tilly and Grandad?

7. They crept carefully toward the door. Was that a sound in the next room? "Get back!" said Frost, "Someone's coming!"....

8. **One way of separating a solute (e.g. sodium chloride) from a solvent (e.g. water) is to use the process of evaporation.**

Different types of writing

A Gospel is a particular type of writing, it is a document of faith. A Gospel is unlike any other type of book. Sometimes it is compared to a history book, or even a biography.

Different types of reading material.

History

However, a Gospel is not a history book about the life of Jesus. In a history book there are dates and exact names of people and places. Events are presented in the order in which they actually happened. In the Gospels there are no dates and the names of people and places are often left out. Furthermore, the events in Jesus' life are not written down in the exact order in which they occurred. Instead, they are often grouped together by topic. For example, Jesus' miracles may be in one section of the Gospel, his parables (stories) in another, and his remaining teaching somewhere else.

Biography

A Gospel is not a biography of Jesus either. A biography is the life story of a particular person. It describes all the events that took place at every stage in that person's life. It fills in all the facts from birth to adulthood. The Gospels on the other hand are mainly about the last three years of Jesus' life. There is very little about Jesus childhood in the Gospels, even less about his schooldays. There is nothing at all about the fifteen years or so he spent working as a carpenter and builder in the village of Nazareth.

Clearly a Gospel is not a piece of writing like a history book or a biography. The Gospel is something quite different.

Evidence

Each Gospel is a document. Documents provide written evidence about something important. The Gospels in the New Testament are our main source of evidence about Jesus. The authors, Mark, Matthew, Luke and John were people of deep faith. They wrote their Gospels with a special purpose in mind. They set out to show that Jesus, the Messiah, is the Son of God.

To this end, the Gospel writers focused their attention on the last three years of Jesus' life, the period when he was a travelling teacher in Palestine. They selected some vital facts such as eye-witness reports of Jesus':

- ❖ Teaching.
- ❖ Miracles.
- ❖ Death.
- ❖ Resurrection.

Then they explained the meaning and importance of these facts. For the evangelists, Jesus' words and actions show who he really is. It is the evidence, the proof, that Jesus truly is the Son of God.

Jesus, the Messiah, the Son of God.

Documents of Faith

The Gospels tell the story of Jesus. The Gospel writers were less interested in giving historical facts about Jesus. They were more interested in explaining the meaning and purpose of Jesus' life, death and resurrection.

The Gospels are called 'documents of faith' because the Gospel writers:

- ❖ Believed that Jesus was the Messiah, the Son of God.
- ❖ Provided evidence to support their belief.
- ❖ Invited others to share their belief.

The purpose of the Gospels

A Gospel is a special type of book. It does not merely tell people about Jesus so that they can admire him. The Gospel invites people to believe in Jesus and to follow him.

The Gospel is not a history or a biography of Jesus, it is more than that. The Gospel is a document of faith written by people who believe Jesus is God in order to help others to believe that Jesus is God.

In his Gospel, John the Evangelist explained the purpose of his writing:

> "...these have been written in order that you may believe Jesus is the Messiah, the Son of God, and that through your faith in him you may have life." John 20:31

Questions

Knowledge

1. Name the authors of the four Gospels.
2. What aspects of Jesus' life did the evangelists write about in the Gospels?
3. What kind of facts about Jesus are barely mentioned in the Gospels?
4. What did the evangelists firmly believe about Jesus?
5. What was the evangelists' purpose in writing the Gospels?
6. Give an example of a document of faith.

Understanding

1. Explain the difference between the way historians and biographers write about famous people, and the way the evangelists wrote about Jesus.
2. In the Gospels, why did the evangelists focus on the last three years of Jesus' life?
3. Why are the Gospels called 'documents of faith'?
4. Give reasons why the story of Jesus in the Gospels is important to Christian people.

Research

- Examine the Gospel of Mark. Find out:
  - How many chapters are in Mark's Gospel.
  - At what stage in Jesus' life the Gospel of Mark begins.
  - How many healing miracles are grouped together in chapters 1-3.
  - How many teaching parables are grouped together in chapter 4.
  - The last week of Jesus' life begins with his triumphant entry into Jerusalem. In Mark's Gospel, how many chapters are devoted to the last week of Jesus' life?
  - Overall, what proportion of Mark's Gospel focuses on the final week of Jesus' life.
  - Can you draw any conclusions from your findings?
  - Discuss your conclusions with the class.

The Kingdom of God

Key Concept

Kingdom of God: Jesus' vision of a way of life that loves God and does good to other people.

Objective

Outline what Jesus meant by the 'Kingdom of God'.

Activity: *"Dreamin' "*

TASK: TO IMAGINE ACHIEVING SOMETHING WORTHWHILE.

- Everyone has dreams. People dream about all kinds of things....
  - Getting to the top.
  - Winning the lotto.
  - Falling in love.
  - Getting good results.
  - Winning the league.

Dr. Martin Luther King, a Baptist minister, spent his life trying to change the way black people were treated in America. He had a dream of a perfect world where everyone would be equal.

"I have a dream that one day all God's children, blacks, whites, Jews, Gentiles, Protestants and Catholics will be able to join hands and sing in the words of the black people's old song 'Free at last..., thank God almighty we are free at last'."

Discuss

- Do you have a dream about something important - some goal that you would really like to achieve?
- Write about your dream.
- Think of a title for this dream.
- Share the dream with others in the class.

Kingdom of God

Jesus had a dream of a perfect world.

The Jewish people waited for centuries for a Messiah to guide them. Many expected a great king, one who would set up a new Jewish kingdom and free them from foreign rule. Jesus of Nazareth - a carpenter - amazed everyone when he announced that the Kingdom was at hand and that he was establishing it. It emerged that Jesus' vision of the Kingdom was very different to what most people expected.

The Baptism of Jesus

(Adapted from Mark 1:1-13)

Jesus had a dream, a vision of a perfect world. He began to follow his dream from the day he was baptised. John the Baptist baptised Jesus in the river Jordan. When Jesus emerged from the water, he felt the peace of God spread over him like a dove. Then God's words came to him "You are my own dear son. I am pleased with you." At that moment Jesus realised what God was calling him to do. His mission was to tell everyone just how much God loved them.

The Baptism of Jesus in the river Jordan.

Jesus' baptism was important. It marked the beginning of his public life as a teacher and a healer. Jesus spent the next three years travelling all over Palestine, telling people about the Kingdom of God.

Jesus' vision of the Kingdom of God

Jesus could see what the world would be like if people would allow the love of God to rule their hearts. It would change everything. It would be like heaven on earth. Everyone would love God, and everyone would love their neighbour as themselves. Jesus called this dream the Kingdom of God.

The Kingdom of God is the central idea in all Jesus' teaching, it is mentioned over a hundred times in the Gospels. The Kingdom of God is Jesus' dream or vision of a way of life that loves God and does good to other people. It is people everywhere living as God wants them to live, in peace, justice, truth and love.

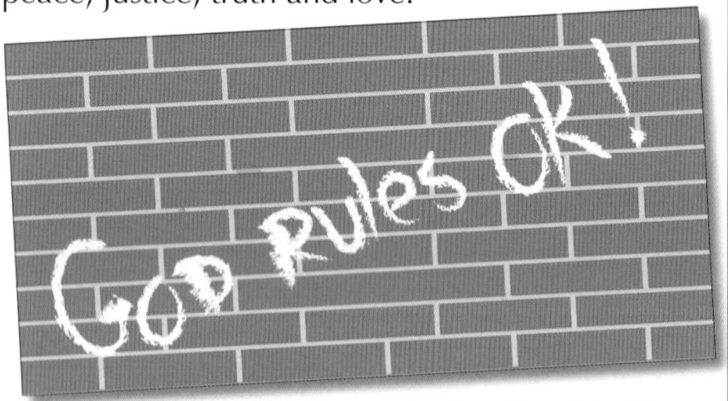
GOD Rules OK!

A modern statement about the place of God in people's hearts.

The Kingdom of God is not a place that can be found on a map. It is found in people, in the goodness of their hearts. Jesus said the Kingdom of God had already begun, it arrived in him.

Jesus used words and actions to help people understand what he meant by the Kingdom of God.

- He told **parables** to teach people about the love of God.
- He performed **miracles** to show people the love of God.
- He shared meals and **table-fellowship** to help all people experience the love of God.
- He called people to **discipleship** so that they could learn from him and follow a way of life based on the love of God.

The things that Jesus said and did were the first signs that the Kingdom of God had arrived.

Questions

Knowledge

1. When did Jesus begin his public life?
2. What happened when Jesus was baptised?
3. Jesus had a dream. What was it called?
4. What does the Kingdom of God mean to Christians?
5. Where is the Kingdom of God to be found?
6. What way of life would bring about the Kingdom of God on Earth?
7. What are the signs that the Kingdom of God has arrived?

Understanding

1. Describe Jesus' dream of a perfect world.
2. Why do you think Jesus' vision is called the Kingdom of God?
3. How did Jesus help people understand what the Kingdom of God is all about?

Research

- Find a copy of the school Mission Statement. This statement expresses the dream or the vision that many people have of the kind of school they want in the community. Examine it for a few minutes.
  - Is it a long statement or a short statement?
  - What does it say?
  - What does it identify as special and important for the life of the school?
  - Now consider what happens in your school to make this dream come true.
  - Discuss how a mission statement can inspire and guide people in human communities.

Parables

Key Concepts

Kingdom of God: Jesus' vision of a way of life that loves God and does good to other people.

Parable: a short story told by Jesus to teach people about the Kingdom of God.

Objective

Identify the characteristics of the Kingdom of God in the parables told by Jesus.

The Kingdom of God in Parable

At the time of Jesus, telling parables or short stories about familiar events was a common way of teaching new ideas. Jesus told parables or stories to teach people about the Kingdom of God. Each parable is a simple story with an underlying message. Jesus invites people to work out the meaning of each parable and then apply its message to their own lives. The parables of Jesus prompt people to stop and think and to live their lives in a better way.

The parables in the New Testament are about ordinary, everyday things such as: farming, minding sheep, housework, leaving home, family celebrations and going on journeys. Jesus' parables showed God's love at work in real everyday situations that everyone knew about. Jesus' parables were therefore easy to understand and easy to remember.

About fifty of Jesus' parables are recorded in the Gospels. A selection of Jesus' well known parables are presented in the table below. Each parable highlights something different about the Kingdom of God. Together they build up a picture of the features, or characteristics, of the Kingdom of God.

Christians believe the messages of the parables are as true today as they were for people in first century Palestine.

Parables of Jesus

Bible Reference	Parable	Characteristics of the Kingdom of God
Mark 4:30-32	***The Mustard Seed.*** It's about planting a small seed that becomes a tall plant.	Shows that God's love is a gift planted in people's hearts where it can grow and mature.
Luke 15:4-9	***The Lost Sheep. The Lost Coin.*** It's about a farmer and a householder searching for something precious.	Shows that God loves every single person without exception.
Matt 13:3-8, 13:18-23	***The Sower*** It's about a farmer sowing seeds on different types of soil.	Shows that people respond in different ways to Jesus' message about the Kingdom of God. Those who accept it try to build the kind of world that God wants for everybody.
Luke 10:25-37	***The Good Samaritan.*** It's about a person in need being cared for by a stranger.	Shows that loving one's neighbour is essential in the Kingdom of God.
Luke 15:11-32	***The Prodigal Son*** It's about a person who regrets leaving home and wants to return.	Shows that in the Kingdom of God, God will always forgive the sinner who is truly sorry.

The parable of The Mustard Seed

(Adapted from Mark 4:30-32)

Jesus once told a parable about sowing a mustard seed. "What shall we say the Kingdom of God is like?" asked Jesus. "What story shall we use to explain it? It is like this. A man takes a mustard seed, the smallest seed in the world, and plants it in the ground. After a while it grows up and becomes the biggest of all plants. It puts out such large branches that the birds come and make their nests in its shade."

the ground... A person's heart.
a seed... God's love.
a small plant... A good action.
a fully grown tree... the Kingdom of God.

The meaning of the parable

The Kingdom of God is compared to the growth of a plant. The seed of love is a gift sown in people's hearts. It grows slowly and silently deep within each person. Each time someone does something good, no matter how small, it is a sign that God's love is in their heart. Jesus promised that from something small, slowly, over time, amazing things will grow.

The fully grown plant stands for the Kingdom of God fully present in the world. Jesus told the parable of *The Mustard Seed* to show that although the Kingdom of God has small beginnings, it will grow slowly and steadily into something wonderful.

Questions

Knowledge

1. What is a parable?
2. Why did Jesus tell parables?
3. What made Jesus' parables easy to remember?
4. Name some parables Jesus told to explain the features or characteristics of the Kingdom of God.
5. In the parable of *The Mustard Seed*, what do the following correspond to in the Kingdom of God?
   a. The ground.
   b. The mustard seed.
   c. The small mustard plant.
   d. The fully grown tree.
6. What is Jesus trying to say about the Kingdom of God in the parable of *The Mustard Seed*?
7. What does the parable of *The Mustard Seed* have to say about:
   a. the scale of the Kingdom of God at the beginning?
   b. the speed at which the Kingdom of God will develop?

Understanding

1. How did Jesus help people understand the concept of the Kingdom of God?
2. What is the difference between a story and a parable?
3. Explain the meaning of Jesus' parable, *The Mustard Seed.*

Research

Find out:

- How many parables are recorded in the Gospel of Matthew, chapter 13.
- List the titles of the parables.
- What ordinary events in people's lives are referred to in each parable.
- What do each of these parables have to say about the Kingdom of God.
- Write a modern day version of any one of these parables.
- Present your composition to the class.

The Lost Sheep

Key Concepts

Kingdom of God: Jesus' vision of a way of life that loves God and does good to other people.

Parable: a short story told by Jesus to teach people about the Kingdom of God.

Objective

To explain how sinners and outcasts are treated in the Kingdom of God.

Activity: *"Lost and Found"*

TASK: TO CONNECT WITH FEELINGS OF CARE AND CONCERN IN PERSONAL EXPERIENCE.

A lost sheep.

Discuss

- Did you ever lose something important?
  1. What was it?
  2. What did you do about it?
  3. Did you find it again?
  4. How did you feel afterwards?

The Kingdom of God in Parable

Jesus told parables to show how God treats those who lose their way in life.

Jesus taught that there is great concern for the lost in the Kingdom of God. Sinners, people who do not follow God's way, are the most lost of all. Jesus told the parable of *The Lost Sheep* and *The Lost Coin* to explain how God treats those who lose their way in life.

When Jesus was teaching about the Kingdom of God, a group of tax collectors and other outcasts gathered around to listen to him. The local Pharisees who were standing nearby began to grumble amongst themselves. They did not agree with Jesus mixing with such sinners, they felt he should know better.

Jesus had different ideas. Jesus wanted people to know that God is a God of love. He wanted them to understand that God loves all people. There are no exceptions. There is a place for everyone in the Kingdom of God. Even if people sin and turn away from God, God will do everything to find them and bring them back again. God does not give up on anyone. Jesus says that when a sinner repents and asks for forgiveness, there will be much joy on his return. Then Jesus told two parables:

- ❖ The parable of *The Lost Sheep*.
- ❖ The parable of *the Lost Coin*.

The parable of The Lost Sheep

(Adapted from Luke 15:4-9)

Jesus said: "Imagine a man has one hundred sheep. One of them wanders off and gets lost." Jesus asked, "What does the man do? He leaves the other ninety nine in a safe place and goes off into the hills, searching everywhere for the lost sheep. When he finds it, he is delighted.

He lifts it up on his shoulders and carries it back home. He can't wait to tell his friends and neighbours: 'Look, he says, I have found my lost sheep! Lets celebrate!'"

The parable of The Lost Coin

(Adapted from Luke 15:8-10)

Jesus said: "Imagine a woman has ten silver coins. One of them falls on the floor and gets lost." Jesus asked, "What does the woman do? She lights the only candle she has and sweeps the house carefully from top to bottom. She searches everywhere for the lost coin. When she eventually finds it, she is delighted. Straight away she calls her friends and neighbours. 'Look', she says 'I have found my lost coin, lets celebrate!'"

In the time of Jesus, a bride on her wedding day often wore an elaborate head-dress of coins and jewels. To lose one of those coins might be like a woman today losing her engagement or wedding ring.

"A Modern Parable"

The parables of *The Lost* apply to people today, their message being just as relevant now as it was at the time of Jesus. The images used now might be different but the message about the immense love of God is still the same.

1.
2.
SPECIAL
OFFER
3.
4.

In the modern parable illustrated above think how parents must feel:

- if a child goes missing.
- when the child is found again.

✦ How would the actions of parents in a story such as this point to the nature of God?

Questions

Knowledge

1. Who was present on the day Jesus was teaching about the Kingdom of God?
2. What parables did Jesus tell that day? What were the stories about?
3. What is the most important moment in the parable of *The Lost Sheep*? Give a reason for your opinion.
4. What is the most important moment in the parable of *The Lost Coin*? Give a reason for your opinion.
5. For whose benefit did Jesus tell both parables?
6. To whom might Jesus address these two parables today?
7. What was the message of these two parables for people at the time of Jesus?
8. What might these parables mean for Christians today?

Understanding

1. What was Jesus trying to explain about the nature of God when he told the parables of *The Lost Sheep* and *The Lost Coin*?
2. What do these parables say about the way sinners and outsiders are treated in the Kingdom of God?
3. Are Jesus' parables of *The Lost Sheep* and *The Lost Coin* relevant to people today? Give reasons for your answer.

Research

- Do you think that signs of the Kingdom of God are visible or absent in the world today?
  - Survey local and national newspapers.
  - Select two articles with a headline, photographs, and a storyline for signs that:
    - a. the Kingdom of God is not accepted in the world today.
    - b. the Kingdom of God is accepted in the world today.
  - Present your case to the class.

The Sower

Key Concepts

Kingdom of God: Jesus' vision of a way of life that loves God and does good to other people.

Parable: a short story told by Jesus to teach people about the Kingdom of God.

Objective

To explain how sinners and outcasts are treated in the Kingdom of God.

Activity: *"Willpower"*

TASK: TO BE AWARE THAT SUCCESSFULLY COMPLETING A TASK REQUIRES EFFORT.

✦ Within a limited timeframe carry out the following tasks. See if you can complete each task without at any time raising your pen off the paper once you have begun.

abcdefghijklmnopqrstuvwxyz

1. Copy the alphabet in joined writing.
2. Draw a picture of twelve trees around a field.

Discuss

- What was easy or difficult about this exercise?
- Did everyone keep going until each exercise was finished?
- What kind of things do we normally put an effort into: - at school? - outside school?

Modern methods of sowing seeds and growing crops.

The Kingdom of God in Parable

Many people make an effort to put their religious faith into practice.

Jesus challenged people to:

- open up their hearts to the Word of God.
- make an effort to live a new way of life.

He told his followers the parable of 'The Sower' to show that people respond in different ways to his invitation to follow him. They can either say 'yes' or 'no' to the way of life that he offers.

In Palestine most of those who listened to Jesus lived in the countryside and worked on the land. They grew their own food, and knew all about the importance of sowing seed and getting a good harvest. When Jesus spoke to them about life in the Kingdom of God he used familiar images from country living to get his message across.

The parable of The Sower

(Adapted from Matthew 13:3-8 and 13:18-23)

Once there was a farmer who went out to sow seed (in those days seed was sown by hand). The seed fell on different types of ground.

Some seed fell on the path. It did not grow and birds flew down to eat it up. Some seeds fell on rocky ground. The soil was not deep enough for the roots to grow. When the sun shone, the young plants dried up and died. Some seed fell among the thorn bushes. As the plants grew, they were choked by the thorns. Other seed fell on good soil. The plants grew well there and produced a good crop.

The meaning of the parable

Jesus explained the meaning of the parable.

The seed represents the message of Jesus about the Kingdom of God.

The ground represents the way the heart of a person is open or closed to the Word of God.

Some people are like the seed that falls on the path. They do not understand the message of the Kingdom of God and fail to take it to heart.

Some people are like seed that falls on rocky ground. At first they are enthusiastic about the message of the Kingdom of God, but they soon give up if it requires extra work or effort.

Some people are like the seed that falls among the thorns. They know about the message of the Kingdom of God but are too busy or too worried about other things to do anything about it.

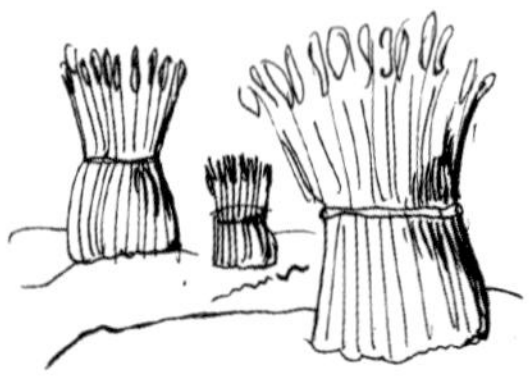

Some people are like the seed that falls on good soil. They understand the message of the Kingdom of God and take it to heart. In following Jesus they try to build the kind of world that God wants for everybody.

In the parable of *The Sower*, Jesus explains that the Kingdom of God can grow and flourish in each person if they live according to his teaching. Jesus never said it would be easy to follow him. He never said it would be a popular choice either. Instead, he pointed out that his way requires an effort, but the effort would be worthwhile.

Questions

Knowledge

1. List the different types of ground mentioned in the parable of *The Sower*.
2. In the parable:
   a. What happened to the seed that fell on the path?
   b. Why did some plants dry up and die?
   c. How did the thorn bushes affect the plants?
   d. Where did the strong healthy plants grow?
3. In the parable, what did Jesus mean by:
   a. The seed? b. The ground?
4. What was the most important moment in the parable of *The Sower*? Give a reason.
5. Select two kinds of people identified in the parable of *The Sower*. Say what their responses are to the Word of God.
6. What was Jesus trying to explain to people in the parable of *The Sower*?

Understanding

1. Why did Jesus use images from farming and country life to explain the idea of the Kingdom of God?
2. In the parable of *The Sower*:
   a. What helps to ensure a good harvest?
   b. What response ensures the arrival of God's Kingdom on Earth?
3. Is the parable of *The Sower* relevant for Christians today, explain your answer.

Research

- Examine another parable about an everyday situation familiar to people at the time of Jesus. The parable of *The Tenants in the Vineyard* is the story of the Jewish people and their relationship with God.
  - Read the parable of *The Tenants in the Vineyard*. Mark 12:1-12.
  - Find out what each of the following elements represent. For example:
    - The vineyard = God's people, the Jews.
    - Vineyard owner =
    - Tenants =
    - Servants =
    - Son =
    - New tenants =
  - What do you think Jesus is trying to tell people in this story?
  - Compare your ideas with those of the rest of the class.

The Good Samaritan

Key Concepts

Kingdom of God: Jesus' vision of a way of life that loves God and does good to other people.

Parable: a short story told by Jesus to teach people about the Kingdom of God.

Objective

Show how love of neighbour is a characteristic of the Kingdom of God.

Activity:

"Kind Hearts, Cold Hearts"

TASK: IDENTIFY SOME OF THE MANY ACTS OF HUMAN KINDNESS PERFORMED ON A DAILY BASIS.

- What kind of thoughtful things do friends, family, neighbours and acquaintances do to make life a bit brighter and a bit easier for us all.
- Brainstorm the type of things kind-hearted people say or do for others.
- How do cold-hearted people behave towards others?

Discuss

- What do kind-hearted people do for others?
- Do people usually treat each other with kindness?
- Tell your own story of receiving a small act of kindness from someone.

The Kingdom of God in Parable

Jesus once told a parable about a kind-hearted man who helped a person in need.

If people want to be part of the Kingdom of God, Jesus said, they must be open-hearted to everyone, even the outcasts of society.

Once when Jesus was teaching about the Kingdom of God, a man asked him about the right way to live. Jesus responded "scripture says 'You must love your neighbour as yourself.'" The man then enquired "Who is my neighbour?" Jesus answered him by telling the parable of *The Good Samaritan*.

The parable of The Good Samaritan

(Adapted from Luke 10:25-37)

One day a Jewish man is going on a journey along a road from Jerusalem to Jericho. A local gang, seeing that he is travelling alone attack him, beat him up, and take all his money. They leave him lying almost unconscious on the side of the road. The poor man is unable to move. Two local people, a Temple priest and a Levite (a Temple official) pass by in a great hurry.

They are on their way to the Temple in Jerusalem. They notice the injured man but choose to ignore him and cross to the other side of the road. They don't want to get involved.

Then a man from Samaria comes along. Jews and Samaritans don't get on. The Jews have always looked down on people from Samaria and treated them as inferior. The Samaritans as a result, hated the Jews. Nevertheless, this Samaritan stops when he sees the man lying at the roadside. He feels sorry for him and goes over to see what is wrong. The injured man groans in pain. The Samaritan immediately gives him first aid and makes arrangements to bring him to the nearest inn. He even stays up all night caring for him. Before leaving the next day, the Samaritan gives the innkeeper some money. "Make sure that man gets everything he needs," he says. "If it costs any more let me know, I'll be back later on to see how he is."

When Jesus finished the parable, he spoke to the person beside him: "Who do you think acted in a neighbourly way to the man who was attacked?" "The person who was kind to him," was the reply.

Samaritans

Samaritans came from Samaria, a province of Palestine. Although the Samaritans were Jewish, other Jews would have nothing to do with them. Both groups had been enemies for centuries, long before the time of Jesus. Samaritans were despised because they mixed freely with Gentiles (non-Jews). Their customs, scripture and religious practices were sufficiently different to convince the majority Jewish population that they were not real Jews anymore. At the time of Jesus, the Samaritans were rejected and despised by everyone. They were treated as outcasts by the rest of the Jewish community in Palestine.

In the parable of *The Good Samaritan*, Jesus teaches that the Kingdom of God is open to everyone, Jew, Gentile, Samaritan, no one is excluded. Our neighbour is anyone at all who needs our help, people we like, even people we don't like. Jesus went out of his way to love and care for people whom others had no time for. He taught his followers to do the same.

Questions

Knowledge

1. What question did Jesus answer by telling the story of *The Good Samaritan*?
2. In the parable, who should have been the first to help the injured man?
3. In the parable, who was the last person anyone would have expected to help the injured man?
4. List the different ways in which the Samaritan showed kindness to a stranger.
5. Who was the hero of the story?
6. How should people treat each other if they want to be part of the Kingdom of God?
7. What is an outcast? Why were Samaritans treated as outcasts in that society?
8. What is the message of the parable of *The Good Samaritan*?

Understanding

1. What do you think is the most important moment in the parable of *The Good Samaritan*? Give reasons.
2. Why do you think Jesus chose a Samaritan to be the 'hero' of this parable?
3. Does this parable have a message for people today?
4. The parable of *The Good Samaritan* is found only in the Gospel of Luke. Why do you think Luke the Evangelist included this parable in his Gospel?

Research

Write a modern version of the parable of *The Good Samaritan.*

Remember: Jesus told parables about events in everyday life. He spoke about ordinary things that everyone knew about. Jesus liked to use familiar situations to get his message across.

A modern parable would be based on ordinary events that are familiar to you. Let the story have a hidden meaning about being kind and thoughtful to one's neighbour - especially people we don't get on with. A neighbour is anyone at all who happens to be in need.

Choose someone unexpected to be the hero.

- Read out your finished work to the class.

The Prodigal Son

Key Concepts

Kingdom of God: Jesus' vision of a way of life that loves God and does good to other people.

Parable: a short story told by Jesus to teach people about the Kingdom of God.

Objective

Show how forgiveness is a characteristic of the Kingdom of God.

Activity: *"First Steps"*

TASK: TO APPRECIATE THE IMPORTANCE OF BEING THE FIRST TO TAKE THE INITIATIVE IN CERTAIN SITUATIONS.

✦ Recruit a group of volunteers. One stands facing the wall.

✦ Six to eight others form a line a short distance behind, facing the same wall.

✦ The first volunteer calls out a letter from the alphabet. The others respond by advancing forward in steps the size of their footwear, ie. - 1 step if their forename contains that letter.
- 2 steps if that letter occurs twice in their name.
- No steps otherwise.

✦ The volunteer quickly repeats another letter etc. The first student to reach the wall gets to be the caller for the next round.

Discuss

- Who took the first steps at the start of the exercise?
- Are you ever the first to do something at home, at school or out of school?
- Have you ever been the first to make up with a friend or someone in your family when you've had a row which wasn't all your own fault.
- What is it like taking the first step in making up with people?

The Kingdom of God in Parable

Christians believe in the forgiveness of God and know they must take the first step and say sorry for any wrongdoing.

Jesus told the parable of *The Prodigal Son* (or *Lost Son*) to help his followers understand that in the Kingdom:

❖ God is a loving God, always ready to forgive.

❖ God's people must be ready to forgive too.

In the parable the father represents God, and the youngest son represents humankind. God the Father is always there for his sons and daughters and never gives up on them, no matter what they do. All a person needs to do is take the first step and say sorry. God will always accept them back. In this parable, Jesus is teaching his followers a new way of living. "Just as God forgives you," he said, "So must you forgive one another."

The Forgiving Parents

(Adapted from the parable of *The Prodigal Son* Luke 15:11-24)

The O'Neills lived in a nice house in a small country town. The parents and their two grown-up daughters worked in the family business. One day Mary, the youngest, complained to her parents. "I'm fed up working here," she said "I want to get away, I want to get a job somewhere else."

Mr and Mrs O'Neill were surprised and indeed a bit worried,

but they didn't want to stop their daughter getting on in life. After some discussion, they went to see their bank manager. They took a large some of money out of their savings and transferred it into their daughters account. The following week, Mary had packed her bags and left home.

She travelled to the city and was soon having a great time. She met an old friend and stayed with her at a really posh address. The girls went out shopping and sight-seeing and spent a lot of money on clothes and make-up. They ate and drank in smart bars and cafes, Mary made lots of new friends. Life was really exciting. They were always going out to a new club or to a party somewhere.

Then the money ran out. One by one, Mary's friends went too. She had to find a place to stay. Eventually she moved into a tiny apartment and tried to get a job. It wasn't easy. She went to the local job centre every day and in the end got a job in a diner called the 'Midnight Express'. She worked the night shift as a cleaner; at least it was a start. It was hard work. The hours were long and the wages were low, in fact it was hardly enough to pay the rent.

Some evenings she was particularly lonely and began to think of everyone back home. She wondered what the family would think of her now. She had made such a mess of everything. Gradually she came to her senses and bravely took the first step and phoned home.

On the journey back she thought about what she would say to her father and mother. "I'll tell them I'm sorry, I'll tell them I made a fool of myself. I'll tell them I'll do anything to make it up to them." Mary opened the gate and walked up the path, her head down. She was anxious, she didn't know what was going to happen. Then the front door opened and there they were. She needn't have worried, her parents ran out to meet her. They stood hugging her for ages. Mary said sorry and tried to explain. She even offered to do her old job for nothing, if only they'd have her back.

Section B

Mary's parents had been very worried, afraid their daughter would never return. She was home again now and that was all that mattered. Everything was forgiven. They all went back into the house, they had a lot to celebrate.

Questions

Knowledge

1. In the parable, what did the young person want to do?
2. What happened when the young person went away?
3. What steps had to be taken in order to receive the parents' forgiveness?
4. What was the parents' attitude on the young person's return?
5. What is the most important moment in the story?
6. Whom do you think Jesus had in mind when he told this parable?
7. What did Jesus challenge people to do in this parable?
8. What aspect of the Kingdom of God is explained in this parable?

Understanding

1. Why was it a brave decision for the young person to return home?
2. Explain why the young person was welcomed back in spite of everything.
3. What is the meaning of the parable of *The Prodigal Son (Lost Son)* for people today?
4. Is it easy or difficult for people to:
   - Say sorry?
   - Show forgiveness?
5. Explain what Christians believe about forgiveness.

Research

- Locate a poem, a short story, or a chapter in a book that, in your opinion, is a good example of one person forgiving another for what he/she has done wrong.
  - Write a summary highlighting the main points.
  - Present your example to the class.

Miracles

Key Concepts

Kingdom of God: Jesus' vision of a way of life that loves God and does good to other people.

Miracle: an amazing cure or deed performed by Jesus to show the power and love of God.

Objective

Identify characteristics of the Kingdom of God in the miracles performed by Jesus.

The Kingdom of God in Miracle

Jesus taught people about the Kingdom of God not only through words, but also through actions. He used miracles to let people see the power and love of God at work in the world. Many amazing cures and deeds were performed during his public life in Palestine.

Jesus worked different types of miracles:

1. Healing miracles - he healed people who were sick or disabled.
2. Nature miracles - he changed something in nature, such as calming a storm, or turning water into wine.
3. Expelling miracles - he got rid of evil spirits from people's lives.
4. Raising to life miracles - he raised the dead to life.

Christians believe Jesus was able to work miracles because he had power from God. The evangelists record thirty-five of Jesus' miracles in the Gospels. A selection of Jesus' well known miracles are outlined below

Jesus fulfils Old Testament prophecies.

In the Old Testament the prophet Isaiah spoke to the Jews, telling them that God would send someone to help them. "When the Messiah arrives," he said, "there will be signs and miracles."

> "The blind will be able to see,
> and the deaf will hear.
> The lame will leap and dance,
> and those who cannot speak
> will shout for joy." Isaiah 35:5-6

In the Gospels, the evangelists point out that Jesus did everything of which the prophet spoke. Jesus travelled all over Palestine and worked miracles wherever he went.

He made:
- ❖ Blind people see.
- ❖ Deaf people hear.
- ❖ Lame people walk.

The evangelists saw the miracles as a sign that Jesus was the Messiah.

1. Healing Miracles • Healing a blind man called Bartimaeus in Jericho. (Mark 10:46-52) • Healing a person with leprosy in Galilee. (Mark 1:39-45)	***3. Expelling Miracles*** • Expelling an evil spirit from a man in Capernaum. (Mark 1:21-28) • Expelling an evil spirit from a man in Gerasa. (Mark 5:1-20)
2. Nature Miracles • Calming a storm on Lake Galilee. (Mark 4:35-41) • Turning water into wine at a wedding feast in Cana. (John 2:1-12)	***4. Raising to Life Miracles*** • Raising Jairus' daughter to life in Galilee. (Mark 5:21-42) • Raising Lazarus to life in Bethany. (John 11:38-44)

Jesus' miracles show the love and power of God at work in the world.

Jesus worked miracles in order to show God's love, show God's power and to strengthen people's faith in God.

The miracles helped people to see **God's love**. Jesus wanted those who were sick or sad or disabled or poor to know that God loves and cares for them. So when he worked a miracle, Jesus was showing people what God is like. God is a God of love who cares deeply for everyone and is with them in all their difficulties.

The miracles helped people to see **God's power**. Jesus made it known that his ability to perform miracles came directly from God. Through God the Father, Jesus has power over disease, over nature, over evil and over death. The power of God is at work in the world and it comes through Jesus.

The miracles helped to **strengthen people's faith**. Jesus did not perform miracles to show off or to amaze people or even to gain acceptance. He worked miracles only for those who had faith in God's presence. Jesus' miracles invited people to open their hearts to the love of God. They were signs that the Kingdom of God is truly present and at work in the world.

Jesus' miracles were an extension of his parables and his teaching about the Kingdom of God. When Jesus performed miracles, he put his words into action.

Questions

Knowledge

1. What is a miracle?
2. Name the different types of miracles worked by Jesus.
3. How many miracles are recorded in the Gospels?
4. What did the prophet Isaiah say about the Messiah that was to come?
5. What did the evangelists think about Jesus' miracles?
6. What was the purpose of Jesus' miracles?

Understanding

1. How do the miracles of Jesus fulfill Old Testament prophecies?
2. Why did Jesus work miracles?
3. What do the miracles tell us:
   a. About Jesus?
   b. About the Kingdom of God?
4. How would miracles help to deepen people's faith in Jesus? Explain your answer.

Research

- Examine the different types of miracles recorded in the Gospels.
  - Select one miracle to begin with.
  - Read the Bible reference.
  - Write down:
    - The title of the miracle.
    - What Jesus said and did.
    - The people's reactions.
    - The place where the miracle occurred.
  - Decide what this miracle demonstrates about the Kingdom of God and share your conclusions with the class.

Healing Miracles

Key Concepts

Kingdom of God: Jesus' vision of a way of life that loves God and does good to other people.

Miracle: an amazing cure or deed performed by Jesus to show the power and love of God.

Objective

Explain how Jesus' miracles show the special place of the poor in the Kingdom of God.

Section B

Activity: *"Role Play"*

TASK: TO KNOW WHAT IT FEELS LIKE TO BE IGNORED.

- Demonstrate an example of poor listening skills to the class.

  Devise a brief scenario.
  Three people, ***A***, ***B*** & ***C*** are together.
  - ***A*** tells the other two about something topical that has just occurred.
  - ***B*** & ***C*** show by their behaviour that they are not really interested in what ***A*** has to say.
- Role play the scenario.
- Afterwards identify any responses used by ***B*** and ***C*** from the list below.

- Pretend to listen.	- Turn up the radio or TV.
- Keep on writing or reading.	- Keep on talking to someone else.
- Glance at the clock.	- Text a message.
- Look at something else.	- Walk away.
- Be dismissive with a wave of the hand.	- Yawn.

Discuss

- Have you ever found yourself talking to someone, only to discover that he/she wasn't listening to you?
- When did this occur last? What happened?
- What is it like to be ignored?

The Kingdom of God in Miracle

In the Gospel of Mark there is a story of a person who was ignored by everyone except Jesus.

Jesus performed a miracle and healed a man who was so poor he had to beg for his living. When Jesus healed the blind beggar in Jericho he was showing people the power of God, and how much God cares for those who are poor and who suffer. He was challenging people's attitude to the poor in that society.

Jesus heals blind Bartimaeus

(Adapted from Mark 10:46-52)

Bartimaeus sat in his usual place by the roadside. The people of Jericho knew him well. He called out as they passed by. Now and then someone stopped and gave him some coins or some food.

Jesus heals a man born blind.

Bartimaeus was blind. He made his living by begging from passers-by. Local people paid little attention to him. He was a nobody. They didn't even call him by his own name. He was known simply as Bar-Timaeus (son of Timaeus).

One day there was a lot of excitement in the town. Bartimaeus heard a group coming towards him. He asked what was happening. "It's Jesus of Nazareth," somebody said, "He's coming this way." Bartimaeus couldn't believe it. He had been told about Jesus, that he was a healer who taught about the love of God. Bartimaeus wanted to meet him.

This was his chance, he just knew Jesus would listen to him. Bartimaeus began to shout - he wanted the Messiah to hear him - "Jesus son of David, take pity on me." The crowd standing in front of the blind man were cross with him and told him to keep quiet. But Bartimaeus shouted even louder, he had a strong voice, he was good at shouting.

When Jesus heard him, he stopped and called him over. Jesus listened carefully as Bartimaeus told him that he wanted to be able to see. He knew Jesus had the power to heal him. "Go, your faith has made you well," Jesus said, and he gave Bartimaeus back his sight. The man was amazed. He looked at Jesus and decided then and there to follow him. The miracle changed his life, it gave him back his sight and opened his eyes to the way Jesus treats everyone.

Bartimaeus realised that he was important and not to be ignored. Poor people have a place in the Kingdom of God.

The Poor in the Kingdom of God

Many people had health problems at the time of Jesus. Blindness was common in Palestine, especially amongst the poor. If a person was poor he had no way of supporting himself or his family. He had to beg in order to live.

Jesus healed several people, many of whom were blind. He healed only those who had faith in him. He used his power to show the love of God for the poor. Through his actions Jesus showed that the poor have a very special place in the Kingdom of God.

Questions

Knowledge

1. In what town did the miracle of healing take place?
2. Who was Bartimaeus?
3. How did the local people treat Bartimaeus?
4. How did Jesus treat Bartimaeus?
5. What is the evidence that Bartimaeus had faith in Jesus?
6. What did Jesus do for Bartimaeus?
7. Did anything else happen that day?

Understanding

1. Why did Bartimaeus think Jesus could help him?
2. Why do you think Jesus worked this healing miracle?
3. What does this miracle tell you about the place of the poor in the Kingdom of God?
4. What does the action of Jesus teach Christians about how to treat the poor and the marginalised in society today?

Research

Jesus performed numerous healing miracles (Matthew 15:29-31), only some of which were recorded in detail in the Gospels.

- Find out about other healing miracles.
  Jesus heals Peter's mother-in-law - Mark 1:29-34
  Jesus cures a sick woman - Mark 5:25-34
  Jesus heals a Roman officer's servant - Matt 8:5-13
  Jesus heals a man with leprosy - Mark 1:40-45
  Jesus heals a paralysed man - Mark 2:1-12
  Jesus heals a deaf man - Mark 7:31-37
  Jesus heals an official's son - John 4:43-54
  Jesus heals ten men with leprosy - Luke 17:11-19
  Jesus heals a man with a paralysed hand - Mark 3:1-6
  Jesus heals a blind man - Mark 8:22-26
  Jesus heals two blind men - Matthew 9:27-31
- Select a Bible reference from the list above. Write down
  - the title of the healing miracle.
  - what Jesus said and did.
  - people's reaction to the miracle.
  - the place where the miracle occurred.
- Discuss what this miracle shows about the Kingdom of God.

Other Miracles

Key Concepts

Kingdom of God: Jesus' vision of a way of life that loves God and does good to other people.

Miracle: an amazing cure or deed performed by Jesus to show the power and love of God.

Objective

Explain how Jesus' miracles show people the meaning of the Kingdom of God.

The Kingdom of God in Miracle

Jesus spent his public life teaching about the Kingdom of God. His words and deeds are recorded by the evangelists in the four Gospels. Jesus did not just tell people about the love of God, he lived it through his actions. When he performed miracles, Jesus showed people what God's love is like so that it would challenge them to love and care for others too.

The miracles were included in the Gospels in order to show God's love and power at work in Jesus. Christians believe the power of God was working through Jesus when he performed:

- ❖ Healing miracles.
- ❖ Nature miracles.
- ❖ Expelling miracles.
- ❖ Raising to life miracles.

Jesus' miracles show that he had power over nature, over illness, even over death itself. People needed to have faith in order for a miracle to happen. Jesus' miracles helped to deepen their faith.

Nature Miracles

Jesus showed his power over the forces of nature when he calmed a fierce storm (Mark 4:35-41), turned water into wine (John 2:1-12) and fed 5,000 people with five loaves and two fishes (Luke 9:10-17). The disciples were totally amazed when Jesus calmed the storm, it made them wonder what kind of a man he really was.

Jesus Calms a Storm
(Adapted from Mark 4: 35-41)

Jesus and his disciples got into a boat and sailed across the lake. Suddenly a fierce storm developed. The waves broke over the side of the boat and it was in danger of sinking. The disciples roused Jesus who had been sleeping. "Save us Lord!" they cried, "we are about to die!" "Why are you so frightened?" Jesus responded. "How little faith you have!" Then he got up and ordered the wind and the waves to stop. The wind dropped and all was calm again. Everyone was amazed. "What kind of man is this?" they said, "even the wind and the sea obey him."

Nature miracles help people understand that God is present with them in times of trouble or great difficulty.

Expelling Miracles

Jesus showed his power over evil when he expelled an evil spirit from a man in Capernaum (Mark 1:21-28), from a man in Geresa (Mark 5:1-20) and a young boy in Galilee (Mark 9:14-29). At that time people believed certain illnesses were caused by demons or evil spirits. At least one of those conditions would be regarded as epilepsy today.

Jesus Heals a Boy with an Evil Spirit
(Adapted from Mark 9:14-29)

A man in the crowd implored Jesus, "Please do something for my son, he is my only child. A demon often attacks him and throws him to the ground, the boy foams at the mouth, grits his teeth and shakes all over. This has been happening since he was born. I begged your disciples to force the demon out of him but they could not do it." Jesus scolded the disciples for their lack of faith and asked for the boy to be brought to him. The demon attacked the boy once more. Jesus ordered the demon to stop, then he healed the boy and returned him to his father. Everyone was amazed at the power of God. When the disciples later asked Jesus why they couldn't drive the demon out, Jesus replied "It was because you didn't have enough faith."

Expelling miracles help people to understand that God accepts everyone no matter what their ability or disability, all they need is faith. Miracles strengthen their faith.

Raising to Life Miracles

Jesus showed his power over death when he raised to life his friend Lazarus (John 11:17-44), a widow's son (Luke 7:11-17) and the daughter of Jairus (Mark 5:21-42). Jesus healed people and worked wonders out of pity and compassion for people's suffering. He wanted to help Jairus and give him back his daughter.

Jesus Raises Jairus' Daughter to Life
(Adapted from Mark 5:21-43)

Jairus, a synagogue official, begged Jesus to heal his daughter. She was twelve years old and she was dying. On the way to the house someone rushed up to Jairus with the news that his daughter had just died. Jesus told him "Don't be afraid, only believe." When they arrived at the house, everyone was crying, they were all very upset. Jesus told them the child was not dead, only sleeping, but they just laughed at him. Jesus ignored this and went with the parents and his disciples into the room where the child was lying. He took her hand and said "Little girl, get up." She got up at once and was able to walk around. Everyone was amazed. He then told them to give her something to eat.

Raising to life miracles help people to understand that God's love and power is stronger than death. With God, nothing is impossible. In the Kingdom of God, miracles happen as long as people have faith, faith is crucial. Jairus had absolute faith that Jesus would heal his daughter.

Questions

Knowledge

1. Name the different types of miracles, giving an example of each.
2. What was the main thing people would learn from Jesus by:
   a. Listening to what he said?
   b. Watching what he did?
3. What needed to happen before any miracle could take place?
4. Select one of Jesus' miracles and state:
   a. What was the situation before the action of Jesus?
   b. Who showed their faith and trust in Jesus?
   c. How did Jesus show his power?
   d. How did people react after the action of Jesus?
   e. What does this miracle show about the Kingdom of God?

Understanding

1. Why did Jesus perform miracles?
2. Give reasons why the evangelists included Jesus' miracles in the Gospels.
3. What do the miracles tell us about Jesus?
4. What do the actions of Jesus show Christians about the way to treat other people?

Table-fellowship

Key Concepts

Kingdom of God: Jesus' vision of a way of life that loves God and does good to other people.

Table-fellowship: the way Jesus shared meals with everyone to show the Kingdom of God is open to all.

Objective

Identify characteristics of the Kingdom of God in table-fellowship.

Activity: *"Food Matters"*

TASK: EXAMINE WHAT IT MEANS TO SHARE A MEAL WITH FAMILY AND FRIENDS.

✦ It's a regular school day, the bell goes, its lunchtime.
  - Where do you usually eat at lunchtime?
  - What do you usually have?
  - Who usually has lunch with you?
  - What do you talk about, usually?

✦ Most people mark important events by sharing a meal. When was the last time your family had a special meal together?
  - What was the occasion?
  - Where did it take place?
  - Who was invited?
  - Was there a special menu?
  - How did the event affect everyone there?

Discuss

What do you think it means to sit down and share food with family and friends?

The Kingdom of God in Table-fellowship

Jesus shared meals with a lot of people.

When we share a meal with family and friends we are not merely sitting down together to satisfy our need for food. When we share a meal it suggests that somehow there is a bond or a connection between us.

Meals were important occasions in Jewish life. Breaking bread and sharing a meal with someone was a sign of closeness and friendship. In first century Palestine, Jews generally shared meals only with their family and friends. Jesus, on the other hand, shared meals with everyone, including those outside his social group such as sinners, tax collectors and other outcasts.

For Jesus, this was table-fellowship. Sharing meals with all kinds of people was a way of showing that the Kingdom of God is open to all. The closeness and unity of table-fellowship helped people to experience the Kingdom of God.

Jesus shared the bread and wine of Eucharist with the disciples at the Last Supper.

The Gospel of Luke records ten occasions when Jesus shared a meal with other people. It indicates that table-fellowship was an important part of the ministry of Jesus.

Characteristics of the Kingdom of God

Jesus was criticised for being a friend to sinners, tax collectors, and other social outcasts.

> *'When the Pharisees saw Jesus eating with sinners and tax-collectors, they said to his disciples, "Why does he eat with such people?" On hearing this, Jesus said, "People who are healthy do not need the doctor, only those who are sick. I did not come to call respectable people, but sinners"'* (Adapted from Mark 2: 15-17)

Jesus showed that the Kingdom of God is open to anyone who turns toward the love of God and away from sin and wrongdoing. Jesus set out to show people what God is like. God is loving and forgiving. Jesus wants his followers to be like that too.

Jesus visits the home of Zacchaeus

(Adapted from Luke 19: 1-10)

One day, when Jesus was passing through the town of Jericho, the chief tax collector joined the crowd waiting to see him. Zacchaeus had heard all about the famous teacher and wanted to see him in person. But the crowd were unfriendly. They stood in front of him, blocking his view. The local people looked down on Zacchaeus. No one liked him because they thought he was dishonest and because he worked for the Romans.

The tax collector suddenly had an idea and climbed a tree by the side of the road. He didn't care if his clothes got torn or if people laughed at him, he just had to see Jesus, nothing else mattered.

Jesus meets Zacchaeus.

When Jesus finally came along, he looked up and saw Zacchaeus. Jesus said his name and then calmly invited himself to Zacchaeus' house for lunch. Zacchaeus couldn't believe it! He slid down from the tree and went over to welcome Jesus. Some people were annoyed and began to complain: "I don't believe it! Look, Jesus is talking to that cheat Zacchaeus." "It's a disgrace, he's a sinner and everyone knows it." "Why is Jesus going to his house? He should be visiting one of us."

Later during the meal, Zacchaeus sat and talked to Jesus for a long time. In the end, the tax collector promised to change his ways. He would stop cheating and pay back anyone he had overcharged. He also promised to help the poor. Jesus assured Zacchaeus that he was saved.

Jesus' act of table-fellowship in the company of a tax collector showed that the Kingdom of God is for everyone. People who are despised and rejected have a special place in the Kingdom of God.

Jesus shares table-fellowship with Zacchaeus.

Ancient mosaic depicting Jesus' miracle of the multiplication of loaves and fishes.

Questions

Knowledge

1. What is table-fellowship?
2. What did Jewish people mean by table-fellowship?
3. What was Jesus' approach to table-fellowship?
4. What was Jesus showing people about the Kingdom of God through his table-fellowship?
5. Who was Zacchaeus?
6. How did people react when Jesus gave all his attention to a social outcast?
7. How did Zacchaeus change his lifestyle after sharing table-fellowship with Jesus?
8. What did Zacchaeus learn about the Kingdom of God?

Understanding

1. How was Jesus' approach to table-fellowship different from the general practice among Jews at the time?
2. a. Why did Jesus share meals with people regarded as outcasts in that society?
   b. Who would be regarded as marginalised in today's society?
3. a. What characteristics of the Kingdom of God are found in Jesus' table-fellowship?
   b. Give reasons why Jesus used table-fellowship to show the characteristics of the Kingdom.
4. Did Jesus' treatment of Zacchaeus contain any message:
   - for Jews in Jericho? - for Christians today?

Research

- Find out about some of the meals Jesus shared with people during his public ministry.
- Select a Bible reference from the Gospel of Luke.
  Luke 9:10-17 - Feeding 5,000 people.
  Luke 5:27-39 - A meal in Levi's house.
  Luke 7:36-50 - A dinner party in Simon's house.
  Luke 10:38-42 - Hospitality in Mary's and Martha's house.
  Luke 11:37-54 - A meal with a Pharisee.
  Luke 14:1-24 - Sabbath meal with a Pharisee.
  Luke 19:1-10 - Hospitality in Zacchaeus' house.
  Luke 22:7-23 - The Passover meal/ The Last Supper.
  Luke 24:13-35 - Supper in Emmaus.
  Luke 24:36-53 - Eating with the disciples in Jerusalem.
- Explore an example of table-fellowship
  - Where did the meal take place?
  - Who was at the meal?
  - What happened during the meal?
  - What did Jesus say?
  - What effect did sharing a meal with Jesus have on the people there?
  - What does this example of table-fellowship:
    - tell us about Jesus?
    - show us about the Kingdom of God?
- Write a report to present to the class.

Discipleship

Key Concepts

Kingdom of God: Jesus' vision of a way of life that loves God and does good to other people.

Discipleship: following Jesus and his teaching.

Objective

Explain the meaning of discipleship in the Kingdom of God.

Activity: *"Friendship diagram"*

TASK: EXPLORE PATTERNS OF FRIENDSHIP IN OUR LIVES.

- On a diagram plot the location of your friendships (add names or initials). Begin by placing yourself at the centre.

Discuss

- Who is your best friend?
- Who are your good friends?
- Do you have other friends?
- What are your friends like? Are they the same or are they completely different from one another?
- Have you been friends long - can you remember how you first met?

The Kingdom of God in Discipleship

Jesus had many friends, he chose twelve of them to be his disciples.

After he was baptised, Jesus travelled all over Palestine, teaching about the Kingdom of God. He went from village to village teaching and performing miracles. As the news spread and the crowds got bigger, Jesus needed others to help him with his work. He chose ordinary people with ordinary jobs to follow him. Jesus called each of his disciples; he chose them, they did not choose him. The first four remained his closest friends.

Jesus calls his first disciples

(Adapted from Mark 1:16-20)

Jesus met his first followers beside Lake Galilee. One day two fishermen, Simon and his brother Andrew, were fishing with a net at the edge of the lake. The two fishermen probably knew about Jesus already and had heard him preach. So when Jesus said to them "Come with me," they both left their work and followed him.

Jesus needed people to help him.

Jesus calls his first disciples.

Further along, two more fishermen, James and John, were mending nets in their father's boat. When Jesus called out to them, they too left what they were doing and followed him. It was a big step. Simon, Andrew, James and John all changed their way of life in order to follow Jesus. He needed their help to bring more people into the Kingdom of God. It is clear from the Gospels that Jesus had a large number of followers, both men and women. One day he picked twelve of them to work more closely with him. The twelve became his disciples. A disciple is someone who learns from a teacher (rabbi). Jesus wanted his disciples to learn from him and follow his example.

Jesus calls twelve disciples

The call to discipleship is a big step. It involves following Jesus and his teaching. In the Kingdom of God, a follower of Jesus is one who puts God and other people first before him or herself. Discipleship involves a total change of heart, a complete break with the way one has lived life up to that point.

Jesus' disciples were twelve ordinary men from all walks of life. A few were well off, but most were poor. They were different ages, some were married, others were not. A number of them were fishermen and tradesmen, some may have been shepherds. One was a tax-collector, another was a zealot. Jesus called each of them to follow him.

Jesus' twelve disciples were:

> Peter (originally called Simon), Andrew, James, John, Philip, Bartholomew (also known as Nathaniel), Matthew (originally called Levi), Thomas, James, Thaddaeus (also known as Jude), Simon and Judas. (Matt 10:1-4)

Jesus needed the disciples to help him establish the Kingdom of God on Earth. He trained them to pass on his teaching and way of life to others. The disciples learned to open up their hearts to God, and to love their neighbour as themselves. The twelve travelled with Jesus all over Palestine. At the start, the disciples saw Jesus as a very holy man, later on they began to think he might be the Messiah. It was only after his death and resurrection that they fully realised Jesus was in fact the Son of God. After Pentecost, the disciples continued Jesus' work; teaching, healing and forgiving members of a new community of faith, Christianity.

Questions

Knowledge

1. What did the crowds see and hear when they came to listen to Jesus?
2. Where did Jesus meet his first disciples?
3. Name two sets of brothers who decided to follow Jesus. How did it change their lives?
4. What sort of people did Jesus choose as his disciples?
5. What is a disciple?
6. What did Jesus call his disciples to do?

Understanding

1. a. What is discipleship?
   b. What does it mean to be a disciple of Jesus?
2. Why did Jesus ask ordinary people and not powerful, wealthy, or holy people to follow him and be his disciples?
3. Why do you think people answer the call of Jesus? How does it change their lives?

Research

- Find out about another person whom Jesus called to follow him.
  - Read Mark 2:13-17
    - Who was this person?
    - Where did he work?
    - What was his job?
    - What did Jesus say?
    - How did the man respond?
    - Outline some major changes that probably took place in this man's life as a result of his decision to follow Jesus.
  - Share your ideas with the class.

The Beatitudes

Key Concepts

Kingdom of God: Jesus' vision of a way of life that loves God and does good to other people.

Discipleship: following Jesus and his teaching.

Objective

Identify the characteristics of the Kingdom of God as preached by Jesus in the Beatitudes.

Activity: *"On the bus!"*

TASK: TO KNOW THE DIFFERENCE BETWEEN CHRISTIAN AND UN-CHRISTIAN ATTITUDES AND BEHAVIOUR.

- Examine the sixteen snippets of conversation on the bus.
- There are eight paired conversations. Try to identify each pair.
- Sort out the attitudes expressed in each conversation into Christian attitudes and un-Christian attitudes

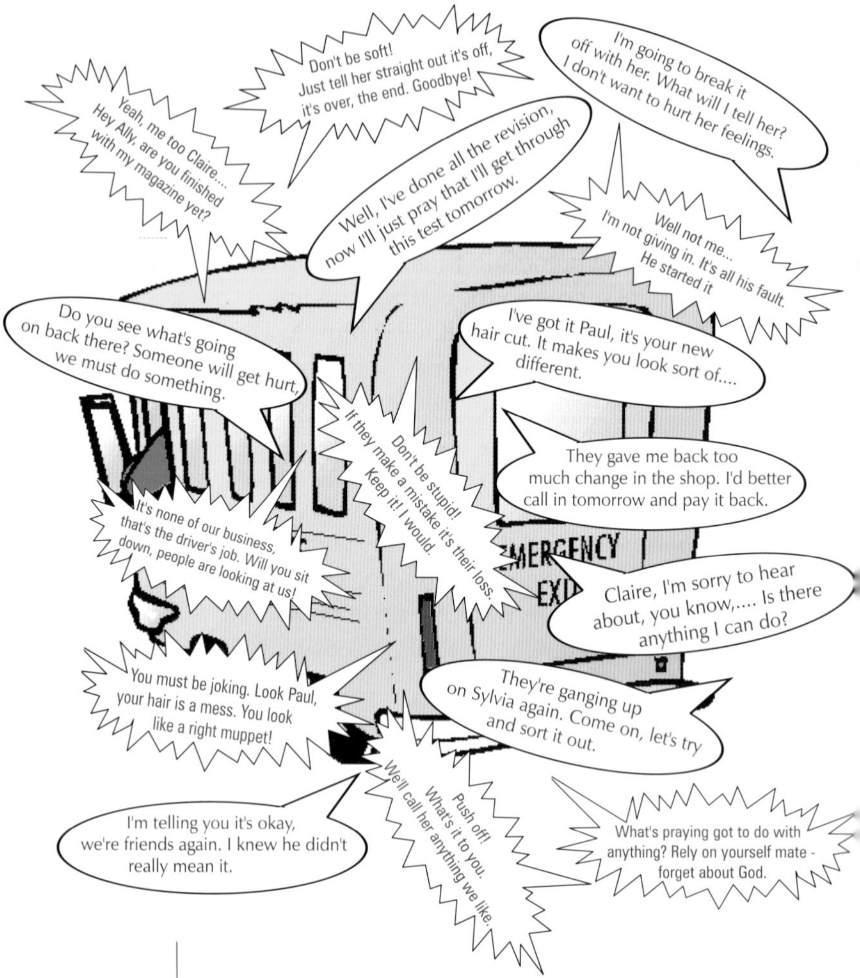
Yeah, me too Claire... Hey Ally, are you finished with my magazine yet?
Don't be soft! Just tell her straight out it's off, it's over, the end. Goodbye!
I'm going to break it off with her. What will I tell her? I don't want to hurt her feelings.
Well, I've done all the revision, now I'll just pray that I'll get through this test tomorrow.
Well not me... I'm not giving in. It's all his fault. He started it
Do you see what's going on back there? Someone will get hurt, we must do something.
I've got it Paul, it's your new hair cut. It makes you look sort of....different.
Don't be stupid! If they make a mistake it's their loss. Keep it! I would.
They gave me back too much change in the shop. I'd better call in tomorrow and pay it back.
It's none of our business, that's the driver's job. Will you sit down, people are looking at us!
EMERGENCY EXIT
Claire, I'm sorry to hear about, you know,.... Is there anything I can do?
You must be joking. Look Paul, your hair is a mess. You look like a right muppet!
They're ganging up on Sylvia again. Come on, let's try and sort it out.
I'm telling you it's okay, we're friends again. I knew he didn't really mean it.
Push off! What's it to you. We'll call her anything we like.
What's praying got to do with anything? Rely on yourself mate - forget about God.

Discuss

- Were you able to differentiate between the Christian attitudes and the un-Christian attitudes?
- Which attitudes do you think are most common today.
- When was the last time someone behaved in a Christian way to you?

The Kingdom of God in Discipleship

People learn Christian behaviour from the teachings of Jesus.

How should we behave at home? How should we treat our friends at school? Does it matter how people behave towards one another? It mattered to Jesus. Through his words and actions, Jesus showed his followers a right way to live. He taught a set of attitudes and behaviours that, if adopted, would bring about the Kingdom of God on Earth. Jesus not only set high standards for Christians to follow, he lived by these standards himself. He showed it could be done.

The Sermon on the Mount (Matt chapters 5-7)

Jesus spent his public life teaching about the Kingdom of God. He used different methods to get his message across: he used parables, miracles and table-fellowship. Jesus also spoke directly to people through sermons. One day he gathered his disciples and his other friends around him. They sat down together on the side of a hill. In the *Sermon on the Mount,* Jesus began by teaching them the Beatitudes. This is a list of qualities Jesus' followers must have in order to be part of the Kingdom of God.

Jesus teaching the Beatitudes.

The Beatitudes

The Beatitudes show people how to be disciples of Jesus. The central message of Jesus is that people love God and love their neighbour as themselves. The Beatitudes show how to put this message into practice. It may not be easy living up to Jesus' way of doing things. Yet Jesus promised that anyone who adopts these attitudes and behaviours would be happy and would receive a special blessing from God.

Discipleship means following Jesus and his teaching and, through good example, passing his message on to others.

The Beatitudes (Adapted from Matt 5:1-10)

Jesus says "Happy are..."	these are people who...	Be-Attitudes
1. The poor in spirit.	have faith and depend on God.	- *Be prayerful.*
2. The mournful.	are sorry for their sins and want to start over again.	- *Be repentant.*
3. The gentle.	treat others with kindness and show care for the Earth.	- *Be gentle.*
4. Those who hunger and thirst for what is right.	try to do what is right and just.	- *Be fair.*
5. The merciful.	forgive those who hurt them or let them down.	- *Be forgiving.*
6. The pure of heart.	are respectful and honourable and won't take advantage of others.	- *Be respectful.*
7. The peacemakers.	work for peace and an end to conflict.	- *Be a peacemaker.*
8. Those persecuted for doing what is right.	can get into trouble because they stand up for what is right.	- *Be brave and have integrity.*

Living the Beatitudes

✦ Select one or more of the Beatitudes and answer the following questions.

1. Be prayerful.

(a.) Describe someone you know who is close to God.

(b.) What happens when a Christian shuts God out of their life?

2. Be repentant.

(a.) What kinds of things might a person regret and be sorry for doing?

(b.) What can happen if a person doesn't care about what they do wrong?

3. Be gentle.

(a.) Describe someone you know who is gentle and kind.

(b.) What happens when a person acts tough all the time?

4. Be fair.

(a.) Describe someone you know who is always fair to others.

(b.) What happens when a person is unfair to someone else?

5. Be forgiving.

(a.) Describe someone you know who forgave another person when it wasn't easy to do so.

(b.) What happens when a person holds a grudge and won't forgive?

6. Be respectful.

(a.) Describe someone you know who always shows respect to other people.

(b.) What happens when a person is disrespectful to someone?

7. Be a peacemaker.

(a.) Describe someone you know who can make people feel at ease.

(b.) What happens when someone behaves like a troublemaker?

8. Be brave.

(a.) Describe someone you know who had the courage to stand up for what is right.

(b.) What happens when a person sees something wrong and decides not to get involved?

Questions

Knowledge

1. Who first taught people a Christian way of life?
2. a. What are the Beatitudes?
   b. How many are there?
3. Where are the Beatitudes to be found in the Bible?
4. According to Jesus, what qualities should people develop in order to be part of the Kingdom of God?
5. Select a Beatitude, state how it could be put into practice today.
6. What promise does Jesus make to Christians who take the Beatitudes seriously?

Understanding

1. What do the Beatitudes tell us about the Kingdom of God?
2. a. What would the world be like if people lived according to the Beatitudes?
   b. Which Beatitude poses the biggest challenge for people today?
3. Can you suggest a person, a group of people, or an organisation that could be identified with each Beatitude? Explain the connection.

Research

✪ Find examples of Christian attitudes in films and on television.

- First identify a hero or heroine in a well-known TV programme, video or film.
- Now select a quality from this list: prayerful, repentant, gentle, fair, forgiving, respectful, peaceful, upright.
- Describe how the hero/heroine portrays this quality on screen for the good of others.
- What is the evidence that behaving in this way was either easy or difficult for him or her?
- Is there a connection between the action on-screen and Jesus' teaching of the Beatitudes in the Gospel?
- Present your findings and ideas to the class.

Discipleship Today

Key Concepts

Discipleship: following Jesus and his teaching.

Vocation: a feeling of being called by God to serve others.

Mission: the specific work carried out by members of a Christian community.

Objective

Identify characteristics of the Kingdom of God in the life of Jesus' followers today.

Activity: *"Charities"*

TASK: DISCUSS WHY PEOPLE SUPPORT THE WORK OF CHARITABLE ORGANISATIONS.

Discuss

- Do fundraising events for charitable causes take place in your school?
- Have you supported any charitable activity in school or out of school this year?
- Why do you think Christians support the work of different charitable organisations?

Discipleship
Vocation

Jesus had a vision of a better world where everyone would help each other out.

The word vocation comes from the Latin 'vocare', which means 'to call'. In the beginning, Jesus called twelve people to follow him and be his disciples. Jesus continues to call people to discipleship today. A vocation is a person's sense of being called by God to live a certain way of life. The Christian way of life involves following the teaching of Jesus "to love God and love one's neighbour as oneself." Matt 22:37-39

The neighbour is everyone, especially the poor, the sick, the lonely, the stranger and the defenseless. Everyone has a place in the Kingdom of God. Catholics, for example, can fulfill their Christian vocation and follow Jesus either as lay people, single or married, as a nun or a brother in a religious community, and as an ordained priest. God's Kingdom can be seen in the lives of all those who strive to do good in the world today.

Herald

Women's Mini-Marathon, Dublin.
Most participants seek sponsorship and raise money for charitable causes.

Mission

All Christians lay and religious, male and female, young and old, answer the call of Jesus in different ways. Each one has a mission, or specific work to do, as a member of the Christian community. This is how God's love is made present and visible in the world today. For example:

Sister Stanislaus Kennedy follows Jesus by establishing 'Focus Ireland', an organisation that ensures young people do not have to sleep rough on city streets. Instead they get help to make a fresh start in life.

Mother Teresa followed Jesus by founding a religious order the Missionaries of Charity to help the poorest of the poor in India and elsewhere.

Brother Roger Schutz followed Jesus by building an ecumenical community in Taize, where Christians of all denominations can meet and pray together.

Archbishop Desmond Tutu follows Jesus by helping to bring peace and justice to people of all races in South Africa.

Christian parents have a special vocation. Their mission is to show the love of God to their children, and to help their friends and neighbours.

Christian teenagers follow their parents' good example and regularly support the work of voluntary organisations such as Trocaire, Christian Aid and the Society of St. Vincent de Paul. These students are packing Christmas gifts for children in Romanian orphanages.

Questions

Knowledge

1. What does the term 'vocation' mean?
2. Who were the first people called to follow Jesus?
3. Whom does Jesus call to discipleship today?
4. What does the term 'mission' mean?
5. a. Give an example of someone called to discipleship today.
   b. What is the work or mission of this modern disciple of Jesus?
6. List the ways in which a Christian today can show that he/she is a true follower of Jesus.

Understanding

1. How is the call to discipleship heard by ordinary Christians today?
2. What is the evidence that the Kingdom of God is present in the lives of Christians today?
3. In Matthew 25:34-40, Jesus tells his disciples "when you do it for them... you do it for me."
   In this country, or in other countries:
   a. Who are those who are hungry, thirsty, a stranger, naked, sick, or in prison?
   b. How do Christians respond to people in need today?

Research

- Invite a Christian to visit the class to discuss their experience of working with, and for, people in need at home or abroad. Choose a person of any denomination whose way of life is inspired by Gospel values e.g. a returned missionary, a member of a religious community, or a lay person involved in a charitable organisation.
- Think about what the visit is to achieve, and agree a set of questions in advance, such as:
  a. Why are you a disciple, a follower of Jesus?
  b. How do you follow Jesus? What do you do?
  c. How did Jesus call you? Did it change you in any way?
  d. What are the challenges of discipleship today? What things do you find difficult?

  Agree a procedure for welcoming, and later thanking the visitor.
- Write a summary of what you learned about Christian discipleship today and discuss it with the class.

Jesus and Outcasts

Key Concept

Conflict with authority: a clash or struggle with people in power.

Objective

Know why Jesus came into conflict with religious authorities when he mixed with social outcasts.

Activity: *"Outsiders"*

TASK: TO BE AWARE THAT IT IS EASY TO LOOK DOWN ON OTHERS.

She's so big-headed.
They're weird.
They wreck your head.
He's useless.
He's so boring.
They're all snobs around here.
Look at the state of her.
Their place is a mess.
She's always moaning about something.
She's so stupid.
Those two are a real pain.
I can't stand him.

Discuss

- Have you ever overheard remarks like these?
- Who might be the target of such remarks?
- Why do some people look down on others and give them a hard time?

Conflict with authority

Jesus mixed with people that others' despised.

Jesus' teaching and miracles attracted a large following in Galilee and other parts of Palestine. His teaching about love and forgiveness was different from that of other Jewish rabbis at the time. Soon Jesus' message brought him into conflict with those in power and authority in the Jewish religion, people such as:

- The Pharisees - Jewish laymen in the local synagogues, and experts on the Law of God.
- The Sadducees - Jewish priests in the Temple in Jerusalem and members of the Sanhedrin.

The Pharisees and Sadducees had considerable power and authority among the Jewish community in Palestine at the time of Jesus.

Mixing with Social Outcasts

Jesus was accused of mixing with outcasts because he was friendly with sinners, Gentiles (non-Jews) and others who were regarded as 'unclean' or unsuitable for Jewish society. People such as tax collectors, Romans, individuals with leprosy and Samaritans were all disliked and treated as outcasts.

The Jewish authorities felt Jesus was unfit to be a rabbi because he mixed with a range of social outcasts. Jesus believed his mission was to show that the love of God is for all people, everyone has a place in the Kingdom of God.

In the Gospels we learn of Jesus' compassion for people suffering from the disease of leprosy. At that time this disease was incurable. People with leprosy were forced to leave their families and live in remote places away from everyone. They had to ring a bell and shout "Unclean!" to warn people not to approach. They were avoided and treated as outcasts because of their illness. Back then there was no cure for leprosy. Today, however, leprosy can be cured by the use of modern drugs.

Jesus heals a man with leprosy
(Adapted from Mark 1:39-45)

A man sat alone on a rocky hillside in Galilee. The sun was high, he shaded his eyes with a deformed hand. He thought he saw someone walking along the road. He looked again and realised he hadn't made a mistake. It was Jesus. It really was Jesus! What was he doing here? "No one ever comes this close, I'd better warn him." He rang a bell and shouted "Unclean! Unclean!"

Jesus did not move away unlike everyone else. Instead, he came closer. "Unclean! Unclean!," the leper shouted more desperately. He stared at Jesus in amazement, then got down from the rocks and moved slowly forward. Because of his disability he stumbled and fell. He was determined however, so he got up and steadied himself with his stick and moved again, shuffling more quickly. His heart was beating fast, he half ran, half crawled to where Jesus was waiting for him. "If you want, you can make me clean," he said. It was a simple prayer and showed great faith.

Jesus looked at the man and had pity on his suffering. Then Jesus did something forbidden by Jewish law, he reached out and touched him. "I want to make you clean," Jesus said, and the man was healed. Jesus asked him to obey Jewish law and go straight to the Temple to show himself to the priest to prove he was cured. Only then would the man be able to go back home to his family and to his community.

The man later told everyone what had happened. The miracle had changed his life; it not only gave him back his health, his whole life was put back together again. Jesus had shown him that he mattered, that he was just as important as anyone else. No one is cast out in the Kingdom of God.

Questions

Knowledge

1. Name two Jewish groups that had power and authority in Palestine.
2. Who were regarded as outcasts at the time of Jesus?
3. What did Jesus do that brought him into conflict with the authorities?
4. How did people treat someone with leprosy at the time of Jesus?
5. How did Jesus treat the man who had leprosy?
6. How did Jesus know the man had faith?
7. Where did the man have to go to show that he was healed?
8. In what ways did Jesus show God's love and care for the man whom others rejected?

Understanding

1. Compare the way Jesus treated the man with leprosy and the way he was treated by everyone else.
2. Give reasons why Jesus would meet and talk to people who were cast out from Jewish society.
3. Why did Jesus' relationship with social outcasts bring him into conflict with the Jewish authorities?
4. What sort of people are rejected in today's society? How would Jesus want his followers to respond to them?

Research

- Find out about Jesus' attitude to other social outcasts in Palestine. Jesus came into conflict with the Jewish authorities because of the way he related to outcasts in that society.
- Select one incident and examine it in detail.
  - Jesus and tax collectors. (Luke 5:27-32)
  - Jesus and Roman officials. (Matt 8:5-13)
  - Jesus and Samaritans. (John 4:1-30)
  - Jesus and people with leprosy. (Luke 17:11-19)

Exploration

1. Where did the incident occur?
2. What did Jesus do?
3. a. Did anyone in authority object to Jesus' action? <u>or</u>
   b. On what basis could someone in authority have objected to Jesus' action?
4. What is Jesus' attitude to this social outcast?
5. How did Jesus explain the meaning of his action?

- Compile a summary for a class discussion.

Jesus Forgives Sins

Key Concept

Conflict with authority: a clash or struggle with people in power.

Objective

To know why Jesus was in conflict with religious authorities when he forgave sins.

Activity: *"Persistence Exercise"*

TASK: TO KNOW THAT PERSISTENCE IS ABOUT MAKING AN EFFORT TO GET SOMETHING DONE.

- Ask a volunteer to go to the farthest corner of the room, and cover his/her eyes and ears.
- The rest of the class select an action for the student to perform (write on the blackboard, close a pencil case, lift a chair, open a window etc...).
- The volunteer returns, and through trial and error makes an effort to establish the correct action to perform.
- Assist the volunteer by giving a quick, loud hand clap the more he/she approximates toward the correct action, and a slower, quieter hand clap the more he/she deviates from it.
- Reward the volunteer with a resounding handclap when he/she performs the correct action.
- Repeat.

Conflict with authority

A group of friends made a big effort to get close to Jesus, who then rewarded their faith.

Jesus' words and actions sometimes brought him into conflict with the Jewish authorities. He travelled throughout Palestine teaching about the Kingdom of God and performing miracles. Jesus had many followers but he also had some enemies. The Pharisees, a powerful group in the Jewish community, were suspicious of Jesus because he mixed with sinners and outcasts, behaviour unbecoming a rabbi. He also annoyed them by some of the things he said, especially his claim to forgive sins.

Jesus heals a paralysed man

(Adapted from Luke 5:17-26)

At the time of Jesus, many people thought that illness and disease was a form of punishment. They believed people who were sick must have done something wrong in their lives. The more serious the illness, the bigger the sin that must have been committed.

When Jesus returned to Capernaum, a large crowd gathered at the house to hear him teach.

Discuss

- How did the class assist the volunteer to carry out the correct action?
- In life, what kind of things do we have to work at in order to succeed?
- Have you ever made a big effort to get something right?

Jesus heals people and forgives sins.

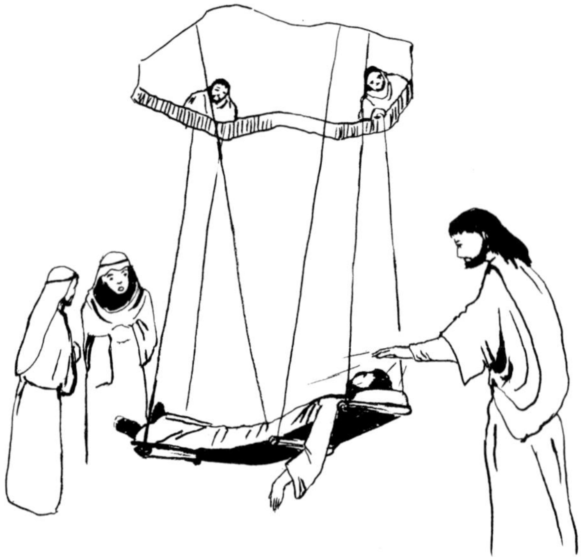

A group of men arrived carrying their friend who was paralysed and could not walk. They were certain that Jesus had the power to heal him. They tried to get their friend inside the house, but the crowd was too big. The men were determined to see Jesus, so they tried to reach him another way.

Carefully, they carried the paralysed man up the steps at the side of the house. It wasn't easy, but they kept going until they got up on the roof. After they caught their breath they set to work and made a hole in the roof. Dust and dirt fell down into the room below. Everyone stood back and looked up in amazement. When the space was big enough for their purpose, the friends told the paralysed man to hold on tight. Then they lowered him down on a mat in front of Jesus.

Jesus heals and forgives sins

It was obvious to Jesus that these men had great faith. He said to the paralysed man, "My son, your sins are forgiven." Jesus' words shocked a group of Pharisees who were standing nearby. Some of them were from Galilee, a few had come all the way from Jerusalem. These Jewish leaders knew that only God had the power to forgive sins. How dare Jesus claim that he too forgives sins! Was he saying that he was equal to God? If so, that was an insult! The Pharisees accused Jesus of blasphemy (serious disrespect of God). The conflict between Jesus and the religious authorities was apparent at that moment.

Jesus turned to the paralysed man and healed him in front of everyone. Then Jesus told him to roll up his mat and go home with his friends. Everyone was completely amazed and praised God. Jesus had shown that he had the power to heal and forgive sins. Jesus did not claim this power as his own, he said it came directly from God.

Questions

Knowledge

1. Who were the people with power and authority in the local Jewish community?
2. What was Jesus doing that was a cause of concern to the Pharisees?
3. Give reasons why a large crowd wanted to meet Jesus.
4. Describe an incident when Jesus came into conflict with the religious authorities.
5. In what two ways did Jesus show God's love for the paralysed man?
6. Of what was Jesus accused?
7. How did Jesus respond to the accusation?
8. With whom was Jesus in conflict that day in Capernaum.

Understanding

1. How did Jesus come into conflict with the authorities in Capernaum?
2. Why did Jesus heal the paralysed man?
3. Why were the Pharisees so outraged by what happened that day?

Research

- Refer to the Gospel account where Jesus forgives sins. (Luke 5:17-26)
  "Your sins are forgiven."
  "I don't believe it! Who does he think he is?"
  "Only God can forgive sins."
  "He's saying that he's equal to God?"
  "But that's blasphemy!"
  "He can't get away with that."
  "It's a scandal!"
  - Find out:
    1. Who were: a. the Pharisees?
       b. the Sadducees?
    2. Why do you think the Pharisees were present in the house in Capernaum?
    3. Did the Pharisees object to Jesus healing people?
    4. What was their main complaint about Jesus that day?
    5. To whom would the Pharisees report their concerns about Jesus?
  - Respond to these questions, and discuss the implications of this incident for Jesus and his mission.

Jesus and Sabbath Laws

Key Concept

Conflict with authority: a clash or struggle with people in power.

Objective

To understand that Jesus came into conflict with the Pharisees and the Sadducees over the Sabbath laws.

Activity: *"TV Soaps"*

TASK: TO EXAMINE THE WAY PEOPLE GET INTO CONFLICT WITH AUTHORITY

Discuss

- What is your favourite TV soap?
- Is there much disagreement or conflict between the characters in TV soaps?
- Can you think of an incident where a character was given a hard time by someone with more power or authority than themselves?
  What happened?
- Who has authority over you?
  Have there been occasions in your life where you were in conflict with authority?
  What happened?
  How did you feel about it all?

Conflict with authority

Jesus came in conflict with Jewish leaders who had a lot of power and authority in Palestine.

The Jewish Sabbath is a holy day, a day of rest and prayer. "Observe the Sabbath and keep it holy." (Exodus 20:8) At the time of Jesus the Pharisees thought that this meant that God did not want people to do any work at all on the Sabbath. There were hundreds of Sabbath laws and the Pharisees applied them very rigidly. For example, people were not allowed to cook, or light a fire, or buy anything in the market. They could not walk more than one kilometre from their home, nor carry a load of any kind.

The Pharisees were anxious to keep God's law in all its exact detail. They believed they were serving God when they encouraged ordinary Jews to obey every tiny detail of the Law. Jesus upset the Pharisees when he challenged their understanding of the Law governing the Sabbath. He believed that too many rules only made people's lives more difficult, and took away from the true meaning of the Sabbath which was about having time to pray and worship God.

Conflict with authority.

Jesus in conflict with the Pharisees

Jesus was accused of breaking Jewish Law when he allowed his disciples to pick ears of corn to eat on the Sabbath.

A cornfield.

In the Cornfield on the Sabbath

(Adapted from Luke 6:1-5)

One Sabbath day, Jesus and his disciples were walking along by a field of corn. The disciples were hungry, so they picked some corn, rubbed it between their hands and ate the grain. It got them into trouble when some Pharisees noticed what happened. They told Jesus that it was against the law of God for the disciples to do something like that on the Sabbath.

Jesus was aware that the Sabbath was holy and a day of rest. He explained to the Pharisees that the disciples were hungry; people must come first, he said, before the detail of the law. The Pharisees were outraged, as they believed the exact opposite.

For the Pharisees, the law came first and must be obeyed in every tiny detail. What gave Jesus the right to change the law, they asked. Jesus replied that he had every right to interpret the law in this way. The Pharisees were no longer the experts about the Kingdom of God, Jesus was the expert.

Jesus was accused of breaking Jewish Law when he healed people on the Sabbath, a day when all physical work was forbidden.

A synagogue.

In the Synagogue on the Sabbath

(Adapted from Luke 6:6-11)

Jesus went into a synagogue on the Sabbath and began to teach the people worshipping there. A man with a paralysed hand came in and sat down. The Pharisees, sitting in the important seats up at the front, waited to see what Jesus would do. Would he heal this man on the Sabbath? If he did, it was against the law of God, and they would have him!

Jesus asked the man to come forward and stretch out his hand. Then he healed him in front of everyone. Jesus believed that it was right to help people, even on the Sabbath. Once again, Jesus said that the needs of the people must come first, before the details of the law.

The Pharisees were horrified. It didn't matter to them that a man had been healed. What mattered was that Jesus had broken God's Law. They left the synagogue in disgust. Later they had a meeting. Jesus was dangerous, he was breaking all the rules. They made plans to get rid of him.

Jesus in conflict with the Sadducees

(Adapted from Mark 11:1-19)

The following account is about Jesus' arrival in Jerusalem and his actions in the Temple.

Jesus' entry into Jerusalem

Jesus and his disciples went to Jerusalem for Passover, the most important feast in the Jewish year. Jesus received a great welcome when he arrived in the city. Crowds lined the streets to wait for him. They shouted and cheered, and even pulled branches from palm trees to wave at him as he passed by.

Jesus in the Temple

Jesus spent the next three days teaching in the Temple. The Temple priests, the Sadducees, were worried at the size of the crowds gathering around him. They became very angry indeed when Jesus defied them and chased the traders and money-changers out of the Court of Gentiles. The Sadducees had allowed them to buy and sell animals and deal in currency in that part of the Temple. The trade was useful and a help to pilgrims.

Jesus was not afraid to challenge the Sadducees about the practice. He said the Temple had become more of a marketplace than a place of worship.

The Sadducees did not want any disturbance in the Temple; the Romans might think things were getting out of control. It might prompt them to make life even harder for the Jews and ban Temple worship altogether. Jesus had to be stopped. Some Sadducees and other members of the Sanhedrin tried to find a way to get rid of Jesus for good.

Questions

Knowledge

1. What is the Sabbath in the religion of Judaism?
2. List three things that the Pharisees said were against Jewish Law on the Sabbath.
3. What was the purpose of the Sabbath, according to Jesus?
4. What did Jesus' disciples do on the Sabbath that annoyed the Pharisees?
5. What did Jesus say about the actions of his disciples?
6. What did Jesus do in the synagogue on the Sabbath that outraged the Pharisees?
7. What did Jesus say about his actions?
8. How did the crowd respond to Jesus teaching in the Temple?
9. List two types of businesses operating in the Temple courtyard.
10. Who allowed these businesses to operate freely in the Temple?
11. Give two reasons why the Temple priests (the Sadducees) became increasingly hostile towards Jesus.
12. Would the Romans have had any reason to be concerned about the disturbance in the Temple?

Understanding

1. Why did the Pharisees object to:
   a. the disciples picking corn on the Sabbath?
   b. Jesus healing someone on the Sabbath?
2. In what way did Jesus' attitude and behaviour conflict with the outlook of the Pharisees?
3. How did Jesus challenge the authority of the Sadducees?
4. a. Explain why traders and money-changers were at work in the Temple.
   b. Why do you think Jesus reacted in the way he did to the business activity in the Temple?
5. Explain why the religious authorities in Jerusalem wanted to get rid of Jesus.
6. Do you think Jesus was aware that these conflicts with the Pharisees and Sadducees put his life in danger?

The Last Supper

Key Concepts

Passover: a Jewish festival to celebrate the Exodus.

Eucharist: a Christian service of thanksgiving. In the Catholic Church the Eucharist is a sacrament.

Memorial: something done to honour and remember someone or something.

Sacrifice: something of value (one's life, for example) offered to God for the sake of others.

Objective

Explain how the Last Supper was a meal in the Passover tradition, in which the Eucharistic sacrifice was central.

Activity: *"Partners"*

TASK: TO NOTICE THAT CONFUSION AND LACK OF UNDERSTANDING CAN OCCUR DESPITE OUR BEST EFFORTS.

- ✦ Everyone select a partner. Sit together back to back. Have a pen and paper ready.
- ✦ Partner A - Draw a simple picture. Now instruct your partner to draw the same picture.
- ✦ Partner B - Listen carefully to the instructions. Try to reproduce your partner's picture without looking at it.
- ✦ Afterwards, compare the two drawings.
- ✦ Swop over tasks and begin again.

Discuss

- Did you both follow the instructions carefully?
- How did your pictures turn out?
- What is it like being asked to do something that you do not fully understand?

Passover

Jesus' disciples were sometimes confused. They did not always understand the meaning of what Jesus said and did.

It is clear from the Synoptic Gospels that the Last Supper was a Passover meal. Jesus and his disciples were Jews so they celebrated Passover every year. Passover is the most important festival in the Jewish calendar. It celebrates the Exodus, when God helped Moses to lead the Jews to freedom from slavery in Egypt. The Passover meal is always the high point of the Passover festival. Each piece of food at the Passover meal helps Jews to remember and re-live what happened to their ancestors at the very first Passover.

Jesus' Last Supper with his disciples.

The Passover Meal

✦ Read about Passover and the first Passover meal in the Old Testament. (Exodus 12:21-28)

The food...	what it symbolises
❖ Lamb bone.	The last night in Egypt when lambs were offered in sacrifice to God. The Jews sprinkled the blood on their door-posts so that the Angel of Death passed over their houses and they were saved.
❖ Horseradish.	The period of bitter slavery in Egypt.
❖ Haroset.	Building work in Egypt.
❖ Green herbs.	To mark the fact that Passover is a Spring festival.
❖ Egg.	New life.
❖ Unleavened bread.	How quickly the people left Egypt (without time for the bread to rise).
❖ Salt water.	Tears shed by the Jews in Egypt.
❖ Wine.	God's promise. (Exodus 6:6-8)

At the annual Passover meal prayers of thanks were offered to God. Roast lamb and bitter herbs were eaten, and a cup of wine was blessed and given to everyone to drink. Unleavened bread was blessed, broken, and shared amongst everyone.

Eucharist

The Last Supper

(Adapted from Mark 14:12-26)

Eucharist means 'to give thanks'. The Eucharist is a Christian service of thanksgiving. Jesus' Passover meal with his disciples became the first Eucharist.

Jesus and his disciples were in Jerusalem for the Jewish festival of Passover. The event attracted thousands of pilgrims to the Temple. Jesus believed that the Sadducees, the Temple priests, were going to have him arrested. Even so, he wanted to share the Passover meal with his disciples. Jesus went ahead and made the arrangements in secret. This was the last meal he ate with them and so it became known as the Last Supper. However the Last Supper became a Passover meal with a difference.

That evening, Jesus hosted a Passover meal for his friends. While they were eating, something out of the ordinary happened. Jesus took the bread, said a prayer of thanks to God, then broke the bread and gave a piece to each disciple saying, "This is my body."

The bread and wine of Eucharist.

Then Jesus the took the cup of wine, again he said a prayer of thanks to God. He handed the cup to each of them and said, "This is my blood." Looking around at all of them he said, "Do this in memory of me."

Jesus gave the Passover bread and wine a new meaning. The bread was his body that would be broken for them. The wine was his blood that would be spilled for them. In this way Jesus connected the Passover meal with his own death. Jesus asked the disciples to continue the table-fellowship of the Last Supper. The Christian Eucharist today is based on the words and actions of Jesus at the Last Supper.

Memorial

A memorial is something that is done to honour or remember someone or something that is important to us. The Jewish Passover meal and the Christian Eucharist are memorials. They not only remember but actually make real what happened.

The Passover meal helps Jews to remember and re-live the events of the Exodus, the time when Moses led their ancestors from slavery to freedom. The Eucharist helps Christians to remember and make present the life, death and resurrection of Jesus Christ.

Jesus asked his followers to remember him by sharing a special meal and repeating the words and actions he used at the Last Supper.

The Eucharist is the Christian memorial meal at which bread and wine is blessed and shared, just as Jesus requested. Catholics believe that Jesus is truly present in the Eucharist under the appearance of bread and wine.

It is important to note that the precise meaning of the Eucharist varies in the different Christian Churches.

Sacrifice

It was only after the death and resurrection of Jesus that the disciples fully understood the meaning of his words and actions at the Last Supper. Jesus tried to tell them that his death would be no ordinary death. His death would be a sacrifice offered to God for the sake of others.

1. Long ago, at the very first Passover, every Jewish family in Egypt sacrificed a lamb to God. It was the most valuable thing they had. They offered the lamb in sacrifice to God to set them free from slavery.
2. Every year after that, Jews travelled to Jerusalem to celebrate the feast of Passover. Jewish families went to the Temple and sacrificed a lamb to God in thanksgiving for their freedom. That evening they shared a Passover meal together.
3. At the Last Supper, Jesus spoke about the most valuable thing he had, his life. He said he was offering his life in sacrifice to God. His death would set everyone free to live in the Kingdom of God. Jesus would be the new Passover lamb.

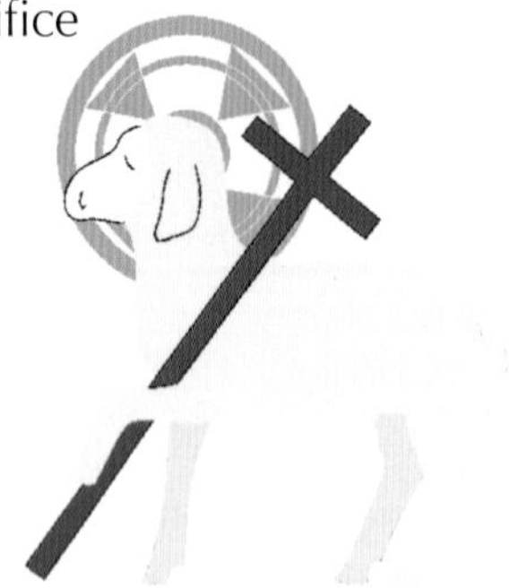

The disciples still did not realise that Jesus was about to die for them. They thought he had travelled to Jerusalem to become king. Was he not the long-awaited Messiah, the one who would set the Jews free from Roman rule? Later that evening, tired and confused, the disciples went with Jesus to the Mount of Olives outside the city.

Questions

Knowledge

1. What important event is celebrated at the Jewish festival of Passover?
2. What happened in the Temple in Jerusalem at every Passover festival?
3. What symbolic food was served at the Passover meal that Jewish families shared together?
4. At the Last Supper, what did Jesus say:
   - about the bread? - about the wine?
5. What did the disciples think about Jesus' words and actions at the Last Supper?
6. What is the link between the Last Supper and the Eucharist?
7. What was sacrificed to God at the first Passover?
8. What sacrifice did Jesus make?
9. What instruction did Jesus give his disciples at the Last Supper?
10. Why was Jesus' Passover meal with his friends called the Last Supper?

Understanding

1. Why did Jesus have to secretly organise a Passover meal for himself and his disciples?
2. Explain what Christians believe is the meaning of the Eucharist.
3. Compare the Jewish Passover meal and the Last Supper. What was the same and what was different?
4. How much did the disciples understand about Jesus' words and actions at the Last Supper?
5. What is a memorial? Explain how the Christian Eucharist is a memorial meal.
6. Describe what you think Jesus and the disciples were thinking and feeling during the Last Supper.

Research

- People have sacrificed their lives throughout history. Many have suffered and died for their beliefs.
- Find out about one Christian martyr past or present, male or female, who sacrificed their life for Christian ideals and the good of others.
- Share the account with the rest of the class.

Arrest and trial of Jesus

Key Concept

Conflict with authority: a clash or struggle with people in power.

Objective

Describe the events leading up to the death of Jesus.

Activity: *"Recall exercise"*

TASK: TO BECOME FAMILIAR WITH THE PRINCIPALS IN THE TRIAL AND SENTENCING OF JESUS.

✦ How many clues do you need to get the correct answer?

1. Who am I?

____

- ✦ I was a fisherman.
- ✦ My wife and family live in Bethsaida.
- ✦ I am a friend and a follower of Jesus.

2. Who am I?

____

- ✦ I am here on duty.
- ✦ I keep law and order.
- ✦ I am in charge of one hundred soldiers.

3. Who am I?

____

- ✦ I am from a wealthy family.
- ✦ I belong to the Jewish court of law.
- ✦ I work in the Temple.

4. Who am I?

____

- ✦ I am thirty three years old.
- ✦ I teach and heal people.
- ✦ I come from Nazareth.

5. Who am I?

____

- ✦ I rule this part of Palestine.
- ✦ I was sent from Rome.
- ✦ I execute anyone who causes trouble for the Romans.

6. Who am I?

____

- ✦ There are seventy of us.
- ✦ We punish those who break Jewish laws.
- ✦ We support the Roman Governor who rules the country.

7. Who am I?

____

- ✦ I used to be a freedom fighter.
- ✦ I looked after the money for my friends.
- ✦ I was a follower of Jesus.

8. Who am I?

____

- ✦ I am an important person in my village.
- ✦ I am strict about the laws of God.
- ✦ I am a leader in the synagogue.

Conflict with authority

Jesus was arrested and put on trial before the Jewish court (the Sanhedrin) and afterwards before Pilate, the Roman governor.

In the Garden of Gethsemane

(Adapted from Luke 22:39-53)

On Thursday evening after dark, Peter and some of the other disciples met at the Garden of Gethsemane. They were afraid. They knew that Jesus' words and actions had brought him into conflict with the Jewish authorities. They made their way to their usual place, at least it was safe and well-hidden.

Jesus knew it was now only a matter of time. He left the disciples and went off by himself. In the silence of the night he fell to his knees and prayed. He was ready if God wanted him. Suddenly there was a lot of noise and torchlight shone all around. Judas had arrived, leading a crowd. In exchange for thirty pieces of silver, he led the Jewish authorities to the disciples' meeting place. He went over to Jesus and greeted him with a kiss. That was the signal.

The arrest of Jesus.

Jesus is arrested

Temple guards armed with swords and sticks rushed forward. The disciples got ready to fight but Jesus stopped them. He said to the Jewish leaders who had come to arrest him "You come here now under the cover of darkness. I was in the Temple every day, you didn't arrest me then." Jesus was aware that there might have been a riot if he was arrested in public, in front of his followers.

The disciples fled, frightened that they too would be arrested, all except Peter, who followed at a distance. Jesus did not resist arrest, he was led away to face his trial alone. It was going to be an unfair trial as the Pharisees and Sadducees had already decided to get rid of Jesus. He had publicly challenged their authority, and also his claim to be the Messiah might cause a revolt against the Romans who could retaliate by closing the synagogues and the Temple. The Jewish leaders were fearful of losing their position of power and influence in Palestine.

Jesus' trial before the Sanhedrin

(Adapted from Matt 26:57-67)

Late on Thursday night, Jesus was brought to the house of Caiaphas, the high priest. He had called together members of the Sanhedrin, the highest Jewish court. They wanted to find out how serious a threat Jesus actually was. The court was full, Jesus stood in front of the high priest and the trial began.

A number of witnesses were called. Jesus was questioned again and again. Finally the high priest asked "Are you the Messiah, the Son of God?" Jesus did not deny it. "So you say", he replied, and added that he had a special relationship with God. The High Priest was shocked. It was blasphemy for anyone to claim he was equal to God. Jesus had broken Jewish law.

The Court of the Sanhedrin gave their verdict. Jesus was found guilty of blasphemy (a religious offence against God) and should be put to death. But the Sanhedrin did not have the power to execute anyone. Only the Roman governor could execute offenders, so they took Jesus to him.

The Jewish authorities knew that the Roman governor would not be interested in the religious verdict of blasphemy so they added another charge that he could not ignore. They would say that Jesus called himself king and that he could cause a revolt against the Romans.

Jesus' trial before Pilate

(Adapted from Mark 15:1-15)

Early on Friday morning Jesus was put in chains and brought before Pilate, the Roman governor of Palestine. Pilate tried to find out if Jesus was a political trouble-maker. "Are you the King of the Jews?" he asked. Jesus replied that he was a king, but his kingdom was not of this earth. Pilate thought the prisoner was innocent and wanted to release him, but under pressure from the Sanhedrin, agreed that he was breaking Roman law by claiming to be a king. The crowd waiting outside, having been won over by the Jewish authorities, shouted "Crucify him! Crucify him!"

The Roman governor did not want a riot, so he made a quick decision. Pontius Pilate gave his verdict. Jesus was found guilty of treason (a political offence against the Roman Empire). Jesus had broken Roman law and was sentenced to death.

Jesus is scourged and beaten.

Roman soldiers took Jesus away to be crucified, but first they mocked him and put a crown of thorns on his head. Then he was tied to a pillar and severely beaten.

Peter denies Jesus three times

✦ Read about this incident in the Good News Bible. What are the missing words below. (Luke 22:54-62)

After Jesus was arrested Peter followed behind at a safe distance. When they arrived at the house of the _____ Peter went into the courtyard and sat down beside a _____ to warm himself.

A young _____ _____ looked at him and said, "This man was with _____." Peter denied it saying "Woman I _____." Then a _____ said, "You are one of them." Peter denied it. "I am not." he replied. Another man, hearing Peter's Galilean accent said, "There is no doubt about it. You must have been with Jesus!" Peter _____ it saying, "I don't know what you are talking about." Just then a _____ crowed. Jesus passed by at that moment and looked straight at _____.

Then Peter remembered. Jesus once told him "You will deny me _____ times before the cock crows." Peter got up and walked away by himself. He _____ bitterly.

Questions

Knowledge

1. What was Jesus doing in Gethsemane before he was arrested?
2. What prompted the Jewish authorities to arrest Jesus?
3. List what happened as Jesus was arrested.
4. Jesus was put on trial twice in 24 hours.
   a. Where did the religious trial take place?
   b. Who questioned Jesus?
   c. What charge was brought against him?
   d. What was the verdict of the Jewish court?
   e. What sentence was passed on him?
5. At a second trial the next morning:
   a. Where did the political trial take place?
   b. Who questioned Jesus?
   c. What charge was brought against him?
   d. What was the verdict of the Roman court?
   e. What sentence was passed on him?
6. What are the meanings of the following terms: a. Blasphemy? b. Treason?
7. What did the Roman soldiers do to Jesus?
8. How did Peter deny his relationship with Jesus? Explain what happened.

Understanding

1. Describe what happened at Jesus' trial:
   a. before the Jewish authorities.
   b. before the Roman authorities.
2. Why did the Sanhedrin send Jesus to Pilate after they had sentenced Jesus to death?
3. Explain why Pilate finally agreed to sentence Jesus to death.
4. What impact do you think the arrest and trail of Jesus had on Peter and the other disciples?

Research

- In the Roman Empire, the torture of prisoners before their execution was a regular occurrence. Check out recent archaeological evidence from excavations at the Antonia Fortress in Jerusalem. Find out about:
  - Games played by crucifixion squads.
  - The game of 'King'.
  - Pavement markings on the site.
- Read Mark 15:16-20. Look again at the way Jesus was tortured by his executioners in light of recent archaeological discoveries.
- Discuss your observations with the class.

Death of Jesus

Key Concepts

Sacrifice: something of value (one's life for example) offered to God for the sake of others.

Martyrdom: a willingness to suffer and die for one's beliefs or a special cause.

Objective

Re-tell the Gospel account of Jesus' death on the cross.

Activity: *"Sacrifice"*

TASK: TO UNDERSTAND THAT SACRIFICE CAN MEAN DEVOTING ONESELF TO WHAT IS WORTHWHILE.

El Salvador is a small country in Central America with a population of five million people. Coffee, cotton and sugar are the main exports. A few rich families own nearly all the land. Most of the population are poor and many work as labourers on the large plantations. They own no land.

Oscar Romeo became Archbishop of the city of San Salvador in 1977. He began to speak out against injustice in his native country. He followed the teaching of Jesus to 'love God and your neighbour as yourself,' and believed in justice for the poor and oppressed. He saw how the army and the government mistreated those who asked for their rights.

ROMERO
MARTIR

Image of Archbishop Oscar Romero outside a building near where he was assassinated.

These people were beaten, their homes and crops burnt, they were put in prison, or even 'disappeared'. The priests, nuns and social workers who tried to help them became victims of violence too.

Although he was a quiet, shy man, the newly appointed Archbishop decided to act. He set up a radio station inside his church. Every Sunday at Mass he spoke out against poverty and injustice in El Salvador. He demanded a better life for the poor. His broadcasts were heard all over the country. People were afraid to listen openly to his message for fear of being beaten, even killed. Oscar Romeo gave people hope, he gave them the courage to demand their rights.

In March 1980 he was in a hospital chapel celebrating Mass for a friend. A gunman walked in and opened fire at point-blank range. The archbishop fell to the ground beside the altar. Oscar Romeo died on 24th March 1980. He made the ultimate sacrifice, giving his life for the good of others.

Discuss

- In what ways did Oscar Romeo sacrifice himself?
- Think about a family. What sacrifices do parents make for their children?
- What do sports people or musicians sacrifice for their sport or their music?
- What kind of sacrifices do you make?
- Have you ever put someone else's needs before your own?

Death of Jesus

Jesus gave up his life for the good of others.

1. Jesus is condemned to death.

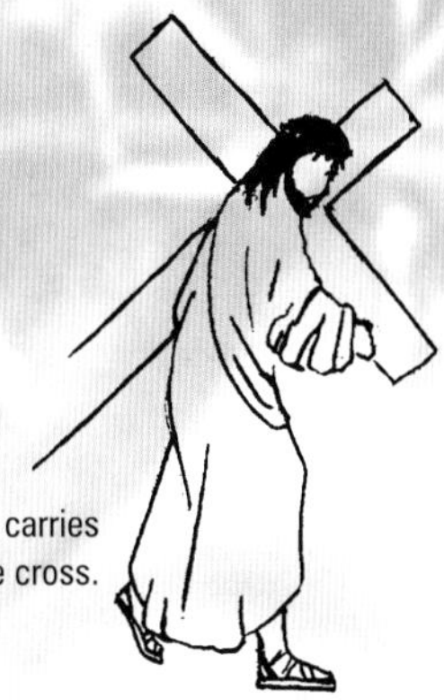

2. Jesus carries the cross.

3. Jesus falls.

4. Jesus sees his mother.

5. Simon helps Jesus.

6. Veronica helps Jesus.

7. Jesus falls again.

8. Jesus speaks to the women.

9. Jesus falls the third time.

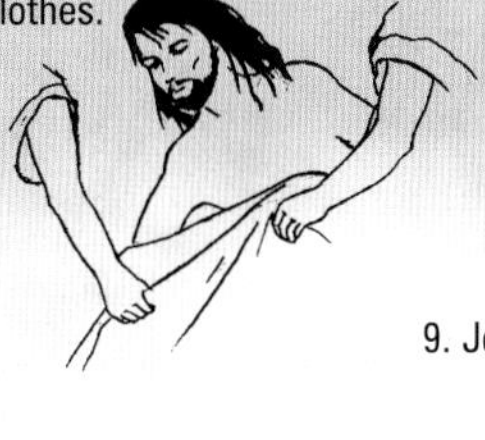

10. Jesus is stripped of his clothes.

11. Jesus is crucified.

12. Jesus dies on the cross.

13. Jesus is taken down from the cross.

14. Jesus' body is put in the tomb.

Way of the Cross

Read about the death of Jesus in the Gospel of Luke 23:24-55.

Inside every Roman Catholic church today you will see a set of pictures displayed around the walls. These images are called the Stations of the Cross, or the Way of the Cross. There are fourteen in all. They tell the story of what happened to Jesus on the day he died. The stations help Christians to pray and reflect on the suffering of Jesus who died to save people from sin.

Jesus died on the cross.

Sacrifice

Crucifixion was a cruel punishment. It involved being nailed to a wooden cross and left to hang until the person died of suffocation. It was used by the Romans to deter people from opposing Roman rule. Jesus was led out to be crucified on the day Christians call 'Good Friday'.

Jesus had to carry his cross through the streets of Jerusalem to a hill outside the city. A large crowd followed, some jeering, some weeping in despair. Jesus was very weak as a result of the beatings he had received and fell several times along the route. Soldiers forced a Jewish by-stander, Simon, a man from Cyrene, to help Jesus carry the cross.

Calvary

At the place of execution, known as Calvary or Golgotha, the soldiers nailed Jesus to the cross. On Pilates orders they attached a notice which read, "This is the King of the Jews." Two criminals were crucified along with Jesus, one mocked him, the other asked for his blessing. Jesus suffered for almost six hours before he gave up his spirit and died. St. Luke's Gospel tells us that Jesus' last words were:

"Father, in your hands I place my spirit."

Luke 23:46.

Jesus offered his life to God for the sake of others. Christians believe his death was a sacrifice. It saved people from sin and enabled them to enter a new life in the Kingdom of God.

Martyrdom

Jesus death was a form of martyrdom. Jesus was willing to suffer and die for his beliefs. His mission was to teach about the love of God and show people how to live in the Kingdom of God.

According to Jewish law, bodies had to be buried before the Sabbath which began at sunset on Friday evening. None of the disciples came forward to claim Jesus' body for burial. They stood watching from a distance, totally aghast that Jesus, the Messiah, had been executed like a common criminal.

The burial of Jesus

So it was that Joseph of Arimathea, a member of the Sanhedrin and a secret follower of Jesus, went to Pilate for permission to bury Jesus (he took a great risk as he was identifying himself as a follower of Jesus, something he felt unable to do earlier). The body of Jesus was taken down, wrapped in a linen cloth and hastily laid in a borrowed tomb near where he was crucified.

Women who stood with Jesus' mother at the cross went with Joseph to see where Jesus' body was placed. They would return after the Sabbath to embalm the body in the customary way. Everything was done quickly. A large stone was then rolled in front of the tomb to seal it. A guard was placed at the entrance to ensure the tomb was not disturbed. The Sanhedrin did not want Jesus' followers to remove the body.

Jesus' body is taken down from the cross.

The Disciples

✚ Imagine how the disciples may have felt after Jesus was crucified.

The End of Everything

Looking back....
We absolutely believed in him you know.
Trusted him completely.
We followed him for three years.
We gave up everything: our jobs, our homes.
Our families rarely saw us, we were always on the road.
We heard his teaching.
We saw the miracles.
We followed the dream.
The Kingdom of God - it meant everything to us.
Jesus, He meant everything to us.
We were proud. Our boss - the Messiah!
We stood by him, when others did not.
When he was arrested we thought he'd turn it around, like he always did.
Not this time.
GOLGOTHA.
The body, the blood.
What was it all about?
What was it all for?
Nothing?
Nothing left.
Everything. Gone.
Still can't believe it!

Questions

Knowledge

1. What is meant by crucifixion?
2. When and where was Jesus crucified?
3. What caused Jesus to be weak and exhausted on the way to Calvary?
4. Who was Simon of Cyrene? What did he do?
5. a. What notice was attached to the cross on Calvary?
   b. How long did Jesus suffer on the cross before he died?
6. Where were the disciples while Jesus was being crucified?
7. Who was Joseph of Arimathea? What did he do?
8. Why was Jesus' burial a rushed affair?
9. Why was a guard stationed at Jesus' tomb?
10. What sacrifice did Jesus make for the good of others?

Understanding

1. a. Describe what happened on the day Jesus died on the cross.
   b. How was his death a form of martyrdom?
2. Jesus was crucified like a common criminal. What impact do you think the crucifixion had on Peter and the disciples?
3. The cross is the symbol of Christianity. What do you think the cross says about the Christian idea of God?

Research

- Read the Gospel accounts of Jesus' death in:
  - Mark 15:21-41
  - Matt 27:32-56
  - Luke 23:26-49
  - John 19:16-37

  a. Find the similarities in the four Gospel accounts.
  b. What differences do you notice in the Gospel accounts?
  c. Can you give reasons why there is some variation in the four accounts of Jesus' suffering and death in the Gospels.

  - Present a summary of your findings and discuss your opinions with the class.

The Resurrection

Key Concepts

Resurrection: the central Christian belief that Jesus rose from the dead three days after he was crucified.

Transformation: a complete change in the appearance and nature of Jesus after the resurrection.

Presence: the fact that Jesus exists and is truly present here and now.

Objective

Describe the impact of the Resurrection appearances on the followers of Jesus.

Activity: *"Transformation"*

TASK: TO BE AWARE THAT PEOPLE CAN BE CHANGED AND TRANSFORMED AS A RESULT OF LIFE'S EXPERIENCES.

- Ask a volunteer to carefully observe everyone in the classroom for a few moments. Then ask him/her to go to the furthest end of the room and turn away.
- Meanwhile one or two members of the class alter their appearance in some way.
- When the volunteer returns he/she has to try and identify what changes have occurred. Repeat.

Discuss

- What changes did people make to their appearance during the exercise?
- Do your relatives comment about the way you have changed if they haven't seen you for a while?
- Do you know of anyone who has been changed or transformed in any way as a result of something that happened in their life?

Resurrection

Jesus was completely transformed after the resurrection. He was different, yet somehow still the same.

The Resurrection of Jesus

(Adapted from Luke 24:1-12)

The resurrection is the fundamental Christian belief that three days after he was crucified, Jesus rose from the dead. Christians celebrate the resurrection of Jesus on Easter Sunday.

Easter Sunday morning.

Jesus rose from the dead three days after he was crucified.

Jesus was completely transformed after the resurrection.

Easter Sunday morning

The Gospel accounts of the resurrection report that when the Sabbath was over, the women mixed spices with oil to embalm the body of Jesus. It was a normal Jewish custom to wash and embalm the body. It was a way of showing respect for the dead.

Very early on Sunday morning they set off. The women were Mary Magdalene, Joanna, and Mary, the mother of James. They were sad and downcast as they walked along carrying the large jars of ointment which they had prepared. It was dawn, the sun was just rising in the sky.

They arrived at the tomb and were surprised to see the large stone had been rolled back. When they looked inside, they got a shock, the tomb was empty! Then a messenger from God spoke to them. "Jesus is not here, he is risen from the dead. Do not be afraid." But they were afraid, and very upset.

They left quickly and rushed to tell the disciples what had happened. The women were the first to witness that Jesus had risen from the dead.

The Disciples

The disciples were still in hiding. They were frightened and on their own, everything had gone wrong. Jesus was dead, his work was over, and now their own lives were in danger. They didn't believe the women, "An empty tomb?" "Nonsense!" they said.

But Peter was unsure so he slipped out and ran to the tomb to see for himself. He was amazed to see that the tomb was completely empty. The body was gone and the burial cloth had been laid to one side. It made no sense at all. It took Peter some time to realise that Jesus was alive, that he had risen from the dead.

Transformation

Presence

Jesus' followers did not immediately recognise him when he appeared to them after the resurrection. It was because Jesus was transformed and his bodily appearance had changed. Jesus was alive but not in the same way as before his death. His followers learnt that although Jesus is now different, somehow everything about him is the same.

Jesus appears to Mary Magdalene
(Adapted from John 20:11-18)

After the resurrection, one of the first people to whom Jesus appeared was Mary Magdalene.

When she had spoken to the disciples, Mary went back alone to the tomb. She began to cry. Jesus appeared beside her. At first she did not recognise him because he had changed. But when Jesus spoke to her and said her name, Mary's eyes lit up, she knew who it was straight away.

"Teacher!" she cried, reaching out to him.

All her sadness turned to joy at that moment. Jesus was alive, he was present, but in a new way, a different way.

Mary Magdalene was the first person to whom Jesus spoke after he had risen from the dead. It changed her life. Jesus gave her a new task, he asked her to go and tell the Good News of the resurrection to everyone she met. Mary Magdalene became the first person to preach the Good News of the risen Jesus.

Questions

Knowledge

1. What is the resurrection?
2. When do Christians celebrate the resurrection?
3. Name the women who went to the tomb on the third day.
4. What did the women discover at the tomb?
5. How did the women know Jesus had risen from the dead?
6. How were the disciples feeling before they were told about the resurrection?
7. What was the disciples' first reaction to the news that Jesus had risen from the dead?
8. What did Peter decide to do?
9. How did Mary Magdalene recognise Jesus when he appeared to her at the tomb?
10. What task did Jesus give Mary Magdalene to do after the resurrection?

Understanding

1. Describe what happened on the morning of the resurrection.
2. In what way was Jesus transformed after the resurrection?
3. Why did the disciples disbelieve the women's story?
4. Jesus appeared to Mary Magdalene. What effect did this experience have on her? Imagine how she felt at different times on the day of the resurrection. How did she feel:
   - On the way to the tomb?
   - When she found the tomb empty?
   - When Jesus appeared to her?
   - After Jesus appeared to her?

   Give reasons why she felt this way.

Research

- Find out about the Church of the Holy Sepulchre and the Garden Tomb. These sites are regarded by Christians as the burial place of Jesus and from where he rose from the dead on Easter Sunday.
- Where is each site located? When was each site discovered? State a few interesting facts about the background of both.
- Which Christian Churches in particular revere each site as the place of the resurrection. How do Christians worship at these sites when they go there?
- Discuss your findings with the class.

Resurrection Appearances

Key Concepts

Transformation: a complete change in the appearance and nature of Jesus after the resurrection.

Presence: the fact that Jesus exists and is truly present here and now.

Objective

Describe the impact of Jesus' appearances on his followers after the resurrection.

Activity: *"Things change"*

TASK: TO BE AWARE OF EXPERIENCES OF CHANGE IN HUMAN LIFE.

- Find others in the class who have experienced one or more of the following changes within the past year.
- The first student to get ten names or initials on their "card" calls out Bingo!

Everything Changes	Sign here
✧ Joined a new club.	________
✧ Family member got ill.	________
✧ Moved house.	________
✧ A pet died.	________
✧ Made a new friend.	________
✧ Changed my bedroom around.	________
✧ Got a new teacher.	________
✧ Changed to a new class.	________
✧ Got a new hairstyle.	________
✧ New baby in the family.	________
✧ Someone close to the family died.	________
✧ Listened to a new type of music.	________

Discuss

- What has been the biggest change in your life so far?
- What effect did it have on you?
  What was different?
  What stayed the same?

Transformation

Presence

After the resurrection everything changed. Jesus was transformed. He was different, yet somehow still the same.

No-one actually saw Jesus rise from the dead. Yet it states in the New Testament that more than five hundred people in Palestine met and talked to him after the resurrection. (1 Corinthians 15:3-8) There are a number of eye-witness accounts from those who met and talked to Jesus after the resurrection, these are recorded in the Gospels.

Jesus was transformed after the resurrection.

After the resurrection, Jesus was different, his bodily appearance changed, he was transformed. The disciples did not immediately recognise him when he appeared to them. At times they found it difficult to explain that Jesus was alive, but in a new way.

Witnesses to the resurrection

In the weeks following the resurrection, the risen Jesus appeared to his disciples many times in different places. Gradually they came to see and believe that he was alive but in a different way. It had an amazing effect on them and they were overjoyed. The disciples realised that they were no longer alone, Jesus had overcome death and was alive and present with them. The disciples finally understood who Jesus really was: Jesus was the Messiah, the Son of God.

After the resurrection, Jesus appeared to:

- ❖ Mary Magdalene at the tomb. (John 20:11-18)
- ❖ Disciples on the road to Emmaus. (Luke 24:13-35)
- ❖ Disciples in a house in Jerusalem. (John 20:19-25)
- ❖ Thomas in a house in Jerusalem. (John 20:24-29)
- ❖ Disciples beside Lake Galilee. (John 21:1-14)

Read about each incident and notice:

- How the disciples were feeling initially.
- Where it took place.
- The disciples' first reaction to the appearance of Jesus.
- The way in which Jesus greets them.
- What Jesus does.
- The disciples response to the presence of Jesus.
- What Jesus asks them to do.

Common themes in eye-witness accounts of the resurrection

Following the resurrection, the risen Jesus appears and is present to the disciples. His presence is experienced by all of them but they were slow to recognise him at first. Common themes in the Gospel accounts of Jesus' appearances after the resurrection include:

1. The disciples are grieving.
2. Jesus appears unexpectedly.
3. Jesus is transformed. The disciples either do not recognise him at first, or are shocked and frightened at seeing him.
4. Jesus comforts them with a greeting.
5. Jesus does something that they recognise.
6. The disciples are overwhelmed with joy and peace because Jesus is with them.
7. Jesus tells them to spread the Good News.

The road to Emmaus

Jesus appeared to his followers on the road to Emmaus. (Adapted from Luke 24:13-35)

Narrator: It is three days since Jesus died on the cross. Two of Jesus' followers are walking towards Emmaus, a small town eleven kilometres from Jerusalem. Both are totally dejected, all their hopes dashed.

Cleo: I still can't believe it. Imagine, Jesus, of all people, put to death on the cross like a common criminal.

Theo: I know what you mean. I can't get over it either. When you think we actually believed he was the Messiah! Now look at us. Three years following him and nothing to show for it. What a waste!

Narrator: A stranger approaches the two men and walks along beside them. It is Jesus, but somehow they do not recognise him.

Jesus: Nice day isn't it?

Theo: Is it? We hadn't noticed.

Jesus: What's up? Have you had some bad news or something?

Cleo: You mean you don't know? You must be the only one around here who isn't talking about it.

Jesus: Tell me, what's happened?

Cleo: Well, you've heard about Jesus of Nazareth - you know, the famous teacher. Everyone thought he was going to lead us to freedom.

Theo: Guess what! He was handed over to the Romans in Jerusalem. They crucified him last Friday!

Cleo: And now there are all kinds of rumours going around.

Theo: Yeah, some women went to his tomb this morning. It was empty, the body is gone!

Cleo: The women are telling everyone that a messenger from God said Jesus is alive!

Theo: Mind you, some of us went along to see for ourselves. It's true, there's no sign of the body anywhere.

Jesus: Why do you sound so surprised? Don't you know it was all meant to happen like this?

Narrator: Then the stranger began to remind them of the Jewish scriptures. He told them how everything in the Old Testament pointed to the suffering, death, and resurrection of Jesus. The men walk along, listening to the words of the stranger. At last they arrived in the town of Emmaus.

Cleo: I must admit, I never thought of it like that before. It's all beginning to make sense now.

Theo: Look, it's getting dark. This is our place. Why don't you come in and have a bite to eat?

Jesus: Well, if you're sure it's no trouble.

The Eucharist.

Narrator: They went into the house together and later sat down to eat. During the meal, the stranger took the bread, said the blessing, then he broke the bread and gave it to each of them. At that moment their eyes were opened. The men understood and knew it was Jesus. He did exactly the same thing when they shared the Eucharist together at the Last Supper.

As soon as the men realised that Jesus was present among them, he vanished. The two got up from the table and went straight back to Jerusalem. Full of excitement, they rushed to tell the disciples the Good News. "He is risen! The Lord is risen!"

"Christ has died, Christ is risen,
Christ will come again."

These are the words that are said at the celebration of the Eucharist in many Christian Churches. The resurrection is important for all Christians and has a major impact on their lives to this day.

Questions

Knowledge

1. What is an eye-witness?
2. How was Jesus transformed after the resurrection?
3. To whom did Jesus appear after the resurrection?
4. Where is Emmaus?
5. How did the two men feel about the death of Jesus?
6. What did the stranger explain to them on the road to Emmaus?
7. How did Jesus' followers recognise him in the end?
8. How did the men feel when they realised Jesus was present among them?
9. What Good News did they have for the disciples in Jerusalem?
10. What did the disciples learn about Jesus' true identity?

Understanding

1. Identify some common themes in the Gospel accounts of Jesus' appearances after the resurrection.
2. Describe what happened:
   - on the road to Emmaus.
   - at the house in Emmaus.
3. What effect did the presence of the risen Jesus have on the men at Emmaus?
4. Identify other witnesses to the resurrection. What impact did meeting the risen Jesus have on each of them?

Research

- Every ten years the entire village of Oberammergau act out a Passion Play about the life, death and resurrection of Jesus. It is a big tourist attraction. The play lasts for about eight hours. Seven hundred local actors are involved. Men grow their beards and even real animals are used in the performance.
- Find out where Oberammergau is located. Find out why the members of the town have acted out a live Passion Play every decade for the past three hundred years.
- Share the outcome of your investigation with the rest of the class.

Ascension

Objective

Explain how the Ascension was a new beginning for the followers of Jesus.

Activity: *"Moving on"*

TASK: TO EXPLORE EXPERIENCES OF CHANGE AND NEW BEGINNINGS.

- Things change.... people:
  - Get married.
  - Move to a new house.
  - Arrive in a new country.
  - Play with a new team.
  - Join a new class.

Discuss

- What kind of changes take place in people's lives from time to time?
- Is it easy or difficult to move on and make a new start?
- What was it like the last time you began something new?

The Ascension

(Adapted from Luke 24:50-53, Acts 1:3-14)

It was the end of Jesus' time on Earth. After the Ascension the disciples had to wait a short time before beginning their new work.

Luke wrote two books to enable Christians to have faith in Jesus. 'The Gospel of Luke' is about the life, death and resurrection of Jesus. 'The Acts of the Apostles' is about the actions of the apostles and the early Church after Jesus ascended to heaven.

St. Luke tells us that three days after Jesus died, he rose again. Jesus appeared to his disciples many times after the resurrection. Jesus was alive again in a new way. The disciples:

- saw him.
- talked to him.
- ate with him.

He continued to teach them about the Kingdom of God.

In Jerusalem

Then, almost forty days after the resurrection, the risen Jesus appeared to his followers for the last time. The disciples were gathered together as usual, behind locked doors in the city of Jerusalem. "Peace be with you," Jesus said, and then told them what he wanted them to do. Jesus asked them to carry on his work. They must go and tell the whole world about the things he said and did, especially his teaching to love God and love one's neighbour. The disciples would not be on their own. Jesus promised to send the Holy Spirit to help them continue the work he had begun. All this would happen very soon he assured them.

At Bethany

Then Jesus led the disciples out of the city as far as Bethany. He stood in front of them, raised his hands, and blessed them. As they watched, a cloud hid him from their sight. Jesus returned to the presence of God the Father.

At that moment the disciples realised something wonderful; Jesus, their friend and teacher, is the Son of God. Joy and happiness welled up in their hearts. Jesus hadn't left them, instead, he was going to be with them forever in a new way. Now all they had to do was wait for the Holy Spirit of God to come and help them spread the Good News.

Jesus' promise filled the disciples with new hope. They went back to Jerusalem and waited patiently for the coming of the Holy Spirit. They went to the Temple and met every day in each others' homes. They prayed together as they waited for the next stage of their lives to begin.

Bible search

✦ Write down the instructions Jesus gave to his followers before his Ascension to heaven.

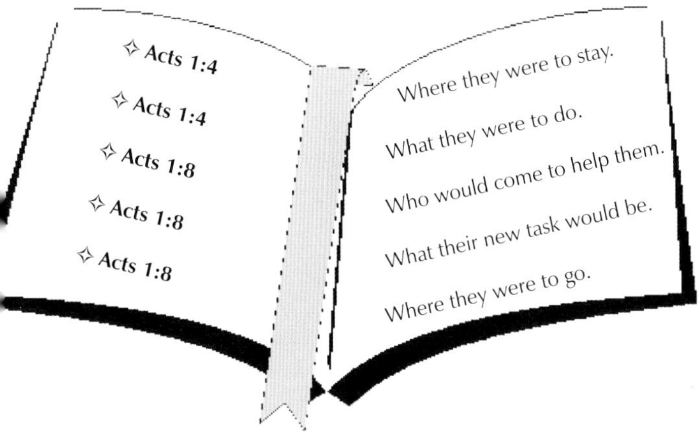

Acts 1:4
Acts 1:4
Acts 1:8
Acts 1:8
Acts 1:8
Where they were to stay.
What they were to do.
Who would come to help them.
What their new task would be.
Where they were to go.

Questions

Knowledge

1. Name the two books written by St. Luke.
2. What did the risen Jesus do during the forty days after the resurrection?
3. How did Jesus greet the disciples when he appeared to them?
4. What new task did Jesus give his disciples to do?
5. What promise did Jesus make to the disciples?
6. Where did the ascension take place?
7. What happened to Jesus at the ascension?
8. What did the disciples realise about Jesus at the ascension?
9. How did the disciples feel after the ascension?
10. What did the disciples do while they awaited the coming of the Holy Spirit?

Understanding

1. What is the ascension?
2. What effect did the ascension have on the disciples?
3. How did the disciples prepare for the coming of the Holy Spirit?

Research

✪ In the Bible when Jewish writers wanted to explain something that was difficult to put into words, they used picture language. For example, Luke used the image of a cloud to express the idea of the presence of God. That was how he communicated the disciples' experience of God being present with them at that moment.

In the New Testament certain images are used to signal the presence of God.

Read and copy out the following Bible reference: Acts 1:9 "After......sight."

a. What picture or image is used to show the presence of God in this reference?
b. What experience is Luke trying to describe by using this picture or image?
c. Is this "picture" to be taken literally?
d. Can you think of an alternative picture or another image to express the same religious experience?

✸ Share your ideas with the class.

Pentecost

Key Concept

Pentecost: the day the apostles received the Holy Spirit and began spreading the message of Jesus.

Objective

Explain how Pentecost prepared the disciples for their new work.

Activity: *"Makeovers"*

TASK: TO DISCUSS CHANGES IN PERSONAL APPEARANCE, AND OTHER CHANGES THAT CAN OCCUR IN ATTITUDE AND BEHAVIOUR.

- ✦ Source a selection of makeover clippings from fashion, sport and music magazines and bring the photographs to class.
- ✦ Examine and discuss the changes that result from the various makeovers.

Discuss

- What kind of changes did people make to their appearance? What might some of those changes cost in terms of money and effort?
- Can people change themselves in other ways?
- Name a person who changed **your** outlook about someone or something.
- Explain how your behaviour changed as a result.

Pentecost

Just as people can change their appearance they can also change their outlook on life. The disciples were completely changed by the arrival of the Holy Spirit at Pentecost.

Ten days after the ascension, on the Jewish feast of Pentecost, Jesus' followers met to pray behind locked doors. It was early morning, just before nine o'clock. The city of Jerusalem was already crowded.

The day of Pentecost

(Adapted from Acts 2:1-42)

People in the street heard a great deal of noise coming from the house in which the disciples were praying. Doors and windows were thrown open, men and women were seen rushing in and out. Everyone seemed happy and excited.

Pentecost.

A crowd began to gather outside, wondering what was happening. *What's going on? What's all that noise at this time of the morning? I can hear singing! Are they all drunk?* they said to one another.

Then a tall, well-built man stepped forward and began to speak to them. He was known locally as Peter the fisherman. "The people in there," he said, "have waited a long time for something special to happen. Well let me tell you, the waiting is over! Today Jesus has sent the Holy Spirit of God to be with us. I tell you, it's amazing, it's hard to put into words. It's like we're on fire with the Spirit of God. We are different...completely changed. We are no longer afraid, we feel brave and strong. Look! We even came out of hiding this morning to tell you the news."

Peter's message

Then Peter told the crowd the Good News. "Jesus, who was crucified, has risen to new life! Jesus is the Messiah, he is the Son of God. The Holy Spirit has given us the power to spread this Good News." The crowd listened, and were amazed. They understood everything that Peter was trying to tell them. Afterwards, some of them went and spoke to him. They wanted to know what they too could do to be filled with the Holy Spirit. Peter said to them:

> *"You must have faith in Jesus. You must turn away from sin. You must be baptised."*

That day in the city of Jerusalem, three thousand people believed his message and were baptised as followers of Jesus.

The Holy Spirit

On the day of Pentecost the Holy Spirit came upon the disciples. The power of the Holy Spirit completely changed their outlook and their behaviour. It gave them the courage to go out in public and teach the Good News. It made them eager to continue the work which Jesus had begun.

Pentecost is regarded as the birthday of the Christian Church. The Church is the community of people who want to live like Jesus. After Pentecost the disciples were called apostles. An apostle is someone who is sent on a mission to do God's work. Christians today believe that the Holy Spirit gives them the confidence to follow Jesus and do God's work in their daily lives.

Questions

Knowledge

1. When did the day of Pentecost occur?
2. What did the disciples do while they waited together in Jerusalem?
3. What happened on the day of Pentecost?
4. How was Peter affected by the arrival of the Holy Spirit?
5. What did Peter preach in Jerusalem on the day of Pentecost?
6. What did Peter say people must do if they wanted to receive the Holy Spirit?
7. How effective was Peter' speech on the day of Pentecost in Jerusalem?
8. What do Christians celebrate at Pentecost each year?

Understanding

1. In what ways were the disciples changed by the arrival of the Holy Spirit?
2. Describe what the disciples experienced on the day of Pentecost.
3. Why is Pentecost important in the life of the Christian Church?

Research

- In the Bible when a writer wanted to explain something that was difficult to put into words he used picture language. That was how he communicated a religious experience such as "The Holy Spirit of God is with us now." Certain images were used to signal the presence of God.

  Read and copy out the Bible reference Acts 2:2-3 "Suddenly......there."

  a. What pictures or images are used to show the presence of the Holy Spirit of God?
  b. Was it a gentle or a powerful experience for the disciples on that occasion?
  c. What are the qualities of wind and fire as they exist in the natural world?
  d. Are there any similarities between the nature of wind and fire and the nature of God?
  e. Are the images in Acts 2:2-3 to be taken literally?
  f. Can you think of an alternative picture or image to express the same religious experience?

- Discuss your ideas with the class.

Early Faith Communities

Key Concept

People of God: Christian communities past and present who believe in God and follow the teaching of Jesus.

Objective

Note the emerging identity and characteristics of the first Christian communities.

Activity: *"Things to Share"*

TASK: TO EXPLORE WHAT SHARING MEANS IN HUMAN RELATIONSHIPS.

✦ Make a list of things you would and would not share with others.

- ✧ *Things I'd share with people...*
- ✧ *Things I'd never share with anyone...*

Discuss

- With whom do you share things?
- What kinds of things do you share?
- Is there anything else, apart from possessions, that we can share with other people?

People of God

The early Christian communities were like one big family, happy to share everything together.

Read about the apostles and the early Christians in Acts 2:43-47 and Acts 4:32-37.

Pentecost gave Peter and the apostles a new understanding of their mission. Guided by the Holy Spirit, they began their work in the city of Jerusalem. They served the followers of Jesus by teaching the Good News and healing illness and disability. They baptised new believers and celebrated the Eucharist in people's homes.

Under the guidance of the apostles, small groups of believers formed themselves into faith communities. They followed Jesus' teaching about the Kingdom of God. Later they became known as Christians, the new People of God.

The early followers of Jesus were called to be the new People of God.

Statue of St. Peter in Rome.

Characteristics of the first Christian communities

Faith The newly baptised firmly believed in the presence of the risen Jesus. They went about their daily activities in the knowledge that Jesus was alive and present among them. They had complete faith that Jesus rose from the dead, that he was the Messiah, the Son of God.

Worship The followers of Jesus met as a group in the Temple in order to pray and to learn from the apostles. On Sunday, the day of resurrection, they gathered with the apostles in one of their homes to pray and share a meal. Together they celebrated the breaking of bread, the Eucharist, as Jesus asked them to do at the Last Supper.

Way of Life The early Christians had a totally new way of life based on the teaching of Jesus. They took seriously Jesus' command to love God and love your neighbour as yourself. They shared everything with each other and helped people in need.

> *"We all try to be friends even though some of us come from very different backgrounds. We make time for each other, we do things together, we help each other out. We share everything we have. None of us thinks that our belongings are just for ourselves. What we have is there for anyone who needs it.*
>
> *Some rich people among us have sold their property. They gave the money from the sale to the apostles who shared it out among people in need. It is important to us that no one goes without."*
>
> Adapted from Acts 4:32-37

Christian Communities

Under the leadership and guidance of Peter and the apostles, small groups of believers formed Christian communities, first in Jerusalem and then in other areas. The early followers of Jesus may not have realised that they were starting a new faith community; they were simply a group of Jews who believed Jesus was the Messiah, and followed Jesus' commandment to love God and love their neighbour.

Slowly, over time, Jesus' followers began to see that their faith, worship and way of life was different from other Jews. The People of God had faith in Jesus Christ. They prayed together and celebrated the Eucharist on Sundays. They shared everything and helped people in need. At a certain point, Jesus' followers realised they could no longer continue being Jews. They became known as Christians, followers of Jesus Christ.

Persecution

In Jerusalem the Sadducees were getting worried about the large crowds gathering around the apostles in the Temple. They did not want the apostles preaching the message of Jesus, healing the sick and disabled, or teaching that Jesus was raised from the dead. At first the Jewish authorities merely warned the apostles to stop their activities. Eventually a number of apostles were imprisoned and tortured before they were let go.

The Arrest of Stephen (Acts 6:8-15, 7:54-60)

Within a short time the persecution of believers became even more severe. Stephen, a senior member of the Christian community, was arrested and brought before the Sanhedrin. He was accused of blasphemy and sentenced to death by stoning. Stephen became the first Christian martyr to die for his faith.

Persecution of the early Christians.

Jerusalem and beyond

It was a difficult time for the Christian community. Its members could no longer meet openly, so they began to meet in secret. However, worries about their safety forced many to leave Jerusalem and move to other towns and villages. Some left Palestine altogether and went to live in other countries. The apostles did not give up, they continued their mission among the People of God. Some left Jerusalem and began to spread the message of Jesus among new Christian communities that were becoming established elsewhere.

The first Christian communities consisted only of Jews. Eventually Gentiles (non-Jews) were welcomed and accepted. Christians came to realise that Jesus' message of the Kingdom of God was not only for Jews, but for all people, in Palestine and beyond.

The early Christians began to use secret signs because it was dangerous to be known as a follower of Jesus. The fish became an important symbol for Christians. It represented the presence of Jesus.

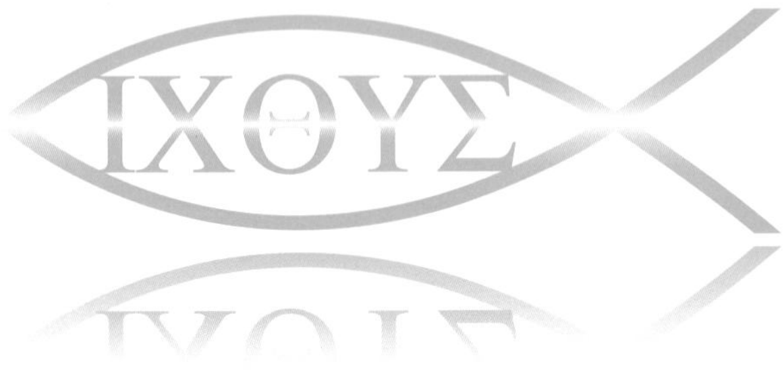
ΙΧΘΥΣ

Questions

Knowledge

1. Where was the first Christian community established?
2. What work did the apostles do among the early Christians?
3. Who were the People of God?
4. What was the faith or religious belief of the early Christians?
5. List three worship practices of the early Christians.
6. What was distinctive about the way of life of the early Christians?
7. What made the first Christians realise they had a separate identity?
8. Who put a stop to the apostles' work in Jerusalem?
9. How were early Christians persecuted in Jerusalem?
10. Who was Stephen? What happened to him?
11. How did the Christian community react to the persecution in Jerusalem?
12. How did the apostles respond as the persecution continued?

Understanding

1. How did Peter and the apostles serve the People of God in the city of Jerusalem?
2. What were the characteristics of the early Christian communities?
3. How was the lifestyle of Jesus' followers different to that of other Jews living in Jerusalem?
4. Why were Christians willing to share everything and help people in need?
5. How did the early Christians respond to the persecution in Jerusalem?

Research

- Find out where archaeologists have found inscriptions like the fish symbol opposite.
  - In what language is the word written?
  - What does the word mean?
  - Can you decode the message for the early Christian communities.
  - Explain the origin and meaning of the symbol for the benefit of the class.

St. Paul

Key Concept

Missionary: one who is sent on a journey to spread the Gospel by preaching, or by example.

Objective

Outline St. Paul's contribution to the development of the early Christian Church.

Activity: *"True Stories"*

TASK: TO IDENTIFY TURNING POINTS THAT CAN MARK A CHANGE OF DIRECTION IN LIFE.

One morning a Mr. Alfred Nobel opened his newspaper and was surprised to see his own death notice on the page in front of him. Of course it was a mistake, but he was curious, so he read it anyway.

The notice said that Alfred Nobel had been a rich businessman. He was the chemist who had invented gelignite and dynamite. He would be remembered as the man who developed the power to blow up the world.

Alfred was shocked; imagine the power of dynamite in the wrong hands! It was unthinkable. He made a decision. If he was to be remembered for anything, it would be for something good and worthwhile. He went straight to his bank and put a large amount of money into a special prize fund. Every year five prizes would be awarded. The prizes would be given to people whose work would be of benefit to the world in some important way.

Today these prizes are called the Nobel Awards. Perhaps the most famous is the Nobel Peace Prize.

Discuss

- What was a turning point in the life of Alfred Nobel?
- In what way did his life change after reading the death notice in the newspaper?
- Do you know of anyone else whose life changed for the better due to some event or experience?
- Has there been a turning point in your life at any stage?

Missionary

The turning point in St. Paul's life happened on the road to Damascus.

St. Paul is the most outstanding Christian missionary of the early Church. He spread the Christian message beyond Palestine to the rest of the Roman Empire. Paul was originally a Jew, a strict Pharisee who persecuted Christians in Jerusalem. He became a follower of Jesus as a result of a religious experience on the road to Damascus.

Fact File	
Name:	Saul: later called Paul.
Date of birth:	10CE (approx.)
Place of birth:	Tarsus, in Asia Minor (known as Turkey today).
Nationality:	Roman Citizen.
Religion:	Jew - a strict Pharisee.
Education:	Well educated. Spoke four languages, including Latin and Greek.
Occupation:	A tent maker.
Personality:	Sincere, full of energy and adventurous.
Major life event:	A religious experience on the road to Damascus. It changed his life.
Famous for:	Missionary work. He brought the Gospel of Jesus to Gentiles (non-Jews) throughout the Roman Empire.
Date of death:	65CE (approx.): possibly beheaded by the Roman Emperor Nero in the city of Rome.

Saul - Enemy of Christians

(Adapted from Acts 8:1-3 and Acts 9:1-25)

Saul opposed the followers of Jesus, he thought they were wrong to believe Jesus was the Messiah. They were wrong to pray to Jesus as the Son of God. Saul was a Jew, a strict Pharisee. He believed the Christians had to be stopped at all costs.

He led house-to-house searches throughout the city of Jerusalem. Captured Christians were imprisoned, many were tortured, some were killed. Saul was present when a Christian named Stephen was stoned to death. He watched it happen, he even looked after the coats of those who carried out the act. Many Christians fled Jerusalem and escaped to other towns and villages. Some went to Damascus. Saul decided to follow them and bring them back to face trial in Jerusalem.

On the road to Damascus

Saul set off for Damascus and was near the city when something very strange happened. Saul had a vision. He later tried to explain what happened.

"There was a blinding flash, I was knocked sideways. Then a clear voice said, 'Saul, Saul, why do you persecute me?' 'Who are you?' I asked. 'I am Jesus, whom you persecute,' was the reply. I was in shock, I felt dizzy. I couldn't see where I was going. My companions brought me to Damascus and got me a place to stay. I was confused. I didn't eat or drink anything for three whole days.

A Christian named Ananias came to see me and explained everything. Jesus had touched my heart, he said. Then Ananias placed his hands upon my head. The healing power of the Holy Spirit went right through me. All of a sudden everything was clear to me. I knew what I had to do. I got up and asked to be baptised, I wanted to be a follower of Jesus."

Paul - Friend of Christians

Saul was a changed man. Before going to Damascus, he was totally against Jesus and his followers. Now he went straight to the synagogue and began to teach about Jesus. The people were naturally a bit suspicious and didn't trust him. After all, Saul had a bad reputation - he had persecuted Christians in Jerusalem. But when they saw how sincere he was, he soon won them over. Paul had changed from being one who persecuted Christians to becoming a Christian himself.

However, his former companions were not as pleased with the turn-about in Saul's life. They plotted against him. At one stage they were ready to kill him, but he managed to escape.

Saul changed his name to Paul. He felt called by God to become a Christian missionary. Paul spent the rest of his life travelling to different places teaching the Good News. He brought the Gospel of Jesus Christ to Gentiles (non-Jews) all over the Roman Empire.

Paul - the Missionary

Paul set out on three missionary journeys, travelling by land and sea to towns and cities around the Mediterranean. As a Roman citizen he could move freely from place to place. Roman roads were good and it was easy to get from one city to another. As Paul could speak both Latin and Greek, people everywhere understood his teaching.

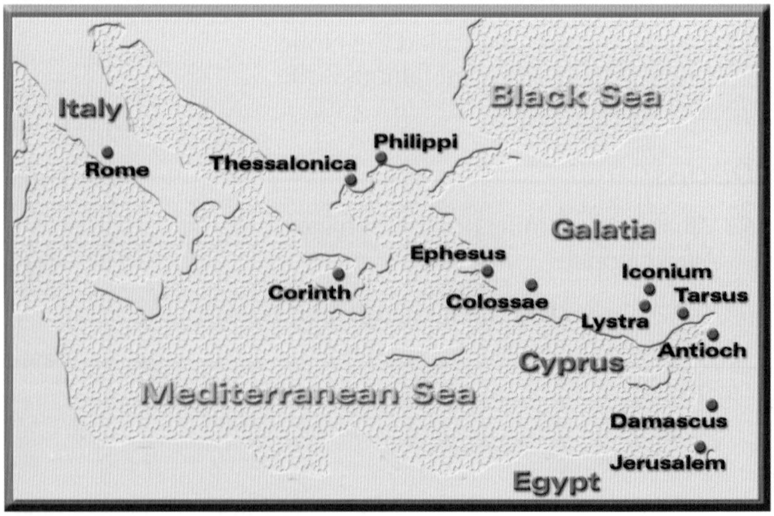
Italy
Rome
Black Sea
Philippi
Thessalonica
Galatia
Ephesus
Iconium
Corinth
Colossae
Tarsus
Lystra
Antioch
Cyprus
Mediterranean Sea
Damascus
Jerusalem
Egypt

St. Paul's missionary journeys throughout the Roman Empire.

Section B

Paul's letters to the Christian communities

Guided by the Holy Spirit, Paul began his mission of teaching the Good News of Jesus Christ. When he baptised new believers, he helped them set up new Christian communities in their local areas. After he moved on, he wrote back to them. His letters, or epistles, were a way of keeping in touch and offering support and advice to each community. His letters to the Christian communities in Corinth, Rome and Ephesus are to be found in the New Testament in the Bible, just after the Gospels and the Acts of the Apostles.

Paul taught each new Christian community to:

Faith:	have faith in Jesus, the Son of God.
Worship:	worship on Sunday, meet in each others homes and celebrate the breaking of the bread.
Way of Life:	follow a way of life that involves sharing everything and helping people in need.

Paul's life certainly wasn't easy and he had many adventures. He was shipwrecked at least twice. He was often hungry and thirsty. Not everyone was glad to see him; sometimes he was called names, stones were thrown at him, he was even chased out of one or two places. He also ended up in prison a few times, but he still kept going!

Finally, Paul went to Rome. Christians in the city were being persecuted by the Romans at the time. Eventually he was caught and put in prison himself. In the year 65CE Paul was put to death for the Christian faith.

Paul of Tarsus, the famous Christian missionary, did more than anyone else to spread the Gospel of Jesus throughout the Roman Empire. By the end of the 1st century CE Christianity had spread beyond Palestine, and Christian communities were established in North Africa, Asia Minor (southern Turkey), Greece and Italy.

Questions

Knowledge

1. What was Paul's religious background as a young man?
2. How did Saul treat the Christians in Jerusalem?
3. Why did Saul travel to Damascus?
4. What happened to Saul on the road to Damascus?
5. Who was Ananias? What did he do?
6. Why do you think Saul changed his name to Paul?
7. What work did Paul do as a Christian missionary?
8. List the characteristics of the new Christian communities founded by St. Paul.
9. What was life like for Paul as a Christian missionary?
10. What prompted Paul to write letters to the various Christian communities?

Understanding

1. Why did Saul persecute Christians in Jerusalem?
2. How did Saul's experience on the road to Damascus change his life?
3. Explain why Paul was such a successful missionary in the early Christian Church.
4. What was Paul's greatest achievement in the development of the early Christian Church?

Research

- Find out more about St. Paul's missionary journeys.
  - Select ***one*** Bible reference.

    Acts 13:4-12 - My time in **Cyprus**.
    Acts 13:13-16, 42-52 - My time in **Antioch**.
    Acts 14:1-6 - My time in **Iconium**.
    Acts 14:8-20 - My time in **Lystra**.
  - Write a short report about Paul's missionary journey to one location. Write the report as if you were Paul.

    Describe: - what happened there.
    - how you were treated.
    - how you felt at the time.
    - what you achieved.
  - Present the report to the class.

Modern Faith Communities

Key Concept

People of God: Christian communities past and present who believe in God and follow the teaching of Jesus.

Objective

Compare early faith communities with modern faith communities.

Activity: *"At your service"*

TASK: TO HIGHLIGHT THE WAY CHRISTIANS CAN USE THEIR GIFTS IN THE SERVICE OF OTHERS.

✦ Connect the following gifts or talents with the behaviour below.

1. Musical.	2. Good listener.
3. Patient.	4. Friendly.
5. Prayerful.	6. Trusting.
7. Compassionate.	8. Playful.
9. Craftsman.	10. Reliable.

- A woman serves her neighbours by being a nice person to talk to.
- An elderly person serves her grandchildren by listening to their jokes and their stories.
- A man serves his family by being good at DIY.
- A person with a physical disability serves the public with her playing and singing.
- A mother serves her children by comforting them when they are upset.
- A boy serves his friends by being someone they can rely on.
- A person with an intellectual disability serves a stranger by the warmth of his smile.
- A sick person serves his family by bringing them to God in his prayers.
- A girl serves her friends by understanding their problems.
- A baby serves his brothers and sisters by simply being lovable.

Discuss

- Did all the gifts and behaviours match up correctly?
- List all the people who have served you in any manner already today.

People of God

Christians follow the example of Jesus by being of service to others.

The Roman Catholic Church is an example of a community of faith. Its members are known as the People of God. Roman Catholics are called by God to follow Jesus and use their gifts in the service of God and others.

The parish is the Catholic Church at local level. It is where priests and lay people work together to love and serve the Lord. A Catholic parish is an example of a modern Christian community.

A parish community is a caring community that follows the example and teaching of Jesus.

Characteristics of the first Christian communities

Under the guidance of St. Peter and the apostles, the first Christian community was established in Jerusalem. Its members followed Jesus' teaching. They wanted to bring about the Kingdom of God on Earth. They all had faith in Jesus, worshipped together on the Sabbath and led a caring and sharing lifestyle.

Members of the early Church known as the People of God had a distinctive:

Faith	They had faith in Jesus, the Messiah, the Son of God.
Worship	On Sunday they met in each others' homes to celebrate the 'Breaking of the Bread', the Eucharist.
Way of Life	They shared everything and helped people in need.

Christian communities today

A parish is an example of a Christian community today. Priests and lay people are the People of God in this faith community.

The priest is the leader of the Christian community in the parish. A lay person is a baptised Christian who is not ordained to the priesthood. Lay people have the right and the duty to spread the message of Jesus. They are called to put Jesus' teaching into practice in their daily lives. Through good example, lay people as well as priests can lead others to God. Both are modern disciples of Jesus, striving to make the message of the Kingdom of God a reality in their own faith communities.

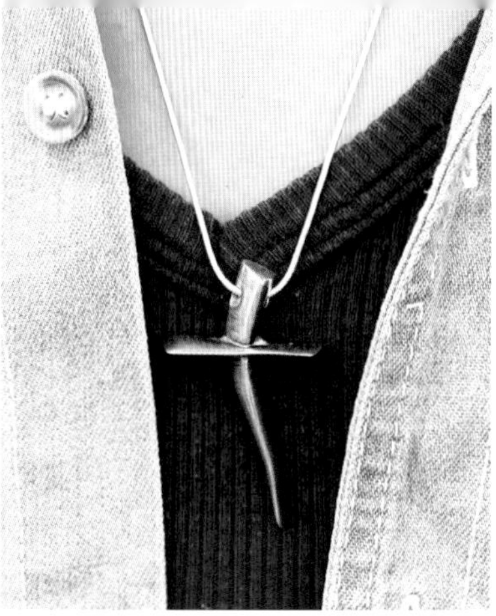

Some people wear a cross or a crucifix as a sign of their Christian commitment.

At work in the parish

Many lay people take an active role in the parish. They express their religious commitment by serving the community in different ways. Various roles are available to people according to their gifts and talents, such as for example:

In parish liturgies as a:
- Minister of the Word.
- Minister of the Eucharist.
- Member of the church choir.
- Sacristan.

In parish development as a:
- Member of the parish council.
- Member of a team preparing children and families for the sacraments of Baptism, Eucharist and Confirmation.

In voluntary organisations as a:
- Member of the St. Vincent de Paul Society.
- Fundraiser for Trocaire and people in need at home and abroad.

There are many ways in which Catholic priests and lay people can work together as members of the local Church.

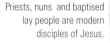

Priests, nuns and baptised lay people are modern disciples of Jesus.

The Christian community at work in the parish

This is St. John's Roman Catholic Church. Meet some members of the parish community.

I'm Father Kennedy, I have been **parish priest** at St. Johns for the past six years. This is a great parish, the people are friendly and work well together. Everyone, young and old, is willing to help out and lend a hand in different ways.

Hello, my name is Liz. I'm a **Minister of the Word**. I read the Bible aloud at Mass on Sunday.

I'm Alice and this is Pat. We're in the **SVP**. We do home visits, and help people who are having money problems.

I am Sister Anna. I am a **Minister of the Eucharist**. I give out Holy Communion at Mass. When people are unable to attend Mass I visit them at home and bring them Holy Communion.

I'm an **altar server**. My name is Karl. I go to St. John's school. I serve at the children's Mass every Sunday.

Kate is my name. I am a **secretary in the Parish Centre**. I work here part-time. I answer the phone and meet people who drop in. Others help out too.

This is Tony and me. He and his friends from the **youth club** come around to cut the grass and tidy the garden for me during the summer.

I'm Sam, last year I joined the **folk group**. We play at Mass on Sunday.

My name is Zainab. I'm new to the parish - we moved here last year. I help with **Trocaire** fund-raising for charity. I'm going on the sponsored walk next week.

Everyone calls me PJ. I'm the **sacristan**. I get the church ready for Mass and the sacraments.

Hello, I'm James Quinn. I'm retired now. I help with the **church collection** at twelve o'clock Mass on Sundays. I sometimes go to the Senior Citizen's Club. I enjoy that.

Parish Newsletter

St. John's Parish, Seatown.

Parish priest: Rev. Peter Kennedy *Parish Centre:* Tel: 001-261801; Fax: 001-250672

Holy Mass

- Saturday - 7.30pm
- Sunday - 9.00am, 10.30am, 12.00 noon.
- Weekdays - 8.00am

Confessions

- Saturday - 10.00-11.00am; 7.00-7.30pm
- Baptisms Sunday - By arrangement.

News

- Please pray for the soul of John Carroll who died yesterday after a short illness. Mass will be held in this church on Monday at 11.00am. Burial will take place afterwards in St. John's graveyard on Newbridge Road.
- The parish welcomes newly baptised twins, Sarah and Rachel, daughters of Ann and James Galvin, Strandhill Road.
- Congratulations to Paul Mitchell and Jessica Coldrick who were married here in St. John's last Saturday. We wish you every blessing in your new life together.
- We welcome two new families who have just moved into the parish. The Disu family and Mr and Mrs Marconi.
- We offer a warm welcome to all the holiday makers who are among us at present. We hope you have an enjoyable holiday here in Seatown.
- Masses will be offered for the following whose anniversaries occur at this time: Tom Lane, James and Eileen Sheridan, Nora Lee, Isabel Dowling. RIP.
- A special word of thanks to everybody who contributed to the church collection last week.

Children's Mass
Every Sunday 10.30 am.
St. John's Primary School.
The school re-opens on Tuesday 2nd September.

Choir
Choir practice on Sunday after 12.00 o'clock Mass. New members welcome.

Folk Group
Music practice on Saturday after 7.30 pm Mass. New members welcome.

Senior Citizen's Club.
Wednesdays and Thursdays in the Parish Centre. For information/transport phone 261801.

The Youth Club
New programme of events on Friday nights. Eight 'till late. The Parish Centre. All welcome.

Notice board this Week

Ministers of the Word:
Eileen Callan, Leo Smyth, Avril O'Brien, Oliver Kearns.

Ministers of the Eucharist:
Michael Tindall, Eliza Lane.

Altar Servers:
Maria Jacobs, Jack Sheridan, Tony Cantwell, Clare McCabe.

Altar Society:
Jane O'Hara, Mary Cantwell.

Flowers:
Carla Morrison.

Cleaning:
Daniel and Mary Shanley.

Collection:
Joe Oldfield, Bill Kent, Anthony O'Rourke.

For your diary

Pilgrimage to Knock
The annual parish pilgrimage to Knock will take place on Monday 29th September. Coaches leave from St. John's Parish Centre at 9.00am, returning to Seatown at 7.00pm.

Cost €20. ***Book early!***

St. Vincent de Paul Society
Help people in need. The next meeting of the SVP will take place in the Parish Centre on Tuesday 2nd September at 8.00pm. New members welcome. The SVP Good-as-New Shop is now in Main Street. Opening hours 10.00am - 5.00pm Mon-Sat. Donations welcome.

Faith Friends
Help prepare children for the sacraments. New leaders welcome (aged sixteen and over). The next training programme begins on Monday night at 7.30pm. For details phone the Parish Centre on 261801.

The Developing World
Help street children in Brazil. Trocaire sponsored walk (5K). Sunday 7th September, 2.30pm start at St. John's. Bring a friend!

The Parish Team
The monthly meeting of all committee members will take place in the Parish Centre on Thursday 4th September at 8.00 pm.

Bible Study
Bible sharing in the Parish Centre every Wednesday morning at 10.30am. Please bring a Bible. All are welcome.

The Parish Newsletter

Reading the parish newsletter is a good way of getting to know the range of services and activities available to the Christian community in the parish. Read St. Johns Parish Newsletter and answer the following questions.

1. List the times of Sunday and weekday Mass in St. John's church.
2. Name four sacraments that are celebrated in the church.
3. Does the parish have its own primary school? What is it called?
4. Where is the parish graveyard?
5. Where is the parish pilgrimage going to this year?
6. Give three reasons why people might phone the Parish Centre.
7. Where is the senior citizen's club held each week?
8. What work does the SVP do in the parish?
9. How does St. John's parish help people in developing countries?
10. What parish activities are open to young people?

Christians - People of God.

Questions

Knowledge

1. What is a parish?
2. Who are the People of God?
3. What were the characteristics of the first Christian community in Jerusalem?
4. Who is the leader of a parish community?
5. a. What is a lay person?
   b. What roles do lay people have in a parish?
6. What motivates people to be involved in their parish?
7. What is the function of a parish newsletter?
8. What evidence is there that members of St. John's parish are committed to the faith?

Understanding

1. How do priests and lay people work together in the parish? Give practical examples.
2. How do the People of God in a Catholic parish today:
   a. show their faith in God?
   b. worship God?
   c. follow a way of life that involves sharing and helping people in need?
3. Compare and contrast the characteristics of a parish community today with the characteristics of the first Christian communities founded by the apostles.
4. Up until recently, priests did everything in the parish. Now lay people are encouraged to serve in the parish community. What are the advantages of this arrangement? Are there any disadvantages?

Research

- There are a number of ministries for lay people in the Catholic Church.
  Find out what is involved in becoming a:
  - Minister of the Word.
  - Minister of the Eucharist.
  - What preparation and training is involved?
  - Is there a commissioning ceremony?
  - What commitment is expected afterwards?
  - Discuss these points with someone who serves as a Minister of the Word or Minister of the Eucharist in a local parish.
  - Perhaps he/she may be available to talk to the class.
  - Discuss a detailed schedule for the visit with the class.

New Titles for Jesus

Key Concepts

Son of Man: a title that shows the human nature of Jesus, and the fact that his suffering and death is a sacrifice to benefit all humanity.

Son of God: a title that shows the divine or holy relationship between Jesus and God the Father.

Christ/ Messiah: a title meaning 'anointed one'; Jesus is a spiritual leader sent by God.

Objective

Explain the meanings attached to the new titles for Jesus.

Activity: *"Identity Parade"*

TASK: TO UNDERSTAND THE MEANING OF THE TERM "IDENTITY".

School Report Date:

Name:

Class:

Best subject(s):

Improvement required in:

Punctuality:

Attendance:

Behaviour:

Achievements:

Teacher's comments:

Discuss

- What basic information does a document like this provide about someone?
- Can friends and team-mates provide any additional information about us?
- Do our families know us in ways that others do not?
- What might we know about ourselves, and our own identity, that others may be unaware of?

A new understanding of Jesus

The apostles tried very hard to express their understanding of Jesus' identity.

After the resurrection the apostles experienced Jesus in a new way. In the early years of the Church they thought a lot about Jesus' true identity and tried to work out exactly who Jesus was. First the apostles needed to understand the connection between God and the risen Jesus. Then they had to find just the right words to tell others what they believed.

The apostles did not use the term 'God' for Jesus straight away. Instead they used certain words from the Old Testament such as Son of Man, Son of God, and Messiah/ Christ. These terms were already familiar to the Jews and that was important. So when the apostles applied them to Jesus, their listeners immediately grasped their significance and understood what the disciples were trying to say. The apostles selected these titles as the best possible summary of Jesus' true identity.

Who is Jesus?
.....Son of Man
.....Son of God
.....Christ/ Messiah

Son of Man

(Mark 10:32-34)

Son of Man was the only title that Jesus actually applied to himself. In Mark's Gospel, Jesus used it fourteen times to indicate who he was.

The Old Testament

The idea of the Son of Man came from the Book of Ezekiel and the Book of Daniel in the Old Testament.

The New Testament

Jesus gave the title a new meaning.
Son of Man means…

- ❖ Jesus is like all humanity. It is like saying 'he is one of us.' He is human, he has feelings, he will suffer and die like any ordinary person, yet....
- ❖ Jesus is different. He is sent by God on a special mission to establish the Kingdom of God on Earth. Out of love he will sacrifice his life, yet his suffering and his death will benefit everyone. God will raise him from death to a new form of life. Jesus will judge his followers on how faithful they have been to his message of the Kingdom of God.

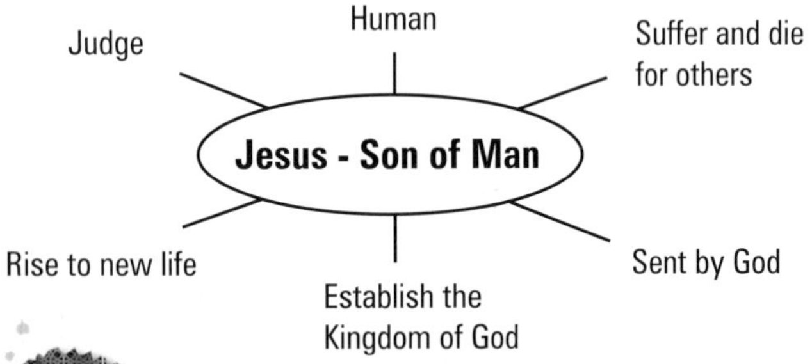
Judge
Human
Suffer and die for others
Jesus - Son of Man
Rise to new life
Establish the Kingdom of God
Sent by God

Son of God

(Mark 15:33-39)

The title of Son of God was first used after the resurrection. The early Christians did not use it for Jesus before that time.

The Old Testament

The idea of the Son of God came from the Book of Hosea and the Book of Psalms in the Old Testament. The phrase 'Son of God' is not to be taken literally. It does not mean someone's actual father or biological son. It is poetic language. It means someone who is extremely good or holy and therefore very close to God.

The New Testament

The term Son of God takes on an extra meaning when applied to Jesus. Son of God means....

- ❖ Jesus is more than just the holiest man who ever lived. Jesus' life and work show he has a unique and very close relationship with God. Indeed, he has the same nature as God. Jesus is not just a Son of God, he is the Son of God.

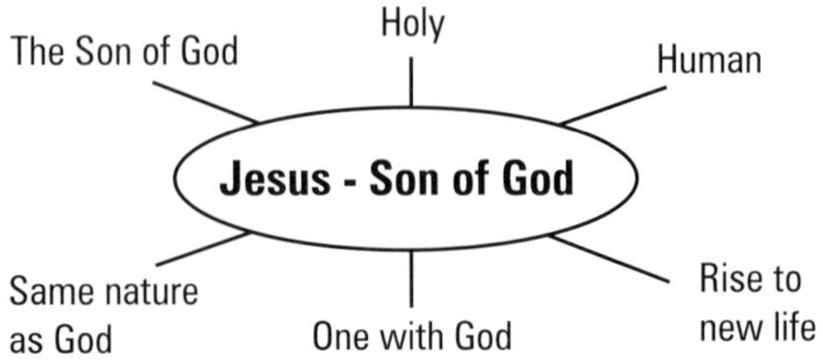
The Son of God
Holy
Human
Jesus - Son of God
Same nature as God
One with God
Rise to new life

Christ/ Messiah

(Mark 8:27-30)

This title came into proper use after the resurrection, although the disciples attempted to use it for Jesus before that. Both words, Christ and Messiah, mean 'the anointed one', that is someone chosen by God to carry out a special task. Christ means 'the anointed one' in Greek. Messiah means 'the anointed one' in Hebrew. Later the title Jesus the Christ was shortened to Jesus Christ. Christ is a title - it is not a surname.

The Old Testament

The idea of 'the anointed one' came from the Book of Isaiah and the Book of Micah in the Old Testament. All Jewish kings including David were anointed at the beginning of their reign. Jews expected the promised Messiah to be another great king who would bring peace and liberty to the Jews in Palestine.

The New Testament

However, Jesus' idea of 'the anointed one' was different from that of the disciples and other Jews at that time.

Christ/ Messiah means…

- ❖ For Jesus, the Messiah is not a political leader who is powerful, famous and warlike. Instead the Messiah is a spiritual leader who must suffer, die, and rise again.
- ❖ His Kingdom will be a spiritual kingdom in people's hearts. It is not an earthly kingdom in a particular place.

After the resurrection the disciples finally understood and believed. Jesus had not come to do battle and overthrow foreign rulers in Palestine. Instead his task was to overcome death itself, an even greater victory. Jesus Christ the Messiah was specially chosen to do God's work not just in Palestine but among all people, everywhere.

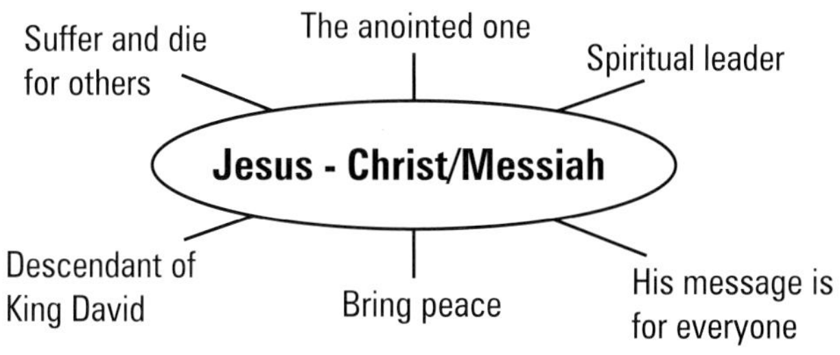
Suffer and die for others
The anointed one
Spiritual leader
Jesus - Christ/Messiah
Descendant of King David
Bring peace
His message is for everyone

Questions

Knowledge

1. a. List three titles that the early Christians used for Jesus.
   b. Which of these titles did Jesus use to describe himself?
   c. Which title was used for the first time after the resurrection?
2. When Jesus called himself Son of Man, what was he saying about his identity?
3. What meaning did 'Son of God' have for:
   - Jews in the Old Testament?
   - Christians in the New Testament?
4. What do the titles 'Christ' and 'Messiah' have in common?
5. What meaning did the title 'Messiah' have for:
   - Jews in the Old Testament?
   - Christians in the New Testament?

Understanding

1. Why did the apostles promote the use of certain titles for Jesus?
2. In what way was Jesus' understanding of the Messiah different to Jewish expectations of the Messiah?
3. What did the apostles mean when they said that Jesus is the Son of God?
4. How did the use of certain titles for Jesus help the early Christians in the practice of their faith?

Research

✪ Find occasions in the Gospels when people use a title for Jesus.

- ✸ Look up the following Bible references.
  - ✢ Son of Man - Mark 2:1-12
    - Mark 10:32-34
  - ✢ Son of God - Mark 15:33-39
    - John 17:1-4
  - ✢ Christ/ Messiah - Mark 8:27-30
    - Matt 9:27-31
- ✸ On each occasion:
  - describe the scene.
  - summarise what is said.
  - was there a reaction or a response from those present at the time?
  - what does this statement say about the identity of Jesus?
- ✸ Share the information and any insights with the class.

Section C - Foundations of Religion: Judaism and Islam

The *Syllabus Aims* in this section are:

- ◆ To explore in detail two major world religions.
- ◆ To examine the impact of these religions on their followers today, and on other individuals and communities.

Concept Checklist (Section C - Judaism and Islam)

Page

- ❑ **Calendar/ Sacred time** - days and weeks set aside every year for a religious purpose. 241, 296
- ❑ **Ceremony** - the solemn or formal actions performed on a ritual occasion. 249, 299
- ❑ **Commitment** - a decision to devote time and energy to the practise of one's religion. 252, 260, 302
- ❑ **Community structure** - the way a community of faith is organised. 266, 307
- ❑ **Creed/ Ethic** - the summary of a religion's deeply held beliefs and moral principles. 225, 284
- ❑ **Cultural context** - the whole way of life of people living in the place where a religion began. 206, 276
- ❑ **Development** - the way a community of faith grows and progresses over time. 252, 302
- ❑ **Dialogue** - open and honest discussion between the major world religions. 266, 307
- ❑ **Education** - the way the faith is passed on within a community of faith. 266, 307
- ❑ **Evidence** - information about a religious tradition collected from different sources. 216, 281
- ❑ **Expansion** - the way a religion spreads out into new territories. 256, 302
- ❑ **Festivals** - sacred time marked by fasting or celebration to remind people of key events and beliefs in their faith. 243, 246, 296
- ❑ **Follower/ Discipleship** - persons called to follow the teaching and way of life of a religious leader. 270, 309
- ❑ **Founder** - the person who established a religion. 209, 212, 278
- ❑ **Inspiration** - the way in which a person is guided by God to pass on a sacred message. 219, 281
- ❑ **Leadership** - the task of a leader in guiding a community of faith. 266, 307
- ❑ **Location** - the part of the world where a religion began. 203, 273, 276
- ❑ **Oral tradition** - stories and religious teaching that a people pass on by word of mouth. 219, 281
- ❑ **Persecution** - making people suffer because of their race or religion. 256, 260
- ❑ **Pilgrimage** - a journey made by a pilgrim to a shrine or a sacred place. 238, 293
- ❑ **Place of worship** - a building or place where people go to pray and worship God or gods. 232, 290
- ❑ **Practice** - customs and rituals that show a person's religious faith. 225, 284
- ❑ **Prayer** - the act of communicating with God. 227, 287
- ❑ **Prophet** - a person chosen by God to give people an important message. 278
- ❑ **Revelation** - the way in which God chooses to make himself known to human beings. 219, 281
- ❑ **Rite** - the pattern of words and actions used in a religious ceremony. 246, 249
- ❑ **Ritual** - an occasion when people use symbolic objects, words and actions to express what is deeply important to them. 229, 235, 238, 246, 249, 293, 299
- ❑ **Sacred text** - the book of holy or sacred writings of a community of faith. 216, 219, 222, 281
- ❑ **Schism** - a division or split within a community of faith. 263, 305
- ❑ **Symbol** - something visible that represents something else that is invisible. 243, 246
- ❑ **Tradition** - the wisdom and teaching of a community of faith handed down from generation to generation. 270, 309
- ❑ **Vision** - a vivid dream or mental image of something important. 209, 212, 278
- ❑ **Worship** - the way people of faith praise and honour God in prayer and at religious services. 235, 290

Judaism - Location

Key Concept

Location: the part of the world where the religion of Judaism began.

Objective

Describe the geographical background at the time of the foundation of Judaism.

Activity: *"Map Work"*

TASK: TO NAME THE COUNTRIES THAT OCCUPY THE REGION ONCE KNOWN AS THE FERTILE CRESCENT.

- ✦ Use an atlas to find the following countries in the Middle East.

  Iraq. Syria. Israel. Jordan.
  Lebanon. Iran. Egypt.

- ✦ Find the following cities and state in what country each is located.

  Jerusalem. Cairo. Damascus.

Discuss

Have you ever (✓)
- Heard about these countries before? ❑
- Visited one of these countries? ❑
- Lived in one of these countries? ❑
- Known someone who has visited or lived in one of these countries? ❑
- Known about a famous person from one of these countries? ❑

State what you know about life in any one of these countries today.

Location

In ancient times part of the Middle East was known as the Fertile Crescent.

Judaism is a major world religion with over eighteen million members in the world today. Jews believe in one God, Yahweh, whom they call 'Lord'. The religion of Judaism was founded by Abraham about 4,000 years ago.

Canaan was the location, or the place, where the religion of Judaism began. Canaan was located in the Fertile Crescent. This was an arc (or crescent) of good land that stretched from Egypt all the way to the city of Ur in Mesopotamia, a distance of over 1,000 miles (1,600 kilometres).

Two rivers, the Tigris and the Euphrates, flowed through the Fertile Crescent. There was plenty of water and the land was fertile. The soil was good for growing crops, and there was enough grass to feed animals such as sheep, goats and camels.

Canaan, later known as Palestine, was located on a highway, or crossroads, between Egypt and Mesopotamia (modern day Iraq).

The Fertile Crescent.

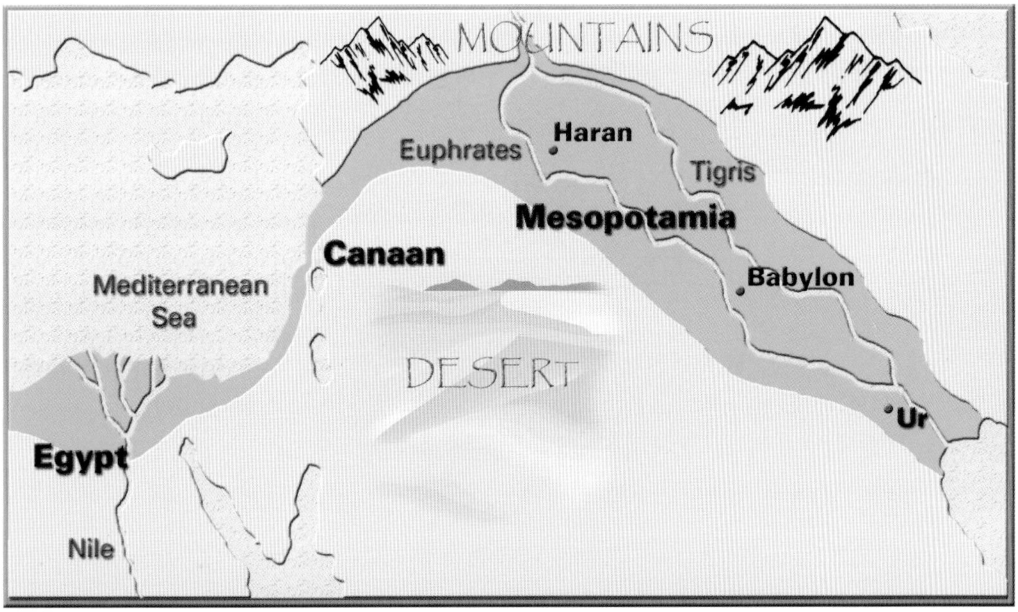
MOUNTAINS
Euphrates
Haran
Tigris
Mesopotamia
Canaan
Babylon
Mediterranean Sea
DESERT
Ur
Egypt
Nile

Section C

Nomads

Long ago different groups of people travelled throughout this vast region. Some were merchants and travellers, most were nomads; large family groups who migrated from place to place in search of pasture for their animals. When they found a good supply of grass and water, they unpacked their camels, pitched their tents and stayed for a few weeks to let their sheep and goats graze on the fresh grass. Afterwards, they packed up and went off to find new grazing somewhere else.

Self-sufficiency

Nomadic families were self-sufficient. They made their tents and their clothes by weaving camel hair and sheeps' wool to make cloth. They had milk and meat from their animals and caught fish in the rivers. They ate wild berries and fruit such as figs and dates. Wild honey was freely available. They also traded their surplus for other goods in the markets along the way.

The tents used by nomadic families today are similar to those used by nomads long ago.

The leader

Nomads moved around in one large family group. Aunts, uncles, cousins and grandparents all travelled together. One person, usually the oldest man, was the *sheik,* or the leader, of the entire group. Everyone looked up to him and had to obey him. The *sheik* decided what was best for the group or the clan.

The *sheik* told them where to take the animals, how to trade in the markets, and with whom it was safe to mix on the journey. The sheik's brothers, sons and nephews worked alongside him as they moved from place to place.

The women raised the children, cooked the meals, made cloth, and provided hospitality to strangers who might need food or water. The children helped their parents with the animals and the preparation of food. The grandparents shared their wisdom about living out in the open, raising a family, and looking after livestock.

Everyone relied on each other. The family, or clan, kept together as they moved about from place to place. The clan was a source of support, wealth and safety for all its members.

Children and animals in the Middle East today.

Abraham

Abraham, the founder of Judaism, became a nomad in later life. He took his family on a long journey, travelling with his wife Sarah, his father Terah, his nephew Lot, their servants and all their goods and animals.

- ❖ They set off from the city of Ur in Mesopotamia and travelled a distance of 600 miles (960km) to Haran.
- ❖ Then they went another 400 miles (640km) to the land of Canaan.
- ❖ Later they visited Egypt before returning once more to Canaan.

Abraham and his family travelled together for a number of years. Their journey from Ur to Canaan took them through the Fertile Crescent, an area that today is made up of Iran, Iraq, Syria, Lebanon, Israel, Jordan and Egypt.

Camels transport people and goods across Middle Eastern countries today, just as they did in Abraham's time.

Questions

Knowledge

1. Name the founding father of Judaism.
2. a. When did Judaism originate?
   b. In what part of the world did Judaism originate?
3. Where is the area known as the Fertile Crescent located on a map of the world?
4. Name two rivers that flow through the part of the Fertile Crescent called Mesopotamia.
5. Explain the meaning of the words - fertile AND - crescent.
6. What is a nomad?
7. Why did Abraham's family not take the short cut straight across from Ur to Canaan?
8. What countries today occupy the area known as the Fertile Crescent?

Understanding

1. What is the location and the physical features of the area known as the Fertile Crescent?
2. Describe the lifestyle of the nomadic people in the Fertile Crescent at the time of Abraham.
3. How would the climate and geographical features of the Fertile Crescent have affected people's lives at the time of the foundation of Judaism?

Research

- Find out more about life in the Middle East today.
- Check *newspapers.... television news programmes.... internet world news websites....* to find a current news item about one of the countries in the Middle East.
- Exchange information and briefly discuss the issues involved.
- Draw a map of the Fertile Crescent. Add the following features:
  - Rivers: the Tigris and the Euphrates.
  - Mountains: to the north of the river valley.
  - Desert: to the south of the river valley.
  - Cities: Ur and Babylon.
  - Countries: Canaan and Egypt.
  - Seas: the Mediterranean Sea.
  - The Fertile Crescent.

Judaism - Culture

Key Concept

Cultural context: the whole way of life of people living in the place where Judaism began.

Objective

Describe the historical situation at the time of the foundation of Judaism.

Activity: *"Codes"*

TASK: TO BE AWARE THAT DIFFERENT CODES TRANSMIT IDEAS AND INFORMATION.

Matching exercise (* ⟷ *)

✦ Match each form of communication with the correct description.

Semaphore	A fast way of taking dictation before writing business letters.
Morse code	A form of writing using a series of raised dots.
Ground to air signals	A method of signaling using two hand-held flags.
Pittman shorthand	The hands are used to make letters and whole words.
Braille	Marks in the snow, sand or on the ground to attract the attention of searching aircraft.
Sign language	Messages sent by flashing a light or sound using a combination of dots and dashes.

Discuss

- Did you match the correct information? Award yourself a mark. [/6]
- Why do you think so many different codes have been invented?
- Do you think it is easy or difficult to invent a form of communication?

Cultural Context

Archaeologists discovered a type of writing called cuneiform invented thousands of years ago. Cuneiform is like an ancient form of shorthand.

Abraham's family came from Ur, a city in Mesopotamia. The word Mesopotamia means 'the land between the rivers'. We will examine the cultural context of this region, which means looking at the way people lived there at the time of the foundation of Judaism.

Archaeology

Archaeologists are scientists who investigate an ancient site and examine what it contains. Their findings can tell us how people lived in that place long ago. Archaeologists found thousands of clay tablets and other objects in the ruins of cities throughout the Fertile Crescent. Their work threw light on the lifestyle of people living there at the time of Abraham, about 4,000 years ago.

Cuneiform was unusual wedge shaped writing on clay tablets. Cuneiform writing developed in Mesopotamia 5,000 years ago. Some people said it looked like 'bird tracks on wet sand'. It was made by pressing a triangular rod, or stylus, into soft clay to make wedge-shaped marks. The clay tablets were then left in the sun to bake hard. When archaeologists first came across cuneiform writing they couldn't understand it. It took a long time to break the code.

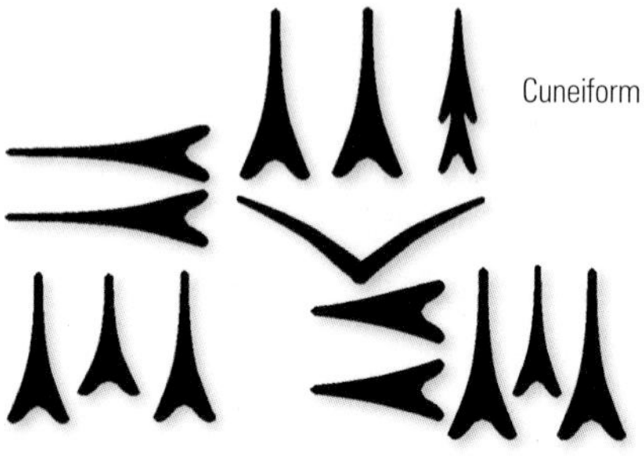

Cuneiform writing.

Section C

Archaeologists at work.

The Political Situation

At one time the majority of people living in Mesopotamia were nomads. Wandering nomads grazed their animals along the banks of the rivers Tigris and Euphrates. Sometimes they stopped to grow crops in the good soil in the river valleys. The nomadic families learned to co-operate, and help each other to harvest the crops. Some stayed on and established settlements and farming villages in different places. A number of villages eventually grew into small towns. Over time some of the towns became important cities. Walls were built around the cities to protect them from invaders.

City States

The leaders in these walled cities became very powerful. Kings and royal families ruled the cities and all the land and villages around in every direction. These became the city states of the ancient world. Ur and Babylon were important city states in Mesopotamia. Some city states became very powerful, and controlled empires.

At the time of Abraham:

- ❖ the Babylonian Empire ruled one part of the Fertile Crescent, including the city of Ur.
- ❖ the Egyptian Empire ruled the other part of the Fertile Crescent, including the land of Canaan.

Life inside and outside the city walls had to be organised. Kings needed to keep track of their armies, their battles, their land and their wealth. Records had to be kept, so there was a need for some sort of writing. Cuneiform, an early form of writing on clay tablets, was invented in Mesopotamia.

The City of Ur

Archaeologists have found hundreds of clay tablets in the city of Ur. It is like a library of poetry, stories, mathematical equations, and business information. This discovery shows that the people of the region were civilised and the city was a place of learning.

Pottery, ornaments and jewellery made of gold, silver and precious stones were also found there. This discovery shows that skilled craft workers, and wealthy families lived in that area.

A number of walls were excavated at the site. These revealed that the city had many good houses and buildings. Its extensive market places suggested it had active trading links with other cities.

We now know that Ur was a very advanced city at the time of Abraham. Ordinary people had a good standard of living, and its rulers were rich and powerful.

The Religious Situation

Archaeologists have also found evidence that people at the time of Abraham were polytheists and worshipped many different gods. Nature gods such as the sun, the moon and the stars were worshipped in temples all over Mesopotamia. In the city of Ur archaeologists excavated a very tall building called a ziggurat. It stood 70ft (20m) high and overlooked the city. In times past there was a temple on top of this building. The temple was dedicated to the moon god Nanna. Ur was a centre of moon worship in Mesopotamia. People came from far and wide to trade in the city and worship in the temple.

Abraham

At the time of Abraham, Ur was an important city for trade and for religion. No one knows how it happened, but Abraham, a citizen of Ur, stopped believing in all the different gods. Instead he started to think there was one God in charge of everything. He felt he had to leave Ur and go in search of the one true God. This meant leaving behind a comfortable home, and a settled way of life in the city he grew up in.

So Abraham, the Father of Judaism, became a nomad in later life. He set out from the city of Ur in Mesopotamia and travelled to the land of Canaan, a distance of over 1,000 miles (1,600km).

His journey took him through Mesopotamia, a land ruled by the Babylonian Empire. After spending some time in the city of Haran, Abraham then travelled to Canaan and finally settled there. Canaan at that time was ruled by the Egyptian Empire.

Questions

Knowledge

1. What do archaeologists do?
2. What is cuneiform writing?
3. Where was Mesopotamia?
4. What does the word Mesopotamia mean?
5. Describe what a city state was like.
6. What two empires controlled different parts of the Fertile Crescent at the time of Abraham?
7. What evidence did archaeologists find to show that Ur was an important city?
8. What religion did people have at the time of Abraham?
9. What did Abraham decide to do in order to find out more about the one true God?
10. In what kind of dwelling would Abraham have lived: a. in the city of Ur?
    b. on his travels?

Understanding

1. How did city states develop in Mesopotamia long ago?
2. Describe the religious situation in Mesopotamia at the time of Abraham.
3. How have archaeologists contributed to our understanding of life in Mesopotamia at the time of Abraham?
4. What do you think it was like for a middle-aged city dweller like Abraham to set off as a wandering nomad 4,000 years ago?

Research

- Find out about some archaeological discoveries that have taken place in this country.
  - Name a local or national archaeological site.
  - What artifacts were discovered during the excavation?
  - What historical period was illuminated by the 'dig' at the site?
  - What did archaeologists learn about the way people lived during that period?
  - Share your findings with the class.

Abraham

Key Concepts

Founder: the person who established a religion.

Vision: a vivid dream or mental image of something important.

Objective

Identify key moments in the life of Abraham, a founder of Judaism.

Activity: *"Circle of trust"*

TASK: TO EXPLORE THE NATURE OF TRUST IN HUMAN RELATIONSHIPS.

- Invite eight volunteers to demonstrate this exercise to the class.
  - Seven volunteers form a close circle around the eighth person, who stands in the centre.
  - The seven must promise to catch and support the volunteer in the centre when he/she falls in their direction. Everyone stands ready, hands held loosely at their sides.
  - The person in the centre stands perfectly still with eyes closed, hands by their side. Then he/she falls in any direction, with the knowledge that members of the circle will offer immediate support.

Discuss

- Write the names of the eight volunteers. Draw a circle around the name of the volunteer who stood in the middle.
- Did the person in the middle trust the others to keep their promise? How do you know?
- What does it feel like to trust people in this way?
- Whom do you trust in life?

Founder

Abraham was willing to trust God. He was a man of faith who set off in a new direction in life.

Abraham (originally called Abram) was a founder of the religion of Judaism. Abraham lived about 4,000 years ago in the city of Ur in Mesopotamia. Like everyone else at the time, he worshipped gods of nature such as the sun, moon and stars. Then a change came over him and he began to wonder about the need for so many different gods. Around this time Abraham's family left Ur, the city where he grew up. They travelled to Haran and decided to settle there. Abraham became head of the family when his father died.

Vision

Abraham's first vision - <u>God calls Abraham</u>

No one really knows how it happened, but Abraham stopped believing in many gods. It came to him that there is one God above all other gods. Then Abraham had a vision. God spoke to him in his heart.

"The Lord said to Abraham, 'Leave your country, your people, and your father's house and go to the land I will show you.'"

Genesis 12:1

Section C

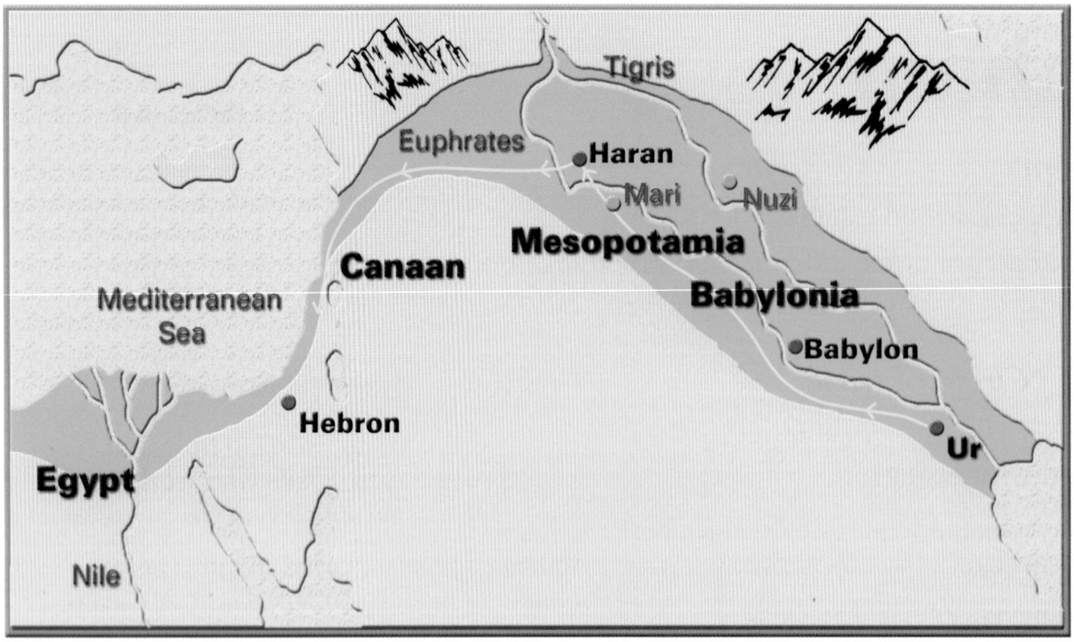
Tigris
Euphrates
Haran
Mari
Nuzi
Mesopotamia
Canaan
Mediterranean
Sea
Babylonia
Babylon
Hebron
Ur
Egypt
Nile

The journey of Abraham.

Abraham's Journey

Deep down, Abraham felt God was calling him to give up his old ways and start a new life somewhere else. Abraham said 'yes' and put all his trust in God even though he was unsure where God was leading him.

Abraham left Haran and set off across the Fertile Crescent with his wife Sarah (originally called Sarai), his nephew Lot and all their goods and animals. Leaving behind their comfortable life, they went in search of the land God would show them.

Abraham and his family travelled south to the land of Canaan. Their long and difficult journey lasted for many years as they wandered from place to place in search of grazing for their animals. Eventually they reached Canaan and settled beside some sacred trees at Hebron. After they pitched their tents Abraham built an altar to the Lord.

At Hebron, Abraham built an altar to the Lord.

Abraham's Second Vision - The Covenant

Soon Abraham had another vision, this time he believed that God made a covenant with him. The covenant was a sacred agreement between God and Abraham. There were two sides to the agreement. God promised to look after Abraham and his family. Abraham promised to worship God and do what God asked. If Abraham did as God asked, God promised him many descendants and the land of Canaan.

> "Then and there the Lord made a covenant with Abraham. He said 'I promise to give your descendants all of this land....'"
>
> Genesis 15:18

The Covenant was the beginning of a special relationship between God and the family of Abraham. Abraham would be the father of a great nation, his descendants would be God's chosen people. God would look after them and guide them, for God had chosen them to be an example of goodness and holiness to the rest of the world. When the Covenant was made, it was sealed with a ritual to show that it was a binding agreement between God, Abraham and all his descendants. The covenant gives rise to two important ideas in Judaism:

- The Chosen People - Abraham's descendants.
- The Promised Land - the land of Canaan, later known as Palestine and Israel.

Abraham's third vision - <u>Sign of the Covenant</u>

Abraham bowed down in prayer and, in another vision, God told him:

> "Your name will no longer be Abram but Abraham." Genesis 17:15

Abraham means 'father of many.' The name was a sign of his new mission in life. From then on Abraham would be the father of many descendants. They would become the 'chosen people' of God.

Then God said:

> "No longer call your wife Sarai. From now on, her name is Sarah." Genesis 17:15

The new name meant she would become the mother of many descendants. Abraham bowed down again to pray. He was worried. Sarah had never been able to have children and now both of them were very old. How could God's promise come true? Abraham had no need to worry. God blessed the couple in their old age. Sarah did indeed have a son and he was named Isaac. Then God told Abraham:

> "You and your descendants must all agree to circumcise every male among you...This will show that there is a covenant between you and me." Genesis 17:12

When the child Isaac was eight days old he was circumcised (the foreskin of his penis was removed). This action was a mark of God's covenant with Abraham and his descendants. Ever since, circumcision is a physical sign that Abraham's descendants have a special relationship with God.

Patriarchs

The Jewish people are the descendants of Abraham. Abraham, his son Isaac, his grandson Jacob and his great grandson Joseph all believed in the one God.

Abraham, Isaac and Jacob are the patriarchs (the father figures) of the Jewish people.

Questions

Knowledge

1. When and where did the religion of Judaism begin?
2. Name the first founder of Judaism.
3. a. Where did Abraham grow up?
   b. Where was Abraham when he had his first vision of God?
4. What did God call Abraham to do with his life?
5. Where did Abraham have his second vision of God?
6. In the covenant between God and Abraham what was:
   a. God's part of the agreement?
   b. Abraham's part of the agreement?
7. How did God and Abraham seal the covenant?
8. Why did Abram and Sarai have their names changed?
9. What sign of the covenant do Jews still carry to the present day?
10. What are the names of the Patriarchs?

Understanding

1. Outline the key moments in the life of Abraham.
2. Describe the changes that occurred in Abraham's religious thinking over time.
3. Why do you think the covenant is so central in the religion of Judaism?

Research

- Find out about Abraham's other son. Read Genesis 16, 17:19-23, 21:9-21 in the Hebrew Bible.

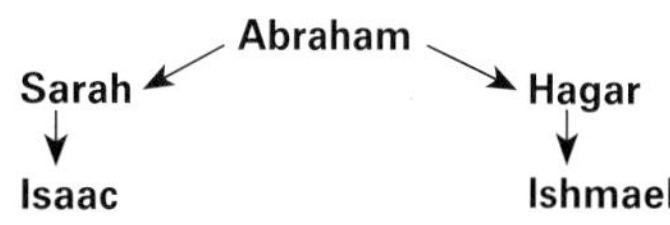

Abraham
Sarah
Hagar
Isaac
Ishmael

- Why do you think some marriage contracts* in ancient times state that a childless wife must provide her husband with another woman to bear his children?
- Why do you think Abraham was happy when Ishmael was born?
- The rules in ancient times** state that an adopted son must defer to a true son, even if he is born later. What were the implications of this ruling for Abraham's two sons?

* & ** These points were noted on documents written on clay tablets found during archaeological excavations at Nuzi and Mari in what was ancient Mesopotamia.

Moses

Key Concepts

Founder: the person who established a religion.

Vision: a vivid dream or mental image of something important.

Objective

Identify key moments in the life of Moses, a founder of Judaism.

Section C

Activity: *"Problems Problems"*

TASK: TO IDENTIFY THE KIND OF PROBLEMS SOME PEOPLE HAVE TO COPE WITH IN LIFE.

You will need: a soft ball or a small cushion.

- Think of a story line about a youth group setting off on a weekend camping trip. A long list of problems and disasters occur.
- During the exercise:
  - The cushion is passed to different people.
  - Each person composes one positive and one negative episode in the story line.
  - After telling the negative episode pass the cushion along to the next person.
  - The cushion journeys around the room as the story unfolds.

Discuss

- What was the funniest thing that happened on the camping trip?
- What was the most unusual problem that had to be dealt with that weekend?
- List the kinds of problems some teenagers have to deal with in real life.
- Who can help young people with their different problems?

Founder

When the Jews lived in Egypt they had to cope with many problems.
God sent Moses to help them.

Moses is a founder of the religion of Judaism. The Jews believe he is a most important person, and the greatest prophet, they ever had.

Early Life (Exodus 1, 2:1-15)

Abraham's descendants left Canaan and migrated to Egypt to escape famine. When a new king came to power, he said the people from Canaan were not to be trusted. He feared they might rise up and refuse to obey him. The Jews* were outsiders, their numbers were getting too big. So the king made their life difficult and forced them to work like slaves on the building sites in Egypt. As a result the Jews lived in constant fear. Their lives were at risk, they were poor, hungry, and in bad health.

To reduce their numbers even further, the king ordered that their first born sons were to be killed at birth. The Jews were heartbroken. They did everything to save their children. One family placed their son in a basket and hid him among the reeds in the River Nile. The baby was saved. He was adopted and allowed to live in the palace. The baby's name was Moses.

Moses grew up and had a good life in the palace, but he was never happy. All about him he witnessed the suffering of the Jewish people. One day he lost his temper and hit a guard who was beating a Jew to death. The guard died and Moses fled for his life into the desert.

Pharaoh's Palace in Egypt.

*NOTE: At different times in Jewish history Abraham's descendants were known as Israelites, Hebrews and Jews.

Moses' Vision - God calls Moses (Exodus 3)

One day, years later, Moses was travelling alone in the desert. He stopped to take some time to think and to pray. On the mountain of Sinai he prayed that the problems of the Jewish people would soon be over. As he prayed a dried bush went on fire nearby. It was then that Moses had a vision. God spoke to him in his heart.

"I am sending you to the King of Egypt so that you can lead my people out of his country." Exodus 3:10

Moses couldn't believe what God was calling him to do. He became nervous and made excuses not to go. Yet he knew it was up to him to do something about the suffering of the Jewish people. Moses prayed even harder.

When God said "I will be with you" (Exodus 3:12) it gave him all the courage he needed. Moses went to the Pharaoh, the King of Egypt, and demanded that God's people be set free. The Pharaoh refused, but was forced to change his mind when a number of disasters, or plagues, occurred in the land.

The Passover (Exodus 12)

On their last night in Egypt, the Jews followed Moses' instructions and sprinkled the blood of lambs on their doorposts. The Angel of Death passed over their houses and they were spared from disaster.

The Jews gave thanks and had a Passover celebration. They ate a special meal of roast lamb, bitter herbs and bread without yeast, but they did not have enough time to enjoy their meal. Their bags were packed and they had to go. So they wrapped up what was left and took it with them. Then they all set off together, a band of ex-slaves with Moses as their leader.

- ✦ Read Exodus 12:1-14 ***The Passover***
- ✦ Write down what the Jews:
  - a. must do before the Passover.
  - b. must eat at the Passover meal.
  - c. must know will happen in Egypt on the night of Passover.
  - d. must do once a year forever afterwards.

The Exodus (Exodus 14)

When the Jews left Egypt they knew God was with them day and night. For a while they travelled without any problems. Then, one morning, they got news that the Pharaoh had sent an army after them. They were trapped. In front was the wet, marshy ground of the Red Sea, behind them were soldiers in armour in horse-drawn chariots. The king's army was racing to catch up with them. The people were terrified and could see no way out. They prayed to God for help. Moses told them to have courage and to keep going, God was with them.

That night, strong winds blew from the east. The winds dried up the wet ground. Moses carefully led the people through the Red Sea. The king's army could not follow. Their horses and chariots got stuck in the mud. The Jews escaped, they were free at last. This is the Exodus, the great event of Jewish history

PROMISED LAND
EGYPT
The Exodus.

Moses' Vision - The Covenant Renewed

(Exodus 19, 20, 24)

The Jews spent the next three months wandering in the desert. When they were hungry and thirsty Moses found food and water for them. He showed the people that God was on their side. God was looking after them.

Then they arrived at the foot of Mount Sinai. Moses needed time to think and to pray so he went up the mountain alone. It was there that he had another vision. God spoke to Moses in his heart. God said;

> "The whole earth is mine, but you will be my chosen people." Exodus 19:5

God renewed the Covenant with Moses and the Jewish people: "I will be your God, you will be my people." This was the basis of the new relationship between God and the descendants of Abraham.

The Torah

To help the Jews keep their part of the Covenant, God gave Moses the Torah containing the Laws and the Ten Commandments. The Ten Commandments gave details of how God wanted his people to live.

They must:

- ❖ Believe in one powerful God.
- ❖ Create a good and just society.

The Jews must obey the Laws and the Ten Commandments in the Torah. The Ten Commandments were written on two tablets of stone. The tablets were placed inside a casket for safe keeping. This casket was known as the 'Ark of the Covenant'.

The Ten Commandments are referred to as the Ten Sayings in the religion of Judaism.

The Ten Sayings

Exodus 20:1-17 (The Jewish Prayer Book)

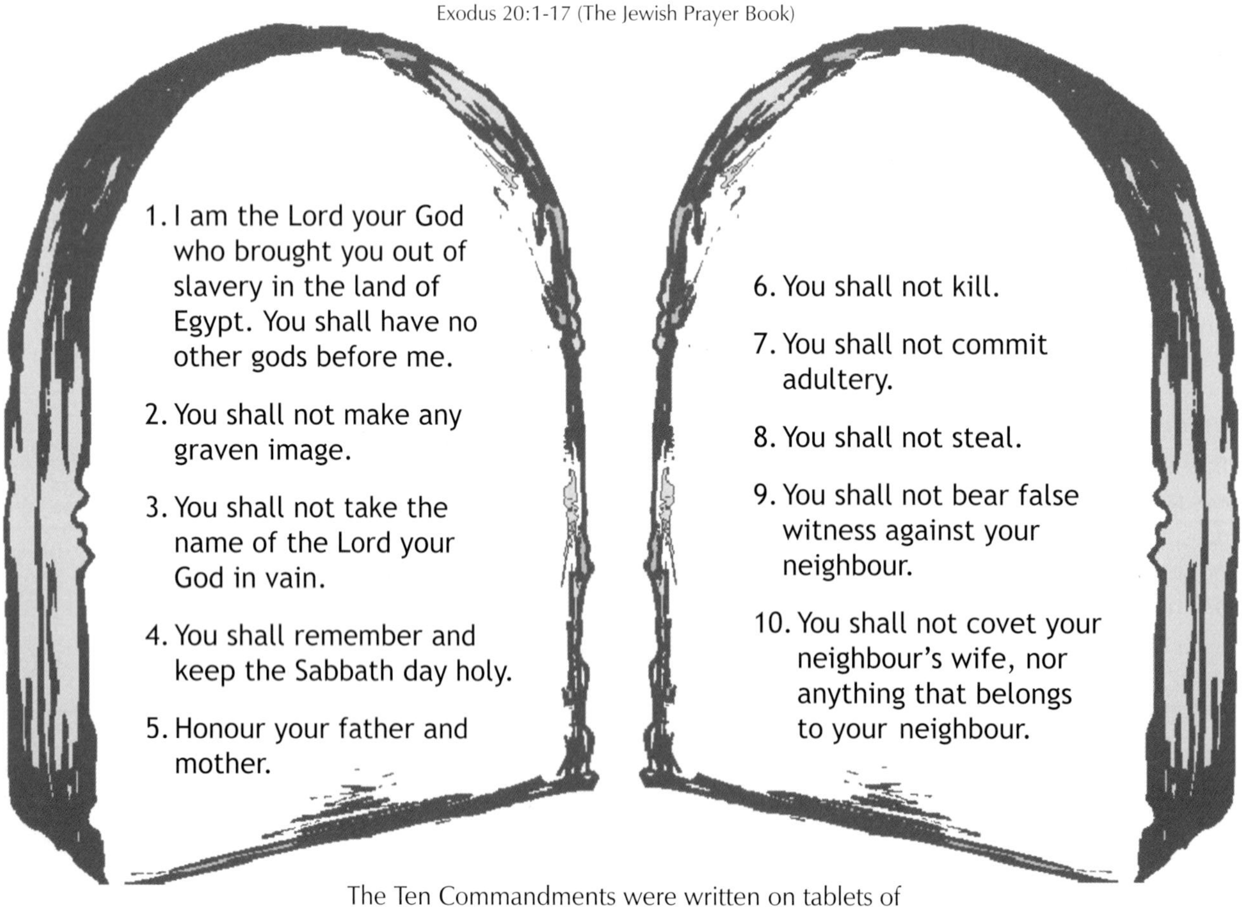
1. I am the Lord your God who brought you out of slavery in the land of Egypt. You shall have no other gods before me.
2. You shall not make any graven image.
3. You shall not take the name of the Lord your God in vain.
4. You shall remember and keep the Sabbath day holy.
5. Honour your father and mother.
6. You shall not kill.
7. You shall not commit adultery.
8. You shall not steal.
9. You shall not bear false witness against your neighbour.
10. You shall not covet your neighbour's wife, nor anything that belongs to your neighbour.

The Ten Commandments were written on tablets of stone and sealed in a casket known as the *Ark of the Covenant*.

The Ten Commandments Exodus 20: 1-17

Many Jews believe that Moses received the Torah directly from God on Mount Sinai. There are over 600 laws in the Torah, the most important are the Ten Commandments. The Torah and the Ten Commandments are the moral code of the Jewish people. This tells them what is right and what is wrong.

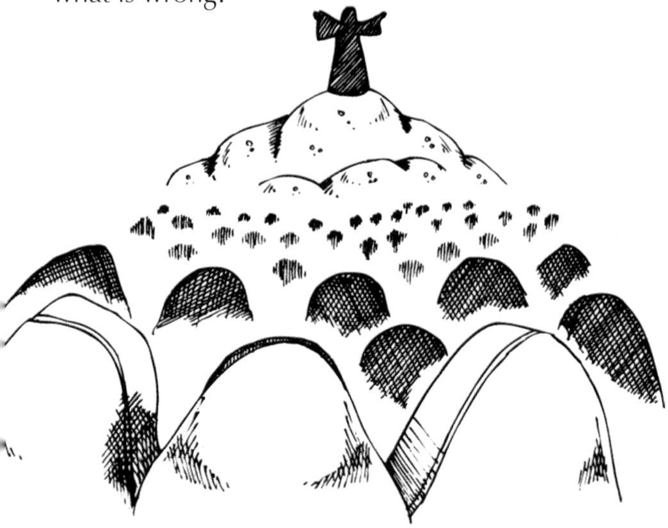

At Mount Sinai Moses speaks to the people and gives them the Law of God.

Moses and the Chosen People

Moses went back down the mountain to tell the people what had happened. The Jews began to realise for the first time who they really were. It dawned on them that they were the only people in the world who believed in one God. Not only that, but God had chosen them to show the world what God is like.

Since leaving Egypt they had learned that God is powerful, God is good, and God is caring. Their God had helped them to escape from Egypt, cross the Red Sea and survive in the wilderness. Their God had given them a clear set of rules to help them live good lives. Other people had gods that were cruel and fearsome. The God of the Jews was different and cared for his people.

When God and Moses renewed the covenant on Mount Sinai it became a binding agreement.

God will look after the Jews,
in return the Jews must obey God's Law.

It was a turning point. The Jews were no longer a band of ex-slaves. They had a new identity. They were a powerful people chosen by God to do his work on Earth.

Questions

Knowledge

1. List the problems the Jews faced in Egypt long ago.
2. What happened during Moses' early life in Egypt:
   a. as a baby?
   b. as a young man?
3. How did God call Moses?
4. How did Moses respond to God's call?
5. How did the Jews spend their final night in Egypt?
6. What food was eaten at the Passover meal?
7. What happened at the Red Sea?
8. How was the Covenant renewed?
9. a. What is contained in the Torah?
   b. What are the Ten Sayings?
10. What did the Jews learn about their identity at Mount Sinai?

Understanding

1. Outline the key moments in the life of Moses.
2. Moses had a number of visions or encounters with God. Describe what happened on two separate occasions.
3. Explain the meaning of *Passover* and the *Exodus* for the chosen people of God.
4. What is the Covenant? Why is it so important in the religion of Judaism?

Research

- Find out more about either:
- The disasters or plagues that struck Egypt.
  Read about:
  The plagues in Egypt. (Exodus 7:14-25, 8, 9, 10)
  OR
  The miracles in the wilderness.
  (The manna, quails, and finding water.
  Exodus 16, 17:1-7)
- Has natural history anything useful to add to our understanding of these events which the Jews see as the guiding hand of God at work in their lives?
- Make a contribution to a class discussion on this issue.

Sacred Text

Key Concepts

Sacred text: the book of holy or sacred writings of a community of faith.

Evidence: information about a religious tradition collected from different sources.

Objective

Name the primary source of information about Judaism.

Activity: *"Evidence"*

TASK: - TO IDENTIFY SOURCES OF INFORMATION ABOUT OURSELVES.
- TO NOTE THE KIND OF EVIDENCE CERTAIN ITEMS CAN PROVIDE ABOUT US.

- A photograph.
- My diary.
- Magazines I read.
- Books I read.
- Computer games I like.
- Clothes I wear.
- My school report.
- Text messages I send.
- Jewellery I wear.
- Trophies or medals I have won.
- My CD or DVD collection.
- Sports shirts I wear.
- Birthday cards I receive.

Discuss

- Examine the list above.
- What kind of information might these items provide about us?
- Which item will provide the best evidence of what someone is really like?

Sacred text

Evidence

The Tenakh is the main source of evidence about the beginning of Judaism.

The Tenakh is the name of the sacred text of Judaism. It is a collection of books and is the primary source of evidence or information about the religion of Judaism. These books are also part of the Old Testament in the Christian Bible.

The Tenakh is a document of faith. It tells the story of how Judaism began and the beliefs and practices that are important in Judaism. The Tenakh, known also as the Hebrew Bible, has three main parts:

1. The Torah.
2. The Prophets.
3. The Writings.

Each part is divided into books. There are thirty nine books in the Tenakh altogether. The Tenakh is like a library of the holy books of Judaism.

Te-Na-Kh

Hebrew is the ancient language of the Jewish people. Most of the Tenakh is written in Hebrew. Tenakh is a word made up of the first letters of Torah, Prophets and Writing in the Hebrew language.

- Torah (the teaching).
- Neviim (the prophets).
- Ketuvim (the writings).

The Torah

The Torah is the holiest and most important part of the Tenakh. It contains five books.

- ❖ Genesis.
- ❖ Exodus.
- ❖ Leviticus.
- ❖ Numbers.
- ❖ Deuteronomy.

The word *Torah* means teaching. The Torah begins with the Jewish teaching on the creation of the world, then it teaches about Abraham and Moses the founders of Judaism. The Torah shows the Jews what God is like and tells them how God wants them to live.

The Torah contains 613 different rules or laws given to Moses on Mount Sinai. The best known are the Ten Commandments. Jewish people read the Torah to learn how to live in a way that is pleasing to God. Most of the Torah is in Hebrew and is handwritten on scrolls for use in the synagogue.

The Prophets

The books of the Prophets are about the history of the Jewish people after the death of Moses. The Jews believe the prophets were men and women who had special powers given to them by God. This meant they were able to speak on behalf of God. At different times in Jewish history the prophets gave messages and warnings, and reminded the Jews of how God wanted them to live. Over the years there were a number of different prophets, including Isaiah, Jeremiah and Ezekiel.

The Star of David placed over the first word of the Book of Genesis in the Hebrew Bible.

The Writings

The Writings are made up of different kinds of books. They tell us more about Jewish history but in a creative way.

There are books of:

- Poetry - love poems.
- Proverbs - wise and witty sayings.
- Short stories - the story of Ruth and the story of Esther, for example.
- Songs - hymns (many composed by King David).
- Chronicles - lists of people and events.

Section C

Scrolls of the Torah on display.

The Christian Bible

The holy books of the Tenakh can be found in the part of the Christian Bible called the Old Testament or Jewish Scriptures. Christianity has its roots in Judaism. The holy writings of Judaism have been part of the Christian tradition since the time of the early Christian communities. However there are certain differences between the composition of the Tenakh and the Jewish Scriptures in the Christian Bible. Examine a copy of both and note the similarities and the differences.

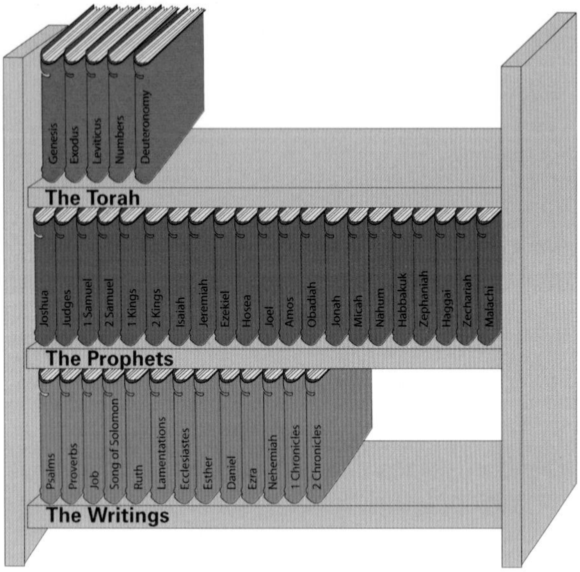

Genesis
Exodus
Leviticus
Numbers
Deuteronomy
The Torah
Joshua
Judges
1 Samuel
2 Samuel
1 Kings
2 Kings
Isaiah
Jeremiah
Ezekiel
Hosea
Joel
Amos
Obadiah
Jonah
Micah
Nahum
Habbakuk
Zephaniah
Haggai
Zechariah
Malachi
The Prophets
Psalms
Proverbs
Job
Song of Solomon
Ruth
Lamentations
Ecclesiastes
Esther
Daniel
Ezra
Nehemiah
1 Chronicles
2 Chronicles
The Writings

The books in the three parts of the Tenakh, the Hebrew Bible.

The Talmud

The Talmud is a sacred text based on the Torah. The laws and commandments that God gave to Moses are found in the Torah. However, the Talmud explains the laws in much more detail. It helps Jews to see how the laws can be applied to all aspects of their daily lives. Long ago some great rabbis (Jewish teachers) studied the Torah very carefully. The rabbis were experts on the Torah and explained how the laws and the Ten Commandments should be kept. For centuries their teaching was passed on by word of mouth. Then in about 500CE all their work was gathered together and written down in the Talmud

The Talmud is regarded as one of the sacred texts of Judaism. It is important because it helps Jews to have an even better understanding of what God is asking them to do. The Talmud is a document of faith that helps Jewish people to better understand and practice their religion.

Questions

Knowledge

1. What is the primary source of information about the religion of Judaism?
2. What do Jews call their sacred text?
3. Name the three main parts of the Tenakh or the Hebrew Bible.
4. How many books are in the Hebrew Bible altogether?
5. What is the Torah?
6. List the books in the Torah.
7. In the Hebrew Bible name the:
   a. Two founders of Judaism.
   b. Two books outlining their stories.
8. What is the Talmud?
9. Who wrote the Talmud?
10. Explain the connection between the Torah and the Talmud.

Understanding

1. Why is the sacred text of Judaism known as the Tenakh?
2. What kind of books are contained in each part of the Tenakh?
3. Why do you think the Torah is regarded as the most important part of the Tenakh?
4. How do you think the Jewish sacred text, the Talmud, helps Jews to practice their faith?

Research

- Find out more about the Talmud.
  a. How many authors contributed to it?
  b. What size is it? How many words/pages does it contain?
  c. When was the task of putting it all together actually completed?
  d. What is the Mishnah?
  e. Who was rabbi Judah 'The Prince' (135-217CE)?
  f. The Talmud is the 'Oral Law'. What does this statement mean?
  - Summarise your findings for the benefit of the class.

Oral and Written Tradition

Key Concepts

Oral tradition: stories and religious teaching that a people pass on by word of mouth.

Sacred text: the book of holy or sacred writing of a community of faith.

Revelation: the way in which God chooses to make himself known to human beings.

Inspiration: the way in which a person is guided by God to pass on a sacred message.

Objective

Trace the development of Jewish sacred texts from the oral tradition to the written word.

Activity: *"Memories"*

TASK: TO CHECK OUR ABILITY TO COMMIT THINGS TO MEMORY.

? The alphabet. ? Class timetable. ?

Recipes. ? Car reg. numbers.

Song lyrics. Phone numbers. ?

? ? ? Sport squads.

Football results. Map directions.

? Birthdays. ? Maths formulae. ?

Discuss

- State at least two things you have committed to memory.
- What is your earliest memory? What age were you then?
- What is your best memory?

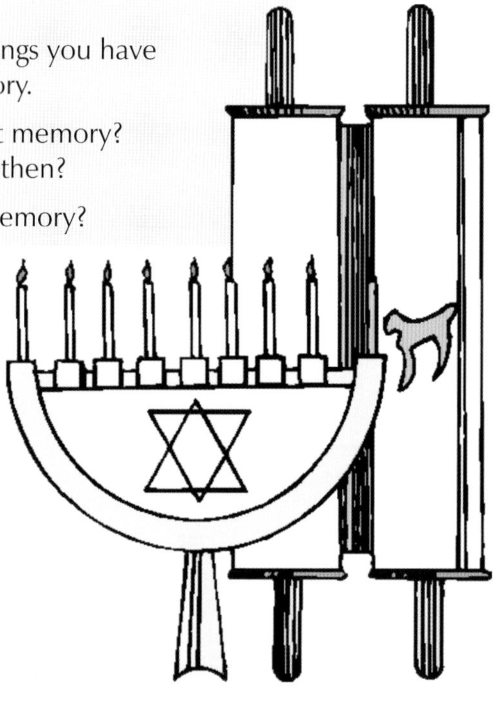

Oral Tradition

The Jews had a lot of memories of God's action in their lives. For centuries the memories were carefully passed on by word of mouth before being eventually written down.

The history of the Jewish people began with Abraham, then Moses, and later the Prophets. For a long time the detail of their story was passed on by word of mouth. Parents told their children the stories of their ancestors. Imagine families sitting together at night around campfires under a desert sky, the children listening to stories about the action of God in the lives of Abraham, Moses, and the chosen people. All the details were carefully remembered.

These memories were handed down as stories, sayings and teachings from one generation to the next. This was the oral stage of Jewish scripture. It was the time when the events of the past were passed on by word of mouth. Most people at that time could not read or write. Precious memories were re-told again and again so the details would not be forgotten. The oral stage lasted for many centuries.

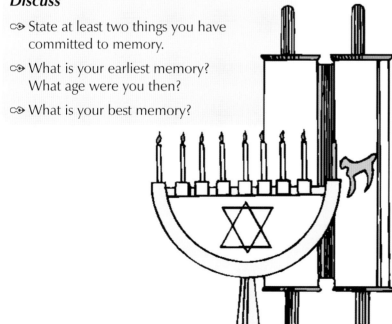

The Written Stage

The history of God's action in the life of God's chosen people was eventually written down. Jewish scripture (sacred writing) was written down between 900BCE and 90CE.

> **Jewish Scripture**
>
> ❖ Stage 1 - handed down orally.
>
> ❖ Stage 2 - set in writing.
>
> ❖ Stage 3 - writings collected together.
> 90CE The Tenakh.
> 500CE The Talmud.

The Hebrew Bible was written by different people from very different backgrounds. The authors had many talents and a variety of writing styles.

- Some were good at story-telling, or writing poetry, songs, or legends.
- More were good at teaching and passing on wise sayings.
- Others were good at legal work that involved facts and figures.
- Many were good at prophesy, being able to show how God was at work in the world.

In this way different authors were inspired to write different parts of the scriptures. The holy writings developed very slowly. They were written down over a period of about 1,000 years.

Sacred Text

The Tenakh

Eventually, some people thought it would be a good idea to have all the scripture together in one volume. They thought it would help the faith of Jewish people in the future. So the work of the different scriptural authors was collected together. God inspired scribes (Jewish writers) to select and edit the sacred writings.

In 90CE the seal of approval was given to thirty nine books. The result was the Tenakh or the Hebrew Bible as it exists today.

The Talmud

The Talmud is another sacred text. It is like a rule book that helps Jewish people to live good lives. The Talmud is based on the Torah - it explains the Torah in more detail.

Jewish rabbis studied all the laws in the Torah. Then they taught the Jews how to put the laws into practice in their daily lives. At first the rabbis' teachings were passed on orally, by word of mouth. Later the teachings were collected together and were finally written down as the Talmud about 500CE.

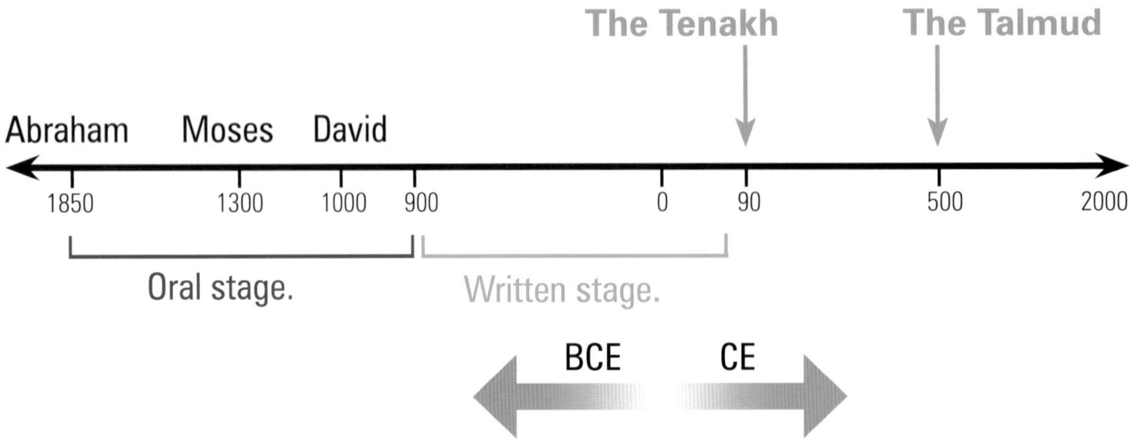
The Tenakh
The Talmud
Abraham
Moses
David
1850
1300
1000
900
0
90
500
2000
Oral stage.
Written stage.
BCE
CE

Revelation

Revelation is the way in which God made himself known to human beings. God made himself known first to Abraham. The founding father of Judaism was the first person to get a glimpse of what God is like (Genesis 15:6-7). Then God called Moses. God revealed himself more fully to Moses than to anyone else.

- ❖ God revealed his holy name - Yahweh. Exodus 3:14-15
- ❖ God revealed that he is good, fair and just.
- ❖ God revealed how he wants people to live when he gave the Law and the Ten Commandments to Moses on Mount Sinai. Exodus20:1-17

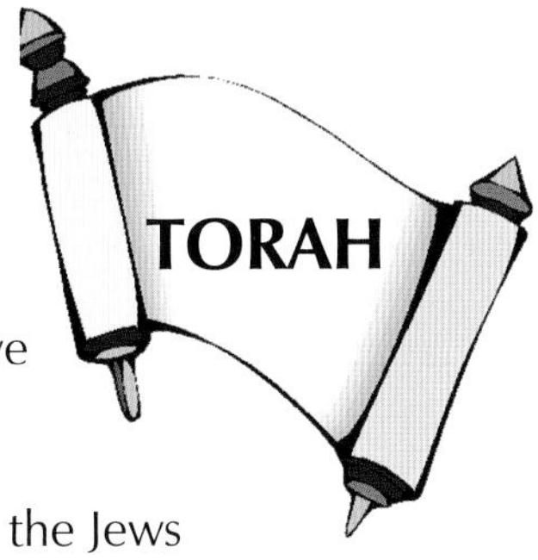
TORAH

All this is written in the Torah. Most Jews believe that the words in the Torah are the words of God himself. The more the Jews study the Torah and live by the Torah the more they will know God. In this way the Jews reveal to the rest of the world what God has revealed to them.

- ❖ God is one and is all-powerful.
- ❖ God is good, fair and just.

Inspiration

Jews believe that all other parts of the Tenakh, the Prophets and the Writings, are inspired by God. This means the human authors of the Prophets and the Writings were guided by God to pass on a sacred message to the Jewish people.

The writers were ordinary people from all walks of life. What they had in common was that God was important in their lives. They were close to God, and God worked through them. Even so, they were free to use their own unique gifts and talents in their writing. In this way they used their own words and style of writing to say what God wanted them to say. This is called biblical inspiration.

Questions

Knowledge

1. Name two important people at the beginning of Jewish history?
2. List the three stages Jewish scripture went through to reach the form the Tenakh has today.
3. What happened during the oral stage of Jewish scripture?
4. What was the written stage of Jewish scripture?
5. What happened to Jewish scripture in 90CE?
6. Who were the authors of the Talmud?
7. What is revelation in sacred scripture?
8. a. What did God reveal to Abraham?
   b. What did God reveal to Moses?
9. Who inspired the authors of both the Prophets and the Writings?
10. What kind of writing styles can be found throughout the Tenakh?

Understanding

1. Describe the three stages through which Jewish scripture passed, to reach the form the Tenakh has today.
2. In Jewish scripture what is meant by:
   a. Revelation? b. Inspiration?
3. Why do you think Jewish scripture:
   a. Was not written down for a long time?
   b. Was eventually written?

Research

- Compare two written accounts of God's action on behalf of the Jews in the Tenakh or Hebrew Bible. For example, *"The Exodus - Moses leads the people out of Egypt to the Promised Land."*
  - Read the story of this event in Exodus 14, 16, 17:1-7
    Read a poem about this event in Psalm 78:1-29
  - Give two reasons why the poet composed the poem.
  - List the ways in which God helped the Jews, the chosen people of God.
  - What do you notice about the style of writing in the two accounts?
  - The Book of Exodus was written almost 700 years after the Exodus itself took place. Can you explain how the detail of the story remained intact for so long?
  - Share your conclusions with the class.

The Dead Sea Scrolls

Key Concept

Sacred text: a book of holy or sacred writings of a community of faith.

Objective

Explain how an archaeological discovery provided more information about Hebrew scripture.

Activity: *"Hebrew"*

TASK: TO KNOW SOME FACTS ABOUT THE HEBREW LANGUAGE.

- Hebrew is the ancient language of the Jewish people.
- Most of the Tenakh was written in Hebrew.
- Unlike English writing, Hebrew is written from right to left.
- The Hebrew language has twenty two letters (English has twenty six letters). Hebrew has no vowels (A, E, I, O and U).
- In the synagogue, the five books of the Torah are handwritten on scrolls in the Hebrew language.
- The Torah is read in Hebrew.

Discuss

- List any five points of information about the Hebrew language.

Jericho
River Jordan
Jerusalem
Qumran
Kidron River
Bethlehem
Dead Sea

Qumran - the site where Dead Sea Scro[lls] were discovere[d]

An Archaeological Discovery

Ancient scrolls written in the Hebrew language were discovered about sixty years ago.

In 1947 some priceless treasure was found by accident near the Dead Sea. It was discovered by a Bedouin shepherd boy in a place called Qumran. He was minding a herd of goats when one of the animals wandered off. The boy went after it, and climbed up the side of a steep hill. He was searching among the rocks when he came across the opening to a cave. He threw a stone into the cave to chase the goat out if it was inside. Instead he heard the sound of something breaking. The young boy got scared and ran off.

The next day he came back with his cousin to investigate. The boys explored the cave and discovered that it was full of large pottery jars. Bundles of scrolls covered in writing were found inside many of the jars.

A segment of a scroll found at Qumran, near the Dead Sea.

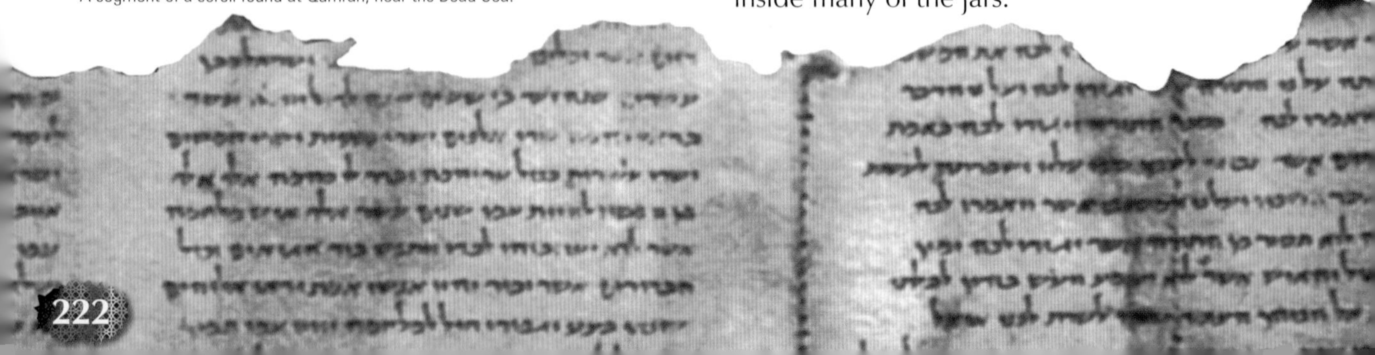

Sacred text

When archaeologists heard about the find in Qumran there was great excitement. The jars contained a lot of ancient documents including copies of Jewish scripture.

A treasure hunt began. Archaeologists searched all the caves in the area. In the end they found two hundred documents of scripture, most of which were in good condition. A scientific process called carbon dating showed that the material was over 2,000 years old. Jewish experts examined the Hebrew writing on the scrolls and discovered that the scrolls were handwritten copies of almost every book in the Tenakh. Before the Dead Sea Scrolls were found, the oldest Hebrew scroll in existence was 1,000 years old. The scrolls from Qumran were 2,000 years old.

Experts later compared scrolls from both periods and found, for example, that two scrolls of the prophet Isaiah were almost identical. This shows the careful way in which Jewish scribes copied the scriptures over the centuries.

Some people think the Dead Sea Scrolls were part of a library that belonged to the Essenes, a community of Jewish monks who lived in Qumran in the first century CE. The monks stored their writing in airtight jars. When the Romans arrived in the region they may have hidden the jars in the caves to keep them safe.

Scrolls

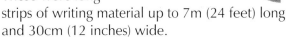

When the Hebrew scriptures were written long ago books had not been invented. Instead people wrote on scrolls. These were long strips of writing material up to 7m (24 feet) long and 30cm (12 inches) wide.

Papyrus The earliest scrolls were made from papyrus (from which we get the word paper). Papyrus is a reed that grows near lakes. Long ago this reed was cut and gathered to make scrolls. The layer on the outside of the reed was peeled off and the inside was cut into strips. The strips were placed side by side and beaten together into long sheets. When the material was smooth enough, the papyrus was ready to be written on. The finished sheet of papyrus was then joined to wooden rods and rolled up from both sides to make a scroll.

Parchment Later on, the scriptures were written on parchment. Parchment is a writing material made from animal hide. Goatskin and sheepskin were scraped clean and made into thin leather sheets. These sheets were sewn together to make one long strip of parchment. The two ends of the parchment were joined to wooden rods and then rolled up from both ends to make a scroll. When not in use, the scrolls were wrapped in a cloth and put in tall jars for safe keeping.

The Scroll Timeline

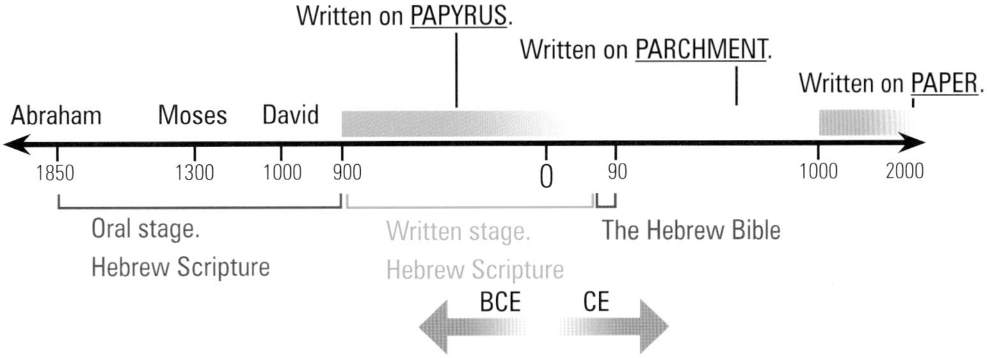
Written on PAPYRUS.
Written on PARCHMENT.
Written on PAPER.
Abraham
Moses
David
1850
1300
1000
900
0
90
1000
2000
Oral stage.
Hebrew Scripture
Written stage.
Hebrew Scripture
The Hebrew Bible
BCE
CE

Scribes

Scribes were Jewish writers who made copies of Hebrew scripture. The scribes wrote on the scrolls with a small reed. The top of the reed was shredded to make a tiny brush. Scribes were very careful when they copied the Hebrew scripture onto the scrolls. They began their work with a silent prayer. Then they looked carefully at the text. They had to say each word aloud before writing it down - this helped the scribes to avoid making mistakes.

When it came to writing a holy name they had to stop and first say the words "I intend to write *the* holy name." If a scribe forgot to say it, even once, then he had to go back to the beginning and start all over again. This made the scribes realise that writing down God's word in scripture was different from all other writing tasks. It must be done carefully and with great respect.

Exercise - "Scribes"

You will need: use of a blackboard and chalk, or a flipchart and markers.

Individually, or in small groups, one or more volunteers will demonstrate the role of the Jewish scribe for the benefit of the class.

1. Adopt the role of a Jewish scribe.
2. Copy down the following verse from the Tenakh.
   "God said, 'Do not come any closer, take off your sandals, because you are standing on holy ground. I am the God of your ancestors, the God of Abraham, Isaac and Jacob.'" Exodus 3:5-6
3. Follow these rules.
   - Pray silently before writing from scripture.
   - Say every word aloud before copying it down.
   - Before writing the name of God say "I intend to write the holy name."
   - If any of these rules are broken, start all over again.
4. Discussion:
   Why is every word said aloud before it is written down? Why say a special sentence before writing the name of God?

Questions

Knowledge

1. Who found the Dead Sea Scrolls?
2. When and where were the Dead Sea Scrolls discovered?
3. How many scrolls of Hebrew scripture were found at Qumran?
4. How old are the scrolls that were found at Qumran?
5. What was written on the Dead Sea Scrolls?
6. Give reasons why the scrolls were in such good condition.
7. What material were scrolls made of around 2,000 years ago?
8. What was the task of a Jewish scribe long ago?

Understanding

1. Why were scrolls hidden at Qumran around 2,000 years ago?
2. Why is the discovery of the Dead Sea Scrolls so important?
3. What evidence is there to show that Jewish scribes have always taken their religious duties very seriously?

Research

- Find out more about the Dead Sea Scrolls from reference books and the Internet.
  - Where are the scrolls kept today?
  - Who examines or studies the scrolls found at Qumran?
  - What is now known about Hebrew scripture after more than sixty years investigating the Dead Sea Scrolls?
  - Share your discoveries with the class.

Belief and Practice

Key Concepts

Creed/ Ethic: the summary of a religion's deeply held beliefs and moral principles.

Practice: customs and rituals that show a person's religious faith.

Objective

Identify the main beliefs of Judaism and how these beliefs are put into practice.

Activity: *"Creeds for Today"*

TASK: TO SHARE BELIEFS ON CERTAIN ISSUES.

✦ What do you believe?

I believe...
I believe God is good.
I believe that if you do the crime you do the time.
I believe charity begins at home.
I believe in love.
I believe that when we die that's it!
I believe...

Discuss

- What beliefs are held by the members of this class?
- What beliefs or convictions are held by members of your family?
- Do you have a strong belief about something important?

Creed/ Ethic

Jews believe in God and put their belief into practice in particular ways.

A creed is a statement that sums up what people believe about something important. The Shema is a Jewish prayer and the nearest thing to a creed in the religion of Judaism. It is a summary of Jewish belief about God.

The Shema Deuteronomy 6:4-5 (Tenakh)

4. "Hear O Israel.
The Lord is our God, the Lord alone.
5. You shall love the Lord your God with all your heart and with all your soul, and with all your might."

Many Jews say this prayer twice daily, morning and evening. The name for God in Hebrew scripture is Yahweh (Yhwh). Yet Jews have such deep respect for God's name that they will not say it aloud. When praying to God the word 'Lord' is used instead.

Main Jewish beliefs

Jews believe:

- In one God, Yahweh, who is good and all-powerful; the creator of the world.
- That they are God's chosen people.
- God made a covenant with Abraham and Moses, and they must be faithful to it.
- God gave Moses the Torah (containing the Law and the ten commandments) to help Jewish people live good and holy lives.

Practice

Jews show their religious belief in the things that they do. Practice is the set of customs and rituals that show a person's religious faith. Jews put their religious beliefs into practice through a range of daily, weekly, annual and life-changing rituals. It is clear that religion affects their lives in many different ways. Jews participate in:

Daily rituals such as...

- Saying the Shema morning and evening.
- Wearing tefillin (small leather boxes containing the Shema) at prayer times.
- Touching the mezuzah (containing the Shema) on the doorframe of their homes.

Weekly rituals such as...

- The celebration of the Sabbath.

Annual rituals such as...

- The celebration of religious feasts and festivals.

Life changing rituals such as...

- The circumcision of a baby boy after birth.
- Bar-mitzvah and bat-mitzvah.
- Wedding ceremonies.
- Death and mourning.

All these customs and rituals are a normal part of life in the Jewish community. It is how Jews express their religious beliefs and their commitment to their faith.

A daily ritual

Touching a mezuzah, as they enter and leave the house, is a daily ritual that reminds Jews of the central creed of their religion. A mezuzah is a small box containing a tiny scroll on which the words of the Shema are hand-written in Hebrew. The box is fitted to the doorframe of a Jewish house, on the right hand side just above eye-level. The mezuzah reminds Jews of the presence of God and that they must follow the law of God in their daily life.

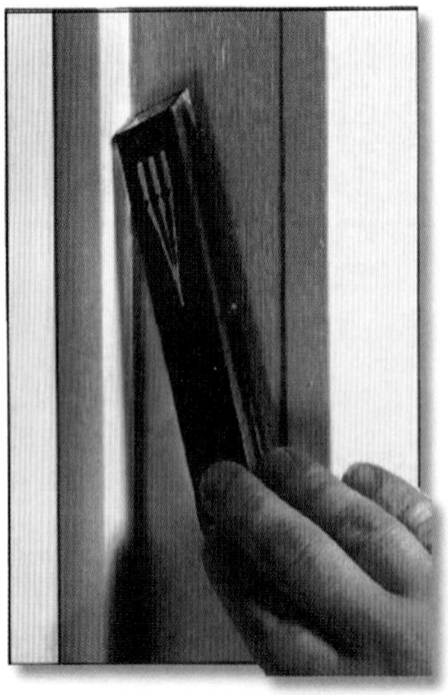

A Mezuzah.

A Jewish man dressed for prayer beside the Western Wall in Jerusalem.

Questions

Knowledge

1. What is a creed?
2. What are the words of the Shema in Deuteronomy 6:4-5?
3. How do Jews show respect for God's name?
4. Name two important Jewish beliefs.
5. Give an example of a daily and a weekly religious practice in Judaism.
6. How do Jews show their commitment to their faith?

Understanding

1. Provide a summary of the main beliefs in Judaism.
2. Explain the connection between a Jewish person's religious beliefs and their daily or weekly religious practice.
3. Give as many reasons as you can to explain why Judaism has a certain creed and code of practice for its members.

Research

- Find out about the creed of one other religious tradition e.g. Christianity or Islam.
  - Does the creed have a title?
  - In what religious text is it written down?
  - What are the words of the creed?
  - Select one belief stated in the creed and show how believers could put it into practice.
  - Discuss the issues with the class.

Prayer

Key Concept

Prayer: the act of communicating with God.

Objective

Outline the importance of prayer in the religion of Judaism.

Activity: *"Keeping in Touch"*

TASK: TO EXAMINE HOW FRIENDS COMMUNICATE WITH ONE ANOTHER.

- Analyse the amount of time you spend communicating with your friends during a typical school day, e.g. on the way to school, at break times, after school etc.
- Do you at any time do any of the following to keep in touch with your friends: (✓)
  - Make a phone call. ☐
  - Send a text. ☐
  - Call around to their house. ☐
  - Send a postcard. ☐
  - Meet for a chat. ☐
  - Use sign language. ☐
  - Send a greeting card. ☐
  - Pass a note during class. ☐
  - Send an email. ☐
  - Use a networking site. ☐

Discuss

- How long do you spend talking to your friends on an average school day?
- When do you talk together?
- What kind of things do you talk about?
- Why do friends spend so much time keeping in touch with each other?

Prayer

Prayer is about keeping in touch with God.

Prayer is how Jewish people communicate with God. Communication with God involves spending time with God. It means talking to God and listening to God.

Abraham and Moses, the founders of Judaism, were able to show the Jews that God is a personal God with whom Jewish people can have a relationship. Abraham and Moses communicated with God through prayer. Jews stay in touch with God through prayer too. The more Jewish people pray, the more their relationship with God will grow and develop.

Jewish men at prayer.

Ways to pray

It is important for Jewish people to spend time with God. Jews can pray at home or in the synagogue.

Personal prayer is when Jews pray by themselves at home during the week.

Communal prayer is when Jews pray with others as part of a community. For example, attending the synagogue on the morning of the Sabbath, and praying together as a family at home on the Sabbath and during religious festivals such as Pesach (Passover).

Clothes for prayer

Male Jews over thirteen years of age are expected to pray three times a day, in the morning, afternoon and evening. Jewish men dress in a special way for weekly prayer. They put on a number of symbolic items, for example, a kippah is a cap that is worn on the head. A tallit is a shawl that is worn around the shoulders. A tefillin is a small leather box that is tied to the forehead and to the left arm, near the heart. The words of the Shema are written on a tiny scroll inside the tefillin. This is a reminder to Jewish people to bring the mind and heart to God in prayer.

When Jewish people pray, they pray aloud reciting prayers from the scriptures and other holy books. The Siddur is the Jewish prayer book. It has the main 'set' prayers, which are said every day and on the Sabbath. The most important Jewish prayer is the Shema (Deut 6:4-6). Jews try to say it as often as possible.

Different types of prayer

The Psalms are the great prayers of Judaism. There are 150 psalms altogether written by people who felt the need to speak to God about what was going on in their lives. Each psalm is a prayer to God. The Book of Psalms contains different types of prayers. There are:

Prayers of Praise and Thanksgiving thanking God for some good thing that has happened.

Prayers of Petition asking God for help with something special.

Prayers of Penitence expressing sorrow for some wrongdoing and asking for forgiveness.

Questions

Knowledge

1. How do people communicate with God?
2. Where and when do Jews communicate with God?
3. How do Jewish men dress for prayer?
4. What is the Siddur?
5. What is the Shema?
6. What is: a. Personal prayer?
   b. Communal prayer?
7. What are the Psalms?
8. Name the different types of prayer in the Book of Psalms?

Understanding

1. Why is prayer important to Jewish people?
2. Explain what is distinctive about the way Jewish people pray?
3. Why do you think there are different types of prayer in the Jewish tradition?
4. How is daily prayer an indicator of a person's religious commitment?

Research

Scripture Search

Long ago, Moses taught the Jewish people the great commandment of God. This is a summary of all the laws of God and is found in the words of the Shema. To make sure the Jews would always remember it, Moses asked them to:

- Repeat it many times a day.
- Pass it on from generation to generation.
- Do something to remind themselves of it.

* Read Deuteronomy 6:1-9
  a. What are the words of the Shema? (Verse 4-6)
  b. How is it to be passed on? (Verse 7)
  c. When is it to be said? (Verse 7)
  d. What must people do to remind themselves of it every day? (Verse 8-9)
* Show the class a summary of these points.

Jewish schoolboys pray at the Western Wall in Jerusalem.

The Sabbath

Key Concept

Ritual: an occasion when people use symbolic objects, words and actions to express what is deeply important to them.

Objective

Describe the ritual of 'Shabbat', the Jewish holy day of the week.

Activity: *"Time out"*

TASK: TO REFLECT ON THE BENEFITS OF HAVING TIME TO REST AND TO WORSHIP.

Imagine if everyone had to work seven days a week with no days off. What would it be like if you had to go to school every day - Saturday and Sunday included? It's thanks to the Jewish community and their idea of a day of rest that everyone now has at least one day off a week.

At the time of Moses, people expected slaves and servants to work every day without rest. The Jews were different. They obeyed a commandment which told them to rest on the Sabbath. It meant the entire household had to rest, slaves and servants included.

The Sabbath was a special day set aside every week for rest and prayer. Today, Jews go to the synagogue on the Sabbath and spend the rest of the time relaxing at home with their families. The Talmud lists thirty nine different types of work that must not be done on the Sabbath. For Jews today this means that on the Sabbath they must not:

- Go out to work.
- Go to school.
- Do housework.
- Do homework.
- Use public transport.
- Cook food.
- Go shopping.
- Answer the phone.

The Sabbath is a holy day, Jews may not do any work at all on this day.

Discuss

- What kind of things do people do at weekends? List the benefits of taking 'time out' of the weekly routine?
- Jews take time out on the Sabbath to pray, to reflect on life and to be with their families. What is helpful about spending a day in this way?

The Jewish Sabbath

People need time for peace and quiet in their lives.

The Sabbath - or 'Shabbat' in Hebrew - is a holy day for Jewish people. It is one day a week set aside for rest and prayer. Shabbat begins at sunset on Friday and ends at sunset on Saturday. Jews celebrate this sacred time with religious services in the home and in the synagogue.

The celebration of the Jewish Sabbath goes back to ancient times. The Torah contains the story of how God created the world in six days. On the seventh day God rested. Much later, when God gave the Ten Commandments to Moses on Mount Sinai, God said:

"Remember the Sabbath day and keep it holy."

Exodus 20:8-11.

The Jews obeyed God and have kept the Sabbath day holy for thousands of years. On the Sabbath, Jews celebrate their special relationship with God. They praise God for his goodness and thank God for caring for the chosen people throughout the ages.

Table set for Shabbat with lighted candle, challah bread and a glass of wine.

Ritual

A ritual is an occasion when people use symbolic objects, words and actions to express what is deeply important to them. Certain things are always said and done on the Jewish Sabbath. The Sabbath rituals help Jews express what is deeply important and matters most in their lives.

Preparing for the Sabbath

On Friday afternoon the family home is tidied, the shopping is done and a nice meal is prepared. Jewish families try to make the Sabbath meal the best they can afford. The table is set with special care. It is covered with a white tablecloth, two candlesticks, a wine glass, a dish of salt and loaves of plaited bread called challah. The bread is specially baked for the Sabbath and is covered with a napkin until the meal begins.

The television and the phones are turned off or taken off the hook. The atmosphere changes, the house becomes quiet and still. Everything is peaceful, it is nearly sunset.

Welcoming the Sabbath

At sunset, the family stand around the table. The mother performs a short ritual. She lights two candles to welcome the Sabbath. She says a prayer and puts her hands over her eyes and asks God to bless the home. Then everyone wishes each other 'Shabbat Shalom', which in Hebrew means 'Have a peaceful Sabbath'. A service is always held in the synagogue on Friday evening. When the men and boys return from the synagogue, the family gather together for the Sabbath meal.

The mother says a prayer to welcome the Sabbath.

The father recites Kiddush at the beginning of the Sabbath meal.

The Kiddush

The Sabbath meal begins with the Kiddush. The father performs this short ritual as the family stand at the table. The father says a blessing over the glass of wine. Everyone drinks from the glass as it is passed around. The wine is a symbol of joy.

Then he says a blessing over the loaves of bread. He breaks the bread and passes a piece to everyone to eat. The plaited bread is a symbol of God, the Torah and the Jewish people united together. Salt from a salt dish is sprinkled on the bread. Salt is a sign of the covenant between God and the Jewish people. (Leviticus 2:13)

The Sabbath Meal

After the Kiddush, the family sit down together to enjoy the Sabbath meal. The food is served, it tastes good, and there is plenty of it. There is a starter, a main course, and a dessert. It is kosher food prepared according to Jewish rules about diet and hygiene. Everyone is calm and relaxed, the family have time to talk and laugh and enjoy each other's company. The meal always ends with a prayer of thanksgiving.

The Sabbath Day

On Saturday mornings Jewish families attend a service in the synagogue. Afterwards they return home to relax and enjoy the day together. The Sabbath is different to all other days. It is a holy day, no work of any kind is done. The Sabbath is a day of rest and enjoyment for all the family. It is a day of prayer when Jews give thanks to God for all their blessings.

The Havdalah

The Sabbath ends at sunset on Saturday. It is marked by Havdalah, a short ritual carried out in the home. This marks the separation of the Sabbath from the rest of the week.

The father says a blessing and lights a special plaited candle. A box of sweet smelling spices is passed around. This ritual symbolises the hope that the sweetness of the Sabbath will light up the week ahead for everyone.

- ✡ A glass of wine: a symbol that the joy of the Sabbath will be carried into the coming week.
- ✡ Spices: a symbol that the sweetness of the Sabbath will spread into the coming week.
- ✡ A plaited candle: a symbol that the unity of God, the Torah and the Jewish people will light up the coming week.

After the blessing a drop of wine is poured over the havdalah candle to put it out.

Questions

Knowledge

1. What is the sacred time of the week for Jewish people?
2. When does the Jewish Sabbath begin and end?
3. What do Jews celebrate on the Sabbath?
4. How do Jewish families prepare for the Sabbath?
5. What is the atmosphere like in a Jewish home on the Sabbath?
6. What does a Jewish mother do at the start of the Sabbath?
7. What does a Jewish father do at the start of the Sabbath?
8. What food do Jewish families eat at the Sabbath meal?
9. When do Jews go to the synagogue during the Sabbath?
10. What ritual brings the Sabbath to a close?

Understanding

1. Why do Jews set aside sacred time every week?
2. Describe the rituals that are performed in a Jewish home:
   a. at the beginning of Shabbat.
   b. at the end of Shabbat.
3. What effect might the Jewish way of celebrating the Sabbath have on Jewish family life, in your opinion?

Research

❂ Find out about kosher food.

The Torah gives no reason for food laws. However they are a mark of Jewish identity. Food laws are a daily reminder of the importance of obeying the will of God.

- What does the Hebrew word "kosher" mean in English?
- Where in the Torah are Jewish food laws written down?
- What foods are kosher?
- What foods ordinarily available in supermarkets are Jews forbidden to eat?
- In Jewish households what foods must <u>not</u> be:
  - cooked together? - eaten together?
  - prepared using the same utensils?
- What is distinctive about the way meat is prepared in a kosher butcher shop?
- Share the results of your research with the class.

Place of Worship

Key Concept

Place of worship: a building or place where people go to pray and worship God or gods.

Objective

Describe a Jewish place of worship.

Section C

Activity: *"Places of Significance"*

TASK: TO IDENTIFY PLACES THAT HAVE SIGNIFICANCE IN OUR LIVES.

✦ Think about the homes in which we live.

Discuss

- What is it about your home that makes it special for you?
- How important is your home to you? Rate it on a scale of 1-10.

1	2	3	4	5	6	7	8	9	10
Not important.									Very Important.

- Is there any other place that has meaning or significance in your life?

Place of Worship

The synagogue is a place of special significance for members of the Jewish community.

A synagogue is a place of worship. It is a building where Jews go to pray and worship God. The word 'synagogue' means 'meeting place'. Jews meet in the synagogue for different reasons:

❖ To worship. ❖ To learn. ❖ To socialise.

The Synagogue

The synagogue is at the centre of Jewish community life. It is a multi-purpose building with space for worship in the main part of the building. There is also space for learning in the classrooms and in the library. Here children are taught Hebrew, the language in which the Torah is written. Adults visit the library to study Jewish scripture. The synagogue also contains a community hall, a kitchen, and some rooms for social gatherings.

There are no rules about what a synagogue should look like on the outside. However, a Jewish symbol such as the Magen David, or Star of David, will usually decorate the front of the building. Synagogues vary in size. Some are big, others are small, it all depends on the needs of the local Jewish community.

A synagogue is usually a plain rectangular building, one wall of which faces the holy city of Jerusalem. The windows may be plain or have stained glass showing images from Jewish festivals. There are no pictures or statues, Jewish law forbids the use of images that depict God. Inside the front door there is a hallway with two doors. One door leads into the main part of the synagogue. The other door leads up a stairway to a balcony overlooking the main worship area.

A synagogue in Dublin.

LAMP
STONE TABLETS
ARK
MEN'S SEATS
BIMAH
MEN'S SEATS
WOMEN'S SEATS UPSTAIRS IN THE BALCONY

Inside a synagogue.

The synagogue interior

The layout of the worship area in a synagogue is based on the ancient Temple in Jerusalem. It has the following features.

The Ark: A special cabinet with a curtain at the front.

Scrolls of the Torah: The books of Moses hand-written on scrolls. Each scroll is covered in a mantle and kept in the Ark.

Everlasting Light: A lamp that burns day and night in front of the Ark.

Stone Tablets: The ten commandments on stone plaques near the Ark.

Bimah: A raised platform in the centre of the synagogue with a reading desk for the scrolls of the Torah.

Seating: Men sit downstairs, women sit upstairs in the balcony.

The Ark

The focal point in a synagogue is the Ark, a special cabinet set in a wall that faces Jerusalem. The Ark in a synagogue is like the Holy of Holies in the Temple in Jerusalem. In ancient times, the entrance to the Holy of Holies was covered by a long veil. Today the front of the Ark in a synagogue is sometimes covered with a beautifully embroidered curtain.

The Ark is named after the Ark of the Covenant, a wooden chest said to contain the tablets of the covenant that God gave to Moses on Mount Sinai. The Temple in Jerusalem was originally built to house the Ark of the Covenant.

Scrolls of the Torah

The Torah scrolls are kept in the Ark. The Torah is the five books of Moses. Each book is handwritten on a scroll in the Hebrew language. Most Jews believe the words in the Torah are the actual words of God himself. The Torah is therefore treated with great respect by Jewish people.

The Sefer Torah, or handwritten scrolls, are looked after very carefully. Each one is wrapped in a special cover when it is put away in the Ark. The cover is usually made of velvet and is called a mantle. Mantles are decorated with tassels and embroidery. Silver ornaments in the form of a crown, tiny bells and a breastplate are sometimes added too.

ואם לא עכשו אימתי

Scrolls inside the Ark.

Jews show respect for their sacred text by having handwritten scrolls of the Torah for use in the synagogue. The sacred scrolls are placed in the Ark for safekeeping. A yad, or pointer, is used to avoid touching the scroll when it is being read.

The Everlasting Light

In front of the Ark is the Everlasting Light. This is a special lamp that is kept burning day and night to remember the menorah that was lit before the Holy of Holies in the Temple in Jerusalem. The Everlasting Light reminds the Jews that God is always with them. A menorah is a seven branched candlestick. Many synagogues have a menorah, it is an ancient symbol of Judaism.

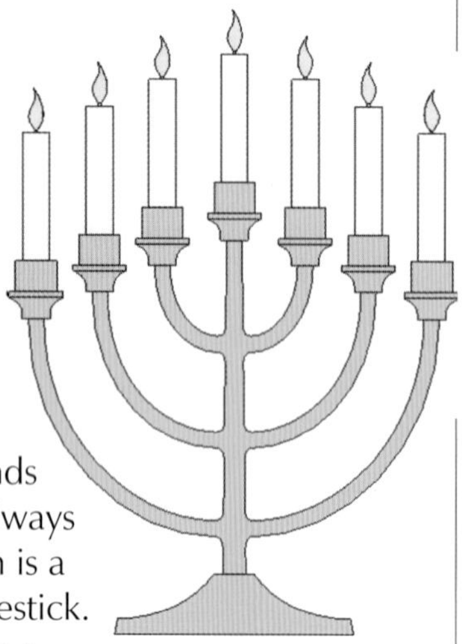

Stone Tablets

Near the Ark are two stone plaques on which are written the Ten Commandments given to Moses on Mount Sinai. The first words of each commandment are written in Hebrew.

The Bimah

The Bimah is at the centre of the synagogue. It is a raised platform with a reading desk on top. The Sefer Torah is placed on the desk when it is taken out to be read at a synagogue service. This happens on the Sabbath and at festivals throughout the year. The leader of the synagogue service stands at the bimah.

Seating

Men and women sit separately in most synagogues. Women sit upstairs in a balcony while men sit downstairs in the main part of the synagogue. There are special seats at the front for the men who lead the service. During the service, everyone faces the Ark. The Ark in turn faces the holy city of Jerusalem.

Questions

Knowledge

1. Where do Jews gather to worship God?
2. What is the Ark? What is kept in it?
3. How are the scrolls of the Torah protected when not in use?
4. What is the Everlasting Light? How might it remind people of God?
5. Where is the bimah in the synagogue? What is its function?
6. Where is an image of the Ten Commandments to be found in a synagogue?
7. What is a menorah?
8. Where do men and women sit in most synagogues?

Understanding

1. Describe the main features of a Jewish place of worship.
2. How do Jews show respect for the sacred scriptures that are kept in the synagogue?
3. Why do you think the Ark is such an important feature in a synagogue?

Research

✪ Read Jewish scripture to find out a little more about some of the features in a synagogue today and what each one symbolises.

On Mount Sinai God instructed Moses how to organise worship to the one God. Worship was carried out initially in a special tent in the desert. Later, when the Jews settled in the Promised Land, the same form of worship was carried out in the Temple in Jerusalem. In 70CE the Temple in Jerusalem was destroyed by the Romans. Local synagogues became the centre of Jewish worship from then onwards.

- The Torah
  The laws given to Moses on Mount Sinai.
  Read Exodus 20:1-17 & Exodus 24:12
- The Ark
  The wooden chest containing the two stone tablets on which the commandments were written.
  Read Exodus 25:10-22
- The Curtain
  The veil that hung like a curtain before the chest containing the two tablets. Read Exodus 26:31-33
- Everlasting Light
  The light kept burning day and night before the Ark of the Covenant. Read Exodus 27:20-21
- Mantle for the Torah
  The ritual clothes worn by the priests represented by:
  - the breast plate - Read Exodus 28:29-30
  - the tiny bells - Read Exodus 28:33-35

✹ Consider what it means that Jews have faithfully kept these symbolic features in their worship for thousands of years.

Worship in the Synagogue

Key Concepts

Worship: the way people of faith praise and honour God in prayer and at religious services.

Ritual: an occasion when people use symbolic objects, words and actions to express what is deeply important to them.

Objective

Outline the main features of Sabbath worship in a synagogue.

Activity: *"In Your Honour"*

TASK: BE AWARE THAT THERE ARE TIMES WHEN WE SHOW CERTAIN PEOPLE HOW MUCH WE ADMIRE AND RESPECT THEM FOR WHAT THEY HAVE ACHIEVED.

✦ When we wish to honour people who have achieved something worthwhile we tend to:

- Organise a special event.
- Invite people to assemble in a certain place at a certain time.
- Request that people dress smartly for the occasion.
- Invite someone to make a speech on behalf of everyone present.
- Say things to praise and thank people for their achievement.
- Do things to indicate our respect and admiration, e.g. stand up, clap, listen attentively, sing (their praises).
- Make a presentation.
- Have a celebration meal.

Discuss

- Think of the last time you were present at an event where a person(s) was honoured for their achievement.
- - What was the occasion?
  - Where did it take place? At what time?
  - Did people dress up or wear special clothes?
  - Who was in charge of the event?
  - What kinds of things were said?
  - What was done to honour the person(s) and to show admiration for their achievement?
  - Was there a meal or a reception?

Worship

Ritual

Jews go to the synagogue to honour God.

Jews praise and honour God both at home and in the synagogue. In Judaism, the home is the more important location for worship. However, many Jews go to the synagogue on Saturday morning for the Sabbath service, it is the main service of the week. Symbolic objects, words and actions are used at this service to give praise and honour to God.

Clothes for Prayer

Jewish men and women cover their heads in the synagogue, it is a way of showing respect for God. Women wear a hat or a scarf. Men and boys over thirteen wear ceremonial clothes such as a kippah (a small round cap worn on the crown of the head). Some men wear a prayer shawl called a tallit around their shoulders. It is white with blue stripes and has tassels at the four corners. Visitors are asked to cover their heads too when they attend a synagogue service.

The Sabbath Service

A ritual is an occasion when people use symbolic actions to express what is important in their lives. The Sabbath service in the synagogue helps Jews express what is deeply important to them. The service is in Hebrew and lasts about an hour. The service includes:

- ❖ Set prayers, including the Shema.
- ❖ Readings from the Torah.
- ❖ Singing the psalms.
- ❖ A sermon. ❖ Private prayer. ❖ A blessing.

The Sabbath service is led by a rabbi or a cantor.

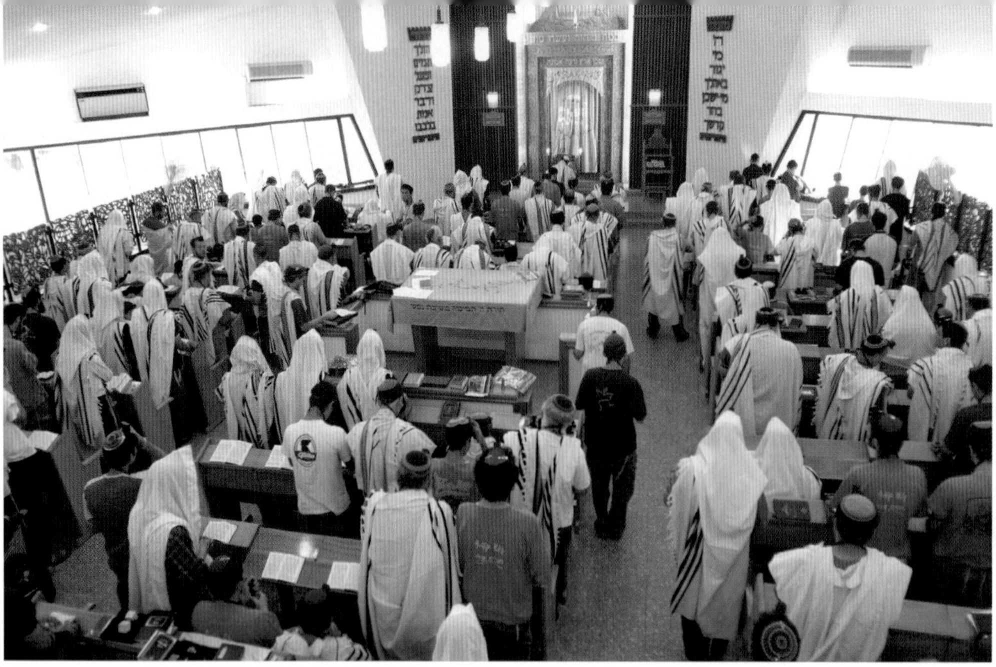

A synagogue service.

The Rabbi

Every synagogue has a rabbi who teaches the Torah. At the Sabbath service the rabbi:

- ❖ Leads the prayers.
- ❖ Reads from the Torah.
- ❖ Gives a sermon.

The Rabbi reading from the Torah.

The Cantor

A cantor is a person with a good singing voice. At the Sabbath service he:

- ❖ Sings the psalms.
- ❖ Chants the prayers.

The cantor leads the congregation in singing the psalms, which are songs of praise to God. The cantor also chants some of the prayers. Chanting is like saying a prayer in a sing-song voice. Jews have chanted prayers for thousands of years. In the synagogue, the chanting and the singing is unaccompanied. Musical instruments are not used in most synagogues.

The Torah

The most important part of the Sabbath service is when the Torah is taken from the Ark and read to the people. It is called the Sefer Torah because a sefer (a scribe) copied it by hand on a scroll of parchment. At the proper time in the service, the ritual begins.

The curtain in front of the Ark is drawn aside. Everyone stands to show their respect for the Law of God in the Torah. The scroll is taken out of the Ark and carried in procession around the synagogue. The bells on the mantle tinkle as it is carried along. The scroll is taken up the steps of the bimah and the mantle is removed.

The scroll is unrolled very carefully. A scroll is about 7m in length. It has a wooden pole at each end. The poles are used for winding the parchment to the reading chosen for the day. The Torah is written in Hebrew, the ancient language of the Jewish people. Everyone sits and listens respectfully as the rabbi reads the Torah aloud. The Torah is the word of God for the Jewish people. A silver pointer called a yad is used to follow the words. The scroll is not touched by hand; it is very precious and this is one way of protecting it.

When the reading and the sermon is over, the scroll is once again carried around the synagogue and put back in the Ark. The service ends with a blessing. After the service, the congregation usually goes to the hall to socialise and have some light refreshments.

לא תרצח
לא תנאף
לא תגנב
לא תענה
לא תחמד
אנכי ״
לא יהיה
לא תשא
זכור את
כבד את

The Ten Commandments written on plaques in a synagogue.

Research

Participation

To participate means to join in and be part of something. People participate in worship as a response to mystery at the heart of human life. Jewish people participate in worship as a response to the mystery of God at the centre of their lives.

- Find out more about Sabbath worship in a synagogue.
  - a. Try to visit a synagogue. It may or may not be possible to observe a form of worship taking place.

  ALTERNATIVELY

  - b. Watch an experience of Sabbath worship on video or DVD to see the different elements of worship in action.

- Observe what happens during the service and answer the following questions.
  1. What is the place of worship?
  2. What day of the week is the service taking place?
  3. What is the occasion?
  4. Who is attending?
  5. Who leads the ceremony?
  6. Do people wear any item of ritual clothing?
  7. What sacred text is used?
  8. Is any kind of music performed as part of the act of worship?
  9. a. List two ritual actions performed during the service.
     b. Who performs these actions?
     c. What is the meaning behind the actions?
  10. a. What was the most memorable part of the service that you just observed?
      b. Can you say why this aspect of the service made an impression on you?

Questions

Knowledge

1. What is the meaning of:
   a. worship?
   b. ritual?
2. Where do Jews worship on the Sabbath morning?
3. What do Jewish men and women wear in the synagogue to show respect for God?
4. What is the role of the rabbi at the Sabbath service?
5. What is the role of the cantor at the Sabbath service?
6. What is the most important part of the Sabbath service in the synagogue?
7. What is the Sefer Torah?
8. List the ways in which the congregation show respect for the Torah at a Sabbath service.

Understanding

1. When Jews gather for worship in a synagogue on the Sabbath:
   a. Whom do they worship?
   b. Why do they worship?
2. Describe what happens at a Jewish Sabbath service in a synagogue.
3. Give reasons why Jews have a day in the week when they honour God in a special way.

Pilgrimage

Key Concepts

Pilgrimage: a journey made by a pilgrim to a shrine or a sacred place.

Ritual: an occasion when people use symbolic objects, words and actions to express what is deeply important to them.

Objective

Identify a Jewish place of pilgrimage and describe how Jews worship there.

Section C

Activity: *"Places of Significance"*

TASK: TO IDENTIFY PLACES THAT ARE IMPORTANT TO US FOR CERTAIN REASONS.

Is there a special place that you like to go to sometimes, maybe by yourself or with others? It might be the the park near your home, or maybe your grandparent's house.

Sometimes I like to visit...

- My friend's house.
- The woods.
- The beach.
- A lake.
- A river.
- The sports grounds.
- The church.
- The park.
- A relative's grave.
- Other...

Discuss

- Identify two places that are special to you in some way. Why do you like to go there sometimes?
- Is there a place that has a special meaning for your whole family? Why do members of your family go there?
- Are there places in this country or elsewhere that are important for other people? Why do you think such places have significance for them?

Pilgrimage

Many people visit places that are important to them for religious reasons.

A pilgrimage is a journey to a holy or a sacred place. Most religions have places that are believed to be sacred and connected to God in a particular way. People who go on pilgrimages to holy places are called pilgrims. They are not tourists who simply want to go somewhere for a holiday; people go on a pilgrimage to pray and get closer to God.

The Western Wall

The Western Wall in the city of Jerusalem is a sacred place and the holiest site in the religion of Judaism. It is a place of pilgrimage for Jews from all over the world even though pilgrimage is not compulsory in Judaism. The Western Wall is the only part of the Temple in Jerusalem that remains standing today. The rest of the building was destroyed by the Romans in 70CE.

Pilgrims gathering at the Western Wall in Jerusalem.

Prayer is the main form of worship at this sacred place. At the Western Wall there is:

- ❖ private prayer - facing the wall.
- ❖ public prayer - in which pilgrims attend services and bar-mitzvahs near the wall.

Praying at the Western Wall in Jerusalem.

The Temple

Jerusalem is the centre of the land that God promised to Abraham and all his descendants. The Temple is believed to be built on the spot where Abraham was prepared to sacrifice his son Isaac. King David's son, Solomon, built a temple on the site to house the Ark of the Covenant, the chest containing the stone tablets of the law given to Moses, by God, on Mount Sinai. Solomon's Temple was destroyed at the time of the Exile, but the Jews rebuilt it again after their return from exile. Years later Herod the Great built an even bigger temple on the same site.

The Temple in Jerusalem was an important place of worship. Jews from all over Palestine travelled there at least once a year, especially on the feast of Pesach (Passover). After it was destroyed by the Romans in 70CE the Temple was never rebuilt again.

There is no rule that Jews must visit the remains of the Temple today, however Jews living outside Israel often make a pilgrimage to the Holy Land to pray at the Western Wall. It is sometimes called the Wailing Wall due to all the pilgrims down the centuries who cried aloud with grief at what happened there.

Ritual

A pilgrimage is a ritual occasion for people of faith. Jewish pilgrims who go to the Western Wall perform symbolic actions which express what is deeply important to them. Pilgrims pray in separate areas in front of the wall, men in one section, women in another. They:

- ❖ Wash their hands before going to pray as a sign of their purity of heart. There are hand basins for washing at the entrance to both prayer areas.
- ❖ Cover their heads as a sign of respect for a holy place. Men wear a kippah, and women tie a scarf around their hair. Men may wear a tallit around their shoulders, and perhaps a tefillin on their arm and forehead.
- ❖ Face the wall to pray.
- ❖ Pray using a prayer book.

As pilgrims offer their prayer to God they can:

- stand near the wall.
- place their hand, or lean their forehead, on the wall.
- press their lips to the stone of the wall.
- push tiny slips of paper containing prayers between the cracks in the wall.

Jewish pilgrims gather in the area directly in front of the wall. Tourists may visit the Western Wall too, but must stand further back behind a low fence. They are able to see everything and may take photographs, as long as they do not disturb the pilgrims who go there to pray.

A view of pilgrims at the Western Wall during a Jewish religious festival.

Place of Pilgrimage

✦ Examine the photograph.

ISRAEL
Jerusalem

1. What is happening?
2. Where is this place?
3. To whom is it special?
4. What do pilgrims do when they go there?
5. Why do people go there on pilgrimage?

Questions

Knowledge

1. What is a pilgrimage?
2. What is a pilgrim?
3. Why do people go on pilgrimages?
4. Name the holiest site in the religion of Judaism.
5. Think of as many reasons as you can why Jews go on pilgrimage to Jerusalem.
6. Why is the Western Wall sometimes called the Wailing Wall?
7. How do Jews worship at the Western Wall?
8. What rituals do Jewish pilgrims perform when they pray at the Western Wall?

Understanding

1. Why is the Western Wall in Jerusalem a sacred place for Jewish people?
2. Describe what usually happens when a Jew goes on pilgrimage to the Western Wall.
3. What do you think is the difference between the experience of...
   a. a pilgrim
   b. a tourist
   ...at the Western Wall in Jerusalem?

Research

✪ Find out what practical arrangements are necessary for a pilgrimage to the Western Wall in Jerusalem. Contact the office of a specialist travel agent and/or visit their website.

- ✸ Prepare a fact sheet for pilgrims.

  Travel details
  - How to get there - airlines, special deals, travel time…
  - Where to stay - hotels, hostels…
  - What to bring - tickets, currency, suitable clothes…
  - Places of interest - map of Jerusalem, Western Wall, on the Mount…
  - What to do - religious rituals at the site…
  - How to make the most of your pilgrimage…
- ✸ Compare your set of travel plans with those of the rest of the class.

The Jewish Calendar

Key Concept

Calendar/ Sacred time: days and weeks set aside every year for a religious purpose.

Objective

Name the sacred times of the year for Jewish people.

Activity: *"Times of significance"*

TASK: TO IDENTIFY TIMES OF THE YEAR WHICH HAVE A SPECIAL SIGNIFICANCE FOR US.

✦ Some days in the year are special to us. What do we remember or celebrate on special days such as:

- Birthdays.
- Anniversaries.
- Holy days.
- Holidays.
- St. Valentine's Day.
- Graduations.

Discuss

- What times in the year are special for you?
- What times in the year have a special significance for your family?
- Why do we remember and celebrate special events?

Calendar/ Sacred Time

Every religion sets aside certain times of the year to remember and celebrate special events.

Jews celebrate many special events. The Jewish calendar is full of religious festivals. There are at least sixteen celebrations every year. A festival is sacred time. It is a day(s) set aside every year to help people focus on their faith. It is a time to think and pray and be united with Jews everywhere past and present.

Some festivals are more important than others. For example, Yom Kippur is the holiest day of the Jewish calendar. Pesach, or Passover, is a major festival and is celebrated by Jews in every part of the world.

Each festival reminds people of an important event in the story of their religion. The festival of Pesach (Passover), for example, reminds Jews of what happened at the time of the Exodus. Moses led their ancestors out of slavery in Egypt to the freedom of the Promised Land.

Time	Festival	To celebrate	Scripture ref.
Autumn	✧ Rosh Hashanah.	The Jewish New Year. A ram's horn is blown to call people to return to God.	Leviticus 23:23-25
	✧ Yom Kippur.	The holiest day of the year. A day of prayer and fasting for the forgiveness of sin.	Leviticus 23:26-32
	✧ Sukkot (Tabernacles).	The time God cared for the Jews in the desert when they escaped from Egypt. They lived in temporary shelters made from leaves and branches.	Leviticus 23:33-43
Winter	✧ Hanukkah.	The time the Jews had a successful protest against foreign rulers in Palestine in 165BCE. The Jews took back the Temple and re-dedicated it to the one true God.	2 Maccabees 10:1-8
Spring	✧ Pesach (Passover).	The time of the Exodus when Moses led the Jews to freedom from slavery in Egypt.	Exodus 12:1-49
Summer	✧ Shavuot.	The time God gave Moses the Torah (the Law and the Ten Commandments) on Mount Sinai.	Exodus 20:1-26

Children play with dreidels at the festival of Hanukkah.

The Jewish calendar is based on the ancient lunar calendar where time is marked by the movement of the moon around the Earth. This means the dates of the Jewish festivals vary from year to year. The calendar is adjusted from time to time to ensure festivals take place during the same season each year.

Jewish Religious Festivals

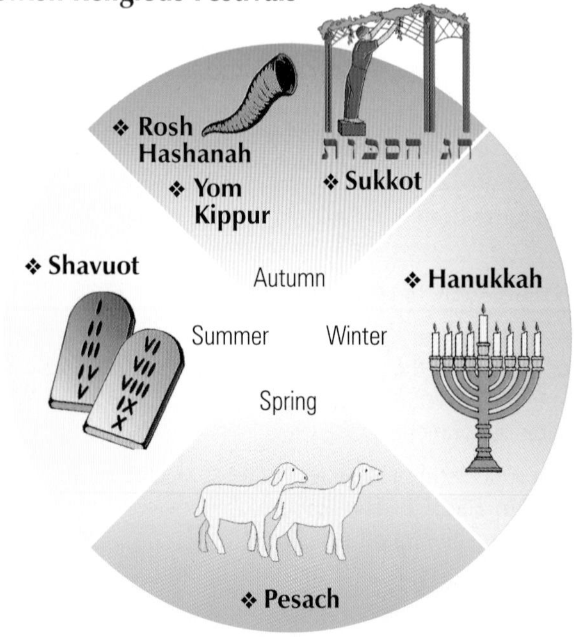
❖ Rosh Hashanah
❖ Yom Kippur
חג הסכות
❖ Sukkot
❖ Shavuot
Autumn
❖ Hanukkah
Summer
Winter
Spring
❖ Pesach

Questions

Knowledge

1. What is the holiest day of the year for Jewish people and when does it occur?
2. Name three festivals that celebrate what happened to Moses and the Jewish people on separate occasions.
3. Name two of the most important festivals in the Jewish calendar.

Understanding

1. Jewish festivals are based on a lunar calendar. How does this affect the timing of the celebrations each year?
2. How does it benefit the Jews to remember and celebrate the events of the past?

Research

- Find out more about the family festival of Hanukkah. When does it take place? How long does it last? What does it celebrate? What customs and traditions are associated with the festival today?
  - Make reference to the following in your summary:
    - Judah the Maccabee, a Jew.
    - Antiochus, a Greek tyrant.
    - Lighting the Hanukkah candles.
    - Playing the dreidel game.
    - Exchanging gifts.
    - Eating doughnuts!
  - Share the details with the class.

Religious Festivals

Key Concepts

Festival: sacred time marked by fasting or celebration to remind people of key events and beliefs in their faith.

Symbol: something visible that represents something else that is invisible.

Objective

Explain how religious festivals remind the Jews of key events and beliefs in their faith.

Activity: *"Abraham and Isaac"*

TASK: TO APPRECIATE THE EXTENT OF ABRAHAM'S FAITH IN GOD.

✦ Read Genesis 22:1-19

Five good readers volunteer to read the story of Abraham and Isaac, taking the roles of:

- Narrator.
- God.
- Angel.
- Abraham.
- Isaac.

Discuss

- What did Abraham believe God wanted him to do?
- How do you think Abraham felt about sacrificing his son?
- How strong was Abraham's faith in God?
- How do people show their faith in God today?

Festival

Symbol

Religious festivals remind people of the beliefs that are important in their religion.

Rosh Hashanah and Yom Kippur are two Jewish festivals celebrated in Autumn.

Rosh Hashanah

Rosh Hashanah is the first day of the Jewish New Year. Jews meeting on this day wish each other well for the coming year. For Jews, Rosh Hashanah is a reminder that God is the creator of the world and everything in it.

The evening before Rosh Hashanah, Jewish families share a meal together at home. Special bread is baked in the shape of a crown; it is a symbol, a way of showing that God is king of the universe. Pieces of apple are dipped in honey and eaten. The fruit and honey are symbols, a way of hoping that the new year will be happy and sweet for everybody.

Apples and honey, symbols of the Jewish New Year.

Section C

Blowing the shofar on Rosh Hashanah.

The Synagogue Service

On new year's morning a special service is held in the synagogue and the shofar is blown. A shofar is a ram's horn that makes a very sharp, shrill sound. Blowing the shofar is a symbolic act, it is a way of reminding people that they must always obey God and try to live good lives.

On Rosh Hashanah every Jew makes a judgement about their behaviour. As they judge themselves before God they look back at what they did wrong in the past and look forward to doing what is right in the future. The story of Abraham and Isaac is read from the Torah at the synagogue service. Abraham was so obedient to God that he was willing to sacrifice his young son Isaac. God was pleased with the strength of Abraham's faith and accepted the sacrifice of a ram instead.

The shofar is blown in the synagogue every day for the following ten days. During this time Jewish people must put right whatever they have done wrong. They ask God to forgive them for their sins and make a promise to do better in the year ahead.

Yom Kippur

Yom Kippur is the holiest day in the Jewish year. It takes place ten days after Rosh Hashanah. The words Yom Kippur mean 'Day of Atonement'. Atonement is about making amends for what people have done wrong. Jews spend this day making amends to God for their sins.

Yom Kippur is a day when Jewish people fast and pray, many fast for the full day. Fasting is a symbolic act. It represents people's sorrow for any wrong they have done and their desire for forgiveness.

Adult Jews spend most of the day of Yom Kippur praying in the synagogue. They pray to God to forgive them for their sins and ask God to help them live better lives in the future.

The Synagogue Service

Everything in the synagogue is covered in white on Yom Kippur. The curtain on the Ark is white. The Torah scrolls are dressed in white. A white cloth covers the reading desk. The rabbi who leads the service wears white too. The colour white is used as a symbol. It shows that when people are sorry, God will forgive their sins. The darkness of sin is taken away and they become pure again, like angels.

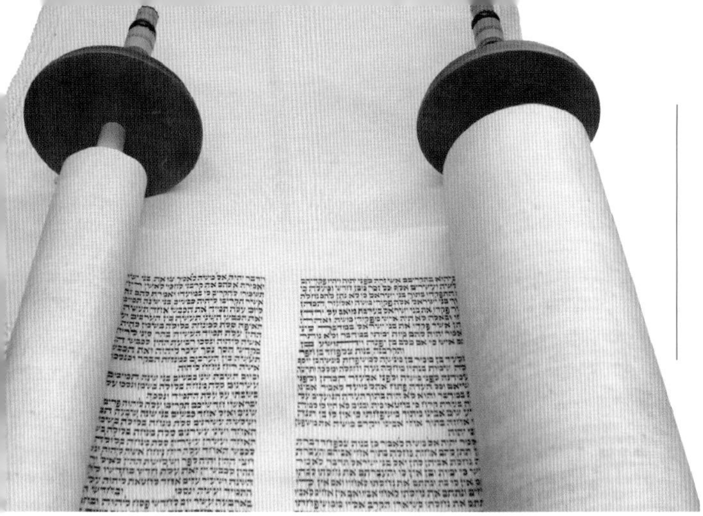

The Sefer Torah in the synagogue.

A reading from scripture tells what happened on the Day of Atonement long ago. Once a year the High Priest went into the Holy of Holies, the most sacred part of the Temple in Jerusalem. There he offered a sacrifice to God to make amends for the sins of the Jewish community.

At the end of the synagogue service, the Shema is said and the shofar is blown one last time. It is a reminder to those present to be faithful to God and to do good in the year ahead.

The dead are remembered on this day too, especially Jews who suffered for their faith in the Holocaust* during World War II. Special candles are lit in their memory.

*Holocaust - the murder of six million Jews by the Nazis during World War II.

The shofar is blown for the last time on Yom Kippur.

Questions

Knowledge

1. What is Rosh Hashanah?
2. What special food is eaten on the eve of Rosh Hashanah?
3. What is a shofar?
4. What story is read from the Torah on Rosh Hashanah?
5. What promise do Jews make to God on the Jewish New Year?
6. What is Yom Kippur?
7. What is atonement?
8. How is the synagogue prepared for Yom Kippur?
9. What do Jews do on Yom Kippur?
10. What happened on the Day of Atonement long ago?
11. What happens at the end of the synagogue service on Yom Kippur?

Understanding

1. Give reasons why the story of Abraham and Isaac is read on Rosh Hashanah.
2. What do the festivals of Rosh Hashanah and Yom Kippur remind Jews about:
   a. God?
   b. their relationship with God?
3. Why do you think so many symbolic words and actions are used in the religious festivals of Rosh Hashanah and Yom Kippur?

Research

- Find out about the use of a scapegoat long ago. A scapegoat ritual took place every year on Yom Kippur (the Day of Atonement).
- Read Leviticus 16:20-24
  The High Priest representing the Jewish nation placed his hands on the goat's head and confessed over it the sins of the people. Then the goat was driven off into the desert.
- Try to explain the meaning behind the different symbolic acts:
  i. Placing both hands on the goat's head.
  ii. Confessing the people's sins over the goat's head.
  iii. Driving the goat off into the desert.
- Share your ideas with the class.

Pesach - Passover

Key Concepts

Festival: sacred time marked by fasting or celebration to remind people of key events and beliefs in their faith.

Rite: the pattern of words and actions used in a religious ceremony.

Symbol: something visible that represents something else that is invisible.

Ritual: an occasion when people use symbolic objects, words and actions to express what is deeply important to them.

Objective

Explain how the festival of Passover reminds Jews of key events and beliefs in their faith.

Activity: *"Freedom"*

TASK: TO EXPLORE WHAT FREEDOM MEANS IN OUR OWN EXPERIENCE.

- When you were five years old, what were you allowed to do?
- When you were ten years old, what were you allowed to do that you couldn't do at five?
- As a teenager, what kind of things are you allowed to do now?
- What can your parents do that you wish you were allowed to do?

Discuss

- List three choices that you freely made today.
- Think of a word or words that best describe what freedom means to you.

  "Freedom is…."
- What symbol would you use to show what freedom is all about?

Ceremonial cup of wine at the Seder or Passover meal.

Festival

Jews have an annual festival to celebrate their freedom.

Pesach (Passover) is a week long festival that takes place in Spring. It is sacred time when Jews remember and celebrate the Exodus, an important event in Jewish history. It is a time when Jews give thanks to God for their escape from slavery in Egypt. The annual festival of Pesach celebrates their freedom.

Their ancestors were in such a hurry to leave Egypt that there was no time to let the bread rise for the thanksgiving meal. As a result the people had to eat flat bread (unleavened bread). Since then, Pesach is often referred to as the festival of Unleavened Bread.

The high point of the festival is the Seder or Passover meal. The Seder is a special meal combined with a religious service. It takes place in the family home on the eve of Pesach. It is a big celebration and relatives and friends are usually invited.

The Seder Table

The Seder table is set with traditional food and drink. It contains:

- A Seder plate.
- Unleavened bread (matzot) covered with a cloth.
- A jug of salt water.
- One large wine glass.
- Wine glasses for all present.
- Two candles.

Rite

A rite is the pattern of words and actions used in a religious ceremony. The Seder meal in every Jewish household always follows the same order of events. This order, or rite, is written in a prayer book called the Haggadah, a copy of which is put in everyone's place at the table before the meal begins.

The father of the family begins the service. He lights the two candles, fills the wine glasses for everyone and says a blessing. A large cup of wine, for the prophet Elijah, is left on the table during the meal and is poured away afterwards.

The youngest child present always asks the same question: "Why is this night different from all other nights?" The father replies by telling the story of Exodus. He teaches the meaning of the Exodus by pointing to the different symbols on the Seder plate.

The Seder Meal.

Symbol

A symbol is something visible that stands for, or represents, something invisible. Each item of food on the Seder plate is a symbol. It stands for, or represents, something in the Exodus event.

The Seder Plate.

The Seder Plate

- **Lamb bone:** a symbol of the Passover lamb that was killed so its blood could be sprinkled on the doorposts of Jewish houses. The Angel of Death passed over their houses and they were saved.
- **Horseradish:** a bitter root vegetable, a reminder of the bitter years of slavery in Egypt.
- **Haroset:** a mix of apples, nuts, honey and spices. A muddy looking mixture that stands for the mud bricks used to make the pharaoh's buildings in Egypt.
- **Green herbs:** parsley and lettuce to remind everyone that Pesach is a spring festival.
- **Egg:** a symbol of new life in a new land.

Other important items on the table are:

- **Matzot:** a reminder of the flat bread eaten on the first Passover night.
- **Salt water:** a reminder of the tears that were shed when the Jews were slaves in Egypt.
- **Wine:** a reminder of the promise God made to Moses (Exodus 6:6-8).

The symbols, words and actions of the Seder meal help Jews to re-live the experience of the Exodus. It brings it alive for everyone.

Everyone reads from a prayer book (the Haggadah) at the Seder meal.

Ritual

A ritual is an occasion when people use symbolic objects, words and actions to express what is deeply important to them. The Seder meal at the festival of Pesach is a ritual. At the Seder meal, readings from scripture are accompanied by certain symbolic actions that help Jews express what is deeply important to them.

- Wine is sipped.
  It tastes of the freedom offered by God
- Parsley is dipped in salt water.
  It tastes of the sorrow that people still suffer from slavery and oppression.
- Matzot is broken and shared out.
  It symbolises the unleavened bread that was quickly prepared in their rush for freedom.
- Bitter herbs are dipped in the haroset.
  It tastes of the bitter misery of working as slaves in Egypt.
- A drop of wine is spilt from the wine glasses.
  It shows sadness for all those who still suffer in the world today.

At this point in the Seder the main meal is served. Everyone enjoys the festive food that has been specially prepared for the occasion. There is a starter, a main course and a dessert. Jews gather together with family and friends at the annual Seder meal to celebrate their freedom and to think of those who still lack freedom in the world today. The service ends with a blessing and the words:

"Next year in Jerusalem,
Next year may we all be free."

Section C

Questions

Knowledge

1. What is Pesach, when does it occur each year?
2. What do Jews celebrate at the festival of Pesach?
3. What is the Seder or Passover meal?
4. What is the Haggadah?
5. At the Passover meal, what is the role of:
   a. the father?
   b. the youngest member of the family?
6. What is unleavened bread, why is it eaten at the Seder meal?
7. In what ways is the Passover meal different from an ordinary family meal in a Jewish household?

Understanding

1. What symbols are used at a Seder service to re-tell the story of Exodus?
2. How do Jewish people celebrate the annual festival of Pesach?
3. Why do you think Pesach is called a festival of freedom?

Research

- Find out about Jewish action for freedom at Masada in 73CE. Masada is the Hebrew word for "fortress".
  - What was the function of the fortress at Masada in Roman times?
  - Where is Masada?
  - Who were the Zealots?
  - What happened to the Jewish Zealots at Masada?
  - Why are the ancient ruins at Masada regarded as a national shrine in Israel today?
  - Discuss your findings with the class.

Rites of Passage

Key Concepts

Ritual: an occasion when people use symbolic objects, words and actions to express what is deeply important to them.

Ceremony: the solemn or formal actions performed on a ritual occasion.

Rite: the pattern of words and actions used in a religious ceremony.

Objective

Show how Jewish beliefs are expressed in the words and actions of a bar-mitzvah ceremony.

Activity: *"Birthdays"*

TASK: TO UNDERSTAND THE NEED FOR RITUAL IN PEOPLE'S LIVES.

✦ Think of a birthday that you celebrated recently (your birthday, a friend's birthday, or the birthday of someone in your family). What rituals are always part of the birthday celebration?

- Sending a birthday card.
- Saying happy birthday.
- Giving presents.
- Having a birthday party.
- Getting a birthday cake.
- Blowing out the birthday candles.
- Singing 'Happy Birthday'.

Discuss

- List the things that always happen on someone's birthday.
- Do you do anything else in your family when it is someone's birthday?
- What deep important things do people express through birthday rituals?
- Choose one symbolic action. What does it mean when we say or do this on someone's birthday?

Ritual

Religious rituals mark important moments in life.

A rite of passage is the name given to an occasion that marks the passing from one stage of life to another. Religions mark important moments in life such as:

✧ Birth ✧ Maturity of faith ✧ Marriage ✧ Death

It is an important event in the Jewish community:

- ❖ when a baby is born into a family.
- ❖ when a person grows up and takes on adult responsibilities in the faith.
- ❖ when a couple fall in love and get married.
- ❖ when a person's life is over at death.

Jews mark all these important moments with religious rituals. A ritual is an occasion when people use symbolic objects, words and actions to express what is deeply important to them. In Judaism, birth, maturity of faith, marriage and death are ritual occasions. Symbolic actions are used to express Jewish beliefs about God's presence in people's lives at such times. Rituals are always carried out the same way each time they are performed.

A Jewish couple standing beneath a special canopy during their wedding ceremony.

Ceremony

Rite

Bar-mitzvah is a rite of passage. Boys in the Jewish community celebrate an important moment in their lives when they are thirteen years old. A boy becomes 'Bar-Mitzvah', which means 'Son of the Law', at a special ceremony in the synagogue. A ceremony is a series of solemn or formal actions performed on ritual occasions.

The bar-mitzvah ceremony marks, in religious terms, the passing from childhood to adulthood. It means a boy of thirteen years is considered old enough to take on adult responsibilities in his faith community.

- ❖ He can now read the Sefer Torah in the synagogue. This is regarded as a great honour.
- ❖ He can be counted on to make up the ten men who must be present before a religious service can take place in a synagogue.
- ❖ He is expected to obey the Law of God, like other Jewish men.

The bar-mitzvah ceremony takes place in the synagogue on the Sabbath following a boy's thirteenth birthday. It is a big day for all the family. Everyone dresses up for the occasion. The boy wears new clothes and looks his best.

The Bar-Mitzvah Ceremony

A special rite, or pattern of words and actions, is used at a bar-mitzvah ceremony. The rabbi welcomes the boy and his family to the synagogue service. Then, for the first time, the boy sits downstairs with his father and the other men. He puts on what Jewish men wear at prayer-time. He will have a new kippah (prayer cap) on his head. A tallit (prayer shawl) will be put around his shoulders. He will be given a tefillin (a box strapped to his arm and forehead) and a siddur (prayer book). The kippah, tallit, tefillin and siddur are all symbols of his new role as an adult Jew.

The boy sits and waits with his father until it is time to read from the sacred scrolls. This is the most important part of the bar-mitzvah ceremony. When his name is called, he walks up the steps of the bimah (a raised platform in the centre of the synagogue) and stands in front of the Sefer Torah, the special handwritten scroll that is kept in the synagogue. He says a prayer and then takes the silver yad in his hand. The passage on the scroll in front of him is in Hebrew. He begins to read it aloud. He has been practising his Hebrew for months to get it right at this moment. He might even be a bit nervous as he is anxious to read without making a mistake. It is an honour to read the Torah in the synagogue in front of his family and the Jewish community.

A Bar-Mitzvah ceremony.

Afterwards the rabbi speaks to him and the rest of the congregation. He reminds the boy of his duty to keep the Law of God like all Jewish men. The rabbi then announces to everyone that the young man is now a 'Son of the Law'. The boy receives a blessing from his father who says a prayer on his behalf.

Later all the family have a meal together to celebrate the boy's bar-mitzvah. The young man must stand up and make a speech. He thanks his parents for all they have done for him. He thanks his friends and relations for all the presents they have given him on this important day in his life.

Hebrew Alphabet and Kabbala Words

א	ב	ג	ד	ה
A	B	G	D	H
ו	ז	ח	ט	י
V	Z	CH'	T	Y / I
כ	ל	מ	נ	ס	ע
C	L	M	N	S	A
פ	צ	ק	ר	ש	ת
P	TZ	K	R	SH	T

אהבה LOVE
תורה Torah
יהדות Judaism
נפש Soul
שמחה Joy
אושר Happiness
קבלה Kabbala
נשמה Spirit

הוד Hod / Steadfastness
ספירות Sefirot / Enumerations
יסוד Yesod / Foundation
תפארת Binah / Understanding
בינה Binah / Understanding
כתר Keter / Crown
מלכות Malchut / Lower Crown
חכמה Chokmah / Wisdom
חסד Chesed / Grace
בינה Binah / Understanding
גבורה Gevura / Determination
נצח Netzach / Persistence

Jewish boys learn Hebrew in preparation for their bar-mitzvah.

Bat-Mitzvah

A girl automatically becomes Bat-Mitzvah when she is twelve years old. It occurs at this stage as Judaism accepts that girls mature earlier than boys. In Hebrew, Bat-Mitzvah means 'Daughter of the Law'.

There is no special Sabbath service to celebrate a girl's bat-mitzvah, as girls do not take part in services in most synagogues. There may be a short ceremony in the synagogue on Sunday afternoon instead. Jews believe women and girls play an important role in keeping a Jewish home. Jewish girls begin to take on this responsibility when they become bat-mitzvah at twelve years of age.

A Jewish boy holding the Torah on the day of his bar-mitzvah.

Questions

Knowledge

1. What is a 'rite of passage'?
2. What are the main 'rites of passage' in the lives of Jewish people?
3. In relation to a bar-mitzvah:
   a. Who is it for?
   b. At what age does it occur?
   c. Where does it take place?
   d. What do the words 'bar-mitzvah' mean?
4. At a bar-mitzvah ceremony:
   a. What ritual dress is worn?
   b. What ritual movements or gestures are used?
   c. What ritual words are spoken?
5. What important things are being expressed through the rituals at a bar-mitzvah?
6. What adult responsibilities does a Jewish boy take on at his bar-mitzvah?
7. What happens directly after the bar-mitzvah ceremony in the synagogue?
8. What is the difference between a bar-mitzvah and a bat-mitzvah?

Understanding

1. Describe what happens at a bar-mitzvah ceremony.
3. Explain how different rituals at a bar-mitzvah help Jews express what is deeply important to them.
4. What do you think is the significance of the bar-mitzvah for young Jewish boys?

Research

- Find out about one other rite of passage in the Jewish community. Select the ceremony held at either birth, marriage or death.
  - What stage in a person's life is celebrated on this occasion?
  - Describe the rituals that are performed at the ceremony.
  - Explain the meaning behind the different rituals.
  - What essential Jewish beliefs are expressed in the rituals of this ceremony?
  - Mention your sources and share your findings with the class.

Development of Judaism

Key Concepts

Commitment: a decision to devote time and energy to the practice of one's religion.

Development: the way a community of faith grows and progresses over time.

Objective

Give an account of important people and key moments in the development of Judaism.

Section C

Activity: *"Me and My Life"*

TASK: TO IDENTIFY IMPORTANT PEOPLE AND EVENTS IN OUR OWN LIVES.

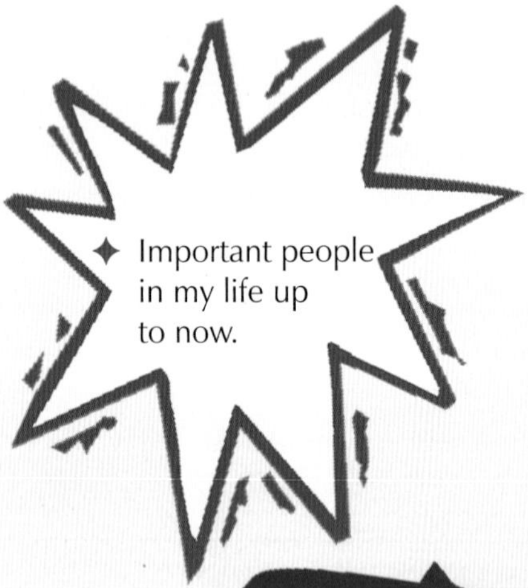
✦ Important people in my life up to now.

✦ Important events in my life up to now.

Discuss

- Who is important to you at the present time?
- Has anyone else been important to you in the past?
- What are some of the key things that have happened in your life so far?

Commitment

Development

There are many important people and key events in the religion of Judaism.

The history of Judaism covers a period of almost 4,000 years. At the beginning there was a covenant (a sacred agreement) between God and Abraham. God promised to look after Abraham and his descendants forever. Abraham promised that his people would worship and obey God forever. The history of Judaism is the story of how the Jewish people have lived up to their part of the covenant down through the ages.

Over the years, the country where Jews have lived has been called: The Promised Land, Canaan, Israel, Judah, Palestine, The Holy Land.

Over the years Jewish people have been known as: God's chosen people, Hebrews, Israelites, Jews.

1. Abraham

THE BOOK OF GENESIS

1850BCE

Abraham grew up in Ur in Mesopotamia where everyone worshipped many gods. People were afraid of the gods because they thought they acted in cruel and evil ways. Abraham had different ideas and came to believe that there was only one God who had power over everything. He believed that God is good and uses his power to do what is right and just. God chose Abraham to show the world what the one all-powerful God is like. Abraham put his trust in God and set off with his wife Sarah on a journey of faith to the land of Canaan. There God made a covenant with him.

Abraham was told "I will be your God… You will be my people." It meant that God would care for Abraham and in return Abraham must worship God and obey him. Then God promised Abraham many descendants and the land of Canaan to belong to them forever. Abraham promised that his people would always worship and obey the one all-powerful God. As a sign of their commitment to the covenant, Abraham's male descendants would bear the mark of circumcision.

Abraham is the first patriarch, or founding father, of God's chosen people. The other patriarchs are his son Isaac and his grandson Jacob.

2. Moses THE BOOK OF EXODUS

There was a famine in Canaan so Abraham's descendants migrated to Egypt. They settled there and their number grew. Then the Egyptians forced the people into slavery. Their suffering lasted almost 400 years.

1250BCE

Moses led the Jews to freedom in an event called the Exodus. He led them out of Egypt, back toward the Promised Land (the Jews celebrate this event every year at Pesach or Passover). At Mount Sinai God renewed the covenant with Moses. God promised to continue looking after the Chosen People if they continued to worship and obey him. Then God gave Moses the Law, which includes the Ten Sayings, or Ten Commandments. In return Moses made a commitment that the Jews would keep the Law of God which would guide them in the right way to live.

This was the beginning of Judaism as an organised religion. Jews now had a clear set of rules for worship and behaviour. Their special task was to make the world a better and a holier place for everyone.

3. Joshua THE BOOK OF JOSHUA

1200BCE

When Moses died, Joshua became leader. He led the Jews back across the Jordan river into the Promised Land. The people wanted a homeland. Joshua was in charge of the army, and he believed God was on their side. They fought and won many battles, yet it took nearly two hundred years before the Jews finally reclaimed control of Canaan.

4. David THE BOOKS OF SAMUEL 1 & 2

1000BCE

God chose David to be king of Israel. He was anointed and grew up to become Israel's greatest king. He reigned for forty years. He won a number of battles and Israel became a great kingdom. He captured Jerusalem and made it his capital city. David was faithful to the covenant and brought the Ark of the Covenant to Jerusalem. This was the casket containing the tablets of the Law given to Moses on Mount Sinai.

When David's son Solomon became king, he built a magnificent temple to honour God. The Ark of the Covenant was placed in the 'Holy of Holies' and was a special sign of God's presence. As a result, the Temple in Jerusalem became the most important centre of worship for the Jewish people.

5. The Prophets THE BOOK OF JEREMIAH. THE BOOK OF EZEKIEL.

860BCE

After Solomon died, Jewish leaders in different parts of the country began fighting amongst themselves. The kingdom soon fell apart. It was then that God called holy men such as Jeremiah and Ezekiel to become prophets. They went on God's behalf to speak to the leaders in the north and south of the country.

The prophets reminded the Jewish leaders to keep the covenant. They told them to change their ways and treat each other fairly and turn back to God. The prophets warned them of what would happen if they did not obey the Law of God. The leaders and the people refused to listen, they had no commitment to the covenant anymore. The country was now divided and less able to defend itself from outside attack.

What the prophets had tried to prevent began to happen. First the north was invaded, most of the people were led away and were never heard from again. Then the south was invaded. The city of Jerusalem was attacked and destroyed. The Temple was looted and burned to the ground. The people were taken away as prisoners to Babylon.

6. The Exile THE BOOK OF LAMENTATIONS

586BCE

The Jews were forced to work like slaves in Babylon. They were heartbroken. They were far from home and the city of Jerusalem was in ruins. They realised it was their own fault; they had disobeyed God's Law. Exile from their homeland was their punishment.

The Jews tried to keep their faith alive. They could no longer go to the Temple so changes had to be made to the way they practiced their religion. They began to meet in small groups on the Sabbath to pray and to study the Torah. This was the beginning of the idea of a synagogue as a meeting place for prayer and learning.

7. Return from Exile THE BOOK OF EZRA

539BCE

Babylon was invaded by the king of Persia and many slaves were set free. The Jews were allowed to go back to their own country. They set out across the desert to return to their homeland after fifty years in exile.

They began at once to rebuild the Temple and the city of Jerusalem. When the Temple was completed, there was a special ceremony to mark the occasion. A holy man named Ezra encouraged the Jews to practice their religion. He told them to go to the Temple to offer sacrifice to God and to go to the synagogue to pray and learn more about their faith. Ezra was a rabbi, an expert on the Law of God. He taught the Jews how to apply the Law to every aspect of their daily lives.

8. Foreign Rulers THE BOOK OF DANIEL

Over the next four hundred years, the Jewish homeland was invaded by one powerful nation after another; first the Persians, then the Greeks, and finally the Romans. The Jews no longer had any power in their own land. The most important thing to them now was their religion. They made a commitment to keep the covenant and obey God's Law. They went to the Temple and the synagogue as often as they could.

The Persians 539BCE
The Persians allowed the Jews to follow their own religion and helped them to rebuild the Temple.

The Greeks 333BCE
When the Greeks invaded they took over the Temple and tried to force their religion on everyone. The Jews fought back and would not give in. One group, led by Judah the Maccabee (nicknamed 'The Hammer') took back the Temple and built a new altar to the one true God (the Jews celebrate this event every year at the festival of Hanukkah).

The Romans 63BCE
When the Romans invaded, they allowed the Jews to practice their religion. Herod, the Roman Governor, enlarged the Temple and made it a magnificent building.

70CE
A group of fervent Jews called Zealots wanted freedom from Roman rule; they led a revolt against the invaders. The Romans responded with force. They destroyed the city of Jerusalem and pulled down the Temple, only the western wall was left standing.

9. The Messiah THE PROPHETS ISAIAH, JEREMIAH AND EZEKIEL.

Throughout the invasions of Palestine by the Persians, the Greeks and the Romans, the Jewish people longed for freedom. They realised that they needed a leader to set them free. Their prophets said that one day a Messiah would lead them to freedom. The Messiah would be anointed by God, meaning he will be someone chosen specially by God, just as King David was long ago. Jews believe the coming of the Messiah will bring peace to their homeland and to the whole world.

10. Diaspora

After the uprising against the Romans in 70CE, many Jews were killed. The rest were driven out of their homeland and were scattered around the lands bordering the Mediterranean Sea. Jewish people living outside the Holy Land became known as the Diaspora.

The destruction of the Temple and the fall of Jerusalem was a terrible loss. Down the centuries the rabbis had a key role in helping the Jews to survive as a nation. They encouraged the people to practice their religion. Jews no longer had the Temple as a place of worship, so the rabbis urged them to pray at home and to meet in the synagogues. There, the rabbis explained to them the teachings of the Law, or the Torah. All their explanations were later gathered together in an important work called the Talmud.

The Jews were in exile for nearly 2,000 years and did not return to their homeland until the middle of the 20th century. In 1948 after World War 2 the Jews went back and founded the modern State of Israel.

Judaism Timeline

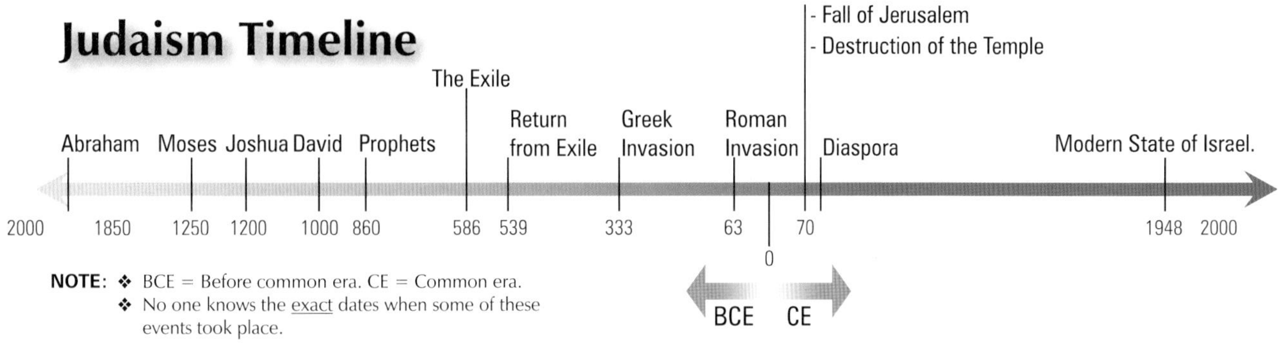
- Fall of Jerusalem
- Destruction of the Temple
The Exile
Abraham
Moses
Joshua
David
Prophets
Return from Exile
Greek Invasion
Roman Invasion
Diaspora
Modern State of Israel.
2000
1850
1250
1200
1000
860
586
539
333
63
0
70
1948
2000
BCE
CE

NOTE: ❖ BCE = Before common era. CE = Common era.
❖ No one knows the exact dates when some of these events took place.

Questions

Knowledge

1. Abraham
a. What religious beliefs did most people have at the time of Abraham?
b. What is a covenant.
c. What covenant did God make with Abraham?
d. Why is Abraham important?

2. Moses
a. What was the Exodus?
b. What covenant did God renew with Moses?
c. What did God give Moses on Mount Sinai?
d. Why is Moses important?

3. Joshua
a. Who was Joshua?
b. What did Joshua do for the Chosen People?

4. David
a. How long was David the king of Israel?
b. What was the name of his capital city?
c. What was the Ark of the Covenant?
d. What did David's son Solomon do for the Jewish people?

5. The Prophets
a. Name two prophets.
b. What did God call the prophets to do?
c. Why did the prophets criticise the Jewish leaders?
d. What happened when the prophets' warnings were ignored?

6. The Exile
a. What was the Exile?
b. Who did the Jews blame for their misfortune?
c. What changes did the Jews make to the way they practiced their religion during their exile in Babylon?

7. Return from Exile
a. How long were the Jews in exile in Babylon?
b. What did the Jews do on their return to Jerusalem?
c. Who was Ezra? How did Ezra help the Jews?

8. Foreign Rulers
a. What foreign armies invaded the Jewish homeland?
b. How did the different foreign rulers treat the religion of the Jewish people?
c. What tragedy took place in Jerusalem in 70CE?

9. The Messiah
a. Why did the Jews need a Messiah?
b. What Jewish leader was anointed long ago?
c. What will happen when the Messiah comes to the world?

10. Diaspora
a. What is the Diaspora?
b. How did the rabbis help the Jews to practice their religion over the centuries?
c. What are the Torah and the Talmud?

Understanding

1. Who are some of the important people, and what are some of the key events, in the development of Judaism?

2. Did the Jews keep their commitment to the covenant throughout their long history? Explain.

3. What do you think the history of the Jewish people tells us about:
- The way of God?
- The ways of people?

Judaism Worldwide

Key Concepts

Expansion: the way a religion spreads out into new territories.

Persecution: making people suffer because of their race or religion.

Objective

Outline the global expansion of Judaism over the centuries.

Activity: *"Where in the World"*

TASK: TO CHECK THE LEVEL OF GENERAL KNOWLEDGE ABOUT WORLD GEOGRAPHY.

- Divide into pairs/groups.
- Agree to use OR not to use an atlas for this exercise.

Can you name:

- 6 countries in the European Union. ___
- 6 states in the USA. ___
- 5 continents in the world. ___
- 4 countries in western Europe. ___
- 4 countries in central Europe. ___
- 3 countries in Asia. ___
- 3 African countries bordering the Mediterranean sea. ___
- 3 European countries bordering the Mediterranean sea. ___
- 3 major cities in Britain. ___
- 3 major cities in Ireland. ___

Total ___ / **40**

Discuss

- What is your standard of general knowledge about places in different parts of the world?

10	20	30	40
Fair	Good	Very Good	Excellent

Expansion

Persecution

There are Jewish communities in many parts of the world today.

Jews do not try to convert people to their faith. They do not set out to get people to join their religion. There are no missionaries who go out to spread the message of Judaism far and wide. Some people do convert to Judaism from other religions, but this is unusual.

A person becomes a Jew by being born into the faith. Anyone with a Jewish mother is automatically counted as a Jew. Some Jewish men and women do get married to non-Jews. In general however Jews are encouraged to find a Jewish partner and raise their children in the Jewish community.

Star of David.

Expansion refers to the way a community of faith grows and spreads to different places over time. After the destruction of the Temple in 70CE the Jews were forced out of Palestine. The Diaspora (Jews outside the Holy Land) were scattered around the Mediterranean. As Jewish families settled in this region they began to form new communities. In this way the religion of Judaism spread slowly across Europe in the centuries that followed.

The Jewish Community in Europe

Some Jews moved to Spain, Portugal, and North Africa. This became a mainly Muslim area in later years and the two cultures mixed. Jews and Muslims managed to live in harmony alongside each other most of the time. This lasted until Islamic control of Spain came to an end in the 15th century. The descendants of those early Jewish settlers are called Sephardi Jews.

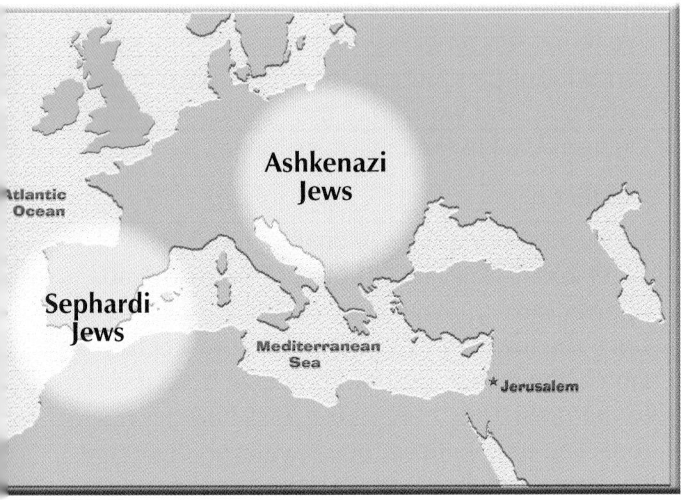
Ashkenazi Jews
Atlantic Ocean
Sephardi Jews
Mediterranean Sea
Jerusalem

Distribution of Jewish communities in Europe and North Africa.

Other Jews moved to countries in central and eastern Europe. These were mainly Christian countries. The two cultures failed to mix and the Jewish minority suffered a lot of persecution. This included being denied the right to live where they wanted. Across Europe Jews were forced to live in a ghetto or the 'Jewish quarter' of towns and cities. As a result, the Jewish community tended to become closed off from the rest of society.

The Jews used their isolation as an opportunity to focus more on the belief and practice of their religion. The descendants of those European Jews are called Ashkenazi Jews.

The Jewish Community in Britain and Ireland

Jews have lived in Britain and Ireland for centuries. The earliest records show that a group of Jews arrived in Ireland in the 11th century, probably from France. According to the Annals of Inishfallen, 1079, "Five Jews came over the sea and....were sent back again."

In Britain the newly arrived Jews were allowed to stay. They soon set up businesses as money lenders and bankers for the leaders of the country. Christians at that time believed it was against their religion to do this kind of work.

In the 15th century Sephardi Jews were expelled from Spain and Portugal. They went to different countries, some arrived in Ireland and settled on the south coast in the towns of Limerick, Cork and Waterford.

Anti-Semitism

In the 18th and 19th centuries there was a major increase in anti-Semitism (hatred of Jews) in eastern Europe. Large numbers of Ashkenazi Jews fled to western Europe and to the United States to escape persecution. Some Jewish families came to Ireland and settled in Dublin and Belfast where they set up synagogues, shops and small businesses.

Belfast
York
Dublin
Leeds
Limerick
Manchester
Cork
Waterford
London

Principal centres of Jewish population in Britain and Ireland.

Jews in Britain and Ireland have not been entirely free from religious persecution. Jews in Limerick experienced the effects of anti-Semitism in the early 1900's. Jews in Britain suffered persecution on and off down the centuries. The most serious incident took place in York in 1190 when many Jews were massacred. In addition, Jews were banned from living in Britain for nearly three hundred years during the Middle Ages.

Today the Jewish population of Britain is about 385,000. London, Leeds and Manchester are important centres of Jewish life in Britain. The Jewish population in Ireland has always been small. It reached its peak of 5,500 in the late 1940s. The number went down partly due to the emigration of Irish Jews to Israel after the Second World War.

Today about 2,000 Jews live in the Republic and Northern Ireland. There is a total of six synagogues serving the Irish Jewish community; four in Dublin, one in Cork and one in Belfast. There is a Jewish school in Dublin that caters for the needs of Jewish children at primary and post-primary level. Again in Dublin, there is a kosher butcher shop and a kosher bakery where Jewish families can buy foodstuffs that meet their special dietary requirements.

The Jewish Community in Israel

After World War 2, many Jewish refugees went to live in Israel. This is the land of Canaan that Jews believe God gave to Abraham and his descendants. The Romans expelled the Jews from this land after the destruction of the Temple in 70CE. The United Nations returned it to the Jews as their homeland in 1948.

The new country was called Israel. Jews from everywhere in the world have a right to go and live there. It is a place where Jews are safe after centuries of persecution. Jewish people can once again pray and worship at their holiest site, the Western Wall in the city of Jerusalem.

Conflict

However there is a lot of conflict today between Israel and its Arab neighbours. Groups of Arabs (mainly Muslim) have lived in Israel (Palestine) since the Jews left in 70CE. They now feel the land is theirs and it should not have been given to the Jews. They believe the Jews have no right to it. The Jews believe they have every right to it because God promised it to Abraham and Jews lived there long before the Arabs settled there.

Leaders of both sides have made many attempts to settle this dispute. Despite violence and bloodshed, efforts are ongoing to find a peaceful solution. Both groups, Jews and Arabs, want an end to the conflict in the Middle East.

The Western Wall in Jerusalem.

A Jewish boy reading from the Torah during his bar-mitzvah at the Western Wall.

The Jewish Community Worldwide

Judaism is one of the oldest religions in the world. It began with Abraham and Moses nearly 4,000 years ago. Yet Judaism is also one of the smallest world religions. There are about eighteen million Jews worldwide - most live in Israel or the USA. The largest Jewish communities in Europe are in France and Britain.

Of Jews in the world today approximately:

- One half live in the USA.
- One quarter live in Israel.
- One quarter live in Europe, Russia, and the rest of the world.

Distribution of Jews Worldwide

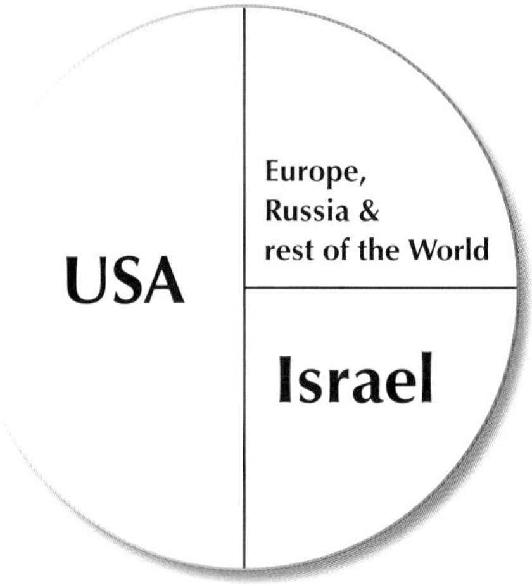
USA
Europe, Russia & rest of the World
Israel

Questions

Knowledge

1. How does a person become a Jew?
2. What happened to the Jews after the destruction of the Temple in 70CE?
3. Who are the Sephardi Jews?
4. Who are the Ashkenazi Jews?
5. When did Jews first come to Britain and Ireland?
6. What is a ghetto?
7. What is anti-Semitism?
8. Where did a large number of Jews go to escape persecution in the 18th and 19th centuries?
9. Where have Jewish communities become established in Britain and Ireland today?
10. When was the State of Israel established as a homeland for Jewish people?
11. What is a cause of the conflict in the Middle East?
12. What is the global distribution of the Jewish population.

Understanding

1. Describe how the Jewish community expanded throughout Europe after being expelled from Palestine by the Romans in 70CE.
2. How did anti-Semitism effect the distribution of the Jewish population in Europe in the 18th and 19th centuries?
3. "The history of the Jewish people is a history of persecution." What do you think of this statement?

Research

- Find out why Jews have been the target of persecution down through the centuries.
  - Identify a historic period when Jews were persecuted.
    - What was the accusation against the Jews?
    - What happened to members of the Jewish community?
    - Who were the perpetrators of accusations and violence against the Jews?
  - Give reasons why people participated in the abuse of their fellow human beings.
  - How did the Jewish community respond at the time?
  - Compile a report and discuss it with the class.

The Holocaust

Key Concepts

Commitment: a decision to devote time and energy to the practice of one's religion.

Persecution: making people suffer because of their race or religion.

Objective

Explain how Jews paid a huge price for their commitment to their faith.

Activity: *"Judgements"*

TASK: TO DISCOVER HOW WE CAN JUDGE AND MISJUDGE PEOPLE BY THEIR APPEARANCE.

- ✦ Assemble in groups and examine pictures A, B and C.
- ✦ Select one picture at a time. Speculate about possible answers to questions 1-10.

Try to imagine…

1. ... what job he or she has.
2. ... what his or her name is.
3. ... how he or she might talk (accent etc.).
4. ... if he or she is married.
5. ... in what kind of house he or she lives.
6. ... what his or her favourite T.V. programmes are.
7. ... how intelligent he or she is.
8. ... is he or she religious.
9. ... is he or she honest.
10. ...which character is:
    - ✧ very different from us?
    - ✧ a bit like us?

A

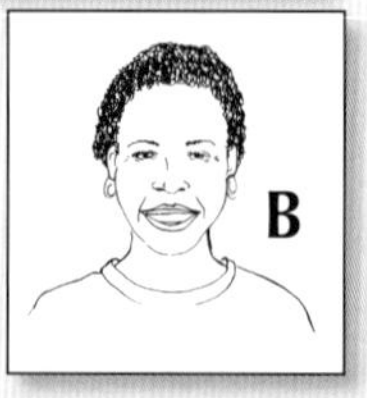
B

C

Discuss

- Did everyone agree or disagree in their opinions about the pictures?
- How did everyone decide on the answers to the questions?
- How do we usually judge people?
- Has anyone ever misjudged you before they got to know you?

Commitment

Persecution

The Jews have been misjudged and mistreated by many individuals and groups down the centuries.

Like people of all religions, Jews have certain beliefs and customs that are different from everyone else's. Yet Jews have been severely persecuted because of their difference. Persecution involves doing something on purpose to make people suffer. Anti-Semitism is the term we use to describe the persecution of Jews because of their religious beliefs.

Down the centuries people of other religions, such as Christians and Muslims, did not always understand the Jews. Sometimes people can be afraid of what they do not understand. However it has happened that certain individuals and groups have used people's ignorance of the Jewish way of life for their own ends.

Anti-Semitism

Jews paid a high price for their commitment to their faith. The worst persecution of the Jews took place in Europe in the 1930s and 1940s under the Nazis. Germany had lost the First World War (1914-18) and there was a lot of poverty and unemployment in the years that followed. Adolf Hitler was the Nazi leader in Germany at the time. He singled out the Jews and blamed them for all the problems in the country. They were made a scapegoat, meaning they were blamed for something that was not their fault.

Hitler and the Nazis hated the Jews. Through their speeches and advertisements they were able to convince the German public that certain people were inferior, especially Jews. They

Sculpture in memory of victims of the Holocaust.

claimed that Jews were not as good as, or as 'pure' as, the rest of the 'Aryan' people, a term used to describe the ethnic German people.

The Nazis began persecuting the Jews by stripping them of their human rights. Jewish men, women and children had to wear yellow badges on their coats to show they were Jews. They were called names and jeered at in the streets. They had to walk everywhere, as they were not allowed to travel on buses or trains, or to own a car.

A curfew was introduced which meant that Jews were not allowed outside after nine o'clock at night. Soon other repressive measures were introduced. Jewish children were not allowed to go to school. Jewish families were evicted from their homes, and their businesses were forced to close. Then the synagogues were burned down.

Auschwitz concentration camp, Poland.

The Holocaust

Then things got much worse. During World War 2, Hitler announced his 'final solution'. Across Europe Jewish people were rounded up and sent to concentration camps. The death camps were surrounded by high walls and barbed wire fences. Nazi soldiers stood on guard with guns and dogs.

On arrival, the men, women and children were divided into separate lines. Many were sent to their death straight away. Others were allowed to live and do heavy work from morning 'till night. They were bullied and beaten. A number was tattooed on their arms. Their hair was shaved off, they got very little food and when they were too sick and weak to work they were sent to the gas chambers. Thousands of Jews were gassed to death every day in the camps. Gypsies, homosexuals, Jehovah's witnesses and communists were put to death in the camps along with the Jews.

Jewish people speak of the suffering and death in the concentration camps as the 'Shoah' or 'the Holocaust'. The word 'Holocaust' means total destruction. Six million Jews died in the Holocaust. Over 1.5 million were children.

> *"I believe in the sun even when it is not shining. I believe in love even when feeling it not. I believe in God even when He is silent."*

This was written on the cellar wall of a house in Germany where Jews hid from the Nazis. The Jews were persecuted by people who were filled with hate and acted with unspeakable cruelty. Many Jews managed to keep their faith in God despite all their suffering.

Anne Frank

A school photograph. Anne aged 13 years.

Across Europe the Nazis were removing Jews and taking them to concentration camps. In Holland Anne Frank, a Jewish schoolgirl, and her family went into hiding in 1942.

Anne wrote a diary during this period. It was found after the family was betrayed and taken to Bergen-Belsen concentration camp. Anne died in 1945, aged sixteen years. Her diary is translated into more than fifty-five languages. It is one of the most widely read books in the world today.

Remembering the Holocaust

Since World War 2, the Jews have tried to keep the memory of the Holocaust alive in different ways. There is an annual Holocaust remembrance day. It is called Tishah'B'av in Hebrew. It takes place in the autumn, on 27 Nisan, the first month of the Jewish calendar. This is a day of fasting and mourning. Special prayers are said in the home and in the synagogue for the victims of the Holocaust.

There are Holocaust memorials. These have been set up in many countries throughout the world. At each place, people can go to discover and talk about what happened to the Jews. Adults and children of all religions visit the memorials. They can watch audio-visual displays, listen to talks and examine symbols and works of art that show the suffering of the Jewish people. The memorials help everyone to reflect on the meaning of the Holocaust for both Jews and the rest of humanity.

There were some people in Europe who did not stand by and let Jews suffer. Some Gentiles (non-Jews) risked their lives to help Jewish people they did not know. Trees are planted in their honour along the "Avenue of the Righteous" at the Holocaust memorial in Jerusalem.

Questions

Knowledge

1. What is anti-Semitism?
2. What human rights were denied to Jews in Germany in the 1930s/40s?
3. What was the Holocaust?
4. How many Jews died in concentration camps in World War 2?
5. Who was Anne Frank?
6. What is Tishah'B'av?
7. What is a Holocaust memorial?
8. Where is the 'Avenue of the Righteous'?

Understanding

1. Give reasons why anti-Semitism was widespread in Europe in the 1930s/40s.
2. What price did Jews pay for their commitment to their faith?
3. Why do you think Jews try to keep the memory of the Holocaust alive today?

Research

- Find out about Holocaust memorials in different parts of the world.
  For example…

  Yad Vashem.

  a. Where is it located?
  b. When was it established?
  c. What is to be found at this memorial site?
  d. Describe any one of the artifacts or features of this memorial.
  e. What is the significance of the 'Avenue of the Righteous'?
  f. Who may visit Yad Vashem?
  g. What do the Hebrew words Yad Vashem mean in English?

  - Members of the class may wish to share information about other Holocaust memorials.

Branches of Judaism

Key Concept

Schism: a division or split within a community of faith.

Objective

Outline the development of the two branches of Judaism that exist today.

Activity: *"The Big Divide"*

TASK: TO BE AWARE THAT DISAGREEMENTS GIVE RISE TO A RANGE OF CONSEQUENCES.

- Dictionary definitions of the word 'schism' include:
  - Dissent.
  - Contradiction.
  - Discord.
  - Disagreement.
  - Difference.
  - Division.
  - Rejection.
  - Split.
  - Separation.

Discuss

- When was the last time you had a difference of opinion with someone?
- Was it a major or a minor disagreement?
- How was the matter resolved?

Schism

In Judaism a disagreement occurred that continues to have consequences to the present day.

Judaism was united for thousands of years from the time of Abraham and Moses. Then, during the period of the Enlightenment in the 17th and 18th centuries, the world changed rapidly. This had an effect on the development of Judaism and a certain division, or schism, occurred.

To be a Jew is to be part of the Jewish community and follow a certain way of life. Jews are descendants of Abraham and follow the Law of God given to Moses on Mount Sinai. The basic beliefs and practices of Judaism remained the same for several millennia.

A painting of a Jewish synagogue in earlier times.

The Enlightenment

Then, in the 17th and 18th centuries, in a period of human history called the Enlightenment, the first changes began to occur. Discoveries in science, literature, philosophy and politics allowed men and women to think in fresh new ways. People began to talk about the equality of all human beings. Some countries eventually made laws that gave rights to minority groups. This meant that at last Jews were free to live and work outside the 'Jewish areas' of cities and towns. This new freedom enabled some Jews to think that even religion itself might begin to adapt and change with the times.

Reform

By the 19th century, some German Jews strongly believed that their religion should keep up with a changing world. They wanted to reform some aspects of Judaism and felt that Jews could try and 'fit in' a bit more with everyone else. Jewish food laws, for example, were very strict and might be re-examined, as sharing a meal with non-Jews was often a problem. They thought that some aspects of worship in the synagogue could also be brought up to date. Maybe some prayers and services could be in Hebrew and in the local language as well. They examined the sacred texts and began to ask questions such as "Who wrote the Torah? How did it come about?"

The Jewish reformers were very committed to their faith, but thought they could make it even better by bringing parts of it up to date with the modern world.

Different Views

While some Jews thought change and reform were a good idea, others thought that change was completely unnecessary. In fact, most Jews at the time thought the old ways, the traditional ways, were best. They had served people well for thousands of years, there was no need to alter them now. Jewish law and ritual was fixed; God had given it to Moses on Mount Sinai, it worked and didn't need to change.

However, the discussion had started and, over time, certain movements or groups began to foster change in the religion of Judaism. These groups became known as Progressive, or Reform, or Liberal Jews. In the 21st century there are now two main branches in the religion of Judaism:

- ❖ Orthodox Judaism (Traditional Judaism).
- ❖ Non-Orthodox Judaism (Reform and Liberal Judaism).

Orthodox and non-Orthodox Jews have different views on certain aspects of Jewish tradition.

Orthodox Jews

- ❖ The Torah
  - The Torah is the literal Word of God.
  - The five books of the Torah were written by Moses.
  - The laws of the Torah cannot change. The laws are fixed for all time.
  - The moral laws of the commandments must be kept.
  - The ritual laws, e.g. food laws, must always be kept.
- ❖ Worship
  - Services are always in Hebrew.
  - The rabbi is male.
  - Men and women sit separately in the synagogue.
  - Men and women have different roles in the synagogue.
- ❖ Rites of passage
  - A Bar-Mitzvah Sabbath service for boys.

Non-Orthodox Jews (Reform/Liberal)

- ❖ The Torah
  - The Torah is people's interpretation of the Word of God.
  - The five books of the Torah were written by different authors.
  - Some laws of the Torah can be changed to fit different circumstances.
  - The moral laws of the commandments must be kept.
  - The ritual laws may be changed or left out.
- ❖ Worship
  - Services are always in Hebrew, prayers may be said in the local language.
  - The rabbi may be male or female.
  - Men and women sit together in the synagogue.
  - Men and women have equal roles in the synagogue.
- ❖ Rites of passage
  - A Bar-Mitzvah Sabbath service for boys.
  - A Bat-Mitzvah Sabbath service for girls.

Both Orthodox and non-Orthodox Jews believe they are true followers of Abraham and Moses. Orthodox means 'right belief'. Orthodox Jews believe their form of Judaism to be correct and true and that non-Orthodox Jews are mistaken. They say the traditions of the past are sacred and no one should try to change them.

The majority of Jews living in Europe today are Orthodox Jews. This is true in the case of Britain and Ireland. There are six synagogues in Ireland; five are Orthodox and one is non-Orthodox. In Britain, one in every six synagogues is non-Orthodox.

Most Jews living in the USA are non-Orthodox. Although Orthodox and non-Orthodox Jews live in Israel, official recognition is given only to Orthodox Jews.

The interior of a modern synagogue in Israel.

Questions

Knowledge

1. What is a schism?
2. When did changes begin to take place in Judaism?
3. What is the Orthodox and non-Orthodox view on:
   a. The Torah?
   b. The use of Hebrew in synagogue worship?
4. What is the Orthodox and the non-Orthodox view on the food laws?
5. What do Orthodox Jews think of the views of non-Orthodox Jews?
6. Where do most Orthodox and non-Orthodox Jews live in the world today?

Understanding

1. What prompted Jews in the 19th century to think of reforming some of the beliefs and practices of Judaism?
2. Outline the main differences between Orthodox and non-Orthodox Jews.
3. Comment on the role of women in the different traditions of Judaism.

Research

- Find out about a group of Orthodox Jews called Hasidic Jews (sometimes called Chasidic Jews).
  - What does the word Hasidism mean?
  - When did Hasidism emerge as a form of Judaism?
  - Who is the founder of this movement within Judaism?
  - In what country did the Hasidic movement begin?
  - What is distinctive about worship in Hasidic synagogues?
  - Who is the Zaddik?
  - Where do communities of Hasidic Jews live today?
  - In what way does the appearance of Hasidic Jews make them stand out from other Jews?
  - Exchange interesting points of information with the rest of the class.

The Jewish Community

Key Concepts

Community structure: the way a community of faith is organised.

Leadership: the task of a leader in guiding a community of faith.

Education: the way the faith is passed on within a community of faith.

Dialogue: open and honest discussion between the major world religions.

Objectives

Describe a key leadership role in the Jewish Community.

Outline the benefits of interfaith dialogue and the links between Judaism and Christianity.

Section C

Activity: *"The Ring Leader"*

TASK: TO LOOK AT THE FUNCTION OF LEADERS IN HUMAN COMMUNITIES.

✦ Divide the class into 2 or 3 groups.

✦ A group may select one of the following statements.
"If I were Taoiseach I would...
"If I were School Principal I would..."
"If I were Sports Coach/ Trainer I would..."

✦ One person in the group will suggest something he/she would do. The next person repeats what has just been said then adds his/her own comment.

✦ Continue this process around the group. The list will get longer! Anyone who forgets a comment is out. Have fun!

Discuss

- What is a leader?
- What do leaders do?
- How do we know when a leader is doing a good job?

Community Structure

The rabbi is the leader of a Jewish community.

Community structure is the way a community of faith is organised. The Jewish community is organised in a certain way with its own network of roles and relationships.

People have certain roles. Each role helps the community to function properly. In Judaism there are no priests, no bishops and no single overall leader, unlike many Christian Churches. Instead the religious needs of the Jewish community are met by a number of different individuals. Each one has a special role and serves the community in a unique way.

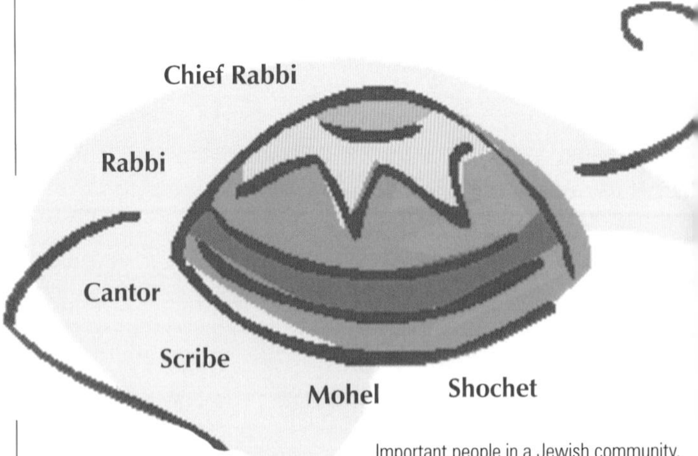
Chief Rabbi
Rabbi
Cantor
Scribe
Mohel
Shochet

Important people in a Jewish community.

The rabbi, the cantor, the scribe, the mohel and the shochet all make an important contribution to the religious life of the Jewish people. This clear structure holds the community together and enables it to run effectively.

Leadership

Leadership is the task of a leader in guiding a community of faith. Each country has a Chief Rabbi who is the senior leader of the Jewish community in that country.

Each synagogue employs its own rabbi. He is a layman with a deep knowledge of the Torah and the Talmud, and a firm commitment to the Jewish way of life.

The Chief Rabbi

The Chief Rabbi is the senior leader of the Jewish community in a particular country. His role is to rule and advise on issues of importance to the Jewish people at a national level. He also acts as an ambassador for the religion of Judaism in the wider community. He may attend meetings of:

The Board of Deputies
- an organisation that represents the interests of Jews living in Britain, for example.

The European Conference of Rabbis
- a meeting of Jewish leaders from all over Europe.

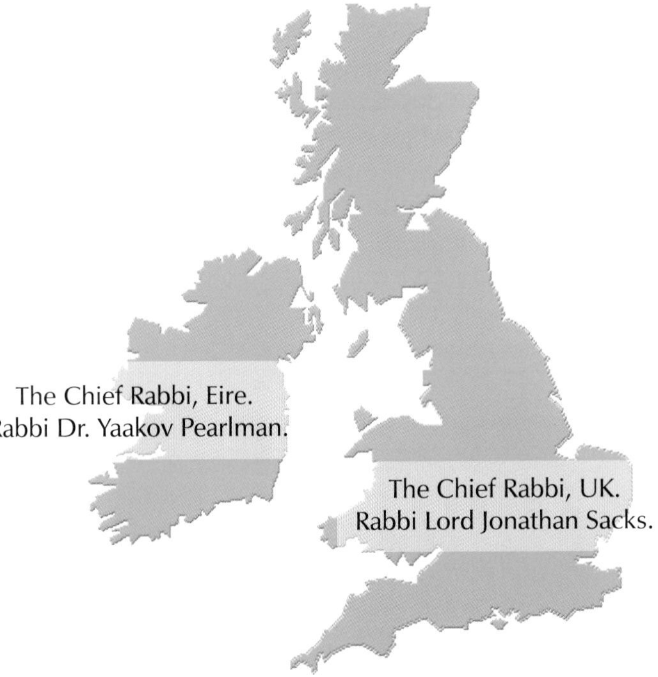
The Chief Rabbi, Eire.
abbi Dr. Yaakov Pearlman.
The Chief Rabbi, UK.
Rabbi Lord Jonathan Sacks.

The Rabbi

The rabbi is the leader of the Jewish faith community and a teacher of the Law. The rabbi is not a priest, a 'go-between' who appeals to God on behalf of the people. In Judaism, each person represents themselves before God. The word 'rabbi' means teacher. Long ago the work of the rabbi was to the study the Torah and teach its wisdom to the Jewish people. Today the role of the rabbi has changed. As religious leader of the Jewish community at local level, the rabbi guides people on both religious and personal matters. A college education, and a long training prepares a rabbi to serve the community.

The Role of the Rabbi

The rabbi has a key role in the Jewish community.

The rabbi:

- Leads the prayers in the synagogue on Shabbat, reads the Sefer Torah in Hebrew, and gives a sermon on the reading.
- Teaches the Law and helps people to apply it to their daily lives.
- Prepares couples for marriage and officiates at wedding ceremonies.
- Conducts funerals and comforts the bereaved.
- Prepares young people to celebrate their Bar-Mitzvah.
- Forms a *bet din* with two other rabbis. A bet din is a Jewish court that makes judgements on issues of Jewish law. It can, for example, issue a *get* (a divorce document), award licences to kosher butchers, and settle disputes among Jewish business people. A bet din does not replace the law courts in any country.
- Advises Gentiles (non-Jews) about Jewish affairs.

The Cantor

A cantor is a person who leads the congregation in singing in the larger synagogues. The cantor's role is important, since no musical instruments (such as organs for example) can be played on the Sabbath. Such activity would be seen as 'work' and is not allowed on the Sabbath day. The cantor's main duty is to chant the prayers in the synagogue on the Sabbath and at festivals throughout the year. He will also take part in wedding ceremonies and funeral services.

The Scribe

The scribe has the important task of copying out the Torah scrolls by hand. A Sefer Torah, or handwritten copy of the Torah, is kept in every synagogue. The work is carried out with great care and attention to detail (if a mistake is made the entire section must be re-written all over again). The role of the scribe also involves handwriting scripture on small pieces of parchment which are placed in Tefillin and Mezuzah.

A scribe at work.

The Mohel

The mohel is a person who circumcises baby boys when they are eight days old. Long ago, the child's father carried out this delicate task. Today, it is performed by a specially trained mohel who goes to the child's home for the ceremony. The role of the mohel is important because circumcision is a physical mark of the covenant between God and the descendants of Abraham. When a child is circumcised, he becomes a member of God's chosen people.

The Shochet

The shochet is a butcher who is specially trained to slaughter animals according to Jewish law. In the process he makes sure that most of the animal's blood is drained away. Jews may only eat meat prepared by a shochet. Such meat is regarded as kosher, which means it is suitable and fit for a Jew to eat. Kosher food can be bought in shops in Dublin and Belfast and in many cities throughout Britain.

Education

Education refers to the way the faith is passed on within a community of faith. Jewish children's religious education begins at an early age, mainly in the home. The home is the centre of Jewish religious life. It is where most prayer and worship takes place. Children join the family in the weekly celebration of Shabbat. Parents are encouraged to explain the meaning of Shabbat, Pesach, and the other festivals held throughout the year.

Children can also attend classes in the synagogue in the evening, or at the weekend. The rabbi teaches the class to read and speak Hebrew. Young boys learn to read the Torah and to study the Law in preparation for their Bar-Mitzvah.

In areas where there is a large Jewish community, children can attend a Jewish school. The ethos of the school will be Jewish, this means the traditions of Judaism will be observed by teachers and pupils at the school. In addition to the ordinary subjects studied for examination, the religious tradition is passed on through the study of Jewish scripture and by highlighting annual Jewish festivals. Many Jewish schools are multi-denominational and students of all religions can attend.

A Jewish school in Dublin.

Dialogue

Dialogue is open and honest discussion between the major world religions. Many believe it is important that people of different religions discuss their religious beliefs and practices. A dialogue is a conversation. When people have a discussion or a conversation they share information about themselves, and talk about things that interest then. People get to know and understand each other when they discuss things together.

Throughout history, Jews and Christians had very few real conversations. Instead there was suspicion and hatred between members of both communities. This resulted in false accusations and the brutal persecution of Jewish people on many occasions. In Nazi occupied Europe there was the ultimate horror of the Holocaust.

Council of Christians and Jews

During the darkest days of World War 2, a small group of Christians and Jews met in England. These peacemakers and people of vision began a series of conversations about what united and what divided the two faith communities. In 1942 the 'Council of Christians and Jews' was formed. It was officially launched by their respective religious leaders, the Archbishop of Canterbury and the Chief Rabbi of Britain. The CCJ was set up to promote good relations between Christian and Jewish communities, and now has over fifty branches throughout Britain and Ireland.

Inter-faith dialogue between Christians and Jews encourages respect and understanding. The hope is that meeting and talking together will help reduce intolerance and bring an end to anti-Semitism. Christians and Jews can learn about each others traditions, they can recognise the similarities and yet be candid about the differences.

Christians and Jews

Believe in:

- One God.
- Life after death.
- God's final Judgement.
- The Ten Commandments.

Have different beliefs about:

- The nature of God.
- The expectation of a Messiah.
- The person of Jesus Christ.
- The status of the Bible and the Tenakh.

Questions

Knowledge

1. List the roles that people have in a Jewish community.
2. What is the title of the leader of the Jewish community in any country?
3. What is the name of the leader of the Jewish community in Ireland?
4. What is the role of the rabbi in a local Jewish community?
5. What is the duty of the cantor in a synagogue?
6. How does the work of the scribe benefit the Jewish community?
7. a. What is a mohel?
   b. What task is performed by a shochet?
8. Who is mainly responsible for the religious education of Jewish children?
9. What is the 'Council of Christians and Jews'?
10. What are the principal links between Christians and Jews.

Understanding

1. Outline the structure of the Jewish community.
2. How does the role of the rabbi support members of the Jewish community in the practice of their faith?
3. Why is the religious education of children important in Judaism?
4. Why is it important for followers of different religions to engage in interfaith dialogue?

Research

- Find out more about primary or post-primary education in the Jewish community.
- Gather information about a Jewish school in Britain or Ireland.
  - Where is the school located?
  - Is it a boarding or a day school?
  - How long is it established?
  - How many students attend the school at present?
  - What subjects are on the curriculum?
  - What facilities does the school have for its activities?
  - What is the school uniform?
  - What is on the school crest?
  - Is there a school mission statement?
  - How does the school mission statement reflect the Jewish ethos of the school?
  - Do non-Jewish students attend this school?
- Discuss any interesting fact that may emerge from this investigation.

Jewish Identity

Key Concepts

Follower/ Discipleship: persons called to follow the teaching and way of life of a religious leader.

Tradition: the wisdom and teaching of a community of faith handed down from generation to generation.

Objective

Describe the faith and practice of Jewish communities past and present.

Activity: *"A Things-to-do List"*

TASK: TO GATHER INFORMATION ON ASPECTS OF JEWISH IDENTITY.

- Individually or in pairs select an item from the list.
- List as many points of information as you can about your chosen topic.
  - ❐ *Mezuzah.*
  - ❐ *Synagogue.*
  - ❐ *Pesach.*
  - ❐ *Kosher.*
  - ❐ *Rabbi.*
  - ❐ *Bar-Mitzvah.*
  - ❐ *Magen David.*
  - ❐ *The Ten Sayings.*
  - ❐ *Jerusalem.*
  - ❐ *Seder.*
  - ❐ *Israel.*
  - ❐ *Talmud.*
  - ❐ *Psalms.*
  - ❐ *Shabbat.*
  - ❐ *Hebrew.*
  - ❐ *Shema.*
  - ❐ *Mohel.*
  - ❐ *The Shoah.*
  - ❐ *Yom Kippur.*
  - ❐ *Sefer Torah.*
  - ❐ *Kippah.*

Discuss

- What topics were chosen by members of the class?
- What does all this information tell us about Jewish identity?

Follower/Discipleship

There are many distinctive features unique to Judaism.

Judaism is a monotheistic religion, founded almost 4,000 years ago by Abraham and Moses. It is the oldest monotheistic faith in the world. Down the ages Jews have learned to remain faithful to the covenant that God made first with Abraham and later with Moses.

To be a Jew is to:

- belong to the religion of Judaism.
- believe in one all-powerful God.
- follow a way of life based on the Torah, the Law of God.

There are over 18 million Jews in the world today, mainly in the United States, Europe, Russia and Israel. The Star of David is a symbol of Judaism. It highlights the reign of David, King of Israel.

Star of David.

Jewish Identity

Identity is the set of distinct characteristics by which a person or group is recognised. Jewish identity is about the many beliefs and customs unique to Jews and the religion of Judaism.

- **Founder.** Abraham is patriarch and founding father of Judaism.
- **Followers.** Orthodox and non-Orthodox Jews follow the teaching that Moses received from God on Mount Sinai.

  The Shema (Deut 6:4-6) is the creed, or main statement, of Jewish belief. God's special relationship with the chosen people was sealed with the covenant.
- **Beliefs.** Jews are monotheistic. They believe in and worship one all-powerful God.
- **Sacred text.** The Tenakh, especially the books of the Torah. The Talmud is a collection of discussions on the Torah that guide Jews in the right way to live.
- **Holy day of the week.** Shabbat, the Jewish holy day, begins at sunset on Friday and ends at sunset on Saturday. It is a day of rest and prayer.
- **Place of worship.** The synagogue, where the scrolls of the Torah are kept in the Ark and read at the bimah. The family home, however, is the more important place of Jewish prayer and worship.
- **Prayer.** Jews pray three times a day. The Siddur is a Jewish prayer book. The Shema is a special Jewish prayer. Jewish men wear a kippah, tallit and tefillin at prayer.
- **Pilgrimage.** The Western Wall in Jerusalem is sacred and a place of pilgrimage for Jewish people.

A kipah can be bought from a shop or a market.

- **Festivals.** Jews celebrate many major and minor festivals throughout the year. Pesach (Passover) is a major festival celebrated by Jewish families in spring time. At Yom Kippur victims of the Holocaust are remembered.
- **Leadership.** The rabbi is the leader of the local Jewish community. He teaches people how to obey the Law in the Torah. Obeying the Law is how Jews show love and respect for God.
- **Life style.** Jews obey moral laws such as the Ten Sayings (Ten Commandments) and follow ritual laws such as eating only kosher food.
- **Rites of Passage.** Ceremonies mark important moments in a person's life, such as birth, marriage and death. Bar-Mitzvah marks a boy's coming of age in the religion of Judaism and entry into adult faith.
- **Symbol.** The Magen (shield of) David is often called the Star of David and is a symbol of Judaism.

Tradition

Tradition is the wisdom and teaching of a community of faith handed down from generation to generation. The wisdom and teaching of Judaism is contained in its sacred texts, the Tenakh and the Talmud. The Torah is the most important part of the Tenakh. Jews believe God gave the Torah to Moses on Mount Sinai.

The Torah is the Law of God and guides the Jews in the right way to live. Over the centuries Jewish rabbis studied the Torah and passed on their knowledge and understanding to the Jewish people. The rabbis taught them how to apply the Law to any given situation in their daily lives.

In every generation religious leaders:

- ❖ Study the sacred texts in great detail.
- ❖ Teach the beliefs, practices and codes of behaviour to the faithful.
- ❖ Show the faithful how to apply these principles to their daily lives.

The beliefs and practices of Judaism have been preserved in the sacred texts, and in the teaching of Jewish rabbis, down the ages to the present day.

A young Jewish man prays at the Western Wall in Jerusalem.

An ancient handwritten scroll of the Torah.

Questions

Knowledge

1. What is a monotheistic religion?
2. What is meant by 'tradition' in Judaism?
3. Who were the guardians of Jewish tradition down through the centuries?
4. What is the main statement of belief in the religion of Judaism?
5. What are some of the main Jewish traditions that constitute Jewish identity?

Understanding

1. What is distinctive about being a Jew, a follower of the Jewish tradition?
2. Outline the similarities and differences between Judaism and two other world religions, in terms of: beliefs, sacred text, prayer, pilgrimage, festivals and lifestyle of believers.

Research

- Find out about a recent initiative to promote good relations between different communities of faith.
  - First, present the facts:
    - What was done?
    - Who was involved?
    - What was the reaction?
  - Second, interpret the facts.
    - How did this initiative promote tolerance and understanding among people in the community?
  - Write a concluding remark based on this experience.

Section C

Ancient Civilisations

Key Concept

Location: the part of the world where a religion began.

Objective

Describe the geographical location at the foundation of the major world religions.

Activity: *"Map Work"*

TASK: TO NAME COUNTRIES AND CITIES THAT TODAY OCCUPY PLACES ASSOCIATED WITH ANCIENT CIVILISATIONS.

✦ Use an atlas to find the following:

a. Continents.
1. Europe.
2. Asia.

b. Countries.
3. India.
4. China.
5. Saudi Arabia.
6. Israel.

c. Regions.
7. The Middle East.
8. The Far East.

d. Cities

9. Karachi.	10. Beijing.
11. Cairo.	12. Jerusalem.
13. Riyadh.	14. Damascus.

Discuss

- Did you find all the places on the map? Award yourself a mark: ___ / 14
- Have you ever (✓):
  - ✧ Heard about these cities before? ☐
  - ✧ Visited one of these countries? ☐
  - ✧ Lived in one of these countries? ☐
  - ✧ Known someone who has visited or lived in one of these countries? ☐
  - ✧ Heard of a famous person from one of these countries? ☐
- State anything you know about life in any one of these locations today.

Location

A location is that place or part of the world where each of the major world religions began.

How do we learn about people who lived in the past? We find out about them through:

- ❖ a study of ancient writing.
- ❖ a study of archaeological objects.

Archaeologists dig up objects left in the ground such as tools, pottery, stonework from buildings and human remains, and examine them carefully. Archaeologists are scientists who can show us how people lived in earlier times, even before writing was invented.

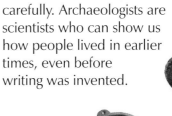

Archaeologists at work.

Section C

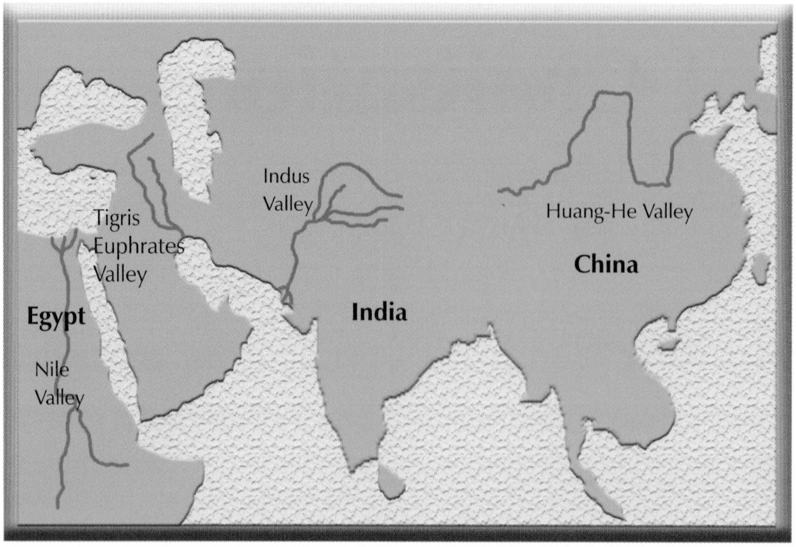
Indus
Valley
Tigris
Euphrates
Valley
Huang-He Valley
China
Egypt
India
Nile
Valley

The valleys of the great rivers.

The first centres of civilisation

The first centres of civilisation were established in the valleys of the great rivers. There was enough water for people and animals and the soil was good for growing crops. Families were able to survive without too much hardship.

It is thought that civilisation began when people began to live and work together in large groups. This occurred in:

- ❖ The Nile Valley in Egypt.
- ❖ The Tigris-Euphrates Valley in the Middle East (it was called Mesopotamia in ancient times).
- ❖ The Indus Valley in India.
- ❖ The Huang-He Valley in China.

Ancient Egyptian hieroglyphics.

How civilisations developed

At one time, all the people in these areas were nomads. Nomads were wandering tribesmen who herded their cattle and sheep along the banks of the great rivers. Sometimes they stopped for a few seasons to grow crops in the good soil in the river valleys. The nomads learned to co-operate and help each other out. They dug canals to bring the river water to their fields and worked together to harvest their crops. Some nomadic groups began to settle and set up farming villages in different places. A number of these villages grew into small towns.

City States

Over time, some towns became important cities. Walls were built around the cities to protect them from invaders. The leaders in the cities became very powerful. Kings and royal families ruled the cities and all the land around in every direction. These became the city states of the ancient world. Some city states were so powerful that they controlled empires. Life inside and outside the city walls had to be organised. Kings needed to keep track of their armies, their battles, their land, and their wealth. Records had to be kept, so there was a need for some form of writing. Every ancient civilisation developed its own form of writing.

Civilisations didn't appear overnight. The entire process took place slowly, over hundreds and, in some cases, thousands of years. Written records, together with archaeological remains, give us an insight into the way life was lived in different places long ago.

Major World Religions

Ancient civilisations were located in the valleys of the great rivers. Each civilisation had its own religious beliefs and religious practices. Religion helped people to make sense of their lives and the world around them.

The major world religions, Hinduism and Buddhism, started in India. Judaism, Christianity, and Islam began in the Middle East, while Taoism emerged in China.

There are many religions throughout the world today. Each started in a different way and at different times in human history. Our focus here is on religions that emerged in the great civilisations of India and the Middle East.

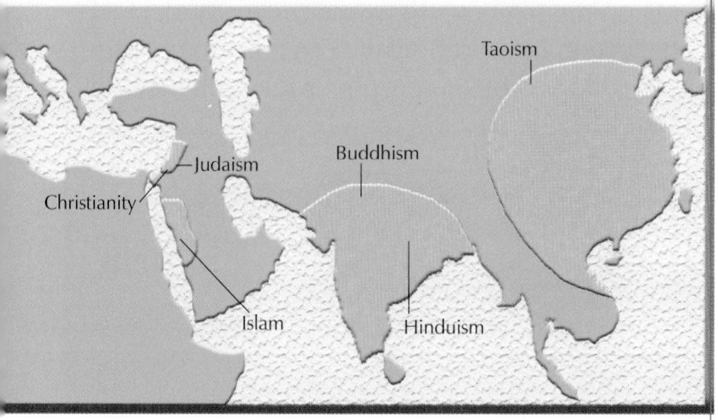

Taoism
Judaism
Buddhism
Christianity
Islam
Hinduism

Location of major world religions

Major World Religions

Religion:	Place Of Origin:	Date:
✧ Hinduism	India	about 4,500 years ago
✧ Judaism	The Middle East	about 4,000 years ago
✧ Buddhism	India	about 2,500 years ago
✧ Christianity	The Middle East	about 2,000 years ago
✧ Islam	The Middle East	about 1,500 years ago

Questions

Knowledge

1. What is archaeology?
2. Where did the first great civilisations develop?
3. Where is the Indus Valley located on a map of the world?
4. What two rivers flow through the area that was called Mesopotamia long ago?
5. a. What are nomads?
   b. Who were the nomads in ancient times?
6. What was a city state?
7. Why was writing important in ancient civilisations?
8. Where did the religion of Hinduism develop?
9. Where did the religion of Buddhism first develop?
10. Where did the religion of Islam begin?

Understanding

1. Explain how the earliest civilisations developed.
2. In what locations did major religions emerge throughout the world?
3. Why do you think many of the major religions began or had their foundation in the valleys of the great rivers?

Research

✪ Find out a little about the religion of Taoism. It emerged in the great civilisation of China.

- Can you explain the meaning of the term "Tao"?
- When did Taoism begin?
- Who were the founders?
- What are the sacred texts?
- What is the meaning of the Ying-Yang symbol?
- What is the role of martial arts in the Taoist outlook on life?
- Share interesting points of information with the class.

Islam - the Context

Key Concepts

Location: the part of the world where the religion of Islam began.

Cultural context: the whole way of life of people living in the place where Islam began.

Objective

Describe the geographical location and the cultural context at the foundation of Islam.

Activity: *"History in the Making"*

TASK: TO FIND OUT WHAT IS HAPPENING IN THE LIVES OF PEOPLE IN SAUDI ARABIA OR THE MIDDLE EAST TODAY.

- Locate the following countries on a map of the world.
  - Egypt.
  - Saudi Arabia.
  - Syria.
  - Iraq.
  - Iran.
- Find a current news item about Saudi Arabia, or another country in the Middle East that might be of interest to the class.
  - *Check:* - newspapers.
    - television news programmes.
    - internet world news sites.
- Exchange information and briefly discuss the facts.

Discuss

- What news items were discussed today?
- What does this information tell us about the life and culture of people living in the Middle East.
- Does anyone have a personal account of what life is like in that part of the world?

Section C

Location

The religion of Islam began in Saudi Arabia.

Islam is a major world religion with over one billion members in the world today. Muslims believe in one God, Allah. The religion of Islam was founded by the prophet Muhammad about 1,500 years ago.

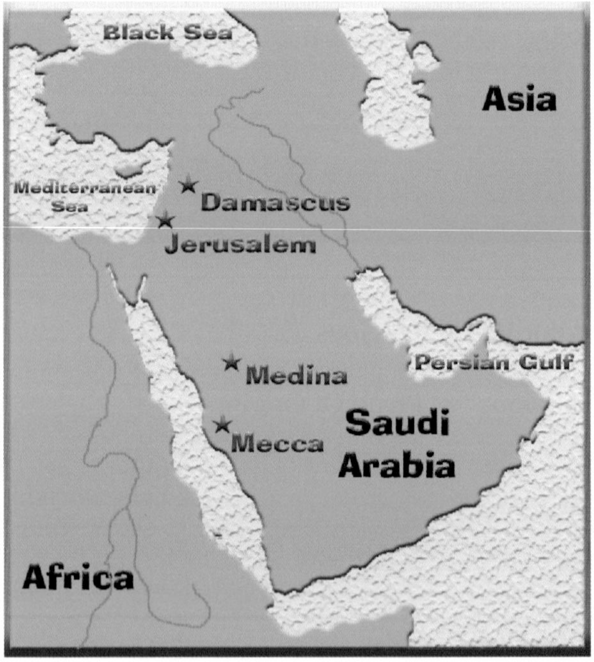
Black Sea
Asia
Mediterranean Sea
Damascus
Jerusalem
Persian Gulf
Medina
Mecca
Saudi Arabia
Africa

The location of Saudi Arabia.

Saudi Arabia in the Middle East is the location, or place, where the religion of Islam began. Arabia is a vast desert land that juts out into the sea between North Africa and western Asia. Mecca and Medina, two cities in Saudi Arabia, are central to the story of the beginnings of Islam.

Cultural Context

The cultural context is the way of life of the people living in Saudi Arabia at the time Islam began. The people of Arabia were known as Arabs. The word 'Arab' means someone who lives in the desert. The nomadic desert people migrated from place to place in search of water and fresh pasture for their animals. It was a harsh life always moving around and trying to cope with shortages of food and water. It made the Arabs tough and warlike. Arab tribes often fought among themselves for control of scarce resources.

Mecca

Some Arabs settled in Mecca, a city that grew up around an oasis on the west coast of Arabia. Mecca was an important trading centre on the path of several trade routes going north to Damascus and the Mediterranean. Traders stopped in Mecca for food and water and to buy and sell goods in the marketplace.

Mecca was also an important religious centre and a place of pilgrimage for the nomadic tribes of the Arabian Peninsula. The Arabs were polytheists and worshipped many gods. Carved images of their gods were kept in the Ka'ba, a shrine in the centre of Mecca. Arab pilgrims arrived in large numbers to worship at this shrine.

Arab traders today.

The Arabs knew of the Jewish and Christian religions because they met Jews and Christians on the caravan routes and at the trading centres across Arabia. But the religious beliefs of Jews and Christians never appealed to them. The tribal people of the desert kept their own beliefs and continued their way of life until the sixth century CE. Everything changed when a child called Muhammad was born to one of the most powerful tribes in the city of Mecca.

Questions

Knowledge

1. Where did the religion of Islam begin?
2. Explain the following terms:
   - Arab. - Polytheist. - Nomad.
3. List as many points as possible about the location and physical features of Saudi Arabia.
4. State one advantage of Mecca's position on the ancient trade routes.
5. What was the religion of the Arab people before the foundation of Islam?

Understanding

1. What impact did the climate and landscape of Arabia have on the Arab people and their way of life?
2. Explain the importance of Mecca in ancient times as:
   a. A trading centre.
   b. A religious centre.
3. Describe the cultural context of Arabia at the beginning of Islam.

Research

- Find out about the Ka'ba in Mecca before the foundation of Islam.
  - What did the structure look like?
  - How many statues or images were kept there?
  - What was contained inside the building?
  - What water source was located near the building?
  - Speculate about the significance of this shrine in the religious life of people in the Arabian peninsula before the establishment of Islam.
  - Discuss your ideas with the class.

Prophet Muhammad

Key Concepts

Founder: the person who established a religion.

Vision: a vivid dream or mental image of something important.

Prophet: a person chosen by God to give people an important message.

Objective

Identify key moments in the life of the Prophet Muhammad, the founder of Islam.

Activity: *"Famous Faces"*

TASK: TO IDENTIFY FAMOUS INDIVIDUALS PAST AND PRESENT.

✦ Can you say why each of the following have become well known beyond their country of origin?

- Napoleon Bonaparte.
- William Shakespeare.
- Isaac Newton.
- Mother Teresa.
- Abraham Lincoln.
- Albert Einstein.
- Marie Curie.
- Martin Luther King.

Discuss

- List some other famous people.
- For what is each person famous?
- Can you name a famous person known to millions of people yet whose face has never been photographed, painted or drawn by anyone?

Founder

The founder of Islam is famous throughout the world.

About 1,500 years ago, a holy man, a prophet named Muhammad, founded the religion of Islam. When Muslims speak or write the name of their prophet, they usually say "Muhammad, peace be upon him". It is a way of showing respect. Furthermore, no image of the Prophet may be painted or drawn or represented in movement or dance.

Early Life

Muhammad is the founder of Islam. He was born in Mecca, in what is now Saudi Arabia, around 570CE. Orphaned as a child, his uncle a rich merchant looked after him until he grew up. Muhammad began work in his uncle's business as a camel driver travelling across the deserts of Arabia. He was such an honest and trustworthy young man that people called him Al-Amin, 'Trustworthy One'.

Throughout his journeys he met traders from other lands, some were Christians, others were Jews. At night around the camp fires they may have sat and talked about their various beliefs and customs.

When he was twenty five years old, Muhammad married a wealthy widow named Khadijah and they had six children. Muhammad became a successful business man in charge of camel caravans that journeyed across the trade routes of Arabia.

Mecca

Mecca in those days was a busy location. Pilgrims crowded around the Ka'ba, traders bought and sold animals and goods in the market place. Muhammad was a good man and became troubled by many things that were wrong in the city. The traders were greedy and dishonest, and they cheated the poor. Too much time was spent drinking and fighting. Women and children were badly treated.

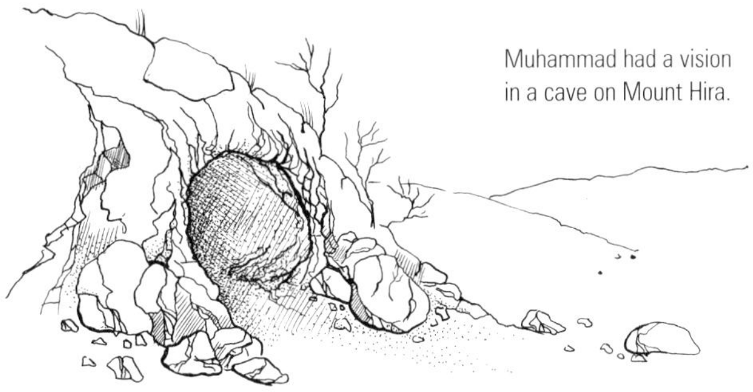

Muhammad had a vision in a cave on Mount Hira.

Mount Hira

Muhammad thought a lot about life and its problems. He went off regularly to the hills overlooking the city. There in the peace and quiet he was able to think and to pray. Muhammad had always been a religious man, yet unlike everyone else he did not worship the gods or idols in the Ka'ba.

Muhammad began to think that idol worhip was the cause of a lot of problems in the city. The worship of many gods was leading people astray. He came to the conclusion that there was only one God, Allah. (Allah is the Arabic word for God.) The same God that was worshipped by Jews and Christians.

Arab traders in a market today.

Vision

Night of Power and Excellence

When Muhammad was about forty years old he went as usual to the hills, just outside the city. One night while praying and fasting in a cave on Mount Hira, something extraordinary happened. Muhammad had a vision. The angel Gabriel appeared to him telling him there was one God, Allah, and Muhammad was chosen to be God's messenger. Muslims celebrate this event as the 'Night of Power and Excellence'.

The experience was unsettling and Muhammad rushed home. His wife assured him that God had indeed called him to be his prophet. Khadijah had great faith and she became the first convert to the new religion of Islam.

Muhammad continued to receive messages from God throughout his life. Khadijah and some other converts learned them by heart until they were all written down. These messages later became the Qur'an, the sacred text of Islam.

Prophet

Muhammad became a prophet, a person chosen to give people a message from God. He began to preach in the city of Mecca.

His message stated that:

- People must worship the one God, Allah, not all the idols in the Ka'ba.
- People must listen to Muhammad because he is the Prophet of Allah.
- Everyone must live good lives, conduct their business honestly, share with the poor, and care for women and children.
- Any wrongdoing in this life will be punished by God in the next.

This message was not very popular with the powerful traders in the city. They relied on the business generated by pilgrims who came to worship at the Ka'ba. Fairness and honesty would reduce their profits even further. They threatened Muhammad and eventually stopped him preaching in the city altogether. Muhammad feared for his life.

The Hijra

In 622CE the Prophet and a group of followers left Mecca secretly in the middle of the night. They travelled across the desert to the city of Medina. The difficult journey from Mecca to Medina is called the Hijra. For Muslims, this event marks the beginning of the religion of Islam. It marks the first day of the first year of the Islamic calendar.

Medina

Muhammad and his followers were made welcome in Medina. The prophet preached his message and made many converts. Under his leadership the first Muslim community was established in Medina. The community grew and the Five Pillars, the moral code of Islam, became accepted throughout the city. The first mosque was built in Medina as a place of prayer and worship. When Muhammad later became the leader of Medina, the rules of Islam became the rules of the city. His power and influence grew stronger and stronger.

The Ka'ba

Eight years later, Muhammad returned to Mecca with a large army. The city was taken by surprise and fell into his hands. He went straight to the Ka'ba and had all the statues and idols removed. He declared that the Ka'ba would instead be the shrine of the one God, Allah.

When Muhammad stated that all Muslims must make a pilgrimage to the Ka'ba, the citizens of Mecca were assured that the valuable pilgrim trade to the shrine would continue. The leaders and the people of the city converted to Islam. Before long, Mecca became the holy city of Islam. Muhammad died in Medina two years later, after returning from a pilgrimage to Mecca. It was the year 632CE, he was around 62 years old. Muhammad is considered by Muslims to be the last, and the greatest, of all the prophets.

Mecca

The Ka'ba.

Questions

Knowledge

1. a. Who founded the religion of Islam?
   b. When and where did Islam begin?
2. What happened in Muhammad's early life?
3. Name the wife of Muhammad.
4. What extraordinary event took place on the 'Night of Power and Excellence'?
5. What is a prophet?
6. What was Muhammad's message to the people of Mecca?
7. What is the Hijra?
8. How did the people of Medina respond to Muhammad's message?
9. What happened when Muhammad returned to Mecca in 630CE?
10. When did the death of the Prophet take place?

Understanding

1. a. List the key moments in the life of Muhammad.
   b. What do Muslims believe about the prophet Muhammad?
2. Why is the Hijra such an important event for Muslims?
3. Compare the way the people of Mecca and the people of Medina responded to the message of the Prophet.

Research

* Identify key moments in the biography of the founder of Islam. On a life-line chart; plot the sequence of events that occurred in the life of the Prophet. The line may be straight or meandering, it may have peaks and troughs to represent the highs and lows in the Prophet's life.
* Use drawings and symbols to complete the task. Remember that out of the tradition of respect no image of the Prophet himself may be printed or drawn.

Section C

Sacred Text

Key Concepts

Sacred text: the book of holy or sacred writings of a community of faith.

Oral tradition: stories and religious teaching that a people pass on by word of mouth.

Evidence: information about a religious tradition collected from different sources.

Revelation: the way in which God chooses to make himself known to human beings.

Inspiration: the way in which a person is guided by God to pass on a sacred message.

Objectives

Name the primary source of information about Islam.

Trace the development of its sacred text from the oral tradition to the written word.

Activity: *"Chinese Whispers"*

TASK: TO DISCOVER WHAT CAN HAPPEN WHEN INFORMATION IS TRANSMITTED ORALLY.

- Organise the class into one or two circles.
- TEACHER: begin by saying something in a low voice to the nearest student.
- STUDENT: pass the sentence around the circle by whispering it to the person on your left.

Rules:
- Whisper the message.
- Do not ask any questions.
- Do not ask for the message to be repeated.

- When the message has travelled around the circle compare what the last person says with the initial sentence.

Discuss

- What message was passed on by the first student?
- How did the final version compare with the first sentence?
- What happened to the message on the way around the circle?
- What could be done to make sure that a message stays exactly the way it was at the start?

Sacred Text

The teaching of Islam was passed on orally before being written down in sacred texts.

The Qur'an is the sacred text of Islam. It is the primary source of information about the beliefs and practices of Islam. The Hadith is another sacred text.

The Qur'an is a document of faith. Muslims believe the Qur'an is the word of Allah, revealed to Muhammad by the angel Gabriel. The Hadith is a collection of sayings and teachings from the life of Muhammad. In Islam, there is a clear distinction between:

- the Qur'an - the direct word of Allah.
- the Hadith - the teaching of Muhammad.

The holy Qur'an.

The Qur'an

The Qur'an is the sacred text of Islam. For Muslims, the Qur'an is a record of the words spoken to Muhammad by the angel Gabriel. It states clearly what Muslims must believe and how they should live.

The Qur'an is written in Arabic, the language spoken by Muhammad. Muslims learn Arabic in order to read the Qur'an. Arabic is written from right to left, so the Qur'an begins at what we would think is the last page. It is not a big book, it is about the same size as the New Testament in the Christian Bible. The Qur'an is divided into 114 surahs (chapters) of different lengths. Most surahs begin with the words "In the name of Allah, the compassionate, the merciful." All Muslims learn several surahs by heart.

Muslims are expected to read part of the Qur'an every day. There is a copy of the Qur'an in every Muslim home, and a special copy is kept in the mosque, the Muslim place of worship. The Qur'an in the mosque is always beautifully bound and decorated.

Revelation

Revelation is the way in which God chooses to make himself known to human beings. Muslims believe that God gave a special message to Muhammad. It was dictated to him word for word by the angel Gabriel. This revelation began on the night Muhammad had a vision in the cave on Mount Hira. The angel's message was that there is one God, Allah, and Muhammad is his Prophet. Further messages were revealed to the Prophet over the next twenty years. These were later written down, word for word, in the Qur'an.

Muslims believe the words in the Qur'an are the exact words of God. This means that Allah, not Muhammad, is the author of the Qur'an. Everything in the Qur'an is the truth because it comes straight from God. It can never be changed. Muslims treat the Qur'an with great respect because they believe it is the very word of God. Muslims show respect for their sacred text by washing their hands before touching it, and placing it on a special stand to read it. It is usually wrapped in a cloth when it is not being read, and it is placed on a high shelf for safekeeping.

Muslim women reading extracts from the Qur'an.

Oral Tradition

Oral tradition refers to the stories and religious teaching that a people pass on by word of mouth. The word Qur'an means 'to recite'. The oral tradition, or oral stage of the Qur'an, lasted for a number of years. The message the Prophet received from the angel Gabriel was initially passed on by word of mouth.

Like many people at the time, Muhammad was unable to read or write, so he learned the angel's words by heart. He repeated them to his wife and followers. They too learned the angel's message word for word. It was not long before scribes began to write some of it down. Although a part of God's revelation was written during the Prophet's lifetime, most of it was passed on orally, by word of mouth. The Qur'an itself was not written during the life-time of Muhammad, it was written after his death.

Evidence

Evidence is the information about a religious tradition collected from different sources. After Muhammad died, all the revelations from oral and written sources were gathered together and written down in one volume. The Qur'an became a complete written record of God's revelations to Muhammad. It was finally written down twenty years after the Prophet's death. The Qur'an was written to ensure the word of Allah was recorded correctly, and to preserve the message of Allah for future generations.

Stages in the development of the Qur'an

- ❖ God's message is revealed to Muhammad through the angel Gabriel.
- ❖ Muhammad recites all the messages word for word.
- ❖ Muhammad passes on each message to his followers and they learn them by heart. Scribes write some of it down.
- ❖ After Muhammad's death the oral and written sources are collected together. The Qur'an is written.

Inspiration

Inspiration refers to the way a person is influenced or inspired by God to pass on a sacred message. Muslims believe Muhammad received messages from Allah through the angel Gabriel. Muhammad received inspiration or guidance to pass on these sacred messages to other people.

Muhammad learned off what the angel told him, he then recited the sacred messages to his followers, passing on the words exactly as he had received them. All the sacred messages were later carefully written down in the Qur'an. This meant many more people were able to know about Allah and what Allah wanted them to do.

Questions

Knowledge

1. What is the primary source of information about the religion of Islam.
2. What do Muslims call their sacred text?
3. In what language is the Qur'an written?
4. What is a surah?
5. What is the Hadith?
6. What message did God reveal to Muhammad?
7. Who do Muslims believe is the author of the Qur'an?
8. How do Muslims show respect for the Qur'an?
9. What is the main difference between the Qur'an and the Hadith?
10. a. What did God inspire Muhammad to do with the messages he received?
    b. When was the Qur'an eventually written?

Understanding

1. Describe the development of sacred writing in Islam from the oral tradition to the written word.
2. Why do Muslims have such a special regard for their sacred text?
3. How might a document of faith such as the Qur'an affect or influence the behaviour of faithful Muslims?

Research

- Find out more about the Hadith, an additional source of evidence about the religion of Islam.

  The Hadith
  - What does it contain?
  - Who is the author?
  - How was the book put together?
  - In what ways does it help people in the Muslim community?
  - How is the book treated by ordinary Muslim people?

  ❋ Discuss these and other findings with the class.

Belief and Practice

Key Concepts

Creed/ Ethic: the summary of a religion's deeply held beliefs and moral principles.

Practice: customs and rituals that show a person's religious faith.

Objectives

Identify the main beliefs of Islam and how these beliefs are put into practice.

Activity: *"Creeds for Today"*

TASK: TO SHARE BELIEFS ON DIFFERENT ISSUES.

✦ What do you believe?

I believe God is good.
I believe charity begins at home.
I believe...
I believe in love.
I believe that if you do the crime you do the time.
I believe...
I believe that when we die that's it!

Discuss

- What beliefs are held by members of the class?
- What beliefs or convictions are held by members of your family?
- Do you have a strong belief about something important?

Creed

Many people have deep religious beliefs that they put into practice in a variety of ways.

A creed is a statement that sums up a religion's deeply held beliefs. The Muslim creed is found in the Qur'an and consists of six main beliefs, or articles of faith.

Main Muslim Beliefs

1. Belief in Allah.
   The basic belief of Islam is that there is only one God - Allah. God is beyond all human understanding and nothing can be compared to him. There are 99 names to describe the qualities of Allah. The list of names include:
   - The Compassionate.
   - The Life-Giver.
   - The Merciful.
   - The Forgiver.

   Muslims use prayer beads to help them to concentrate when they are reciting the names of Allah.

A Muslim using prayer beads.

2. Belief in angels.
   Angels have an important place in the religion of Islam. God does not speak directly to humans. God gives messages to angels who pass on God's words to the prophets. The angel Gabriel revealed God's message to the Prophet Muhammad.

3. Belief in a sacred text.
   Muslims believe the words in the Qur'an are literally the words of Allah. The sacred text of Islam is therefore treated with great respect in both the home and the mosque.

4. Belief in prophets.
   Muslims believe that Muhammad is the last and the greatest of all the prophets. Adam was the first of twenty eight prophets who passed on the message of Allah. These include:
   - Abraham (Ibrahim).
   - Isaac (Ishaq).
   - Ishmael (Isma'il).
   - Moses (Musa).
   - David (Dawud).
   - Jesus ('Isa).
   - Muhammad.

   In Islam, Jesus is seen as an important prophet, but not as the Son of God. Muslims believe that the words of Muhammad sum up everything taught by the other prophets. He is 'The Seal of the Prophets'.

5. Belief in a Day of Judgment.
   Muslims believe that after death there will be a final Day of Judgement. Depending on how people lived, they will either:
   - Be rewarded and go to heaven.
   - Be punished and sent to hell.

6. Belief in pre-destination.
   Muslims believe that God has already decided what is going to happen. God already knows what choices people will make. So it is better for everyone to obey the will of Allah rather than go their own way in life.

A young Muslim girl holding a copy of the Qur'an.

Practice

Practice is the set of customs and rituals that show a person's religious faith. Followers of all religions put their religious beliefs into practice through performing certain daily, weekly and annual rituals, alone and in the company of others.

Muslims put their religious beliefs into practice when they carry out certain duties known as 'The Five Pillars'. It is what Muslims believe Allah wants them to do. A pillar, as we know, is something solid which supports a building. The Five Pillars help and support people in leading a Muslim way of life.

The *Dome of the Rock*, a mosque in the city of Jerusalem.

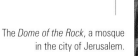

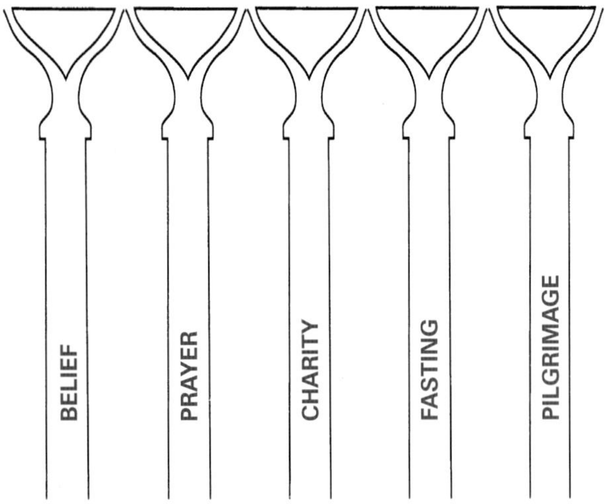
BELIEF
PRAYER
CHARITY
FASTING
PILGRIMAGE

The Five Pillars of Islam

These Five Pillars are a normal part of the Muslim way of life.

1. Belief (Shahadah).
   "There is no god but Allah and Muhammad is the Prophet of Allah." This is a statement of faith. Muslims say this creed as often as possible every day.
2. Prayer (Salat).
   Pray five times a day.
   On Friday, pray in the mosque.
3. Charity (Zakat).
   Give 2.5% of all savings every year to help those in need.
4. Fasting (Sawm).
   Fast from sunrise to sunset during the month of Ramadan. This is the time of year when Muslims make an extra effort to pray and read more of the Qur'an, practice self-denial, and give money to charity.
5. Pilgrimage (Hajj).
   Make a pilgrimage, a holy journey, to Mecca at least once in a lifetime.
   Mecca is the birthplace of Muhammad and the site of the Ka'ba, the most sacred shrine in Islam.

The star and crescent moon, the symbol of Islam.

Questions

Knowledge

1. List the main beliefs of Islam.
2. What do Muslims believe about Allah?
3. What do Muslims believe about angels?
4. What do Muslims believe about the Day of Judgement?
5. What are the main religious practices of Islam called?
6. Name the Five Pillars of Islam.
7. How often are Muslims expected to pray to Allah each day?
8. What is Zakat?
9. What do Muslims do during Ramadan?
10. What is the Hajj?

Understanding

1. Select one of the names of Allah. What things does this name suggest about Allah?
2. Why do you think Muslims regard Muhammad as unique among the prophets?
3. Provide examples of what Muslims might and might not do because of their religious beliefs.
4. Explain how the Muslim creed affects the daily life of Muslim people.

Research

- Make a list of the main religious practices of your own religion.
  - Compare some aspects of religious practice in the Muslim tradition and in one other community of faith.
  - Explore the similarities and differences.
  - Share your observation with the class.

Prayer

Key Concept

Prayer: the act of communicating with God.

Objective

Outline the importance of prayer in the religion of Islam.

Activity: *"Keeping in touch"*

TASK: TO EXAMINE HOW FRIENDS COMMUNICATE WITH ONE ANOTHER.

✦ Analyse the amount of time you spend communicating with your friends during a typical school day, e.g. on the way to school, at break times, after school etc.

Do you at any time do any of the following to keep in touch with your friends? (✓)

- Make a phone call. ❑
- Send a text. ❑
- Call around to their houses. ❑
- Send a postcard. ❑
- Use sign language. ❑
- Pass a note during class. ❑
- Meet for a chat. ❑
- Send a greeting card. ❑
- Send an email. ❑
- Use a networking site? ❑

Discuss

- How long do you spend talking to your friends on an average school day?
- When do you talk together?
- What kind of things do you talk about?
- Why do friends spend so much time keeping in touch with each other?

Prayer

Prayer is about keeping in touch with God.

Muslims communicate with God through prayer. Prayer is the second pillar of Islam. The Qur'an states that Muslims must pray five times a day. This is special time set aside for Allah.

Salat is a formal prayer that follows a set pattern of words and actions. The Qur'an states that it is important to pray to Allah at fixed times every day. Muslims pray in the morning, at midday, during the afternoon, after sunset, and before going to bed at night. Prayer is obligatory for men and women, and for boys and girls over twelve years of age. If a prayer time is missed it can be made up later.

Muslim boys at prayer.

Salat is a ritual that can be performed alone or with others. It can be offered up anywhere, at home, in a quiet place at work, or in the company of other Muslims in the mosque. When it is time for prayer, Muslims stop what they are doing and turn their mind and heart to God.

Salat

Before Salat, a Muslim must:

- Get ready to worship Allah.
  Remove shoes.
- Perform wudu.
  Become ritually clean by washing the hands, arms, head and feet in a certain way. This makes people pure and clean to enter the presence of Allah.
- Stand on clean ground.
  A prayer mat is used if not praying in the mosque.
- Face Mecca.
  A small compass will locate the direction of Mecca from most places in the world.

Salat is a series of prayers that use words and actions. Muslims pray using their whole body. The Rak'ah is a sequence of body movements; a different movement is used for each part of the prayer. The prayers are mainly verses from the Qur'an that praise Allah and ask for his guidance. All the prayers are said in Arabic.

The Rak'ah

The Rak'ah are ritual actions. Each prayer position has a special meaning:

- The person stands:
  - a sign of listening to God.
- The person bows:
  - a sign of respect for God.
- The person bows low touching the forehead to the ground:
  - a sign of obedience to the will of God.

Between each bow, the person sits back to say certain prayers. The number of Rak'ahs in the prayer varies according to the time of day. At the end of Salat, the Shahadah (creed) is said in order to give thanks for the greatness of God.

> "There is no god but Allah and Muhammad is his Prophet" -
> The Shahadah

The movements of the Rak'ah

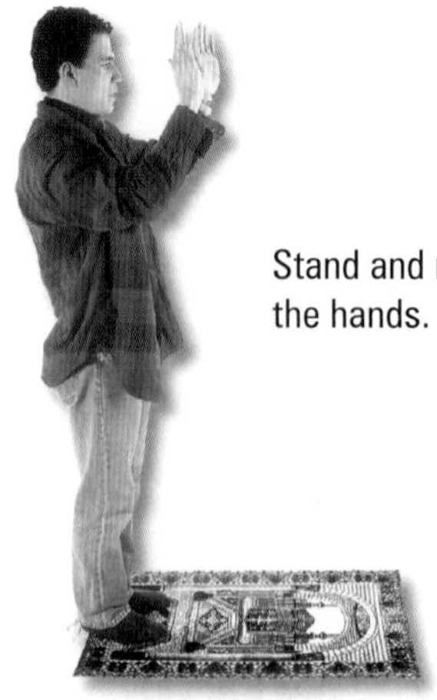

Stand and raise the hands.

Bow and straighten up again.

Bow low, touch the ground with the forehead.

Sit back on the heels.

Ways to pray

- **Personal prayer** - when Muslims pray alone during the week.
- **Communal prayer** - when Muslims pray together as part of a community, for example in the mosque on Friday at mid-day prayer. Salat is the ritual prayer performed by the Muslim community in the mosque.

Different types of prayer

Du'ah are informal personal prayers with no set pattern of words or actions. A person can say them anywhere, anytime, facing any direction, using their own words. Personal prayers may be:

- Prayers of **praise and thanksgiving** to Allah for some good thing that happened.
- Prayers of **petition** asking Allah to help with something special.
- Prayers of **penitence** that express sorrow and regret for some wrongdoing.

Du'ah ends with the person drawing their hands across their face to show that they have received Allah's blessing. The Prophet Muhammad said:

> "Prayer said in a congregation is twenty five times more excellent than prayers said by a person alone."
>
> The Hadith.

Meeting in one place, facing the same direction and performing prayer rituals together is very important in Islam. It reminds Muslims that they all belong to one worldwide community of faith. Joining together in communal prayer is a sign of unity and solidarity between Muslims everywhere.

Questions

Knowledge

1. How do Muslims communicate with Allah?
2. When are Muslims expected to pray each day?
3. Where do Muslims face when they pray?
4. How does a Muslim prepare for prayer?
5. What is wudu?
6. How do Muslims pray?
7. What is Rak'ah in Islam?
8. What is the meaning of the different movements of the Rak'ah?

Understanding

1. How does daily prayer show a person's religious commitment?
2. List the advantages and disadvantages of praying five times a day.
3. In Islam, is communal prayer as valuable as personal prayer? Give reasons for your answer.
4. How does Muslim prayer differ from prayer in your own or another religious tradition?

Research

- Find out about the use and the design of prayer mats in the tradition of Islam.
  - A prayer mat is used when a Muslim person is unable to attend the mosque for prayers. Locate some examples of prayer mat designs.
  - Share your findings and interesting points of information with the class.

Communal prayer outdoors.

Place of Worship

Key Concepts

Place of worship: a building or place where people go to pray and worship God.

Worship: the way people of faith praise and honour God in prayer and at religious services.

Objectives

Describe a Muslim place of worship. Outline the main features of Friday worship in the mosque.

Section C

Activity: *"Places of Significance"*

TASK: TO IDENTIFY PLACES THAT HAVE SIGNIFICANCE IN OUR LIVES.

✦ Think about the homes in which we live.

Discuss

- What is it about your home that makes it a special place for you?
- How important is your home to you?

1	2	3	4	5	6	7	8	9	10
Not important.									Very Important.

- Is there any other place that has meaning or significance in your life?

A mosque, the Muslim place of worship.

Place of Worship

The mosque is a place of special significance for members of the Muslim community.

A mosque is a place of worship. It is a building where Muslims go to pray and worship Allah. Prayer is the second pillar of Islam. The Prophet Muhammad told his followers to bow down and pray to Allah five times a day.

The Mosque

The word mosque means a place where people bow down in the presence of God. In Ireland and the UK some mosques are converted houses, halls or churches. A specially built mosque is a rectangular building with a dome shaped roof. The dome represents the universe over which Allah has control. It may have the symbol of the star and crescent moon on top.

At the corner of the mosque there is at least one minaret. This is a tall, narrow tower with a small balcony at the top. A muezzin (a crier) stands on the balcony and calls Muslims to prayer five times a day.

Wudu

When people arrive at the mosque they enter a partially covered courtyard. Everyone removes their footwear and covers their heads as a sign of respect. Every mosque has either a fountain outdoors or a cloakroom indoors with taps of running water. This is the wudu area for ritual cleansing. Muslims wash their feet, hands, arms and head before going inside to pray.

Muslim men performing wudu before entering the mosque to pray.

Inside the mosque

The main prayer hall inside the mosque is almost bare. There is no altar, and there are no seats, pictures, statues, flowers or candles. The Prophet Muhammad did not want images of any kind in the Muslim place of worship. They were to be avoided in case some people began to worship them instead of worshipping Allah.

The walls in some mosques are covered with beautifully decorated patterns and sentences from the Qur'an. The floor is usually covered with a deep carpet. A small arch is built into one wall, this alcove is called the mihrab. It points in the exact direction of Mecca. The mihrab is an important feature in a mosque as Muslims must pray facing the Ka'ba in Mecca.

The only piece of furniture in the mosque is the minbar. This is a small platform just like a pulpit. It is from here that sermons are preached at Friday prayer. Near the minbar is a bookstand containing a copy of the Qur'an, the sacred text of Islam.

Worship

Worship is the way people of faith praise and honour God in prayer and at religious services. Friday is the holy day of the week for Muslims. In Islam the main form of worship is Friday mid-day prayer in the mosque. Everyone gathers in the mosque to worship as a community. All Muslim men attend Friday mid-day prayer. Women can go too or they can pray at home. Men and women do not pray together in the mosque, women gather in a separate room.

Friday mid-day prayer

The imam is the leader in the mosque; there are no priests in Islam. The people choose their own imam to lead the prayers. He is a man whom everyone believes is a good Muslim and who knows the Qur'an very well. At the mihrab, the imam faces Mecca to lead the prayers. Worshippers stand shoulder to shoulder in long straight rows. There are faint lines on the carpet to help people find their place. Together they chant the creed in Arabic and perform the prayerful ritual, the Rak'ah. Muslims worship Allah with movements that involve their whole body. The imam then stands at the minbar and gives a sermon based on the Qur'an.

Muslims at prayer in a mosque.

Muslim men at prayer.

Muslims go to the mosque to worship Allah. All Muslims have a deep respect for the Prophet Muhammad, but do not worship him. Although they believe he is the last and the greatest of the prophets, he is not God.

The Mosque in Community Life

The mosque is the centre of the Muslim community in a local area. In a specially built mosque, many activities take place under one roof. The community prays together in the prayer hall. In the library and the study rooms, men and women study the Qur'an and the Muslim way of life. Children attend classes to learn Arabic in order that they too can read the Qur'an. There may be a canteen where people go to eat, and a shop where they can buy certain goods.

Questions

Knowledge

1. Name the Muslim place of worship.
2. What is the meaning of the word mosque?
3. What is a minaret?
4. How does a Muslim show respect on entering a mosque?
5. How do Muslims prepare for prayers at the mosque?
6. What are each of the following and what is its purpose in the mosque:
   a. Mihrab?
   b. Minbar?
   c. Wudu area?
7. Why are there no pictures or images in a mosque?
8. What are the roles of the following people in a mosque:
   a. Imam?
   b. Muezzin?

Understanding

1. Identify some similarities between a mosque and a place of worship in another community of faith. List some differences.
2. Describe the different elements of Friday worship in a mosque.
3. Why do Muslims worship together in the mosque?

Research

Participation

To participate means to join in and be part of something. People participate in worship as a response to mystery at the heart of human life. Muslims participate in worship as a response to the mystery of Allah who is the centre of their lives.

Try to visit a mosque. It may, or may not, be possible to observe a form of worship taking place. Alternatively watch an excerpt of Muslim worship on video/ DVD to see the different elements of worship in action.

Observe what happens during an act of worship and answer the following questions.

1. What is the Muslim place of worship called?
2. On what day of the week is the act of worship taking place?
3. What is the occasion?
4. Who is attending?
5. Who leads the worship?
6. Do people wear any item of religious clothing?
7. What sacred text is being used?
8. Is any type of music performed during the act of worship?
9. a. List the ritual actions performed during worship.
   b. Who performs these actions?
   c. What is the meaning behind the actions?
10. What was the most memorable part of the act of worship you just observed? Can you say why it made an impression on you?

Pilgrimage

Key Concepts

Pilgrimage: a journey made by a pilgrim to a shrine or a sacred place.

Ritual: an occasion when people use symbolic objects, words and actions to express what is deeply important to them.

Objectives

Describe a Muslim place of pilgrimage and how Muslims worship there.

Activity: *"Places of Significance"*

TASK: TO IDENTIFY PLACES THAT ARE IMPORTANT TO US FOR CERTAIN REASONS.

- Is there a special place that you like to go to sometimes, either by yourself or with others? It might be the park near your house, or maybe it's your grandparents' house.

Sometimes I like to visit...

- My friend's house.
- A lake.
- The beach.
- A relative's grave.
- A river.
- The sports grounds.
- The church.
- The park.
- The woods.
- Other...

Discuss

- Identify two places that are special to you in some way. Why do you like to go there sometimes?
- Is there a special place that has meaning for your whole family? Why do members of your family go there?
- Are there places in this country or elsewhere that are important for other people? Why do you think such places have significance for them?

Pilgrimage

Many people visit places that are important to them for religious reasons.

A pilgrimage is a journey to a holy or a sacred place. Most religions have places that are believed to be sacred and connected to God in a certain way. People who go on pilgrimages to holy places are called pilgrims. They are not tourists who simply want to go somewhere for a holiday. People go on a pilgrimage to pray and get closer to God.

Mecca

Hajj, the pilgrimage to Mecca, is the fifth pillar of Islam. Every Muslim is expected to go to Mecca at least once in their lifetime if they can. The pilgrimage lasts for five or more days. Each year, about two million Muslims from all over the world go on pilgrimage to Mecca.

Pilgrims praying at the The Ka'ba at the centre of the Great Mosque in Mecca. Pilgrims arriving home from Mecca can adopt the title Hajj (man) or Hajjah (woman).

Ritual

A ritual is an occasion when people use symbolic objects, words and actions to express what is deeply important to them. During the Hajj, pilgrims perform a range of symbolic actions that express important Muslim beliefs. Many of the rituals of Hajj are carried out in places Muslims believe are associated with the prophet Abraham, his wife Hagar, and his son Ishmael. Going to the different places makes the story 'come alive' for Muslim people. Mecca, the most sacred place in Islam, is where the Prophet Muhammad lived and began to teach about the one God, Allah.

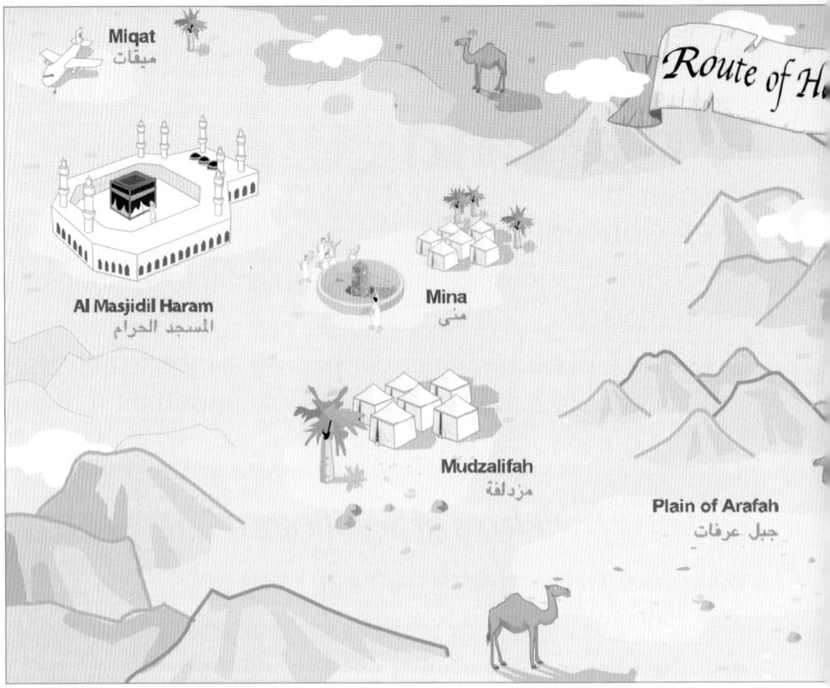

Route of H
Miqat
ميقات
Al Masjidil Haram
المسجد الحرام
Mina
منى
Mudzalifah
مزدلفة
Plain of Arafah
جبل عرفات

The route of the Hajj.

Stages of the Hajj

1. **Mecca.** Pilgrims arrive in Mecca and ritually wash themselves and change into white robes to begin the Hajj.
2. **The Ka'ba.** Pilgrims circle the Ka'ba in the courtyard of the Great Mosque. They drink water from the Zamzam (holy well) nearby.
3. **Hills of Safa and Marwa.** Pilgrims walk or run between the two small hills which today are joined by one long corridor.
4. **Plain of Arafat.** Pilgrims travel to the wide plain of Arafat outside Mecca for a day of prayer. Tents are provided for their use on a vast campsite.
5. **Pillars at Mina.** Pilgrims throw stones at three large pillars. Later, animals are sacrificed as part of the festival of Eid-ul-Adha.

Newly arrived pilgrims in Mecca wearing white robes.

Mecca

Pilgrims stop just outside the city of Mecca and ritually wash themselves to prepare for the pilgrimage. People change their clothes and put on long white tunics to show that everyone is equal before Allah. A special prayer is said to focus the mind and heart on the Hajj.

The Ka'ba

Pilgrims arrive in Mecca and go straight to the Ka'ba. They walk around it seven times in procession. The Ka'ba is a cube-shaped building in the courtyard of the Great Mosque in Mecca. A 'Black Stone' that Muslims believe came from heaven is kept inside the Ka'ba. A dark cloth on which are written words from the Qur'an covers the outside of the shrine from top to bottom. Muslims believe the Ka'ba was first built by Abraham and his son Ishmael. It was later restored by Muhammad as a place of worship to the one God, Allah.

Hills of Safa and Marwa

Pilgrims then hurry seven times between two small hills near the Ka'ba. Today the two hills are connected by a long wide corridor. Muslims believe that God once told Abraham to leave his wife Hagar and son Ishmael alone in the desert. When their water supply ran out, Hagar ran up and down the hills praying and looking for water. Her prayers were answered when Ishmael found a well, which is now called the Zamzam, or holy well. Pilgrims take water from the Zamzam which is located near the Ka'ba.

Plain of Arafat

Pilgrims go to Arafat which is about 24km from Mecca. They stand there for a full day listening to sermons and praying to Allah to forgive their sins. This is where Muhammad preached his last sermon. Muslims believe this is also the place where Adam was forgiven for his sin in the Garden of Eden.

Pillars at Mina

Pilgrims throw stones at three pillars in Mina. Muslims believe that Abraham took his son Ishmael to Mina to offer him as sacrifice. The devil tempted Abraham not to sacrifice the boy, but he refused to listen and threw stones at the devil to drive him away. Pilgrims re-enact this event, it is their way of showing that they too reject evil, and wish to follow Allah.
Eid-ul-Adha, the festival of sacrifice, marks the end of the pilgrimage. Sheep are sacrificed. This recalls Abraham's sacrifice of a sheep to God in place of his son. Pilgrims return to Mecca and circle the Ka'ba for the last time.

In Islam, going on pilgrimage is like going on a special journey to God. Muslims believe that if they undertake the Hajj in the right spirit, Allah will forgive them for everything they have done wrong in their lives.

✦ Examine the photograph.

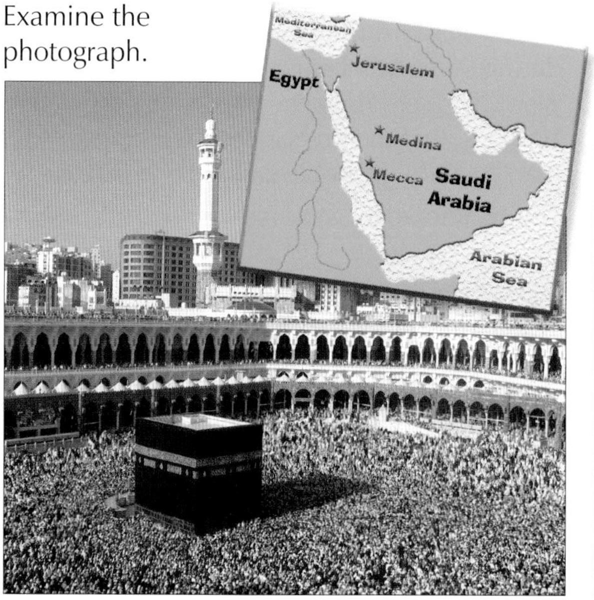
Mediterranean Sea
Jerusalem
Egypt
Medina
Mecca
Saudi Arabia
Arabian Sea

1. What is happening?
2. Where is this place?
3. To whom is it special?
4. What do pilgrims do when they go there?
5. Why do people go there on pilgrimage?

Questions

Knowledge

1. What is:
   a. a pilgrimage?
   b. a pilgrim?
2. Give one reason why people go on pilgrimage.
3. Name the most sacred place in the religion of Islam.
4. a. What is the Hajj?
   b. Where do pilgrims go to on the Hajj?
   c. How long do pilgrims spend on the Hajj?
5. What happens when pilgrims arrive at Mecca to begin their pilgrimage?
6. Why do pilgrims all wear the same type of clothes during Hajj?
7. What are the different stages of the Hajj?
8. a. What rituals do Muslims perform at:
   i. the Ka'ba?
   ii. Safa and Marwa?
   iii. Arafat?
   iv. Mina?
   b. What occurs at the end of Hajj?

Understanding

1. Give reasons why Muslims may wish to go on pilgrimage to Mecca.
2. How did the Ka'ba in Mecca become a sacred place for Muslim people?
3. Explain the significance of the different places a pilgrim visits during a pilgrimage to Mecca.

Research

✪ Find out what practical arrangements are necessary for a pilgrimage to Mecca. Try contacting the office of a specialist travel agent and/or visit their website.

✸ Prepare a factsheet for pilgrims.

Travel Details
- How to get there, airlines, special deals, travel times.
- Where to stay, hotels, hostels.
- What to bring, tickets, currency, suitable clothes.
- Places of interest, map of Mecca, transport arrangements to Arafat.
- What to do, religious rituals at each site.
- How to make the most of your pilgrimage.

✸ Compare your set of travel plans with those of the rest of the class.

Religious Festivals

Key Concepts

Calendar/ Sacred time: days and weeks set aside every year for a religious purpose.

Festivals: sacred time marked by fasting or celebration to remind people of key events and beliefs in their faith.

Objective

Explain how religious festivals remind Muslims of key events and beliefs in their faith.

Activity: *"Times of significance"*

TASK: TO IDENTIFY TIMES OF THE YEAR THAT HAVE A SPECIAL SIGNIFICANCE FOR US.

✦ Some days of the year are more special than others. What do we remember or celebrate on special days such as:

- Birthdays.
- Anniversaries.
- Holy Days.
- Holidays.
- St. Valentine's Day.
- Graduation.

Discuss

- What times in the year are special to you?
- What times in the year have a special significance for your family?
- Why do we remember and celebrate special events?

Calendar/Sacred Time

Every religion sets aside certain times of the year to remember and celebrate special events.

Sacred time refers to days and weeks set aside every year for a religious purpose. In Islam, sacred time is set aside each year to remind Muslims of what is important in their religion. Islam follows a lunar calendar, and the Muslim year is eleven days shorter than the western year. This means Muslim festivals and holy days vary from year to year.

Ramadan

The holiest month is Ramadan. It reminds Muslims of the time Allah revealed himself to the Prophet Muhammad through the angel Gabriel. Muslims fast from sunrise to sunset each day during Ramadan. Fasting is one of the pillars of Islam. The self-discipline of fasting is a sign to Muslims, that their religion is more important than everything else, even food and drink.

During Ramadan, Muslims spend extra time:

❖ at prayer.
❖ reading the Qur'an.
❖ attending the mosque.
❖ giving money to charity (Zakat).

Jan | Feb | Mar | April | May | June | July | Aug | Sept | Oct | Nov | Dec

Islam - RELIGIOUS FESTIVALS

Eid-ul-Fitr

Festival at the end of Ramadan.

Eid-ul-Adha

Festival at the end of Hajj.

Section C

Dhu-al-Hijjah

The other important month is Dhu-al-Hijjah. This is when the Hajj, the annual pilgrimage to Mecca, takes place. Muslims are reminded of the time Abraham was willing to sacrifice his son. Then Allah intervened providing him with an animal to sacrifice instead.

The pilgrimage to Mecca is one of the pillars of Islam. The pilgrimage begins and ends at the Ka'ba, a shrine believed to have been built by Abraham and his son.

Festivals

A religious festival is sacred time usually marked by fasting or celebration. It reminds Muslims of the key events and important beliefs in their faith. The two major Muslim festivals celebrated each year are:

- ❖ Eid-ul-Fitr - at the end of Ramadan.
- ❖ Eid-ul-Adha - at the end of Hajj, the pilgrimage to Mecca.

Both of these major festivals were started by the prophet Muhammad. They are a time to think and pray and be united with Muslims everywhere.

Eid-ul-Fitr

This is a three day festival that takes place at the end of the holy month of Ramadan. Muslims fast every day from sunrise to sunset during Ramadan. The prophet Muhammad taught his followers the importance of fasting. It is one of the Five Pillars of Islam.

Eid-ul-Fitr is a joyful festival to thank Allah for a successful fast. On the last night of Ramadan, everyone goes outside to see the new moon appear in the sky. It marks the beginning of a new month and the festival can begin.

The next morning Muslim families attend the mosque for prayers, all wearing their best clothes. Special prayers are said in thanksgiving to Allah following the fast. An amount of money is given to the poor on the same occasion.

After prayers, families return home for a big breakfast and to spend the rest of the day visiting friends and relatives. People wish each other 'Eid Mubarak' which means 'the blessing and joy of Eid'. There are parties, especially for children. Homes are decorated, people give presents and send Eid cards to each other. Special cakes and sweets are eaten.

Over the following days, Muslims visit the cemetery to pray at the graves of their dead relatives. No one is forgotten during the festival.

The interior of a mosque.
Muslims spend extra time praying in the mosque during Ramadan.

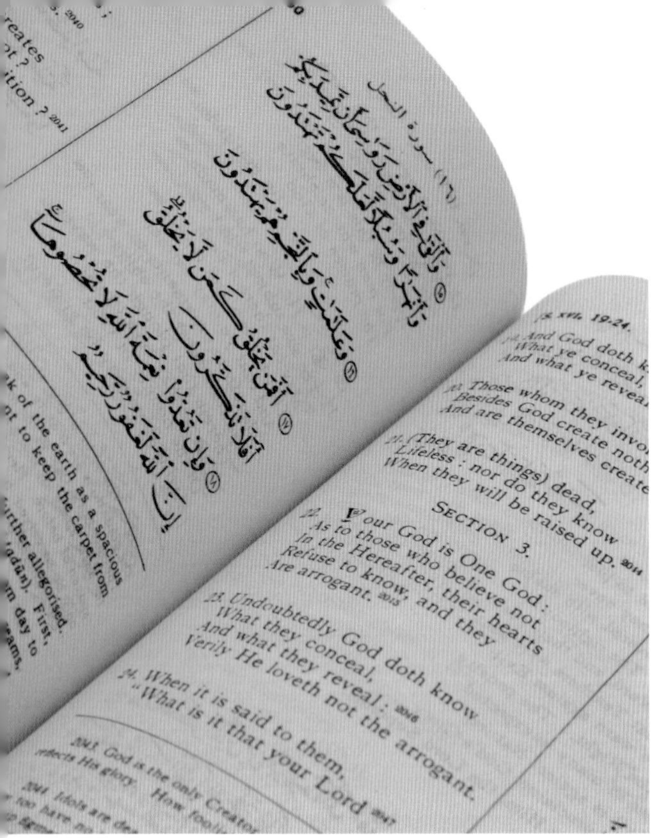

Pages from a translation of the holy Qur'an.

Eid-ul-Adha

The festival of Eid-ul-Adha takes place two months after Eid-ul-Fitr. It is celebrated at the end of Hajj, the Muslim pilgrimage to Mecca. It is a festival recalling Abraham's willingness to sacrifice his son to Allah.

At Eid-ul-Adha Muslims not in Mecca attend their local mosque for special prayers, and listen to a sermon recalling the story of Abraham. He was ready to sacrifice his son because he believed that was what God wanted of him. At the last moment, God provided a sheep to be sacrificed instead.

The sacrifice of an animal is the main feature of the festival of Eid-ul-Adha. The sacrifice is a sign that Muslims are themselves willing to give up everything for Allah. After the sacrifice, a portion of the meat is given to the poor.

After prayers, families gather together to share a special meal. Over the following three days, friends and relatives visit each other exchanging cards and gifts.

Questions

Knowledge

1. Why are Muslim festivals celebrated on different dates each year?
2. Name the holiest month in the Islamic calendar.
3. What important event is remembered at Ramadan?
4. What happens during Ramadan?
5. Name the two main festivals in the Muslim calendar.

Understanding

1. Choose one major festival in Islam:
   a. When does it occur?
   b. What religious event is remembered at this sacred time?
   c. What do Muslims do during the festival?
2. a. Why is Eid-ul-Fitr important for Muslims?
   b. How do Muslims celebrate this festival?
3. a. Why is Eid-ul-Adha known as the festival of sacrifice?
   b. How do Muslims celebrate this festival.
4. How can a Muslim's faith be strengthened by taking part in a religious festival?

Research

- Find out about one other festival in the Islamic calendar:
  - Al-Hijra.
  - Milad un Nabi.
  - Lailat al Miraj.
  - Lailat al Qadr.

  * When does this festival occur?
  * What does it celebrate?
  * How does this festival strengthen the faith of Muslim people?
  * Discuss this and other interesting findings with the class.

Rites of Passage

Key Concepts

Ritual: an occasion when people use symbolic actions to express what is deeply important to them.

Ceremony: the solemn or formal actions performed on a ritual occasion.

Objectives

Show how Muslim beliefs are expressed in the words and actions of one Muslim ceremony.

Activity: *"Birthdays"*

TASK: TO UNDERSTAND THE NEED FOR RITUAL IN PEOPLE'S LIVES.

✦ Think of a birthday that you celebrated recently (your birthday, a friend's birthday, or the birthday of someone in your family). What rituals are always part of the birthday celebration? (✓)

- Sending a birthday card. ❑
- Saying happy birthday. ❑
- Giving presents. ❑
- Having a birthday party. ❑
- Getting a birthday cake. ❑
- Blowing out the birthday candles. ❑
- Singing happy birthday. ❑

Discuss

- List the things that always happen on someone's birthday.
- Do you do anything else in your family when it is someone's birthday?
- What deep important things are expressed through birthday rituals?
- Choose one symbolic action. What does it mean when we say or do this on someone's birthday?

Ritual

Ceremony

Religious rituals mark important moments in life.

A rite of passage is the name given to a ritual occasion that marks the passing from one stage of life to another. Religions mark important moments in life such as:

◆ Birth. ◆ Marriage. ◆ Death.

It is an important event in the Muslim community:

- when a baby is born into the family.
- when a couple fall in love and get married.
- when a person's life is over at their death.

Muslims mark all these important moments with religious rituals.

A Muslim mother and child.

A ritual is an occasion when people use symbolic objects, words and actions to express what is deeply important to them. In Islam, birth, marriage and death are ritual occasions. Symbolic actions can be used to express Muslim beliefs about the presence of Allah in people's lives at such times. Rituals are always carried out the same way each time they are performed. A ceremony is the solemn or formal actions performed on a ritual occasion.

Birth

Muslims believe a child is a gift from Allah. When a baby is born, the father whispers words from the Qur'an into the child's ear:

> '...I witness there is no god but Allah and that Muhammad is the messenger of Allah.'

Among the very first words a child hears is the name of Allah. After the Shahadah (creed) is recited, a tiny piece of sugar or honey is placed on the child's tongue by its oldest relative. This may be done as a sign of hope that the child will grow up 'sweet' and kind, and become a good person.

The Aqiqah

When the baby is seven days old the Aqiqah, a naming ceremony, takes place. The baby is dressed in beautiful clothes and the event is a great family occasion.

- ❖ The baby's hair is cut. In the past, its weight in gold or silver was given to the poor. Today a donation is given to charity. This act brings Allah's blessing on the child.
- ❖ The baby is given a name. The name chosen is very important. It may be one of the ninety nine names of Allah, or a name associated with the Prophet Muhammad.
- ❖ An animal is sacrificed to give thanks for the birth of the baby. The meat is shared among relatives and friends, but most of it is given to the poor.
- ❖ Male children are circumcised. In some countries this is performed later, at the age of four years. Circumcision is the removal of the foreskin of the penis. This mark is a sign that the child has joined, or is now initiated into, the Muslim community.

Marriage

In Islam, a marriage ceremony is more of a legal event than a religious occasion. A legal agreement is made between two families, not two people.

Muslim marriages are usually arranged by parents who suggest a suitable partner for their son or daughter. No one is forced to marry against their will. The final decision lies with the young man and the young woman themselves. When a couple agree to marry, a contract is drawn up and a dowry is decided. This is a gift of money that the groom's family gives to the bride. The engagement is announced, and the wedding date is set.

The wedding day

The wedding may be held at the bride's home, or at the local mosque. Parents, relatives, and friends are invited to attend. The bride and groom wear ceremonial clothes. The ceremony is short and simple. It may be conducted by the imam, or any qualified male Muslim. Verses are recited from the Qur'an. The imam prays for the health and happiness of the couple, who then exchange rings.

The couple make their vows in front of two male witnesses, and sign copies of the marriage contract. This is the most important part of the ceremony. Afterwards there is a special meal or wedding reception to celebrate the occasion.

A Muslim couple on their wedding day.

Section C

A Muslim man can marry up to four wives but that rarely occurs nowadays. In any case, polygamy (which means having more than one wife) is illegal in this country and many other places throughout the world. Divorce is allowed in Islam but is very rare. Instead, families try their best to help couples sort out any problems that may arise.

Death

All Muslims hope to recite the Shahadah, the creed, as they approach death: 'There is no God but Allah, and Muhammad is his messenger.' It was the first thing they heard at birth, they hope it is the last thing said at death.

When a person dies, burial takes place soon afterwards, within twenty four hours. First the body is washed as a sign of respect, this is done by the relatives. Then it is wrapped in white sheets and brought to the mosque. Everyone gathers around for the funeral prayers. Prayers of petition are said that the dead person may be judged mercifully and gain a place in paradise. The prayers may be led by the imam or a member of the family.

Beliefs about death and the after-life

Afterwards, the body is taken in procession to a Muslim cemetery for burial. Muslims are always buried, never cremated. It is believed that the body will be raised from the dead when it is resurrected on the Day of Judgement. In Muslim countries, the body is placed directly into the earth without a coffin. The body is buried on its right side with the head facing toward Mecca.

Muslims believe that the soul of the person who has died will be carried to Allah by an angel. They also believe that every person will be judged on Judgement Day. The good will be rewarded and go to heaven. The bad will be punished and sent to hell.

Muslims visit graves and pray for their dead relatives, especially during Eid-ul-Fitr at the end of Ramadan.

Questions

Knowledge

1. What is a rite of passage?
2. Name three Muslim rites of passage that are celebrated through ritual.
3. What ceremony takes place to mark a child's entry into the Muslim community of faith?
4. Select a rite of passage that marks a key moment in the life of a Muslim person.
   a. What special actions or gestures mark the occasion?
   b. What special words are spoken?
   c. What special clothes are worn?
5. What deep important things are expressed through Muslim rituals on one of the following occasions?
   a. Birth.
   b. Marriage.
   c. Death.

Understanding

1. a. How do Muslims celebrate key moments in life such as birth, marriage or death?
   b. What is the most important part of the ceremony on one of those occasions?
2. What do Muslims believe about:
   a. birth?
   b. death?
3. How are Muslim beliefs evident in the rituals conducted at ceremonies for birth and death in Islam?

Research

- Find out more about one particular rite of passage in the Muslim community. Select the ceremony held at either birth, marriage or death.
  - Describe in detail the rituals performed at the ceremony.
  - Explain the meaning behind the different rituals.
  - Identify the essential Muslim beliefs expressed in the rituals of this ceremony.
  - Mention your sources and share your findings with the class.

Islam Worldwide

Key Concepts

Development: the way a community of faith grows and progresses over time.

Commitment: a decision to devote time and energy to the practice of one's religion.

Expansion: the way a religion spreads out into new territories.

Objective

Describe key moments in the development and expansion of Islam.

Activity: *"Snapshots"*

TASK: TO IDENTIFY KEY MOMENTS IN PEOPLE'S LIVES.

✦ What do you consider are the key moments in most people's lives?

Discuss

- What have been some of the key moments in your life so far?
- Select one occasion and describe what happened.
- How did life change afterwards?

Muslim men and women.

Development

There are a number of important people and key events in the religion of Islam.

Development is the way a community of faith grows and progresses over time. Muslims believe that Islam has always existed. The last and most complete revelation of God's will was made through the Prophet Muhammad. The development of Islam took place rapidly during the lifetime of the Prophet Muhammad.

Key moments in the beginning of Islam

- 570CE Muhammad is born in the city of Mecca in Arabia.
- 595CE Muhammad and Khadijah get married.
- 610CE The angel Gabriel appears to Muhammad in a vision in a cave on Mount Hira. Over the years Muhammad had other visions and received many messages from the angel. He learned everything by heart and repeated it to his wife and his followers. He began to teach in the city of Mecca saying that there is one God, Allah. He condemned the worship of idols in the Ka'ba.
- 622CE The Hijra. Muhammad and his followers are forced to flee from Mecca to Medina. This event marks the beginning of Islam.
- 630CE Muhammad returns to Mecca with an army. The people are converted to Islam, and the Ka'ba is established as a place of worship to Allah.
- 632CE The prophet Muhammad dies after returning from a pilgrimage to Mecca.

Commitment

The messages the Prophet received from Allah through the angel Gabriel were written down in the Qur'an, twenty years after his death.

The history of Islam is the story of how Muslims have been faithful to the Qur'an down through the centuries. Muslims show their commitment to the Qur'an, and the religion of Islam, in the way they devote time and energy to carrying out duties known as the Five Pillars:

Belief, Prayer, Charity, Fasting and Pilgrimage.

The Five Pillars are the foundation of the Muslim way of life.

Expansion

Expansion refers to the way a religion spreads out into a new territory. The religion of Islam expanded and spread into countries beyond Arabia. By the time of Muhammad's death, most of Arabia was converted to Islam. The prophet had been both a religious and a political leader. With a powerful army he united all the Arab tribes into a single state. It was his dream to win the whole world for Allah.

His followers shared the same dream. Within a century of Muhammad's death, Islam had spread eastwards as far as India. It spread west throughout northern Africa and across the Mediterranean Sea into Spain and Portugal. Islam later went north and gained control of parts of Eastern Europe.

The Golden Age of Islam

By the tenth century, three hundred years after Muhammad, the cities of Baghdad in Iraq, Cairo in Egypt and Cordoba in Spain were the main centres of Muslim civilisation. They were places of learning for Muslim scholars of science, medicine, mathematics and the arts. This period from 800-1200CE is regarded as the Golden Age of Islam.

The Middle Ages

Islam spread to Palestine, a country that was sacred to Jews and Christians, as well as Muslims. In the Middle Ages, at the time of the Crusades, fierce battles were fought around the city of Jerusalem. The city was holy to all three religions and each one wanted to control it. There was violent persecution of Muslims living in the city.

Eventually the victorious Muslim forces built a mosque on the site of the ancient Jewish Temple in Jerusalem. The Dome of the Rock is the most important Muslim shrine in the city, and the third most important place of pilgrimage in Islam.

Muslim Empires

The great Christian centre of Constantinople was conquered by Muslim forces in the 15th century and was re-named Istanbul. By the 17th century, the power and wealth of three Islamic Empires in the Middle East was at its height. The Ottoman Empire spreading out from Turkey was the largest. It also lasted the longest, from the 14th century until just after the First World War (1914-18).

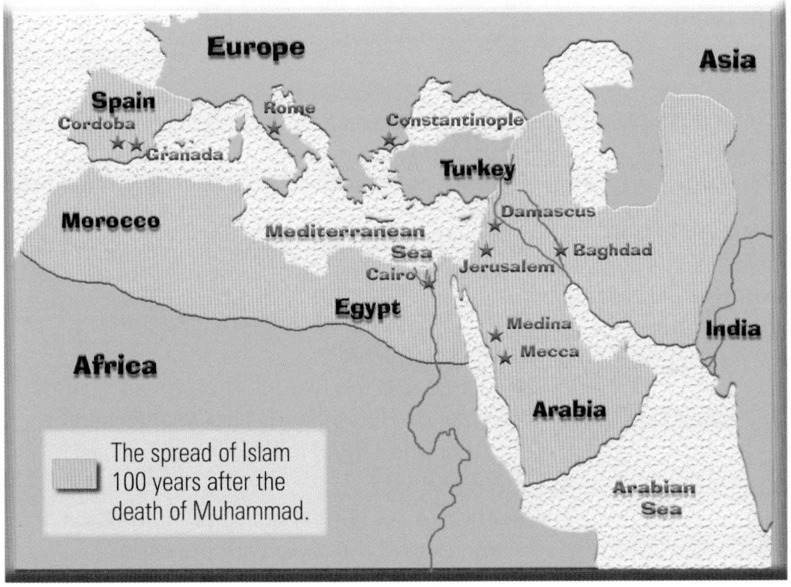
Europe
Asia
Spain
Cordoba
Granada
Rome
Constantinople
Turkey
Morocco
Mediterranean Sea
Damascus
Baghdad
Jerusalem
Cairo
Egypt
Medina
Mecca
India
Africa
Arabia
Arabian Sea
The spread of Islam 100 years after the death of Muhammad.

Islam was not just spread by wars and fighting. Many Muslim traders travelled all over the known world, buying and selling goods. They brought the message of Islam to new countries in the East. Local people were impressed by the religious fervour of Muslim merchants and traders, their advanced knowledge and culture, and the fact that they lived good lives. They converted to Islam in large numbers and inter-marriage between religions became acceptable.

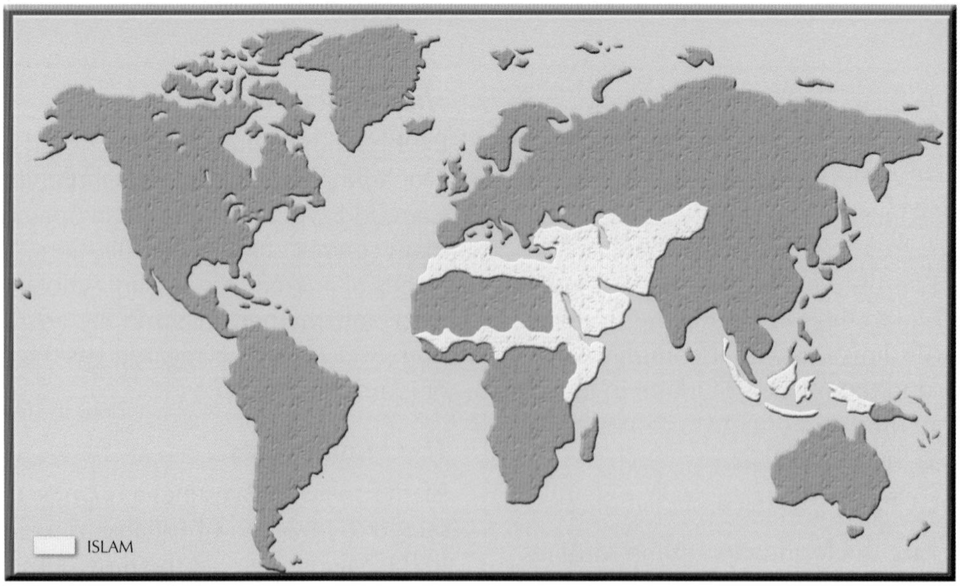
ISLAM

Global distribution of Islam today.

Islam Today

Today there are over one billion followers of Islam. The highest population of Muslims live in Saudi Arabia, Iran, and Iraq in the Middle East, and in countries in north and west Africa. There are about two million Muslims living in Britain, and about twenty thousand Muslims living in Ireland. In Islam, the worldwide community of Muslims is known as Umma.

Jihad

There were times in the past when Islam was spread by fighting and the force of war. The Prophet Muhammad had taught his followers that a jihad (holy war) was allowed under strict conditions:

- ❖ To defend a country that had been attacked.
- ❖ In the name of Allah to spread Islam and encourage people to follow the way of Islam.

Today, many Muslims use the term jihad in two ways.

1. The first kind of jihad is an inward spiritual struggle to obey Allah and be a good Muslim.
2. The second kind of jihad is an outward struggle against poverty and injustice. Part of this is to defend Islam against its enemies. For Muslims, killing is wrong, unless it is in self-defence.

Questions

Knowledge

1. Who is the most important figure in the early development of Islam?
2. What are some key moments in the life of the founder of Islam?
3. What happened to Islam after the death of Muhammad?
4. How far had Islam expanded in the first hundred years after the prophet's death?
5. What is meant by the Golden Age of Islam?
6. What happened in Palestine at the time of the Crusades?
7. When was the Ottoman Empire in power?
8. Where do the majority of Muslims live today?

Understanding

1. Where were the earliest Muslim communities established?
2. How did Islam spread so quickly and so extensively throughout the world?
3. Explain the meaning of jihad in Islam.

Research

- Find out more about the Muslim community in Ireland.
  - Where is the largest mosque in Ireland? When was it opened?
  - What happens at the Islamic Cultural Centre in Dublin?
  - Where was the first Muslim primary school established in Ireland? How many children attend the school and what subjects are they taught?
  - Add any additional points of information and discuss the topic with the class.

Division in Islam

Key Concept

Schism: a division or split within a community of faith.

Objective

Outline the factors that contributed to the schism that divided the religion of Islam.

Activity: *"The Big Divide"*

TASK: TO BE AWARE THAT DISAGREEMENTS GIVE RISE TO A RANGE OF CONSEQUENCES.

✦ Dictionary definitions of the word 'schism' include:

- Dissent.
- Discord.
- Difference.
- Rejection.
- Separation.
- Contradiction.
- Disagreement.
- Division.
- Split.

Discuss

- When was the last time you had a difference of opinion with someone?
- Was it a major or a minor disagreement?
- How was the matter resolved?

Muslim man at prayer.

Schism

In Islam a disagreement arose that was never resolved.

A schism is a division or a split within a community of faith. A division occurred in the religion of Islam following the death of the Prophet Muhammad. A disagreement arose about who should succeed him as leader of the Muslim community. Muhammad had left no instructions about how to choose his successor. So there was a difference of opinion as to how it should be done.

Disagreement

One view was that the leader should come from Muhammad's own tribe. The person must be elected, not simply given the role. A man called Abu Bakr was chosen - he was given the title Caliph which means 'successor' in Arabic. Abu Bakr was one of Muhammad's closest friends and a member of his tribe.

This decision was not unanimous. The other view was that the leader should come from Muhammad's own family. It must therefore be Ali, Muhammad's cousin and son-in-law (Muhammad's sons had died in childhood). The next leader should be Ali's son and then his descendants after him. Ali eventually became the fourth leader appointed after the death of Muhammad. Before long, Ali was assassinated, and his son who succeeded him was killed in battle.

Division

There was a bitter dispute. Supporters of Ali's family broke away and became known as Shi'ah Muslims. The rest were known as Sunni Muslims. Shi'ah and Sunni formed separate groups; these divisions still exist today.

Shi'ah Muslims

Shi'ah Muslims make up about 10% of the Muslim population of the world today. 'Shi'ah' comes from an Arabic word which means 'separate'. They are faithful to the Qur'an, but interpret every word in a strict literal manner.

Shi'ah Muslims believe that Ali was chosen by Muhammad to lead the Muslim community. They believe that God gave Ali the ability to correctly interpret the Qur'an. His teaching was thought to be free from error and always right. This ability was passed on to his son.

Today, leaders who guide the Shi'ah community are called Ayatollahs. Most Shi'ah Muslims live in Iran, The Lebanon, Afghanistan and India. They follow the teaching of the Qur'an, the Hadith (the sayings) of Muhammad, as well as the Hadith of Ali. The Shi'ah pay special attention to Ali and his sons. They celebrate the anniversaries of their deaths and make pilgrimages to places associated with their lives.

Sunni Muslims

Sunni Muslims make up about 90% of the Muslims in the world today. 'Sunni' comes from an Arabic word which means 'the path shown by the prophet'. They regard themselves as orthodox, the true followers of Muhammad and his teaching.

Sunni Muslims believe Muhammad was the final 'Seal of the Prophets'. God did not reveal his truth to anyone else. No one after Muhammad received special knowledge from God. They do not accept that Ali and his sons were holy men; their family ties with Muhammad did not give them special powers. Sunnis think this belief takes too much attention away from Allah, and the Prophet Muhammad, and this is wrong. Sunni Muslims are the most powerful group in Islam.

Sunni and Shi'ah formed separate groups in Islam fifty years after the death of Muhammad, and have been in conflict with each other ever since. They have some different interpretations of the Qur'an and have developed different customs and traditions. They disagree on many points, especially over control of the sacred shrine, the Ka'ba, in Mecca. There are Sunni and Shi'ah Muslims living in all parts of the world today, including Britain and Ireland.

The holy Qur'an, sacred text of Islam.

Questions

Knowledge

1. What is a schism?
2. What are the two main groups within Islam? Which one is in:
   a. the majority?
   b. the minority?
3. What issue caused the division in Islam in the beginning?
4. When did the followers of Islam eventually split into two different groups?

Understanding

1. Why did a schism occur in the Muslim community?
2. Explain what is distinctive about either:
   a. Sunni Muslims, OR
   b. Shi'ah Muslims.
3. Outline the effects you think a schism would have on a community of faith.

Research

- Find out more about the Shi'ah tradition in Islam.
  - Who was Husayn?
  - Why is the anniversary of his death remembered by Shi'ah Muslims each year?
  - What is the connection between Husayn and the Shi'ah tradition in Islam?
  - Why do Shi'ah Muslims cover themselves with red paint on the anniversary of his death?
  - Add your findings to a file of information on the Sunni and Shi'ah compiled by the class.

The Muslim Community

Key Concepts

Community structure: the way a community of faith is organised.

Leadership: the task of a leader is guiding a community of faith.

Education: the way the faith is passed on within a community of faith.

Dialogue: open and honest discussion between the major world religions.

Objectives

Describe a key leadership role in the Muslim community.

Outline the benefit of inter-faith dialogue and the links between Islam and Christianity.

Activity: *"The Ring Leader"*

TASK: TO LOOK AT THE FUNCTION OF LEADERS IN HUMAN COMMUNITIES.

- Divide the class into 2 or 3 groups.
- A group may select one of the following statements.

  "If I were Taoiseach I would..."

  "If I were School Principal I would..."

  "If I were a sports coach/ trainer I would..."
- One person in the group will suggest something he/she would do. The next person repeats what has just been said then adds his/her own comment.
- Continue this process around the group, the list will get longer! Anyone who forgets a comment is out. *Have fun!*

Discuss

- What is a leader?
- What do leaders do?
- How do we know when a leader is doing a good job?

Community Structure

Leadership

The imam is the leader of a Muslim community in the Mosque.

Community structure is the way a community of faith is organised. The Muslim community is organised in a certain way with its own network of roles and relationships. People have certain roles, each role helping the community to function properly. In Islam there are no priests and no single overall leader, unlike in many Christian Churches. Instead the religious needs of the Muslim community are met by the local imam.

The imam

The imam makes an important contribution to the religious life of Muslim people. Leadership is the task of a leader in guiding a community of faith. The imam is the religious leader in the mosque. Each community elects its own imam. He is a well-respected layman with a good knowledge of the Qur'an and a deep commitment to the Muslim way of life.

An imam leads Muslim worshippers in prayer at an outdoor event.

The imam has a key leadership role in the Muslim community. He leads the prayers and gives the sermon at Friday mid-day prayer in the mosque. He teaches the Qur'an, and assists at marriages and funerals.

Education

Education is the way the faith is passed on within a community of faith. Muslim children's religious education starts at an early age. Children attend the mosque for special classes after school and at the weekend. In the mosque, Muslim children are taught Arabic in order to read the Qur'an and study the beliefs and practices of Islam.

In areas where there is a large Muslim community, children can attend a Muslim school. The ethos of the school will be Muslim; this means the traditions of Islam will be observed by teachers and pupils at the school. In addition to the ordinary subjects studied for examination, the religious tradition is passed on through the study of Muslim sacred texts and by highlighting annual Muslim festivals.

Dialogue

Dialogue is open and honest discussion between the major world religions. Many believe it is important that people of different religions have open and honest discussion about religious belief and practice. In Ireland the Three Faiths Forum has established links between the three monotheistic religions: Judaism, Christianity and Islam. Members, for example, participate in inter-faith services to mark special occasions.

Interfaith dialogue between Christians, Jews and Muslims encourages respect and understanding, and helps to reduce prejudice and intolerance. The different faith communities can learn about each other's traditions. They can recognise the similarities and yet be candid about the differences.

Christians and Muslims

Believe in...	Have different beliefs about..
◆ One God.	◆ The nature of God.
◆ Life after death.	◆ The person of Jesus Christ.
◆ God's final Judgement.	◆ The role of the Prophet Muhammad.
◆ Prayer, fasting and charity.	◆ The status of the Bible and the Qur'an.

Questions

Knowledge

1. What is the title of the leader in a local Muslim community?
2. What is the role of the imam in a Muslim community?
3. Where do Muslim children receive an education in the traditions of their faith?
4. What is inter-faith dialogue?
5. What is the Three Faiths Forum?
6. What are the principal links between Christians and Muslims?

Understanding

1. How does the role of the imam support members of the Muslim community in the practice of their faith?
2. Why is children's religious education important in Islam?
3. Why is it important that followers of different religions engage in inter-faith dialogue?

Research

- Find out more about primary or post-primary education in the Muslim community.
  - Gather information about a Muslim school in Britain or Ireland.
    - Where is the school located?
    - Is it a boarding or a day school?
    - How long is it established?
    - How many students attend the school at present?
    - What subjects are on the curriculum?
    - What facilities does the school have for its activities?
    - What is the school uniform?
    - What is on the school crest?
    - Is there a school mission statement?
    - How does the school mission statement reflect the Muslim ethos of the school?
    - Do non-Muslim students attend this school?
  - Prepare a fact sheet and report to the class.

Muslim Identity

Key Concepts

Follower/ Discipleship: persons called to follow the teaching and way of life of a religious leader.

Tradition: the wisdom and teaching of a community of faith handed down from generation to generation.

Objective

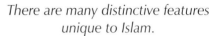

Describe the faith and practice of Muslim communities past and present.

Activity: *"Things-to-do List"*

TASK: TO GATHER INFORMATION ON DIFFERENT ASPECTS OF MUSLIM IDENTITY.

- Individually or in pairs select an item from the list.
- List as many points of information as you can about your chosen topic.

1. Prophet Muhammad.
2. Angel Gabriel.
3. Allah.
4. Khadija.
5. Qur'an.
6. Mecca.
7. Wudu.
8. Medina.
9. Imam.
10. Aqiqah.
11. Ramadan.
12. Ka'ba.
13. Mosque.
14. Shahadah.
15. Arabic.
16. Halal.
17. Hajj.
18. Rak'ah.
19. Sunni.
20. Eid-ul-Fitr.
21. Five Pillars.
22. Hijra.
23. Caliphs.
24. Mihrab.
25. Eid-ul-Adha.
26. Zakkat.

Discuss

- What topics were chosen by members of the class?
- What does all this information tell us about Muslim identity?

Follower/ Discipleship

There are many distinctive features unique to Islam.

Islam is a monotheist religion founded almost 1,500 years ago by the prophet Muhammad. To be a Muslim is to:

- Belong to the religion of Islam.
- Believe in the one God, Allah.
- Follow a way of life based on the Qur'an and the teaching of the Prophet Muhammad.

A Muslim girl.

There are over 1 billion Muslims in the world today, mainly in the Middle East, North Africa and parts of Asia. About twenty thousand followers of Islam live in Ireland. The first mosque opened in Dublin in 1975. As the Muslim community grew, other mosques were established in Cork, Galway, Limerick and Belfast. The Islamic Cultural Centre in Dublin caters for the religious, educational and social needs of the Muslim community.

Muslim Identity

Identity is the set of distinct characteristics by which a person or group is recognised. Muslim identity is about the many beliefs and customs unique to Muslims and the religion of Islam.

- ✧ Founder: The most important teacher in the religion of Islam is the Prophet Muhammad.
- ✧ Followers: Sunni and Shi'ah Muslims follow the teaching of the Qur'an and the Prophet Muhammad. The word Muslim means 'people who bow down to God'.
- ✧ Beliefs: Muslims are monotheistic. They believe in and worship one God, Allah, and believe that Muhammad is his Prophet. The main beliefs are the Articles of Faith and the Five Pillars.
- ✧ Sacred text: The Qur'an is the sacred text of Islam. For Muslims, it is the word of Allah.
- ✧ Holy day: Friday is the holy day of the week. All Muslim men are expected to attend the mosque on Friday for mid-day prayer.
- ✧ Place of Worship: The mosque is the Muslim place of worship. It features: a wudu area for washing; a mihrab facing Mecca; a minbar for preaching sermons.
- ✧ Prayer: Muslims pray five times a day, kneeling on a prayer mat facing Mecca. Rak'ah is a ritual prayer which involves standing, bowing and kneeling to show their willingness to submit to the will of Allah.
- ✧ Pilgrimage: The Ka'ba in the city of Mecca is the holiest site and place of pilgrimage in Islam. Every Muslim aspires to go on pilgrimage to Mecca at least once in their lifetime.
- ✧ Festivals: Eid-ul-Fitr takes place at the end of Ramadan. Eid-ul-Adha celebrates the end of Hajj, the Muslim pilgrimage to Mecca.
- ✧ Leadership: The imam is the religious leader in the mosque. There is no single overall leader in Islam.
- ✧ Lifestyle: Muslims strictly follow the Five Pillars and eat only halal or lawful food. Men and women do not mix socially and women follow a strict dress code.
- ✧ Rites of Passage: Ceremonies, such as the aqiqah naming ceremony at birth, mark important times in a person's life.
- ✧ Symbol: The star and crescent moon is the symbol of Islam. It highlights the Five Pillars and the lunar calendar of the Islamic year.

Star and Crescent Moon on top of a mosque.

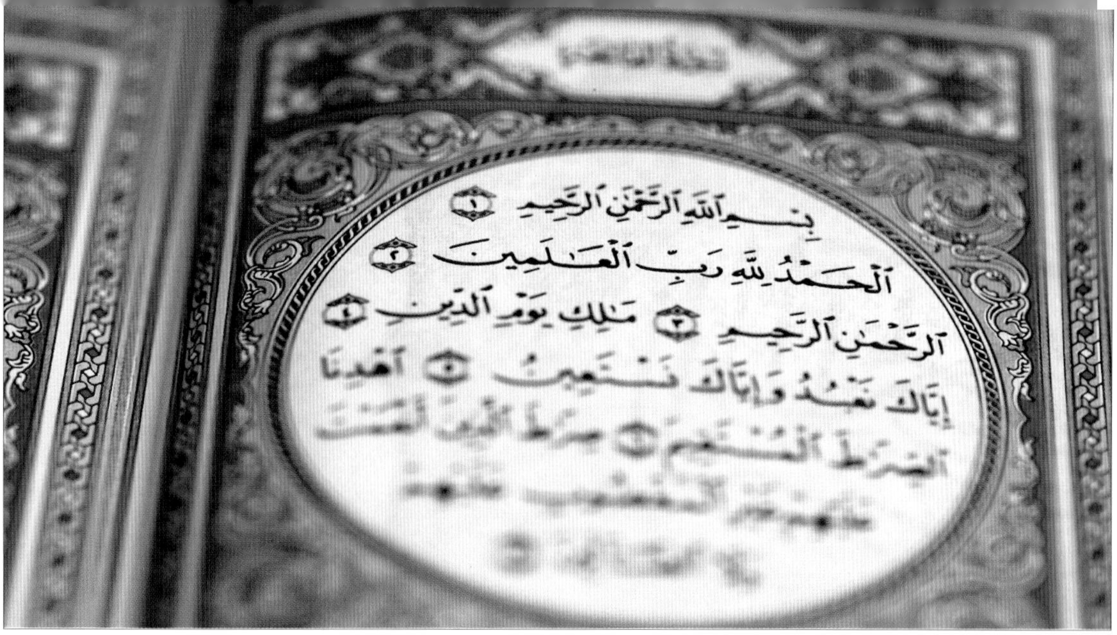

A page from the holy Qur'an.

Tradition

Tradition is the wisdom and teaching of a community of faith handed down from generation to generation. The wisdom and teaching of Islam is contained in the Qur'an, and in the Hadith another sacred text. Down the centuries, Muslim imams have studied the sacred texts and passed on their knowledge and understanding to the Muslim people, guiding them in the right way to live.

In every generation religious leaders:

- ❖ study the sacred texts in great detail.
- ❖ teach the beliefs, practices, and codes of behaviour to the faithful.
- ❖ show the faithful how to apply these principles to their daily lives.

The beliefs and practices of Islam have been preserved in the sacred texts and in the teaching of Muslim imams down the ages to the present day.

Questions

Knowledge

1. What is a monotheistic religion?
2. What is meant by tradition in Islam?
3. Who were the guardians of the tradition of Islam down through the centuries?
4. What is the central belief in the religion of Islam?
5. What are some of the main traditions that constitute Muslim identity?

Understanding

1. What is distinctive about being a Muslim, a follower of the tradition of Islam?
2. Outline two similarities and differences between Islam and two other world religions in terms of:
   - Beliefs.
   - Sacred text.
   - Prayer.
   - Pilgrimage.
   - Festivals.
   - Lifestyle of believers.

Research

- Find out about a recent initiative to promote good relations between different communities of faith.
  - ✹ First, present the facts:
    - What was done.
    - Who was involved.
    - What was the reaction.
  - ✹ Second, interpret the facts:
    - How did this initiative promote tolerance and understanding among people of different faiths in the community.
  - ✹ Write a concluding remark based on this experience.

Section D - The Question of Faith

The *Syllabus Aims* in this section are:

- To explore the situation of faith today.
- To identify the beginning of faith in the asking of questions and the search for meaning.
- To recognise expressions of human questioning in modern culture.
- To identify the characteristics of religious faith.
- To examine challenges to religious faith today.
- To offer opportunities for the exploration of, and reflection on, personal faith positions.

Concept Checklist (Section D - The Question of Faith)

Page

- ❑ **Agnosticism** - the view that people cannot know for certain whether or not God exists. 364
- ❑ **Atheism** - a view that denies the existence of God. 364
- ❑ **Awe and wonder** - feelings inspired by mysterious aspects of life. 329
- ❑ **Childhood faith** - a simple trust in God and an acceptance of one's parents' faith. 347
- ❑ **Creation** - a view on the origin of the world and life on Earth. 359
- ❑ **Experiencing God** - being aware of God's mysterious presence. 364
- ❑ **Faith** - a strong inner belief and trust in God. 347
- ❑ **Fundamentalism** - the view that a sacred text is a factual account to be taken literally. 359
- ❑ **Humanism** - a belief system that rejects religion and makes sense of life through human reason alone. 336
- ❑ **Materialism** - the view that only material things are real. 364
- ❑ **Mature faith** - a close relationship with God and an active commitment to one's faith. 347
- ❑ **Meaning** - to find or to have a sense of purpose in life. 336
  Meaninglessness - failing to find meaning or purpose in life. 336
- ❑ **Monotheism** - the belief in one God. 355
- ❑ **Personal faith** - a person's own religious beliefs and response to God.. 344
- ❑ **Prayer** - the way people of faith communicate with God. 352
- ❑ **Polytheism** - the belief in many gods. 355
- ❑ **Question** - the act of asking questions e.g. about the meaning of life. 332
  Questioner - the person who asks questions and seeks the truth. 332
- ❑ **Reflection** - thinking deeply about certain aspects of life.. . . . . 329, 364
- ❑ **Religious belief** - a set of ideas about God, or gods, that people accept as true. 315, 322, 326
- ❑ **Religious practice** - the things people do to express their religious belief. 315, 319, 322, 326
- ❑ **Search** - the deep human need to find meaning in life. 336
- ❑ **Secularism** - the view that organised religion should have no direct influence on society. 364
- ❑ **Stages of faith** - the development of a person's relationship with God from childhood faith to mature faith. 347
- ❑ **Trust** - being able to rely on a person with complete confidence. 347
- ❑ **World view** - a set of ideas about what the world is like. 359, 364
- ❑ **Worship** - the way people of faith praise and honour God in prayer and at religious services. 352

Religion Today

Key Concepts

Religious belief: a set of ideas about God, or gods, that people accept as true.

Religious practice: the things people do to express their religious belief.

Objective

Give an account of the changing patterns of religious belief and practice in Ireland and elsewhere.

Activity: *"Class Survey"*

TASK: TO DISCUSS OUR PERCEPTIONS OF THE LEVEL OF RELIGIOUS BELIEF AND PRACTICE IN OUR LOCALITY.

- What do you imagine the people in this area feel about religion.
- Do they have religious beliefs? If so, what are their religious practices?
- Examine the topics in the survey.
  - Vote on each topic.
  - Discuss the results.

Discuss

- What are the main findings in the survey?
- Did any of the results surprise you?
- Would people in other classes in the school agree with the findings in this survey?
- What might people in other parts of the country think of the findings in this survey?

Religious Belief and Religious Practice

A survey of religious belief and practice can be undertaken in class, or extended to include all members of the year group.

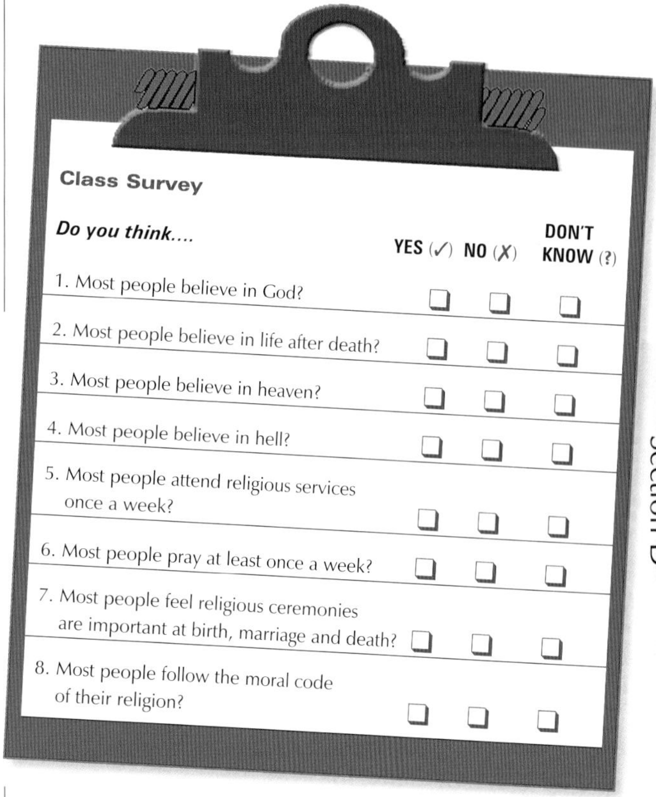
Class Survey

Do you think....	YES (✓)	NO (✗)	DON'T KNOW (?)
1. Most people believe in God?	❑	❑	❑
2. Most people believe in life after death?	❑	❑	❑
3. Most people believe in heaven?	❑	❑	❑
4. Most people believe in hell?	❑	❑	❑
5. Most people attend religious services once a week?	❑	❑	❑
6. Most people pray at least once a week?	❑	❑	❑
7. Most people feel religious ceremonies are important at birth, marriage and death?	❑	❑	❑
8. Most people follow the moral code of their religion?	❑	❑	❑

As an alternative to the questions above you can also personalise the survey by asking:

- *Do you - believe in God?*
- *Do you - believe in life after death? etc.*

Religious Belief

Everyone has beliefs but not all beliefs are religious. Religious belief is the set of ideas people have about God or gods that they accept as true. The central beliefs in Christianity, for example, are summarised in a special prayer called 'The Apostles' Creed'.

Most religions have a creed. A creed sums up what all the followers of a religion believe. The word creed comes from Latin 'credo' meaning 'I believe'. The earliest Christian creed is known as the Apostles' Creed. It was not actually written by the apostles, but is based on their teaching. The Apostles' Creed is a list of the most important beliefs in the religion of Christianity. These beliefs include:

- ❖ Belief in God the Father, Son and Holy Spirit.
- ❖ Belief in life after death.
- ❖ Belief in a final Judgement that involves heaven and hell.

The Apostles' Creed

I believe in God, the Father Almighty,
creator of heaven and earth.

I believe in Jesus Christ, His only Son, our Lord.
He was conceived by the power of the Holy Spirit, and born of the Virgin Mary.
He suffered under Pontius Pilate,
was crucified, died, and was buried.
He descended to the dead.
On the third day He rose again.
He ascended into heaven,
and is seated at the right hand of the Father.
He will come again to judge the living
and the dead.

I believe in the Holy Spirit,
The Holy Catholic Church,
The communion of Saints,
The forgiveness of sins,
The resurrection of the body,
And life everlasting. Amen.

Some Christian Churches differ slightly as to how these beliefs may be understood. The Apostles' Creed is a short statement of Christian belief that can be easily learnt by heart. There is another longer creed called the Nicene Creed. It is recited at Mass in the Catholic Church and at Communion Services in Anglican churches.

Religious Practice

All religions have their own beliefs and practices. Religious practices are the things people do to express what they believe. When people have a deep faith in God, they often feel the need to express it. They find ways to show how important God is in their lives. People with deep religious beliefs do things to show their beliefs. Christians, for example, express their religious beliefs through:

- ❖ Praying.
- ❖ Participating in weekly church services.
- ❖ Celebrating annual religious festivals.
- ❖ Going on pilgrimage to sacred places.
- ❖ Obeying the moral code of their religion ie. to love God and their neighbour.

INRI
Praying in church.

Going on pilgrimage.

Helping one's neighbour.

Surveys of Religious Belief

Social surveys routinely investigate levels of religious belief in Ireland and in other countries. Two European-wide values surveys, for example, found a consistently high level of religious belief among Roman Catholics in Ireland over the period 1981-1999.

Republic of Ireland
Religious Beliefs

	Belief in God.	Belief in life after death.	Belief in heaven.	Belief in hell.
1981:	95%	76%	83%	54%
1999:	96%	80%	86%	54%

European Values Study 1981, 1999.

Questions

1. What do the figures say about Irish people's belief in God?
2. Had belief in God gone up or gone down in the twenty year period?
3. Do Irish people believe in life after death?
4. What religious belief remained the same?

Surveys of Religious Practice

Social surveys also investigate the levels of religious practice in Ireland and elsewhere. Two European-wide values surveys found a decline in attendance at religious services in Ireland over the period 1981-1999.

Republic of Ireland
Attendance at Religious Services

	Once a week or more.		Once a month or more.
	All age groups.	*18-26 age group.*	*All age groups.*
1981:	83% (87%)	75% (79%)	89% (92%)
1999:	59% (65%)	23%	70%

European Values Study 1981, 1999.
(Mass attendance for Catholics in brackets.)

Questions

1. What do these figure say about the level of religious practice in Ireland?
2. Did attendance at religious services go up or go down in those twenty years?
3. Which age group has shown the biggest change in religious practice in that time?

Religious Belief and Practice in Ireland

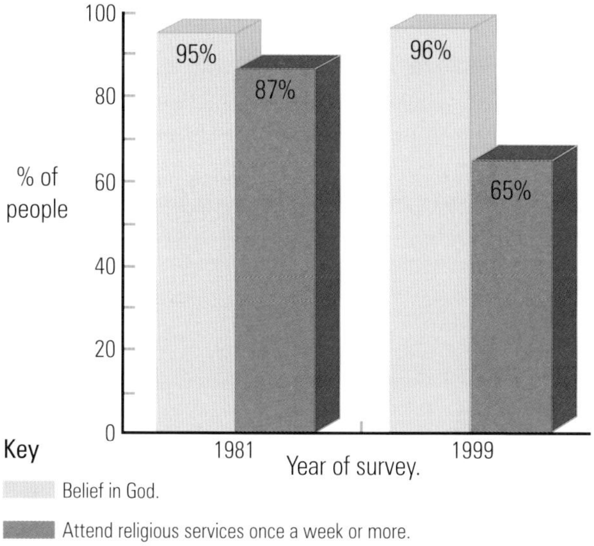
100
80
60
40
20
0
% of people
95%
87%
96%
65%
1981
1999
Year of survey.
Key
Belief in God.
Attend religious services once a week or more.

The surveys show that in Ireland, over a twenty year period...

- ❖ religious belief had not changed.
- ❖ belief in God remained consistently high.

But...

- ❖ religious practice had changed.
- ❖ church attendance had dropped by almost a quarter.

Religious belief remains strong among Roman Catholics in Ireland but this is not reflected in equally high levels of church attendance. Although it is a fact that religious practice is falling in Ireland, at 65% it is still one of the highest rates of religious practice in the world.

Religious Belief and Practice

People's faith, and their belief in God, is a personal interior experience. Religions provide a way to outwardly express the beliefs people hold in their hearts. Religious belief and religious practice are therefore connected, but they are not the same. Recent surveys show that most Irish people believe in God, yet they attend religious services less often than they did in the past. Do current patterns of religious practice mean there is some kind of crisis in the Irish Church?

If we look at the data, we can see that religious behaviour in Ireland has changed, church attendance is dropping. Yet the level of religious belief has not changed, it has been the same over the twenty year period. Irish people continue to believe in God, believe in life after death, pray and attend weekly Mass at the highest rate in Europe. There is no crisis. Church attendance may be falling, but this is not a crisis of faith. Religious belief remains strong in Ireland. What needs to be examined is why this is no longer reflected in higher levels of church attendance.

International Comparison

A sample from a world wide survey of thirty two countries carried out in 1998.

Church Attendance

Two or three times a month or more often.

Country:	0 10 20 30 40 50 60 70 80 90 100%
R.of Ireland	73%
Poland	62%
N. Ireland	51%
Italy	44%
Portugal	41%
USA	39%
Austria	33%
Norway	Below 10%
Japan	Below 10%

(International Social Survey Programme 1998.)

Questions

Knowledge

1. What is religious belief?
2. What is a creed? Name one Christian creed?
3. Give two examples of Christian religious belief.
4. What is religious practice?
5. Give two examples of religious practice from:
   a. Christianity.
   b. One other religion.
6. According to international surveys (1981-1998):
   a. What proportion of Irish people believe in God?
   b. What proportion of Irish people attend religious services?
7. Is the number of people attending church in Ireland rising or falling at present?
8. How does church attendance in Ireland compare with church attendance in other countries?
9. How is religious belief different from religious practice?

Understanding

1. Choose one belief from the Apostles' Creed and explain how it could influence the way a Christian might behave.
2. Describe the changing pattern of religious belief and practice in Ireland in the twenty year period 1981-1998.
3. How do the findings of your own class survey on religious belief and practice compare with the results of major international surveys.
4. How do trends in religious practice in Ireland compare with that of other countries?

Religion in the Past

Key Concept

Religious practice: the things people do to express their religious belief.

Objective

Describe aspects of Catholic religious practice in Ireland over the past century.

Activity: *"Sundays"**

TASK: TO BE AWARE OF CHANGES IN RELIGIOUS PRACTICE OVER TIME.

✦ Think about what you do on Sundays at present.

How do you imagine your parents spent Sundays when they were your age?

ABOUT US:
What we do on Sundays now?
ABOUT OUR PARENTS:
What they did on Sundays years ago.

Discuss

- What do members of the class do on Sundays?
- What do the class think their parents did on Sundays when they were growing up?
- Compare the way people spend Sundays now and the way people spent Sundays thirty years ago.
  a. What is the same? b. What is different?

*NOTE: Sunday is the holy day of the week for Christians. Saturday and Friday are holy days for Jews and Muslims respectively. Adapt the exercise to fit the religious affiliation of class members.

Religious Practice

Patterns of religious practice have changed since our parents' and our grandparents' time.

In the following account, a young teenager asks his mother about religious practices when she was a girl. Ursula and her son are Roman Catholics.

Religious practice in our parents' generation

Mam, what prayers did you say when you were young?

Well, when I was your age, I said the Our Father, the Hail Mary, the Gloria and my night prayers. I said these prayers every day. When Granny came to visit us, the T.V. would be turned off in the evening and we would all kneel down and pray the Rosary together.

Did you say any other prayers?

We always said the Angelus. At school the class would stand up at mid-day and say the Angelus together. At home we said it again at six o'clock in the evening. Sometimes we said it aloud. Mostly though, we prayed it silently to ourselves.

Did you have any holy pictures or things like that in your house?

We did. Upstairs there was a holy picture or a crucifix in every room. Downstairs there were statues of Our Lady and the saints. In the kitchen there was a framed picture of the Sacred Heart of Jesus. There was a little red light in front of it; the light was on all the time. Also on the wall, just inside the front door, there was a holy water font. Before we went out to school, to town or on a journey, we blessed ourselves with the holy water.

Did you always go to Mass when you were my age?

I did. We went every Sunday. We all went in the car, it was too far to walk. We all wore our good clothes. Everyone went to Mass, the church was always full. We went with our parents, of course we went over to talk to our friends afterwards.

Did you like going to Mass?

I didn't mind, it was part of my life. Every week I went to Mass, every month I went to Confession. Sometimes I went to Benediction. I liked the hymns and the incense, it was always special.

Did you ever go on a pilgrimage?

We did, every year the family went to Knock. We walked in procession around the church saying the Rosary, then we did the Stations of the Cross. In front of Our Lady's shrine we knelt to say our private prayers. We were allowed to buy medals, beads or holy pictures at the souvenir stalls afterwards.

You know I'm glad that some of those practices have survived and are still part of what it means to be a Catholic today.

Ursula Doyle

Religious practice in our grandparents' generation

The Station

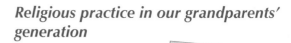

I grew up in the 1950's in a rural part of Ireland. The custom of 'The Station', as it was called, was very popular back then. Once a year a priest came to one of the houses in the parish to celebrate Mass. Hosting the Station was a great honour.

The family would begin immediately to do up the house inside and out in preparation for the big event. Painting gates and whitewashing the walls outside, and wallpapering, cleaning windows, dusting and waxing the furniture indoors. Everyone helped to get the house in spic and span order. The major face-lifting began several months in advance. Anyone passing would notice the new lace curtains in the windows, the clean white walls and newly painted gates that led up to the front door.

A few days ahead of time the woman of the house would begin baking bread and cakes. Butter was freshly churned and moulded into fancy shapes. The fine china, serving dishes and freshly polished silverware was taken out of the cabinet. This was for the priest's breakfast that would follow the Station Mass.

Praying the rosary.

The Station Mass

The morning of the Station my father arose early and started the fire in the parlour where Mass would be celebrated. When he was satisfied that the turf was burning brightly he went outside to make sure everything was looking all right. Then the neighbours started to gather. Everyone came dressed up in their best clothes in honour of the occasion.

The priest usually arrived at around 8am. He was escorted to the parlour where he robed and got ready to hear confession. After everyone had been to confession the Mass began. It was said in Latin at that time.

Table prepared for Mass.

The Mass was a very happy and holy occasion. All the neighbours were there together in a spirit of prayer and worship. They were gathered in our house to pray to God and to receive Holy Communion. Afterwards they brought the blessing of the Station back with them to their own house and family. When the Mass was over there was a collection. The money was given to the priest; the family hosting the Station always gave the biggest donation.

The priest then blessed the bucket of spring water that had been placed beside the table where he had celebrated Mass. Everyone took a bottle of the holy water home with them to bless their family and the farm animals. The priest also blessed rosary beads, medals, holy pictures, scapulars and other religious objects brought by the neighbours. After his breakfast the priest left the house to bring Holy Communion to old and infirm people in the parish.

Agnes McKenna-Cagney

Questions

Knowledge

1. List the prayers the mother said daily when she was young.
2. When did the family:
   a. say the Rosary? b. say the Angelus?
3. What religious objects were in the house?
4. Describe one holy picture found in most Catholic homes in the past.
5. List the religious practices undertaken by the mother when she was a young girl.
6. How often did the mother go to confession?
7. Is the mother describing religious practice in Ireland 30, 60 or 100 years ago?
8. a. What is the custom of 'the Station' in rural Ireland?
   b. How did a family prepare for the Station?
   c. Who attended the Station?
   d. Why was it regarded as an honour to have the Station in the house?

Understanding

1. How important was religion in family life in your parent's time, and in your grandparents' time?
2. Have religious practices changed much in this country in recent years?
   a. What has changed?
   b. What has stayed the same?
3. What do you think is the biggest change that has taken place in Roman Catholic practice in the last thirty years?

Research

Find out about religious customs and practices that were common in this country 30-60 years ago. Grandparents or older relatives may be a useful source of information.

- Write a descriptive paragraph on one of the following from the Roman Catholic tradition.
  - Benediction. - The Station.
  - The Latin Mass. - Fasting during Lent.
  - The Rosary. - The Parish Mission.
  - A wake for the dead. - The Angelus.
- What are the similarities and differences between older people's experience of religion when they were growing up, and the experience of people today?
- Discuss your ideas with the class.

ALTERNATIVELY

- Select a custom or a practice that was prevalent in another Christian Church in Ireland some time ago and discuss that.

Religion in a Changing World

Key Concepts

Religious belief: a set of ideas about God, or gods, that people accept as true.

Religious practice: the things people do to express their religious belief.

Objective

Identify factors that influence the changing pattern of religious belief and practice.

Activity: *"Brainstorm"*

TASK: TO IDENTIFY SOME IMPORTANT ASPECTS OF MODERN LIFE.

- Life today is not the same as it was one hundred years ago, or even fifty years ago. A lot of change has occurred in recent times.
- Brainstorm some of the major changes that have taken place over the last century that have a direct effect on the way we live today.

Discuss

- List some changes that have taken place in the world in the last one hundred years?
- How do these factors affect the way we live today?
- In your opinion, what change has had the biggest effect on modern life?
- Do you think any of these changes affect the way people practice their religion?

Religious Belief
Religious Practice

Major historical events and technological developments have affected people's lives in different ways, including what they believe and how they practice their religion.

Modern Life

The world has changed in many ways over the last century. This has contributed to changing patterns of religious belief and practice in Ireland and elsewhere. Factors that have contributed towards this change include:

The influence of **migration**. There was a huge movement of people from the countryside to towns and cities in search of work. The move to urban centres led to a decline in religious practice in rural areas.

The influence of the **media**. Film, television and the internet presented images, values and behaviours that were different from people's religious values and way of life.

The influence of **materialism** and economic prosperity. People work longer hours and may not have the time, energy or inclination to practice their faith. Success is increasingly viewed in material terms as people focus on earning more money, having a good lifestyle and acquiring lots of possessions.

NEXT
GAP

A busy town centre.

Section D

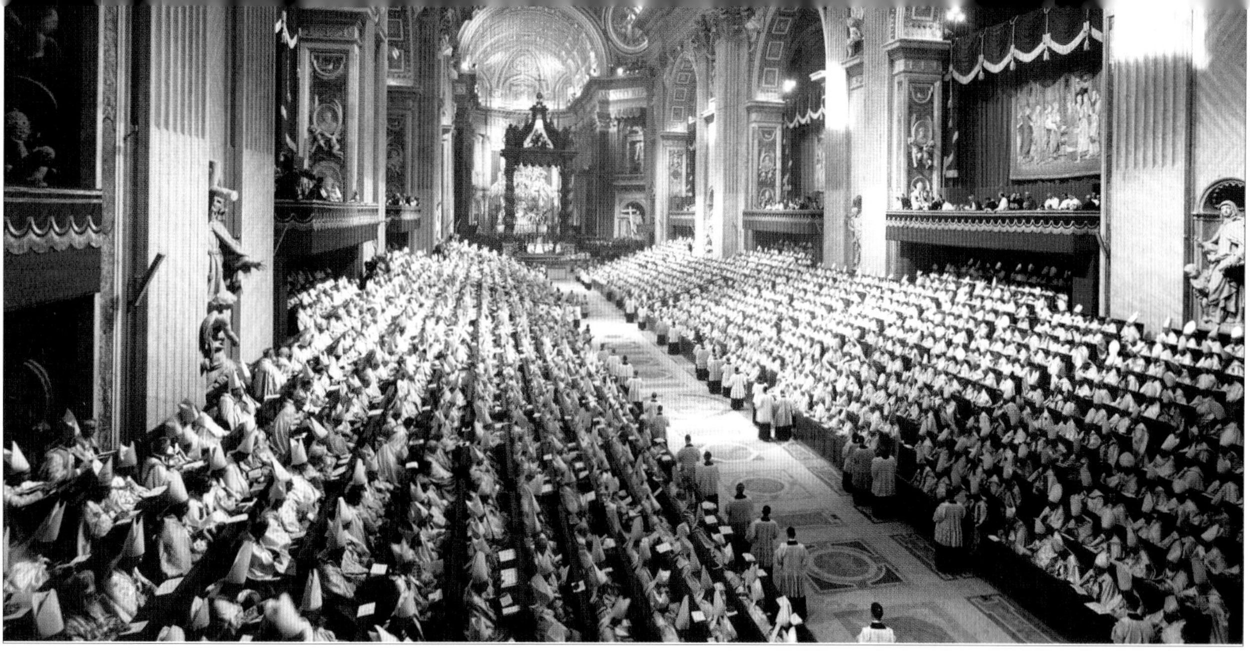

The Second Vatican Council meeting in Rome.

The response of the Roman Catholic Church

The Roman Catholic Church has tried to respond to the way people live in modern times.

About fifty years ago the Church elected a new leader, Pope John XXIII, to become head of the Roman Catholic Church throughout the world. He was quite old when he became Pope and nobody expected him to do anything new, but they were wrong. Pope John XXIII surprised everyone by introducing more changes in the Catholic Church than had happened for hundreds of years. The new Pope believed the Church was behind the times and needed to be brought up to date. He said it was important that the teaching of Jesus be made more relevant to people in the modern world.

Vatican II

To begin this process of change, the Pope organised a meeting at the Vatican in the city of Rome. Bishops and religious leaders from every country in the world were invited; over 2,600 people attended. There were many things to discuss and the gathering lasted three years - from 1962-1965. This meeting was called the Second Vatican Council, or Vatican II for short.

A lot changed in the Roman Catholic Church as a result of Vatican II. Pope John XXIII said it was like opening the windows of the Church to let in some fresh air. Every aspect of Church life had to be examined. The bishops set to work. First they looked at the way the world had developed in terms of technology, politics, economics and sciences. Then they had to figure our how the Catholic Church could respond. Their job was to find new ways of bringing the teaching of Jesus closer to people in the modern age.

The bishops came up with a lot of fresh new ideas to improve aspects of Church life. Their suggestions were written down in sixteen separate documents. When all the documents were bound together in one book it came to almost 700 pages!

The work of Vatican II continues to guide the Catholic Church in the world today. As a result of Vatican II:

- ❖ Catholics became more willing to work toward Christian unity with members of other Christian Churches.
- ❖ Catholics became more open and understanding of other world religions.
- ❖ Catholics make a greater effort to put their faith into practice by standing up for human rights, working for justice and peace and helping the poor.
- ❖ Catholics became more actively involved in the life of the Church. The sacraments were revised so that lay people would have a greater role, for example, in the celebration of the Mass as ministers of the Word, ministers of the Eucharist, and in liturgy preparation groups. Lay people also took on a greater role in the parish as members of the Parish Council.

Changes in the celebration of the Mass

The Mass before Vatican II

- ✧ The words of the Mass were in Latin.
- ✧ The design of the church meant that the priest had his back to the congregation.
- ✧ The congregation watched the priest at the altar and quietly said their own private prayers.
- ✧ People knelt at the altar rails to receive Holy Communion. The priest placed the host on the tongue of each person.
- ✧ The Mass was celebrated by the priest who was assisted by the altar boy(s). Lay people were not actively involved.
- ✧ Women covered their heads with hats or scarves at Mass.

Pre-Vatican II - a congregation attending Mass.

The Mass after Vatican II

- ✧ The Mass is in English, or in the language of the country in which it is celebrated.
- ✧ Churches are re-designed so that the priest faces the congregation.
- ✧ The congregation say the responses aloud with the priest and everyone prays together as a community.
- ✧ People stand to receive Holy Communion. The priest or the minister of the Eucharist places the host in the hands of each person.
- ✧ The Mass is celebrated by the priest and the people. Lay people are actively involved, for example, as Ministers of the Word and ministers of the Eucharist, and as ushers, collectors and altar servers.
- ✧ Women's head covering is optional at Mass.

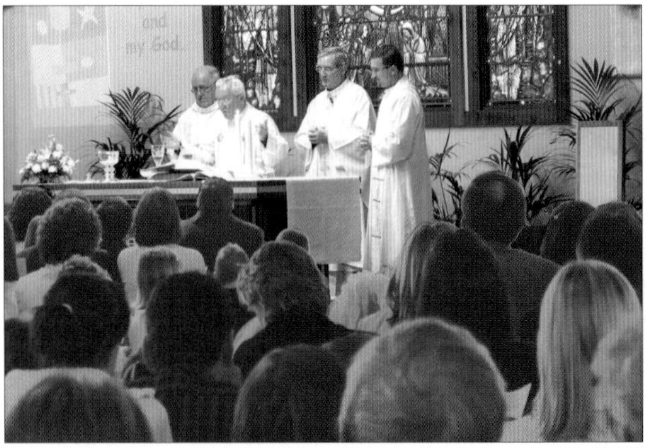

Post Vatican II - a congregation attending Mass.

The People of God

Vatican II helped the Catholic Church to adapt to the needs of the times. Modern life left many people isolated and cut off from one another in their homes, their cars, in their jobs and inside their churches. Men and women needed to belong. They wanted to be part of something worthwhile. They wanted to share their talents and belong to a community where they actually mattered.

The Sacristan.

A new model of Church

The Catholic Church responded by developing a new model of Church called the People of God. This is a new way of looking at the life of the Church, especially the role of lay people within the Church. The emphasis in this model is on building a community.

The Church is the People of God, a community of baptised Christians where everyone has a place and a task to perform for the benefit of all.

Boys' and girls' choir.

Lay involvement

Vatican II gave lay people a new role in the Church. It created new ways for Catholics to become involved in their parish communities. Although there are less people attending Mass today than in the past, there are more lay people actively involved in Church life than ever before.

The Children's Liturgy.

Minister of the Eucharist.

Questions

Knowledge

1. What factors weakened people's religious belief and practice in recent times?
2. Vatican II
   a. Who started it?
   b. When did it take place?
   c. Where did it take place?
3. What work did the bishops carry out at the Second Vatican Council?
4. Name one sacrament where a lot of changes were made at Vatican II.
5. a. What changes took place in the language of the Mass after Vatican II?
   b. What changes were made to the design of Catholic churches after Vatican II?
6. How did lay people become more involved at Mass after Vatican II?
7. What changes helped to make Sunday Mass more of a community celebration?
8. Who are the People of God?

Understanding

1. What could be the main reason people are not practicing their religion as much as before?
2. Explain how you think the media could affect a person's religious faith.
3. What changes did Catholics experience at Mass after Vatican II?
4. How has the role of lay people in the Catholic Church developed since Vatican II?
5. Why do you think Vatican II is regarded as a major event in the Catholic Church?

Research

- Find out about the role of lay people in other Christian Churches.
  How do lay people serve the community in Churches where priests, pastors or ministers have an established role? For example, in the Church of Ireland, in the Methodist Church, or in the Baptist or Presbyterian communities.
  - Select one of these Christian traditions.
    - What duties do lay people fulfill?
    - What is the title of their respective roles?
    - How long have lay people been actively involved in these ministries?
  - Discuss any interesting findings with the class.

Religion and Young People

Key Concepts

Religious belief: a set of ideas about God, or gods, that people accept as true.

Religious practice: the things people do to express their religious belief.

Objective

Identify factors that influence the religious belief and practice of adolescents.

Activity: *"Under the Influence"*

TASK: TO LIST THE VARIETY OF INFLUENCES ON THE LIVES OF YOUNG PEOPLE TODAY.

✦ We are all influenced by many things, although we might not be fully aware of this all the time.

List all the people and things you think have an influence on young people today.

Discuss

- Rank the influences in order of priority
- Who or what is the strongest influence on young people today?
- Who influenced you most when you were a child?
- Who is the greatest influence on your life now?

Religious Belief

Religious Practice

Teenagers are aware of the variety of influences on their lives.

Life is a bit like a journey. We do not travel alone, we are connected to other people along the way. We are part of a web of relationships that began right back when we were born.

Our primary, or first, relationship is with our parents and our family. At school we have relationships with friends and classmates, and with adults such as teachers and sports coaches. We may be involved with a community of faith in the parish. We are also connected with our neighbours and maybe with certain clubs or organisations.

People we meet face to face can have a direct influence on us. Those we see and admire from a distance on TV, in sport, and the music business can have an impact on us too. There may also be outstanding people, alive or dead whom we look up to and admire for what they achieved in their lives.

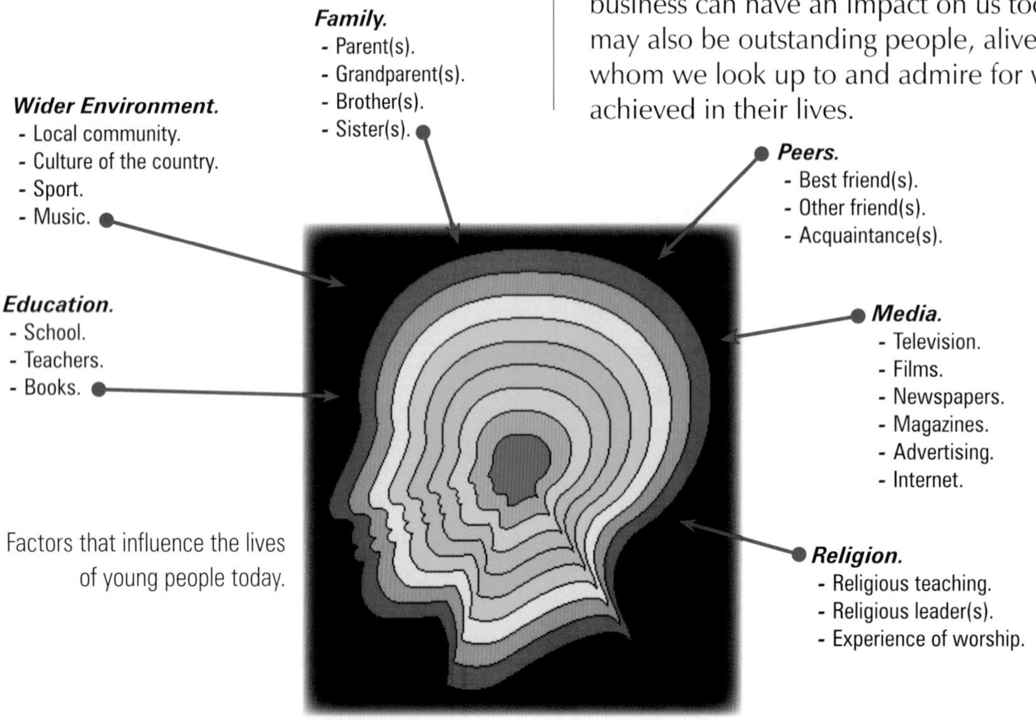

Family.
- Parent(s).
- Grandparent(s).
- Brother(s).
- Sister(s).
Wider Environment.
- Local community.
- Culture of the country.
- Sport.
- Music.
Peers.
- Best friend(s).
- Other friend(s).
- Acquaintance(s).
Education.
- School.
- Teachers.
- Books.
Media.
- Television.
- Films.
- Newspapers.
- Magazines.
- Advertising.
- Internet.
Religion.
- Religious teaching.
- Religious leader(s).
- Experience of worship.

Factors that influence the lives of young people today.

Religion in adolescence

Adolescence is a time when young people struggle to form their own identity. Everyone wants to be their own person and to stand on their own two feet. This effort does not occur in isolation, it happens in the midst of a whole set of relationships.

Adolescents become more and more aware of what it is that influences their ideas and actions. They may know that some things have a greater influence on them than others. According to social research, the greatest influences on the religious belief and practice of young people are:

a) The family. b) The peer group.

Research carried out in the UK and Australia shows that parents have the strongest influence on the religious belief and practice of young people. In Ireland research found that young people's outlook on religion was usually shared by their peers.

Parents

The values of parents are a critical factor in young people's attitude to religion. Children from an early age pick up whether or not religion is valued in the home. Parents may encourage or discourage religious belief and practice.

If parents pray with their children and take them to religious services, children will learn that religion matters in life. If, on the other hand, God or religion is rarely mentioned in the home, children will pick up that religion is unimportant and matters little in life. The religious influence of parents and the family lasts throughout childhood and continues into adolescence.

Family saying a short prayer before their meal.

Girl praying.

The example of parents, what they say and do, has more of an influence on the religiousness of their teenage sons and daughters than any other factor. Research shows that the example of parents is critical. If teenagers see that their parents value religion, they are more likely to value it themselves. However if parents do not pray or attend religious services, it is less likely that their sons or daughters will find a place for such religious practices in their own lives.

Peers

The values of the peer group also affects the way teenagers express their religious beliefs. The peer group consists of boys and girls of one's own age, this includes friends, classmates, team-mates and acquaintances. How friends and classmates view religion, and whether or not they practice it, has implications for the young person's attitude to religion.

The influence of the peer group is strong in adolescence. Young people value the opinion and seek the approval of their friends. This can lead to peers sharing a similar outlook on religious belief and practice. Teenagers for example find it easier to participate in religious services in church or at school if their friends also take part.

Case Study

The Year Head announces at assembly that the school retreat for each class group is coming up soon. It is optional again this year. Nearly everyone in your class went on it last year and said it was good. It's on Tuesday, a normal school day.

Students not participating in the retreat attend class as usual. The Year Head wants the list of names of those going on retreat to be handed in by Friday.

NOTE: Non-Christians may attend and observe if they wish.

People who shape your life

You are thinking about the retreat next week: 'To go or not to go' is the question! What might the following people have to say about the matter:

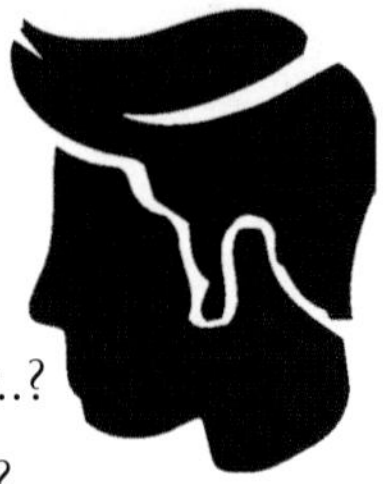

- My parents might say…?
- My religion teacher might say..?
- My best friend(s) might say…?
- Others in the class might say…?
- What else might influence your decision?

✦ Discuss:

1. What do you think each group might urge you to do?
2. Rank the influences in order of priority (1-5).
3. What do you think you might decide to do? Why?
4. Which is better: to have retreats optional or compulsory? Give a reason.

Questions

Knowledge

1. a. Name one religious belief.
   b. Name two religious practices.
2. List all the main influences on the religious belief and practice of young people.
3. What is the biggest influence on young people's religious belief and practice according to recent research?
4. In what ways could parents encourage the religious belief and practice of their children?
5. How might parents discourage the religious belief and practice of their children?
6. In what ways can one's peers have a positive effect on one's religious belief and practice?
7. How might peers have a negative effect on each others religious belief and practice?

Understanding

1. What are the main factors that influence the religious belief and practice of the adolescent? Select two factors and explain their influence in detail.
2. What degree of influence do you think the following have on the religious outlook of teenagers in different faith communities?
   School. Friends. Parents. Church.
   Synagogue. Mosque. Temple.
3. What do you think of the research finding that parents have by far the greatest influence on the religiousness of adolescents?

Research

- Find out who are the heroes and heroines of members of the class. Is there any trend in the feedback from the group?
  - Think about your own hero or heroine. Select someone you look up to and admire; someone who has or had a positive influence on you. Is this person famous? Or is it someone known to you now, or whom you once knew in the past?
  - Write a summary containing a few biographical facts about your chosen hero or heroine. What is it you like and admire about him/her? What is the extent of his/her influence on your life? In what ways would you like to be like him/her?
  - Present you statement to the class. (Supporting artifacts, pictures or photographs optional.)

Looking at Life

Key Concepts

Awe and wonder: feelings inspired by mysterious aspects of life.

Reflection: thinking deeply about certain aspects of life.

Objectives

Examine experiences of awe and wonder.

Show the importance of stopping to reflect on these experiences.

Activity: *"Journey to the Stars"*

TASK: PARTICIPATE IN AN IMAGINATION EXERCISE.

- All that is required is that you give this exercise your full attention and have paper and pens ready to write with afterwards.
- Settle down quietly, be comfortable and alert. First there will be a quietening exercise to settle the body. Then there will be an imagination exercise to engage the mind.

- - - - - - - - - - - - - - -

- Sit comfortably with your back straight, feet firmly on the floor, hands unclasped and placed lightly in your lap.

  Take a good deep breath. Let your body relax. Be aware of your breathing, the in-breath and the out-breath. Now close your eyes. Let your eyes relax. Let your face relax. Now be aware of the rest of your body. Starting with the feet... legs... thighs... stomach... chest... shoulders... arms... hands... face...

  Your eyes remain closed.

- Now be aware of your body sitting in this room… Take in the fact that we share a building with many other people who at this very moment are doing other things…
  Be aware that the school we are in is only one of a number of buildings in the area... there are houses… shops…. roads… fields where people are all doing their own tasks.

- In your mind's eye be aware of (name the town/ village you are in). Imagine yourself rising above it… See what is going on down below… People out for a walk… Going into shops… Cars and vans on the streets… Notice the different landmarks….

- Now rise further until you can see the whole county…. With its towns…. fields…. rivers…. hills…. and be aware that you are part of that….

- Higher still you can now see the entire country as if you were looking down on it from space…. Continue to rise up…. until you can see the continent of Europe…. Gradually the whole world comes into view…. The other continents: Asia, Africa, North and South America, Australia…. the white of the polar ice caps. Be aware of all the people on the planet and that you are part of that...

- Moving further away you see the Earth becoming smaller…. with the moon circling around it…. then the other planets…. All of them circling around a vast bright sun…. to form a solar system of which you are a part….

- And now you are so far away that the Earth has vanished and our sun is one small star among the billions forming the galaxy of the Milky Way…. You become aware of other galaxies…. Stars all around you, stretching to infinity…. You are part of all that….

- Take some time to be aware of this infinity…. and when you are ready…. return here.... gently open your eyes and be aware that you are now back in this room.

- Stay quiet for a little while longer (stretch if necessary).

- - - - - - - - - - - - - - -

A. Now, on your own, try to express what you experienced during the exercise. Do this through a drawing, a symbol, a poem, a paragraph, or any other way you can think of. Add an appropriate title to your finished work.

B. Share your experience with a partner.

C. Discuss with the class.

i. Was it easy or difficult to do this exercise?

ii What sort of things did you see and feel during the exercise?

iii What are your thoughts as a result of doing this exercise?

Awe and Wonder

Awe and wonder are feelings inspired by the more mysterious aspects of life. People can experience deep joy and admiration at the mysterious nature of:

- ❖ The universe.
- ❖ The natural world.
- ❖ Other human beings.

There are moments when we are awestruck by the wonder of creation. People of all ages can feel a sense of wonderment at the vast scale of the universe.

One small part of the universe.

The Universe

When was the last time you stopped to stare at the sky on a starry night? The stars above us are part of a galaxy called the Milky Way. Astronomers estimate that our galaxy contains over a hundred billion stars. Add to that the millions of other galaxies elsewhere in the universe - its immense! It is barely possible even to imagine just how big it is. As human beings we are struck with awe and wonder at the enormous size of the universe.

The Natural World

There are many glories in nature that can lift the heart and mind in a special way.

In the natural world there are large-scale wonders such as:

- the Grand Canyon in the USA.
- the Great Barrier Reef in Australia.
- the Aurora Borealis of the Northern Hemisphere.

The Northern Lights.

And small-scale wonders such as:

- the detail of a spiders web on a frosty morning.
- the beauty of a rainbow.
- sunlight sparkling on water.
- the colours of a sunset.

There are a lot of things to marvel at if we take the time to stand and notice them. Ordinary things become extraordinary when we stop and give them some attention.

Human Beings

Moments of awe and wonder occur to us as we stand in silence before the vastness of the universe and the wonders of nature, big and small.

We can also have moments of rapture in relation to other human beings. There may be times when we stop and marvel at the gift of someone's existence, especially if that person is somehow part of our life. We might find ourselves stopping to marvel at the gift or special reality of:

- a new born baby.
- a good friend.
- a loving parent or grandparent.
- a person who has achieved some amazing feat.

New born baby.

Section D

Reflection

Everyone can recall a moment when they felt awe and wonder at some aspect of life. Such a moment may lead us to reflect on the mystery of:

- ❖ The universe.
- ❖ The natural world.
- ❖ Human life itself.

Reflection means taking time to stop and examine something in our experience, and to think deeply about it. In the following extract a man remembers an experience which took place years earlier, when he was a teenager.

"One day during my last term at school I walked out alone in the evening... I heard the birds singing... a chorus of song which can only be heard... at dawn or at sunset. I remember now the shock of surprise with which the sound broke on my ears. It seemed to me that I had never heard the birds singing before and I wondered if they sang like this all the year around and I had never noticed it.

As I walked on I came upon some Hawthorn trees in full bloom and again I thought that I had never seen such a sight or experienced such sweetness before. I came then to where the sun was setting over the playing fields. A lark...poured out its song above my head. Then everything grew still as the sunset faded and the veil of dusk began to cover the Earth.

I remember now the feeling of awe which came over me. I...wanted to kneel on the ground as though I had been standing in the presence of an angel. I hardly dared look at the face of the sky because it seemed as though it was but a veil before the face of God."

Bede Griffiths, "The Golden String", Fontana.

Questions

Knowledge

1. What feelings might people have if they stopped to think about the sheer scale of the universe?
2. What things in the natural world might fill people with a sense of awe and wonder?
3. Give examples of how other human beings can fill us with a sense of awe and wonder.
4. Suggest three other words to describe this feeling of awe.
5. What is the meaning of reflection? What does it mean to reflect?
6. In the story, what did the teenager appear to notice for the first time that evening?
7. What feelings came over him as he walked alone through the school grounds?
8. How did the events of the evening affect him?

Understanding

1. a. Describe a time when you were filled with awe and wonder about something in life.
   b. How did the experience affect you?
   c. Did it prompt you to reflect? What thoughts came to you then?
2. Is it important to stop occasionally to reflect on life? What is your opinion?

Research

- Talk to someone you know well; it may be someone your own age, or someone older. Ask the following questions:
  a. What kind of experiences fill you with awe and wonder?
  b. What kind of questions do these experiences prompt you to ask?
  - Write a summary of the person's response and, with their permission, share the account with the class.

Questions about Life

Key Concepts

Question: the act of asking questions, e.g. about the meaning of life.

Questioner: the person who asks questions and seeks the truth.

Objective

Show that human beings tend to ask questions about the meaning of life.

Activity: *"All living things"*

TASK: TO BE AWARE OF DISTINCTIVE HUMAN CHARACTERISTICS

All living things share certain characteristics. This means plants, animals and human beings have a number of elements in common. However this does not mean that they are all equal in every respect. The list below shows some of the characteristics of living organisms.

✦ What elements are characteristic of plant life, animal life, and human life? (✓)

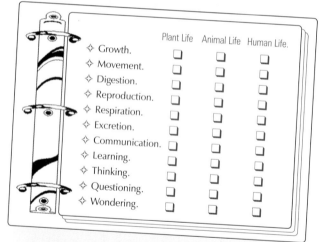

	Plant Life	Animal Life	Human Life.
✧ Growth.	❑	❑	❑
✧ Movement.	❑	❑	❑
✧ Digestion.	❑	❑	❑
✧ Reproduction.	❑	❑	❑
✧ Respiration.	❑	❑	❑
✧ Excretion.	❑	❑	❑
✧ Communication.	❑	❑	❑
✧ Learning.	❑	❑	❑
✧ Thinking.	❑	❑	❑
✧ Questioning.	❑	❑	❑
✧ Wondering.	❑	❑	❑

Discuss

- What characteristics do all living things have in common?
- What characteristics are unique to human beings?
- Can you explain how the ability to ask questions is of value to human beings?

Question

Questioner

The ability to ask questions is an essential human characteristic.

People ask a lot of questions; it is part of being human. Human beings ask all kinds of questions. We ask people for information when we want to learn something. We ask people for directions if we are lost. We ask people for their opinion when we are having a discussion. Or we may ask someone how they feel after something has happened.

Not all questions have the same significance or have equal value. We need to be able to distinguish between different types of questions. It is important to know the difference between small ordinary questions, and the bigger, more fundamental questions about the meaning of life.

✦ Examine the list below, distinguish between the small ordinary questions and the bigger fundamental questions about life.

Questions (✓)	**Small Qs**	**Big Qs**
✧ What time is it?	❑	❑
✧ What homework do we have?	❑	❑
✧ How much is it?	❑	❑
✧ Do people matter?	❑	❑
✧ Should I do transition year?	❑	❑
✧ Can I have some money?	❑	❑
✧ What class do we have next?	❑	❑
✧ What happens when we die?	❑	❑
✧ What film is on?	❑	❑
✧ Why do I have to go to school?	❑	❑
✧ Where do you keep the biscuits?	❑	❑
✧ Why do people suffer?	❑	❑
✧ Who won the match?	❑	❑
✧ Will I get a job?	❑	❑
✧ Are we there yet?	❑	❑

✦ Discuss

1. Which type of questions are asked...
   a. more often? b. less often?
2. Which type of questions are...
   a. easy to answer?
   b. more difficult to answer?
3. What do you think is one of the most important questions to try and answer? Give a reason for your choice.

The Meaning of Life

One important difference between human beings and other creatures is that we have the capacity to question and to seek the truth. There are different types of questions, some are more difficult to answer than others. The questions that we might see as difficult or complex are often questions about the meaning of life. Everyone, whether they are religious or not, has questions about the meaning and purpose of life.

Reflecting on life.

When you stop to wonder about life do you ever find yourself asking questions to which there are no simple answers, such as:

- Why is there a universe?
- Why does anything exist?
- Who am I?
- How can I be happy?
- What happens when we die?
- Why do people suffer?
- What is the right thing to do?
- Why is the world the way it is?
- What do I want to do with my life?

Deep questions such as these help us to explore the mystery of life. Each question is important, yet difficult to answer. All are questions about the meaning of life.

Questions at different stages of development

We think and wonder about life at all stages of our development from childhood, through adolescence into adulthood. People ask questions in order to make sense of what they see and experience in the world around them. Children's questions tend to be concrete and down to earth. Adolescents and adults are able to think about life at a deeper level and can ask more abstract questions.

Small children.

Try to imagine the kind of questions children ask about life.

✧ For children the big questions might be...

1. ____________________
2. ____________________
3. ____________________

Teenagers.

Try to imagine the kind of questions teenagers ask about life.

✧ For teenagers the big questions might be...

1. ____________________
2. ____________________
3. ____________________

Parents.

Try to imagine the kind of questions parents ask about life.

✧ For parents the big questions might be...

1. ____________________
2. ____________________
3. ____________________

Retired people.

Try to imagine the kind of questions retired people ask about life.

✧ For retired people the big questions might be...

1. ____________________
2. ____________________
3. ____________________

Youth Culture - Search for Meaning

From time to time we stop and think about our lives and wonder why things are as they are. We have a need to understand what our life, and life in general, is all about. At such times we might listen to our favourite music, finding inspiration in the words of a song. Seeing a film, reading a book or watching a favourite T.V. show might also express questions about life that concern us at a particular moment.

A Study Group exercise

✦ Form groups to discuss music, films, T.V. programmes and books or magazines that are popular and relevant to young people today.

✦ Divide into groups.
a. A music group. b. A film group.
c. A T.V. group. d. A book/ magazine group.

✦ Each group elects:
- a leader to keep the group on task.
- a record keeper to take notes of the discussion and report back to the class.

✦ Afterwards write a paragraph on the questions of meaning that arise in the facet of contemporary youth culture that you explored.

Music
1. What songs are popular at the moment?
2. Pick one song. Say what the song is about.
3. What questions of meaning are raised in this song?
4. What answers does the song give to these fundamental questions?

Films
1. What recent films have you seen?
2. Pick one film. Say what the film is about.
3. What questions of meaning are raised in this film?
4. What answers does the film give to these fundamental questions?

T.V.
1. What are your favourite TV programmes?
2. Pick one programme. Say what the programme is about.
3. What questions of meaning are raised in this programme?
4. What answers does the programme give to these fundamental questions?

Books/ Magazines
1. What books/magazines do you read?
2. Pick one book or magazine. Say what the book/magazine is about.
3. What questions of meaning are raised in this book/magazine?
4. What answers does this book/magazine give to these fundamental questions?

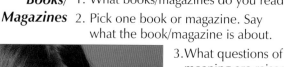

Making sense of life

Sometimes people have experiences such as birth, death, success, failure, an accident or an illness that make them stop and reflect on life. Here some young people share their thoughts and their questions about life based on their own experience.

"An experience that made me think about life was when my Nana died. I was very close to her and I would see her every weekend. Then she got sick. My grandad phoned and told us she had died and we were all upset. It was strange and weird. I thought about what will happen when I die, and when will I die. I thought about how long will I have to live, and what will I do when I am older, and will I have a good job."

Mark

"Last year my aunt had her first child, a baby boy. She named him John Charles after his two grandads. When he was only a few days old he already had a nickname, we called him 'Little Digger', as his initials were JCB! The first time I saw the baby it made me stop and think about life. His little fingers and his little toes were so tiny. It was wonderful how God had made them like that. I got to hold the baby. I was very careful. Babies make you think about being careful and gentle and good things like that. Babies make people smile and be happy. I think babies bring happiness into the world."

Niamh

"My sister has a serious illness. She is only young, it makes me worry and makes me think deeply about life. I think life should be enjoyed and that your time should be used wisely, doing something you want to do. It makes me wonder what life is all about and that I don't know what will happen next. I now pray to God more frequently and say special prayers for people that I know are ill. My prayers to God have increased. This experience has changed my life and all our lives. It has made me think deeper about my own life."

Emma

Questions

Knowledge

1. What is one of the main differences between human beings and other creatures?
2. List some common questions that people ask about life.
3. When you think deeply about life what sort of questions do you ask? Make a list.
4. What is the difference in the way children and adults ask questions about life?
5. Give examples of questions of meaning asked by:
   a. Children. b. Teenagers. c. Adults.
6. What questions of meaning are expressed in teenage music, film, T.V. programmes, books and magazines?
7. What kind of experiences may prompt people to ask questions about the meaning of life?

Understanding

1. Do you agree or disagree with the statement "asking questions is an essential human characteristic"? Give reasons for your answer.
2. Why do human beings ask questions about the meaning and purpose of life?
3. What are the similarities and differences about the questions people ask at various stages in their lives?
4. How could music, for example, shed meaning on our lives?

Research

- Write a paragraph or a short poem about some of the questions that you ask about the meaning of life?

  Invite members of the class to share their work.

  Rules:
  - Everyone listens with respect.
  - No discussion or comments necessary.
  - Everyone gets a turn.
  - Anyone may pass if they choose.

Search for Meaning

Key Concepts

Search: the deep human need to find meaning in life.
Meaning: to find or to have a sense of purpose in life.
Meaninglessness: failing to find meaning or purpose in life.
Humanism: a belief system that rejects religion and makes sense of life through human reason alone.

Objective

Identify evidence of the search for meaning in contemporary culture.

Activity: *"A Wish List"*

TASK: TO BE AWARE THAT STRIVING TO BE HAPPY IS PART OF THE HUMAN CONDITION.

A Wish List

- All I want is…
  - to get that MP3 player.
  - to have nice hair.
  - to win the match.
  - to do well in the exams.
  - to be allowed to go to…
  - to have a boy friend/ a girl friend.
  - to finish school.
  - for them to get back together again.
  - to be picked for the team.
  - to buy the things I want.
  - for people to like me.
  - to live somewhere else.
  - for him/her to get better.
  - to be friends with them again.

Discuss

- What do you think people long for most?
- How might it make them happy?
- What happens when people get what they want?
- Have you ever really longed for something? Explain.

Search

Meaning

Human beings have a built-in need to search for happiness.

We all know what it is like to look forward to something; to want something very badly indeed. We also know that when the moment arrives the delight is short lived, and then we want something else. We seem to be unable to reach the point where we are totally satisfied. We are constantly searching for more. No matter what we set our heart on, it is never enough. We are restless and full of longing. This kind of restlessness is part of being human. We want to be happy, and we think we know what will make us happy.

If we accept that human beings have a built-in need for happiness, but nothing we buy ever makes us really happy, then what are we to do? Where can human beings find happiness? How can people be truly happy? These are big questions. In fact these are fundamental questions about the meaning of life. To be able to ask questions like these is the first step in what is known as the search for meaning.

People try to make sense of life.

Section D

The search for meaning

The basic difference between human beings and other creatures is our ability to think and ask questions. From time to time we stop and think about life. We wonder why things are as they are. We ask deep questions about the meaning of our lives. Sometimes we even ask questions about the meaning of life itself; questions such as why do we exist?, what is life for?, what is the right way to live?, what happens when we die?

Human beings have a profound need to understand what life is all about. The ability to ask endless questions about the meaning of life is part of the human search for happiness. It is like being on a quest or a mission. People will search for answers until they find one that satisfies them and makes them truly happy.

One's family is an important source of meaning for many people.

Sources of meaning

When people search for meaning, they are looking for something that makes sense of life. In our society, people find meaning and purpose in life by devoting themselves to one or more of the following:

- their family.
- their friends.
- their music.
- their religion.
- their education.
- their work.
- their sport.
- their politics.
- their social life.
- their voluntary activities.

These are the main ways in which people find some meaning in life. However there are people who fail to find meaning or purpose in any human activity. For them everything is meaningless, nothing has any meaning or value at all.

Sources of meaning in my life

✦What is important and gives meaning to your life?

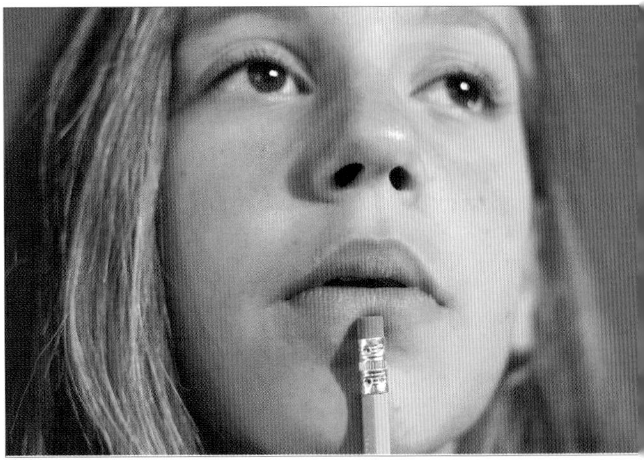

- Having friends.
- Doing well at school.
- Having good health.
- Being a good person.
- Keeping fit.
- My religion.
- Getting a good job.
- Being liked by everyone.
- Making the world a better place.
- other...
- Having fun.
- My family.
- Helping others.
- Being good at what I do.
- Being on the team.
- Doing what's right for me.
- Looking good.
- Having money.
- Having a boyfriend/ girlfriend.
- other...

✦ Exercise

1. Select your top five sources of meaning from the list above.
2. Are your sources of meaning the same or different to the rest of the class.
3. Finish the following sentences:
   - Two important sources of meaning for me are....
   - Two important sources of meaning for my class are....
4. Name three things that give most meaning to your life. Describe how these had an influence on your attitude or behaviour sometime in the past week.
5. Write a paragraph on your philosophy or outlook on life. Think about what is important in life. Think about what really matters to you. Understand that what matters most is what gives meaning to your life.

   "What matters most to me is...."

Religion - a source of meaning

People who believe in God think religion can show the way to true happiness. People who do not believe in God think the way to true happiness lies elsewhere. There are religious and non-religious answers to the question of what is important in life.

A Christian Orthodox priest.

A Muslim girl.

A Jewish family at the Sabbath meal.

St. Augustine

St. Augustine was one of the greatest thinkers in the history of Christianity. When he was sixteen years old Augustine got into a lot of trouble. His mother worried constantly about how he was going to turn out. Her son was restless, always trying something new. He made many false starts before finally turning his life around.

In his autobiography Augustine writes about his desperate search to find happiness in life. Everything he tried left him feeling empty and dissatisfied. Nothing was ever enough; he always wanted more. Then he realised that this search for happiness was in fact his search for God. Only God can satisfy the longing, the restlessness of the human heart. St. Augustine wrote:

"You have made us for yourself O Lord,
Our hearts are restless until they rest in Thee."

✦ This is a famous quotation from the writings of Saint Augustine. In your own words explain what you think it means.

✦ Discuss your insights with the class.

Religious answers

Religion helps many people to find answers to the big fundamental questions in life.

Jews, Muslims, and Christians each:

- Belong to a community of faith,
- Believe in one God, and
- Follow a code of behaviour that comes from God.

The monotheistic religions, Judaism, Islam and Christianity, teach people that they are not alone. God is there to help them. God guides each person as he/she tries to understand what life is all about. People of religious faith believe their relationship with God is the answer to their questions about the meaning of life.

People who believe in God find their religion gives the most meaning to their lives.

- ❖ For Jews: belief in the Lord God and following the Torah gives meaning to their lives.
- ❖ For Muslims: belief in Allah and the teaching of the Qur'an gives meaning to their lives.
- ❖ For Christians: belief in Jesus and his teaching in the Gospels gives meaning to their lives.

Jews, Muslims and Christians believe their faith gives true meaning and purpose to life.

Non-religious answers

Humanism

Jews, Muslims and Christians have faith in God, and rely on their religious beliefs to give meaning to their lives. However, some people do not believe in God and do not belong to any community of faith. They do not look to religion or religious beliefs to give meaning to their lives. Religious ideas are rejected in favour of making sense of life through the power of human reason alone. Such people are called Humanists. Their belief system is called Humanism.

A Humanist is a person who believes that life on Earth is the only reality. There is no God or gods or any power greater than the human person. Humanists do not turn to God or religion for answers to life's big questions. Humanists believe reason and human experience alone is sufficient.

Every religion has its own set of answers to life's big questions. Humanists have answers to life's questions too.

Questions of Meaning	*Religious Answers*	*Non-Religious Answers*
1. Why are we born?	Jews, Muslims and Christians believe life is a gift from God. *For example*, Christians believe God loves the world and creates human beings out of love. Human life is sacred and is to be respected because it comes from God.	Humanists say God is not involved in human life. Human life is born from nature and is to be respected for its own sake.
2. What happens when we die?	Jews, Muslims and Christians believe in life after death. *For example*, Christians believe that after death the souls of good people go to heaven to be with God forever.	Humanists say that after death there is nothing. There is no heaven or after life. The world and this life is all that there is. Death is the end.
3. What is right and what is wrong?	Jews, Muslims and Christians have rules for right and good behaviour. The code of behaviour comes from God. It is written in the sacred text of each religion. *For example*, the Christian code of behaviour is the teaching of Jesus in the New Testament in the Bible.	Humanists have guidelines for right and good behaviour. This code of behaviour does not come from God. It comes from reason and human experience.

Questions

Knowledge

1. What questions do people sometimes ask about life?
2. What sort of things can make a person's life meaningful?
3. Name three things that make you happy and give meaning to your life.
4. Who was St. Augustine and how did he find true happiness in life?
5. What community of faith believes the person and teaching of Jesus gives meaning to life?
6. What do Humanists believe about God and religion?
7. Where do Humanists find meaning in life?

Understanding

1. 'The human heart is restless.' What does this statement say about the nature of human beings?
2. How important do you think family and friends are as a source of meaning in our lives?
3. How can religion help people find meaning in life?
4. What do you think of the Christian and the Humanist outlook on either:
   a. The issue of life? b. The issue of death?
5. Is there any point in searching for answers to the big questions about life?

God in Scripture

Objective

Describe the various images of God and their sources in the Old and New Testament.

Activity: *"Metaphors"*

TASK: USE THE IMAGINATION TO INTRODUCE THE NOTION OF METAPHOR.

✦ Use your imagination to complete the sentences below.
- Try to attempt as many as you can.
- Figure out what each image might be saying about you.

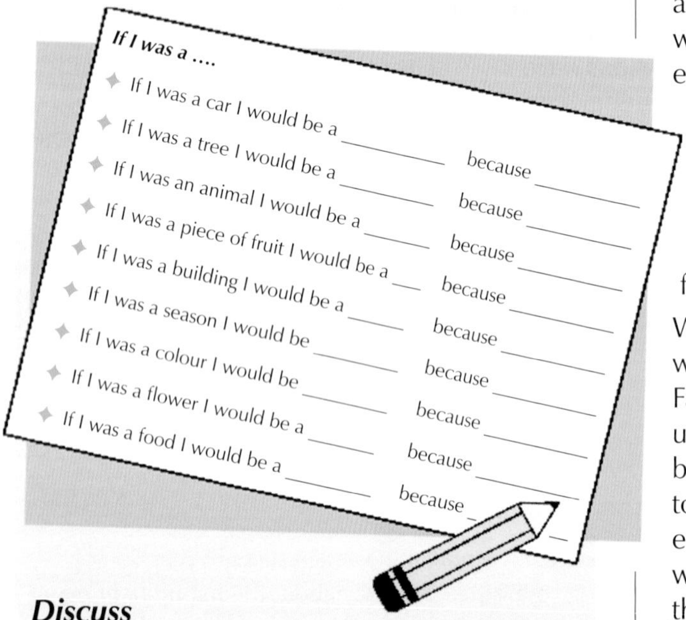

If I was a ....
If I was a car I would be a ________ because ________
If I was a tree I would be a ________ because ________
If I was an animal I would be a ________ because ________
If I was a piece of fruit I would be a ________ because ________
If I was a building I would be a ________ because ________
If I was a season I would be ________ because ________
If I was a colour I would be ________ because ________
If I was a flower I would be a ________ because ________
If I was a food I would be a ________ because ________

Discuss

- What was easy or difficult about doing this exercise?
- What made you choose particular things?
- Did any of the ideas surprise you?
- Which idea did you like best?

Images of God

Images of God from the Old and New Testament enable people to form their own image of God.

We use metaphors to stretch our imagination to see things in a different way. Comparing one thing with another gives us a hint about the nature of something, although it cannot describe it completely. The sacred texts of many world religions are full of metaphors.

God is at the centre of religion. People wonder about God and try to say what God is like. When we think of God we try to find the right words to express what we mean, but soon discover that words fail us. We realise that the mystery of God is beyond our understanding. No matter how hard we try, the words we use cannot capture all that is God. So we do what we can. We compare God with what we already know from our own experience.

When we speak of God, we use metaphors. Familiar images give us a sense of God and bring us a bit closer to knowing God. Yet even the best images will never fully grasp the true nature of God. People will always need to use metaphor to talk about God because:

❖ God remains a mystery to the human mind.

❖ Language is limited when it comes to expressing the mystery of God.

G
O
D

Section D

The Bible

Christians believe in one God. They believe every good thing in the world comes from God. Yet no one knows for sure what God is really like. People have certain ideas of what God must be like. These ideas are like pictures or images that come into people's minds when they talk about God, think about God, or pray to God.

Christians believe that scripture reveals or shows what God is like. There are many images of God in the Bible. The Christian Bible is divided in two parts: the Old Testament or Jewish scriptures, and the New Testament.

The Old Testament

In the Old Testament when people speak of God they use metaphors comparing God to what they already know from their own experience.

In the Old Testament familiar images...

- ❖ from nature,
- ❖ from human life,

...help people to know what God is like.

Images of God from nature.

God is like:

- ✧ An eagle... that is powerful.
- ✧ The rain... that nourishes.
- ✧ A tree... that shelters.
- ✧ A rock.. that protects.
- ✧ Fire... that is a guiding light.
- ✧ A lion... that defends.

Images of God from human life.

God is like:

- ✧ A king... who reigns.
- ✧ A judge... who is fair and just.
- ✧ A mother... who comforts you.
- ✧ A father... who created you.
- ✧ A shepherd... who guides you.
- ✧ A potter... who moulds you.

In the Jewish scriptures of the Old Testament, God is the one all-powerful Yahweh, who created the universe and formed a special relationship with his chosen people, the Jews.

Quotations from the Old Testament

"He protected them and cared for them... like an eagle teaching its young to fly, catching them safely on its spreading wings." Deut 32:11

"I will be to the people of Israel like rain in a dry land. They will blossom like flowers." Hosea 14:5

"Like an evergreen tree I will shelter them. I am a source of all their blessings." Hosea 14:8

"The Lord is my protector. He is my strong fortress." (rock) Psalm 18:2

"He went in front of them in a pillar of fire to give them light." Exodus 13:21

"My people will follow me when I roar like a lion at their enemies." Hosea 11:10

"God is the King over all the world. Praise him with songs." Psalm 47:7

"You are the judge of all mankind. Judge in my favour O Lord." Psalm 7:8

"I will comfort you in Jerusalem as a mother comforts her child." Isaiah 66:13

"He is your Father, your Creator. He made you into a nation." Deut 32:6

"The Lord is my shepherd,... he guides me on the right path." Psalm 23:1-3

"You are in my hands like the clay in a potter's hands." Jeremiah 18:6

A potter at work.

The New Testament

Christian scripture teaches that the best image of God is an actual person, Jesus the Son of God. Christians believe Jesus came on Earth to show people who God is. Jesus told his followers:

"Whoever has seen me has seen the Father."
(John 14, 9-11)

In the New Testament Jesus shows people what God is like by:

- ❖ The things he said - his parables.
- ❖ The things he did - his miracles.

The Parables of Jesus

Jesus told parables to help people understand the goodness of God. Jesus said God is like:

- ❖ A good shepherd. (Luke 15:4-6)
- ❖ A good housekeeper. (Luke 15:8-10)
- ❖ A generous host. (Luke 14:15-24)
- ❖ A good father. (Luke 15:11-32)

Jesus told these stories to help people feel what the goodness of God is really like. When a shepherd discovers one of his sheep missing, he leaves everything and goes off to look for the one that is lost. When a housekeeper discovers a coin is missing, she searches everywhere until it is found. The little lamb and the small coin are precious to their owners, so too each person on Earth is even more precious to God.

The Good Shepherd.

Jesus said God is like a person who gave a great banquet and invited the poor, the crippled, the blind and the lame to attend.

Jesus said God is like the ideal parent and taught his followers to call God 'Abba' meaning 'Dada' or 'Daddy'. Jesus encouraged his followers to pray to God. The prayer said by all Christians today begins with the words "Our Father who art in heaven".

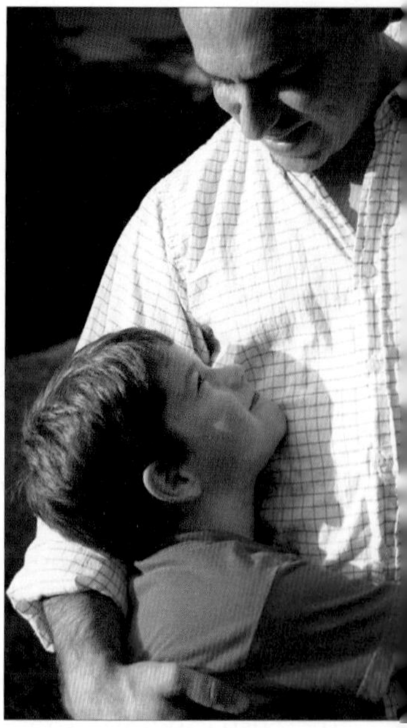

Jesus wanted his followers to think of God as a loving caring parent.

We know from experience that good parents love and care for their children. They are close to them, protect them and give them what they need. Parents are always ready to forgive a child who says "sorry" for what he/she has done wrong. Jesus said God is just like that. God is very near, always looking after us and helping us. God loves and cares for us more than we can imagine.

The Miracles of Jesus

When people looked at Jesus they could see what God is like.

Jesus:
- ❖ Healed people who were sick. (Mark 1:29-34)
- ❖ Forgave people who had done wrong. (Mark 2:1-12)
- ❖ Was friendly to outcasts and people whom nobody liked. (Mark 2:13-17)
- ❖ Was compassionate to those who had problems. (Mark 8:1-10)
- ❖ Gave up his life out of love for everyone. (Mark 15:1-47)

Jesus wanted his followers to think of God as good, loving and caring. Someone close to them, always looking after them. A God they can trust.

Christian teaching about God

Two key Christian teachings about God that are central to Christian faith are:

- ❖ The Incarnation.
- ❖ The Trinity.

The Incarnation

The Incarnation is the Christian belief that, in Jesus, God became a human being. In other words Jesus is fully God and fully human. This is called the mystery of Incarnation.

"Whoever has seen me has seen the father."
John 14:9-11

The Trinity

The Trinity is the Christian belief that in the one God there are three distinct and equal persons; the Father, Son and Holy Spirit. So when Christians speak of God they mean the Father, the Son, and the Holy Spirit.

The mystery of the Trinity can be confusing and hard to understand. Different metaphors and images have been used to help people grasp the idea that there are three distinct and equal persons in the one God. It is said St. Patrick used a three leaved shamrock to explain how there are three persons in one God. Each person of the Trinity is a special aspect of God.

God is...

- ✧ **The Father** who creates the world.
- ✧ **The Son** (Jesus) who saves the world.
- ✧ **The Holy Spirit** who helps people to follow the way of Jesus.

Questions

Knowledge

1. What is a metaphor?
2. What do we mean when we say we have an image of God?
3. How did people picture God in Old Testament times?
4. Which images of God in the Old Testament do you like best? Why?
5. Where do Christians get the best insight into the nature of God?
6. List three parables Jesus told to show what God is like.
7. Pick an image from one parable and describe what it tells us about God.
8. What did the word 'Abba' mean at the time of Jesus?
9. When Jesus used the image of a good father, what was he saying about God?
10. Name the three persons in the Trinity.

Understanding

1. Select one of the images in the Old Testament and say why it is a suitable image for God.
2. Why do Christians speak about God in images and metaphor?
3. "Whoever has seen me has seen the father." John 14:9-11. What do Christians believe Jesus meant by this statement?
4. Select an image of God from the New Testament. Explain how this image can help Christians understand what God is like.
5. "When Christians think about God they think about the Trinity."
   Can you explain what this means?

Research

- Jews and Muslims believe in God but are forbidden to draw or to make images of God. Christians frequently draw pictures and images to show their understanding of God.
  - Can you think of another image for the Trinity? Draw the image and write an explanation beside it. Display your work for the benefit of the class.

Our image of God

Key Concept

Personal faith: a person's own religious belief and response to God.

Objective

Describe your own image of God and identify its source.

Activity: *"Forced Choice"*

TASK: CHOOSE A METAPHOR FOR GOD.

✦ Use your imagination to think about God in unusual ways.

Is God more like....
1. A daisy... or a rose...?
2. The mountains... or the sea...?
3. A painting... or a jig-saw...?
4. A whisper... or a shout...?
5. Summer... or winter...?
6. Red... or green...?
7. A song... or a dance...?
8. Candlelight ... or sunlight...?

✦ Select a pair of words.
  - Ask yourself: is God more like, for example, a daisy or a rose? You have two options - you may choose only one.
  - Pick the one you think God is more like, not the one you happen to like best yourself.
  - Give a reason for your choice. Think of all the qualities of, for example, a daisy or a rose. Say how these qualities remind you of the nature of God.

✦ Compare your answers with everyone else.

✦ Select another pair of words and again force yourself to choose between them.

Discuss

- Is it easy or difficult to think of the qualities of different things?
- What was it like when you compared your ideas with everyone else?
- What do you think is the best metaphor for God? Why?

Personal Faith

Using metaphors can help people to think about their image of God.

No one has ever seen God, yet millions of people believe in God. Everyone has certain ideas of what God is like, although it can sometimes be difficult to find just the right words to say what we mean.

Christians for example, find it useful to form an image or mental picture of God in their mind. It brings the idea of God to life and makes it more real for them. Everyone can have an image of God whether or not they believe in God.

Our images of God are important because they help us to imagine what God is like. But our images cannot describe God completely as God is a mystery to the human mind.

When Christians pray to God they hold a certain image of God in their mind.

My image of God

Personal faith is a person's own religious belief and response to God. It is our relationship with God arising out of our own personal experience of everyday life; its joy and sorrows, hopes and disappointments. Our image of God is part of all this.

My image of God - what is it exactly?

Over to you

What is your image of God? What picture or image comes into your mind when you think about God? If you are not sure what image of God you have:

- ❖ Begin by listing experiences.
- ❖ Then use words.
- ❖ Then move on to images.

Get in touch with your image of God.

a. List some *experiences* that you had in life that give you a hint of what God is like.

b. Pick one *word* that sums up your sense of God from these experiences.

c. What picture or *image* of God comes into your mind because of these experiences?

Sources of my image of God

The source of our image of God has to do with where our image of God comes from. Our idea of God could be based on:

- ❖ Stories from scripture told in church and read to us by parents and teachers.
- ❖ Pictures we have seen.
- ❖ Songs and hymns we have listened to.
- ❖ Our own personal experience of everyday life; its joys and sorrows, hopes and disappointments.

This is a list of people and things that can shape our image of God.

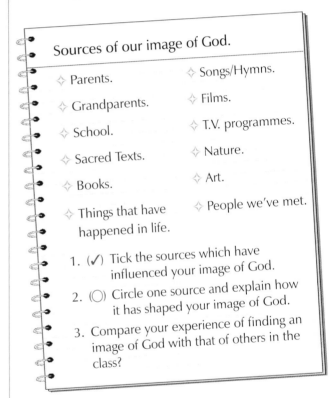

Sources of our image of God.

- ✧ Parents.
- ✧ Grandparents.
- ✧ School.
- ✧ Sacred Texts.
- ✧ Books.
- ✧ Things that have happened in life.
- ✧ Songs/Hymns.
- ✧ Films.
- ✧ T.V. programmes.
- ✧ Nature.
- ✧ Art.
- ✧ People we've met.

1. (✓) Tick the sources which have influenced your image of God.
2. (◯) Circle one source and explain how it has shaped your image of God.
3. Compare your experience of finding an image of God with that of others in the class?

We can use words to describe the nature of God, and we can use images to imagine what God looks like. Yet it is important to realise that our words and images will never fully capture who God is. The mystery of God is too great for the human mind to understand.

One artist's image of God.

Art as a source of our image of God

✦ Discuss

1. Name this famous work of art showing an image of God.
2. Who was the artist?
3. Where is this painting on view to the public?
4. What do you think the artist is trying to say about God?
5. What might have influenced the artist to depict God in this manner?
6. Do you think this image is an accurate portrayal of what God is like?
7. Can you name or describe any other famous works of art that show images of God?

Questions

1. Name some experiences that you have had in life that give you a hint of what God is like.
2. a. List all the words you can think of to describe the nature of God.
   b. Which of these words do you associate with God the most?
3. a. What is your present image of God?
   b. Why do you think this is a good image of God?
4. Where do people generally get their ideas about God? Identify as many sources as possible.
5. From what sources do you get your ideas about God?
6. Has your religious tradition influenced your image of God in any way? Explain.
7. Where do you think small children get their ideas about God?
8. 'No one knows what God is like.'
   Why? Why not...?

Research

- Try to express your own image of God through an artistic medium.
  You will need: paper and pens, a CD player, a CD of reflective music, index cards and modelling clay (optional).
  - Play reflective music and work quietly.
  - Think about what God means to you.
  - Can you draw a picture or mould a piece of clay to show your image of God?
  - When the work is completed take an index card and on it:
    - Compose a title for your work.
    - Write a statement beginning with the words "My God is...".
    - Sign the card with your name, initials, or code mark.
  - Display the completed work in a suitable location.

Stages of Faith

Key Concepts

Trust: being able to rely on a person with complete confidence.

Faith: a strong inner belief and trust in God.

Stages of faith: the development of a person's relationship with God from childhood faith to mature faith.

Childhood faith: a simple trust in God and an acceptance of one's parents' faith.

Mature faith: a close relationship with God and an active commitment to one's faith.

Objectives

Differentiate between the faith of the child and that of the adult, and have a sense of the development from one to the other.

Activity: *"Steps and Stages"*

TASK: TO BE AWARE THAT PEOPLE EXPERIENCE THINGS AT DIFFERENT STAGES IN LIFE.

✦ Number the stages below in the correct order, starting with the earliest.

- ❑ Learning to talk.
- ❑ Learning to read.
- ❑ Breathing.
- ❑ Learning to drive.
- ❑ Drinking from a glass.
- ❑ Crying.
- ❑ Getting married.
- ❑ Learning to walk.
- ❑ Joining a club.
- ❑ Leaving home.
- ❑ Doing exams.
- ❑ Cycling a bicycle.
- ❑ Making friends.
- ❑ Learning to pray.
- ❑ Buying clothes.
- ❑ Getting a part time job.
- ❑ Buying a house.
- ❑ Starting primary school.

Discuss

- Compare your answers with everyone else. Are they the same, or different?
- What other experiences could be added to the list? Where would they be placed on the list?
- Why do you think that things happen in stages as people go through life?

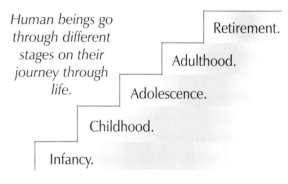

Human beings go through different stages on their journey through life.

Retirement.

Adulthood.

Adolescence.

Childhood.

Infancy.

As we grow older we change and mature in different ways. We change:

- ❖ Physically - our bodies develop.
- ❖ Intellectually - our minds develop.
- ❖ Emotionally - our feelings develop.
- ❖ Spiritually - our faith develops.

In this lesson we will look at the way religious faith can grow and develop throughout a person's lifetime.

Parents, grandparents and children.

Trust and Faith

Trust is being able to rely on a person with complete confidence. People learn about trust early in life. When small children feel loved by their parents it gives them the assurance, as they get older, that they can trust other people and life in general. Being able to trust a person, and rely on him/her with complete confidence, comes from an experience of being loved and cared for by others.

Parent and child.

Faith is a strong inner belief and trust in God. When a person is able to put their trust in God, this is faith. Someone who trusts God believes:

- ❖ God loves them.
- ❖ God will always be there for them.
- ❖ God will not let them down.

Having faith in God is about trusting God. Faith is a gift from God. People are free to accept or reject the gift of faith. A person may choose to put their trust in God or not. Sometimes it is hard for people to accept that God loves them, and is always there for them. We cannot see or touch God, and this can make it more difficult to have faith in God. That is why people often find it helpful to have an image or a picture of God in their mind.

Questions

1. What does it mean to trust someone?
2. How do most of us learn to trust other people?
3. What does it mean to have trust in God?
4. What is religious faith?

Stages of Faith

People's religious faith can grow and develop throughout their lifetime. Experts who study religious faith tell us that people go through a series of different stages in their relationship with God. The stages of faith are:

- ❖ Childhood faith - an imitative faith.
- ❖ Adolescent faith - a questioning faith.
- ❖ Mature faith - an active commitment to one's faith.

Each stage is necessary and has its own unique characteristics.

Everyone's image of God, and their relationship with God, changes and develops as they grow older and become more mature. The faith of a child is different to the faith of an adolescent, which in turn is different to the faith of an adult.

In most cases people make an effort and their faith and religious ideas move forward from one stage to the next. It can happen however that a person gets 'stuck' at a certain point, and their faith does not progress any further. We might see this, for example, where a young person passes their exams at school, graduates from college, gets a good job, maybe has a nice boy or girl friend, but still has an image of God that he or she had at ten years of age!

Most well-rounded people grow and develop physically, intellectually, emotionally and spiritually at the same time. But spiritual development does not happen automatically. It too needs to be updated and worked at like everything else.

Questions

1. Name the different stages of faith.
2. A well-rounded person grows and develops physically, intellectually, emotionally and spiritually.
   a. What does this mean?
   b. What might happen if a person's spiritual development did not keep pace with their physical, intellectual and emotional development?
3. People view God differently at different stages in their lives. Do you agree or disagree with this statement?

Childhood Faith

Childhood faith is a simple trust in God and an acceptance of one's parents' faith. Children's image of God as a father or grandfather figure is based on their experience of the love of parents and family members.

Image of God

"When I was small I used to think that God was a very old man with a long white beard and a happy face. He lived somewhere up in the sky, above the clouds. He wore a long robe and sat on a golden throne. God is good. You could ask him for anything (but only if you were good yourself and asked in the right way). God was in charge of everyone and everything on the Earth."

Gary

Children have a very definite image of God, they also have a very active imagination. They like to listen to all kinds of stories, including parables or religious stories. It makes sense for children to imagine that God must be very old - after all, they understand that he has been around since the beginning of the world! He must be up in the sky somewhere since he's in charge of everything that is going on down here. He must smile a lot too since he likes people and is always helping them.

Children trust people who are good to them, such as their parents and their grandparents. They learn to trust God who is both very good and very powerful. Children learn to trust God in the same way that they trust good people around them. Their image of God is based on their experience. It is also based on their ability to think about things in a concrete, matter of fact manner.

Children's pictures of God.

Children learn about their faith from their parents, their teachers and from religious leaders in their place of worship. Childhood faith might be described as an imitative form of faith. Children accept the religious belief and practice of their parents, imitating what they do without question. If parents belong to a particular faith community, children tend to feel that they belong there too.

Ross age 4.

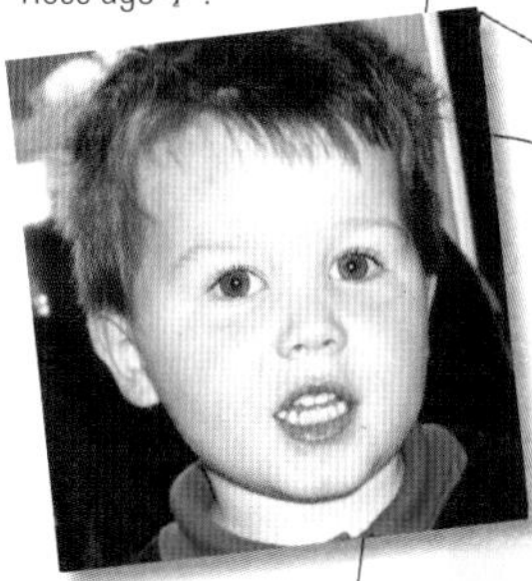

Hannah age $7\frac{1}{2}$.

Questions

1. What was Gary's image of God when he was a child?
2. Where do children get their images of God?
3. How do children learn to trust in God?
4. Did anyone talk to you about God when you were young? If so, whom?
5. Were you taught any prayers and religious practices as a child? If so, what were they?
6. 'Childhood faith is an imitative faith.' What does this statement mean?

Adolescent faith

The adolescent's image of God is more like that of a friend; someone to turn to, talk to, and who can always be relied upon. This image is based on the adolescent experience of friendship and acceptance in the peer group.

Image of God

"What is my image of God? Well, in religion class we learn that Christians believe Jesus came on Earth to show people what God is like. So I think it makes no sense to think of God as an old man up there in the sky. I don't buy into that anymore. Now I think God is more like a friend than anything else. God is someone to turn to, someone to talk to. Someone who will never let you down. I suppose God is like an invisible friend. Maybe he looks a bit like Jesus."

Paul

When you were in primary school, you took your religion for granted and didn't think too much about it, you just accepted it. Things are different now. Your mind is developing and you are able to think at a deeper level. You are beginning to ask some challenging questions about religion and religious ideas and you want some reasonable answers. This is a good sign. It shows you are growing and developing in mind and spirit. Your ideas about religion will grow and develop too.

Adolescents realise that the world is not always a good place; there is evil and injustice, and bad things do happen to good people. Adolescents begin to question how God can allow this to happen. Doubts and questions are important and necessary at this stage of faith development. A person who cares enough to ask deep questions about life, will care enough to search for the answers. He/she will eventually arrive at a deeper understanding of their own faith.

Friends and Peers

Friendship is very important at this stage in life. You may find that you and your friends share the same ideas and opinions about most things, including religion. In matters of faith, young adolescents are often content to accept the views of friends and peers. This changes later on when they are older and ready to leave school.

In senior cycle you may find that you don't need to agree with your friends all the time. You will be able to make up your own mind about things, religion included. For example, if you choose to believe in God, and if you choose to live a good moral life, it is because you believe it is a worthwhile choice. It will be your own personal decision. You will be confident enough to take responsibility for your own faith and your own lifestyle.

This is a long way from the imitative faith of your childhood. Back then you tended to copy what your parents did without giving it too much thought. That was the right thing for you to do at the time. However in adolescence you are beginning to stand on your own two feet. You can actively make a choice to have a religion.

Questions

1. What is Paul's image of God?
2. What is one of the main influences on adolescent faith?
3. Teenage faith is a questioning faith. What does this statement mean?
4. What is the main difference between a child's and an adolescent's:
   a. Image of God?
   b. Attitude to religion?
5. Explain how a person's image of God can change and develop over time. (You may refer to your own experience if you like).

Mature Faith

Mature faith involves an active commitment to one's faith and a close personal relationship with God. A person can reach the stage of mature faith any time between the late teens and middle age.

A person's image of God at this stage is that of a loving presence surrounding them and being close to them. This image is based on personal experience of knowing that what matters most in life is love of God, and the love and care of other people.

Image of God

"When I'm an adult, I'll probably know a lot more about God than I do now. Maybe I'll be more religious as well. Take my Nana for example; she prays all the time. She can pray anywhere, even when she's out walking the dog. 'The goodness of God is all around us, you know.' She's always saying things like that. She told me once that she thinks God is like a loving presence who is with us all the time. Nana is a really good person. She likes all of us and gives us things, and she always remembers my birthday. She's very good to the neighbours as well and helps them out whenever she can. I'd say my grandmother is closer to God than anyone I've ever met."

Gina

Adult life is different from your own experience of life at the moment. Just think of your parents and other adults around you. They are responsible for looking after children, keeping a nice home, going out to work and helping in the community. They do their best and take their responsibilities seriously. Many adults continue to grow in faith throughout their lives. It is also true that some adults give up their faith.

Christians of mature faith follow the teaching of Jesus to love God and their neighbour as themselves. They like to pray and try to live as God wants them to live. People of mature faith, while aware that suffering and injustice exists in the world, are able to trust in the goodness of God. They know that there are things they will never fully understand. They can accept that mystery is part of life. People of mature faith have a very close relationship with God. They have worked out what they believe and have made an active commitment to their faith. They have made the decision to set time aside for God and to live good moral lives caring for others.

The Journey of Faith

As we grow older and learn more about God, our image of God and our relationship with God changes and develops. When we were children, our image of God as someone 'up above' meant we were always asking God to do things for us. When we get older, an image of God as a loving presence can lead us to be less focused on ourselves and more able to love and care for people around us.

Questions

1. What is Gina's grandmother's image of God?
2. What are the characteristics of mature faith?
3. How can people of mature faith show the love of God:
   a. to their family?
   b. to their neighbours?
   c. to their colleagues at work?
4. What is the difference between childhood faith and mature faith in terms of:
   a. image of God? b. relationship with God?
5. Mature faith involves an active commitment to one's faith. What does this statement mean?

Research

- Interview a person of mature faith about his/her image of God. This can be an adult of any age. The person may be known to you or recommended to you as someone who has an obvious commitment to their faith.

  Conduct the interview along the following lines.
  1. Do you feel close to God or far away from God? Explain.
  2. What is your image of God at the present time?
  3. Have you ever felt differently about God at any other time in your life?
  4. Do you communicate with God? If so: When? How?
  5. Does your relationship with God have any effect on the way you live your life?
- With the interviewee's permission compile a summary of the interview and present it to the class.

Section D

Signs of Religious Faith

Key Concepts

Prayer: the way people of faith communicate with God.

Worship: the way people of faith praise and honour God in prayer and at religious services.

Objective

Explain how religious belief finds expression in prayer, worship and a way of life.

Activity: *"On Show"*

TASK: TO BE AWARE THAT WE SHOW OR EXPRESS OUR FEELINGS IN DIFFERENT WAYS.

Counselling psychologists have identified four primary human feelings.

We can be:
✧ *HAPPY* ✧ *SAD* ✧ *ANGRY or* ✧ *AFRAID*.

These feelings are the basis of the emotional life of all human beings. When a person is feeling happy, sad, angry, or afraid they will show it in certain ways. So what a person is feeling inside will often show itself in their outward behaviour.

- ✦ How would you know if a person was feeling sad, for example. What would you notice about their behaviour?
- ✦ List all the ways people show their feelings. If they are:
  - Feeling happy, how do they show it?
  - Feeling sad, how do they show it?
  - Feeling angry, how do they show it?
  - Feeling afraid, how do they show it?

Discuss

- How does your list compare with that of others in the class?
- Do you agree that inward feelings are usually expressed in outward ways?
- Why is it that people cannot help but express their feelings?

Expressing our feelings

People show their feelings and their beliefs in a variety of ways.

We all use words and actions to express our inner feelings. It is natural for people to express feelings of happiness, sadness, fear and anger. These feelings are expressed through words, facial expressions, bodily gestures and a variety of actions and behaviours.

- ✦ What do you think this person is feeling?
- ✦ How do you know? What is the evidence?

In the same way, if a person has a feeling of deep trust or faith in God, he/she will want to express that too. People show their religious faith through prayer, worship, and the way they live their lives.

A person's inner faith in God will always find expression in outer ways. In other words, if a person has faith, it shows! It is natural that a person's inner faith in God will find expression in outer ways, such as wanting to:

- ❖ Pray to God.
- ❖ Worship God.
- ❖ Live the way God wants.

All such behaviours are signs of religious faith.

Section D

✦ Examine the way one girl's faith in God can be seen in her behaviour.

"My name is Rebecca and I am fourteen years old. All my family are fairly religious. From a very young age my parents brought me and my brothers to Mass every Sunday. Gradually as I got older I became more involved. Now I'm in the choir. Some of my friends are in the choir too. I learned to pray as soon as I could talk. I try to pray to God every day; I always say prayers at night.

If I go to the shops or for a walk I sometimes call into the church to pray and light a candle. God is very important to me. But I have a few questions about life - like why do people have to suffer? My aunt is in hospital and we are all worried about her.

I try to help people. I do small simple things that you normally wouldn't notice, like calling my friend if she's sick and chatting to her about what went on at school. I often help out around the house without being asked. For example, I might hang out the washing or brush the kitchen floor. I sometimes help my brothers with their homework. The other thing is I would never steal or do stuff like that. I just don't think it's right. I try not to tell lies either.

I don't understand God fully, but my image of God is of a very good and caring friend. I believe God is always listening to my prayers, and that he is always there for me when times are hard."

Discuss

1. Does Rebecca have faith in God? Give a reason for your answer.
2. Who influenced Rebecca's faith, and in what ways have they done so?
3. How does Rebecca's faith in God affect her behaviour?
4. Give an example of how Rebecca's faith in God is expressed through:
 - prayer - worship - and the way she lives her life.

Prayer

Religious faith is expressed through prayer. People of religious faith believe in God and trust in God. They have a relationship or a friendship with God. To keep any relationship going, people need to:

- ❖ Spend time together.
- ❖ Talk to each other.
- ❖ Listen to each other.

Prayer is the way people of faith keep their relationship going with God. Prayer is the way people communicate with God. In order to build a strong relationship with God people need to communicate with God often. This involves spending time talking and listening to God. When people pray it brings them closer to God.

Discuss

1. What is the person doing in this picture, how do you know?
2. What questions could you ask her about her actions?
3. Have you ever noticed someone praying by themselves? What did you observe?
4. Do you at any time pray by yourself or with other people?

AVE·MARIA
RATIA·PLENA
Waiting for Mass to begin in a Roman Catholic church.

Worship

Worship is the way people praise and honour God at religious services, for example in churches, synagogues and mosques. People show their faith when they worship God.

A religious service may involve reading from a sacred text, praying, singing hymns or participating in sacred rituals. When a person attends a religious service to worship God, it is a sign that their relationship with God really matters to them.

Way of Life

Religious faith is expressed in the way people try to live good moral lives. When people have faith in God it influences the choices they make and the way they live. For Christians this means following the teaching of Jesus and obeying his commandment to 'love God and love your neighbour as yourself' (Matthew 22:37-39). Christians who are sincere about their faith try to follow this commandment in their daily lives.

A boy reading a story to his baby sister.

Questions

Knowledge

1. What is religious faith?
2. What do people need to do to keep their relationships going with each other?
3. What do people of religious faith need to do to keep their relationship going with God?
4. Why do people of faith pray to God?
5. What is worship?
6. How do people worship God?
7. How does Jesus want his followers to live their lives?
8. Give examples of what Christians might and might not do because of their faith.

Understanding

1. Compare the way people keep a relationship going with each other and the way people keep a relationship going with God.
   a. What is the same? b. What is different?
2. *"I only pray in emergencies, like before an exam or if I'm in trouble."*
   Comment on the kind of relationship this person has with God.
3. Can you explain why people who have a genuine faith in God tend to express it in prayer, worship and the way they live their lives?
4. How do people show their religious faith in the way they live?
5. Do you know anyone who makes it a priority to put their religious faith into practice on a daily basis? Provide some examples of their behaviour in your answer.

Research

- Find out about someone who is honoured in their religious tradition as a person of faith. This person can be a Roman Catholic, past or present - a saint perhaps. Or this could be a significant person in another Christian Church.
  - Try to discover what the person's faith meant to them, and how their faith found expression in prayer, worship and way of life.
  - Write a report and present it to the class.
    - What were his/her main religious beliefs?
    - How often did he/she pray?
    - When did he/she attend religious services?
    - How did the person's faith affect the way he/she lived.

Faithful People

Key Concepts

Monotheism: the belief in one God.

Polytheism: the belief in many gods.

Objective

Show how religious belief influenced the lives of faithful people from two religious traditions.

Activity: *"World Religions"*

Monotheism

Polytheism

TASK: TO KNOW THE MEANING OF THE TERMS MONOTHEISM AND POLYTHEISM.

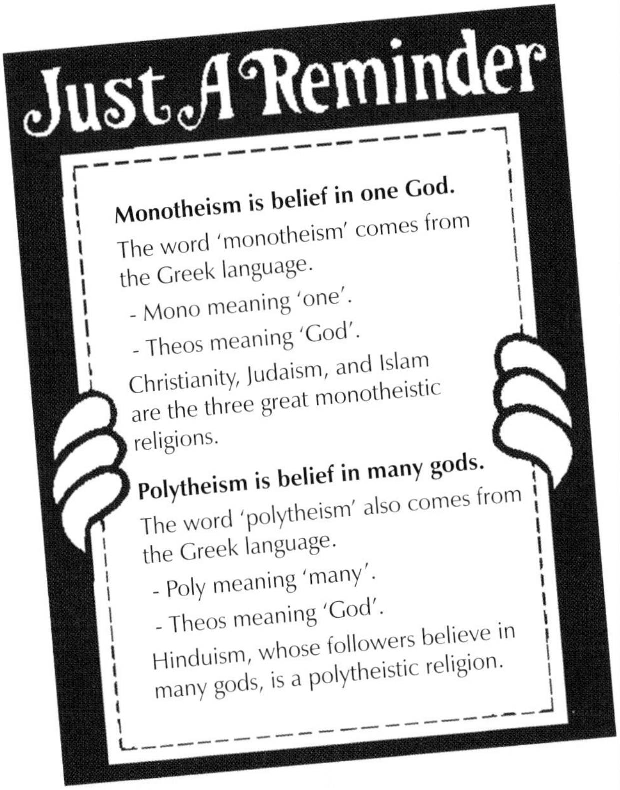

Just A Reminder
Monotheism is belief in one God.
The word 'monotheism' comes from the Greek language.
- Mono meaning 'one'.
- Theos meaning 'God'.
Christianity, Judaism, and Islam are the three great monotheistic religions.
Polytheism is belief in many gods.
The word 'polytheism' also comes from the Greek language.
- Poly meaning 'many'.
- Theos meaning 'God'.
Hinduism, whose followers believe in many gods, is a polytheistic religion.

Discuss

1. What is monotheism?
2. Name a religion whose followers believe in one God.
3. What is polytheism?
4. Name a religion whose followers believe in many gods.
5. From what language do we get the terms monotheism and polytheism?
6. Do you know the name for God in:
   a. Christianity? b. Judaism? c. Islam?
7. Do you know the name of any gods in the religion of Hinduism?
8. Name three monotheistic world religions.
9. Name a polytheistic world religion.
10. All religions have rules to help their members to live good moral lives.

    Fill in the details:

    In ***Judaism*** these moral rules are called the ____________.
    They were given to __________ on Mount Sinai. They are written down in the ___________ which is the sacred text of Judaism.

    In ***Islam*** these moral rules are called ________. They were given to the prophet __________ and were later written down in the __________ which is the sacred text of Islam.

    In ***Christianity*** Jesus gave his followers one great _________. He said to them "Love ___ _____ and love _______________________".
    This is written in the __________ which is the sacred text of Christianity.

What follows are the life stories of two faithful people from different religious traditions.

- ❖ Martin Luther King - a Christian.
- ❖ Mahatma Gandhi - a Hindu.

Mahatma Gandhi (1869-1948)

Mahatma Gandhi, a devout Hindu, was a lawyer who spent his life campaigning for human rights. His religious beliefs had a great influence on everything he did. Mohandas Gandhi (Mahatma was a title he received later) grew up in India at a time when the country was under British rule. His family were well off. He was sent to London to further his education and study for a law degree.

On his return, Gandhi started to practice as a lawyer. He was soon able to support his wife and their young children. The family moved to South Africa when he got a job offer in the legal office of a shipping company.

> In South Africa, Indians were regarded as inferior and were badly treated. Gandhi had many first hand experiences of what that was like. On one occasion he took the train to go on a business trip. A European passenger complained when he found Gandhi sitting in a first class compartment. When he was told to move to another carriage Gandhi objected, saying he had bought a first class ticket. Nobody listened and the police were called. Gandhi was pushed out at the next station and the train left without him. He spent the night shivering in the cold on the station platform.
>
> This experience was a turning point in his life. No Indian should suffer that kind of humiliation. Gandhi made a decision. He would fight for the civil rights of all people. It became a lifelong quest.

Hindu faith

Gandhi's strong Hindu faith led him to believe that love and truth were important and that all forms of violence were wrong. All his life he had a deep faith in the Hindu god Rama. The Bhagavad Gita was one of his favourite sacred texts. Gandhi developed a new method of non-violent protest called Satyagraha (meaning "way of truth"). The theory and practice of Satyagraha was greatly influenced by Gandhi's religious beliefs.

Peaceful protests in South Africa and India

Gandhi set out to improve the situation of Indians in South Africa, but in a peaceful way. He made speeches, led demonstrations and encouraged Indians in acts of civil disobedience, refusing for example to pay unjust taxes. All this took great courage; Gandhi and his followers were often arrested and put in prison. Their peaceful protests did eventually result in change.

After spending twenty years in South Africa, Gandhi moved back to India and began to campaign for the rights of Indian people in their homeland. He led a campaign of passive non-co-operation with the government of British India. He encouraged a boycott of British goods and led thousands of people on a famous 'salt march'. The marchers walked together to the Arabian Sea to collect their own salt instead of paying an unjust salt tax.

Mahatma Gandhi and his grand-daughters.

Gandhi also used fasting as a form of protest and he frequently ended up in prison. Gandhi gave up his profession as a lawyer and became a Hindu holy man, devoting himself full-time to the cause of human rights. He no longer wore European business suits, but put on the simple clothes of a poor Indian worker. He went barefoot, and ate one vegetarian meal a day. He spent a lot of time in silent prayer, believing it brought him inner peace. He became known as Mahatma Gandhi (Mahatma meaning 'great soul').

A man of truth, non-violence and courage, Gandhi never received the Nobel prize for peace, although he was nominated five times. Gandhi's peaceful protests helped to bring an end to British rule in India in 1947. The following year he was shot by an assassin while attending a prayer meeting in New Delhi. Gandhi's last words were "He Rama" and he gave his assassin the Hindu sign of forgiveness. He died as he had lived, every act dedicated to God.

Martin Luther King (1929-1968)

Martin Luther King, a committed Christian, was a civil rights leader in the U.S.A., and a man of deep religious faith. Martin Luther King lived in the United States of America at a time when there was a lot of prejudice against the black community. Members of the black community were treated as second class citizens.

- ❖ Black people earned half the wages of white people doing the same job.
- ❖ Black people were not allowed to vote.
- ❖ Black people were not allowed into certain places that were for 'whites' only.

Black people had to sit in the back seats of buses, and had to give up their seat if it was wanted by a white person. One day in 1955, a black woman got on a local bus in Alabama. She was glad to sit down; the weather was hot and she was tired. When she refused to give up her seat to a white person, she was arrested. This action sparked off a bus boycott. Black people refused to use the buses, they did not want to be treated as second class citizens by the bus company, or by anyone else. The leader of this protest was a young Baptist minister called Martin Luther King.

Peaceful protests across the United States

Martin Luther King said racial prejudice was wrong. He believed everyone was created equal in the eyes of God. He wanted equal rights for all people - black and white. He soon became leader of the Civil Rights Movement in America, and travelled throughout the US leading marches and speaking at rallies. Dr. King wanted things to change. Yet he wanted change to take place peacefully, not through violence. He organised petitions, sit-ins, and demonstrations, all of which were non-violent forms of protest.

Christian faith

Martin Luther King believed in the teaching of Jesus. He said the Christian way of love and peace was better than hatred and violence. "We must meet hatred with love," he said. He once led a peaceful march of a quarter of a million people through the city of Washington. The marchers wanted equal rights for all people of colour. Standing on the steps of the Lincoln Memorial he made one of his most famous speeches. *"I have a dream,"* he began.

Dr. Martin Luther King.

"I have a dream that one day my children will not be judged by the colour of their skin, but by the content of their character. I have a dream that black and white, boys and girls will be able to join hands together as brothers and sisters. When we let freedom ring, we will be able to speed up that day when all of God's children black and white, Jews and Gentiles, Protestants and Catholics, will be able to join hands and sing in the words of the old Negro spiritual 'Free at Last. Free at Last. Thank God almighty, we are free at last!'"

In their home the King family began to receive threatening phone calls. Threatening letters began to arrive. On one occasion their house was bombed. However his strong faith in God gave Martin Luther King the courage to carry on, no matter what happened.

In 1964 a Bill was passed in Congress (the American parliament) granting civil rights to all people of colour in America. Soon afterwards Dr. Martin Luther King was awarded the Nobel prize for peace.

Four years later the world was shocked to hear the news that Dr. King was dead, shot by an assassin in Memphis, Tennessee. He was thirty nine years old. Martin Luther King had dedicated his life to doing God's will. His beliefs and ideals live on today through the work of his friends, his four children and his wife, Coretta Scott King.

Questions

Knowledge

Mahatma Gandhi

1. Where did Gandhi grow up?
2. To what religious tradition did he belong?
3. What did Gandhi protest about in South Africa and in India?
4. What form of protest did Gandhi encourage people to use?
5. Why was the 'salt march' organised?
6. What happened on the 'salt march' to the Arabian Sea?
7. What impact did Gandhi's work have on people in India and South Africa?
8. What happened to Gandhi in 1947?
9. What religious beliefs influenced Gandhi's way of life?
10. Give examples of how Mahatma Gandhi expressed his faith through prayer, worship and way of life.

Dr. Martin Luther King

1. Where did Dr. King grow up?
2. To what religious tradition did he belong?
3. What did Dr. King protest about in America?
4. What form of protest did Dr. King encourage people to use?
5. Why was the Washington march organised?
6. What happened at the march to the Lincoln Memorial in Washington?
7. What impact did Dr. King's work have on people's lives in America?
8. What happened to Dr. King in 1964?
9. What religious beliefs influenced Dr. Martin Luther King's way of life?
10. Give examples of how Dr. King expressed his faith through prayer, worship and way of life.

Understanding

1. Why are people such as Mahatma Gandhi and Martin Luther King regarded as people of faith?
2. How did religious belief influence the life of Mahatma Gandhi and Martin Luther King? What is the evidence?
3. a. Do you think it was easy for Mahatma Gandhi or Martin Luther King to do what they believed God was calling them to do? Why? Why not?
   b. What do you admire most about either man?

Section D

Research

- Find out more about other famous people of religious faith. Choose someone from the group of people below, or select someone else whose life and work you admire.

Jean Vanier
- founder of L'Arche.

Sister Stanislaus Kennedy
- founder of Focus Ireland.

Mother Teresa
- founder of the Missionaries of Charity.

Dame Cicely Saunders
- founder of the Modern Hospice Movement.

Archbishop Desmond Tutu
- defender of human rights in South Africa.

- What has this person achieved in life that is worthy of public attention?
- How has this person's religious faith influenced his/her choices and way of life?
- Compile a profile of the person you have selected.

Science and Religion

Key Concepts

World view: a set of ideas about what the world is like.

Creation: the origin of the universe and life on Earth.

Fundamentalism: the view that a sacred text is a factual account to be taken literally.

Objective

Identify points of conflict and points of contact between the scientific and religious world views of creation.

Activity: *"The Solar System"*

TASK: TO NAME THE DIFFERENT PLANETS IN OUR SOLAR SYSTEM.

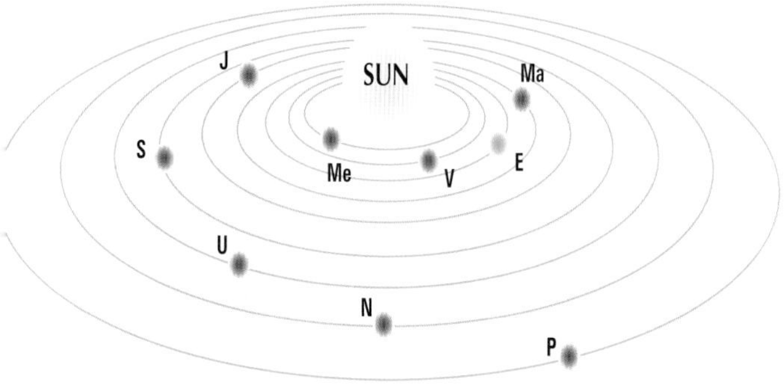
SUN
J
Ma
S
Me
V
E
U
N
P

Discuss

- Name the planets in our solar system starting with the planet nearest the sun.
- What is the third planet nearest the sun?
- Highlight any words that describe how you feel when you stop to think about the size of the world in which we live.
  - Sad... scared... small... excited... lonely... weird... bored... amazed...
  - Add some words of your own.

World view

Both science and religion help us to know and understand the world.

A world view is a set of ideas about what the world is like. Science and religion have a different outlook and different views on life and the universe.

- Science is about examining things that can be seen, weighed and measured.
- Religion is about belief in things that cannot be seen but can be experienced.

Science and religion have been regarded as rival forms of knowledge since the time of the Enlightenment in the 17th century. Up to that time people saw the world in religious terms. God was behind everything and only God could understand it all. From the time of the Enlightenment people began to see the world in scientific terms. Natural laws governed everything and these laws could be understood by human reason alone.

The idea that religion and science are opposed took hold when the Catholic Church banned the work of two scientists whose discoveries affect the way we understand the world.

- Galileo Galilei in the 17th century.
- Charles Darwin in the 19th century.

A view of the Earth from space.

Scientific World View

Galileo

Galileo Galilei (1564-1642) was an Italian astronomer, a scientist who studied the planets and the stars. He built a powerful telescope and discovered mountains and craters on the moon. Then he discovered four moons circling, or orbiting, the planet Jupiter. On the basis of this observation he was soon able to prove, as Copernicus had noted before him, that the Earth orbited the sun.

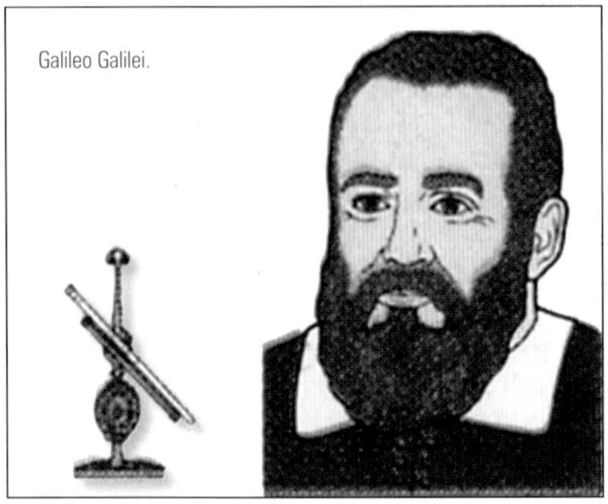

This was exciting news. Up to that point, everyone believed the Earth was the centre of the universe. Galileo's information turned that idea upside down. He later wrote a book outlining his discoveries.

Important people in the Catholic Church at the time became worried by these new developments. The Church had always taught that God has a special relationship with humanity. The Bible therefore seemed to say that the Earth was the centre of the universe. Galileo's new ideas contradicted that view. Church leaders reacted quickly and Galileo was put on trial in Rome. As a result his writings were banned and he was kept under house arrest for the remainder of his life.

Years later the Church apologised and went on to accept Galileo's findings, but the damage was done. People now had the idea that science and religion were opposed to each other, that somehow there was a major conflict between the world of science and the world of religion.

Darwin

Charles Darwin (1809-1882), a British scientist, wrote a book entitled "On the Origin of Species." In this book he put forward a theory of evolution. It stated that all life on the planet, including human life, had developed from much simpler forms of life over millions of years. Some life forms were able to adapt to the environment in which they lived, they were flexible and able to change to suit their surroundings.

If a species was able to adapt then it survived, otherwise it died out and became extinct. Darwin called this process 'natural selection'.

Darwin's ideas caused a sensation. Up to that point people understood that life according to the Bible was created in six days. Darwin's new theory stated that life developed slowly, over millions of years. This scientific theory of evolution seemed to contradict the religious view of God as creator. As such, Darwin's work was seen as a challenge to the wisdom and authority of the Bible and the Church. His writings were quickly condemned.

One of the main concerns at the time was what Darwin's theory seemed to imply about the place of human beings in the world. The Church had always taught that human beings were created in a special way and were different from all other creatures. In Darwin's theory all life had evolved from simpler forms. Human beings appeared, therefore, to have no special status, but were on the same level as everything else.

In the clash between religion and science it seemed that faith and reason were once again opposed to each other.

A Religious World View

The Story of Creation (adapted from Genesis 1:1-31, 2:1-4)

God says
let there be light.
And so there is.
God names the light 'day' and
the darkness 'night'.
God sees it is good.

Evening comes and morning comes the first day.

God says
let there be a roof over the land.
And so there is.
God names it the 'sky'.
God sees it is good.

Evening comes and morning comes the second day.

God says
let there be water all around the land,
and plants to grow on the land.
And so there is.
God names the water 'sea',
and the land 'earth'.
God sees it is good.

Evening comes and morning comes the third day.

God says let there be lights in the sky
to shine day and night.
And so there is.
God names the lights 'sun', 'moon' and 'stars'.
God sees it is good.

Evening comes and morning comes the fourth day.

God says
let there be water filled with
every kind of living thing,
and air filled with birds
and so there is.
God names all the birds of the sky.
God sees it is good.

Evening comes and morning comes the fifth day.

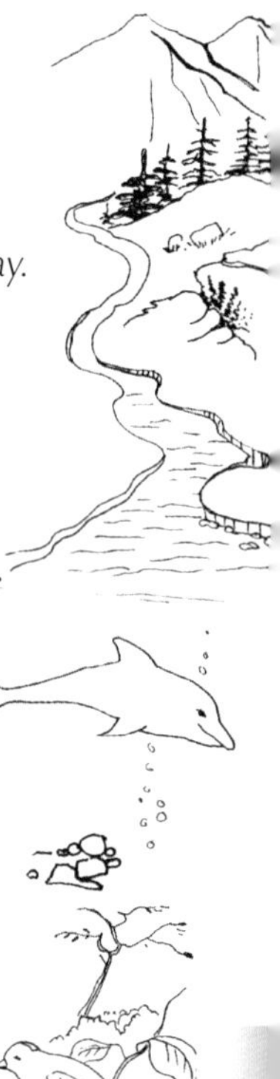

God says
let the earth be filled with
every kind of animal.
And so it is.
God names all the animals of the earth.
God sees it is good.

God says
let there be men and women
and children to help Me care for
everything on the earth.
And so there is.
God knows the name of every
person on the earth.
God sees they are good.

Evening comes and morning comes the sixth day.

On the seventh day God rests.
God looks at everything.
God sees it is all very good.

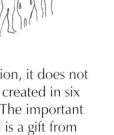

Creation

The Book of Genesis in the Bible

Christian views on the origin of the world and life on Earth are contained in the Bible, in the Book of Genesis.

Genesis is not a scientific account of how the world began. The purpose of the creation stories in Genesis is not to give a factual account of the origin of the world, or how animal and plant life came to be, that is the role of science. The creation story in Genesis is a religious account explaining why the world came to be. The world was created out of the goodness and love of God.

From the point of view of religion, it does not matter whether the world was created in six days or over millions of years. The important religious truth is that the world is a gift from God. The writers of Genesis were not scientists but religious Jews who used poetic language to convey important religious truths such as:

- ❖ God created the world.
- ❖ God's world is created by design.
- ❖ God's world is good.
- ❖ God created human beings as the high point of creation.

GENESIS
God created the heavens
formless and void
surface of the deep;
moving over the
Let there be

The opening page of the Book of Genesis.

Fundamentalism

Fundamentalism is an outlook among some religious groups that their sacred text is a factual account to be taken literally word for word. Fundamentalists reject scientific discoveries that do not match a literal interpretation of their sacred text.

Christian fundamentalists believe that everything in the Bible is literally true. They believe for example that the Genesis account of creation is factual: the world was created in six days and each "day" was a twenty-four hour period. While a minority of Christians take the Bible literally today, most people took the Bible literally at the time of Galileo and Darwin in the 17th and 19th centuries.

Today new advances in Bible research show that the creation accounts in Genesis are not factual accounts of how the world was made. The writers of Genesis were not scientists. They were not trying to answer the question of *how* the world was made. That is a scientific question. The writers of Genesis had another purpose in mind altogether. Genesis was written to help people understand *why* the world was made, and that is a religious question.

Science and Religion

Science explains *how* the world was made. Religion explains *why* the world was made. Science and religion are two separate disciplines, asking different kinds of questions and providing different types of answers. We cannot judge one by the standards of the other.

Science and religion are two distinct and equally valuable forms of knowledge. One is not better than the other, they are simply different. There is room for both. We now know that the Bible is not a book of science, and the creation account in Genesis is not to be taken literally as scientific fact. The Bible is a religious book, and the creation account in Genesis teaches an important religious truth - that God created the world out of goodness and love.

There has been a big effort in recent years to heal the conflict and misunderstanding that has arisen between science and religion. In 1979 Pope John Paul II admitted the wrong done to Galileo long ago. In his statement the Pope quoted Galileo's own words. "The Bible teaches us how to go to heaven and not how the heavens move."

Partnership

Many Church leaders today see little conflict between religion and science. Darwin's theory of evolution explains how life began, the book of Genesis explains why it began. Most Christians can now accept some form of Darwin's theory of evolution.

Religion and science see the world from different points of view. The two forms of knowledge can work together, and need not contradict each other. Both add something valuable to our understanding of the world.

A scientist at work.

Points of Contact

The main point of contact between science and religion is that both accept that there is order and design in the universe. The world is just too complicated and too beautiful to have happened merely by accident.

Visual System

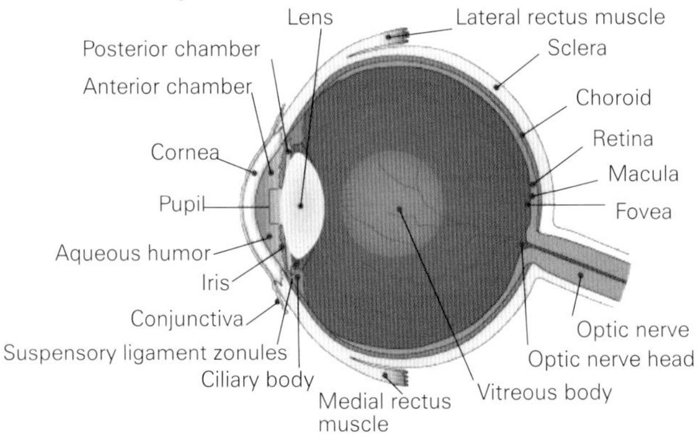

Lens
Lateral rectus muscle
Posterior chamber
Sclera
Anterior chamber
Choroid
Retina
Cornea
Macula
Pupil
Fovea
Aqueous humor
Iris
Conjunctiva
Optic nerve
Suspensory ligament zonules
Optic nerve head
Ciliary body
Medial rectus muscle
Vitreous body

Take for example the human eye. The eye is a wonder of creation. A scientist can examine it and explain its internal workings in minute detail. The interdependency of all its parts are a matter of awe and amazement.

A person of religious faith will have the benefit of all this information. He/she can then reflect on the perfection of the human eye and see the hand of God in its creation. The response of the religious person is to marvel and give thanks to God.

Pierre Teilhard de Chardin

Teilhard de Chardin.

Pierre Teilhard de Chardin (1881-1955) was a French Roman Catholic priest and a renowned scientist. He was highly respected for his work in physics, geology, palaeontology (the study of ancient things), and theology (the study of God). Teilhard de Chardin spent a great deal of his life in scientific research. He was part of a team that excavated ancient sites in China, resulting in the discovery of "Peking Man", thought to be nearly 500,000 years old.

Teilhard de Chardin believed scientific work enriched his religious understanding of God as creator. The more he discovered about the world of nature, the more he saw the creative hand of God at work. For him, science and scientific research were ways of getting closer to God. He wrote about his insights in two famous books, 'The Phenomenon of Man' and 'The Hymn of the Universe'.

Questions

Knowledge

1. Who was Galileo? What scientific discovery did he make in the 17th century?
2. How did Galileo's ideas conflict with the Christian story of creation in Genesis?
3. Who was Darwin? What scientific discovery did he make in the 19th century?
4. How did Darwin's ideas conflict with the Christian story of creation in Genesis?
5. How does the Genesis account in the Bible explain creation?
6. According to Genesis, how and why are human beings different to other creatures?
7. What is fundamentalism?
8. What is the main difference between the ways science and religion approach the topic of creation today?
9. a. What are the similarities and differences between the scientific and religious views of creation?
   b. Give an example of a point of contact between science and religion.
10. a. Who was Pierre Teilhard de Chardin?
    b. What did experience teach him about the connection between religion and science?

Understanding

1. What were the main points of conflict between the scientific and religious views of creation in times past? In your answer refer to the case of either Darwin or Galileo.
2. What do Christians believe about creation? Explain the difference between the way Christians understood the biblical account of creation in the past, and the way it is understood by most Christians today.
3. What do you think of the comment: "Genesis is out of date, it took a lot more than six days to make the world!"?

Research

- Find out more about the connection and points of contact between science and religion.
  - Science and religion share the belief that the universe is ordered, it is not chaotic. Can you show where order is obvious in the world of nature?
  - Identify things in the natural world that are wonderful and awe inspiring in their order, design and complexity.
  - Discuss some examples with the class.

World Views

Key Concepts

Reflection: thinking deeply about certain aspects of life.

World view: a set of ideas about what the world is like.

Experiencing God: being aware of God's mysterious presence.

Atheism: a view that denies the existence of God.

Agnosticism: the view that people cannot know for certain whether or not God exists.

Materialism: the view that only material things are real.

Secularism: the view that organised religion should have no direct influence on society.

Objectives

Display an awareness of the variety of world views in today's culture,

and show how some pose a challenge to religious belief.

Activity: *"A think in"*

TASK: REFLECT ON SOME OF THE BIG ISSUES IN LIFE.

Have you ever wondered... (✓)

- ❑ How the world began?
- ❑ What it means to be human?
- ❑ What keeps people and societies together?
- ❑ Why the world is the way it is?
- ❑ How the problems of the world could be solved?
- ❑ What's going to happen in the future?

Discuss

- How many of these issues have you thought about from time to time?
- What issue(s) have you reflected on a lot recently?
- In your view how important is it to reflect on life?

Reflection on life is:

Not important.
Important
Very important.

- Can you give a reason for your answer?

Reflection

Our world view affects the way we see the world.

Reflecting.

Reflection is about taking time to think deeply about certain aspects of life. Some of life's big questions, such as whether or not God exists, and what is the meaning and purpose of life, require careful thought and reflection. The answers we give to these questions is influenced by our world view.

World View

When we look at life and try to understand it, we tend to see it through the prism of a particular world view.

Our world view is like a prism through which we look at life.

A world view is a set of ideas about what the world is like. It is the framework we use to organise our thoughts about life. Our world view helps us to tie all our ideas together in order to make sense of life.

Experiencing God

Some ways of understanding the world are based on religious belief. Members of the great world religions have a religious or spiritual outlook on life. Most believe in the existence of God even though they cannot see God. They believe God is present everywhere.

Experiencing God is about being aware of God's mysterious presence in a deep and quiet way. People who make sense of the world from a religious viewpoint are quietly aware of the mysterious presence of God in their lives.

Religious World Views

Theism is belief in God. Christians, Jews and Muslims are monotheists. They believe in one God who created the world and who guides and sustains the world out of love.

- ❖ Christians believe God revealed himself through Jesus Christ the Son of God.
- ❖ Jews believe God revealed himself through Abraham and Moses.
- ❖ Muslims believe God revealed himself through the messages given to the prophet Muhammad.
- ❖ Polytheism is belief in many gods. Hindus believe in many gods, and in their gods' benign influence on the earth.
- ❖ Buddhists do not believe in God or gods, but they do believe in something that is 'timeless and formless'.

The Christian World View

Christians believe in God and see the world from a religious point of view. Christians believe:

- ❖ God is the creator of the world.
- ❖ Human beings are created in the image of God.
- ❖ God speaks through the Bible.
- ❖ Jesus the Son of God entered human history as saviour of the world.
- ❖ Jesus taught his followers 'to love and respect God and their neighbour' as the guiding principle in life.

Looking at life from a Christian point of view.

- ❖ The Holy Spirit helps people to follow the teaching of Jesus.
- ❖ God is near and cares for each person.

Non-Religious World Views

While some ways of understanding the world are based on religious belief, other ways of understanding the world are unrelated to religion. A growing number of people in our society make sense of the world from a non-religious viewpoint.

The question of God

To the question 'Does God exist?' there are different responses:

- Theism - Yes. There is a God.
- Atheism - No. There is no God.
- Agnosticism - Don't know. It's impossible to answer that question.
- Materialism - Of course not. Only material things exist, nothing else.
- Secularism - Don't care. God is irrelevant.

The materialist world view is becoming more prevalent in our society.

Atheism

Atheism is a view that denies the existence of God. Atheists do not believe that God or gods exist. From an atheist's point of view there is no God. God is not real.

Agnosticism

Agnosticism is the view that human beings cannot know for certain whether or not God exists. There is simply not enough evidence to prove it one way or the other. Agnostics claim that no one can say for definite that there is a God or that there is no God.

Materialism

Materialism is the view that only material things are real. Something is real if it can be physically seen, touched, weighed and measured. The physical world is the only reality, nothing else exists. God does not exist.

Materialism also has another related meaning. A materialistic way of life is about having lots of money, lots of possessions and enjoying oneself as much as possible. Accumulating material things becomes important when it is accepted that only material things matter in life.

Secularism

Secularism is the view that organised religion should have no direct influence on society. Secularists are opposed to the influence of religion in public life. Secularism claims that God and religion are simply not relevant anymore.

From a secularist point of view, if someone has religious beliefs then it should be a private matter. Religious activity should not enter the public domain. Religion should not in any way be supported by the State. In fact, Church and State should be completely separate. This means that religions, or religious groups, should not receive any kind of special treatment from the State.

Challenges to Religious Experience

The Example of Materialism

Materialists claim that the only real things are material things. Something is real if we can see it, touch it, hear it, taste it or smell it. If something can be examined by the senses then it is real. If it cannot, then it is not real and does not exist.

Everything around us, in a classroom for example, is real in the materialist sense. The chair, the desk, the book, the wall, the window, can all be examined by the senses. The people around us are material too. We can see and hear ourselves and others: we are real.

However there are things about us that we cannot see, touch or hear. We cannot see, hear or touch our ideas, our beliefs or our feelings, yet most people would agree that they are real and are a very important part of our lives. Humans therefore are not simply material beings, we are both material and spiritual beings.

God, on the other hand, is quite different. We cannot see, hear or touch God. God is not material; God is totally spiritual. Human beings communicate with God through the spiritual aspect of their own nature. Religion is the way that people connect with the spiritual side of life.

A challenge to religious faith

Materialism poses a challenge to religion and religious experience. It claims that only material things are real. On that basis the spiritual nature of human beings is not real. God is not real. Religion doesn't matter.

The materialist outlook is very pervasive and has been the basis of scientific thought for over 300 years. Materialists claim that the scientific way of looking at things is the only way. Scientific truth is the only truth. The materialist outlook can undermine people's confidence in religious truth as a valid form of human knowledge. There are vast areas of human experience that are not suited to testing by the scientific method. From the point of view of religion, the spiritual dimension of life and the search for God is no less real than other aspects of life.

Questions

Knowledge

1. When a person stops to reflect on life, what is he/she actually doing?
2. "There are a variety of world views in today's culture." What does this statement mean?
3. How do people of faith experience God in their daily lives?
4. What is atheism?
5. What is agnosticism?
6. What is materialism?
7. What is secularism?
8. What world views are a challenge to religious belief in our society?

Understanding

1. Describe some of the elements of a Christian outlook on life.
2. Belief in God is central to Judaism, Christianity and Islam. Explain how materialism poses a challenge to religious faith.
3. What is your world view at this time? If you think you have a religious world view, can you describe a time when you were aware of the presence of God in your life?
4. In what ways do you think society has become more secular and less religious?

Research

- Find out more about secularism.
  - In the secularist's desire to separate the sacred and the secular, what is their position on one of the following issues?
    - Religious schools.
    - Religious education.
    - Religion and Public Broadcasting.
  - What is the position of some Church authorities on the same issue?
  - Prepare a comment sheet for discussion in class.

Section E - The Celebration of Faith

The *Syllabus Aims* in this section are:

- To show how ritual and worship have always been part of the human response to life and to the mystery of God.
- To identify how communities of faith express their day-to-day concerns in various forms of ritual.
- To explore an experience of worship.

Concept Checklist (Section E - The Celebration of Faith)

Page

- ❑ **Actions of significance** - actions that have a special meaning for people. 371, 377, 382, 390
- ❑ **Celebration** - a religious ceremony performed in public for a community of faith. 413
- ❑ **Communal prayer** - praying to God with others as a community. 437
- ❑ **Communication with God** - a prayerful exchange between God and human beings. 437, 440
- ❑ **Communicating experience** - experiencing an invisible reality and expressing it clearly in symbolic words and actions. 432
- ❑ **Contemplation** - a form of deep silent prayer that does not use words or thoughts. 447
- ❑ **Encountering mystery** - connecting with something mysterious that is beyond human understanding. 409
- ❑ **Encounter with God** - connecting with the mysterious presence of God in acts of worship. 413
- ❑ **Icon** - a sacred image used as an aid to prayer mainly in the Orthodox Churches. 424
- ❑ **Identity** - the distinct characteristics by which a person or group is recognised. 432
- ❑ **Meditation** - a form of silent prayer based on the use of an icon, a repeated word or a passage from scripture. 447
- ❑ **Participation** - being actively involved in an act of worship. 405
- ❑ **Penitence** - prayer admitting to wrongdoing and asking God for forgiveness. 443
- ❑ **Personal prayer** - praying to God by oneself. 437
- ❑ **Petition** - prayer asking God for help with one's own needs or the needs of others. 443
- ❑ **Places of significance** - places or buildings that have a special meaning for people. 371, 377, 382
- ❑ **Praise and thanksgiving** - prayer to praise and thank God for blessings already received. 443
- ❑ **Reflection** - thinking deeply about some aspect of life. 409
- ❑ **Ritual** - an occasion when people use symbolic objects, words and actions to express what is deeply important to them. 401
- ❑ **Sacrament** - a sacred ritual that is a visible sign of God's presence with people at key moments in their lives. 427, 432
- ❑ **Sacredness** - a thing or a place that is holy and set apart from ordinary life.. 371, 382
- ❑ **Sign** - something that communicates a brief message or a piece of information.. 417
- ❑ **Symbol** - something visible, i.e. an object or action, representing something invisible that is difficult to put into words. 417, 420
- ❑ **Times of significance** - times of the year that have a special meaning for people. 390
- ❑ **Wonder** - a feeling inspired by some mysterious aspect of life. 409
- ❑ **Worship** - the way people of faith praise and honour God in prayer and at religious services. . . 397, 401, 405
- ❑ **Worship as a response to mystery** - people responding to mystery by gathering together to perform acts of worship. 413

Places of Pilgrimage

Key Concepts

Sacredness: a thing or a place that is holy and set apart from ordinary life.

Places of significance: places or buildings that have a special meaning for people.

Actions of significance: actions that have a special meaning for people.

Objective

Explain why certain places have religious significance for people.

Activity: *"A Special Place"*

TASK: TO IDENTIFY PLACES WHICH HAVE SOME IMPORTANCE IN OUR LIVES.

Last year we went on a school trip to France. Part of it involved going to see the war cemeteries in Flanders. Before we left, my Mam told me about my great grand-uncle, who was buried there. She said that if she was able to find the exact location of the grave, would I go and visit it? I felt a bit weird about that, but I could see that it meant a lot to her, so I told her that I would.

When we got there, I noticed the place was neat and well kept. Everything seemed very bright, mainly because the sun was glinting on all the white gravestones. There were hundreds, maybe thousands of gravestones stretching forever in all directions. It was totally quiet. We were quiet too, like it was the right thing to do.

The teacher gave the guide my Mam's information. A short while later I stood alone in front of my great grand-uncle's grave. I looked at the words carved on the white headstone. We even had the same name, James McDermott. Then his regiment; he was a private, aged 17. I'll be seventeen in two years time. I suppose I was a bit upset. It was a strange feeling, sort of good and bad at the same time. I was relieved the teacher had left me by myself for those few minutes, and I'm glad I went there, it's a really special place.

Cemetery for the war dead, Flanders, France.

Discuss

- What did the group find when they went to Flanders?
- How did the journey affect one person in particular?
- Is there a place that means a lot to you? Can you say why is it special for you?

Special places

Certain places can be very important to us.

There may be some places we like to visit occasionally, such as our grand-parents house, a woodland, or a lake near our home. Maybe it is somewhere we went as children or perhaps it is a place connected with a friend or a member of the family. We may not go there very often, but it somehow holds a special meaning for us. Places that are significant and meaningful for us, while they are important, are not necessarily sacred. A sacred place is a location where people can encounter God. For Christians, this means somewhere connected with Jesus, the Virgin Mary, or one of the Saints (holy men and women of the Church).

Sacredness

Sacredness refers to a place that is holy and set apart from ordinary life. In the Christian tradition, it can be a place associated with Jesus, the Virgin Mary, or the Saints. Christians believe God is present in some mysterious way in a sacred place. God's presence makes it holy. Sacred places are therefore different from all other places.

Pilgrimage

A pilgrimage is a journey made by a pilgrim to a sacred place. Pilgrims are not tourists or sightseers on a holiday or a day out. Their journey is made for religious reasons and involves taking part in prayer and acts of worship.

A pilgrimage is a break from routine. People take time away from their busy everyday lives to devote special time to God. Travelling a distance from everything that is familiar can help pilgrims to become more aware of the presence of God in their lives. Christians have made journeys to sacred places from earliest times.

There are many places of pilgrimage all over the world. Every country has its sacred sites. Christians believe that, while God is present everywhere, he is present in a special way in places made holy by the life of Jesus, a vision of Mary, or the actions of the saints. Christians honour these places because they are touched by God. They believe God has communicated with people in a special way in these locations. Pilgrims travel there to pray and feel closer to God. Places of pilgrimage have been prayed in for centuries and continue to be great centres of prayer today.

Graffiti in Jerusalem, a city sacred to three religions.

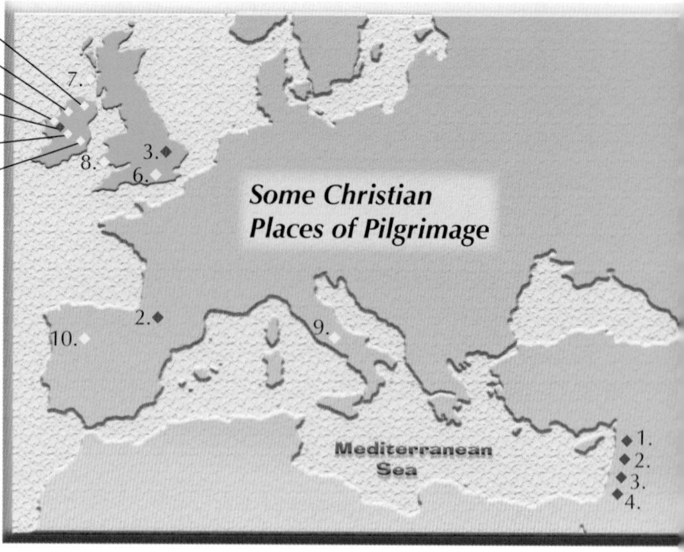
Some Christian Places of Pilgrimage
Mediterranean Sea
5.
2.
1.
1.
3.
4.
7.
8.
3.
6.
2.
10.
9.
1.
2.
3.
4.

Jesus
- ◆ 1. Holy Land.
- ◆ 2. Nazareth.
- ◆ 3. Jerusalem.
- ◆ 4. Bethlehem.

Mary
- ◆ 1. Knock.
- ◆ 2. Lourdes.
- ◆ 3. Walsingham.

Saints
- 1. St. Patrick - Croagh Patrick.
- 2. St. Patrick - Lough Derg.
- 3. St. Ciaran - Clonmacnoise.
- 4. St. Kevin - Glendalough.
- 5. St. Patrick - Downpatrick.
- 6. St. Thomas Beckett - Canterb
- 7. St. Columba - Iona.
- 8. St. David - St. David's.
- 9. St. Peter and St. Paul - Rome
- 10. St. James the Apostle - Santiago de Compostela.

Reasons why Christians go on pilgrimage

- ❖ To pray for themselves, their family, and their friends.
- ❖ To thank God for a particular blessing.
- ❖ To seek God's forgiveness for a particular sin.
- ❖ To ask God for help.
- ❖ To strengthen their faith in God.

It is customary for Christians to go on pilgrimage but it not something they are obliged to do. The Catholic Church has always accepted pilgrimage as a form of worship. It is one way of getting closer to God. The Protestant Churches on the other hand, do not have a tradition of going on pilgrimage.

For details of places of pilgrimage in: Judaism see p238. Islam see p293.

Places of Significance
Actions of Significance

A place can have religious significance for people because it is associated with an important person in a religion. He/she may have been born there, lived there, visited there, or be buried there. In Christianity, a place becomes a centre of pilgrimage because it is associated with either the life of Jesus, a vision or apparition of the Virgin Mary, or the life or death of a saint.

Places of pilgrimage associated with Jesus

The Holy Land

The Holy Land is the name Christians give to the country where Jesus lived 2,000 years ago. Pilgrims journey to the places made holy by the events of Jesus' life; where he was born, lived, died and rose again. Following his footsteps, and seeing the places he knew, helps people to feel closer to Jesus and understand him better. Shrines and church buildings now mark the three most important sites associated with Jesus; Bethlehem, Nazareth and Jerusalem.

Bethlehem

The Church of the Nativity stands over the place in Bethlehem where Jesus was born. Once inside, the pilgrims go down a few steps into the grotto of the Nativity. A star on the ground marks the spot where it is thought Jesus was born. People pause here to pray in silence. The site is protected by what is said to be the oldest church on Earth. It was originally built by Emperor Constantine in the fourth century CE.

The grotto of the Nativity in Bethlehem.

Nazareth

Jesus lived in the village of Nazareth with Mary and Joseph. It was where he grew up and worked until he became a travelling teacher. A church is now built over the place where it is thought the family home and workshop once stood. A shrine marks the spot inside the church.

Pilgrims walk the route to Calvary through the narrow streets in Jerusalem, stopping to pray the Stations of the Cross along the way.

Jerusalem

Many pilgrims visit Jerusalem and go to places linked to the crucifixion and resurrection of Jesus. They walk the road to Calvary, known as the Via Dolorosa. This is the route Jesus took when he carried his cross to the place of execution on Good Friday. Pilgrims carry their own cross and stop at fourteen points along the way. The readings and the prayers at the fourteen Stations of the Cross help them to reflect on Jesus and his journey.

ויאה דולורוזה
طريق الآلام
VIA DOLOROSA
V

Via Dolorosa in Jerusalem, the fifth station.

The Church of the Holy Sepulchre is at the end of the Via Dolorosa. It is built on what is thought to be the site of Jesus' crucifixion and the place where he was buried in a borrowed tomb. Originally the two sites would have been separate but near each other, they are now honoured under one roof.

Pilgrims waiting to visit the site of Jesus' death and resurrection inside the Church of the Holy Sepulchre in Jerusalem.

Pilgrims stop to pray at the place where the body of Jesus was laid to rest after his crucifixion. A sheet of marble covers the stone on which his body would have rested. There is a sense of wonder among pilgrims who gather there. Each one reaches out to touch or kiss the sacred place where Jesus rose from the dead on Easter Sunday.

Places of pilgrimage associated with Mary

Lourdes

Lourdes is in the Pyrenees mountains in the south of France. It is a popular place of pilgrimage for Christians in search of healing. Here, in 1858, a fourteen year old girl named Bernadette Soubirous had a vision of Mary the Mother of God. It took place in a grotto in the middle of a wood near her home.

'The Lady' as Bernadette called her, appeared eighteen times over a six month period. On one occasion, she pointed to the ground nearby and asked Bernadette to dig. A spring of water appeared, which is believed to have sacred healing powers. The Pope later declared that the visions were genuine and Lourdes became an important centre of pilgrimage. Several million people make the journey there each year to pray for healing. Even if they do not find physical healing, they say their pilgrimage is still worthwhile. Pilgrims get an inner peace there that gives them the courage and strength to face their difficulties.

Pilgrims at Lourdes perform special rituals or actions that have a religious significance. They:

- Pray and light candles in front of the grotto where Our Lady appeared.
- Bathe in one of the baths fed by the spring well in front of the grotto.
- Attend Mass in a church near the grotto.
- Pray the Stations of the Cross.
- Join in the candle-lit procession after dark.
- Fill bottles and flasks with holy water to take home to their relatives and friends.

Pilgrims visit the grotto in Lourdes.

The shrine at Knock.

Knock

Knock is a centre of pilgrimage in Co. Mayo in the west of Ireland. On a dark, wet night in August 1879, fifteen people, aged six to seventy five years of age, claimed they saw an apparition outside the parish church. The group stood for two hours in the driving rain gazing at the vision and praying the Rosary together. Today there is a full size replica on the church wall of what the group of men, women and children saw that night.

There were three figures. In the centre was Our Lady, dressed in white robes with a crown on her head. She was praying, her hands and eyes raised to heaven. To her right stood St. Joseph. He also wore white robes. He was turned toward Our Lady in an attitude of respect. St. John the Evangelist stood on her left. He wore white vestments and looked like a bishop. He seemed to be preaching as he held an open book in his hand. Beside St. John there was an altar with a cross and a lamb. It was surrounded by angels.

The Catholic Church examined the evidence and later announced that the people's account was genuine. Thousands of pilgrims began to arrive at Knock. At present, one and a half million people visit annually to pray at the place where Our Lady appeared. Pilgrims at Knock perform special rituals or actions that have a religious significance. They:

- Pray in front of the shrine.
- Visit the Blessed Sacrament Chapel.
- Go to Confession.
- Attend Mass.
- Pray the Stations of the Cross.
- Walk in procession around the church, praying the Rosary.

Walsingham

Walsingham in Norfolk, eastern England, is the location of Anglican and Roman Catholic shrines to Mary, the Mother of God. Pilgrims have been visiting this place since the Middle Ages when a noblewoman built a replica of the home in Nazareth here in 1061. The shrine, known as 'England's Nazareth', and the monastery attached to it were destroyed at the time of the Reformation. The site was restored and rebuilt again at the beginning of the twentieth century.

Thousands of Catholic and Anglican pilgrims have flocked here every year since. They visit the 'Holy House' in the shrine church. The house acts as a reminder of the central Christian belief of the Incarnation: that God entered human history in a particular time and place and became part of the Holy Family in Nazareth. A special statue of Our Lady of Walsingham has place of honour within the holy house.

Catholics, Anglicans and Orthodox Christians have their own churches and shrines in Walsingham. Ecumenism is an important feature of this pilgrimage centre where all Christians are welcome to pray and share together.

Catholic pilgrims at Walsingham perform special rituals or actions that have religious significance. They:

- Pray before the shrine of Mary.
- Go to Confession.
- Attend Mass.
- Pray the Stations of the Cross.
- Join in processions with other pilgrims.
- Spend time in quiet prayer.

The High Altar in the church of Our Lady of Walsingham.

Pilgrims in St. Peter's Square in Rome.

Places of pilgrimage associated with the Saints

Rome

Rome in Italy is an important centre of pilgrimage for all Christians. The catacombs underneath the city are where the early Christians, trying to avoid persecution, met in secret and worshipped together. The leaders of the early Church, St. Peter (Jesus' first disciple), and St. Paul (the first great missionary), are buried in Rome. Pilgrims visit the church of St. Peter in Rome which was built on the site of St. Peter's tomb. They also go to pray in the church of St. Paul, which was built on the site of St. Paul's tomb.

Rome has additional importance for Roman Catholics. The Pope, whom they see as St. Peter's successor as head of the Church, lives within the Vatican. The Vatican is an independent city state in the centre of Rome. Hundreds of pilgrims from all over the world visit the Vatican every day of the year.

Catholic pilgrims who arrive in the Vatican city perform special rituals or actions that have a religious significance. They:

- Visit St. Peter's Basilica to pray.
- Go to Confession.
- Attend Mass.
- Attend one of the Pope's regular public audiences and receive his blessing.

For details of pilgrimage in:
Judaism see p238. **Islam** see p293.

Questions

Knowledge

1. Identify two places of significance in your life. State why these places are important to you.
2. Provide an example of a secular place in Ireland or elsewhere that is of significance to many people. Can you say why this place is important to them?
3. a. Provide an example of a sacred place in Ireland or elsewhere that is of significance to many Christians.
   b. What makes a place sacred to Christians?
4. a. What is a pilgrimage?
   b. How does a place become a Christian centre of pilgrimage?
5. Give three reasons why Christians go on pilgrimage to sacred places.
6. a. List three places of religious significance in the Holy Land and describe one of them.
   b. What happened there to make it a sacred place?
   c. What actions of religious significance do pilgrims perform when they go there today?
7. a. Name two places of religious significance associated with Mary the Mother of God and describe one of them.
   b. What happened there to make it a sacred place?
   c. What actions of religious significance do pilgrims perform when they go there?
8. What makes Rome an important place of pilgrimage for Christians?

Understanding

1. What do Christians mean when they describe a particular place as sacred?
2. Why do Christians go on pilgrimage to sacred places?
3. Account for the different impact a visit to a sacred site might have on:
   a. A tourist. b. A pilgrim.
4. Explain how going on pilgrimage can strengthen a person's faith.

Research

- Find out about a Christian place of pilgrimage.
  - Select one of the pilgrimage sites from the map on page 372. State:
    - Where it is located.
    - Why it became a sacred place.
    - What pilgrims do when they go there.
    - How a pilgrim benefits from going there on pilgrimage.
  - Prepare a fact sheet for presentation to the class.

Local Pilgrimages

Key Concepts

Places of significance: places or buildings that have a special meaning for people.

Actions of significance: actions that have a special meaning for people.

Objective

Show how places connected to St. Patrick have religious significance for many people in Ireland.

Activity: *"About water"*

TASK: TO COMPILE A LIST OF TEN FACTS ABOUT WATER.

- ✦ Establish a time limit for completion.
- ✦ Omit unnecessary repetition.

Fascinating facts about water:

1. The human body is made up of 90% water.
2. Without water, a person would die within five days.
3. Water covers three quarters of the Earth's surface.
4. 'Speedo' swimwear helped people swim faster because it was specially constructed to reduce water resistance.
5. The first life form on the Earth emerged in the sea 440 million years ago.
6. A shower uses 7 gallons (32 litres) of water per minute.

Discuss

- What additional facts can be added to the list?
- How important is water for human life?
- What important qualities can water represent or symbolise?

Places of Significance

Actions of Significance

Water has life-giving qualities. Wells and springs have historically been of great significance in the lives of all peoples.

"Going on pilgrimage without a change of heart brings no reward from God." This is a quotation from an ancient Irish manuscript, the Book of Lismore. The 'Aithri', or change of heart, was something very deep in Irish spirituality. It was the hope and the dream that, by leaving home and travelling to a special place, one might return somehow changed and renewed. Thus the practice of going on pilgrimage to holy places developed in Ireland. These places were often wells, rivers or mountains, many of which were places of significance long before the coming of Christianity. Wells were particularly important, as water was regarded as the greatest gift provided by the Earth.

The Celts

The pre-Christian Celts thought of the well as one of the entrances to the 'otherworld'. This was a kind of parallel universe, whose gods and goddesses had the power to control the natural forces of this world. It was believed that water which filled springs, wells and rivers had its source in the 'otherworld'. People visited the wells at special times of the Celtic year to make offerings. It was thought that the gates of the 'otherworld' were unlocked at such times.

St. Patrick and the Saints

St. Patrick and his followers took over many of the practices of the Celtic people and used them to spread the Christian faith. Saints used the fresh water of the existing wells to baptise new Christian converts. A saint often left a blessing on a well and it became known afterwards as a place of healing.

Some wells therefore became associated with:

❖ Baptism,
❖ Healing, *and*
❖ A particular saint.

In this way the sacred wells were incorporated into the new religion. Monasteries and centres of learning later grew up around the site of these ancient wells. This occurred, for example, at St. Kevin's well in Glendalough, and at St. Ciaran's well in Clonmacnoise.

Tobernalt, a holy well in Co. Sligo.
An inscription at the entrance reads:
"Pilgrim walk softly, this is holy ground."

Holy Wells

It is estimated that there are about 3,000 holy wells throughout Ireland. There are 118 holy wells in Co. Dublin alone. These became the focal point of local pilgrimages on 'Pattern Days'. The Patterns (after 'patron saint') took place on the eve of the feast of the saint associated with the well or the parish.

People who went on pilgrimage to a holy well did so with a purpose. They were concerned for themselves, their families, their communities, their crops, or their livestock. They gathered at the well to pray for healing, for forgiveness, or for a special blessing. They prayed to God, and asked the patron saint to help them obtain everything they needed.

Catholic pilgrims who visited holy wells on Pattern days performed special rituals or actions of religious significance. They:

- Arrived barefoot.
- Knelt beside the well for private prayer.
- Prayed the Rosary aloud together.
- Took a drink of water and blessed themselves in the name of the Trinity.
- Walked in a circle around the well and the tree that was usually beside it.
- Placed a thread or piece of cloth on the tree, or threw a coin or pin into the well. This symbolised leaving one's troubles behind at the end of the pilgrimage.

Tobernalt

Tobernalt is a holy well in the diocese of Elphin. It is located a few miles outside Sligo town near the shores of Lough Gill. The water in the well is believed to have curative powers for head and back pains. Pilgrims go there regularly for prayer and reflection. There is a special pilgrimage to the holy well each year on "Garland Sunday", the last Sunday in July.

Places of Pilgrimage associated with St. Patrick

St. Patrick, patron saint of Ireland.

Croagh Patrick

Croagh Patrick is a place of pilgrimage in Co. Mayo in the west of Ireland. Ireland's patron saint is said to have climbed this mountain to pray and fast during Lent 441CE. Pilgrims follow his footsteps on 'Pilgrimage Sunday' at the end of July each year. They kneel and pray where Patrick prayed and attend Mass on the summit. Over 25,000 pilgrims climb the mountain on that day alone, many in bare feet as an extra penance.

On pilgrimage to Croagh Patrick.
Pilgrims who climb Croagh Patrick perform special rituals or actions of religious significance.

The rituals of the pilgrimage

❖ 'The Rounds' at St. Patrick's statue.

The pilgrimage begins at the foot of the mountain beside the statue of St. Patrick. Here, pilgrims do 'the rounds' while praying a set number of 'Our Fathers' and 'Hail Mary's'. A round is a circular walk around a sacred object or place. Seven rounds are undertaken at this stage.

❖ Climbing the Reek.

Then the climb begins - it can take two hours or more to reach the summit. People pray silently and support each other as they make their way up. The path is four kilometres long and is steep and covered in loose stone near the top.

❖ Mass at the summit.

At the very top there is a church. All the building materials used in its construction were carried up by a team of men and donkeys in the past. On 'Pilgrimage Sunday' the pilgrims go to confession, and attend Mass, on the top of Croagh Patrick.

At other times, when it is less crowded, people do the rounds of the church praying a set of 'Our Fathers' and 'Hail Marys'.

❖ The Descent.

Pilgrims endure the hardship of the climb and the steep descent in order to walk in the footsteps of St. Patrick. He made this place holy by his peaceful presence. Christians have felt drawn to it as a place of prayer ever since.

Lough Derg

One of Ireland's oldest pilgrimage sites is a small island in the middle of Lough Derg in Co. Donegal. St. Patrick is believed to have paid frequent visits to the island to pray and fast before continuing his missionary activities in the region. This island has been a place of pilgrimage since earliest times.

Lough Derg.

The rituals of the pilgrimage

Hundreds of pilgrims go to Lough Derg each year. They cross to the island by boat and remain for three days. The style of pilgrimage here is unique. Everyone removes their shoes, as the pilgrimage is undertaken in bare feet. Pilgrims go without proper food and sleep while on Lough Derg. The focus is on prayer and receiving the sacraments.

❖ Fast - pilgrims fast from midnight the night before they arrive. Fasting means no food or drink except water. There is one 'meal' of dry toast and black tea or coffee each day. The fast continues until midnight on the day they return home.

❖ Vigil - pilgrims stay up the first night praying in the church. There are set times for public and private prayer throughout the night. Everyone helps each other stay awake. By the second night most people are sound asleep in bed by lights out at ten o'clock.

Pilgrims on Lough Derg perform special rituals or actions of religious significance.

Walking barefoot around the 'beds', praying the Rosary.

❖ The Stations - pilgrims complete nine 'stations' during their stay on the island. The stations are a series of prayers that are said while walking barefoot around penitential 'beds' and standing and kneeling at the waters edge. The penitential 'beds' are large rings of stone, probably the remains of monastic cells built long ago.

❖ Confession - many pilgrims receive the sacrament of Reconciliation.

❖ Mass - pilgrims attend Mass each day and receive the sacrament of the Eucharist.

❖ Prayer - in addition to the stations, pilgrims pray the Rosary, and follow the Way of the Cross. There is time for further private prayer and meditation inside the church, or outside in the fresh air.

❖ Benediction - pilgrims attend Benediction and join in the night prayer each evening.

Pilgrims attending Mass.

The Meaning of Pilgrimage

What makes hundreds of people undertake the journey to Lough Derg each year? Most will say that deep down it is the love of God that draws them to this sacred place. Leaving the distractions of the material world behind gives people the chance to spend time in prayer and reflection. Having to do without food and sleep tends to focus the mind on what really matters in life.

On the island there is a greater awareness of God, and there is more time for getting closer to God in the stillness. Going barefoot can be difficult, but it makes people more attentive to what they are doing and why they are doing it. It is also a sign that there are no barriers or divisions on the pilgrimage. Everyone is equal, rich and poor, young and old alike.

Although the pilgrim is alone before God, he or she is not on their own, others are on the same journey. People can get strength and encouragement from talking to each other and sharing their experience.

Sharing a quiet moment after a day of prayer.

Questions

Knowledge

1. In what ways were wells and rivers places of significance in pre-Christian Ireland?
2. How did St. Patrick and the saints incorporate those wells into the Christian tradition?
3. What was a 'Pattern Day' and how was it celebrated in parishes throughout Ireland?
4. What rituals or actions of religious significance were performed by pilgrims on a visit to a holy well?
5. a. Where is Croagh Patrick?
   b. Why is it a sacred place?
   c. What do people do when they go on pilgrimage to Croagh Patrick?
6. a. Where is Lough Derg?
   b. Why is it a sacred place?
   c. What do people do when they go on pilgrimage to Lough Derg?

Understanding

1. Why do Christians go on pilgrimage to Croagh Patrick, Lough Derg, or to a holy well in their locality?
2. Describe one Christian place of pilgrimage. Why do you think pilgrims are prepared to undergo a bit of hardship while there on pilgrimage?
3. How does going on pilgrimage to sacred places in Ireland or elsewhere strengthen a person's religious faith?

Research

- Find out about a holy well in your parish, near your home or near your school. Older people in your family or in the community might be willing to share their knowledge and experience with you.

1. What saint is associated with the holy well?
2. Was there ever a 'Pattern Day' or a pilgrimage associated with this well?
   a. If so, does it continue today?
   b. If it was once held, when did it stop?
3. What rituals and religious practices are associated with the holy well?
4. Is the water at the well believed to have any special healing powers; such as for eyes, headaches, backpain, childbirth etc.?
5. What are the stories and myths surrounding the holy well near you?
6. Do people continue to visit the holy well for prayer and reflection today?
7. Is the well and its environs well maintained?
8. Do you think holy wells which go back so far in our past should be allowed to be forgotten?
9. If you think they are worth preserving, what do you think should be done to preserve them?
10. Who should help in the preservation of a holy well in the parish?

Places of Worship

Key Concepts

Sacredness: a thing or a place that is holy and set apart from ordinary life.

Actions of significance: actions that have a special meaning for people.

Places of significance: places or buildings that have a special meaning for people.

Objective

Describe Christian places of worship and their significance in the different Christian traditions.

Activity: *"Places of Significance"*

TASK: TO IDENTIFY BUILDINGS THAT HAVE A CERTAIN MEANING OR SIGNIFICANCE IN PEOPLE'S LIVES.

This year my grandfather took me on the trip of a lifetime. We went to New York for St. Patrick's weekend. When he suggested that we should visit Ellis Island and the Statue of Liberty, I was only too keen to go. We took the ferry from Battery Park over to the island. We stood out on deck and looked up in awe at the massive building rising up ahead of us. For Grandad, it brought back all the old memories of sailing up the Hudson in the 1950's. "This is where it all happened," he said softly.

We got off at Ellis Island. There was a huge crowd there that day, all trying to trace their roots. He told me that this was the place where thousands of immigrants from all over the world first landed when they reached the U.S.A.

The brochure said that 40% of Americans can trace their ancestry to the registry room on Ellis Island. The building itself closed down in 1940, the whole place is now turned into a museum. We went up to the third floor, looking for the Irish section. It was a massive area, covered in names all in alphabetical order. We moved around until we found what we were looking for:
John McGowan, Kinlough.
William J. Eames, Rossinver.

My great grandfather and great granduncle. It was fascinating, This is where they landed. Two young men all on their own set off on their adventures from this very spot. We stood together in silence. The plaque on the wall before us said it all.

My grandfather told me later that he was glad we went. It was something he always meant to do.

Ellis Island.

Discuss

- What did the visitors find when they got to Ellis Island?
- What is it about the building that makes it special for them?
- Is there a building somewhere that has a special significance for you or for members of your family.
  What is special about it?

Sacredness

Some buildings are significant for religious reasons. A building can be a sacred place where people go to pray and worship God.

Christians believe that God is with them at all times, in all places. Yet people also build churches where they can meet together and worship God as a community. For many Christians, their church building is a holy and sacred place.

Sacredness refers to a thing or place that is holy and set apart from ordinary life. When a church is first opened, there is a special ceremony and the building is dedicated to God. From then on, the church is holy ground. While Christians believe the whole Earth is holy, a church is a building specifically set aside to honour God. People maintain a respectful silence when they enter a church. It indicates that the building has a special purpose.

A Christian church.

Actions of Significance

People of faith use certain actions in order to reach out and communicate with God in sacred places. Catholics, for example, believe their place of worship is sacred. Catholics perform special actions when they enter a church. They:

- ❖ Bless themselves with holy water.
- ❖ Genuflect before the Blessed Sacrament.
- ❖ Kneel in a pew and bow their head.
- ❖ Join their hands together in prayer.

This behaviour marks the church as a place that is significant and out of the ordinary. Such actions have a special meaning or religious significance. Their actions show that when they are in a Catholic church, Catholics believe they are in the presence of God.

Places of Significance

A church is a place of religious significance for members of the Christian community. Churches are places where Christians go to worship and get closer to God. We often come across churches built in the middle of a village or a town, or in the busier parts of large cities. Churches look distinctive and are quite unlike other buildings built alongside them. The height of churches makes them impressive. Many have a tower or a spire that can be seen from a distance. Churches are landmarks visible in every direction and are an indicator of the Christian faith of people in that community.

A church may have a clock and bells. These were important in the days when people had no clocks or watches of their own. The bells were rung to call people to Mass and church services. Today they are rung to announce special occasions such as a wedding or a funeral. Some churches have graveyards around them. These are burial places for members of the community. A Catholic church may have a cross, or an image of the Virgin Mary or the patron saint outside. Such Christian symbols indicate that the building is a place of Christian worship.

Inside a church

A church building is designed as a place of worship. The design and layout of churches varies in the different Christian traditions. Every church will have at least one focal point. A focal point is a place inside the building that draws everyone's attention. The focus of a church's interior will, in general, be on either:

❖ the pulpit *or* ❖ the altar.

The pulpit is the central feature in Methodist, Presbyterian and Baptist Churches, because the main emphasis in Sunday worship is reading and preaching the Word of God in the Bible.

The altar is the focal point of Catholic, Anglican* and Orthodox church buildings because the Eucharist is the main form of Sunday worship.

The focal point for the Salvation Army and the Society of Friends (Quakers) in their place of worship is not a pulpit or an altar, but the assembly of people gathered together.

* Church or Ireland.
Church of England.

A Roman Catholic church

Roman Catholic churches are usually built in the shape of a cross or a rectangle. The altar is the central feature of the church. The priest stands at the altar to celebrate Mass.

The interior of a Catholic church.

Diagram of a Roman Catholic church interior.

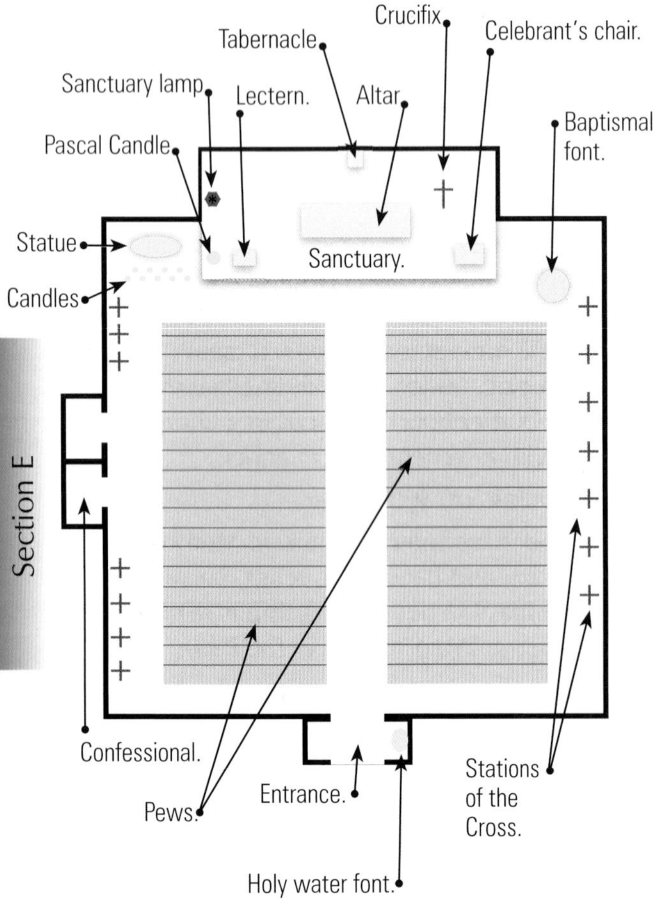

Crucifix
Tabernacle
Celebrant's chair.
Sanctuary lamp
Lectern.
Altar
Baptismal font.
Pascal Candle
Statue
Candles
Sanctuary.
Confessional.
Pews
Entrance.
Stations of the Cross.
Holy water font.

Features of a Roman Catholic church

- **Sanctuary:** The sanctuary, which means 'holy place', is where the Eucharist is celebrated. It is usually one or two steps higher than the main body of the church. It is raised so the everyone can see what is happening there. A crucifix hangs above the sanctuary.
- **Altar:** The altar stands to the front of the sanctuary and can be seen from all parts of the church. The word 'altar' is connected with sacrifice. It refers to the sacrifice Jesus made for all. When the community gathers to celebrate the Eucharist, they remember and make present the life, death and resurrection of Jesus. The priest stands at the altar and faces the community during the celebration of Mass.
- **Tabernacle:** The tabernacle is a small safe that is free-standing or built into the wall of the sanctuary. It is where the consecrated communion hosts, the Blessed Sacrament, is kept or reserved. When people enter the church they bow or genuflect toward the tabernacle in honour of the presence of Jesus in the Blessed Sacrament.
- **Sanctuary lamp:** The sanctuary lamp is a red lamp located near the tabernacle to alert everyone to the presence of Jesus in the Blessed Sacrament.
- **Celebrant's chair:** The priest has a special chair where he sits at Mass. It indicates his role as leader of the celebration of the Eucharist.

An open Bible on a lectern.

Lectern: The lectern is a tall stand that holds the Bible. It is the place from where the Word of God is read at Mass. The priest delivers his homily from here.

Baptismal font: The baptismal font is in a small area set aside for the sacrament of Baptism. It is near the sanctuary so that everyone can see and welcome the newly baptised members into the Christian community.

Pascal candle: The Pascal Candle is a large candle that is usually located near the baptismal font. It is first lit during the Easter Vigil. It is a symbol reminding people that Jesus Christ is the light of the world.

A
2 0
1 2
Ω

A Pascal candle.

Stations of the Cross: The stations of the cross are fourteen images around the walls of the church. Each illustrates an event on Jesus' final journey to his death on Calvary. People walk from station to station, stopping at each one to pray and meditate on the suffering of Jesus.

Statues: Statues are images of Jesus, Mary, or the saints. People light candles and pray in front of statues of their favourite saints. The statues are not objects of worship in themselves; people use them to focus their prayer on the person the statue represents. The votive candles are a sign of the prayer that has been offered to God.

Confessional: This is a place in the church where people can go to confess their sins. The priest will offer them God's forgiveness in the sacrament of Reconciliation. There are two styles of confessional:

1. A penitent (the person confessing sins) can enter a small cubicle and kneel down. A screen separates him/her from the priest. Although they can hear each other, the penitent cannot be seen by the priest.

2. Many church buildings now have a reconciliation room. The priest and the penitent sit together and talk face to face.

Pews: The main body of the church contains lines of benches called pews. It is where people sit or kneel facing the altar.

Stained glass windows: Stained glass windows show scenes from the Bible or represent the lives of various saints. In the past they were teaching aids for people who were unable to read the Bible for themselves.

Holy water font: A font containing holy water is attached to the wall just inside the main entrance. People dip their fingers in the holy water and make the sign of the cross as they enter the church.

An Anglican church

Anglican churches* are usually built in the shape of a cross. The altar is the central feature of the church. The minister or rector stands behind the altar to lead the service of Holy Communion.

The interior of a Church of Ireland church.

Diagram of an Anglican church interior.

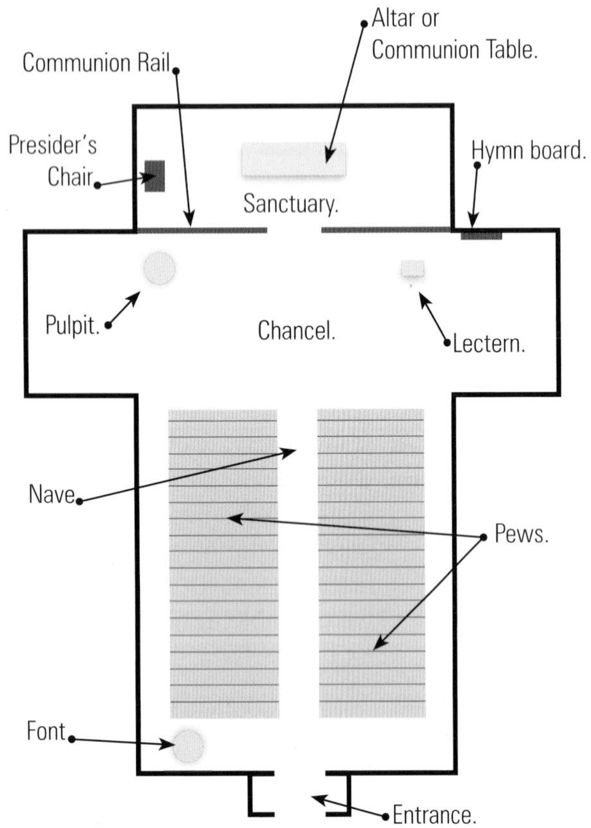
Altar or Communion Table.
Communion Rail
Presider's Chair
Hymn board.
Sanctuary.
Pulpit.
Chancel.
Lectern.
Nave
Pews.
Font
Entrance.

* Church or Ireland.
Church of England.

Features of an Anglican church

Altar:	The altar or communion table is the focal point of the church. It is raised so that people can see the actions of the minister (rector). There is a cross on the altar.
Sanctuary:	The area around the altar is called the sanctuary.
Chancel:	The area between the sanctuary and the rest of the church is called the chancel. The choir may sit here.
Communion rail:	The communion rail divides the sanctuary from the chancel. People kneel at the communion rail to receive Holy Communion.
Lectern:	The Bible is read from the lectern. Some lecterns are in the shape of an eagle, and the Bible rests on the eagle's wings.
Hymn board:	The hymn board lists the numbers of each hymn in the hymnal for that day's service.
Pulpit:	The sermon explaining the Bible reading is preached from the pulpit. It is a small raised platform from where everyone can see and hear the minister.
Presider's chair:	The chair indicates the role of the minister as leader of the service.
Pews:	People sit on seats facing the altar; these seats are called pews.
Font:	The font contains the water used for Baptism. It is usually placed near the main door because being baptised means entering the Christian Community.

A Methodist church

Methodist churches are usually built in the shape of a rectangle. The pulpit is the central feature of the church. The minister may lead the entire Sunday service from the pulpit, including the Bible readings and the sermon.

GIVE PRAISE TO OUR GOD

The interior of a Methodist church.

Diagram of a Methodist church interior.

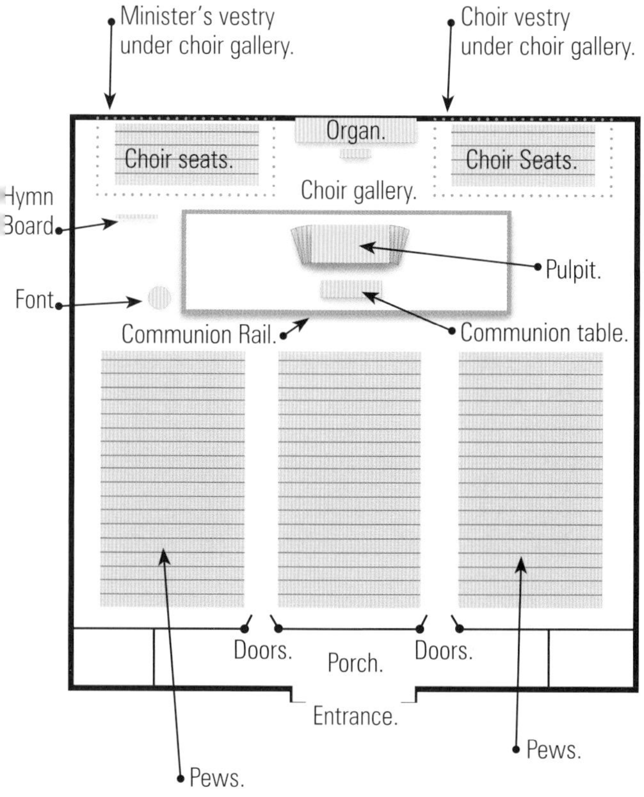
Minister's vestry under choir gallery.
Choir vestry under choir gallery.
Organ.
Choir seats.
Choir Seats.
Choir gallery.
Hymn Board
Pulpit.
Font
Communion Rail.
Communion table.
Doors.
Porch.
Doors.
Entrance.
Pews.
Pews.

Features of a Methodist church

- **Pulpit:** The pulpit is the focal point of the church. It is in a prominent position because reading and teaching the Word of God in the Bible is the main form of worship in a Methodist church.
- **Communion table:** The communion table is in front of the pulpit. It is called a table to stress the idea that Communion is a shared meal uniting people with their fellow Christians and with Jesus himself.
- **Choir gallery:** Hymn singing and organ music have always been characteristic of worship in the Methodist tradition. Many of Charles Wesley's hymns are still sung at church services today. Charles and his brother John were the founders of the Methodist movement.
- **Hymn board:** The hymn board lists the numbers of the main hymns for that day's service.
- **Font:** Baptism takes place at the font. It is located at the front of the church to enable everyone to see and welcome the new member into the Christian community.

A Methodist church (or chapel) is usually very simple in design. It is quite plain, with few if any ornaments or symbols. A plain cross may be the only symbolic object to be seen inside.

Methodist, Presbyterian and Baptist churches look very similar. They are plain with few ornaments or symbols. The central feature is the pulpit. It emphasises the importance of the Bible in the act of worship.

The baptistry is an important feature in Baptist churches. It is a special pool in the floor of the church where adults are baptised by being fully immersed in water at Baptism.

A Quaker Meeting House

Some Christians place very little emphasis on the buildings they use as places of worship. The Society of Friends (Quakers) worship in a building referred to as a meeting house. The Quakers do not regard their place of worship as sacred or holy. For them, the assembly of people gathered together is what matters most. It is more important than the altar or the pulpit.

Quakers do not refer to the meeting house as a church. Their place of worship is plain and simple without signs or symbols of any kind. Seats are arranged in a circle, facing each other. A Bible is placed on a table in the centre of the gathering. It is an ordinary table and is not seen as an altar or a communion table. At a Quaker meeting everyone sits in silence, awaiting the Holy Spirit to inspire one of the members to speak.

A gathering in a Quaker Meeting House.

Diagram of a Quaker Meeting House interior.

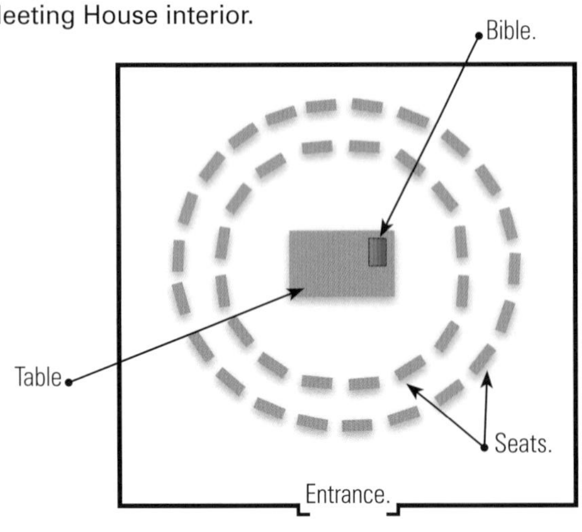
Bible.
Table
Seats.
Entrance.

Cathedrals

Exterior of a Roman Catholic Cathedral.

A church is a specially designed building where the Christian community meets to worship God. Christian traditions which have priests and bishops will have cathedrals. A cathedral is the bishop's church and is the main church in a diocese. There are Anglican and Roman Catholic cathedrals throughout Ireland and the United Kingdom.

The word 'cathedral' comes from the Latin 'cathedra', meaning 'high seat' or 'throne'. There is a cathedra in every cathedral for the bishop of that diocese. A cathedral has all the features of a parish church, but is usually larger, more ornate, and is designed to cater for a greater number of people. Everything in a cathedral is on a bigger and grander scale than in a parish church.

Interior of a Roman Catholic cathedral during the season of Lent.

The Roman Catholic basilica in Knock.

A modern cathedral, like a modern church, is designed in a different way from older, more traditional church buildings. This can be clearly seen in the design of the new basilica in Knock, in the west of Ireland. Although not a cathedral, this very large church caters for thousands of pilgrims who go to Knock each year to pray at the Marian shrine.

Congregation at Mass at the basilica in Knock.

The internal layout of the church reflects the new thinking that emerged at the Second Vatican Council. The altar is the focal point, and is located in the centre. Seats are arranged in a circle around the altar. This new style emphasises that God is close to people and part of everyday life. When the congregation gathers around the altar for Mass, everyone can see each other. The priest stands at the altar amongst the people to celebrate the Eucharist. There is a sense of togetherness, with God at the centre.

For details of places of worship in:
Judaism see p232. **Islam** see p290.

Questions

Knowledge

1. What is the purpose of church buildings in the Christian community of faith?
2. a. What do Catholic Christians do when they enter their place of worship?
   b. What is the meaning or significance of these actions for the persons concerned?
3. What distinctive features set a church apart from other buildings in a town or district?
4. What is the focal point inside:
   a. A Roman Catholic church?
   b. A Church of Ireland church?
   c. A Methodist or Presbyterian church?
   d. A Quaker meeting house?
5. Select a church building or a place of worship known to you:
   a. To which denomination does it belong?
   b. What is the focal point in the building?
   c. List the main features inside the building and explain their purpose.
6. Identify the ways in which a Methodist church is different to a Catholic church.
7. What is a cathedral?
8. What aspects of the design of the Roman Catholic basilica in Knock show the influence of new thinking from Vatican II on modern church buildings?

Understanding

1. Why is it important for Christian communities to set aside a special place for worship?
2. How do Catholics show by their actions that their churches are sacred places?
3. How does a Catholic church and a Methodist church reflect the beliefs of the people who worship there?
4. What do you think of the layout of modern church buildings compared to the style of older more traditional churches?

Research

- Name and describe a place of worship in your community of faith. Draw a labelled diagram to support the description.
  - Display the work for the class.

The Liturgical Year

Key Concepts

Times of significance: times of the year that have a special meaning for people.

Actions of significance: actions that have a special meaning for people.

Objective

Identify times of the year that have a special significance for Christians.

Activity: *"The cycle of time"*

TASK: TO REFLECT ON THE PASSING OF TIME, AND HOW THE YEARLY CYCLE IS MARKED BY EVENTS OF PERSONAL SIGNIFICANCE.

- On a diagram mark in some of the ways in which we divide time over a calendar year.
  - The four seasons: Spring, Summer, Autumn, Winter.
  - School events.
  - School holidays.
  - Family birthdays.
  - Family anniversaries.
  - Sporting events.
  - National events.
  - Other dates that are important.

Discuss

- What key events are remembered and celebrated in your family every year?
- Select a special event in your family, in your school, or in your country and describe how it is remembered and celebrated annually.
- Why do you think it is important to remember and celebrate special times in one's family, one's school, or one's country?

Times of Significance
Actions of Significance

Special times in family life are remembered and celebrated during the calendar year, while special times in the life of Jesus are celebrated during the Liturgical year.

Time is divided up into night and day, weeks and months, and the seasons of the year. Just as the seasons come and go, each calendar year begins in January and ends in December. The school year starts in September, and ends when the holidays begin in June. Our birthdays indicate that we are now a year older. Birthdays, anniversaries and other special occasions give shape to the year. The yearly cycle makes us aware of the rhythm of our lives and the passing of time.

When we celebrate special occasions, we are not simply remembering something that happened in the past. These are celebrations of the present and future as well. Think of a birthday for example; birthdays are about remembering the past, rejoicing in the present and having hopes for the future.

When young people celebrate their birthdays, they are the centre of attention for a day. Their parents remember the time when their children were born into the world, how small and vulnerable they were and how much they loved them. Now they look at their sons and daughters and marvel at how much they have grown and changed over the years. This prompts parents to think forward to the future and imagine what life will be like in the years ahead.

Sacred time

A religion, like a family, has important dates to remember. Every religion sets aside special times each year to recall important people and events in the faith. Christianity has a religious calendar that marks special times in the life of Jesus. Each year the Church remembers and celebrates:

- ❖ The birth of Jesus at Christmas.
- ❖ The death and resurrection of Jesus at Easter.
- ❖ The sending of the Holy Spirit at Pentecost.

The annual cycle of Church seasons is sacred time set aside to honour God. During the seasons of the Church's year, Christians remember the events of Jesus' life in the past and celebrate the fact that the risen Jesus is here now in the present. They also look forward to the Second Coming of Christ in the future, at the end of time.

The Liturgical Year

The seasons of Advent, Christmas, Lent and Easter are sacred time set aside to honour God. The Christian Churches place different emphases on the seasons of the Liturgical Year. The calendar on this page is used by Roman Catholics and most Anglicans. All Christians observe Christmas and Easter.

Liturgical Colours

The most important events in the Christian tradition are remembered and celebrated at special times in the Liturgical Year. Some Churches pay particular attention to the environment within church buildings during the Christian seasons. The use of colour, for example, on the priests' vestments (clothing) and on altar cloths and church banners, remind people of the meaning of each season. It also helps them to feel the difference in the seasons.

1. Purple.
   This colour is used during Advent and Lent. Purple is a sign of penance and fasting.
2. White/Gold.
   These colours are used at Christmas, Easter and Ascension. White and gold are signs of light and joy.
3. Red.
   This colour is used at Pentecost. Red is a sign of goodness and strength.
4. Green.
   This colour is used in Ordinary Time. Green is the colour of growth and hope.

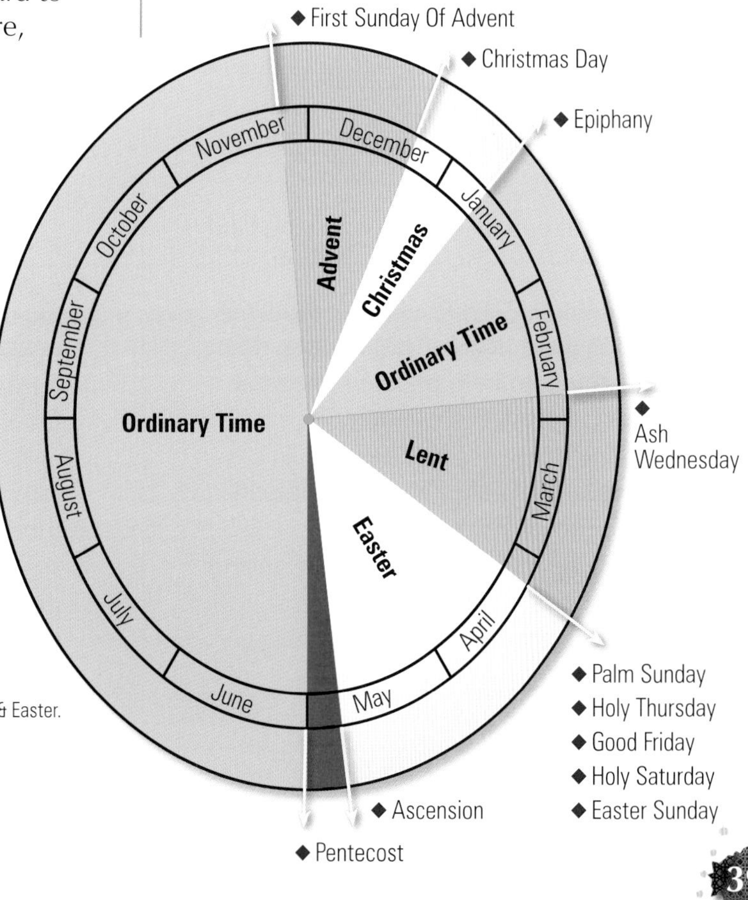
◆ First Sunday Of Advent
◆ Christmas Day
◆ Epiphany
◆ Ash Wednesday
◆ Palm Sunday
◆ Holy Thursday
◆ Good Friday
◆ Holy Saturday
◆ Easter Sunday
◆ Ascension
◆ Pentecost
November
December
January
February
March
April
May
June
July
August
September
October
Advent
Christmas
Ordinary Time
Lent
Easter
Ordinary Time

The Liturgical or Church Year

Colour Key
Purple: Advent and Lent.
White & Gold : Christmas & Easter.
Red: Pentecost.
Green: Ordinary Time.

Times and Actions of Significance

Advent

The Liturgical Year begins on the first Sunday of Advent. The season of Advent begins four Sundays before Christmas and ends on Christmas Eve. Roman Catholics and Anglicans observe the season of Advent.

The word 'Advent' comes from the Latin 'adventus' meaning 'the approach' or 'the coming'. For Christians, there are three aspects to the coming of Jesus at Christmas.

- ❖ It means looking back to the past and thinking about the coming of Jesus 2,000 years ago in a stable in Bethlehem.
- ❖ It means the risen Jesus coming into people's lives now and being present in the Christian community at Christmas.
- ❖ It means looking forward to the Second Coming of Jesus in the future.

Advent is a time of waiting and preparation for the coming of Jesus at Christmas. Christians are encouraged to actively prepare for the birth of Jesus, not merely wait for it to happen. During Advent Catholics, for example, get ready for the festival of Christmas by examining their lives in a thoughtful way. For a Catholic person this means:

- ❖ Reflecting on their life as a Christian and seeing what improvements can be made in order to become a better person, living as Jesus lived.
- ❖ Prayer and attendance at Mass, asking God to help him/her to change for the better.
- ❖ Receiving the sacrament of Reconciliation.
- ❖ Performing good deeds. This involves doing practical things to help people in need at home and abroad. For example:
  - preparing Christmas hampers for St. Vincent de Paul to give to people in need in the local community.
  - undertaking a sponsored fast for Concern to raise funds for projects in the developing world.

An Advent wreath.

The Advent Wreath

The Advent wreath is a religious symbol. The wreath is a circle of evergreen branches decorated with candles and ribbon. The candles are lit consecutively each week during Advent. Lighting candles on the Advent wreath is a way of looking forward to the coming of Jesus at Christmas. It reminds Christians that Jesus said:

"I am the light of the world." John 8:12

The Symbols

- ❖ **Circle:** The wreath is a circle with no beginning and no end. It symbolises the unending love of God.
- ❖ **Light:** Candlelight symbolises thousands of years of waiting in hope for the coming of Jesus.
- ❖ **4 purple candles:** Purple symbolises the need for people to prepare themselves for the coming of Jesus by being sorry and asking forgiveness for their sins.
- ❖ **1 pink candle:** The pink candle is lit on Christmas day to mark the coming of Jesus. Pink symbolises the joy of living a good life as a follower of Jesus.

Lighting the Advent candles.

Section E

Christmas

The Christmas season begins on Christmas day and celebrates the birth of Jesus. The season lasts until the third Sunday after Christmas. The word 'Christmas' comes from the old English term meaning the 'Mass of Christ's birth'. It was later shortened to 'Christ's Mass', and then to 'Christmas'.

A Christmas nativity scene.

All Christians celebrate Christmas, although the form of worship varies in the different Christian Churches.

The Incarnation

Christmas is the time when Christians focus on an important aspect of their faith, that God became human in Jesus Christ. This Christian belief is called the Incarnation. The mystery of the Incarnation is that Jesus is truly God and truly human. For Christians, the birth of Jesus is a sign of God's great love for the world.

The festival celebrating Jesus' birth is therefore a joyous occasion and a time of thanksgiving. Christians thank God for sending his only son to the world to be born as a human being.

Christmas Day

The story of Jesus' birth is told in the Gospels of Matthew (Matt 1:1-25) and Luke (Lk 2:1-20). The Gospel writers show that Jesus was no ordinary baby; Jesus is the Messiah, the saviour of the world. All the carols, hymns, and readings at Mass and church services at Christmas relate to Jesus and give thanks for his birth. For Catholics, the celebration of Christmas begins at the Vigil, or evening Mass, on 24th December.

Christians decorate their homes and workplaces in preparation for Christmas. On Christmas day they attend Mass and religious services, share a special meal and exchange gifts with family and friends.

Epiphany

The Feast of the Epiphany takes place twelve days after Christmas on 6th January. During the Epiphany, Christians remember the arrival of the Magi (wise men) to honour the child Jesus. The Magi were non-Jews and their visit shows that Jesus is the saviour and Messiah of the whole world and not just the Jewish nation.

The Christmas season ends on the Sunday after the Epiphany when Christians celebrate the feast of the Baptism of Jesus. This marks the beginning of Jesus' public ministry and the start of Ordinary Time in the Christian calendar.

Gift-giving is a feature of celebrating Christmas.

Lent

The season of Lent lasts for forty days and is a time of preparation for Easter. Christians remember that, after his Baptism, Jesus spent forty days in the desert. He fasted and prayed in preparation for the work that he was going to do next. During Lent, Christians think about their lives and try to focus on Jesus and his message. It is a time when they try to change their ways and develop a closer relationship with God.

Catholics, for example, make a renewed effort to pray and fast and do good deeds.

- *Prayer:* getting closer to God - going to daily Mass, receiving the sacrament of Reconciliation, visiting a church to pray and light candles.
- *Fasting:* giving something up - luxuries such as sweets, chocolate, crisps, biscuits, sugar in tea or things we enjoy such as going to the cinema, playing computer games etc.
- *Good deeds:* doing something positive - making a special effort to help others, especially people in need, both locally and in the developing world.

Setting time aside for prayer, making small sacrifices and trying to help others enables Christians to focus on God and what God wants. It makes them more aware of the presence of God in their lives. When people are attentive to deeper things, they are more likely to change their lives for the better.

The day before Lent begins is called Shrove Tuesday. Pancakes were traditionally made and eaten on Shrove Tuesday to use up rich ingredients such as eggs, butter and sugar before Lent began. Hot cross buns are another favourite in Lent, and were traditionally eaten on Good Friday.

Hot Cross buns.

The sign of the cross being made on the forehead with blessed ashes on Ash Wednesday.

Ash Wednesday

Ash Wednesday is the first day of Lent. Roman Catholics and some Anglicans attend church and are signed with ashes on their forehead. The blessed ashes are a sign that:

- People are sorry for their sins.
- People will turn away from sin and make a new start for the better.

On Ash Wednesday, Christians promise to make an extra effort to live a good Christian life. The ash is made by burning some of the palm saved from Palm Sunday the previous year. Ash Wednesday and Good Friday are fast days during Lent. For Catholics this means having smaller meals and eating no meat on these two days.

Christians spend extra time in prayer and reflection during Lent.

Holy Week

The final week of Lent is called Holy Week; it is the most important time in the Liturgical Year. Holy Week begins on Palm Sunday and ends a week later on Easter Sunday. The last days of Holy Week are called the Easter Triduum (from the Latin word for 'three days'). Holy Thursday, Good Friday and Holy Saturday link together the seasons of Lent and Easter.

During Holy Week, Christians remember and celebrate the events surrounding the death and resurrection of Jesus.

- ❖ *Palm Sunday:* Jesus triumphantly entered Jerusalem; people joyfully waved palm branches in his honour.
- ❖ *Holy Thursday:* Jesus shared the Eucharist with his disciples at the Last Supper.
- ❖ *Good Friday:* Jesus carried his cross and was crucified on Calvary.
- ❖ *Holy Saturday:* Jesus' body lies in the tomb. The people wait.
- ❖ *Easter Sunday:* the resurrection of Jesus from the dead. He appeared to Mary Magdalen, to the women and to the other disciples.

The empty tomb.

The Easter Triduum

For Catholics, the Easter Triduum (the last three days of Lent) begins on Holy Thursday night with the evening Mass of the Lord's Supper. On Good Friday a liturgy at three o'clock in the afternoon recalls the Passion (the term for Jesus' suffering) and death of Jesus on the cross. On Holy Saturday night the Easter Vigil celebrates the resurrection of Jesus and the Pascal candle is lit.

Jesus rose from the dead on Easter Sunday.

Easter

The season of Easter begins on Easter Sunday and lasts for fifty days. Easter is significant because all the other events in Jesus' life, from his birth to his Ascension, are important precisely because Jesus died and rose again from the dead. Christians believe the resurrection makes it possible for Jesus to be alive and present with his followers today.

The resurrection of Jesus is celebrated by all Christians everywhere. Catholics, Orthodox and some Anglicans begin the celebration at the Easter Vigil on Holy Saturday evening. Most Christian Churches have a Communion service on Easter morning.

While the date of Christmas is fixed, the date of Easter changes from year to year as it is based on a lunar cycle. Easter falls on the first Sunday after the first full moon following the Spring Equinox, Easter Sunday can therefore be 'early' or 'late'. The season of Easter ends on the feast of Pentecost.

Ascension

Ascension takes place forty days after Easter. It celebrates the return of Jesus to God the Father in heaven and his promise to send the Holy Spirit.

Pentecost

Pentecost takes place ten days after the feast of the Ascension. It celebrates the coming of the Holy Spirit to the disciples as Jesus promised. The gift of the Spirit gave them the courage to publicly speak about the resurrection for the first time. For this reason Pentecost is known as the birthday of Christianity. Pentecost is the last day of the season of Easter.

Ordinary Time

The remainder of the Christian year outside Advent-Christmas and Lent-Easter is called Ordinary time. There are two periods of Ordinary time.

- ❖ The first is between Christmas and the beginning of Lent.
- ❖ The second is between Easter and the beginning of Advent.

Each week during Ordinary time, the Gospel readings focus on key events in the life and teaching of Jesus. There are thirty three weeks in Ordinary time and this covers about sixty percent of the Liturgical Year.

For details of sacred time in:
Judaism see p241. **Islam** see p296.

Cross of the resurrection.

Questions

Knowledge

1. a. List times of significance in the life of your family, your school and the country in which you live.
   b. How are any two of these important times marked or celebrated?
   c. Why is it important to mark significant times in our lives?
2. a. What is the Christian Liturgical Year?
   b. How is the Christian calendar divided?
   c. Name the colours of the seasons in the Liturgical year.
3. a. When does the Liturgical year begin?
   b. Name the most important Christian festival.
4. a. What is Advent?
   b. When does it start and finish?
   c. What do Christians look forward to during the season of Advent?
   d. What is an Advent wreath? Explain the meaning of its various elements.
5. a. What do Christians celebrate on Christmas day?
   b. What is the meaning of the Incarnation in the Christian faith?
   c. How do Christians celebrate this sacred time of year?
6. a. When does Lent begin? How long does it last?
   b. What happens on Ash Wednesday?
   c. What is the purpose of the Lenten season?
7. a. Name the important days of Holy Week.
   b. What event is recalled on Palm Sunday?
   c. What is the Easter Triduum in the Christian tradition?
   d. List the events that are remembered and made present at the Easter Triduum.
8. a. What do Christians celebrate at Easter?
   b. Why is Easter a time of great religious significance for Christians?
9. What do Christians celebrate at Pentecost?
10. What is Ordinary time in the Church year?

Understanding

1. Name the main times of significance in the Christian religion and when they occur. Select any two and explain how Christians celebrate this sacred time.
2. Explain why the following times are significant in the Christian tradition.
   a. Christmas. b. Easter. c. Pentecost.
3. Explain, and give examples of, how actions of religious significance undertaken at certain times in the Church year can strengthen a person's faith.
4. Why is there a time of preparation before the seasons of Christmas and Easter each year?
5. Why do you think Christians regard Easter as the most important event on their religious calendar?

Worship

Key Concept

Worship: the way people of faith praise and honour God in prayer and at religious services.

Objective

Identify the elements of worship at religious services.

Activity: *"In your honour"*

TASK: TO BE AWARE THAT WE NORMALLY SET TIME ASIDE TO HONOUR PEOPLE FOR THEIR ACHIEVEMENTS.

When we wish to honour people who have achieved something worthwhile we tend to:

- Organise a special event.
- Invite people to assemble in a certain place at a certain time.
- Expect that everyone will dress appropriately for the occasion.
- Invite someone to make a speech on behalf of those present.
- Say things to praise and thank the person(s) for their achievement.
- Do things to indicate our respect and admiration eg. stand up, clap, listen attentively, sing (their praises), make a presentation, and perhaps share a celebration meal.

Discuss

Think of the last time you were present at an event where a person(s) was honoured for what he/she had achieved. It might be a school event such as an awards ceremony, a presentation night at your sports club or a family occasion.

- What was the occasion?
- When did it occur?
- Where did it take place?
- Did people dress up?
- Who was in charge of the proceedings?
- What kinds of things were ***said***?
- What was ***done*** to show admiration for the person(s) concerned?
- Was there a meal or a reception afterwards?

Worship

People of all religions set time aside to gather together to honour God.

Worship is the way people of faith praise and honour God in prayer and at religious services. Christians worship God. They believe:

- *God is almighty* - the creator of the world and the creator of all life.
- *God is good* - he so loved the world that he sent his only son, Jesus Christ, to save everyone from sin.

Christians worship God when they pray and attend religious services.

People feel the need to acknowledge God for who he is and all he has done for them. Worship is their way of saying 'thank you' to God. Christians can worship God privately by themselves or publicly in the company of others.

- Examples of private worship are individual prayer, meditation and Bible reading.
- Examples of public worship are the Mass, Holy Communion and church services, sacraments and pilgrimages.

Going into a church to worship God.

Christian worship

The main form of worship for many Christians is the Eucharist. It is collective worship celebrated by members of a church community united together in honouring God.

- ❖ The Eucharist is celebrated every day in the Roman Catholic and Orthodox Churches.
- ❖ In the Anglican Communion most Churches celebrate Holy Communion at least twice a month.
- ❖ In the Methodist Church Holy Communion, or the 'Lord's Supper', takes place about once a month.
- ❖ The Presbyterian Churches hold a Communion service about four times a year.

World Religions at Worship

Members of each of the great world religions honour God or gods in their place of worship.

Christians singing hymns in a Methodist church.

A Jewish community at worship in a synagogue.

A Muslim man at prayer in a mosque.

A Hindu woman worshipping in a mandir.

Buddhists worshipping in a temple.

Christian Worship

Collective worship can be either liturgical or non-liturgical.

Liturgical Worship

(Roman Catholic, Anglican, Orthodox.)

The worship is altar-centred. The Eucharist is the principal act of worship. In liturgical worship there is:

- A set ritual with a fixed pattern of words and actions.
- A book containing the order of service.
- Vestments for the priest.
- Use of symbolic objects and ritual actions to express beliefs.

Interior of an Anglican church in preparation for a service of Holy Communion.

Non-liturgical Worship

(Methodist, Presbyterian, Baptist.)

The worship is pulpit centred. Bible reading and preaching is the main act of worship. Set rituals are avoided, there is no book with a fixed order of service. In non-liturgical worship there are:

- Bible readings.
- Preaching.
- Hymn singing.
- Prayers.

Interior of a Methodist church in preparation for Morning Prayer.

Sunday Worship in an Anglican church

Sunday Service is the main form of Sunday worship in the Church of Ireland.

An Anglican church.

The Service is led by the minister (rector) who leads the prayers and gives a sermon based on the Bible readings. The congregation listens to the lesson from scripture and reflects on its meaning in their lives. They respond to the prayers and sing the hymns together.

Holy Communion

On the first and third Sunday of every month, there is a Holy Communion service. This has two main parts. During the Ministry of the Word there are scripture readings, a sermon and prayers. During the Ministry of the Sacrament bread and wine are presented at the altar (or communion table). The bread and wine are blessed and the words that Jesus spoke at the Last Supper are repeated. Members of the congregation kneel before the altar and receive, first the bread, and then the wine from a chalice (or cup). Only full members of the Church (i.e. those that have been baptised and confirmed) may receive Communion.

The bread and wine.

Sunday Worship in a Methodist church

Morning Worship is the main form of Sunday worship in the Methodist tradition. The minister leads the worship but there is no fixed order of service. The Assembly listens to readings from the Bible and to the sermon preached by the minister. Everyone sings the hymns, and prayers are said, especially for those in need.

Holy Communion (or the Lord's Supper)

Holy Communion is celebrated once a month as part of the morning or evening service. Holy Communion may be the last part of the service; it is not the main part as it is in Churches that have an altar-centred liturgy. Methodists believe that hearing God's Word in a sermon is just as important, and time is needed to reflect on it in depth.

During Holy Communion, the minister recalls the Last Supper and says the prayer of thanksgiving over bread and wine. After the bread is broken there is a period of silence. Then the minister and the people eat the bread and drink the wine together. This is done in memory of the life, death and resurrection of Jesus Christ.

Bread and individual cups of wine.

The bread used for the communion may be ordinary bread. The wine in individual glasses may be unfermented grape juice as many Methodists do not drink alcohol. The service ends with a hymn and a blessing to 'Go in peace' and to live and work 'to God's praise and glory'.

For details of worship in:
Judaism see p235. **Islam** see p290.

Questions

Knowledge

1. What is worship?
2. Why do Christians worship God?
3. What is the difference between private worship and collective worship?
4. How often is the Eucharist or Holy Communion celebrated in different Christian Churches?
5. What Christian denominations have:
   a. A liturgical form of Sunday worship?
   b. A non-liturgical form of Sunday worship?
6. What is distinctive about:
   a. Liturgical worship?
   b. Non-liturgical worship?
7. a. What is the main form of Sunday worship in an Anglican church?
   b. When does Holy Communion take place in an Anglican church?
8. a. What is the main act of Sunday worship in a Methodist church?
   b. When does Holy Communion take place in a Methodist church?

Understanding

1. Why do Christians gather together at certain times, and in certain places, to worship God?
2. Give reasons why a Christian might:
   a. Prefer to worship alone.
   b. Want to worship with others.
3. Explain the difference between liturgical and non-liturgical forms of Christian worship.
4. Describe what happens at a Holy Communion service in:
   a. An Anglican church, *OR*
   b. A Methodist church where Holy Communion is part of the act of worship.

Research

- Find out about the origin of the term 'worship'.
  - What language does it originally come from?
  - How was the word spelled?
  - What is the root meaning of the word?
  - What is the meaning of worship in a religious sense today?
  - Summarise the information in a written statement.

Ritual

Key Concepts

Worship: the way people of faith praise and honour God in prayer and at religious services.

Ritual: an occasion when people use symbolic objects, words and actions to express what is deeply important to them.

Objective

To identify elements of worship in the celebration of the Eucharist at Mass.

Activity: *"Birthdays"*

TASK: TO IDENTIFY THE TYPE OF BEHAVIOUR THAT IS ALWAYS PART OF BIRTHDAY CELEBRATIONS.

✦ Think of a birthday that you celebrated recently. (Your birthday, a friends birthday, or the birthday of someone in your family)

✦ What words or actions were part of the birthday celebrations? (✓)

- ❑ Sending a birthday card.
- ❑ Saying 'Happy Birthday'.
- ❑ Giving presents.
- ❑ Having a birthday party.
- ❑ Getting a birthday cake.
- ❑ Blowing out the candles.
- ❑ Wearing the party hats.
- ❑ Other: ____________________

Discuss

- List the things that always happen on someone's birthday.
- Do you do anything else in your family when it is someone's birthday?
- Select one action. What does it mean when we say or do this on someone's birthday?
- How do we celebrate other important events such as anniversaries, weddings and graduations?
- What is expressed on these occasions?

Worship

Ritual

Certain words and actions are used to help people express matters of religious importance.

A ritual is an occasion when we use symbolic objects, words and actions to express what is deeply important to us. Rituals are always done in the same way every time they are performed. The words and actions of religious rituals have a special meaning for those involved. Religious rituals help people of faith to express deep beliefs about their relationship with God. Christians take part in rituals when they gather in sacred places to worship God.

The rituals in an act of worship are always carried out in the same way every time they are performed. Rituals may involve wearing special clothes, saying special words and using special actions or gestures. Religious rituals are an integral part of Christian acts of worship at Mass, Holy Communion services, sacraments and pilgrimages.

Celebrating the Eucharist.

A Christian Act of Worship

The Mass in the Catholic Church is an example of an act of worship that involves participation in religious rituals.

A Catholic church.

The Sacrament of the Eucharist

The Mass is a ritual meal that has its origins in the Last Supper. The words and actions of Jesus are remembered and made present to the Christian community at Mass. Catholics refer to the sacrament of the Eucharist simply as the Mass. The word probably comes from a shortened version of the Latin phrase 'Ite, missa est' (Go, you are sent) spoken when the Mass was originally said in Latin.

At Mass the priest wears ceremonial clothes, reads the Word of God in the Bible and repeats the words of Jesus at the Last Supper

> *"This is my body...This is my blood...*
> *Do this in memory of me."*

He performs the actions of Jesus at the Last Supper, taking the bread and wine, blessing it and sharing it with those present.

The sacrament of the Eucharist is the central act of worship in the Roman Catholic Church. The word 'Eucharist' means 'thanksgiving'. Catholics attend Mass to give thanks to God for the gift of life and for what Jesus did in sacrificing his life to save people from sin.

The different parts of the Mass include the:

- Introductory Rite.
- Liturgy of the Word.
- Liturgy of the Eucharist.
- Concluding Rite.

The priest leads the celebration.

1. Introductory Rite

◆ Entrance Procession and Greeting:	The community gathers together as the People of God. They make the Sign of the Cross.
◆ Penitential Rite:	Penitence is sorrow for sin. The people reflect on what they have done wrong and ask for God's forgiveness.
◆ Kyrie:	The congregation repeats the words of the Kyrie (Lord / Christ have mercy) after the priest.
◆ Gloria:	The Gloria is a prayer of praise.
◆ Opening Prayer:	The theme of the celebration is outlined in the opening prayer.

The priest greets the congregation at the beginning of Mass.

2. Liturgy of the Word

The Bible is the Word of God. On Sunday there are three readings from the Bible, the first two are read by ministers of the Word.

- **First Reading:** The first reading is from the Old Testament.
- **Responsorial Psalm:** The responsorial psalm is one of the 150 psalms in the Old Testament.
- **Second Reading:** The second reading is from the New Testament, often from one of the letters of St. Paul to the early Christians.
- **Gospel:** The congregation stands for the Gospel which is solemnly read by the priest. It contains the message of Jesus to "love God, and love your neighbour, as yourself".
- **Homily:** The priest gives a homily or a sermon based on the Bible readings. He will explain how the message of the Gospel can be applied in daily life.
- **Creed:** Everyone stands to say the Creed which is a summary of what Catholics believe about God and the Church.
- **Prayers of the Faithful:** Some members of the congregation say the prayers of the faithful for the needs of the Church, the world, and the local community.

The Bible.

3. Liturgy of the Eucharist

- **Presentation of the Gifts:** The gifts of bread and wine, and the collection, are brought to the altar in a procession. The bread and wine are blessed and the people pray that their sacrifice will be acceptable to God.
- **Eucharistic Prayer:** The Eucharistic prayer is a prayer of praise and thanks to God for Jesus Christ. At the consecration the priest prays that by the power of the Holy Spirit the bread and wine will become the body and blood of Christ. The priest then repeats the words and actions of Jesus at the Last Supper. He consecrates (makes sacred) the bread and wine with Jesus' words:

  'This is my body...
  this is my blood...
  Do this in memory of me.'

  Jesus is now truly present under the appearance of bread and wine.

  All the people express the mystery of their faith by saying together, *'Christ has died. Christ has risen. Christ will come again'*.
- **The Lord's Prayer:** The congregation stand and say the Lord's Prayer together.
- **Sign of Peace:** They offer each other a sign of peace and unity by shaking hands and saying, *'Peace be with you.'*
- **Communion:** The congregation receives Holy Communion from the priest and the ministers of the Eucharist. Catholics receive the host with great reverence because the risen Jesus is truly present. The Eucharist is spiritual nourishment to give them the strength to be true followers of Jesus.

4. Concluding Rite

- Final Blessing: The priest blesses the people and says 'Go in peace to love and serve the Lord.'
- Dismissal: All are sent out to love and serve the Lord during the rest of the week. God is loved and served when people help their neighbour, especially if he/she is in need. Christians today are called not only to believe in the risen Jesus, but also to actively follow his teachings in their daily lives. The Eucharist gives them the strength and confidence needed to do this.

Catholics believe...

Jesus is truly present at Mass:

- In the gathering of the priest and the people. Jesus said "Whenever two or three of you gather in my name, I am there with you." (Matt 18-20)
- In the Word of God in the Bible.
- In the bread and wine of the Eucharist. The bread and wine becomes the body and blood of Jesus Christ at the consecration of the Mass. Jesus' sacrifice on the cross is made present each time the Eucharist is celebrated.

"Whenever two or three of you gather in my name, I am there with you." (Matt 18-20)

Questions

Knowledge

1. What is a ritual?
2. What rituals are usually part of important events such as birthdays, anniversaries, graduations and weddings?
3. a. When do people participate in religious rituals?
   b. What do religious rituals help people to express?
4. a. What is the Mass?
   b. Explain the origin of the word 'Mass'.
   c. What are the four main parts of the Mass?
5. What is the purpose of the Penitential Rite at Mass?
6. What happens during the Liturgy of the Word?
7. In the Gospel, what does Jesus say about the way in which his followers should treat God and each other?
8. a. Find two examples to show that Mass is a service of thanksgiving.
   b. What did Jesus say and do at the Last Supper?
   c. What happens during the consecration at Mass?
9. a. Why do Catholics act reverently when they go to receive Holy Communion?
   b. How are Catholics expected to 'love and serve the Lord' when they are sent out at the end of Mass?
10. a. List the ways in which Catholics believe the risen Jesus is present at Mass.
    b. What do Catholics believe about the presence of Christ in the Eucharist?

Understanding

1. What important things do you think are expressed through the words and actions of important events such as birthdays, anniversaries, graduations and weddings?
2. a. What is the difference between liturgical and non-liturgical forms of Christian worship?
   b. In what ways would you expect Sunday worship in a Catholic church to be different from Sunday worship in a Methodist church?
3. Mass is an example of an act of worship in which people participate in religious rituals.
   - Why do Catholics go to Mass?
   - What religious rituals do people participate in at Mass?
   - What is the meaning of the rituals for those involved?

Participation

Key Concepts

Participation: being actively involved in an act of worship.

Worship: the way people of faith praise and honour God in prayer and at religious services.

Objective

To participate in/observe an experience of worship to see the elements of worship in action.

Activity: *"Be involved"*

TASK: TO KNOW THE MEANING OF DIFFERENT RITUALS IN WHICH WE HAVE PARTICIPATED.

✦ Examine the list of rituals below.

- Shaking hands when meeting someone.
- Standing to attention for the national anthem.
- Making the sign of the cross.
- Singing 'Happy Birthday to you'.
- Wearing the colours of your favourite team.
- Lighting a candle in front of a statue.
- Cutting the ribbon at the opening of a new building.
- Genuflecting in front of the Blessed Sacrament.
- Getting ashes on the forehead on Ash Wednesday.
- Clapping after a performance.
- Receiving a diploma at graduation.

Discuss

- Have you participated in any of these rituals? Which ones?
- Which of these are:
  a. secular rituals? b. religious rituals?
- What is the meaning of each secular ritual?
- What is being expressed in each religious ritual?

Participation in Worship

Participation in ritual is central to all acts of worship.

Participation in religious rituals means being actively involved in an act of worship with others. Catholics, for example, are encouraged to take a full and active part in the celebration of the Mass.

The Second Vatican Council:

- ❖ Encouraged everyone to take a full and active part in the Mass.
- ❖ Recommended changes in the layout of churches: the altar was moved to the centre of the congregation.
- ❖ Called for a change in the language used in the celebration: the use of Latin was replaced by the language spoken by the people.

Catholics gather in Jesus' name to share in the celebration of the Mass. The Eucharist is a communal celebration. All the changes at Vatican II were introduced to make people conscious and more aware of the communal spirit of the Eucharist.

A congregation attentively watches the presentation of the gifts at a First Holy Communion Mass.

The People of God

The Church, that is the People of God, actively participate in Mass in different ways.

◆ Priest:	The role of the priest is to lead the prayers and perform the ritual of the Eucharist on behalf of the Christian community.
◆ Lay ministers:	Lay people participate by taking on the role of: - Minister of the Word. - Minister of the Eucharist. - Altar server. - Choir member. - Participant in processions. - Usher. - Collector. - Flower arranger. - Sacristan.
◆ Congregation:	Members of the congregation give their full attention but do not have to perform a specific task in the celebration of the Eucharist.

Full participation in the Mass means receiving the Blessed Sacrament in Holy Communion.

The Congregation

The full and active participation of every member of the congregation involves:

❖ Gathering.
Catholics are expected to fast for one hour before receiving Holy Communion. This encourages respect for the sacrament they are about to receive. People are encouraged to arrive in church early for Mass. This allows time for private prayer and reading the missalette before Mass begins.

❖ Listening.
People are expected to listen carefully to the prayers and readings at Mass. This means paying close attention to what the priest is saying. When people listen actively, they open their minds and hearts to the Word of God.

❖ Responding.
People participate in the Mass by what they say. Prayers and responses are spoken by the entire congregation. They recite certain prayers together such as the Gloria, the Creed and the Lord's Prayer. They respond aloud to other prayers such as the Prayers of the Faithful. Joining in the hymn singing is another way of uniting together to worship God.

❖ Gesturing.
People can participate in the Mass by what they do. Certain gestures or ritual actions performed at Mass carry a deep meaning. When people think about the meaning of these gestures and perform them in a conscious way, they are participating in the Mass.

Blessing	- Making the sign of the cross is a public statement of their belief in the Blessed Trinity.
Kneeling	- When people kneel, bow, or genuflect, they are acknowledging the greatness of God.
Standing	- People stand as a sign of respect for the importance of what is taking place.
Shaking hands	- When people shake hands at the sign of peace, it shows their hope that the peace of God will be with each one in the community.

Section E

- ❖ Communion.
  The high point of participation in the Mass is receiving Holy Communion. The priest or the Eucharistic minister offers the host to each person saying 'The body of Christ.' When the person responds 'Amen', it means that he/she believes:
  - Jesus Christ is really present.
  - The body of Christ gives him/her the strength to follow Jesus in daily life.

All baptised Catholics are called to serve God as members of the Christian community. At Mass they gather together to worship God. Active participation in the Mass, as lay ministers or members of the congregation, is a way of honouring and serving God.

Elements of Worship

A collective act of worship in any religion will have certain features. It will involve a gathering of a community of faith in a sacred place, at a sacred time, led by a religious leader. There will be at least one reading from a sacred text, prayers will be said, and sacred rituals will be performed with the full participation of the community. These elements can be observed in Christian acts of worship such as:

- ❖ Sunday Mass and Holy Communion services.
- ❖ Sacraments.
- ❖ Pilgrimages.

For elements of worship in:
Judaism see p235. **Islam** see p290.

ELEMENTS OF WORSHIP

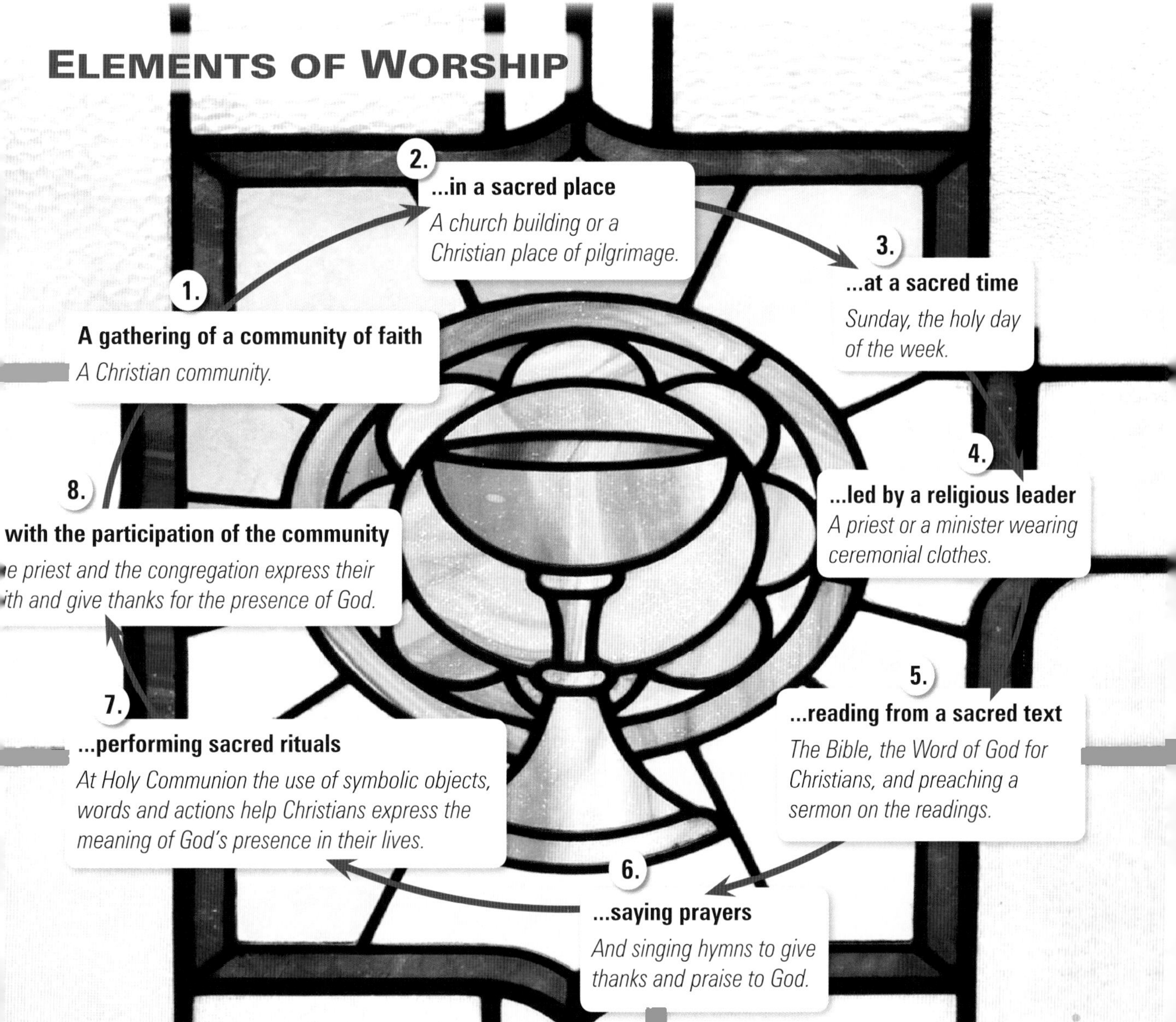
1.
A gathering of a community of faith
A Christian community.
2.
...in a sacred place
A church building or a Christian place of pilgrimage.
3.
...at a sacred time
Sunday, the holy day of the week.
4.
...led by a religious leader
A priest or a minister wearing ceremonial clothes.
5.
...reading from a sacred text
The Bible, the Word of God for Christians, and preaching a sermon on the readings.
6.
...saying prayers
And singing hymns to give thanks and praise to God.
7.
...performing sacred rituals
At Holy Communion the use of symbolic objects, words and actions help Christians express the meaning of God's presence in their lives.
8.
with the participation of the community
e priest and the congregation express their
ith and give thanks for the presence of God.

Questions

Knowledge

1. What does it mean to participate in an act of worship?
2. 'The Mass is a communal celebration.' What does this statement mean?
3. a. What is the role of the priest at Mass?
   b. What is the role of the minister of the Word and the Eucharistic ministers at Mass?
4. List the ways in which members of the congregation can actively participate in the Mass.
5. What effect should the Eucharist have on Catholics in their daily lives?
6. List the key elements of collective worship in all religions.
7. What are the key elements of collective worship at Mass in the Catholic Church?
8. What are the key elements of collective worship in one other Christian Church?

Understanding

1. How do baptised lay people participate in the celebration of the Mass?
2. What religious beliefs do Catholics express by participating in the rituals of the Mass?
3. Why do you think all Christian worship includes at least:
   - One period of prayer?
   - One reading from a sacred text?

Research

- Identify the key elements of worship in one other major world religion.
  - Create a diagram listing all the elements of worship under the relevant headings 1-8.
  - Outline the main similarities and differences in the way Christians and members of this other religion worship God or their gods.
  - Discuss any points raised in this exercise.

Activity

- See the elements of worship in action.

  Describe either a liturgical or non-liturgical church service:

  a. in which you have participated and experienced the elements of worship in action.

  OR

  b. which you have observed and seen the elements of worship in action.

Answer the following questions to guide your response.

1. What is the place of worship?
2. What day of the week is the religious service taking place?
3. Is it a special occasion?
4. Who has gathered to worship?
5. Who leads the act of worship?
6. Is any item of ceremonial clothing being worn?
7. What sacred text is being used?
8. Is any kind of music performed as part of the act of worship?
9. a. List two ritual actions being performed during the service.
   b. Who performs these actions?
   c. What is the meaning behind these actions?
10. a. What was the most memorable part of the service you just observed, or in which you participated?
    b. Can you say why this aspect of the service made an impression on you?

Mystery

Key Concepts

Encountering mystery: connecting with something mysterious that is beyond human understanding.

Reflection: thinking deeply about some aspect of life.

Wonder: a feeling inspired by some mysterious aspect of life.

Objective

Show an awareness of the impact of mystery in human life.

Activity: *"Listening Exercise"*

TASK: TO DEVELOP THE ABILITY TO LISTEN AND BE AWARE OF WHAT IS HAPPENING AROUND US.

Directions

- ✦ Direct students to be *quiet and still* for a few minutes, and to close their eyes or look down.
- ✦ When everyone is settled invite them to take time to listen to:
  - the *sounds of their own body.* (i.e. their breathing.)
  - the *sounds inside the room.* (i.e. the breathing of others, window or door rattling, creaking of furniture, shuffling of feet, etc.)
  - the *sounds outside the room.* (i.e. the sounds outside the window, next door, in the corridor, etc.)
- ✦ Direct students to slowly turn their attention back to the room.
- ✦ Close the exercise.

Discuss

- What kind of things did you hear around you during the exercise?
- What does it feel like to be quiet and still?
- What are the benefits of taking time to be silent? Does it help us to be more aware of things?

Encountering Mystery

When we are quiet and still we become more aware of the sense of mystery at the heart of life.

The word mystery refers to something that is beyond human knowledge. It is something real, but with a meaning so deep the human mind cannot fully understand it. God is a mystery. Christians believe it is possible to encounter the mystery of God within human experience. If people are attentive to what is happening in their lives, they can become aware of the mysterious presence of God.

Prayerful reflection.

Section E

Reflection

Reflection involves taking time to think deeply about some aspect of life. Christians believe in:

- ❖ The invisible presence of God in the world.
- ❖ The Incarnation, that is the Christian teaching that God became human in Jesus Christ.

For Catholic Christians these beliefs mean God's loving presence is everywhere, if people have the eyes to see. It is their belief that God tries to reach us through the people, events and ordinary things we experience every day. When people of faith stop to reflect on life, they can see how God is present among the people they meet and in the world of nature around them. God is also present in a special way in the rituals of the sacraments in which they participate.

God's presence among people.

✱ God is present ***among people*** in:

- ✱ the innocence of a child.
- ✱ a kind or thoughtful gesture.
- ✱ a close conversation with a friend.
- ✱ being able to say sorry when we are wrong.
- ✱ a smile of acknowledgement.
- ✱ coping with a loss or a failure.
- ✱ a hug from a friend.
- ✱ sharing a meal with those we love.

The world of nature is full of God's presence.

✱ God is present ***in nature*** in:

- ✱ the beauty of a sunset.
- ✱ the sound of the sea.
- ✱ the smell of freshly cut grass.
- ✱ the first flowers of Spring.
- ✱ the faithfulness of a pet.
- ✱ the warmth of sunshine.
- ✱ the sight of new lambs.
- ✱ the silence of falling snow.

God is present ***in the sacraments.***

The sacrament of Baptism.

The sacrament of the Eucharist.

People encounter mystery in the company of each other, in the world of nature and on ritual occasions such as the sacraments. For a person of faith, these are graced moments when the love of God touches their life.

Wonder

To be filled with wonder is to be filled with awe and amazement at some mysterious aspect of life. Religion arose out of people's deep sense of wonder at the mystery of the world around them. From earliest times, people were in awe of the movement of the sun and moon, the changing of the seasons, and the cycle of birth, life and death. They struggled to find an explanation for these mysterious events. This is how religion most likely began.

Mystery

The word 'mystery' refers to something that is beyond human understanding. Encountering mystery is to experience something so deep and profound that the human mind cannot fully grasp it. Our early ancestors experienced life as deeply mysterious.

At first, the ancients believed the sun and the moon had special powers that were somehow able to affect nature and life on earth. They looked at the sun and the moon and regarded them as gods.

Then the ancients' understanding changed. They began to believe that behind the sun and the moon were much higher powers which controlled even these forces of nature. There were unseen powers living in an invisible spirit-world beyond the physical world. Ancient peoples were probably polytheists - believing in many different, unseen gods.

In time, people's ideas about the spirit world developed yet again. Some came to believe that the great power or spirit of the unseen world is one God only. This was the basis of the monotheistic belief of Judaism, and later of Christianity and Islam.

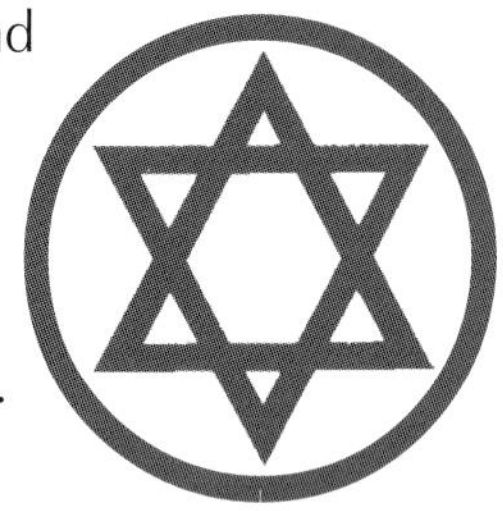

The Jews came to understand that the power behind the universe is a personal God, not an impersonal force. God revealed himself to be good as well as powerful.

Thousands of years later Christians came to believe that the one God so loved the world that, in Jesus, God became human. Jesus lived and died on Earth and rose again. Jesus bridged the great distance between God and human beings. He helped people to understand that God is not far away in a distant place. God is near. Christians believe God's caring presence is with each person in the world today.

Stonehenge - England.

Newgrange in Co. Meath is one of the most impressive Stone Age passage tombs in Europe. It was built about 5,000 years ago by people who seemed to consider the sun to be a god. Newgrange appears to have been designed as an observatory to capture the movement of the sun on the shortest day of the year, the winter solstice, on 21st December. Archaeologists believe that this monument and the stone circles in Stonehenge in Britain were used to calculate the movement of the sun, moon and stars.

Newgrange - Ireland.

Encountering mystery.

The Spiritual World

Human beings since the dawn of time have experienced a mysterious dimension to life, and have sought to understand what it means. They have responded to mystery with acts of worship and sacrifice.

People of religious faith believe there is more to life than the physical world. They find meaning and purpose in their lives through belief in something extra beyond the physical world. This something is just as real as anything they can see and touch. For some it is even more real than the physical world. It is the absolute or ultimate reality, it is a spiritual reality.

People communicate with the spiritual world through prayerful acts of worship. God cannot be seen and is even harder to describe, but for a person of faith God's presence is everywhere.

Questions

Knowledge

1. 'Mystery.' What does the word mean?
2. How is God a mystery?
3. What is the Incarnation?
4. What does it mean to reflect on something?
5. How do Christians benefit when they take time for reflection on life?
6. What kind of experiences might prompt you to reflect on the mystery of life?
7. What things filled ancient people with awe and wonder about life?
8. What did our early ancestors believe about the sun and the moon?
9. How did people's religious ideas develop after the period of sun and moon worship?
10. List the religious beliefs that distinguished the early Jews from all other people at that time.
11. What is distinctive about the religious belief and practice of Christians?
12. How have people responded, throughout the ages, to the mysterious dimension of life?

Understanding

1. Do you think we need to take time for reflection on life? Why? Why not?
2. Explain how the doctrine of the Incarnation affects the way Catholics think about the presence of God in their lives.
3. Explain how our early ancestors' understanding of the mysterious dimension of life evolved or developed over time.

Research

- Find out about the kind of experiences that fill your peers with awe and wonder about life.
  - Do such experiences prompt people to stop and reflect on the mystery of life.
  - With permission, describe one person's experience and how it caused him/her to reflect on life.

Response to Mystery

Key Concepts

Worship as a response to mystery: people responding to mystery by gathering together to perform acts of worship.

Encounter with God: connecting with the mysterious presence of God in acts of worship.

Celebration: a religious ceremony performed in public for a community of faith.

Objective

Identify participation in worship as a response to encounters with mystery.

Activity: *"Experience of God"*

TASK: TO ACKNOWLEDGE SOMEONE'S PERSONAL ACCOUNT OF THEIR EXPERIENCE OF GOD.

"The first time we could see the whole Earth we saw it as a ball in the sky. It was about the size of a basketball and the most beautiful thing you could ever want to see in all your life. Then as we got farther and farther away, it diminished in size. We saw it shrink to the size of a baseball, and then to the size of a golf ball, and finally to the size of a marble, the most beautiful marble you can imagine. The Earth is uncommonly lovely. It is the only warm object that we saw on our flight to the moon.......

On the moon the total picture of the power of God and his Son Jesus Christ became abundantly clear to me. I felt an overwhelming sense of the presence of God..... I felt his spirit..... right there beside me..... it was amazing."

Adapted from Jim Irwin 'To Rule the Night'.

Discuss

- How was the author affected by what he saw on his space flight to the moon?
- Have you ever had an experience that made you think about the mystery of life. Maybe it was something to do with nature, travel, art, birth, death, illness, music or sport.
- Were you ever moved to express how you felt at special moments such as these?

Worship as a response to mystery

Worship expresses the belief that God is at work in the world of nature and in the lives of human beings.

When people encounter mystery, they respond by gathering together to perform acts of worship.

Down the ages human beings:

- became aware of powers greater than themselves.
- acknowledged their dependence on such powers.
- sought to connect with such powers.

A dolmen:
the site of an ancient Celtic burial ground.

The Celts

In Ireland, the Celts are an example of a people who had a religious response to the mystery of the world around them. The Celts came to Ireland and parts of Britain around 500BCE. They were an agricultural people, and skilled metal workers, who depended on animal rearing and crop growing for their livelihood. They cleared vast tracts of forests and lived in scattered homesteads up and down the land. Their daily life revolved around the natural world and the pattern of the seasons.

The Celts believed in an otherworld of gods and goddesses. Moon and sun worship was also part of their belief system. Small communities gathered together in woodland groves, on hilltops, and beside rivers and wells, to honour the forces of nature. The Celts, by worshipping in sacred places, actively sought to communicate with powers greater than themselves.

The Celtic Year

People in Ireland and Britain not only enjoy long summer days, but also endure long winter nights. The coming and going of sunlight has always been important to people living in this part of the world. The Celts counted time from the cycle of dark to light. They looked on the year as having two parts:

- the dark half (Winter/Spring).
- the light half (Summer/Autumn).

The movement of the sun was marked by the solstice.

❖ The winter solstice, the shortest day of the year, occurs on 21st December.

❖ The summer solstice, the longest day of the year, occurs on 21st June.

The Celtic year began with the return of the sun. The winter solstice on 21st December was the turn of the year; the days start getting longer from then on. The sun begins to regain its strength, and darkness is left behind. The Celts were in awe at the wonder of night following day and the cycle of the seasons. The sun's energy would ripen new crops and ensure a good harvest. This guaranteed the survival of the people and their animals. The Celts responded to the mystery of the sun by holding a festival with various forms of worship. The annual sun festival celebrated the passage of darkness to light.

The Christian Year

The Christian festival of Christmas takes place at the darkest time of the year. Christians gather in churches to celebrate the birth of Jesus as the light coming into the world. Jesus referred to himself as the 'light of the world'.

> "I am the light of the world," he said. "Whoever follows me will have the light of life and will never walk in darkness." John 8:12

No one knows exactly when Jesus was born; the date of the 25th of December was fixed by the Emperor Constantine in the fifth century. The date was set to coincide with the pre-Christian festival devoted to the worship of the sun. Christians took over this ancient festival and gave it a new meaning. Instead of celebrating the return of the sun, the Christian festival celebrates the coming of the Son of God as the light of the world. Jesus is the light that overcomes the darkness in the world, and in people's hearts.

The transition from pre-Christian to Christian worship is reflected in the design of the Celtic Cross:

- the circle represents the sun.
- the cross represents the Son of God, the light of the world.

A Celtic cross.

Celebrating the passage of darkness to light.

Participation in worship as a response to mystery

The Celts responded to the mystery of the world around them with acts of worship.

The Celts

Believed in:	• The sun and moon as gods and in an 'otherworld' of invisible gods and goddesses.
Gathered in sacred places:	• Woodland groves, hilltops, beside rivers and wells.
Gathered at sacred times:	• The winter solstice, the shortest day of the year. • The summer solstice, the longest day of the year.
Were led by a religious leader:	• A druid.
Participated in sacred rituals:	• The sun festival, when offerings were made to the gods to celebrate the passage of darkness to light.

Encounter with God

Today people of faith, Christians for example, communicate with the mysterious and invisible presence of God through acts of worship.

Christians

Believe in:	• The invisible presence of God, and that God became human in Jesus Christ.
Gather in sacred places:	• Churches and places of pilgrimage.
Gather at sacred times:	• On Sunday, the holy day of the week. • At Christmas, the Christian festival of thanksgiving celebrating the birth of Jesus Christ. • At Easter, the Christian festival celebrating the Pascal Mystery. • At other times in the Liturgical Year.
Are led by a religious leader:	• A priest or a minister.
Participate in sacred rituals:	• In the sacrament of the Eucharist - a service of thanksgiving. • In the other sacraments e.g. baptism at birth, anointing of the sick at death. • On pilgrimage.

Celebration

A celebration is a religious ceremony performed in public for a community of faith. The Eucharist is a religious celebration. It is the central act of worship for many in the Christian community of faith.

Celebrating the Eucharist in a Catholic church.

The Mass

For Catholic Christians, the words and actions of Jesus at the Last Supper are remembered and made present at the Sacrament of the Eucharist. The Eucharist is a prayerful act of thanksgiving for God's presence in the world. Participation in worship is the way Christians respond to the mystery of God's presence in their lives.

Questions

Knowledge

1. How did ancient peoples respond to mystery in life?
2. Who were the Celts?
3. Where did the Celts gather for worship?
4. At what times during the year did the Celts have special religious celebrations?
5. Give reasons why Christians came to celebrate the birth of Jesus on 25th December.
6. Where, and at what sacred times, do Christians gather for worship throughout the year?
7. What is the purpose of sacred rituals in the Christian tradition?
8. What is the principal act of worship for many Christians?

Understanding

1. Why did the Celts gather to honour the sun in their religious celebrations?
2. Explain why the winter solstice is a good time to celebrate the Christian festival of Christmas.
3. Why did people from earliest times down to the present day feel the need to participate in acts of worship?
   OR
   'Worship is a response to mystery.'
   Explain the meaning of this statement.

Research

- Find out about any one of the following festivals of the Celtic year.
  - Samhain.
  - Imbolc.
  - Bealtaine.
  - Lughnasa.
  - When did the festival take place?
  - What did it celebrate?
  - How was it transformed into a Christian event or practice in early Christian Ireland?
  - Share the results of your research with the class.

Section E

Sign and Symbol

Key Concepts

Sign: something that communicates a brief message or a piece of information.

Symbol: something visible, i.e. an object or action, representing something invisible that is difficult to put into words.

Objective

Outline the place of sign and symbol in everyday life.

Activity: *"Charades"*

TASK: TO COMMUNICATE USING SIGNS.

- ✦ Briefly discuss the procedure involved in the well known game of charades. Offer the title of a popular film, book or television programme to a volunteer who will mime it for the class.
- ✦ Establish signs to indicate whether the title refers to a film, book or a television programme.
- ✦ The class will try to identify what is being mimed. The first to identify the title correctly is the winner.

Discuss

- Was it easy or difficult to know what was being mimed?
- What signs were the easiest to understand?
- What signs are generally used to communicate the following messages?

  'Look at that.'

  'Silence.'

  'Wait here.'

  'Come back.'

  'Follow me.'

  'Don't know.'

  'What time is it?'

  'Well done.'

  'Hello.'

Sign

Signs and symbols are frequently used to communicate important messages.

The spoken and written word are the most common forms of communication, yet they are often supplemented with the language of sign and symbol.

A sign is something that communicates a brief message or a piece of information. A sign can be a word, a picture, an object or an action. A specific sign gives the same message to everyone. We see signs every day, road signs on the way to school, signs on shop-fronts in towns and villages, wiring instructions on electrical goods, laundry labels on our clothes. A sign gives a clear, quick message that can be easily understood.

✦ Examine the following signs from everyday life.
  a. What does each one communicate?
  b. Check that everyone agrees the meaning of each sign.

1.
2.
3.
4.
5.
6.
7.
8.
9.

Section E

The Function of Signs

The sole purpose of a sign is to pass on a short, clear message that is easily understood by everyone. Many signs are international and can be understood by people even when they cannot speak the language. Think of all the signs to be seen at bus stations, railway stations and airports. People see the signs and immediately recognise what they mean. The most successful signs are those that communicate a brief message that is easily understood. People glance at a sign, decide whether or not to act on the information and then move on thinking no more about it.

A sign does not affect us in any significant way. It merely offers a simple message that has the same meaning for everyone. It is precisely these characteristics that distinguish a sign from a symbol.

Symbol

Symbols are more powerful than signs, they touch people at a deeper level. A symbol is something visible, i.e. an object or action, which represents something invisible that is difficult to put into words. Symbols are powerful and touch us deeply. They can actually affect the way we think and feel. We respond to symbols not only with the head, but with the heart as well.

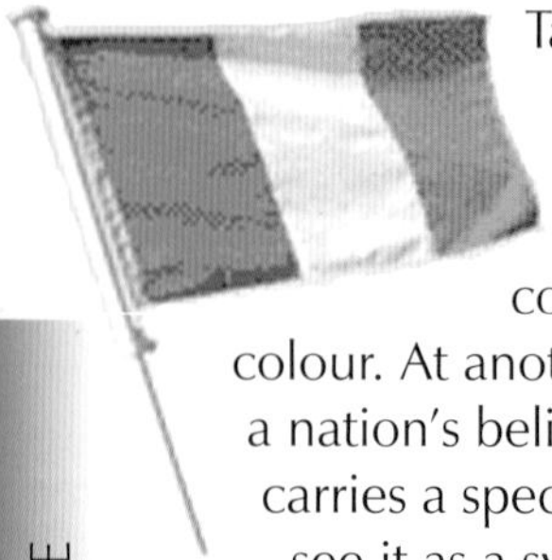

Take a national flag for example. On the surface it is a piece of material decorated with a combination of design and colour. At another level, it tells the story of a nation's beliefs and dreams. The flag carries a special meaning when citizens see it as a symbol of their national identity. It can generate a sense of pride, respect, loyalty and patriotic fervour. As a national symbol it has the capacity to tap into deep emotional responses that no words can express.

A national flag and a national anthem are symbols of a country's identity. A citizen, by acknowledging the flag, and standing for the national anthem, conveys feelings of pride, respect and loyalty that are beyond words.

The Function of Symbols

A symbol can express feelings or ideas that are not always easy to communicate. Deep feelings like loyalty, respect, love, joy or grief are sometimes difficult to express in words alone.

Wedding rings.

When a couple are in love, they can talk endlessly about their feelings for one another, yet their deepest feelings will be expressed in a kiss or the exchange of rings.

When a baby is born, family members can be speechless with delight. They express their joy by going to see the child and bringing cards and gifts. Similarly, when a person dies, it can be hard to find the right words to say how we feel. The depth of our grief is expressed in an embrace, in shared moments of silence, in the lighting of candles, and in laying down offerings of flowers. The purpose of symbols is to give people a way of communicating feelings and ideas when words alone are not enough.

Grieving at a candle-light vigil.

Symbolic objects such as wedding rings, floral wreaths, lighted candles, cards and gifts, and symbolic actions such as a kiss, an embrace or a moment of silence, all express powerful emotions that words alone cannot capture.

Natural Symbols

Symbols have two aspects, one visible, the other hidden or invisible. A symbol is something we can see which helps us to imagine something else that we cannot see.

When we see or think about something tangible from nature such as a rock, for example, it can 'speak' to us about such abstract ideas as reliability, strength, solidity, permanence and endurance. Symbols go beyond the obvious. They have layers and layers of meaning. A rock can be a symbol when it stands for something else.

High up on a rocky outcrop.

The word 'symbol' comes from the Greek 'symballein' which means 'to bring together'. Every symbol brings together something visible (that we can see) and something abstract or invisible (that we cannot see but that is real). Symbols have hidden meanings. Think about other natural elements such as water, food or fire. They too are often used as symbols. Their hidden meanings are recognised by people everywhere.

Questions

Knowledge

1. What is a sign? Give three supporting examples.
2. What is the value or purpose of having signs?
3. What is a symbol? Give two supporting examples.
4. What meaning is conveyed by:
   a. Wearing a wedding ring?
   b. Standing for the national anthem?
   c. Lighting candles at a vigil.
5. Give an example to show how symbols, such as a wedding ring and a national flag, can affect people deeply.
6. a. Give three examples of natural symbols.
   b. What meanings are associated with one of these symbols?
   c. What is it about a natural object that gives it the ability to convey certain meanings to us?

Understanding

1. Why are signs an important means of communication?
2. Why do people use symbols?
3. How is a symbol different to a sign?
4. How is it that symbols are able to communicate things that words frequently cannot?

Research

- Find out more about the use of natural symbols.
- What meanings do you associate with the following: water, food, light/fire?

The Symbol *Visible object* *(what you see)*	The meaning behind the symbol *Invisible reality* *(what the symbol stands for)*
Water:	
Food:	
Light/Fire:	

- Make a list of the thoughts and feelings that are often connected with these symbols.
- Discuss your ideas with the class.

Religious Symbols

Key Concept

Symbol: something visible, i.e. an object or action, representing something invisible that is difficult to put into words.

Objective

Describe the power and meaning of religious symbols.

Activity: *"Symbols"*

TASK: TO IDENTIFY VARIOUS RELIGIOUS SYMBOLS IN A CATHOLIC CHURCH.

Walk into a sacred place such as a Catholic church and you will be surrounded by religious symbols. Imagine two friends decide to visit their local parish church on their way home one afternoon. They push open the heavy entrance door and then bless themselves with holy water from a font in the porch.

Once inside the church, they look toward the altar with the tabernacle and the sanctuary lamp flickering beside it. They genuflect slowly and reverently before going to kneel in front of a statue of Our Lady. Making the sign of the cross they join their hands in prayer.

After several minutes they light some candles. Before turning to leave they glance at the crucifix suspended above the altar, it catches the light from the stained glass window nearby.

They both know they will be back again sometime soon.

Discuss

- What religious symbols can be seen inside a Catholic church?
- What symbolic gestures or actions are used when Catholics go into a church to pray?
- Can you explain the meaning of:
  a. each symbolic object?
  b. each symbolic action?

Symbol

Religious symbols are plentiful in sacred places.

The world of the sacred is an invisible reality. God is invisible, yet is very real for people of faith. People use the language of symbol when they want to communicate with God. The experience is so special that ordinary language, by itself, cannot fully express everything that needs to be said. Christians therefore communicate with God through symbols.

Kneeling to pray and light candles before a statue in a Catholic church. A statue is not an object of worship in itself, but a reminder of how to follow Jesus.

A religious symbol is an object or action that helps people express their religious beliefs. Religious symbols bring together:

- Something visible that can be seen, *and*
- Something invisible that cannot be seen, but which is real.

Symbolic actions and symbolic objects are frequently used in Christian prayer and acts of worship.

Religious symbols

Natural elements such as:

- Water
- Fire/Light
- Food

are used as religious symbols in the rituals of many of the great world religions. Although these natural elements are commonly used, they have a different meaning within each religion.

Take water for example. All life depends on water for its very existence. The life-giving properties of water make it a powerful religious symbol. In Christianity water is used at the sacrament of Baptism, an initiation ceremony into the Christian faith. Water symbolises the start of a new life as a follower of Jesus.

The Sacraments

The most important symbols of the Catholic Church are the seven sacraments. A sacrament is the experience of God's presence made visible in a person's life. It can be difficult to explain or describe such sacred moments, words are simply not enough. The various symbols used in the sacraments convey a depth of meaning that goes beyond mere words.

The Cross

The cross is the most widely recognised symbol of Christianity; it is the central symbol of the Christian faith. A cross is found in almost every Christian place of worship. Christians believe that Jesus, the Son of God, was put to death on the cross. He was buried, and rose again from the dead. The crucifixion and the resurrection are the central events in the Christian faith. The cross is a symbol of these major Christian beliefs.

2 0
1 2

The Pascal candle

The Pascal candle is the great Christian symbol of Easter. It is a special candle representing the risen Jesus, the light of the world. The Pascal candle is lit at the Easter Vigil to celebrate the resurrection of Jesus Christ.

The Pascal candle has several distinctive features and each one has a special meaning. The cross in the centre represents the crucifixion of Jesus. The brass markers around the cross represent the wounds on Jesus' body, the crown of thorns, the nails in his hands and feet, and the spear that pierced his side. The letters Alpha (A) and Omega (Ω), the first and last letters of the Greek alphabet, represent Jesus as the beginning and end of all things. The date on the candle shows that Jesus is Lord of all time.

The Christian symbol of the cross.

The Power and Meaning of Religious Symbols

The power and meaning of religious symbols is evident, for example, in the Easter Vigil. This Christian ceremony is held on Holy Saturday night to celebrate the resurrection of Jesus. There are several stages in the Easter Vigil, most of which are symbolic. Symbolic words and actions express a deep spiritual reality at the heart of the Christian faith. It is the Pascal Mystery that Jesus died, rose from the dead, and will come again at the end of time.

The Easter Vigil in Roman Catholic, Anglican and Orthodox churches takes place after dark. Natural elements such as fire/light, water and food take on religious significance at the Easter Vigil.

Important features of the ceremony include:

- Lighting the Easter fire.
- Lighting the Pascal Candle.
- Pouring the water of Baptism.
- Sharing the gifts of bread and wine in the Eucharist.

The Easter Vigil

The Service of Light

- ❖ All the lights in the church are put out and the service begins in darkness. This darkness symbolizes death and Jesus lying in the tomb.
- ❖ A fire is lit outside the church. It represents the moment of resurrection: Jesus is risen.
- ❖ The priest lights the Pascal candle from the Easter fire. The candle will be used at baptisms and funerals throughout the year. It is a symbol of the risen Christ, the light of the world.
- ❖ The Pascal candle is brought in procession into the darkened church. As it is carried toward the altar the congregation light their own individual candles from it, and pass the light along to those near them. The passing of the light symbolises the spreading of the Good News of Jesus' resurrection to all parts of the world.
- ❖ The Pascal Candle is placed on a high stand near the altar. It will be lit at every liturgy over the following fifty days of the Easter season.
- ❖ The congregation stand to hear the 'Easter proclamation.' This joyful hymn gives praise and thanks to God for the resurrection of Jesus Christ.

Liturgy of the Word

- ❖ Readings from scripture tell of God's saving action on behalf of the People of God. Everyone listens to the accounts of God's love and care down through the ages, from the time of Abraham in the Old Testament, to the resurrection of Jesus Christ in the New Testament.

Liturgy of Baptism.

- ❖ The water of baptism is blessed. Water symbolises life. The congregation renew, or re-make, the promises made at their own baptism. In the early Church, baptisms always took place at Easter. Christians believe that the water of baptism symbolises the beginning of a new life in Jesus. That is why Christians remind themselves of their baptismal promises at Easter. The renewal of baptismal promises unites the Christian community. Everyone states their Christian beliefs. They promise to say 'no' to sin and 'yes' to new life as followers of Jesus Christ.

Liturgy of the Eucharist

- The priest and the congregation give thanks to God for the sacrifice Jesus made for the sake of all. They offer gifts of bread and wine. They bow their heads to acknowledge his suffering and death.

  They say prayers and sing hymns of joy to celebrate his resurrection. They gather around the altar to receive the body and blood of the risen Jesus in Holy Communion.

- Easter bells ring out. The church is adorned in fresh flowers, candlelight and colourful banners. The priest wears white and gold vestments. The choir joyfully sing Glorias and Alleluias. These, together with the Easter fire, the Pascal candle, the water of Baptism, and the celebration of the Eucharist, symbolise the reality of the Pascal Mystery. For Christians, the meaning is clear:

  'Christ has died,
  Christ is risen,
  Christ will come again.'

For details of religious symbols in:
Judaism see p246. In **Islam** the use of symbols in acts of worship is less common.

Easter liturgies celebrate Jesus, the "Light of the World".

Questions

Knowledge

1. What are religious symbols?
2. What is the purpose of religious symbols?
3. What natural elements tend to be used in the rituals of many world religions?
4. a. Why is water often used as a religious symbol?
   b. How is water used as a symbol in the Christian sacrament of Baptism?
5. a. List three symbolic objects you would expect to see in a Catholic church.
   b. What religious meaning do you think these symbols have for members of the Catholic community?
6. What religious beliefs are expressed in the following Christian symbols:
   a. The cross?
   b. The Pascal Candle?
7. What natural elements are used as religious symbols at the Easter Vigil?
8. a. What do Christians celebrate at Easter?
   b. What do the symbols of darkness and light represent at the Easter Vigil?

Understanding

1. Why do religions make use of symbols in acts of worship?
2. How do religious symbols help people express their religious beliefs?
3. Describe how symbolic objects and actions are used to communicate religious beliefs in one Christian ceremony.

Research

- Find out about the first Pascal Fire lit by St. Patrick in 5th century Ireland.
  - Who was St. Patrick?
  - Where did he light the fire?
  - What Christian event was he celebrating?
  - What did the symbolic fire represent?
  - Who objected to his action?
  - Why was there a major objection to Patrick's action?
  - What was the outcome for all concerned?
  - Present an account of your findings to the class.

Icons

Key Concept

Icon: a sacred image used as an aid to prayer, mainly in the Orthodox Churches.

Objective

Describe the power and meaning of religious symbols in the Orthodox tradition.

Activity: *"Art Appreciation"*

TASK: TO EXAMINE AN ICON.

✦ Look at the icon closely and reflectively, then answer the questions.

Discuss

1. Who is in this icon? How do you know?
2. Is the child (☑):
   - ❐ leaning against the woman looking content?
   - ❐ leaning forward and looking worried?
   - ❐ sitting up looking sure of himself?
3. What do you notice about the face of the mother and the child?
4. Where is the woman's gaze directed?
5. Describe the relationship between the two figures in the icon.
6. What are the different colours used in this icon?
7. Are the figures in the icon painted in (☑):
   - ❐ a style that is flat and one-dimensional?
   - ❐ a style that is varied and multi-dimensional?
8. Are the figures in the icon(☑):
   - ❐ lively and full of energy?
   - ❐ quiet and peaceful?
9. Do the figures in the icon(☑):
   - ❐ look real and life-like?
   - ❐ look unreal and mysterious?
10. The icon has a message. What do you think it might be?

ΘΥ
IC XC

A religious icon.

Icon

Icons are religious symbols.

Icons are sacred images of Jesus, Mary and the saints. They have an important place in worship in the Orthodox Churches. In recent years the use of icons has become more evident in the Roman Catholic Church, and in some Anglican Churches as well.

An icon is not meant to be a life-like portrait of a sacred person. Icons are a particular type of religious painting, very different from other works of art. Indeed they may appear strange or unusual to people who are unfamiliar with them.

An icon is a religions symbol and points to another reality beyond itself. Orthodox Christians use icons to help them communicate with the world of the sacred.

For Orthodox Christians, looking at icons of Jesus, Mary, or one of the saints is to see something of the 'Kingdom of Heaven' made visible. This is because each icon is believed to be filled with the spirit of the person whose image it represents. As such, icons are regarded as sacred and are treated with great respect. Although Orthodox Christians treat icons with the greatest respect, they do not pray to them. The icons are a means of helping the person to focus their prayer and attention on God.

Praying in front of icons

When people enter an Orthodox church they buy a candle and light it before an icon. They make the sign of the cross and kiss the icon as a mark of respect. They then stand and gaze at the icon in prayerful silence. The image helps the person to focus their mind and heart on the presence of God.

Icons direct prayerful attention to the presence of God.

When a person prays before an icon, he/she becomes quiet and still in response to the stillness of the image before them. The image slowly draws the person into its world. An Orthodox Christian describes it like this: "We gaze at the eyes in the face of the icon. We believe the eye of the icon is like the eye of God. God gently reaches out and draws us near. God reaches right into our hearts. The icon brings us closer to God."

An iconographer at work.

The Iconographer

Artists who create icons are called iconographers. Painting icons is a spiritual activity and iconographers believe that the inspiration for their work comes from God. Before painting an icon, the artist will spend time in prayer and meditation, go to confession and receive Holy Communion. Icons are symbolic paintings that have layers of meaning. Iconographers are not free to paint what they like, they must follow certain rules laid down by tradition. The aim of their work is to capture the spiritual nature of the person they are painting.

Creating an icon

All icons are painted on wood in a distinctive style. The artist will distort or exaggerate certain features so that some parts are enlarged and some parts reduced. The eyes, for example, tend to be bigger and wider than normal. This suggests that they see beyond this earthly world to another reality. The rest of the face has a somewhat noble aspect. The nose is long and narrow, the mouth is small and the lips are closed. The head and rest of the body is elongated. The hands are important too. Hands are presented as long and thin and may be holding something, pointing towards something, or raised in a blessing. All the details are designed to convey important religious truths.

Everything about an icon has a special meaning, including the use of certain colours. Gold and silver represent holiness and the power of God. Blue represents heaven. Red represents royalty, and white represents the presence of God.

While we can easily recognise the figure in an icon, it is somehow not very real or lifelike. The body is perfectly still and there is no suggestion of movement. The figure is simply present. The image communicates a mysterious stillness, a perfect peace. The deep border around the edge of the image symbolises the connection between the human world and the spiritual world of the icon.

The Iconostasis

Many things in an Orthodox church have a symbolic meaning. The most distinctive feature inside a church is the iconostasis. This is a solid screen, in front of the altar, which divides the church in two. The iconostasis separates the sanctuary from the area in front where the congregation gathers for worship. The iconostasis symbolises the separation between the world of heaven and earth.

The iconostasis inside an Orthodox church.

The word 'iconostasis' means 'the place of the icons or pictures', and it is usually decorated with important icons. There is an icon of Jesus and one of Mary, the mother of God. The icon of the church's patron saint and some other saints cover the remainder of the screen. The 'Royal Doors' are in the centre. They are opened during Divine Liturgy to reveal the altar and the sanctuary beyond.

Icons cover the walls and pillars inside the church. Some are placed on special stands inside the entrance and in the worshipping space in the middle of the church. Ornate oil lamps often hang in front of the icons.

On Sunday morning, during Divine Liturgy, the doors of the iconostasis are opened after the prayer of thanksgiving at the consecration. The priest walks through from the sanctuary into the body of the church symbolically bringing heaven closer to earth. He distributes the bread and wine of Holy Communion to each member of the congregation assembled in the church.

Questions

Knowledge

1. What is an icon?
2. What is the purpose of icons in the Orthodox Churches?
3. How do Orthodox Christians pray in front of an icon?
4. Who paints religious icons?
5. What preparations do icon artists make before painting an icon?
6. What techniques do iconographers use to capture the spiritual nature of the person they are painting?
7. What is an iconostasis?
8. What is done to show that icons are an important part of the interior of Orthodox churches?

Understanding

1. Why are icons referred to as religious symbols?
2. How are icons different to other types of religious art?
3. Why do you think iconographers regard their work as sacred?
4. Explain the meaning or significance of icons for members of the Orthodox Churches.

Research

- Find out about one of the most famous icons - the Rublev Icon.
  - What is the full name and nationality of the iconographer?
  - When was the icon created?
  - What sacred image is on the icon?
  - Which story in the Bible was the inspiration for this icon?
  - Why is the icon also referred to as the Holy Trinity icon?
  - What Christian teaching or message is contained in this icon?
  - Compile a report with this and any additional information and present it to the class.

Sacraments

Key Concept

Sacrament: a sacred ritual that is a visible sign of God's presence with people at key moments in their lives.

Objective

Outline the Christian understanding of sacrament.

Activity: *"Love is everything"*

TASK: TO BE AWARE OF HOW WE COMMUNICATE A MESSAGE OF LOVE.

The most important message any person can communicate is the message of love.

- Love is real.
- We can experience it.
- We know what it is.
- Yet, love is invisible.

Love exists, but it is not a physical reality. We cannot see it, hear it or touch it. We cannot break a bit off and give it to someone like we would divide up and share a bar of chocolate.

✦ So how do we communicate our love to another person? We might:

- Send a card.
- Bring flowers.
- Give a present.
- Share a hug or a kiss.
- Spend time with him/her.
- Help him/her in any way we can.

There are many ways in which people can express their love. Yet this is not the same as love itself. We show our love through what we say, what we do, and the things we give to one another. These are all symbols of our love. We communicate an invisible reality such as love, through a series of visible symbols. These symbols might be words, actions or carefully chosen gifts.

Discuss

- How do parents show their love for a child?
- Love is invisible, how do we know that it is real?
- How can offering a gift to someone communicate the fact that we love them and care about them?

Sacrament

The love of God is communicated to people through the sacraments.

Christians believe in the invisible and mysterious presence of God in their lives. Before his ascension into heaven Jesus promised his apostles that he would never leave them.

'I will be with you always' Matthew 28:20.

Christians believe that Jesus kept his promise. The risen Jesus is present in the world today. Many Christians believe that Jesus reaches out to them in a special way through the words, actions and symbols of the sacraments. The sacraments are sacred rituals. They are a visible sign of God's loving, invisible presence with people at key moments in their lives, such as:

- the birth of a child,
- arriving at religious maturity,
- getting married, or
- preparing for death.

When a sacrament is celebrated, it is a visible sign of something sacred and invisible happening. God is present, communicating his love for the persons involved.

Parents express their love for a child in many different ways.

Sacraments in the Christian Churches

Christianity is divided into three main parts.

- ❖ The Roman Catholic Church.
- ❖ The Orthodox Churches.
- ❖ The Protestant Churches.

The Orthodox Churches

Orthodox Churches celebrate seven sacraments.

- ❖ Baptism.
- ❖ Confirmation.
- ❖ Eucharist.
- ❖ Reconciliation.
- ❖ Marriage.
- ❖ Holy Orders.
- ❖ Anointing the Sick.

Baptism in the Orthodox tradition

In the Orthodox Churches the first three sacraments, Baptism, Confirmation and Eucharist, are administered together in infancy.

A family brings their newborn baby to the church when he/she is eight days old. The child is baptised by total immersion in the water of the font. He/she is then confirmed with holy oil; this is called Chrismation. Finally he/she receives Holy Eucharist, the body and blood of Christ. It is given to the child on a spoon from the chalice.

Marriage in the Orthodox tradition

Marriage is a sacrament in the Orthodox tradition. Two people make vows before God and witnesses that they will love and cherish each other all the days of their lives.

Marriage ceremony in an Orthodox church.

The Protestant Churches

Many Protestant Churches recognise only two sacraments, Baptism and Holy Communion (the Lord's Supper). A few Protestant Churches, such as the Society of Friends (Quakers) and the Salvation Army, do not celebrate any sacraments. They believe that outward signs are unimportant. To them, what matters more is the relationship with God within the heart of each person.

Pastor handing out communion bread during a church service.

Sacraments in the Anglican tradition

Anglicans believe that a sacrament is an outward visible sign of an inward spiritual grace. Anglicans believe Jesus instituted only two sacraments while he was on Earth, namely:

- ❖ Baptism.
- ❖ Holy Communion.

The other sacraments, Confirmation, Ordination, Holy Matrimony, the Ministry of Absolution (Penance) and the Ministry of Healing (Extreme Unction) emerged later in the early Christian Church. As such they are celebrated as 'sacramentals', or special occasions. Anglicans believe they are important, but do not have the same importance as the two sacraments instituted by Jesus during his public ministry in Galilee.

In the Church of Ireland people are usually baptised in infancy, are confirmed at around fourteen years of age and receive Holy Communion for the first time shortly afterwards.

The Roman Catholic Church

In the Roman Catholic Church the word 'sacrament' is understood in three ways.

1. *Jesus as sacrament* - When Jesus was on Earth he was the love of God made visible. Jesus was the fundamental sign or sacrament of God.
2. *Church as sacrament* - Members of the Catholic Church are meant to be Jesus-like for those around them. The Church is a sign of the continuing presence of Jesus in the world today.
3. *The seven sacraments* - The sacraments are the Church's way of showing that Jesus reaches out to people with God's love at significant moments in their lives. The seven sacraments of the Catholic Church are divided into:

Sacraments of Initiation
- ✦ Baptism.
- ✦ Confirmation.
- ✦ Eucharist.

Sacraments of Healing
- ✦ Reconciliation.
- ✦ Anointing the Sick.

Sacraments of Vocation
- ✦ Marriage.
- ✦ Holy Orders.

Sacraments of Initiation

When Jesus was on Earth he called his disciples to follow him. Today, the risen Jesus calls people in the sacraments of initiation. Through these sacraments a person becomes a full member of the Christian community. In the Roman Catholic Church people are usually baptised in infancy, receive Holy Communion at eight years of age, and Confirmation at twelve years of age.

❖ Baptism
Through the waters of Baptism the risen Jesus unites the person with God. The child is called to be a Christian, a follower of Christ.

❖ Confirmation
Through the oil of chrism the risen Jesus sends the Holy Spirit to give each young person the strength and courage to follow him.

❖ Eucharist
Through the bread and wine the risen Jesus gives himself to his followers so that they may be more fully united with him and with one another. The Eucharist helps a Christian to be better able to live a Christian life in the world.

Sacraments of Healing

Jesus healed and forgave many people during his time on Earth two thousand years ago. He not only healed their physical ailments, he also healed their spirit and forgave their sins. The risen Jesus brings comfort and forgiveness to people today through the Church's sacraments of healing.

❖ Reconciliation
Through the words of the priest the risen Jesus forgives the sins of those who are sorry for what they have done wrong. Jesus reconciles, or heals, their relationship with God and with each other. The sacrament of reconciliation gives people the strength and encouragement to begin again to live a Christian life.

❖ Anointing the Sick
Through the holy oil the risen Jesus offers inner healing and peace of mind to those who are seriously ill. The sacrament assures the sick person that he/she is not alone in their pain and suffering.

Sacraments of Vocation

Jesus called his disciples to serve the community in different ways. He gave them special roles to perform for the benefit of all. Sacraments of vocation are special ways in which Christians are called to serve in the Church today.

❖ Marriage
Through the words of the priest, and the exchange of rings, the risen Jesus helps the love of a married couple to grow and deepen all the days of their lives. The love and commitment they have for one another, their family and their community, will reflect the love of God for all his people.

❖ Holy Orders
Through the oil of chrism and the priestly vestments the risen Jesus gives priests, bishops, and deacons the authority to be leaders of a Christian community. They serve God's people by preaching the Gospel and administering the sacraments.

Sacrament	Significant Words	Significant Actions	Key symbols
✦ Baptism: 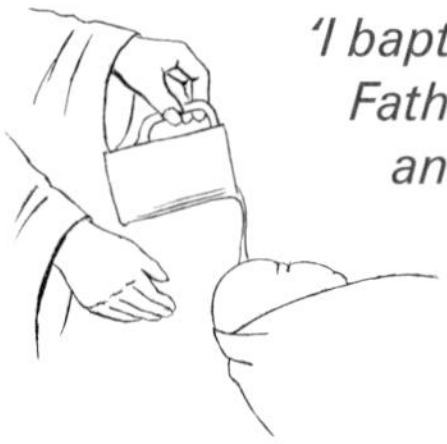	*'I baptise you in the name of the Father, and of the Son, and of the Holy Spirit.'*	✧ Pouring of water. ✧ Anointing with oil. ✧ Lighting baptismal candle. ✧ Clothing in a white garment.	- Water. - Oil of Chrism.
✦ Confirmation: 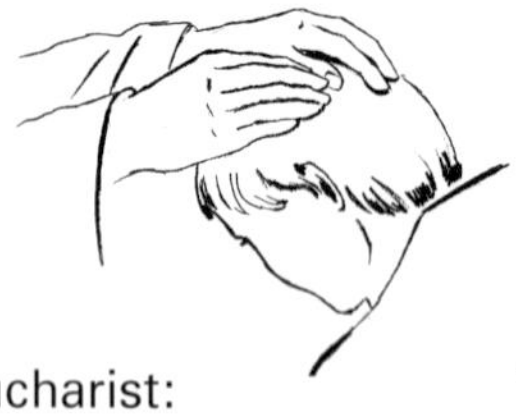	Prayer of the bishop. *'Be sealed with the Holy Spirit.'*	✧ Laying on of hands. ✧ Anointing with oil.	- Oil of Chrism.
✦ Eucharist: 	The Eucharistic Prayer (the words of consecration). *'This is my body... This is my blood... Do this in memory of me.'*	✧ The offering of bread and wine. ✧ The distribution of Holy Communion.	- Bread and Wine.
✦ Reconciliation: 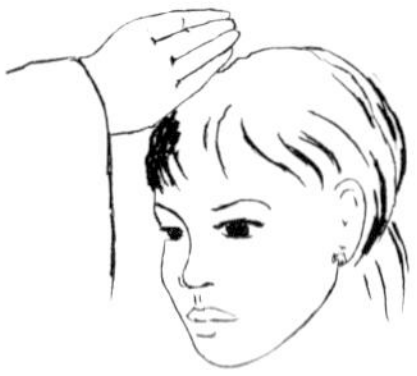	The confession of sin (the words of absolution). *'...I absolve you from your sins in the name of the Father, and of the Son, and of the Holy Spirit.'*	✧ The priest stretches out his hand and says the prayer of absolution.	- None.
✦ Anointing the Sick: 	The prayer of anointing. *'Through this holy anointing may the Lord in his love and mercy help you with the grace of the Holy Spirit.'*	✧ Laying on of hands. ✧ Anointing with oil.	- Holy oil.
✦ Marriage: 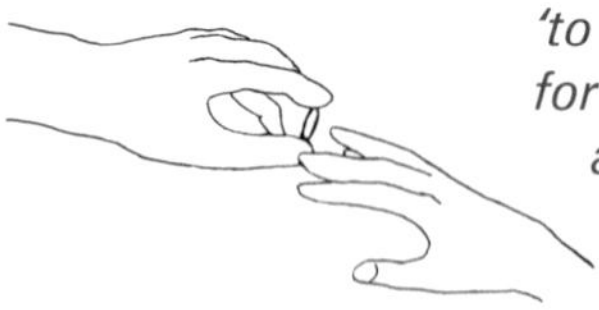	The exchange of vows. The couple promise each other *'to love... for better for worse, for richer for poorer, in sickness and in health, all the days of our lives'.*	✧ The exchange of rings.	- Wedding rings.
✦ Holy Orders: 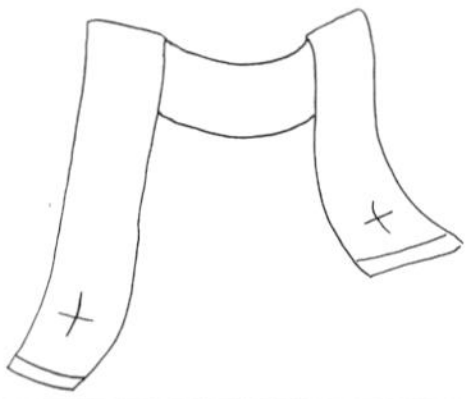	Prayer said by the bishop. *'Almighty Father, grant to this servant of yours the dignity of the priesthood...'.*	✧ Laying on of hands. ✧ Anointing with oil. ✧ Putting on vestments for Mass.	- Oil of Chrism. - Vestments.

Experiencing the love of God

Each sacrament has its own set of significant words, actions and religious symbols. Catholics use ordinary material things such as bread, wine, water and oil to symbolise the presence of Jesus. It is through these things that God reaches out and touches them at key moments in their lives. In the sacraments God's love is made present and real for those who believe.

The Sacrament of Marriage in a Catholic church.

Sacraments are communal celebrations. When a sacrament is celebrated, members of the Christian community gather together in small or large numbers to participate fully in what is taking place. While one or two persons may be 'receiving' the sacrament, the whole community actually celebrates the sacrament. This means all who attend benefit from the loving presence of God. The sacrament changes everyone. The presence of the risen Jesus strengthens people's faith, and their commitment to follow the example of Jesus in their everyday lives.

For details of rites of passage:
In **Judaism** see p249. In **Islam** see p299.

Questions

Knowledge

1. What is a sacrament?
2. Name two key moments in life when a sacrament is celebrated.
3. What do Christians believe happens when a sacrament is celebrated?
4. a. List the sacraments celebrated in the Orthodox Churches.
   b. Name the sacraments celebrated in infancy in the Orthodox Churches.
5. a. How many sacraments are celebrated in the Protestant Churches?
   b. What are 'sacramentals' in the Anglican tradition?
6. a. What is distinctive about the Catholic understanding of the term 'sacrament'?
   b. Name the seven sacraments of the Catholic Church.
7. a. In the Catholic Church name:
   - The three sacraments of initiation.
   - The two sacraments of healing.
   - The two sacraments of vocation.

   b. State when each of the sacraments is celebrated.
8. Select one sacrament of initiation.
   a. What is the purpose of this sacrament?
   b. What words, actions and key symbols are used in this sacrament?
   c. What is communicated through the use of these symbols?
   d. How does this sacrament affect the way a person lives their life?

Understanding

1. What is the Christian understanding of sacrament?
2. Outline the place of sacraments in any two Christian denominations.
3. How do Christians benefit by being present and participating fully in the celebration of a sacrament?

Research

- Find out about sacramental ceremonies attended by members of the class.
  - Have you participated in/attended the celebration of a Christian sacrament?
  - Name the sacrament(s).
  - Describe what took place during the ceremony.
  - Explain the significance or meaning of the sacrament for the person(s) involved.
  - Share your experience and insights with the class.

Sacrament of Baptism

Key Concepts

Identity: the distinct characteristics by which a person or group is recognised.

Communicating experience: experiencing an invisible reality and expressing it clearly in symbolic words and actions.

Sacrament: a sacred ritual that is a visible sign of God's presence with people at key moments in their lives.

Objective

Explain the place of the sacrament of Baptism in two Christian traditions.

Activity: *"That's Life"*

TASK: TO DEMONSTRATE THAT WATER IS ESSENTIAL FOR LIFE.

- Water can be used in a variety of ways.
  - To wash ourselves.
  - To make things grow.
  - To drink.
  - To obtain food.
  - To relax.
  - To cook.
  - To listen to it.
  - To clean.
  - To cool down.
  - To swim.
  - ....
  - ....

  Can you add to the list?

Discuss

- List the ways in which you have made use of water already today.
- What scientific facts do you know about water?
  - Where did life first emerge on the planet?
  - How much water covers the surface of the earth?
  - What is the proportion of water in the human body?
  - How long can a human being survive:
    a. without food?
    b. without water?
- How important is water for life?

Identity

Every living thing needs water.
In Baptism water is a symbol of life.

Identity, in religious terms, is the distinct characteristics by which a person is recognised as belonging to a community of faith. Baptism is a ceremony of initiation at which a person officially becomes a member of the Christian community. Baptism establishes a person's identity as a follower of Jesus and a member of a particular Church.

People are baptised in most Christian Churches. Roman Catholic, Orthodox and the Churches in the Anglican Communion baptise babies, as do Methodists and Presbyterians. This is called Infant Baptism. Other Churches will only baptise adults. This is the practice in the Baptist Church; it is called Believer's Baptism.

Water is an important symbol in both Infant Baptism and Believer's Baptism. It shows that all sin is washed away and forgiven. In Baptism a person joins other Christians to start a new life following the teaching of Jesus.

Water is essential for life.

Communicating Experience

Christians believe in the invisible presence of God. God is real, God exists. The sacraments communicate the experience of God's presence in people's lives. In the Roman Catholic Church, the invisible presence of God is expressed in the symbolic words and actions of the different sacraments people receive during their lifetime.

In the sacrament of Baptism symbols that communicate the experience of God's presence are:

- ❖ The pouring of water.
- ❖ The anointing with oil.
- ❖ Lighting the Baptismal candle.
- ❖ Clothing in a white garment.

Symbols of Baptism

Water

Water is vitally important for life; we cannot live without it for more than five days. All life depends on water for its very existence. Water has a special meaning for the Christian community. Its life-giving qualities make it a powerful symbol in the sacrament of Baptism.

Baptism is the start of a new life following Jesus and doing the will of God. Human beings have a tendency to turn away from God and commit sin. In Baptism a promise is made to reject sin and become united with God in a special way. The pouring of water symbolises, and brings about, the end of sin and the start of a new spiritual life in the heart of the child.

The priest speaks aloud the child's name, as to have a name is to have an identity. The water of Baptism, and the new name, signal the child's new Christian identity and new life as a follower of Jesus.

Oil

Two kinds of oil are used in Baptism, the oil of catechumens and the oil of chrism. The oil of catechumens is used to anoint the baby before Baptism. At the time of the Roman Empire, soldiers and gladiators used oil to make their bodies strong and supple. The oil also had healing properties and it helped the body resist infection from cuts and bruises. Modern athletes use oil for much the same reasons today. At Baptism the baby is anointed on the chest with oil to symbolise God strengthening the child against sin and temptation.

Oil of chrism is used to anoint the baby after Baptism. This same oil was used in Old Testament times to anoint kings and prophets. For example, King David was anointed with oil of chrism to show that he was specially chosen to serve God. At Baptism the baby is anointed on the head with chrism to show that he/she is chosen to serve God too.

Candle

Light helps us to see clearly and without it we would be unable to find our way. The symbolism of light is very important in the Christian faith. Jesus is the 'Light of the World' bringing light to people's lives by teaching them to love God and each other. The child's parents hold a baptismal candle lit from the large Pascal candle in the sanctuary. The Pascal candle is a sign of the risen Jesus present in the Church. The light of the baptismal candle symbolises the new life of Christ present in the heart of the child.

White Garment

People tend to wear special clothes on special occasions. In the early Church people presenting themselves for Baptism wore white robes as a sign of their new life of faith in Jesus Christ. When a baby is baptised today he/she is wrapped in a white shawl to symbolise being clothed in Christ. The white garment points to the child beginning a new life as a follower of Jesus and a member of the Church.

> "And when you were baptised, it was as though you had put on Christ in the same way you put on new clothes." Galatians 3:27

Infant Baptism in the Catholic Church

Infant Baptism in the Catholic Church is a sacrament, a sacred ritual. The sacrament is a visible sign of God's loving, invisible presence with the child as he/she joins the Christian community.

The Ceremony

The family gather at the church to present the child for Baptism.

1. *Welcome*
   The priest meets the child, the parents and godparents at the entrance to the church. He welcomes the child on behalf of the whole Christian community. The parents are asked the name of the child, and about their understanding of what is involved in bringing up their son/daughter in the Christian faith. The priest traces the sign of the cross on the child's forehead and invites the parents and godparents to do the same. The role of the godparents is to support the mother and father in helping their child to live a Christian life. The sign of the cross symbolises that this child belongs to God.
2. *Bible Readings and Sermon*
   Those present listen to the Word of God in the Bible. The reading from the New Testament may describe the Baptism of Jesus. The priest gives a short sermon to explain the reading and the meaning of Baptism. This is followed by the Prayers of the Faithful for the child, parents and godparents.
3. *Exorcism and Anointing*
   The priest anoints the child on the chest with oil of catechumens and prays that he/she will be protected from evil. The oil is a symbol of strength and healing. It symbolises God strengthening the child to face life's challenges and be able to do good and avoid evil.
4. *Baptismal promises*
   The priest blesses the water in the baptismal font. Then he invites the parents and godparents to express their own faith and make promises on behalf of the child. In a question and answer format they agree to all the Christian teaching found in the words of the Apostles' Creed.

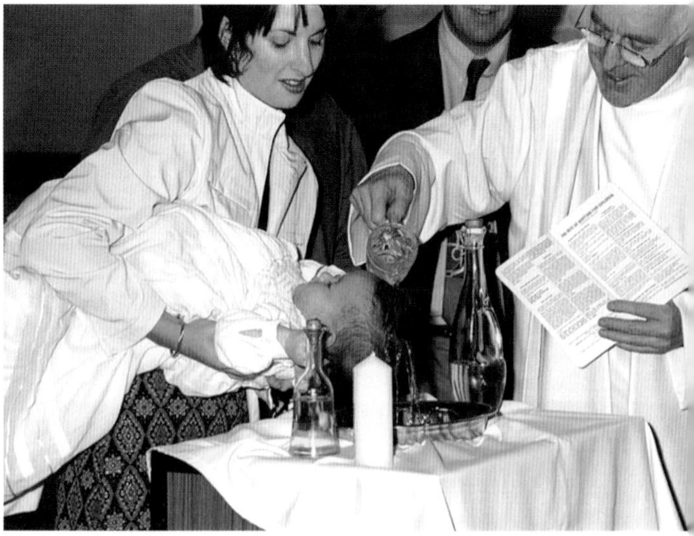

Pouring water onto the head of an infant at Baptism.

5. *Baptism*
   Water from the baptismal font is poured three times over the baby's head. While this is being done, the priest says '___(NAME)___, I baptise you in the name of the Father, and of the Son, and of the Holy Spirit'. This is the sacrament of Baptism. All other parts of the ceremony led up to this important moment. The pouring of water symbolises the child entering a new life in the family of God.
6. *Anointing with Chrism*
   The child is anointed on the head with oil of chrism. It symbolises that the child is chosen by God to live a Christian life.
7. *White Garment and Baptismal Candle*
   A white shawl is wrapped around the baby. It symbolises a new life clothed in Jesus Christ. A candle is lit from the Pascal Candle and given to the child's parents. The priest says 'receive the light of Christ'. This symbolises that the child has the guidance of Christ to believe and practice the Christian faith.
8. *The Lord's Prayer and Final Blessing*
   Everyone says the Lord's prayer. The child has become a member of the Christian community, now he/she too can call God 'Father'. The priest gives his final blessing to the parents and asks God to help them bring up their child in the faith. Then he blesses all who attended the baptismal ceremony.

Believer's Baptism in Baptist Churches

Some Christian Churches only baptise adults. They think it is better to wait until a person is old enough to make the decision for themselves. Believer's Baptism, as it is called, takes place when a person is ready to make a commitment to become a Christian and asks to be baptised.

The Baptism is by total immersion. This means the person's whole body is immersed, or dipped, into the baptismal water. Believer's Baptism is practised in Baptist Churches. Baptism can take place outdoors in a river, or indoors in a baptistry (a waist-high pool of water built into the floor of the church building). Baptists follow the example of the New Testament in which Jesus was an adult when he was baptised, and he was baptised by total immersion in the waters of the river Jordan.

The Baptism of Jesus by John the Baptist in the river Jordan .

Baptists wish to follow the example of Jesus' baptism. Their Baptism is an outward sign that the person believes in Jesus and has chosen to be a Christian. Once a person decides to be baptised, he/she is taken through a period of preparation by an elder of the Church. These meetings take place several weeks before the Baptism itself.

Baptist churches follow a non-liturgical form of worship, so there is no fixed form of service at a Believer's Baptism. The service of Baptism will vary a little from one church to another.

At a Believer's Baptism

1. The congregation is present and witnesses the Baptism. They sing hymns and say prayers. Readings from the Bible are followed by a sermon explaining the importance of Baptism.
2. Candidates wearing white robes are called forward in turn. Each one expresses sorrow for their sins.
3. The candidate may read a short passage from the Bible, and give a testimony, which is a short statement in their own words. They tell everyone present how they came to believe in Jesus and why they wish to be baptised.
4. The pastor and the candidate then step down into the baptismal water. The pastor says the person's name and baptises him/her in the name of the Father, Son and the Holy Spirit and carefully immerses the person in the water.
5. The congregation sing a hymn as the baptised person emerges from the water. He/she is offered a towel by a sponsor, someone who has been particularly supportive of him/her on this spiritual journey. The believer leaves to change and then returns to the service.

The Baptism is a symbol of:

- ❖ *Spiritual cleansing*
  That is forgiveness and washing away of sin.
- ❖ *Renewal*
  That is beginning a new life of faith in Jesus, and a commitment to follow his teaching.

At Baptism the believer is admitted to full membership of the Church.

Total immersion in the water of a river at a Believer's Baptism.

Questions

Knowledge

1. What part of a person's identity is established at Baptism?
2. What is a sacrament of initiation?
3. Name the Christian Churches that practice:
   a. Infant Baptism.
   b. Believer's Baptism.
4. What symbols are used in Baptism in the Catholic Church?
5. In the sacrament of Baptism:
   a. What does water symbolise?
   b. What does light symbolise?
6. What are the roles of the following people in the sacrament of Baptism:
   a. The priest?
   b. The godparents?
7. a. List the different parts of the sacrament of Baptism in the Catholic Church.
   b. Write two sentences describing what happens at each stage.
8. What is meant by the term 'Believer's Baptism'?
9. What aspects of the Baptism of Jesus influenced the form of Baptism in the Baptist Churches?
10. What happens at a Believer's Baptism in a Baptist church?

Understanding

1. a. When does a Christian receive their religious identity?
   b. In your opinion how important is religious identity for a person of faith.
2. What spiritual experience is communicated in the sacrament of Baptism?
3. Explain why water is an important symbol at baptismal ceremonies in all Christian Churches?
4. What are the similarities, and the differences, in the celebration of Baptism in two Christian traditions.
5. Outline the effect of Baptism on a person in the Christian community of faith.

Confirmation

Being confirmed by a bishop.

Research

- Find out about or recall the ceremony in which Confirmation is celebrated as:
  - A sacrament (in the Roman Catholic Church)
  - A sacramental or special occasion (in the Church of Ireland).
- Where did the sacrament take place?
- Who attended the ceremony?
- What was the average age of the candidates?
- What was the role of:
  a. The bishop?
  b. The sponsor?
- List the different parts of the ceremony.
- At the moment the sacrament was administered:
  a. What symbolic objects and actions were used?
  b. What symbolic words were spoken?
- Explain the significance of the sacrament for those who were confirmed that day.
- Discuss the place of Confirmation in the life of a community of faith.

Section E

Prayer

Key Concepts

Communication with God: a prayerful exchange between God and human beings.

Personal prayer: praying to God by oneself.

Communal prayer: praying to God with others as a community.

Objective

To explore the idea of prayer as a need to communicate with God.

Activity: *"True or False"*

TASK: TO CLARIFY SOME MISCONCEPTIONS ABOUT PRAYER.

✦ Identify which of the following statements are true or false.

- God likes formal prayers better than people's made-up prayers.
- You can talk to God just like you talk to a friend.
- You can pray about anything. God is interested in everything you do.
- You can pray with other people or by yourself.
- You can think silent prayers inside your head.
- Praying means talking to God.
- The best prayers have big words and long sentences.
- You can pray anywhere - on the bus, in the take-away, at home, out cycling...
- God only listens to people who are good all the time.
- You must always make the sign of the cross and say "Amen" for a prayer to work.
- God will only listen if you kneel down, join your hands and close your eyes.
- You can only really pray in a church.

Discuss

- What did you already know about prayer?
- Did you learn anything new about prayer from doing this exercise? What did you learn?
- When do Christians pray to God?

Communication with God

Prayer is about talking to God about anything, anywhere, at any time.

Human beings are social creatures, we cannot live in isolation. It is part of our nature to seek out the company of others. We all need a family and friends to help us, to care about us and to give us a sense of our value and worth.

We are in regular contact with those who matter to us. We can be in touch with some people several times a day, with others it may be several times a week. We make time to talk and listen to one another, to help each other out, or simply to enjoy each other's company.

Experience tells us that we cannot afford to take our relationships for granted. We need to stay in touch with people and keep the lines of communication open. That is how we maintain a relationship with those who are important to us. To keep any relationship going people need to spend time talking and listening to each other.

People communicate with God through prayer.

Prayer

People communicate with God through prayer. Christians, for example, tend to look on God as a good parent, a good friend, or a loving presence. They have a need to communicate with God, spending time talking and listening to God in prayer. Prayer is the way people keep a relationship going with God.

People of faith keep in touch with God through prayer. This is how they keep God up to date with what is going on in their lives. They can tell about the things that make them happy or sad, anxious or disappointed. Talking often about things that matter strengthens people's relationship with God. Making the effort to pray regularly helps Christians to be aware of the loving presence of God in their lives.

Reasons why people pray

- ❖ To express joy at the wonder of creation and the mystery of life.
- ❖ To give thanks when things turn out well.
- ❖ To ask for help or guidance in times of need.
- ❖ To say sorry when they know they have done something wrong.

There are two general approaches to prayer: vocal prayer, and silent prayer such as meditation (the topic of another lesson). Vocal prayer is when people use words to communicate with God. The words may be said aloud, or said quietly in the mind.

Personal Prayer

Personal prayer is private. Catholics, for example, sometimes pray alone when they want to have a private conversation with God.

- ❖ Their prayer can be formal - using the fixed prayers of the Church such as the 'Lord's Prayer' and the 'Hail Mary'.
- ❖ Their prayer can be informal - using a prayer that they have made up or composed themselves.

Personal prayer can take place anywhere, for example on the way to school, before a test, after training, or in one's room.

Communal prayer

Communal prayer is public. Christians gather in a church or a sacred place to pray to God as a community. Together they say the formal prayers of the Church that everyone knows. This is evident at church services such as Mass for example, when Catholics gather to pray and worship God, not as individuals but as a community.

A Catholic community walk in prayerful procession on the feast of Corpus Christi.

Personal Prayer:
a private conversation with God.

The Rosary

The Rosary is an example of a form of vocal prayer. It is a traditional prayer in the Roman Catholic Church. People often find it helpful to focus their attention on something while they are praying. Using rosary beads helps Catholics to concentrate on their prayers.

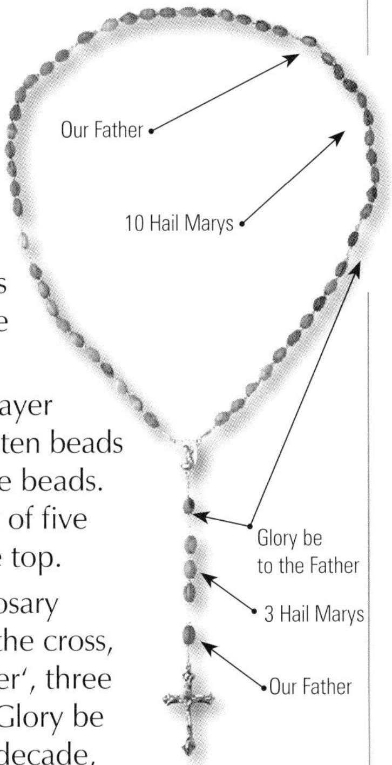

Our Father
10 Hail Marys
Glory be to the Father
3 Hail Marys
Our Father

A rosary is a circle of prayer beads. It has five sets of ten beads separated by single large beads. A crucifix on a short set of five beads is attached to the top.

A person praying the Rosary begins with the sign of the cross, and says one 'Our Father', three 'Hail Marys', and one 'Glory be to the Father'. At each decade, the person who is praying says one 'Our Father', ten 'Hail Marys', and one 'Glory be to the Father'. The beads are passed through the fingers at each prayer. Catholics pray the Rosary at home or in the church, they can say it silently by themselves, or say it aloud with others in a group.

For details of prayer
In **Judaism** see p227. In **Islam** see p287.

Questions

Knowledge

1. What kind of things do people normally do to maintain their relationship with family and friends?
2. How do people communicate with God?
3. What is prayer?
4. What are the benefits of prayer?
5. What is the nature of:
   a. Personal prayer?
   b. Communal prayer?
6. Give reasons why people might pray on their own.
7. Give reasons why people might join others and pray as a group.
8. How do Catholics pray the Rosary?

Understanding

1. Why do you think people feel the need to communicate with God?
2. Explain the difference between personal prayer and communal prayer in the Christian tradition.
3. How does prayer strengthen a person's faith?

Research

- Find out about one person's experience of prayer. Talk to a person you know well who prays regularly. Ask him/her some of the following questions:
  - When do you pray?
  - Where do you pray?
  - To whom do you pray?
  - How do you pray?
  - Why do you pray?
  - How important is prayer in your life?
  - Thank the person for telling you about their experience of prayer. With their permission, present a summary to the class.

Jesus and Prayer

Key Concept

Communication with God: a prayerful exchange between God and human beings.

Objective

To look at the importance of prayer in the life of Jesus in the Christian tradition.

Activity: *"Prayers"*

TASK: TO APPRECIATE THE IMPORTANCE OF PRAYER IN DIFFERENT RELIGIOUS TRADITIONS.

✦ Read the following prayers.

1. "There is no God but Allah, and
   Muhammad is his prophet."

2. "In the name of the Father,
   and of the Son,
   and of the Holy Spirit. Amen."

3. "I take refuge in the Buddha.
   I take refuge in the Dharma.
   I take refuge in the Sangha."

4. "Hear, O Israel!
   The Lord is our God,
   the Lord alone."

5. "I see in thee
   all the gods O my God
   and the infinity of the beings
   of thy creation."

Discuss

- To what religious tradition does each prayer belong?
- Do you know what some of these prayers are called, or when they are said?
- Can you name an important person in the spiritual tradition of each religion.

Communication with God

There are important people in the spiritual traditions of all religions. Jesus is the most important figure in the spiritual tradition of Christianity.

Prayer had a central place in the life of Jesus, the founder of Christianity. We know from the Gospels that Jesus often prayed to God; prayer was important to him. Christians try to follow his example and his teaching on the value of prayer.

Christians frequently light candles when they pray.

Jesus prayed often. He prayed alone. He prayed in small groups with friends. He also prayed with the rest of the community in the synagogue and in the Temple.

St. Luke tells us that:

- 'He would go away to lonely places where he prayed.' Luke 5:16
- 'Jesus took Peter, John and James with him and went up a hill to pray.' Luke 9:28
- 'On the Sabbath he went as usual to the synagogue. He stood up to read the scriptures.' Luke 4:16
- 'It was almost time for the Passover festival so Jesus went to Jerusalem. There in the Temple...' John 2:13

Prayer in the life of Jesus

Jesus prayed at important moments in his life. Before any major decision and in times of stress Jesus took time out to communicate with God.

❖ *At his Baptism:*
'Jesus was also baptised. While he was praying, heaven was opened and the Holy Spirit came upon him.' Luke 3:21-22

❖ *Before beginning his teaching ministry:*
'The Spirit made him go into the desert where he stayed for forty days.' Mark 1:12-13

❖ *Before choosing his twelve disciples:*
'Jesus went up a hill to pray and spent the whole night there praying to God. When day came, he called his disciples to him and chose twelve of them.' Luke 6:12-13

❖ *Before preaching about the Kingdom of God:*
'Very early the next morning, long before daylight, Jesus got up and left the house. He went out of the town to a lonely place where he prayed. He travelled all over Galilee preaching in the synagogues.' Mark 1:35-39

❖ *Before working miracles:*
'Jesus took the five loaves and two fish, looked up to heaven, thanked God for them, broke them, gave them to the disciples to distribute to the people.' Luke 9:16

❖ *Before his arrest in the Garden of Gethsemane:*
'Then they came to a place called Gethsemane and Jesus said to his disciples "sit here while I pray."' Mark 14:32

❖ *Before his death on the cross:*
'Jesus cried out in a loud voice, "Father in your hands I place my spirit." He said this and died.' Luke 23:46

INRI

Jesus' death on the cross.

Jesus' teaching on prayer

The disciples frequently observed Jesus at prayer. Eventually one of them approached him and said,

'Lord, teach us how to pray.' Luke 11:1

Jesus responded to this request in two ways.

1. He told them parables about prayer.
2. He taught an actual prayer, 'The Lord's Prayer'.

Jesus is the most important person in the spiritual tradition of Christianity.

Parables on Prayer

Jesus told three parables to teach his followers important lessons about prayer.

❖ The Friend at Midnight Luke11:5-8
Jesus taught that people should have faith, to keep on praying and never give up.

❖ The Widow and the Judge Luke 18:1-8
Jesus taught that people should always pray and never lose heart.

❖ The Pharisee and the Tax Collector Luke 18:10-14
Jesus taught that people should be humble, not full of pride when they pray. It is better to be open and honest with God at all times.

The Lord's Prayer

Jesus taught his followers to address their prayer directly to God. He told them to call God 'Father'. This shows that it is possible to have a close personal relationship with God. People can approach God in the way they would approach a loving parent, confident of receiving help and protection in times of need. Their prayer should contain words of:

- **Praise and thanksgiving** - to thank God for caring so much that he brought about the Kingdom of God on Earth.
- **Petition** - to ask God to meet one's own needs and the needs of others.
- **Penitence** - to say sorry for any wrongdoing and to ask God for forgiveness.

The Lord's Prayer

Our Father who art in heaven,
Hallowed be thy name,
Thy Kingdom come,
Thy will be done on Earth as it is in Heaven.

Give us this day our daily bread.

And forgive us our trespasses,
As we forgive those who trespass against us,
And lead us not into temptation,
But deliver us from evil, Amen.

(The Sunday Missal)

This version of the Lord's Prayer is based on the teaching of Jesus in the Gospel (Matt 6:9-13). Jesus composed this prayer to show his followers the best way to pray. It is the model for all Christian prayer of praise and thanksgiving, petition and penitence. Christians of all denominations share this prayer today.

Jesus wanted people to follow his example. He taught them to:

- ❖ Set aside time for prayer.
- ❖ Pray often, both alone and in the company of others.
- ❖ Pray to God using words of praise and thanksgiving, petition and penitence.

Questions

Knowledge

1. Who is the most important person in the Christian spiritual tradition?
2. Give three examples from the Gospel when Jesus:
   a. Prayed alone.
   b. Prayed with others.
3. What important moments in Jesus' life were preceded by prayer?
4. How did Jesus teach his followers to pray?
5. What point was Jesus making in each of his three parables about prayer?
6. What 'model prayer' did Jesus teach his followers?
7. How can calling God 'Father' help Christians to pray?
8. What phrases in the Lord's Prayer reflect praise and thanksgiving, and praise and penitence?
9. Who says the Lord's prayer today?
10. What did Jesus teach his followers about prayer?

Understanding

1. How did Jesus communicate with God?
2. How important was prayer in the life of Jesus?
3. Explain why the 'Lord's Prayer' is the model for all Christian prayer.
4. Give reasons why the Lord's prayer is important in the spiritual tradition of Christianity.

Research

- Find out more about the place of prayer in other religious traditions. Select a world religion and answer the following questions.
  - Who was an important figure in the spiritual tradition of that religion?
  - How often are people of that religion expected to pray?
  - Do people have to make special arrangements before they pray?
  - Do people have to wear any special clothing before they pray?
  - What exactly do people do when they pray?
  - Is there a special day of worship in the week?
  - How do people worship God on that day?
  - Prepare a report and offer your opinion on the importance of prayer in the religion investigated.

Types of Prayer

Key Concepts

Praise and thanksgiving: prayer to praise and thank God for blessings already received.

Petition: prayer asking God for help with one's own needs or the needs of others.

Penitence: prayer admitting to wrongdoing and asking God for forgiveness.

Objective

Differentiate between the various types of prayer and explore some difficulties with prayer.

Activity: *"Praying"*

TASK: TO EXAMINE THE WAY PEOPLE PRAY.

- People of faith pray, but how and why do they pray? Individually or in groups address the following questions.
  - Do you take time to pray?
  - When do you pray?
  - How often do you pray?
  - What do you pray about?
  - How exactly do you pray?
  - Do you think your prayers are answered?

Discuss

- Whose approach to prayer is similar to your own?
- Whose approach to prayer is different from yours?
- How important is prayer in people's lives?

Different types of prayer

People use different types of prayer at different times.

When they pray, Christians are following the example of Jesus. Their way of praying is often affected by what is going on in their lives at a particular time.

Sometimes they will want to communicate their joy and delight at an event made possible by God's action in the world.

At other times they may want to say how deeply grateful they are for something good that has just taken place.

Then there will be occasions when problems arise. This is when they will request God's help either for themselves or for someone else.

Now and again they will let themselves down and do something wrong. When this happens they can own up, express sorrow and ask God to forgive them for their sin.

Lighted candles in a church.

Prayer in the Christian tradition

The following are the four types of vocal prayer that Christians use from time to time.

- ❖ Prayer of Praise.
- ❖ Prayer of Thanksgiving.
- ❖ Prayer of Petition.
- ❖ Prayer of Penitence.

All these types of prayer come together in the 'Lord's Prayer'. Each type of prayer is also evident in the prayer life of Jesus.

Praise

This prayer focuses on praising God.

Christians look around and marvel at the world in which they live. They want to praise God for the wonder of creation, for the gift of human life, and for the natural order of things.

Jesus praised God when poor, ordinary people welcomed his teaching.

> 'Jesus was filled with joy by the Holy Spirit and said "Father, Lord of Heaven and Earth, I thank you because you have shown to the unlearned what you have hidden from the wise."' Luke 10:21

Thanksgiving

This prayer focuses on thanking God for things.

Christians bring to mind the many gifts they have been given. While it is easy to take these things for granted, it is only right to give thanks to God for the blessings they have received.

Jesus *thanked* God the Father when Lazarus was raised from the dead.

> 'They took the stone away. Jesus looked up and said "I thank you Father, that you listen to me. I know that you always listen to me."' John 11:41-42

Petition

This prayer focuses on asking God for something.

Christians request God's help when they are in trouble, or have a problem of some kind. It may have to do with illness, exams, relationships, or making big decisions. When they ask God for help it may be for themselves or for other people.

Jesus *asked God to help him* when he was in anguish in the Garden of Gethsemane.

> 'He went a little further on, threw himself face downwards on the ground and prayed; "My Father, if it is possible, take this cup of suffering away from me, yet not what I want but what you want."' Matthew 26:39

Penitence

This prayer focuses on saying sorry to God for wrongdoing.

Christians believe it is important to be sorry and admit when they have done something wrong. They can ask God for forgiveness, knowing that God's love is so great he is always ready to forgive their sin.

Jesus told the parable of the Lost Son to show that God welcomes the sinner when he is *sorrowful* and prays for *forgiveness*.

> "Father," the son said, "I have sinned against God and against you. I am no longer fit to be called your son." Luke 15:21

Different types of prayer at Mass

The different types of prayer can be seen in the celebration of Mass in the Catholic Church.

Prayers of Praise

The 'Responsorial Psalm' is a prayer to praise the goodness and greatness of God. It is said during the 'Liturgy of the Word' at Mass.

Prayers of Thanksgiving

The 'Eucharistic Prayer' is a prayer of thanksgiving. It is one of the most important prayers of the Church. It gives praise and thanks to God for the gift of creation, the gift of life, the gift of Jesus Christ, and the gift of the great love of God.

Prayers of Petition

The 'Prayers of the Faithful' are prayers of petition in which people pray for the needs of others. The congregation unites in prayer for the needs of the local and global community, and for the needs of the Church.

Prayers of petition at Mass.

Prayers of Penitence

The 'Penitential Rite' is a prayer of confession. People confess their sin and appeal to God for forgiveness. This prayer is said at the beginning of Mass.

Difficulties with prayer

People's relationship with God is different to their other relationships. When people speak to God in prayer, God doesn't answer them in words. This can sometimes lead them to wonder if God has heard them at all.

Praying to God in times of need.

Although Christians believe that God is present and always answers their prayers, they do not expect prayer to work like magic. Sometimes they get what they ask for, at other times they do not. The way God answers prayer is mysterious, and not always obvious. Prayers, for example, are frequently offered for those who are seriously ill. Sometimes sick people are healed, sometimes they are given the strength to cope with their illness.

Jesus taught his followers to go ahead and ask, and be full of hope when they pray to God. He told them not to be ashamed to keep on asking:

> "For everyone who asks will receive, and he who seeks will find, and the door will be opened to anyone who knocks." Luke 11:10

God will respond. God will care not only for those who pray, but also for those for whom they pray. God will answer everyone's prayers, often in ways they least expect or imagine.

Asking God for help

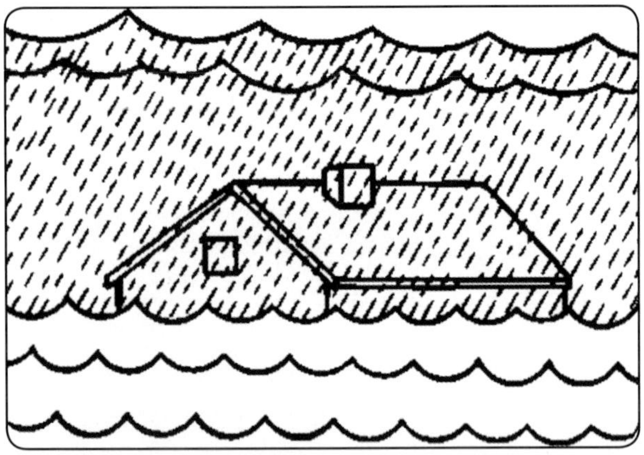

A story is told of something that happened in a small town during a particularly bad storm.

Heavy rain poured down for days and the main street became flooded. Rescue teams from the local council arrived with sandbags. Householders did their best but by nightfall the river had burst its banks. Everyone had to be evacuated.

A rescue truck pulled up beside the last house in the street, but the owner refused to leave. "I'm staying here," he said, "God will save me." However the flood water kept rising, and the man had to move upstairs. The council sent out a motorboat. He shouted to the crew from the window above "It's alright, I don't need to be rescued, God will save me."

The floodwater continued to rise. Eventually the man had to climb out on to the roof. The council made one last bid to reach him. This time they sent a helicopter and lowered a rope ladder down to him. "Quick, grab that!" they cried, "And hang on!" "No need," replied the man confidently, "God will save me." With that, the floodwater swamped the house and the man disappeared.

Later there was a loud knock on the gates of heaven. The man stood outside demanding to know why God hadn't answered his prayers. A Voice called out: "I sent you a truck, a motorboat and a helicopter. What more did you want?!"

Christians accept that God works and speaks in mysterious ways through the people and events around them.

For details of prayer
In **Judaism** see p227. In **Islam** see p287.

Questions

Knowledge

1. In what kinds of situations would a person feel the need to:
   - Praise God?
   - Thank God?
   - Petition God?
   - Be penitent and ask for God's forgiveness?
2. Name the four different types of prayer.
3. State the purpose of each type of prayer.
4. In what kinds of situations did Jesus use different types of prayer?
5. How are different types of prayer used in religious services such as the Mass?
6. Give reasons why some people might find it difficult to pray.
7. What do Christians believe about the way God answers people's prayers?
8. What did Jesus say about the frequency of prayer?

Understanding

1. Describe the four types of prayer.
2. Why is it that when people pray, more often than not, it is to ask God for something rather than to give praise or offer thanks?
3. What would a person of faith say to someone who told them "I prayed, but I didn't get what I prayed for."

Research

- Find out about the use of music and song in prayer.

  "To sing is to pray twice" (St. Augustine)

  - Write down the name and some of the words of:
    - your favourite hymn or
    - a song appropriate for use in a prayer service.
  - Are these hymns/songs about praise, thanksgiving, petition or penitence?
  - Compile a presentation of the words and music of your favourite hymn for the class.

Section E

Silent Prayer

Key Concepts

Meditation: a form of silent prayer based on the use of an icon, a repeated word, or a passage from scripture.

Contemplation: a form of deep, silent prayer that does not use words or thoughts.

Objective

To examine meditation and contemplation, and look at the life of an important person in the Christian spiritual tradition.

Activity: *"Relax"*

TASK: TO RELAX THE BODY AND QUIETEN THE MIND IN PREPARATION FOR A GUIDED MEDITATION.

✦ For the Teacher.

Direct the following exercise in a gentle modulated tone, pausing frequently. Students may stand for the first exercise, and may sit for the second and third exercises. In all instances request that they close their eyes or look down to avoid interacting with others in the room. The third exercise, the guided meditation, may be directed on a separate occasion, if preferred.

1. Relax - attend to body muscles.

Stand upright in a comfortable position, arms hanging loosely by the sides. Close the eyes or look down. Make a tight fist of one hand... notice what happens to your arm... let go. Relax. Make a tight fist of the other hand... Notice what happens to this arm... let go. Relax. Tighten up your face... let go. Relax. Tightly tense your entire body... hold it a moment... let go. Relax.

2. Relax - attend to breathing.

Sit upright in a comfortable position. Close the eyes or look down. Place one hand on the upper part of your stomach. Notice how it rises and falls with every breath.

- Pay attention to your breathing. Breathe slowly in and out..., in and out...
- Breathe in slowly and count to four. One... two... three... four... Breathe in, count. Breathe out, count. Repeat several times.
- Now as you breathe in, imagine light and goodness coming into your body... Breathe in, imagine...
- As you breathe out, imagine worries and problems leaving your body... Breathe out, imagine... Repeat several times.
- Slowly return your attention to the classroom..., gently open your eyes... stretch if necessary.

3. A guided meditation.

Sit upright in a comfortable position. Close the eyes or look down. Imagine you are far away from here in another place. Imagine you are on a beach... It is a summer's day. Feel the warmth of the sun on your face... You have taken off your shoes and are walking slowly toward the waters edge... look out to sea... feel the texture of the sand beneath your feet... listen to the sound of the waves... watch the sunlight glinting on the water... smell the fresh sea air... breathe in deeply... you are at peace...

Now imagine bending down to write a name in the sand... What have you written?... A small wave comes in and flows around your feet... it spills over the name and gently washes it away... taking a deep breath you turn to continue your journey along the water's edge... When you are ready, return here to this room.

Gently open your eyes... Stretch if necessary.

Discuss

- How are you now, after the guided meditation?
- What was easy or difficult about doing the meditation?
- Why do you think it is necessary to relax the body and quieten the mind before meditating?

Ways of Praying

Prayer is time spent communicating with God. Most Christian prayer relies on words, the words of formal set prayers such as the 'Lord's Prayer', or the words of informal prayers composed by each individual themselves.

Meditation is a way of praying that uses very few words. Contemplation is a way of praying that uses no words at all. Christians believe God is within each person as well as all around them. Meditation and contemplation clear a path within, enabling each person to experience the presence of God at the centre of their being.

Meditation

Christian meditation is silent prayer of the mind. The person quietly gives their attention to God using their thoughts, their feelings and their imagination.

The first step involves calming the body and the mind. This means:

- ❖ Finding a quiet place.
- ❖ Adopting a prayerful posture.
- ❖ Relaxing the body.
- ❖ Breathing deeply.
- ❖ Becoming still and calm.

A person meditating.

Getting ready to Meditate

A Quiet Place

Christians can meditate anywhere. They meditate at home, in the prayer room at school, in a church, or even outdoors. Any place might work, as long as it is somewhere quiet and comfortable where they will not be disturbed. If people meditate regularly indoors in the same place, a prayerful atmosphere can be created with candles, an open Bible, a cross or crucifix and maybe an icon and some incense.

A Prayerful Posture

A person can meditate sitting on the floor or sitting on a chair.

- ❖ On the floor - the legs are folded, the back straight, the hands resting on the knees.
- ❖ On a chair - the back straight, the feet together on the floor, the hands resting in the lap.

Relax the body

When the person is sitting comfortably, it is helpful to calm the body by relaxing the muscles. Tension can build up in muscles and joints without us even realising it. The tension in the various muscle groups is relieved by tightening and relaxing one part of the body at a time. When the body is relaxed, close the eyes. Distractions are eliminated when the eyes are closed. It allows the person to begin entering their own personal world.

Breathe deeply

Taking a series of slow, deep breaths at the start of a meditation helps the person to be more focused and calm. Sitting quietly, the person becomes aware of his/her breathing, inhaling slowly through the nose and exhaling slowly through the mouth.

Become still and calm

Once the mind and the body are relaxed, the person becomes still and calm. He/she is now ready to focus on being in God's presence in prayer.

The next step is the act of meditating. Focus on something that will draw the mind closer to God. An icon, a religious symbol or a passage from scripture can be used for that purpose. In meditation, the person calmly thinks about Jesus as he/she gazes at an icon, or imagines the scene in a passage from scripture.

Guided Meditation

Guided meditation relies on people's ability to imagine a scene in which they encounter Jesus. Guided meditations are usually undertaken in groups. A teacher or chaplain will direct a class or a retreat group to become quiet and still. Then he/she will read aloud a story from the Gospel, or from some imaginary event.

Everyone gets enough time to follow the script and make it their own. Each one imagines themselves entering the scene and meeting Jesus, and perhaps talking to him. Participants take what they need from the encounter; for some it might be comfort, for others it might be forgiveness, strength, or maybe courage.

Steps in a Guided Meditation

- ❖ Find a quiet place.
- ❖ Sit in an upright position, close the eyes.
- ❖ Relax the body.
- ❖ Breathe deeply.
- ❖ A script is read aloud in a slow relaxed voice.
- ❖ The reader stops frequently to allow those meditating to imagine the scene as it develops; "Now imagine yourself.."
- ❖ Those meditating fill in their own reactions to what is being read.
- ❖ At the end the leader says "When you are ready, return from the scene and open your eyes." Stretch if necessary

After undertaking a guided meditation it can be helpful to spend some time writing down one's thoughts about the experience.

Praying with Scripture

Praying with scripture involves reading a passage from the Bible and meditating on what it means in our lives today. Christians believe the Bible is the Word of God. When they read the Bible in a thoughtful way they believe they are listening to God speaking in their hearts.

A person reading about an event in the life of Jesus can use their imagination to picture the scene as it might have happened. The person can put themselves into the scene in the role of one of the characters. Then he/she takes time to reflect on what Jesus might be saying to them through the reading.

Steps in Praying with Scripture

- ❖ Find a quiet place.
- ❖ Sit comfortably.
- ❖ Relax the body.
- ❖ Breathe deeply.
- ❖ Select a passage in the Gospel and read it slowly once or twice.
- ❖ Imagine entering the story to meet Jesus; go slowly and deeply into the scene.
- ❖ Pretend you are there on that day.
  - What is happening around you?
  - Who are you (a disciple, a bystander)?
  - What are you doing?
  - You approach Jesus.
  - What do you say to him?
  - What does Jesus say to you?
  - What is it like meeting Jesus?
- ❖ Gently return to the present, the meditation is over. Stretch if necessary.

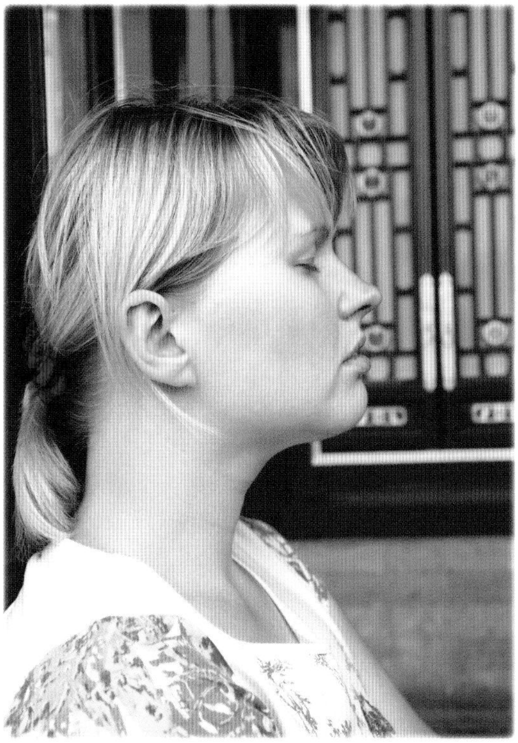

Meditating.

When Christians read and meditate on a passage from scripture they reflect on how its message can be applied to their daily lives.

Contemplation

Contemplation is deep prayer of the heart. It is a higher and more advanced form of silent prayer. Contemplation is communication with God without the use of words or thoughts of any kind. The person goes beyond words and thoughts to an awareness of God's presence deep within the core of their being.

Vocal Prayer:
Is a prayer of the lips. There is an emphasis on the use of words in both formal and informal prayers.

Meditation:
Is a prayer of the mind. The lips are quiet but the mind is active. There is an emphasis on the use of the imagination and the process of thought to gain insight and understanding.

Contemplation:
Is a prayer of the heart. The lips and the mind are at rest. The person goes beyond words and thoughts to an awareness of God's presence deep within the heart.

For a long time contemplative prayer was associated with monks and nuns living in monasteries. Such people dedicated their lives to this method of communicating with God. Although contemplation is seen as the highest form of prayer, this does not mean that only special 'holy' people can avail of it. It is a way of praying that is for any ordinary happy person who is content to spend time alone with God.

Steps in Contemplative Prayer

Contemplation is a sense of being quiet and still in the presence of God.

The person:

- ❖ Finds a quiet place.
- ❖ Quietens the body, is calm and silent.
- ❖ Quietens the mind, sheds all thoughts, all feelings, all imaginings.
- ❖ Journeys inward to the centre, to silence.
- ❖ Waits and listens.
- ❖ God does the rest.

An important person in the spiritual tradition of Christianity

St. Teresa of Avila (1515-1582)

St. Teresa of Avila is an important person in the spiritual tradition of Christianity. Prayer had a central place in the life of St. Teresa, the founder of a religious order of Carmelite nuns. She discovered the practice of contemplative prayer and taught it to the nuns in her convents throughout Spain, her native land.

St. Theresa of Avila.

St. Teresa had been brought up to think of prayer only in terms of vocal prayer, but then realised there was a whole world of silent prayer waiting to be discovered. It was completely different to anything she had known before and appealed to her greatly. She valued it so highly that she founded a new religious order dedicated to contemplative prayer and a simple way of life.

St. Teresa of Avila is the founder of the Discaled Carmelites (discaled means barefoot; the sisters wore sandals instead of shoes worn by other Carmelites). The order was soon followed by a similar order for men who also followed the contemplative way of life. St. Teresa also wrote several books; her way of prayer was the main topic in all her writings.

The writings of St. Teresa of Avila

The books written by St. Teresa of Avila, especially the 'Interior Castle', describe the way a person can learn and progress in the method of contemplative prayer. Her writing has influenced the practice of Christian contemplative prayer to the present day.

In her book the 'Interior Castle', St. Teresa compared a person's interior prayer life to a castle with many rooms. All the rooms are inter-connected, each one inside the other. She used the image of the castle to describe the way a person progresses in prayer. One begins by entering the outer room, then gradually moves further and further inward. Deep within, at the very centre, is God.

St. Teresa's entire approach to prayer was based on the conviction that God is within each one of us at the very core of our being.

St. Teresa's Way of Prayer

- She closes her eyes and makes a journey to inner silence.
- No words have to be said.
- Nothing has to be thought.
- She waits in silence.
- God seeks her out.
- She rests in God's presence.

When St. Teresa prayed she simply let herself be quiet in God's presence. She fully believed that God is present deep within the heart and soul of each person.

Questions

Knowledge

1. What is prayer?
2. What is Christian meditation?
3. How do Christians prepare themselves to begin meditation?
4. What is involved in quietening the body for meditation?
5. What is guided meditation?
6. How do Christians pray and meditate on scripture?
7. What is contemplation?
8. What is the main difference between vocal prayer, meditation and contemplation?
9. How do Christians pray in a contemplative way?
10. a. Name one important person in the spiritual tradition of Christianity.
    b. What was his/her teaching on prayer?
    c. What is the title of one book on prayer written by this person?

Understanding

1. Describe an ideal setting for Christian meditation in the home or at school.
2. Explain why quietening the body is important before beginning meditative prayer.
3. Explain what happens when a person prays as part of a group doing a guided meditation.
4. Outline the contribution of St. Teresa of Avila to the development of contemplation in the spiritual tradition of Christianity.
5. Compare meditation and contemplation as forms of prayer.
   a. What are the similarities?
   b. What are the differences?

Research

- Find out about the importance of prayer in the lives of other people in the spiritual tradition of Christianity
  - Identify one person, giving his/her name, date and nationality.
  - Mention key aspects of his/her life story.
  - Explain how this person's life and work is an expression of his/her religious faith.
  - What is the evidence to suggest that prayer was very important in his/her life?
  - Compile a fact sheet and present it to the class.

Section F - The Moral Challenge

The *Syllabus Aims* in this section are:

- To explore the need to order relationships at the personal, communal and global levels.
- To explore how this need can be expressed in a variety of ways.
- To identify how this need is expressed in civil and other legal codes.
- To show how religious belief is expressed in particular moral visions.
- To explore the moral visions of two major world religions, one of which should be Christianity.
- To analyse the impact of these visions on the lives of believers and non-believers in considering some current moral issues.

Concept Checklist (Section F - The Moral Challenge)

Page

- ❑ **Action and consequence** - what people do and the effect it can have on themselves and others. 462
- ❑ **Authority** - the power of sacred texts and religious leaders to guide people on moral issues. 481
- ❑ **Choice** - looking at different options in a situation and selecting one. 459
- ❑ **Civil law** - the laws of a state that regulate the behaviour of people within the state. 523, 527
- ❑ **Conscience** - the ability to know and judge what is right and wrong in a particular situation. 490
- ❑ **Constitution** - a document outlining the fundamental political principles by which a state is governed. 523
- ❑ **Decision-making** - the process of making up one's mind about moral issues. 498
- ❑ **Forgiveness** - to have pity and be willing to excuse someone's mistake or wrongdoing. 518
- ❑ **Freedom** - the liberty to say, do or think what one wants. 459
- ❑ **Influence** - something that shapes or affects a person's behaviour. 455
- ❑ **Integrity** - being upright and honest and sticking to one's moral principles. 494
- ❑ **Judgement** - the belief that, in the end, God will judge each person on their moral behaviour. 514
- ❑ **Justice** - to treat all people fairly and respect their rights. 501
- ❑ **Laws** - codes of behaviour enforced by the state. 472
- ❑ **Libertarianism** - the view that people should be free to behave as they choose, without undue interference from the state. 530
- ❑ **Life** - the state or quality of being alive. 506
- ❑ **Morality** - a set of principles or rules to help us know the difference between right and wrong behaviour. 455
- ❑ **Moral growth** - the process by which people learn to distinguish right from wrong, and then do what is right. 485
- ❑ **Moral maturity** - the stage beyond self interest where people take the needs of others into account when making moral decisions. 485
- ❑ **Moral vision** - an awareness of what is right and wrong. 468, 472
- ❑ **Peace** - harmony between people instead of disorder or conflict. 501
- ❑ **Pluralism** - the view that all groups in society must have equal representation. 530
- ❑ **Reconciliation** - making the effort to heal and restore a broken relationship. 518
- ❑ **Relationships** - ways in which people are connected to one another. 464
- ❑ **Religious Fundamentalism** - the view that the laws of a state should be based on the moral laws of its dominant religion. 530
- ❑ **Religious moral vision** - an awareness of what is right and wrong shaped by religious beliefs. 475, 478
- ❑ **Respect** - to have a high regard for someone or something, and to treat each with great care. 506, 510
- ❑ **Sin** - any deliberate thought, word or action that damages a person's relationship with God and other people. 514
- ❑ **Society** - the entire web of relationships that binds communities together. 464
- ❑ **Stewardship** - the way people care for the Earth on behalf of God. 510
- ❑ **Tradition** - religious belief and practice handed down from generation to generation. 481
- ❑ **Truth** - being honest with oneself, others and God. 494

Morality

Key Concepts

Morality: a set of principles or rules to help us know the difference between right and wrong behaviour.

Influence: something that shapes or affects a person's behaviour.

Objectives

Be aware of different descriptions of what it means to be moral.

Identify key influences on moral behaviour.

Activity: *"Words and Meanings"*

TASK: TO KNOW WHEN A WORD IS BEING USED IN A MORAL AND A NON-MORAL SENSE.

✦ Divide the following statements into two categories to indicate when a word is being used in a moral and in a non-moral sense.

- Their take-out pizza is really <u>good</u>.
- There is a <u>bad</u> bend in the road.
- It is <u>wrong</u> to tell lies.
- It is <u>good</u> to have a warm-up before a match.
- Mahatma Gandhi was a <u>good</u> man.
- It is <u>right</u> to give to charity.
- She got all the answers <u>right</u>.
- It is <u>bad</u> to call them names like that.
- He phoned the <u>wrong</u> number.
- If someone is hurt it is <u>right</u> to help them.
- She said it was <u>good</u> of them to hand in the money that they found.
- It is <u>good</u> to have a hobby.

Discuss

- Which statements have a moral meaning?
- Can you explain the difference between moral statements and non-moral statements?

Morality

The words 'right', 'wrong', 'good' and 'bad' are part of the language of morality.

Morality has to do with the way we live our lives. It is about what is right and wrong, good and bad. Morality is a set of principles or rules to help people know the difference between right and wrong behaviour. It is the basis on which moral choices are made. Morality helps people to judge the difference between right and wrong. It also helps people to act on that judgement and do what is right and avoid what is wrong.

❖ Morality can tell us, for example, that:
a. Honesty is right and stealing is wrong.
b. Caring is right and angry outbursts are wrong.
c. Truthfulness is right and cheating is wrong.

❖ Morality guides our actions. Once we know the difference between right and wrong, we can do what is right and avoid what is wrong.

As human beings we are able to think about our behaviour. We can decide what to say and what to do in any given situation. From a moral point of view, we can either act in a way that we know is right, or we can do the opposite and act in a way that we know to be wrong.

See no evil,
hear no evil,
speak no evil.

5 EURO

Finding money on the ground - what to do?

✦ In the following scenarios:
- i. What is the moral issue?
- ii. What is the right thing to do?
- iii. What do you think happened in the end?

A. Kevin and Thomas rush out to the local take-away at lunchtime for sausages and chips. Even though their class got out a bit early, the place is already crowded. The staff are busy trying to serve everyone. When the boys finally collect their order, they realise they have been given the wrong change. They were only charged for the chips and nothing else.

✦ What should they do: keep the money or give it back?

B. Angie is at home in the kitchen trying to finish her technical drawing homework. The page is taped to the kitchen table and she is trying to get the measurements exactly right. Her little brother wanders in, making noise and distracting her from her work. She feels very annoyed.

✦ What should she do: shout at him and chase him away, or speak to him and give him something to do until she is finished?

C. Jane and the rest of the class are revising for another test. The teacher says he expects them all to do much better than they did last time. When a knock on the door distracts him for a minute Jane, who is sitting in the front row, gets a quick glance at the test paper on top of his books. She sees one of the questions that will be coming up the next day.

✦ What should she do: go ahead and cheat in the test, or revise everything and do her best?

Different descriptions of what it means to be moral

People sometimes have different notions or ideas of what it means to be moral. For example when judging whether an action such as stealing, drunk-driving, lying, vandalism or cheating is right or wrong, they might say it depends on...

1. Their emotions - how they might feel about it afterwards. "I'd feel guilty about it."
2. The consequences - what could happen if they do it. "I might get caught."
3. Laws and rules - if it's against the law or a rule. "It's against the rules."
4. Their conscience - knowing that it's right or wrong. "Something tells me it's wrong."
5. The situation - the background, what led up to it. "It depends on what was going on at the time."
6. Common practice - whether everyone is doing it or not. "It's no big deal, everyone's doing it."
7. Authority - if someone orders them or forces them to do it. "They told me to do it."

The following adjectives can be applied to people when a moral issue is involved.

A <u>moral</u> person.
Someone who knows the difference between right and wrong and chooses to do what is right.

An <u>immoral</u> person.
Someone who knows the difference between right and wrong and chooses to do what is wrong.

An <u>amoral</u> person.
Someone who has no regard for any standards of right or wrong, and just does what he/she likes.

Influence

We all have certain ideas about right and wrong behaviour. However, we do not reach these conclusions entirely on our own. Our morality, our sense of right and wrong, is influenced by a number of factors.

Where does our morality come from? Who influences what we believe is right and wrong, good and bad, in human actions? Our moral outlook, our sense of what is right and what is wrong, is influenced by many factors such as:

- ❖ Our family and the way we are brought up.
- ❖ Our peers and what matters to them.
- ❖ The type of society in which we live.
- ❖ The education we receive.
- ❖ The religion to which we belong.
- ❖ The media, in its many forms.

All these things are mixed up inside us as we struggle to know the difference between right and wrong, and do what is right and avoid what is wrong. These influences can be positive or negative. All have the power to shape or affect our moral behaviour. These factors influence our behaviour to varying degrees at different stages throughout our lives. For example, the family has a big influence on our moral behaviour in childhood, while friends and peers tend to have a considerable impact on our moral behaviour in adolescence.

✦ In the following scenario try to identify the various influences at work as a moral decision is being made.

Ciara has a Saturday job in the local supermarket. She has worked there for almost six months and was hoping to get extra hours over the school holidays. But she missed out, the manager gave the job to someone else. "It's not fair," Ciara complained, "She hasn't been here half as long as I have." Ciara was really annoyed and went straight up to the office. "They owe me," she thought to herself as she knocked on the door. There was no reply so she went inside. "Still on their break probably," she thought as she looked around. Glancing at a nearby desk, an opportunity suddenly presented itself...

a. What opportunity may have arisen?

b. What do you think Ciara might do?

c. Identify the influences at work as Ciara struggles to make a moral decision.

d. What factors might have the strongest influence on Ciara's moral choice?

Major influences on our moral behaviour

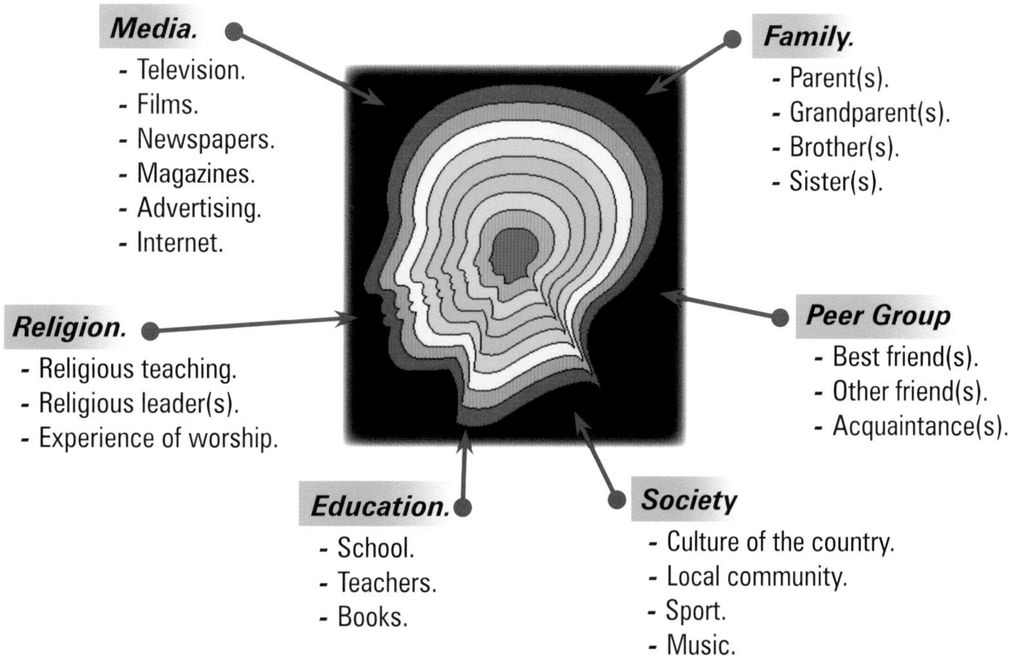

Media.
- Television.
- Films.
- Newspapers.
- Magazines.
- Advertising.
- Internet.
Family.
- Parent(s).
- Grandparent(s).
- Brother(s).
- Sister(s).
Religion.
- Religious teaching.
- Religious leader(s).
- Experience of worship.
Peer Group
- Best friend(s).
- Other friend(s).
- Acquaintance(s).
Education.
- School.
- Teachers.
- Books.
Society
- Culture of the country.
- Local community.
- Sport.
- Music.

The Golden Rule

Morality is a universal characteristic of people everywhere. Morality is about how we live and how we treat the people around us. The way we behave toward each other is an issue for societies in every part of the world. We might wonder then if there is any universal agreement on what is the right way to behave. Is there any rule or guideline that is common to everyone?

The great world religions speak for millions of people, past and present, in all parts of the world. These religions appear to agree on one common rule for human behaviour. This rule is known as 'The Golden Rule'. Although each religion expresses this rule in slightly different words, the meaning is the same: all people must behave toward each other in the right way.

The Golden Rule

- Christianity:
  "Do for others what you would want them to do for you." (Luke 6:31)
- Judaism:
  "What is harmful to you, do not do to your fellow men." (Talmud Shabaat 3id)
- Islam:
  "None of you is a true believer if you do not desire for your brother what you desire for yourself."
  (Hadith 13 Al Bukhari)
- Hinduism:
  "Do not do to others what would make you suffer if it were done to you."(Mahabharata 5:1517)
- Buddhism:
  "Hurt not others in ways that you yourself would find hurtful."
  (Udana-Varga 5,18)

In 'The Golden Rule' the great world religions appear to agree on one common guideline for human behaviour:

We should treat other people the way we ourselves would like to be treated.

Questions

Knowledge

1. What is morality?
2. What are moral decisions? Give examples?
3. a. Make a list of three things that you personally think are morally right to do.
   b. Try to explain why you think these things are right.
4. a. Make a list of three things that you personally think are morally wrong to do.
   b. Try to explain why you think these things are wrong.
5. List some of the different notions or ideas people have about making moral judgements.
6. a. Give an example of a character that you have read about in a book, seen on television, or in a film or video game, who fits the description of one of the following: i. A moral person. ii. An immoral person. iii. An amoral person.
   b. Try to explain why you place the character in that particular category.
7. Factors that influence moral behaviour.
   a. Who or what influences our understanding of right and wrong?
   b. What was the strongest influence on our moral behaviour when we were younger?
   c. What can be the strongest influence on our moral behaviour now:
      - In a positive way?
      - In a negative way?
   d. What might be the strongest influence on our moral behaviour as we get older?
8. a. What is the Golden Rule?
   b. Imagine what the world would be like if people were to live by the Golden Rule.
      - What would there be much more of?
      - What would there be much less of?
   c. If you decided to treat people as you would like to be treated:
      - What kind of things would you always try to do?
      - What kind of things would you never do?
   d. Why is it called 'The Golden Rule'?

Understanding

1. What is the difference between right and wrong moral behaviour?
2. Why do people have different notions or ideas about what it means to be moral?
3. What do you think has the biggest influence on our moral behaviour?
4. Does morality matter?

Free to Choose

Key Concepts

Choice: looking at different options in a situation and selecting one.

Freedom: the liberty to say, do or think what one wants.

Objective

Show that freedom and choice are aspects of morality.

Activity: *"Bottle Bank"*

TASK: TO BE ABLE TO THINK ABOUT ALTERNATIVE OPTIONS.

- Display a collection of empty containers, for example:
  - a soft drinks can.
  - a ketchup bottle.
  - a butter tub.
  - a spice jar.
- In pairs, list as many uses as possible for each item. Afterwards, compare all the lists made by the class.

Discuss

- For which item did you find the most uses?
- List the different ways this item could be used.
- Was it easy or difficult to think up different ways of using things?
- Are you used to looking at things in different ways?

Choices about right and wrong are called moral choices.

Choice

Making a decision involves looking at all options in a situation.

Human beings are unique. We are able to think and make up our minds about things, unlike creatures in the natural world that react to things purely by instinct. We can think for ourselves, we have choices.

Choice involves looking at the different options in a situation and selecting one. People make choices about all sorts of things every day. Most choices are easy to make and are just a matter of routine, such as:

- What time to get up.
- What to have for breakfast.
- Who to sit beside in class.
- Where to go at lunchtime.

Moral Choices

Deciding what is right and wrong is more demanding and can take more time. Choices about right and wrong are called moral choices. For example, deciding whether to:

- Cheat in a test - or not.
- Gossip about someone - or not.
- Lie to get oneself out of trouble - or not.
- Stand by as someone is being bullied - or not.
- Pay the correct fare on the bus - or not.

In all cases there are usually a number of options available to us. So before making a moral decision it is a good idea to examine the options; to look at the different ways of working something out.

Moral Dilemma

✦ Discuss the following moral dilemma.

The issue

The class is in the Home Economics room. Everyone is tidying up after a cookery lesson. John and Paula notice that once again Karl is slipping something into his school bag. This time it is a small sharp knife from the cutlery drawer. What can they do?

The options

- ❑ Tell the teacher at once.
- ❑ Say nothing.
- ❑ Tell Karl to put it back.
- ❑ Talk to the class tutor as soon as possible.
- ❑ Discuss it later with your parents.
- ❑ Tell the Principal.
- ❑ Tell some other people in the class.
- ❑ Speak to the Home Economics teacher when everyone else has left the room.
- ❑ Other.

Questions

1. What is the issue?
2. What is the best option?
3. Why would the two students choose that option?
4. What do you think other people might do in that situation?

Activity

Find out a bit more about the choices we make on a daily basis. Divide into pairs or groups (optional).

- ❖ List the various choices you have made so far today.
- ❖ Are there any "moral choices" on the list? (A moral choice is a choice between good and bad, right and wrong.)
- ❖ In the case of one moral issue,
  - what options were available?
  - what moral choice was made?
  - what influenced your choice?

Personal freedom and responsibility go together.

Freedom

All people have a desire to be free. This can mean being able to act in the way we choose.

We might like to:

- ✧ Say what we want.
- ✧ Do what we want.
- ✧ Go where we want.
- ✧ Get what we want.
- ✧ Be all that we want to be.

Freedom and Responsibility

However, we soon realise that no one is completely free in this sense. Our society could not function if everyone just did what they wanted and ignored the effect of their actions on other people.

When we make choices we have to take other people into account. We must think of their needs too. So our freedom is possible only if we respect the freedom of others. Personal freedom and responsibility towards others go hand-in-hand. Freedom means that we can do what we choose, but only within certain limits.

Limits to freedom

Our freedom is limited by factors that are both outside and inside ourselves.

Limits from outside

- ❖ The laws of the country; what is legal and illegal.
- ❖ The rules of the school; what we must do, and what we are forbidden to do.
- ❖ The guidelines of Church and religion; what it is right and wrong to say and to do.
- ❖ The expectations of parents; what we are allowed and not allowed to do.
- ❖ The attitude of our friends; what they might think and say.

Limits from inside

- ❖ Our freedom might be limited by our shyness or maybe even by our laziness. On the other hand, it could be a deep fear or certain worries that stop us from doing what we want. It might even be not having enough self-confidence, or it might simply be a lack of knowledge or information about something. We can see the way our personal freedom is limited if we think about the following examples:
  - ✧ If I want to go bungee-jumping, but I am afraid of heights, my freedom is going to be limited.
  - ✧ If I want a CD or a DVD, and I don't have the money to buy it, my freedom is limited if I believe stealing is wrong, and I know taking something without paying for it is illegal anyway.
  - ✧ If I like someone and want to go out with him or her, but my text messages are never answered, this puts a limit on my chances of making something happen.

As human beings we can think and make choices, and can choose between different courses of action. However, there are certain limits on our freedom to act. Our freedom is limited by factors inside and outside ourselves. This is especially true in cases where moral issues are involved.

Questions

Knowledge

1. What are moral choices?
2. Consider the scenarios below.
   In each instance:
   a. What is the issue?
   b. What are the options?
   c. Choose the best thing to do.
   d. Explain why you chose that option.
   i. You are ready to go out with your friends when your mother asks you to baby-sit. What can you do?
   ii. Your friends are smoking behind the gym and they ask you to join them. What can you do?
   iii. You are walking down the corridor when someone calls you a name. What can you do?

Understanding

1. Why would we look at the range of available options before making moral choices?
2. Provide some examples of external and internal limitations on the personal freedom of individuals.
3. Explain the connection between freedom and responsibility.
4. Imagine what a perfect day would be like. List five things that would make a day really special for you...

   Now ask yourself:
   - Are you free to do what you want?
   - Are you free to be where you would like to be?
   - What limits your freedom?
   - What enhances your freedom?
   - How perfect is a perfect day after all?
   - In real life, freedom is....

Consequences

Key Concept

Action and consequence: what people do and the effect it can have on themselves and others.

Objective

Show that people's moral choices have consequences for themselves and others.

Activity: *"Pros. and Cons."*

TASK: TO CONSIDER THE POSITIVE AND NEGATIVE EFFECTS OF CERTAIN CHOICES.

✦ Respond to the list of statements below.

This action may have:
\+ positive consequences. (✓)

This action may have:
− negative consequences. (✓)

Choices	+	−
1. David's bicycle has a slow puncture. He cycles to school on it anyway.	❑	❑
2. Shirley climbs a gate into a field. There is a sign: 'Beware of the bull'.	❑	❑
3. Joe is wrongly accused of fighting. He goes to find his tutor to explain what happened.	❑	❑
4. Ken sets off for the cinema but is unsure what time the film starts.	❑	❑
5. Tanya puts a lead on the dog and takes him for a walk.	❑	❑
6. Fiona's parents argue a lot. She phones her grandmother to chat about it.	❑	❑
7. Ray finds a way to let the teacher know who took the caretaker's keys.	❑	❑
8. Lucy is being bullied at school but tells no-one.	❑	❑

Discuss

- Which choices may have...
  a. positive consequences
  b. negative consequences
  ... for those involved?
- How can a choice made by one person have consequences for other people? Discuss an example.
- How can we judge whether our choices will be good or bad for someone.

Action and Consequence

Our actions have consequences for ourselves and others.

Everything we say or do affects someone else. This is certainly true in relation to moral choices concerning right and wrong. When we make a choice to do something, we know that it is going to affect us in some way and may also affect others.

Consequence is the word used to describe the result, or the effect, of our action on ourselves and other people. When we choose to do something our actions can have good consequences for us, and for those around us. Sometimes though, our actions can have bad consequences. This is the case wherever we are. At school, for example, what we say and do affects others around us, such as the teachers, other students and our friends. Similarly, what we say and do at home affects other people in the family.

Moral Choices

When people make a choice and act on it there are consequences, some positive, others negative.

MORAL CHOICE
↓
ACTION
↓
CONSEQUENCES
↙ ↘
POSITIVE **NEGATIVE**

When people make moral choices they are choosing between right and wrong. A moral person knows the difference between right and wrong and chooses to do what is right. Consider the actions and consequences in the following moral dilemma.

Actions have consequences.

Moral Dilemma

Steve has met up with a few friends in town, they all go along to the video shop. While they look around at the new releases, Steve wanders over to the games section. The one he is going to get next is already in, in fact a 'demo' copy has been left in one of the consoles. No-one is looking...

What might he decide to do? First, think of the options. Then, look at the consequences.

a. Which option might he select?

b. What consequences might this option have: i. for him. ii. for others.

c. Are any of these consequences good or bad for someone?

d. Could any of these consequences be anticipated beforehand?

e. Are there any other options available that might have a different set of consequences?

f. In your experience, do people tend to think ahead, or do they do the first thing that occurs to them?

To be a moral person means to know the difference between right and wrong, and choose what is right and avoid what is wrong. Sometimes it is hard to know what is the right thing to do. Sometimes it is easy to know the right thing to do but it might not be easy to do it. That is part of the challenge everyone faces when making a moral decision.

Questions

Knowledge

1. All actions have consequences - what are consequences?
2. Using personal examples, explain the connection between action and consequence.
3. Imagine it was you in the video shop; you took the game and you were caught. What effect do you think this would have on:
   a. Your parents?
   b. Your friends?
   c. Other people?
   d. Yourself as a person?
4. If you took the game and did not get caught, would your action have an effect on anyone?
5. Give an example of another situation involving a moral choice.
   Identify the consequences of making:
   (a) a right choice. (b) a wrong choice.
   Explain how each choice might affect relationships with:
   (a) Family and friends. (b) The community.

Understanding

1. Everything we say and do causes something else to happen. In other words there is a chain reaction.
   Think about the following scenario.
   Natalie and a group of friends meet at the cinema on a Friday night. When everyone arrives they go inside to queue for their tickets. Natalie's brother is also there that night, he has a part-time job checking tickets. Natalie goes over and speaks to him. They talk for a minute, then she is back whispering something to her friends.
   a. What you think happens next?
   b. Draw a diagram of the chain of events that might follow from the choices Natalie has available to her. Consider Natalie's options and the consequence of each option.
   c. How might Natalie's choices affect her relationship with those around her?

Relationships

Key Concepts

Relationships: ways in which people are connected to one another.

Society: the entire web of relationships that binds communities together.

Objective

Explain how our moral choices affect our relationships at every level.

Activity: *"In the Frame"*

TASK: TO IDENTIFY SOME IMPORTANT RELATIONSHIPS IN OUR LIVES.

- ✦ Draw a diagram placing yourself in the centre.
- ✦ Around you, write the names or initials of people who are important in your life.

Discuss

- Why did you choose these people?
- In what ways have they made a difference to your life?
- List some positive ways in which you have made a difference to their lives.
- Select one or two of these people. What do you think they might say about what you mean to them?

Human relationships.

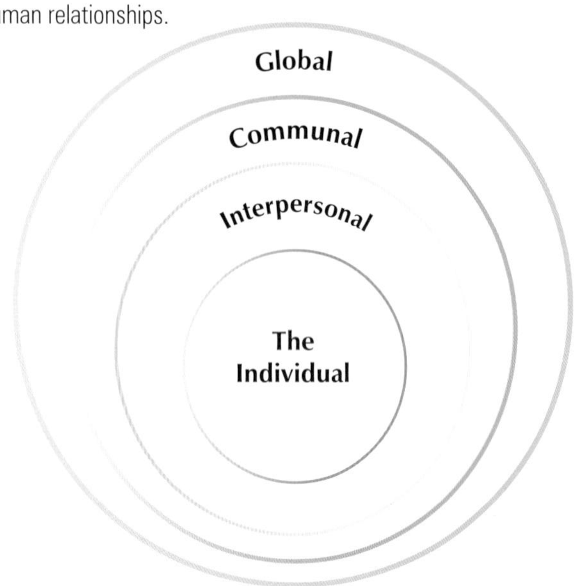
Global
Communal
Interpersonal
The Individual

Relationships

Our moral choices affect our relationships with others.

Human beings do not live in isolation but are connected to other people through a network of relationships. Our relationships are the different ways in which we, as human beings, are connected to one another. Our relationships are not all the same because we interact with people in a variety of ways. We have:

- ❖ **Interpersonal relationships** - at an individual level with family and friends.
- ❖ **Communal relationships** - at a group or community level with a class, a team, a school, a parish or a neighbourhood.
- ❖ **Global relationships** - at a worldwide level with the rest of humanity.

Moral Choices

The moral choices we make have consequences for everyone. The right choice will strengthen our relationships in a positive way. The wrong choice will weaken and damage those relationships. When we make a moral choice we need to think of the impact it will have on others; people close to us, and people further away.

We have to ask ourselves:

- ✦ How will my decision...
  - i. affect me?
  - ii. affect my family and friends?
  - iii. affect my community?
  - iv. affect the world?

Interpersonal Relationships

These are the relationships we have with people on an individual basis. We are quite close to some people and know them very well. For example, we have interpersonal relationships with our parents, our brothers and sisters and our friends.

Other people we meet only occasionally and don't know them well at all. We can also have a one-to-one relationship with such people, for example a neighbour, a teacher, the bus driver, or a shop assistant.

A close personal relationship exists between family members.

How we behave, what we choose to say and do, has an impact on all the people we know and meet on a daily basis.

Communal Relationships

This is the relationship that exists between an individual and a group of people. Each of us belongs to a number of different groups or communities. For example, as young people we are members of a class and a school. We may also belong to a neighbourhood, a parish, a team, a club or society, a county and a country. We can have relationships with all these communities.

Team members share a communal relationship.

The choices we make, the things we say and do, can have an impact on one or all of these groups. It may be something positive and helpful that brings honour to the group. It could also be something negative and hurtful that dishonours the group or disrupts the harmony within the group.

Global Relationships

These are the relationships that connect us to the world at large. The choices we make can have an impact on people everywhere. The question is, how can the actions of one person, or even a few people, make a difference to everyone else? If we accept that every action has a reaction, we can understand how the ripple effect works. Our actions can have consequences for a whole series of relationships. Every decision we make has an effect on the world around us, close to and far away. For example, a careless act such as dropping litter can have consequences for our relationship with an entire range of people.

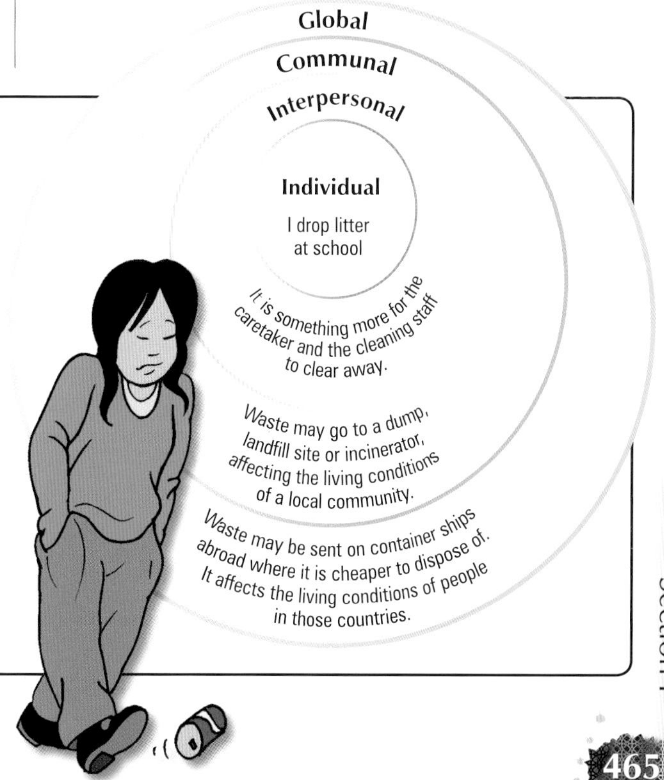
Global
Communal
Interpersonal
Individual
I drop litter at school
It is something more for the caretaker and the cleaning staff to clear away.
Waste may go to a dump, landfill site or incinerator, affecting the living conditions of a local community.
Waste may be sent on container ships abroad where it is cheaper to dispose of. It affects the living conditions of people in those countries.

Section F

We now recognise that no one is totally independent. Just about every decision we make and everything we do affects someone else.

- It might be someone we know who is near to us (family, friends, the local community).
- It could be someone we've never met, living in a place we've never been.

The story of Louis Braille shows how the decisions and actions of one person can have a positive effect on the lives of other people at an interpersonal, communal and global level.

Louis Braille

Louis Braille was born in 1809 in a small town near Paris. As a child he had an accident that left him disabled for the remainder of his life. The bright, inquisitive little boy liked to play in his fathers workshop. On one occasion he wandered in and began examining some items on top of a work bench. Somehow he stumbled, and one of the sharp tools injured his eye. The wound became infected. Soon the infection spread to both eyes, damaging his eyesight. At four years of age Louis was completely blind.

Louis' parents sent him to the local school along with his brothers and sisters. The teacher allowed him to sit in the classroom and Louis tried to learn what he could by listening. He was eager to learn and, although he was unable to read or write, at ten years of age he was awarded a scholarship to attend a school for blind boys in Paris.

At school in Paris

The school in Paris was new and the first of its kind at that time. It was better than the village school but, even here, the teachers just talked to the students. They were taught practical skills such as caning chairs and making slippers that would be useful ways of earning a living afterwards. The boys were intelligent and as smart as anyone else, they just couldn't see. Louis felt that blind people should be able to get on in life like sighted people. Learning to read and write was one way to make it happen; he decided to do something about it.

The challenge

The idea of 'finger reading' had been around for some time. However the methods that were available were too cumbersome, and of little use

Reading braille.

to people who were blind. Louis thought that there must be a better way, and the idea that he could read by feeling the words on the page began to capture his imagination.

Louis began to experiment. A system of raised dots punched into heavy paper was the most promising direction to follow. He set himself the goal of making a raised-dot alphabet that was quick to read. He made hundreds of patterns on pieces of cardboard, spending every spare moment trying to work it out. Everyone around him said it was impossible; blind people would never be able to read. However, Louis' parents encouraged him and he kept on punching holes into cardboard. He frequently felt tired and discouraged, but he never gave up.

The breakthrough

After three years Louis made a breakthrough. He worked out an alphabet made up entirely of six dots. The position of the raised dots was different for each letter. Better still, with proper training it could be read at speed. This was an exciting discovery. All blind people could learn to read using this method. Louis Braille was only fifteen years old at the time of this achievement and the new system of touch-reading was later named after him.

Braille is now used in almost every language throughout the world. It enables blind and partially sighted people everywhere to take control of their lives and be independent. Today, many years after his death, Louis is honoured in his native country. He is buried in the Pantheon in Paris, the resting place of France's national heroes.

Society

As human beings we are members of small family groups and larger communities. Good relationships must exist for a group of any size, large or small, to function properly. Society is the entire web of human relationships that binds communities together. It is the way people manage to live together as a group.

All groups tend to be organised, otherwise there is chaos. Each group works out a way of behaving that benefits all its members. This is true of societies in every part of the world, including the society in which we ourselves live. Irish and British society is organised in a way that is for the good of all its citizens.

If we look at our society, we see, for example, that the welfare of children is a top priority. Children are well cared for in families, they are educated in schools, and get medical attention in hospitals and clinics. Children are taught to obey the rules of the road and the laws of the land because it protects them and ensures their personal safety.

The role of the family

Within families parents prepare children for life in society. A child is taught how to relate to people such as parents, grandparents, brothers, sisters, friends and neighbours. The home is where the child first learns the difference between acceptable and unacceptable behaviour. It is where the child learns the moral standards of the family and the customs and traditions of the society in which they all live.

The family links the child to society. The family, and later the school, prepares the child for life as a responsible member of society. The family, the school and the Church are units of society. Each has an important role in preparing children to be responsible members of society by teaching and showing them good moral behaviour.

Questions

1. Name three different types of human relationships and give examples of each.
2. a) Think about the following situation and decide what you would do in this case.
   b) Consider how others might be affected by your decision.

   The year didn't get off to a good start, Carla hates school now. She could easily take a day off and go into town. Of course she would make sure she got home at the usual time. No one need find out.
3. Describe how a player's behaviour can affect a club or a school team.
   a. What happens if he/she always turns up for training and plays his/her best every time?
   b. What happens if he/she turns up when it suits and makes an effort only now and again?
4. a. Who was Louis Braille?
   b. What were the consequences of his decision to find a way for blind people to read?
   c. How did Louis' decision affect his relationships:
      - at an interpersonal level with those around him?
      - at a communal level with those in his own community in France?
      - at a global level with people the world over?
   d. How would you describe the personality and character of Louis Braille? What is your evidence?
5. What is society?
6. What is the function of the family in our society?
7. "There is no such thing as society." Respond to this statement.

Research

A. Find out about Amnesty International's letter writing campaign for prisoners of conscience.

The campaign works on the principle that, although an individual or a community action may appear small, the more of it there is, the more likely national governments and international bodies will take notice.
- What is Amnesty International?
- Who are prisoners of conscience?
- How does a letter campaign work?

B. Describe how an individual letter writing action can affect relationships between people at the following levels:
- Interpersonal. - Communal. - Global.

✱ Source an example to illustrate your points. Present the results to the class.

Sources of Morality

Key Concept

Moral vision: an awareness of what is right and wrong.

Objective

Explain 'moral vision' and identify sources of morality in our lives.

Activity: *"Way to go!"*

TASK: TO BE AWARE OF WHERE WE STAND ON CERTAIN ISSUES.

✦ You will need:
- space to move around.
- labels for three areas of the room. Mark each area:

RIGHT
WRONG
Not sure

✦ The teacher reads a statement from the list opposite.
- Students respond by moving to a position which reflects their outlook on the matter.
- Each student must be ready to give one reason why he/she made this choice.

✦ The teacher invites responses from two or three students in each position.

✦ If a student reconsiders, he/she is free to move to another position.

Discuss

- What made it easy or difficult to undertake this activity?
- Are people generally aware of their position on moral issues?
- Are you fully aware of your own standpoint on certain moral issues?

Is it Right or Wrong to...(✓)	Right.	Wrong.	Not sure.
✧ Keep a secret.			
✧ Talk about someone behind their back.			
✧ Neglect animals.			
✧ Help people out if they need it.			
✧ Drink alcohol and drive.			
✧ Steal bars of chocolate from the shop.			
✧ Borrow stuff without asking.			
✧ Be vulgar.			
✧ Tell a lie to get out of trouble.			
✧ Buy alcohol for underage friends.			
✧ Stick up for your friends.			
✧ Break up a fight before it gets out of hand.			
✧ Smoke in public places.			
✧ Keep money if you find it.			
✧ Do something for a good cause.			

Moral Vision

Our standpoint on moral issues is influenced by our moral vision.

Our moral vision is our view or awareness of what is right and wrong, fair and unfair. It's the way we see life and how we think it should be lived. Our moral vision has a powerful influence on the choices we make. It affects what we say and do. It shapes how we behave morally.

A moral vision is like a pair of sunglasses, it affects the way we see the world.

Sources of Morality

The source of something means the origin or the place from which it comes. When we talk about the source of our morality, we are asking where our ideas about right and wrong actually come from. The main sources of morality are the family, the peer group, the school, religion and the state.

The Family

One of the most important sources of morality is the family. The family is the first place where people learn about right and wrong. Parents regard it as their duty to teach their children good moral behaviour. They want their children to know that it is good to share, to tell the truth, and to treat others with respect.

At first children learn by imitation and copy what they see and hear around them. Then they begin to notice how others respond to them. They quickly learn what behaviour is acceptable, and what behaviour is out of line. In this way parents, and quite often grandparents, come to have a big influence on a child's moral outlook.

The family is therefore one of the principal sources of a person's morality. The family can influence one's sense of what is right and wrong, good and bad, through a range of formal and informal rules and expectations. These might restrict individual freedom, but are there for the benefit of family members and the good of the community as a whole.

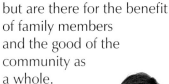

The family is a key source of our moral vision - our sense of right and wrong.

Friends have an impact on our moral vision - our sense of right and wrong.

The Peer Group

Another important source of morality is the peer group, ie. those who are the same age and share the same interests as ourselves. Mixing with friends and classmates makes us aware that there are alternative ways of behaving.

Our friends are very important to us, they are people we know and like, and who are easy to get on with. We tend to value their opinion and try to fit in with them. Friends therefore can have a big influence on us. This can be positive and may help us, for example, to be good listeners, to be loyal and trustworthy, to be thoughtful and considerate. Friendships can also influence us in the opposite direction, sometimes resulting in dishonest, cruel or insensitive behaviour.

The peer group is a significant source of morality for adolescents. This becomes clear when we see its influence on the decisions we make about right and wrong behaviour.

The School

The school can influence our sense of right and wrong through the words and actions of teachers, the content of lessons, the code of discipline, school wide activities and the general interaction of students and staff.

During our teenage years the school community is one of the most important groups to which we belong. School prepares us to enter adult life as mature, well rounded, responsible individuals.

School exposes us to a range of people and situations that have an important influence on our behaviour. Interacting with classmates, teachers and other members of staff, shows us the value of working in co-operation with other people. In class we learn the importance of respecting the rights of others, making an effort and working to the best of our ability. In a club or society, or as a member of team, we learn important lessons in teamwork, loyalty and fair play.

The school is therefore a significant source of morality and its effect can remain with us for the rest of our lives.

Religion

Religion is a very important source of morality. People's moral outlook can be strongly influenced by the religion in which they have been brought up.

Moral teaching on what is right and wrong is found in the sacred texts of the great world religions. Christians, for example, follow the teaching of Jesus in the Bible. Roman Catholics, in addition, are guided by their Church's teaching on moral issues. The moral teaching of a community of faith can have a major influence on the behaviour of believers.

The Golden Rule is a statement from each world religion about what it means to be moral. It guides the followers of each religion in making a judgement about right and wrong behaviour.

The teaching of Jesus in the Bible is the fundamental source of morality for Christians.

The State

The State can influence our moral behaviour. The State makes laws to protect the rights of individuals and their property. The laws are enforced and must be obeyed; this ensures that citizens behave in a responsible manner.

Irish government buildings.

We live in a democratic state. Our system of government is a democracy, which means we vote to elect people to run the country on our behalf. The elected government makes laws to protect the rights and well-being of everyone living here.

State laws are designed to ensure that everyone acts responsibly. For example, theft is against the law. It is illegal to steal because it interferes with a person's right to own property. On the roads, speeding and drunk-driving are offences because of the danger to the lives of others. To supply alcohol and cigarettes to those underage is illegal because it is a threat to the health and development of young people. When people fail to obey the laws of the state, they are usually brought to court; if found guilty, they can be punished.

In this way the state can be a source of morality. People obey the laws of the state because they believe the laws are just.

Questions

Knowledge

1. What is a moral vision?
2. What are your views on the following moral issues? Name the people in your life who influence your views on these matters.
   i. To take something that does not belong to you: - is right. - is wrong.
   ii. To own up if you have made a mistake: - is right. - is wrong.
   iii. To get your own back on someone who has done something against you: - is right. - is wrong.
3. a. Who has the most influence on your moral viewpoint?
   b. How does this person or group influence your moral behaviour?
4. List in order of priority the main sources of influence on your moral vision.

Understanding

1. Explain how parents can be a source of morality for their sons and daughters.
2. In what ways can the peer group have:
   a. a positive influence, and
   b. a negative influence,
   on a young person's moral behaviour.
3. How can classmates, teachers, and other members of the school community influence a person's moral behaviour?
4. How might a person's religious beliefs affect their moral behaviour?
5. Provide two examples to show that the laws of the state can influence or shape our morality.
6. Is it possible that we could be a source of morality for someone else? Why? Why not?

Research

- Find out a bit more about our moral vision.

A. Imagine what it would be like if you and your friend found something valuable such as:
- A wallet with a sum of money inside.
- A sports bag with a complete kit.
- A mobile phone (the latest model).

Compose a short dialogue based on the incident. Entitle it 'Finders Keepers'.

B. Discuss the moral vision at work among the characters in the script? Do both characters have:
i. the same view on what is right and wrong?
ii. different views on what is right and wrong?

C. Identify a possible source of their moral outlook. Where might it come from?

Codes of Behaviour

Key Concepts

Laws: codes of behaviour enforced by the state.

Moral vision: an awareness of what is right and wrong.

Objective

Examine the evolution of formal and informal codes of behaviour.

Activity: *"Guess the Rule"*

TASK: TO IDENTIFY A RULE OPERATING IN A GROUP.

- Ask a volunteer to go to a distant part of the room. He/she must turn away and prepare two questions to ask each student about their interests, favourite food, subject, colour, etc.
- Meanwhile, the class agree on a rule they will employ when the volunteer returns. The rule could be, for example, that each respondent will fold their arms, smile, etc.
- When the volunteer returns, he/she is to interview a number of students and must guess the rule on which the class is operating.
- When successful he/she gets a clap from everyone.

Discuss

- How did the class decide on the rule for the exercise?
- Did the class keep the rule? Explain.
- How did the volunteer know which rule was being used?
- Most groups who do things together have rules. Why do groups have rules?

Laws

Moral vision

Rules direct behaviour in a positive way for the well-being of everyone.

We live in an organised society. Most of the groups to which we belong have a code of behaviour. A code is a set of rules that point out acceptable ways to behave in a particular situation.

Formal and informal codes of behaviour operate in schools.

School Rules

What are the rules of the school?

Ask everyone to write down one school rule from memory.

Discuss a few examples.

- Who agrees that this is a school rule?
- Is it written down anywhere?
- How did you know about this rule?
- If it's not written down, what makes you think it is a rule?

Formal and informal rules

There are formal and informal codes of behaviour.

A formal code - is a written rule.
It's an official rule that is written down and must be accepted by everyone.

An informal code - is an unwritten rule.
It's an unofficial rule that is not written down, but is nonetheless accepted by everyone.

Formal and informal rules operate in schools and in any situation where people have to work and live together. Examine a copy of the official school rules. Compare the list of formal rules with the list of informal rules suggested by the class.

Formal and informal codes of behaviour operate in team sports.

Rules in Team Sports

Select a team sport.

1. List at least three formal and three informal rules that enable everyone to play together.
2. Why are these formal rules necessary in this sport?
3. Why do informal rules exist alongside the formal rules of the game?
4. What would happen in team sports if no formal or informal rules were established?

The Evolution of Codes of Behaviour

Formal and informal codes of behaviour do not appear overnight, but develop gradually over a period of time. They are usually put in place as a result of people's experience of certain situations.

✦ What do you imagine was the background behind the following rules being put in place?
- The wearing of seatbelts in cars and buses.
- The ban on smoking in public places.
- The purchase of pit-bull terriers being disallowed.
- The need to have a licence to own a gun or firearm.

What may have started as an informal guideline evolves into a formal rule when the needs of the community require it. Rules evolve into laws when they serve the needs of the wider community, and are upheld by the wider community.

State Laws

Laws forbid or promote certain behaviour. Laws are enforced by the state and people must obey them. There are sanctions if a law is broken.

GARDA
TRAFFIC CORPS

It is against the law to go over the speed limit.

Moral vision behind State laws

The moral vision behind many state laws is the idea of 'the common good'. This moral vision influences the way a government, for example, sees society and how it thinks it should be. The government will make laws according to its vision of what is best for society as a whole. The existence of these laws will have an influence on the moral behaviour of citizens.

Laws are codes of behaviour enforced by the state, and citizens are expected to obey state laws. Codes of conduct to ensure orderly behaviour go back to ancient times. No society ever allowed its members unlimited freedom of action. Early codes of behaviour were not very complex. Over time these codes developed and became more structured to become the state laws that we have today.

The following written codes evolved over thousands of years and set out how people must act if they are to get on together.

The **Code of Hammurabi**, King of Babylon, is almost 4,000 years old. It is the first written account of a ruler making laws to govern his people. Strict punishments ensured the strong would not oppress the weak.

The **Brehon Laws** was a system of ancient Irish Law, written down by 'judges' in the fifth century CE. It was in continuous use in Ireland until it was abolished in the 16th century. The Laws upheld the values of equality and fairness central to Irish society.

The **Magna Carta**, introduced in England in 1215CE by King John, established the individual's right to freedom and equality under the law of the land. Its principles form the basis of the constitution and state laws of many countries throughout the world today. The Irish Constitution was adopted by the Irish people in 1937.

State Laws are laws made by governments; they are introduced to keep order and protect the rights of citizens. Most laws are fair and are designed for the common good and the welfare of the whole society. Key principles of human liberty, fairness and equality form the basis of the *Universal Declaration of Human Rights*, adopted by the United Nations after the Second World War. This Declaration has influenced state laws in many countries and the constitutions of many new democracies.

Questions

Knowledge

1. What do we mean by a 'code of behaviour'?

2. a. What is an informal code of behaviour?
b. What are formal codes of behaviour? Provide examples of each.

3. a. List three formal and informal rules that enable everyone to work together in school.
b. Why was this set of formal rules established in the school?
c. Why do informal rules exist alongside formal rules in the school?
d. What would your school be like without such formal and informal rules?

4. Identify another group to which you belong.
a. List two of its formal rules.
b. What other kind of behaviour is expected but not actually stated as a formal rule?
c. What might happen if these formal and informal rules were ignored?

5. a. What are laws?
b. Describe how any one of our state laws may have evolved or come about.
c. What is the moral vision behind the state laws of this country?

6. Select one of the following codes of behaviour and answer the questions that follow: the Code of Hammurabi; the Brehon Laws; the Magna Carta; Irish Civil Laws; the Universal Declaration of Human Rights.
a. Who wrote the code?
b. When was the code written?
c. How do people benefit from the existence of the code?
d. What would happen if the behaviour outlined in this code was not valued in society?

Understanding

1. a) Why do you think rules are made?
b) Suggest some rules that would improve life at school and in the home.

2. Explain the difference between formal and informal codes of behaviour.

3. Describe how laws and codes of behaviour evolve over time.

4. Select one of the following: the Code of Hammurabi; the Magna Carta; the Brehon Laws; Irish Civil Laws; the Universal Declaration of Human Rights.
a. What would life be like for people in a society, past or present, without this set of laws or code of behaviour?
b. What moral vision or way of seeing the world comes across in the code or set of laws?

The Ten Commandments

Key Concept

Religious moral vision: an awareness of what is right and wrong shaped by religious beliefs.

Objective

Explore the characteristics of a religious moral vision.

Activity: *"Ground Rules"*

TASK: TO IDENTIFY SOME BASIC RULES WHICH ENSURE THE WELL-BEING OF A GROUP.

Imagine the following scenario. The entire class is shipwrecked on a desert island and everyone must get on together in order to survive.

- Begin by thinking about the following behavioural issues.
  - a. How could some people make life difficult for others?
  - b. List ways in which people could make life easier for everyone.

  Take feedback and compile two lists on the board for all to see. Discuss and clarify as required.
- Divide into groups, four or five members to a group. Using the list as a guide:
  - Draw up five ground rules to help everyone get on together.
  - Try to reach a consensus about the rules.
  - List the rules in order of priority 1-5.
- A spokesperson from each group gives feedback to the class.

Discuss

- What rules did your group think would help people to survive together on a desert island?
- How did your group get on together while doing the task? What happened?
- In your opinion, what is the most basic ground rule for getting on with people in any given situation?

Religious moral vision

The ten commandments are the basic rules that ensured the survival of Judaism as a community of faith.

A moral vision is a person's awareness of what is right and wrong. A moral vision may be:

- *Religious* - shaped by a religion such as Judaism or Christianity, for example.
- *Non-Religious* - shaped by a belief system such as Humanism, for example.

A religious moral vision is a person's view of right and wrong shaped by their religious beliefs. Jews for example have a moral vision shaped by the Jewish faith, while Christians have a moral vision shaped by their Christian faith.

Having a religious moral vision in the case of a Christian or a Jew is about knowing and doing what God wants. All people of faith look to their religion for guidance when faced with moral issues. Each religion influences the way its followers see the world and how they think it should be.

The Star of David, ancient symbol of Judaism.

Jewish Moral Vision

The Tenakh is the sacred text containing the religious beliefs and moral vision of Judaism.

The Covenant

A key feature of the Jewish moral vision is the Covenant. The Covenant is the promise, or sacred agreement, between God and the Jewish people (Genesis 15:5). In the Covenant:

- ❖ God made a promise to look after the Hebrews* and to care for them.
- ❖ The Hebrews for their part made a promise to worship God and to live the way God wants.

The Covenant signalled that a special relationship exists between God and the Jewish people. The Covenant is a religious belief at the very heart of the moral vision of Judaism. It influences the way Jews see the world and how they think it should be.

The Ten Commandments

On Mount Sinai, God gave Moses the Torah which is the Law and the Ten Commandments. (Exodus 20:2-17). The Torah outlines how Jews must live if they are to be faithful to the Covenant. The Ten Commandments are the basic moral code of Judaism and Christianity. Both Christians and Jews follow the Ten Commandments.

This is the way the Commandments are written by some Christian Churches today:

The Ten Commandments

1. I am the Lord your God, you shall not have other gods before me.
2. You shall not take the name of the Lord your God in vain.
3. Remember to keep holy the Sabbath day.
4. Honour your father and mother.
5. You shall not kill.
6. You shall not commit adultery.
7. You shall not steal.
8. You shall not bear false witness against your neighbour.
9. You shall not covet your neighbour's wife.
10. You shall not covet your neighbour's goods.

* Hebrews - the ancient name for the Jewish people.

The Commandments
(in modern language)

1. Put God first in your life before everything else.

2. Respect God's name, never swear or curse.

3. Worship God and keep the Sabbath day holy.

4. Help and obey your parents.

BULLY!!

5. Never hurt a person in any way.

6. Be faithful in marriage.

7. Never take or damage anything that belongs to someone else.

8. Never tell lies, cheat or spread gossip.

9. Do not try to possess a person who already belongs with another.

10. Don't be jealous of things that belong to other people.

Following the Ten Commandments

The first three commandments show the importance of having love and respect for God. The next seven commandments show the importance of having respect for other people.

People of faith are motivated to honour and respect God because they believe God is good and all-powerful. They are respectful of one another because they believe everyone is made in the image of God. For Christians and Jews the commandments are the will of God for the world, it is the way God wants the world to be.

Judaism

The moral vision of Jewish people, their view of right and wrong, is shaped by:

- ❖ The Covenant.
  (The sacred agreement between God and the Jewish people.)
- ❖ The Torah.
  (The part of the Tenakh containing the Law and the ten commandments.)
- ❖ The Talmud.
  (Teachings of the rabbis down the centuries.)

All of the above shape the moral vision of Jewish people; it influences how Jews see the world and how they think it should be.

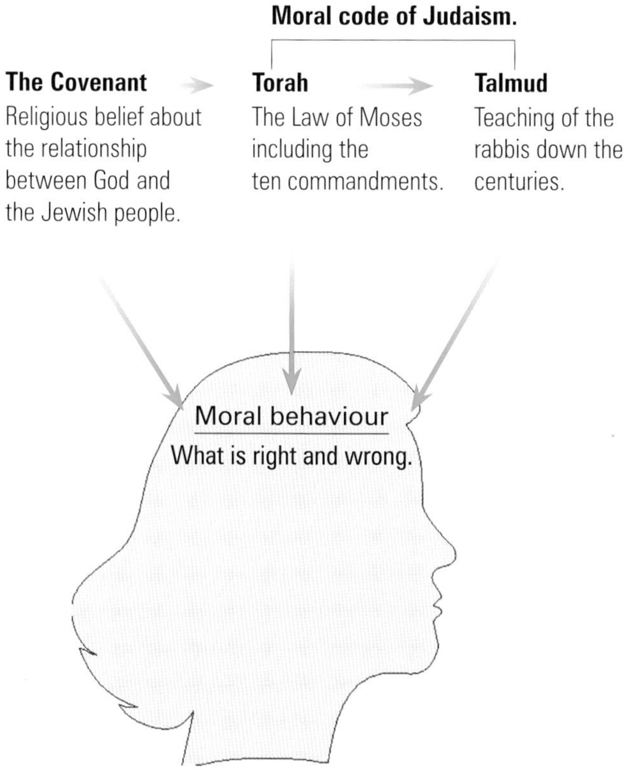
Moral code of Judaism.
The Covenant
Religious belief about the relationship between God and the Jewish people.
Torah
The Law of Moses including the ten commandments.
Talmud
Teaching of the rabbis down the centuries.
Moral behaviour
What is right and wrong.

Questions

Knowledge

1. What is a moral vision?
2. What is a religious moral vision?
3. What is the source of the religious beliefs and moral vision of Judaism?
4. What were the details of the Covenant between God and the Jewish people?
5. How important is the Covenant in the moral vision of Judaism?
6. What are the Ten Commandments?
7. In the Ten Commandments list the Commandments that focus on:
   a. People's relationship with God.
   b. People's relationship with one another.
8. What core religious beliefs motivate Jews and Christians to live good moral lives?
9. What are the Torah and the Talmud?
10. What shapes or influences the moral vision of Jewish people?

Understanding

1. Explain what is different or distinctive about a religious moral vision.
2. How did the religious belief of the Covenant shape the moral code of Judaism, especially the Ten Commandments?
3. Describe how people in the Jewish or Christian faith communities can by following the Ten Commandments:
   a. Show respect for God.
   b. Show respect for other people.
4. Describe the main features or characteristics of the Jewish moral vision.

Research

- Find out how people's religious moral vision can influence their way of life.
  - Identify a person (maybe known to you personally, or perhaps whom you have read about) who's choices clearly indicate a strong religious moral vision at work in their life.
  - Has his/her life been easy?
  - What challenges did he/she encounter?
  - Did prayer have any part in sustaining his/her commitment to live a good moral life.
  - Summarise the story and re-tell it to the class.

Commandment of Love

Key Concept

Religious moral vision: an awareness of what is right and wrong shaped by religious beliefs.

Objective

Explore the characteristics of a religious moral vision.

Activity: *"Love is...."*

TASK: TO EXPLORE WHAT ST. PAUL HAD TO SAY ABOUT LOVE IN THE FIRST CENTURY CE.

St. Paul wrote one of the best known passages on love in the New Testament. It was part of a letter written to the Christian community in Corinth in Greece. Today it is often selected by couples as a Bible reading on their wedding day.

"Love is patient and kind, it is not jealous or conceited or proud. Love is not ill-mannered or selfish or irritable. Love does not keep a record of wrongs. Love is not happy with evil but is happy with the truth. Love never gives up, and its faith, hope and patience never fail."
1 Corinthians 13:4-7

Discuss

- According to this passage state:
  - What love is.
  - What love is not.
- Reflect on what love means in our own lives.
  - Am I: patient? kind? truthful?
    Am I: jealous? conceited? proud? ill-mannered? selfish? irritable?
  - Do I keep a record of wrongs?
  - Do I give up easily?
- Is it possible for any of us to live up to the ideal of love outlined by St. Paul?

Religious Moral Vision

Christians believe Jesus is the only one who fulfils the ideal of love. Jesus' teaching on love is found in the Gospels in the New Testament.

A moral vision is a person's awareness of right and wrong. A moral vision may be religious or non-religious. A religious moral vision is an awareness of right and wrong shaped by religious belief. Christians have a moral vision shaped by their Christian beliefs.

The Bible is the sacred text containing the religious beliefs and moral vision of Christianity. Key features of the Christian moral vision are:

- The teaching of Jesus.
- The life of Jesus.

Jesus' commandment of love is the foundation of the Christian moral vision.

The Moral Vision of Jesus

Jesus was born a Jew and he was grounded in the tradition of Judaism. One day Jesus was asked which commandment of Jewish law was the most important of all. He replied:

> "The most important one is this...Love the Lord your God... and love your neighbour as yourself." Mark 12:28-34.

Jesus spelled out his moral vision when he said that the Ten Commandments, and all the laws of the Jewish tradition, could be summed up in one great commandment, the commandment of love. Love of God and one's neighbour is the basis of Jesus' moral vision and the very foundation of Christian morality.

To love God means:

- ❖ To make sure God comes first before all else in life. Do what God wants.

To love one's neighbour means:

- ❖ To be concerned about the well-being of other people. Do good to others without expecting anything in return.

The commandment of love gives Jesus' followers a way of measuring what is right and what is wrong. Before making a moral decision, Christians can ask themselves if what they are about to do shows love and respect for God and their neighbour, or not. The words of Jesus can guide their choice. The Christian ideal is for people to have the same moral vision - the same sense of right and wrong as Jesus.

DON'T ATTACK IRAQ
NO WAR ON IRAQ

Students protesting against the injustice of war.

The Teaching of Jesus

The moral vision of Christians, their sense of right and wrong is shaped by the life and teaching of Jesus.

The Sermon on the Mount

Jesus main teaching on morality is found in the Sermon on the Mount, in the Gospel of Matthew, chapters 5 and 6. Here Jesus teaches his disciples what loving one's neighbour actually means in practice. He said you must love all people because God loves them, that is God's way, so it must be yours. You must love everyone, not just your friends and those you like or who like you - anyone can do that. As disciples you must go further and show goodwill toward those you don't like, including your enemies.

> "I say to you, love your enemies and pray for those who persecute you." Matthew 5:44

This means be good to those who hate you. Pray for those who hurt you. God loves everyone, and so Jesus' followers must do so too. Jesus set very high standards and he wanted his followers to be as good as possible.

> "Be perfect just as your Father in Heaven is perfect." Matthew 5:48

Christians must try to live up to this ideal, even if they don't always reach it. From the teaching of Jesus in the Sermon on the Mount we learn that love is absolutely central to the Christian moral vision.

The Life of Jesus

Jesus taught his followers the right way to live. But he did more than simply use words to get his message across; he taught by both word and by example. Jesus used his own life to show people how to love as God loves. When Jesus saw people in need he felt a deep sympathy and compassion for them, and always did something to help.

- ❖ He helped the son of a widow in the village of Nain because he felt pity for her. Luke 7:11-17
- ❖ He fed a large crowd who were hungry and thirsty after spending the whole day listening to his teaching. Mark 8:1-10
- ❖ He was friendly to people that nobody liked because he was touched by their loneliness and isolation. Luke 19:1-10
- ❖ He performed a miracle at a wedding feast in Cana because he felt pity for the family when the good wine ran out. John 2:1-12
- ❖ He healed the ear of a slave when it was cut during a struggle. Luke 22:47-51

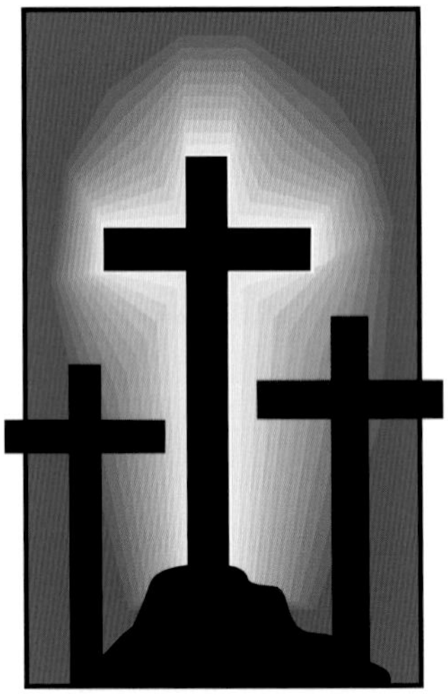

- ❖ He showed the greatest love of all when he gave his life and died on the cross to save the world from sin. John 3:16

In the life and teaching of Jesus, Christians can see God at work in the world. Christians respond to the person of Jesus. They see him as the model of the person they ought to be. They follow his example and try to live as he did, full of love and care for everyone.

Jesus' life and teaching is central to the Christian moral vision. Following Jesus and living in a relationship with him is the basis of the Christian moral life. In Christianity, being a moral person is a lot more than obeying rules and regulations. It means following the example of Jesus by living a life based on love.

Questions

Knowledge

1. What is the difference between a moral vision and a religious moral vision?
2. What is the source of the religious belief and moral vision of Christianity?
3. What is the key feature of the Christian moral vision?
4. What did Jesus say is the greatest commandment of all?
5. How do Christians show their 'love of God'?
6. What do Christians think 'love your neighbour' means?
7. What is the Sermon on the Mount?
8. State one important lesson Jesus taught his followers in the Sermon on the Mount.
9. How did Jesus live his life while he was on Earth?
10. How can Christians follow Jesus' example in the way they live their lives today?

Understanding

1. What does Jesus teach about:
   a. Love of God?
   b. Love of neighbour?
2. How is the teaching of Jesus and the life of Jesus central to the moral vision of Christians today?
3. If all Christians lived according to the moral vision of Jesus what effect would it have on the world?
4. Mother Teresa once said "Christianity = Love". Explain what you think she meant by this equation.

Research

- Find out how the moral vision of Jesus influenced the life of one Christian person.
  - Who was Fr. Jerzy Popieluszko? What was his nationality?
  - How would you describe his religious moral vision?
  - How did his religious moral vision affect the choices he made in life?
  - What were the consequences of his moral choices for himself and for others?
  - Discuss the details of his story with the class.

Wisdom of Others

Key Concepts

Authority: the power of sacred texts and religious leaders to guide people on moral issues.

Tradition: religious belief and practice handed down from generation to generation.

Objective

Explain how authority and tradition are sources of morality.

Activity: *"Morality Matters"*

TASK: TO BRIEFLY RECAP ON PREVIOUS LEARNING ABOUT MORALITY.

✦ In the mix…

The mixing bowl contains ingredients associated with the topic of morality.

ELIGIOUS MORAL VISION
SOURCES OF MORALITY
MORAL VISION
MORALITY
RELATIONSHIPS
MORAL CHOICES
CONSEQUENCES

Discuss

- What is morality?
- Provide examples of:
  a. good moral choices.
  b. bad moral choices.
- Identify the different sources of morality.
- What impact might a person's religious moral vision have on their moral behaviour?
- How do our moral choices affect our relationships with others?
- What is your moral vision?
- Fill the bowl with your ideas of how people should behave toward one another.

Authority

Authority is the power of sacred texts and religious leaders to guide people on moral issues. People of faith believe that this authority, where it exists, comes from God.

When Christians, for example, need guidance on moral issues, they believe it is important to turn to God and find out what God wants them to do.

They can learn what God wants by:

- ❖ Reading their sacred text.
- ❖ Following the teaching of Church leaders.

Sources of Moral Guidance in different religions

Members of all faith communities look to their sacred texts and religious leaders for moral guidance.

Religion	Sacred Texts	Leaders
✧ Judaism:	- Tenakh. - Talmud.	Rabbi.
✧ Christianity:	- Bible.	Priest, Minister, Bishop, Pope.
✧ Islam:	- Qur'an. - Hadith.	Imam.
✧ Hinduism:	- Vedas.	Priest.
✧ Buddhism:	- Tipitaka.	Monk, Dalai Lama.

The authority of sacred texts

People of faith believe that their sacred texts contain:

- Words spoken directly from God.
- Words written by authors who were inspired by God.

Most religions believe that their sacred texts have a special authority that comes from God.

The authority of religious leaders

Some religions select or ordain certain people to:

- Conduct worship.
- Act as official teachers of the faith.

They believe that the authority of religious leaders, such as priests and bishops, comes from God.

Christians have different opinions about the best way to look for guidance on moral issues. Some Christians look to Scripture alone for authority. Others believe that Scripture, together with the teaching of Church leaders, are sources of authority on moral issues. Different Churches put more emphasis on one source of authority than another.

The 'Scripture-only' approach

The 'Scripture-only' approach is adopted by many Protestant denominations. When people need guidance on a religious or moral question, they turn to God's word in the Bible.

In the Old and New Testaments people find all they need to know about how a Christian should respond to moral issues. Scripture is the authority and the main source of guidance. It alone shows people how to follow Jesus and do God's will in the world.

The Bible contains general principles for moral behaviour. Christians prayerfully read the Bible and try to work out how its teaching applies to their particular situation. This is one reason why Bible study is an important part of Protestant religious life.

In some Churches people meet regularly in small groups for Bible study. A Bible passage is studied and the group tries to work out how its message applies to their daily lives. This helps them to understand how God wants them to live. Christians believe that they are guided by the Holy Spirit in their search for answers.

Christians studying the Bible.

The Vatican and
St. Peter's Square in Rome.

The 'Scripture and Church Teaching' approach

The 'Scripture and Church Teaching' approach is adopted by Roman Catholics, Orthodox Christians and many Anglicans. These faith communities believe that their religious leaders have a special authority to teach and guide people on moral issues. Leaders interpret the message of Scripture and help people to apply it to the concrete situations of their daily lives.

The Catholic Church, for example, believes that Scripture and Church teaching are not separate, but are inter-related. The teaching of the Church is firmly rooted in Scripture. Its guidance on Christian living is based on the Bible, especially the teaching and example of Jesus in the New Testament. The role of Church leaders is to interpret Jesus' teaching for those who want to live a moral life in today's world.

In the Roman Catholic tradition, the authority of religious leaders goes back to the apostles. Jesus gave Peter, the first of the apostles, the authority to teach (Matthew 16:13-20). The Pope and the bishops take the place of Peter and the apostles. The Church says that whoever listens to them, listens to Christ. Jesus promised the disciples and their successors that the Holy Spirit would be with them in their teaching ministry.

> 'Anyone who listens to you, listens to me.'
> Luke 10:16

The Holy Spirit is present is a special way in those who are called to be Church leaders. What they have to say, therefore, deserves special attention.

Tradition

When Catholics need guidance on moral issues they turn to:

- ❖ The teaching of Jesus, and
- ❖ The teaching of the Church.

Church teaching is carried out by the leaders of the Catholic Church. When the Pope and the bishops teach about faith and morals they are not expressing their own opinions, they are expressing the tradition of the Church. The word tradition comes from a Latin word meaning 'to hand over'.

Tradition is the body of belief and religious teaching that has been handed down from generation to generation since the time of Christ. It is the collective wisdom of the Church of the past 2,000 years. Tradition is a process, it is not static and unmoving but grows and develops over time.

In each generation the Church tries to follow the example and teaching of Jesus. The Church then reflects on its own experience. As a result it learns and deepens its understanding of Jesus and his message. Today the Church arrives at its teaching after centuries of thinking and living according to the vision of its founder. The Church does not achieve this learning by itself. It takes place under the guidance of the Holy Spirit.

The Magisterium

The word 'magisterium' comes from a Latin word meaning 'to teach'. The Magisterium consists of the Pope and the bishops; it is the official teaching voice of the Catholic Church. The task of the Magisterium is to:

- ❖ Decide what is essential for the faith.
- ❖ Teach what is essential to the faithful.

The teaching of the Magisterium is passed on to Catholics mainly in the form of:

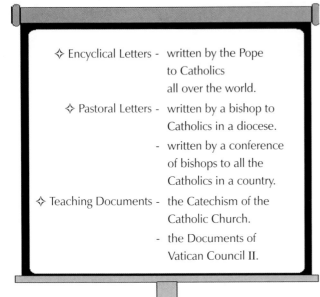

- ✧ Encyclical Letters - written by the Pope to Catholics all over the world.
- ✧ Pastoral Letters - written by a bishop to Catholics in a diocese.
  - written by a conference of bishops to all the Catholics in a country.
- ✧ Teaching Documents - the Catechism of the Catholic Church.
  - the Documents of Vatican Council II.

The teaching in Church documents guides people in making moral decisions. This is especially helpful when a person wants to know what Catholic teaching is on a particular issue. The Church today advises its members on issues such as abortion that highlight respect for life, and on issues of justice such as poverty, racism and care for the environment. Catholics learn Church teaching in different ways. They may hear it from the priest during the sermon at Mass, and study it during religion class at school. They may also learn it at home from their parents.

Down through the centuries Christians have wanted to love God and love their neighbour in a wholehearted way. In their struggle to live a moral life Catholic Christians look for guidance to both:

- ❖ Scripture - the teaching of Jesus.
- ❖ Tradition - the teaching of the Church.

Questions

Knowledge

1. Name the titles of the:
   a. sacred texts and
   b. religious leaders
   of the five major world religions.
2. How do Christians find out how to live a moral life?
3. What do many Protestant Christians believe is the only source of authority to guide moral behaviour?
4. What do Catholic Christians believe is the source of authority that guides moral behaviour?
5. What does tradition mean in the Catholic Church?
6. What is the Magisterium in the Catholic Church?
7. How is Church teaching on moral issues passed on to Catholics?
8. How do Catholics learn the Church's teaching on moral issues?

Understanding

1. Why do Christians use the Bible to help them decide what is right and wrong?
2. Why should Catholics listen to the teaching of Church leaders on moral issues?
3. Explain how authority and tradition influence a Christian's judgement of right and wrong.

Research

- Find out about the subject of infallibility in the Catholic Church.
  - What does the term 'infallible' mean?
  - To whom does this term apply in particular instances?
  - In what circumstances is a statement deemed to be infallible?
  - According to the Church, where does the power to speak infallibly come from?
  - What is the name of Church teachings regarded as infallible?
  - Discuss the details of your research with the class.

Developing Morality

Key Concepts

Moral growth: the process by which people learn to distinguish right from wrong, and then do what is right.

Moral maturity: the stage beyond self interest where people take the needs of others into account when making moral decisions.

Objective

Explore the development of personal morality.

Activity: *"Habits"*

TASK: TO KNOW THAT A HABIT IS A TENDENCY TO ACT IN A PARTICULAR WAY.

✦ Invite three or four volunteers to stand in front of the class. Give each one a sugared doughnut and ask them to eat it without licking their lips. The class will judge how they get on!

Discuss

- How did the volunteers get on? Did anyone automatically lick their lips?
- A habit is something we do, almost without thinking. There are good habits and bad habits.
  - ✧ Give examples of *bad* habits that are:
    a. anti-social. (e.g. picking one's nose.)
    b. harmful to health.
    c. immoral.
  - ✧ Give examples of *good* habits that are:
    a. socially appropriate.
    (e.g shaking hands to greet an adult.)
    b. beneficial to health.
    c. moral.
- St. Paul wanted Christians to get into the habit of living a good moral life.
  - ✧ Read Colossians 3:5-10.
    List the immoral selfish behaviour he told them to give up.
  - ✧ Read Colossians 3:12-17.
    List the moral un-selfish behaviour he encouraged them to practice.

Moral Growth

Good habits practiced regularly help us to grow toward moral maturity.

Human beings grow:

- ✧ Physically.
- ✧ Intellectually.
- ✧ Emotionally.
- ✧ Spiritually.
- ✧ Morally.

Moral growth is the process by which people learn to distinguish right from wrong, and then do what is right. We learn about right and wrong from experience and the guidance of others.

Moral growth takes place gradually. People are born with the basic ability to know the difference between right and wrong. Over a period of time we learn from our own experience and the guidance of others that some actions are good and others are bad. Then there follows a slow process of development from moral immaturity to the stage of moral maturity.

Moral Immaturity → Moral Maturity

Stages of Moral Development

Moral growth is age-related and takes place gradually over time.

Childhood

Young children are self-centred. They learn quickly that good behaviour leads to praise and reward, while bad behaviour leads to punishment. Reward and fear of punishment influences moral choice in childhood.

Moral choice in childhood is influenced by reward and punishment.

Reward and punishment

When a child does something good, he/she is rewarded. The reward may be that the parent is pleased, smiles and offers praise. If it is a particularly good deed, the child may be offered one of his/her favourite things, an extra story, some sweets, or to get to watch another cartoon.

On the other hand, if the child does something wrong, he/she is punished. The punishment may mean that there are no smiles, the parent is disappointed, and the child is scolded. If he/she has behaved very badly some privileges may be taken away; this could mean no more television, being sent to bed early, or being given 'time-out'.

Children quickly learn the outcomes of good and bad behaviour. They will naturally seek reward and avoid punishment. This tendency influences their behaviour. Children will obey their parents because they want to be rewarded and don't want to be punished. The motive for their moral behaviour lies outside themselves. From a child's point of view, rules and codes of behaviour are laid down by parents and by teachers. The rules are to be obeyed because parents, teachers, or someone in authority says so. Good children simply do what they are told and follow the rules.

Adolescence

Pre-teens start to apply reason to moral situations and begin to understand the idea of consequences. However, moral choices continue to be made in the expectation of reward, or the avoidance of punishment.

Teenagers apply the use of reason to most moral issues. A greater awareness of the positive and negative consequences of moral choice is now developing. Moral choices, however, tend to be influenced by the desire to seek approval from others, either at home or at school, but especially from friends and peers.

Influence of the peer group

The behaviour of teenagers is, to a great extent, the result of their desire to fit in and be the same as the people around them. It is natural for adolescents to want to be well-liked and accepted by their friends and peers. Belonging to the group offers security and a sense of identity.

Moral choice in adolescence can be influenced by the desire to seek approval.

Membership of the group can have an impact on one's morality. Decisions about what to think and how to act are influenced by one's peers. In order to be well-liked and accepted, some teenagers may adopt the outlook of the group without examining it too closely. Many of the group's opinions and practices are influenced by the media, through television shows, films, the internet and popular music. In adolescence, what a boy or a girl chooses to do is affected greatly by what everybody else does.

Moral Maturity

Moral maturity is the stage beyond self-interest, where people take the needs of others into account when making moral decisions. A person who has reached a level of moral maturity is aware of the consequences of their actions for themselves and for others. As people get older they use their ability to reason when dealing with moral issues. They are able to think about moral choices and analyse them in terms of their consequences. They can clearly see the effects their choices will have:

❖ on themselves. ❖ on others. ❖ on the world in general.

It is a mark of moral maturity when a person can take other people into account when making moral decisions. This means a person moves on from being selfish to being altruistic (un-selfish), and is willing to put the interests of others first above their own.

The morally mature person

The morally mature person is influenced more by their inner convictions and maybe religious faith, and less by reward and punishment or social approval. For the morally mature person the motive for their behaviour comes from within themselves, not from outside. This means that when they make a moral decision to do something that is right, it is not because they want others to think well of them, but because doing the right thing is worthwhile in itself.

Similarly, when they avoid doing something wrong it is not simply because they are afraid of the punishment if they get caught. It is because they see the sense of doing what is right and feel it is so important that they cannot do otherwise.

Morally mature people drive responsibly on the road.

Examples of morally mature behaviour

■ *Morally mature people will not drink alcohol and drive.* They will always try to keep within the speed limit when driving on the road. They do so not because they fear getting penalty points if they are caught drinking or speeding, but because they realise that both actions are dangerous and a threat to themselves and to the lives of other motorists.

Morally mature people are well aware of the effect that road accidents can have on victims and their families, so they obey the law because they see the sense behind it and think it is right. Furthermore, if they belong to a community of faith, they will have respect for human life because it is the law of God. They do not want to be the type of person who would endanger the life of another.

Morally mature people always try to do what is right.

EUROPEAN UNION

Morally mature people will not steal.

■ *Morally mature people will not steal anything big or small.* This is not because they are afraid of what will happen if they are caught. It is because they believe that stealing is wrong. It is against the law of the land and against the law of God.

The morally mature person knows the effect that theft can have on people and the hurt it can cause. This leads them to the firm belief that stealing is always wrong. Stealing is habit-forming when people get away with it. Morally mature people would prefer to develop good habits, not bad habits. They believe that it is better to be an honest person rather than one who is dishonest.

The difference between moral immaturity and moral maturity

Moral Immaturity

The morally immature person is affected by influences that are outside the self. His behaviour is determined by desire for reward, fear of punishment or the need for social approval. He obeys the rules because he has been told to do so. He keeps obeying them so people will be pleased with him, or because they will punish him if he doesn't.

Moral Maturity

The morally mature person on the other hand is affected by influences that are inside the self. His behaviour is determined by deep personal convictions and perhaps by religious belief. He always tries to do what is right because it is the best and most worthwhile thing to do. The morally mature person moves beyond simply obeying the rules. He takes the rules on as his own and makes them part of himself. They become part of his own personal conviction, his moral vision.

Many people remain at a level of moral immaturity all their lives, while others go on to become morally mature individuals.

The morally **immature** *person*:

- ❖ Acts out of a desire for reward or the fear of punishment.
- ❖ Is selfish and considers only his/her own needs.
- ❖ Ignores the consequence of his/her behaviour on others.

The morally **mature** *person*:

- ❖ Acts out of a deep personal conviction about what is right, and what is good.
- ❖ Is altruistic and considers the needs of others.
- ❖ Will stop to think of the consequences before deciding to act.
- ❖ Has the courage of his/her convictions and will actually do what he/she believes to be right.

People can grow from the level of moral immaturity to the level of moral maturity. This transition to a stage of moral maturity can take place during adolescence for some people. Discuss the following dilemmas. Try to decide what is the morally mature thing to do.

A. You are in the classroom in your usual location down the back. Today the class is doing a test for which you haven't studied. You can see others cheating around you. Nearly everyone is doing it. Do you think you should too?

B. You are in the changing rooms after PE. You see money falling out of someone's pocket. With all the noise and commotion the student didn't notice it happening, and is heading out the door. Should you run up and point it out to him, or should you say nothing, pick it up, and keep it yourself after he's gone?

C. You are back in class after lunch. A guy with long hair is sitting a few seats in front. When the teacher turns to write on the board, all your mates start flicking stuff into his hair. What do you do?

D. You are passing the newsagents on your way home from school. A bunch of first years are hanging around outside asking older lads to get them some cigarettes. What do you think you will do if they approach you?

The transition to moral maturity for some people can take place during adolescence.

Moral growth in adolescence

Change begins to occur when young people move:

FROM: - making decisions based on the opinions of their peers, "that's the way everybody does it..."

TO: - making decisions based on their own judgement, "this is the way I do it."

FROM: - making choices that are designed to please their friends and get approval from them...

TO: - making choices that come from within themselves, choices that are based on their own judgement and their own convictions.

As they grow older, young people become more confident and begin to trust their own judgement. They rely less and less on the opinions and outlook of their peers and begin to discover reserves of moral courage within themselves. This enables them to stand apart and do what they know is right. Gradually as their moral courage develops they find they are becoming a person who:

- ❖ wants to do what is right.
- ❖ is able to do what is right.

Standing on one's own two feet when it comes to moral issues shows that a person is becoming morally mature.

Questions

Knowledge

1. What is moral growth?
2. Where do children learn about right and wrong?
3. What effect does reward and punishment have on children's moral behaviour?
4. Provide examples to show how a young person might do something good or bad to gain the approval of friends and peers.
5. What is moral maturity?
6. a. Give examples of selfish and non-selfish behaviour.
   b. How could a person's selfish behaviour affect themselves, their community and the world at large.
7. What influences a morally mature person to act in the right way?
8. a. What are the characteristics of a morally mature person?
   b. When does the transition from moral immaturity to moral maturity begin for some people?

Understanding

1. a. What are the different stages of moral development?
   b. As people grow older, how does their sense of right and wrong change and develop?
2. What is the difference between moral immaturity and moral maturity?
3. Do you think that it is inevitable that everyone will reach a level of moral maturity?
4. What would be the consequence for society if the majority of people remained at an early stage of moral development?

Research

- Find out about someone whose life demonstrates that he/ she acted with conviction and moral maturity.
  - Create a profile of the person - does he/ she live now or in times past?
  - Say why you think he/ she is (or was) a morally mature person.
  - What finally became of this person?
  - The class might be willing to share and discuss the profiles of the people researched.

Conscience

Key Concept

Conscience: the ability to know and judge what is right and wrong in a particular situation.

Objective

Explain the meaning of conscience and its importance in moral maturity.

Activity: *"An ordinary day"*

TASK: TO DISTINGUISH BETWEEN INSTANCES OF RIGHT AND WRONG BEHAVIOUR.

Everyone makes numerous moral decisions during the course of a single day. People struggle to do what is right, and sometimes they succeed. At other times, they just let themselves down.

"Time to get up!" his mother calls from the bottom of the stairs. Mark pulls the sheet over his head, pretending not to hear. He eventually arrives down to the kitchen and gets himself a bowl of cereal. The two younger children are arguing over the cereal box. Mark quietens them down, he can see his mother doesn't need the noise. He looks at the clock...he's going to be late. He rushes out, banging the door behind him.

Mark reaches the bus stop just on time. His friend Jeff pushes past everyone to get to the back seat. Mark follows. They both copy the last bit of science homework from someone nearby. As they get near the school Jeff looks up and makes some smart remarks about two girls sitting in front; luckily, the girls didn't hear. Mark tells his friend to 'shut up' and leave them alone. Jeff laughs and pushes against the girls as he gets off the bus. The homework copy is forgotten and left behind on the seat.

After assembly the two friends go on a tour of the corridors and arrive late to class. Jeff says another teacher sent them on a message. Both boys walk noisily down to their seats. They can see the teacher is annoyed. Jeff doesn't care, Mark isn't so sure.

The next class is English, with a stand-in teacher. Jeff gives a wrong name when corrected for in-attention and everyone laughs. Mark is moved away from Jeff and told to sit beside Lee, who is

Conscience is our ability to judge what is right and wrong.

new to the class. Lee hasn't made many friends yet. Later on, during PE, Mark offers to partner Lee for one of the activities. At break Mark and Jeff allow Lee to hang around with them for a while.

The class are in French after break. Mark notices Jeff scraping the desk with a compass. Later, during science, the French teacher comes in to ask whoever ruined the desk to own up. Jeff says nothing. At the end of class Mark offers to help the science teacher to move some equipment. He knows that he can get off at least one class if he takes his time.

Discuss

- How many examples of right behaviour did you find in the story?
- Pick one example of:
  a. right behaviour and say why it is right.
  b. wrong behaviour and say why it is wrong.
- Where does our strong sense of right and wrong come from?

Conscience

Our conscience tells us what is right and wrong.

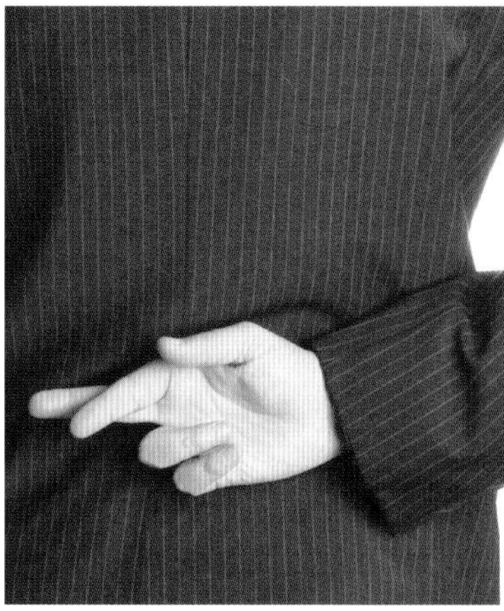

Making good moral choices helps each of us to become a better person. The ability to know and judge what is right and wrong in a particular situation is called conscience. The word conscience comes from a Latin word meaning 'to know'. Conscience is an in-built ability that we all possess. It is what helps us to figure out what is right and wrong, good and bad.

Conscience is our ability to use our knowledge in order to judge what is right and wrong in a particular situation. It is our moral sense, our sense of what we ought to do. We rely on our conscience to guide us when we have to make a moral decision. Our conscience helps us in two ways:

- To judge what is right and wrong.
- To act on that judgement and do what is right.

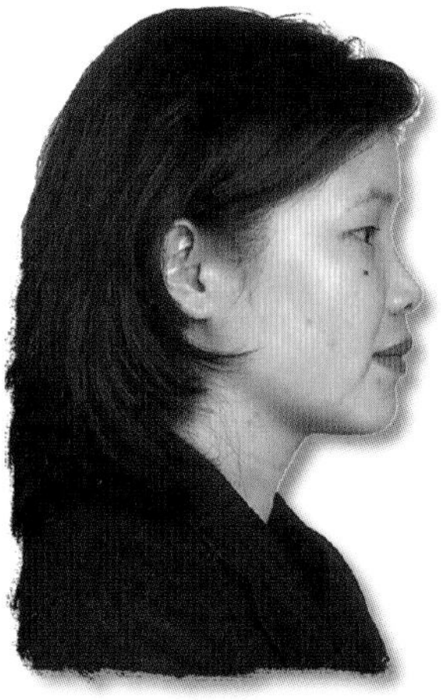

- We use our conscience when we stop and think about an action and judge if it is right or wrong.
- We follow our conscience when we decide to do what is right.
- We ignore our conscience when we decide to do what is wrong.

Different views on conscience

People have different views on the meaning of conscience. Some describe their conscience as 'a little voice' that tells them what is right or wrong. Others say that it is a peculiar guilty feeling they get, especially when something they are doing is wrong. There is some truth in both sets of ideas, but it is not the full story.

The *small inner voice* is partly related to conscience, but is not what we mean by conscience. It is only one aspect of what conscience is all about.

Feelings of guilt are related to conscience in that they can be a sign that our conscience is alive and well. Yet these feelings are not what we mean by conscience either, they are only another aspect of what conscience is all about.

A religious view of conscience

Conscience is not simply a 'little voice' that advises us from inside. Nor is it a guilty feeling that we get about things from time to time. Such ideas make it appear that our conscience is an 'it', or a 'thing' that is somehow apart and separate from us. In fact our conscience is not separate from us at all. It is at the very core of our being, an essential part of who we are. It is that deep part of us that is directed towards goodness and truth.

A person of faith would say that our conscience is a gift from God. It is God's word printed in our heart, urging us to do good, and avoid evil.

"Deep within our conscience,
God calls us to love
and do what is good
and to avoid evil...
Within our conscience
we are alone with God
whose voice echoes in our depths."

(Paraphrased from 'Pastoral Constitution on the Church in the Modern World' Vatican II.)

Developing a conscience

Nearly everyone accepts that human beings have a conscience. Having a conscience is one of the things that separates human beings from the animal world. Animals behave purely by instinct. Human beings can rationalise, and are able to decide for themselves how to behave. It is their conscience that tells them whether their actions are right or wrong. Even though people have the basic ability to know right from wrong, that capacity has to be developed. Our conscience does not grow or develop by itself; it needs help to develop fully.

This process begins in childhood when parents teach their children about moral behaviour. It continues as children grow older and parents, teachers, priests and ministers give advice when difficult decisions have to be made. Gradually, a young person begins to have a deeper understanding, not only of what is right and wrong, but why something is right or wrong. The home, the school and the church have a vital role in helping people to develop a healthy and informed conscience.

Many believe the school has a role in helping people develop an informed conscience.

An informed conscience

Christians agree that people should follow their conscience and do what is right. Sometimes, however, it may not be clear what is right and what is wrong. It could happen that despite someone's best intentions, he or she might end up doing the wrong thing without knowing that it is wrong. For this reason, Christians believe that they have a duty to find out the right thing to do; they must inform their conscience.

Informing one's conscience involves gathering the necessary facts and information about a moral issue, and using that information to make a moral decision. This will enable the person to make a better and more informed judgement about what is right and wrong.

Catholic Teaching

> *Conscience is not merely somebody whispering in my ear, it is not just a feeling or an instinct. It is my judgement of what is the best thing to do in a particular situation.*
> (The Irish Bishops Conference 1998)

Catholics learn the moral teaching of the Church during sermons at Mass.

The Catholic Church teaches that people should follow their conscience and do what is right. Catholics have a duty to inform their conscience and find out the right thing to do. But where do people get all the facts that are needed to inform their conscience? How do they arrive at good moral decisions? Catholics, for example, take a number of steps in order to inform their conscience.

Catholics are guided by:

- The teaching of Jesus in the Bible.
- The teaching of their Church.
- Prayer.
- Trustworthy people who give good advice.

People of faith turn to God, and to others outside themselves, for help and guidance in making moral decisions. Paying attention to this guidance will inform a person's conscience and will enable him/her to make morally mature decisions.

If people rely solely on themselves and nothing else to distinguish right from wrong, they run the risk of being mistaken and making the wrong decisions. A person's 'inner voice' and 'feelings' are a private matter; no one is sure that such a voice and such feelings will always be correct. That is why people turn to God and to others outside themselves for help and guidance in moral decision-making. This explains why Christians turn to the teaching of Jesus, the teaching of their Church, to prayer and to trustworthy people for good advice.

Trustworthy people can help us to inform our conscience.

People who care for us at home, at school, and in church, can help us to inform our conscience by:

- listening to us.
- explaining new facts to us.
- offering us good advice.

After that, it is up to each one of us to make our own decisions.

Questions

Knowledge

1. What is conscience?
2. How do people use their conscience?
3. When do people follow their conscience?
4. What happens when people ignore their conscience?
5. a. Give examples of situations in which young people have to use their conscience.
   b. Selecting one example, state what the person would do:
      i. if they followed their conscience.
      ii. if they ignored their conscience.
6. a. Is it easy or difficult to follow one's conscience?
   b. Make a list of reasons why people don't always follow their conscience.
7. State two different views on conscience.
8. State one religious view of conscience.
9. How do people develop their conscience?
10. Do you think that teenagers have a more developed conscience than children who are half their age? Explain your answer.
11. What is an informed conscience?
12. List the steps a Roman Catholic might take to inform or guide his/her conscience.

Understanding

1. Explain what it means:
   - to have a conscience.
   - to follow one's conscience.
2. Does conscience have the same meaning for everyone?
3. Do people automatically know what is right and wrong, or do they have to learn the difference between right and wrong?
4. What do you think are the signs that a person has a well developed conscience?
5. Why is it necessary to develop an informed conscience?

Research

- Find out about developing your own conscience. Every skill and talent we have needs to be developed to reach its full potential. It's the same with conscience, that ability within ourselves that guides our moral choices.
  - List some things that might help your own conscience to grow and develop.
  - Write about a person or an incident that helped your conscience to develop.
  - Share your story with the class (optional).

Moral Values

Key Concepts

Truth: being honest with oneself, others and God.

Integrity: being upright and honest, and sticking to one's moral principles.

Objective

Know the place of values in moral decision making.

Activity: *"Values"*

TASK: TO IDENTIFY STUDENT'S OWN VALUES, AND DISCUSS HOW THESE VALUES HAVE BEEN FORMED.

A value is something that we think is very important and worthwhile.

- Arrange the values, on the chart opposite, according to their importance in your own life. Select the six most important values for you.
- Organise these six values in order of priority.
- Put the letter P beside any value you think you got from your parents.
- Put the letter F beside any value you think you got from your friends.
- Put the letter E beside any value you got elsewhere, e.g. school, church, media.
- What are the top three values of the class?
  - what are the similarities between your chosen values and those of the class?
  - what are the differences?

Discuss

- Were you surprised at the choice of values in your class?
- How do people get to have such values?
- Make a list of people you admire (in your family, in school, or in public life) and identify the values they stand for.
- Do those values feature in your life?

Examples of values:

- ☐ To be popular.
- ☐ To have a nice house.
- ☐ To have lots of money.
- ☐ To be honest.
- ☐ To have lots of friends.
- ☐ To be fit and healthy.
- ☐ To care for the environment.
- ☐ To be truthful.
- ☐ To have a happy family.
- ☐ To work hard.
- ☐ To have a strong faith.
- ☐ To look well.
- ☐ To be good at sports.
- ☐ To be fair.
- ☐ To have a few good friends.
- ☐ To be generous.
- ☐ To be independent.
- ☐ To be respected.
- ☐ To get a good job.
- ☐ To be well organised.
- ☐ To be trustworthy.
- ☐ To get good exam results.
- ☐ To have a nice car.
- ☐ To feel happy and content.
- ☐ To have a sense of humour.
- ☐ To be kind.

Personal values

Our values affect the way we think, what we say, and how we behave.

Our values are what we believe is important and worthwhile in life, such as friendship, honesty and loyalty for example. Our values are not acquired by accident. We get our values from other people; we learn them from our parents, our friends, our school, our church, the media and society in general.

It is necessary that people be aware of what they value, because values are a critical factor in moral decision-making. A person will make decisions according to what he or she values.

Christian values

Christians need to examine their values occasionally. All Christian values are based on Jesus' teaching on love in the New Testament. In the Gospel of Matthew we read that Jesus taught his followers to:

> Love God... and love your neighbour as yourself. Matthew 22:37-39

This is the basis of Christian moral teaching. Being a Christian means trying to love God and other people at all times, in all circumstances. The following are examples of Christian values that help people to put love into practice in everyday situations.

Christian values

- Love.
- Peace.
- Forgiveness.
- Truthfulness.
- Honesty.
- Respect.
- Gentleness.
- Self control.
- Courage.
- Patience.
- Prayer.
- Tolerance.
- Helping others.
- Fairness.
- Caring for the Earth.
- Compassion.
- Freedom.
- Sacrifice.
- Service.
- Preventing suffering and harm.

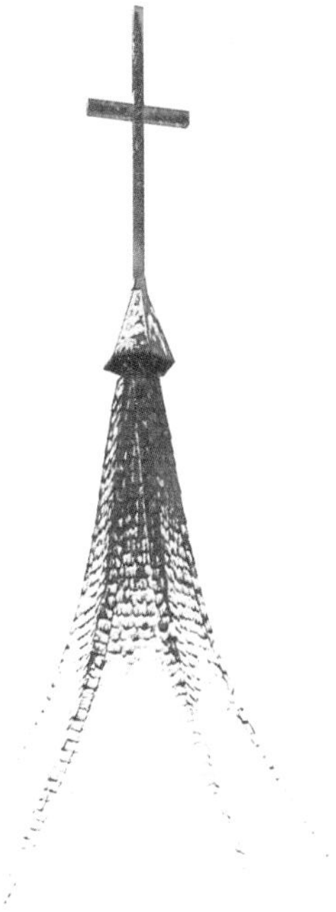

As young people reflect on the values they receive from their family and other sources, they can work out what is important and what really matters in life. They are able to identify their own set of priorities, and in so doing become aware of their own system of values.

Truth

Truth and honesty are important values for many people, and especially for Christians. To tell the truth is the eight commandment of God.

Truth and honesty are the basis for all social relationships in the family, among friends and in the wider community of business, politics, and the professions. Honest people tell the truth, are trustworthy and always keep their word. Everyone can rely on them.

Truth and honesty are important values for Christians.

Jane has a weekend job in the local supermarket. She is paid the minimum wage. When she gets home on Saturday night she discovers that she is €20 overpaid. "Well, they won't miss it," she thinks, "and anyway, I'm worth it." When her father realises what has happened, he says that she must give the money back. "But why?" she protests, "They won't even know." "That's probably true," he replies, "but we do."

A person's value system is apparent, even in the ordinary decisions that are made every day. To be a morally mature person able to make moral decisions, a person must be fully aware of the values by which he/she lives.

Dishonesty is very common. People often deceive others, or tell a lie instead of telling the truth. Telling lies can get someone out of a tight situation where he/she might face blame, criticism and maybe punishment. This could encourage him/her to act in the same way on another occasion. Being dishonest could then become a habit and part of their character.

Integrity

Being honest and truthful is not always easy, it often costs us something. A person of integrity is one who is upright and honest and sticks to their moral principles, even when it costs. People of integrity have a high level of moral maturity. They have deep convictions about what is right and wrong. They follow their conscience and do what is right, even if it is at some cost to themselves.

St. Thomas More (1478-1535)

Sir Thomas More was Chancellor (Prime Minister) at the time his friend, King Henry VIII, ruled England in the 16th Century. Thomas was a deeply religious person. He was also a scholar and one of the best educated and most respected men in Europe at the time.

Everything changed when the King decided to leave his wife Catherine and marry another woman called Anne Boleyn. When the Pope refused permission, the King broke away from the Catholic Church and named himself the head of the Church in England. Thomas could not, in conscience, support the King's decision. He resigned from his post as Chancellor and went back to live quietly with his family in the English countryside.

The king's ministers tried to force Thomas More to make a public statement and accept King Henry VIII as head of the English Church. When Thomas refused he was arrested and put in prison in the Tower of London.

Thomas was accused of treason. He was charged with betraying his country and was put on trial. If found guilty, he would be executed. His family and friends came to visit him in prison and begged him to change his mind.

Thomas felt that he must remain true to his conscience. He refused to swear an oath that the child of King Henry VIII and Anne Boleyn was heir to the throne. The court eventually found him guilty, and he was sentenced to death. On the day he was to be beheaded, he told the people who stood there watching "I die the King's good servant, but God's first."

In 1936, the Catholic Church declared Thomas More a saint and a martyr (a person who died for his beliefs).

Franz Jeagerstaetter (1907-1943)

- Austrian farm worker, married with three children.
- Did not want to join the German army in World War 2.
- As a Christian he believed he could not, in conscience, be part of the Nazi war effort.
- Refused to take the oath of loyalty to Hitler.
- Was sentenced to death in August 1943 for disloyalty to the state.

Franz Jaegerstaetter.

The Tower of London.

Section F

Being honest and truthful often costs us something.

Exercise

Imagine a situation at school, where a friend is in trouble over one of the following incidents.

- Being late.
- Breaking a window.
- Hiding someone's bag.
- Cheating in a test.
- Skipping classes.
- Copying homework.
- Setting off the fire-alarm for fun.
- Not wearing full uniform.
- Other…

Compose a short dialogue in which you try to convince your friend that telling the truth and owning up is the right thing to do, even if it costs.

Questions

Knowledge

1. Name some people who have a big influence on your life. What values did you learn from them?
2. Give an example of how a Christian value can influence the behaviour of a person of faith.
3. Give examples of values that are un-Christian, that is they encourage people to be selfish and unloving.
4. How do the values you have now compare with the values you had five years ago?
5. Some of the values you have now may change in the future. Do you have any values which you hope will never change? If so, give examples.
6. What is the meaning of:
   a. Truth?
   b. Integrity?
7. Does the story of St. Thomas More or Franz Jaegerstaetter suggest any values that were important to them? If so, list them.
8. What values matter most to you?
   a. Make a list.
   b. State why they are important to you.

Understanding

1. Does it matter what we value? Why? Why not?
2. Why is truth an important value for Christians?
3. Describe an occasion when you saw the values of truth and integrity at work in the choices made by a public figure, or by someone known to you personally.

Research

- Find out about the values inherent in certain newspaper stories.
  - What are the main news stories this week?
  - What values are evident in one of the main news stories?
  - Do these values concur or conflict with your values and what you stand for?
  - What do you think about this?
  - Is there anything to learn from this?
  - Share your reflections on a particular news item with the rest of the class.

Moral Decision-Making

Key Concept

Decision-making: the process of making up one's mind about moral issues.

Objective

Explain the process of moral decision-making.

Activity: *"Decisions"*

TASK: TO APPRECIATE THAT ALL DECISIONS MATTER, BUT SOME MATTER MORE THAN OTHERS.

✦ Consider the following statement.

"First they came for the Jews and I did not speak out because I was not a Jew. Then they came for the communists and I did not speak out because I was not a communist. Then they came for the trade unionists and I did not speak out because I was not a trade unionist. Then they came for me and there was no one left to speak out for me."

Martin Niemoller (1946)

Discuss

- Moral decision-making is about making up one's mind about moral issues.
  What helps people to act in the right way?
- "For evil to triumph, it is only necessary for good people to do nothing."
  In what circumstances can in-action be wrong?

Decision-making

Morality is about deciding between what is right and wrong, good and bad.

Learning how to make moral decisions is an important part of growing up and becoming morally mature. Moral decision-making is a complex activity. When the process is analysed, we can see that it involves a number of different steps. Christians, when faced with a moral decision, are encouraged to take the following steps:

Steps in moral decision-making

1. Stop, look at the **facts** of the situation.
2. List the **options**, work out the **consequences** of each option for oneself and others.
3. Get good **advice**.
4. Be aware of one's **values**.
5. **Pray** for guidance to do what is right.
6. Follow one's **conscience**. Make a **decision**.

Normally the six elements in the decision-making process run together and overlap with each other. Here we are simply separating everything out in order to look at each element more closely. We must remember that decision-making in real life is rarely, if ever, as neat and tidy as this.

Moral decision-making involves a number of steps.

"Jennifer's story"

The mock exams are not far off. Jennifer makes up her mind: it's decision time! She knows that she is not a genius, but she is going to work hard and try to get good results. She writes out a revision timetable for herself and pins it to the notice board in her room.

The first few days go well enough. A pattern is established: she gets in from school, has her tea, watches the television for a while, then goes up to her room. She plays some music in the background as she thinks it helps her to study better. By Friday, though, she is beginning to lose her resolve. Her mother knocks on the door as usual. "Just a treat to keep you going," she says with a smile.

Jennifer feels guilty. She has done nothing for the past half hour, just sat there listening to music and daydreaming. She gets another text message. Her friends want to know if she's going to go into town with them the next day. They could go around the shops, some of the sales are still on.

Jennifer thinks that maybe she should have a day off. She glances at the revision timetable again. On Saturday she had planned to do Geography; should she meet up with them or stay in and do her work?

She decides to go downstairs and chat to her mother. It might help to talk to her about how things have been going so far.

Making Moral Decisions

1. Look at the facts.

Ask - what is the issue?

✦ The exams are coming up, Jennifer wants to do well. She needs to study.

✦ She'd like to go out with her friends.

---

2. List the options.

Ask - what choices does Jennifer have?
- what are the consequences of each choice: ✧ for herself.
✧ for others.

---

3. Get good advice.

Talk to a wise person who is able to offer good advice. Get help from family, professional people and reliable friends.

✦ Jennifer talks to her mother who is supportive and understanding.

---

4. Be aware of one's values.

Ask - what values are at issue here?

✦ Jennifer's values are reflected in her moral vision.

✧ She values hard work - she tries to keep to a revision schedule.

✧ She values truthfulness - she felt guilty about accepting treats from her mother who thought she was studying.

✧ She values respect - she respects her parents and wants to be honest with them.

✧ She values self-respect - she wants her family to be proud of her.

✧ She values friendship - she tries to maintain her friendships.

---

5. Pray for guidance.

Be open to God's help.

✦ As a Christian, Jennifer would be aware of God's presence as she tries to do the right thing.

---

6. Make a decision.

Follow one's conscience. Do what is right.

✦ Jennifer makes a decision. She does not put it off. She accepts full responsibility for her actions.

DECI ION

It can sometimes be difficult to make a moral decision. Yet we usually know what we should do, even if we don't always do it. What do you think you would do in each of the situations outlined below. Use the decision-making process. Go step-by-step through each stage of the process.

1. A school trip is coming up. Everyone is looking forward to it. There is a visit to an exhibition and then a stop at a leisure centre on the way back. The teacher reads out the list of those who have paid so far. Your name is called out, but you know you haven't paid. The money is still in your pocket as you just brought it in that morning. What do you do?

2. The class organise a school fundraising event for victims of a natural disaster. Everyone works hard, and it is a great success. You and your friends are the principal organisers. You count and bag the money, and a teacher drives you down to the bank. The cashier weighs the bags and tells you the total. There is a shortfall of €25, and you realise one bag is missing. You have your suspicions, although you didn't actually see anyone take it. The gift cheque must be presented to the relief organisation by the end of the week. What do you do?

3. One of your friends is in trouble. Pornographic images were viewed on the internet in the computer room at lunch time. He says it wasn't him, he wasn't even there as he was down town at the time. Someone else must have used the password to log on. He asks you to back him up. What do you do?

✦ Make up your own worked example. Think of another moral decision that a person might have to face. Incorporate each element of the decision-making process in order to arrive at a solution.

Questions

Knowledge

1. List the elements in the moral decision-making process.
2. What kind of facts does a person need to look at before making a moral decision?
3. a. Think of a moral decision that you made recently. List at least two options that were available to you.
   b. What were the consequences of each option for yourself and for others?
4. Where should Christians look for help and advice in moral decision-making?
5. What are your top three values?
6. What do Christians pray for when making moral decisions?
7. What does it mean to follow one's conscience and take responsibility for one's decision?
8. In what ways might a person's religious beliefs influence their moral decision-making?

Understanding

1. Explain the process of moral decision-making in the Christian tradition.
2. What do you think might happen if some of the steps in the process were left out?
3. Do you think that the process of decision-making outlined here would help a Christian teenager to make a good moral decision? Why? Why not?
4. Why is it important to turn to others for advice when faced with a difficult moral decision?

Research

- Find out about the Lutheran pastor Martin Niemoller (1892-1984).
  - Provide details of his:
    - Nationality.
    - Navy career.
    - Decision to oppose Hitler.
    - Imprisonment.
    - Life and work after the Second World War.
  - Discuss his life and moral vision with the class.

Social Justice

Key Concepts

Justice: to treat all people fairly and respect their rights.

Peace: harmony between people instead of disorder and conflict.

Objective

Show how a religious moral vision can influence decisions on issues of justice.

Activity: *"Where in the world..."*

TASK: TO EXPERIENCE WHAT IT IS LIKE TO BE TREATED UNJUSTLY.

✦ Divide up the class.
- Three quarters of the group go to one end of the room, they are called group B.
- The remaining quarter stay at the front, they are called group A.

✦ Explain to the class that you are going to call out the names of different countries. The first group to name the capital of each country will get a prize.
- If group A gets it right, everyone in that group will get a sweet.
- If group B gets it right, one sweet will be given to the whole team.

✦ Begin the activity and continue for a few minutes.
- If group B begins to question the rules, explain that the rules can be changed. However, only people with sweets can vote. One sweet is worth one vote.

Discuss

- How did it feel to be in group A or B? Were you surprised by your reactions?
- Would you have liked the activity to be different in any way?
- How would someone with a Christian moral vision respond to the situation?
- Who do the A and B groups represent:
  i. in the world today?
  ii. in this country today?

Is there justice for everyone in the world today?

Justice

Peace

Justice is about right relationships between all people.

Justice is the first step in developing good relationships between people. Justice is about treating all people fairly and respecting their rights.

Injustice, on the other hand, is a lack of concern for people which can result in them being treated unfairly. A sense of justice involves treating others in the same way that we would like to be treated ourselves.

Justice is an important part of the religious moral vision of both Christianity and Judaism. A religious moral vision is a person's view of right and wrong, shaped by their religious beliefs.

Human Rights

Justice is based on human rights. Rights are something to which we are all entitled - because we are human. In 1948, the United Nations (UN) passed the Universal Declaration of Human Rights. It outlined thirty basic rights to which all people are entitled. For example, everyone has the right:

- ✧ To life.
- ✧ To work.
- ✧ To education.
- ✧ To proper medical care.
- ✧ To vote in choosing a government.
- ✧ To fair wages.
- ✧ To a fair trial.
- ✧ To own property.
- ✧ To freedom of conscience.
- ✧ To an adequate standard of living.

The UN Declaration is universal, it applies to everyone throughout the world. The fact that people have rights means that their rights must be respected. I have rights, my rights must be respected; I in turn must respect the rights of others.

Relative poverty and absolute poverty

Yet injustice persists; the world is divided between the rich and the poor, the "haves" and the "have not's". In our own country, being poor means not being able to afford the things that others take for granted. This is referred to as relative poverty.

In developing countries, being poor means struggling to survive and not having the basic necessities of life such as: enough food or clean water, adequate health care, somewhere decent to live, an education or a job. This is referred to as absolute poverty.

The Big Picture

The big picture:
is it one of social justice, or social injustice?

If we could shrink the world's population to a village of 100 people, there would be:

- ✧ 57 Asians.
- ✧ 21 Europeans.
- ✧ 14 North, Central and South Americans.
- ✧ 8 Africans.

In that village 50% of the worlds wealth would belong to only six people - all six would be US citizens.

- ✧ 70 people would be unable to read.
- ✧ 50 would suffer from malnutrition.
- ✧ 80 would live in sub-standard housing.
- ✧ 1 would have a college education.

Rich world, poor world.

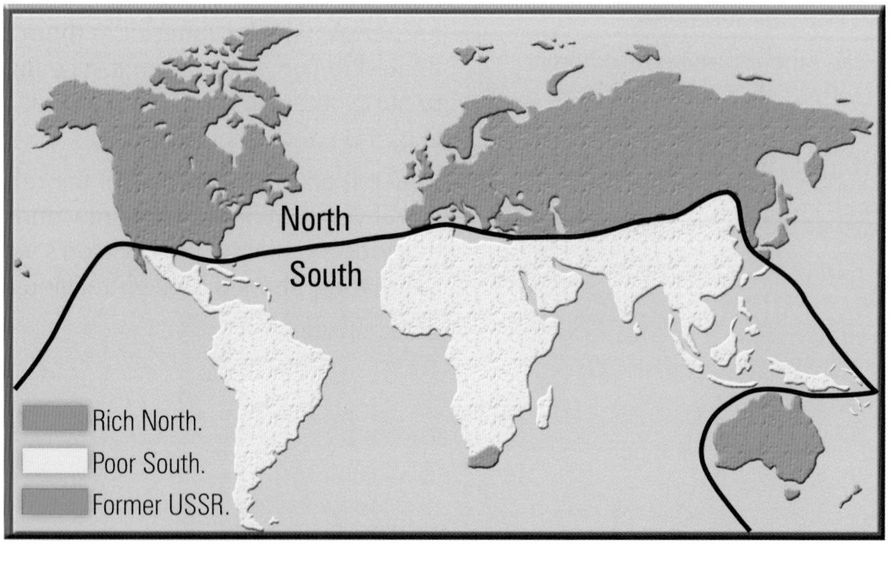
North
South
Rich North.
Poor South.
Former USSR.

Christian Moral Vision

Christians believe that a person has rights not simply because a human law says so, but because he/she is created by God. Human beings are made in the image of God, their worth and dignity comes from God. It is for this reason that their dignity must be respected and their rights protected.

The Christian Churches each have their own outlook on the subject of human rights and human dignity. For example, the teaching of the Roman Catholic Church on human rights is contained in a document entitled "Peace on Earth" (Papal Encyclical Pope John XXIII). This document outlines the rights the Church considers vital in order to preserve human dignity and maintain social justice. Catholic bishops point out that Church teaching strongly supports the UN Declaration on Human Rights.

Irish bishops' teaching on social justice states that Christian love begins with respect for the rights of others. Justice, like many values, the bishops point out, is first learned in the home where it is done much more effectively by example than by talk ('The Work of Justice' Irish bishop's pastoral letter).

Jesus and Justice

Christians learn about Jesus' teaching on love and justice in the New Testament. Christians must act justly, treat people fairly and respect everyone's rights. But the teaching of Jesus is about more than justice, it is about love. To act justly is good, but Christians must do more. They have to go beyond what is just and act in the same caring, compassionate way Jesus did in the Gospels.

Parables of Jesus

The parable of the Good Samaritan (Luke 10:25-37) is a story about love and justice. Jesus wanted to teach his followers that there are no limits to love. Love reaches out with care and compassion to everyone, it would never walk by and look the other way. Love stops to help no matter who the person is. Anyone, anywhere, should be helped if they are in need.

Jesus' message to 'love others as you love yourself' is also found in the parable of the Rich Man and Lazarus (Luke 16:19-31). The rich man failed to get to heaven because he ignored the beggar at his door. He was rich but he did not help the person suffering in poverty.

Jesus identifies with the suffering of the poor.

Actions of Jesus

During his public ministry, Jesus spent a great deal of time among poor people and social outcasts. He identifies so closely with those in need, that he considers what has been done to them as having been done to himself.

> "I was hungry and you fed me,
> thirsty and you gave me a drink.
> I was a stranger, and you received me
> in your house,
> naked and you clothed me.
> I was sick and you took care of me,
> in prison and you visited me…
> when you did it for one of these…
> you did it for me."
> (Matthew 25:31-48)

Feeling sorry for people is not enough, Christians have a duty to act justly and help people in need.

Homeless people asleep on the pavement.

Jewish Moral Vision

The Hebrew word for charity also means justice. Down the centuries Jewish rabbis have taught that, not only is it fair and just to help the poor, it is a duty required by God. They have also taught that people should be helped in a sensitive way that allows them to keep their dignity and self-respect.

Helping the poor is a duty required by God.

Jews learn about love and justice in the Tenakh. Jewish scripture outlines practical things that can be done to ensure that everyone has enough. For example, land owners must leave part of the annual harvest in the fields for the poor and the stranger to collect.

"When you reap the harvest of your land do not reap to the very edges of your field, or gather what has fallen. Do not go over your vineyard a second time or pick up the grapes that have fallen. Leave them for the poor and the stranger."
(Leviticus 19:9-10)

Ruth, a poor woman and a foreigner, is allowed to gather grain at harvest time.
Ruth 2:1-23

The Prophets and Justice

In the Tenakh, the prophets had an important role. They were people called by God to speak out against injustice in Jewish society. When they saw the poor being exploited or badly treated they spoke out on their behalf. It took great courage to be a prophet, because they were demanding that the rich and powerful change their ways and act justly towards the less well off.

Amos

God called Amos to be a prophet and gave him a message for the people of his time. Amos was a farmer who lived in the 8th century BCE. He looked after a small herd of sheep and goats and tended some fig trees. His plot of land was not far from the city of Jerusalem.

Several times a year, pilgrims passed his gate praying and singing hymns on their way to offer sacrifice in the Temple. Amos believed their outward show of religion was totally insincere. Beneath it all there was widespread injustice and oppression of the poor. Wealthy merchants overcharged people, sold useless goods at high prices, gave the wrong measure, and got people into debt. Even the judges in the courts were corrupt and took bribes. Amos warned them all that it was wrong to be selfish and greedy. He told them to change their behaviour. He called for......

"justice to flow like a river throughout the land."
Amos 5:10-15, 21-24

Tzedek

Today Tzedek is a Jewish agency working in some of the poorest countries in the world. It educates the Jewish community about world poverty and raises funds to help people in poor communities. Disaster relief is provided in emergencies, but the main work is supporting long-term projects that help people to help themselves.

Justice in Action

When a Christian or a Jew makes a decision to act justly and help people in need, they are likely to be influenced by the moral vision of their religious tradition. When a person takes their faith seriously, their religious moral vision should be evident in their behaviour.

Students helping to deliver gift boxes for children in need.

There are many ways to help people in need at home and abroad.

1. **Pray.** When a person of faith is concerned about others, he or she will place their problems before God in prayer.
2. **Be thankful.** Remind ourselves of all the blessings we have received, and our duty not to waste our talents or opportunities.
3. **Buy Fair-Trade products.** Buying Fair-Trade tea, coffee, or chocolate ensures that poor farmers get a fair price for their products. Greeting cards and craft items bought from reputable charities ensures that all the funds go to needy communities.
4. **Be label-aware.** Many designer goods are made in sweatshops in developing countries. Asking how and where clothes, footwear, and sports goods are made challenges this practice.
5. **Get involved.** Fundraising for charitable organizations through sponsored events provides aid for emergency appeals. Fundraising for longer term projects helps people in poor communities to become self-sufficient.
6. **Raise awareness.** Tell others what is going on in the world; give talks, put up posters, write articles, send emails and text messages.

Questions

Knowledge

1. What is the meaning of justice?
2. What are human rights?
3. List the ways in which you can respect the rights of others:
   i. At home.
   ii. At school.
   iii. In your local area.
   iv. In other parts of the world.
4. Describe an incident where your rights were not respected and you were treated unjustly.
5. "We live in a 'divided world'."
   a. What does this statement mean?
   b. How is it an unjust situation?
6. What is the Christian outlook on human rights and human dignity?
7. How did Jesus teach his followers about love and justice?
8. What did Jesus teach about helping people in need?
9. What have Jewish rabbis taught about social justice?
10. Who were the prophets in Jewish scripture?
11. How did Amos respond to the injustice he saw around him in his society?
12. How can people with a religious moral vision people help in need?

Understanding

1. What religious beliefs and teachings encourage:
   a. Christians, b. Jews,
   to act justly and help people in need?
2. How would you expect someone with a:
   a. Christian moral vision.
   b. Jewish moral vision.
   to respond to people in need in their local community and in the world at large?
3. Whose responsibility is it to provide for the needs of the poor at home and abroad?

Research

- Find out about 'Trocaire', 'Christian Aid' or 'Tear Fund', three Christian organisations that raise awareness about justice issues and support many short and long-term projects in the developing world.
- Compile a fact file and make a presentation to raise awareness in the class.

Respect for Life

Key Concepts

Respect: to have a high regard for someone or something, and to treat each with great care.

Life: the state or quality of being alive.

Objective

Show how a religious moral vision can influence decisions on abortion.

Activity: *"It's my life"*

TASK: TO RATE THE WAY WE LOOK AFTER OUR BODIES.

How do you treat your body? (✓)	YES	NO	SOMETIMES
✧ Do you buy snack food and soft drinks?			
✧ Do you eat fried food?			
✧ Do you have a balanced diet?			
✧ Do you smoke cigarettes?			
✧ Are you fit? Do you exercise?			
✧ Do you brush your teeth every day?			
✧ Do you hang around with people who use drugs?			
✧ Do you get enough sleep at night?			
✧ Do you keep safe and wear a seatbelt in the car?			
✧ Do you drink alcohol?			
✧ Do you take a shower regularly?			
✧ Do you practice calming techniques when you are worried or under pressure?			

Discuss

- How do you rate the way you treat your body?
- Is there room for improvement: can you respect your body a bit better?
- Do people generally respect the life that they have?

Respect for Life

Human life is precious;
it should be treated with care and respect.

The major world religions teach that life, especially human life, is sacred or holy. Respect for life is important in Christianity and Judaism because it is believed that human life:

- Is a gift from God.
- Is sacred and deserves to be treated with great care and respect.

The word 'respect' means 'to look again'. To respect human life means taking another look, a deeper look, at each person in order to see what God sees. God looks on each human being and sees every one as sacred and valuable in themselves. In the moral visions of Christianity and Judaism all persons are sacred and must be cherished and respected.

Respect for life is central to the moral vision of both Christianity and Judaism.

Abortion

An abortion is an operation to end a pregnancy by removing a foetus, an unborn child, from the womb. Abortion is carried out by medical staff who use surgery or drugs to remove the foetus from the mother's womb. Abortions are legally carried out in many countries. In the United Kingdom it is legal to carry out an abortion up to the 24th week of pregnancy under certain conditions. Abortion is not legal in Ireland under any conditions.

When does life begin?

In a discussion about abortion, one of the crucial issues is when exactly life begins.

- Is it at conception, when the male sperm joins the female egg to form an embryo?
- Is it at the first heartbeat, around day 23?
- Is it when the arms and legs begin to form, around day 28?
- Is it when brain activity can be detected, around day 40?
- Is it when all organs begin functioning, around day 56?
- Is it when a baby becomes viable (able to survive outside the womb), around week 24? (Medical science is improving on this all the time.)
- Is it at birth, sometime between weeks 36-40?

Some people believe that human life begins at conception. From the moment of conception a separate human life begins to grow inside the mother's body. To deliberately end a pregnancy means causing the death of another human being.

Other people believe that human life does not really begin until the baby is born, or at least until it can survive outside the womb. Up to that point it is part of the mother, and she has the right to decide what to do with her own body.

Although abortion is now legal in many countries, most religions teach that abortion is morally wrong.

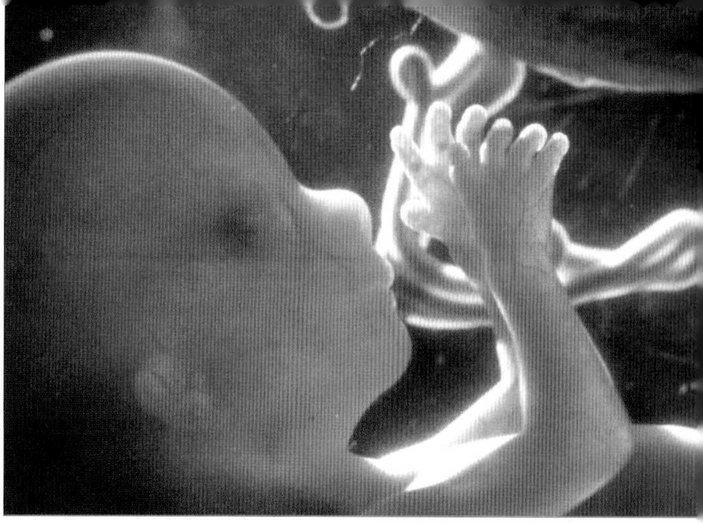

A foetus in the womb.

Right or Wrong

The Christian Churches do not share the same outlook on the issue of abortion. Some Christians believe abortion is always morally wrong. Abortion is murder, there are no exceptions.

Other Christians believe that abortion is wrong, but that it could be allowed under certain circumstances. For example in the case of rape, if the mother's life is at risk, or if the baby is seriously disabled. The decision would not be taken lightly but would be seen as the lesser of two evils. To end the pregnancy would be regarded as the most loving thing to do in the circumstances.

The case for abortion

- Every woman has the right to decide what happens to her own body.
- If a woman becomes pregnant due to rape or incest, abortion is seen as a way of helping her deal with the problem.
- If there is a high risk that the child will be born with a disability, abortion may be the answer, as quality of life is important.
- A young woman who becomes pregnant, and who is not married or in a stable relationship, may be lonely and confused; she may also be worried about being unable to cope financially. Opting for an abortion might seem a practical solution.
- If there is a risk to the physical or mental health of an expectant mother, abortion would be considered acceptable.
- Every child should be a wanted child. A woman should not be forced to carry a child that is unwanted.

The case against abortion

- The foetus (the baby in the early stages of life), has a right to life. It is not just another part of a woman's body, it is a separate human being sacred to God. The Catholic view is that God creates life, and therefore only God can take it away.
- If a woman conceives a child as a result of a terrible crime such as rape or incest, she will need a lot of help and support. Yet the trauma does not alter the fact that the child developing in her womb is a new human being. The child has done no harm. Its life is sacred and must be protected.
- The certainty that a child will be physically or mentally disabled is not a good enough reason for taking its life. All children need love and care, those with a disability need extra care. Their life is a precious gift and can bring a special joy to their family and friends.
- Hardships such as poverty and single parenthood do not give women a reason for having an abortion. Catholic organizations like 'Cura' have been set up to support women and girls who have unplanned or crisis pregnancies. It provides an information and counselling service and also gives practical assistance when required. Cura exists to help women make an informed decision about their pregnancy.
- If complications arise during pregnancy, and the life of the mother and her unborn child are at risk, the doctor will always try to save the life of both patients. The Catholic Church teaches that if a pregnant woman has a life threatening condition, such as cancer for example, she will always be given medical treatment, even if it results in the death of the unborn child. Such a tragic outcome is considered to be morally acceptable if the intention of the surgery is not deliberately to end the life of the child.
- Children are a gift from God to be treated as a blessing, not as a burden. If a child is unwanted, there are many childless couples who would gladly adopt the child and raise it as their own.

The Catholic Moral Vision

The Roman Catholic Church is against abortion. It teaches that abortion is morally wrong in all circumstances. Although abortion is legal in the United Kingdom for example, Catholics believe the law is wrong and abortion should not be allowed. Catholics base their beliefs on the Bible and the teaching of the Church.

- All life is a gift from God. Human life is created in the image of God; it is sacred and must be treated with deep respect. (Genesis 1:27)
- God creates life; only God can take it away. Taking innocent life is murder. It breaks the commandment of God. (Exodus 20:13)
- Human life begins at conception. From the moment the egg is fertilized a new life begins and must be protected. The unborn child is a separate human being and has a right to life. (Gaudium et Spes, Document of Vatican II)

Human life is sacred.

The Jewish Moral Vision

Judaism teaches that abortion is morally wrong but is allowed in certain circumstances. Abortion is legal in the Jewish state of Israel.

Jews believe:

- All life is sacred as it is a gift from God. God created life in the beginning and each new life comes from God.
  "God created human beings, making them to be like himself." (Genesis 1:27 The Tenakh)
- Some rabbis teach that life does not begin until the moment of birth. The Talmud is a sacred text containing important Jewish teachings on moral issues. It states that the foetus does not become a human being until the forty-first day of the pregnancy - the day on which God plants the soul in the human body. Other rabbis added to Jewish teaching by saying that human life does not begin until the actual moment of birth.
- Abortion is wrong as the taking of life is against the law of God.
  "You shall not murder." (Exodus 20:13 The Tenakh)
- Abortion is not totally forbidden.
  Some rabbis say that, although it is sad and regrettable, abortion is allowed in certain circumstances.
  - If the mother's life is at risk.
  - If the child will be severely disabled.
  - If a woman is the victim of rape or incest.

Making a moral decision

A woman's religious moral vision is likely to influence her decision as to whether or not to have an abortion. In a situation where a young woman discovers that she has an unplanned pregnancy, it is better to:

✦ Stop and think before doing anything.

1. Look at the facts.
2. List the options. Ask:
   - what choices does she have?
   - what are the consequences of each choice for - herself? - the baby? - others?
3. Get good advice.
4. Be aware of one's values.
5. Pray for guidance.
6. Follow one's conscience and make a decision.

Questions

Knowledge

1. What is the meaning of respect?
2. a. Describe someone who makes you feel respected.
   b. Describe an occasion when you were not treated with respect.
3. What religious belief influences both Christians and Jews to have a deep respect for life?
4. What is abortion?
5. What is conception?
6. Do all the Christian Churches share the same view on abortion?
7. Give three reasons why someone might think of having an abortion.
8. What is the Roman Catholic position on abortion?
9. What religious teaching would a Catholic use to support his or her view that abortion is morally wrong in all circumstances?
10. What is the Jewish position on abortion?
11. What religious teaching would a Jew use to support his or her view that abortion is morally wrong, but may be allowed in certain circumstances?
12. What appears to be the main reason for:
    a. Catholics opposing abortion?
    b. Jews considering abortion?

Understanding

1. What does it mean to have respect for life, and why is this important?
2. What teachings of the Catholic Church might influence a Catholic's decision to oppose abortion?
3. What teachings of the Jewish faith might influence a Jew to consider abortion as a last resort?
4. 'If abortion is legal then it must be all right.' Do you agree or disagree with this statement?

Research

- Find out about a group that argues in favour of abortion, and one that argues against it.
  - What are the different groups called?
  - What advice might each one offer someone who is considering having an abortion.
  - Assemble the information for a brief presentation to the class.

Care for the Earth

Key Concepts

Respect: to have a high regard for someone or something, and to treat each with great care.

Stewardship: the way people care for the Earth on behalf of God.

Objective

Show how a religious moral vision can influence decisions on the environment.

Activity: *"Close Encounter"*

TASK: TO GET IN TOUCH WITH A SMALL PART OF THE NATURAL WORLD.

- ✦ Gather enough leaves to fill three to four containers, one leaf for each student in the class. Select dry fallen leaves with prominent veins - all from the same variety of tree.
- ✦ Divide the class into three to four groups, and give each group a container. Everybody in the group is invited to take a leaf and examine it closely.
- ✦ Look closely at the leaf in your hand.
  - What colour is it? What size is it? What shape is it?
  - What does the edge of the leaf look like?
  - What shape is the tip of the leaf?
  - Are there any spots, marks, holes or tears on the leaf? How many large veins are on the underside of the leaf? What does the topside of the leaf feel like?
  - What does the leaf smell like?
  - Draw a picture of the leaf you have examined, then return it to its container.
- ✦ Invite each group in turn to gather round and empty out their container. Ask each member of the group to find their own leaf and explain how they recognised it.

Discuss

- What did you discover while examining the leaves during this exercise?
- Do you know why trees are important to the environment?
- Do people need to have closer contact with nature in order to appreciate it? What is your opinion?

Respect

Everything in the environment deserves our care and respect.

The environment is everything around us on the Earth. Originally there was enough clean air, fresh water and good food for everyone to share.

Now:

- ❖ The Earth's atmosphere is badly damaged.
- ❖ Rainforests are being destroyed.
- ❖ Rivers and seas are polluted.
- ❖ The quality of the land, and the welfare of animals, are casualties in modern methods of food production.

There is a lack of respect for the Earth.

To respect the Earth means to have a high regard for it and to treat it with care. An attitude of deep respect is the starting point of any action to protect the Earth. Christians and Jews believe the Earth is worthy of respect because it is a gift from God.

Stewardship

A steward is like a caretaker who looks after someone else's property. Stewardship in a religious sense is about caring for the Earth on behalf of God. People do not own the Earth, but are its caretakers. It is everyone's responsibility to pass it on in perfect condition to the next generation. It appears however that we have not taken this responsibility very seriously. We seem to have slipped further and further away from our role as stewards of creation. In fact we have become careless caretakers.

A sea bird caught in an oil slick, stranded on a beach.

World Religious Leaders

In 1995 the leaders of the world's major religions met in Japan to raise awareness about the need to care for the Earth. They issued a joint statement agreeing that:

- ❖ It is a person's religious duty and responsibility to care for the Earth.
- ❖ The root cause of environmental problems is greed.

All the major world religions share a common religious moral vision to care for the Earth.

Jews and Christians share the same creation story in Genesis in the Bible. They believe God created the Earth and put humans in charge to look after it.

> "God blessed them (male and female) and said, 'have many children so that your descendants will live all over the earth and bring it under their control. I am putting you in charge of the fish, the birds..., the plants..., and all living creatures'." Genesis 1:28-30

The Christian Moral Vision

The Bible teaches that:

- ❖ God created the Earth.
- ❖ God put humans in charge to look after it.

The Christian attitude to the environment therefore should be one of good stewardship. Leaders of the Christian Churches have each spoken out about environmental issues in recent times. On World Peace Day 1999, Pope John Paul II reminded people again that the present and the future of the world depends on safeguarding the environment. It is part of the moral vision of Christianity to respect and care for the environment.

The Bible

The idea of Christian stewardship is found in the book of Genesis, where God settles the man in the Garden of Eden, and tells him to cultivate it and protect it. The Earth is on loan to us, it does not belong to us, it is a gift from God. We respect it and care for it because of its essential goodness, not just because of its usefulness to us.

In the New Testament, Jesus was aware of the goodness of God all around him in the natural world.

To care for the Earth is part of the moral vision of Christianity.

The Jewish Moral Vision

The Tenakh teaches that:

- ❖ God created the Earth.
- ❖ God put humans in charge to look after it.

The Jewish attitude to the environment is one of good stewardship and involves looking after it in very practical ways. It is part of the moral vision of Judaism to respect and care for the environment.

Genesis

The idea of stewardship in Judaism is found in the Book of Genesis. Jews believe that when God put humans in charge of life on earth, he wanted them to use the earth's resources wisely. Jewish sacred texts, especially the Torah, stress the importance of looking after nature. Jews are aware that they depend on the natural world and that it needs to be treated with care.

Jewish respect for nature, and especially for the land and for trees goes back to Abraham, the Father of Judaism. In Genesis 21:33 we learn that Abraham planted a tree and then worshipped the Lord.

In Israel today there is an annual tree planting festival called Tu B'Shevat. Trees are planted at the edge of the desert and in marshy areas all over the country. Parents take their children out to plant a sapling where it is needed. Trees are also planted in Israel to celebrate important occasions such as weddings and Bar-Mitzvahs.

What to do about the environment

A person's religious moral vision is likely to influence his/her decision to do something positive to help the environment. The Biblical idea of good stewardship involves:

- ❖ Having an attitude of respect for the environment.
- ❖ Doing something to care for the environment on a daily basis.

'Reduce, re-use, recycle' is a good place to begin.

Making a moral decision

- ❖ When we stop and look at the **facts** we can see the problems facing the planet today. The choices we make as individuals and groups can have a positive or negative effect on the environment.
- ❖ If we want to do something to help, there are a number of **choices** or options available. All have **consequences** in terms of the degree of commitment involved and the impact of the action overall. Because it is not possible to do everything, some people might be tempted to do nothing. It is essential to do something, no matter how small, as long as it is done faithfully and often. Christians know that God does not expect them to do the good they cannot do, only the good they can do.
- ❖ Keeping oneself informed about environmental issues on an on-going basis is also part of the process. Being concerned enough to seek **advice** and discuss the matter with teachers, family and friends helps to clarify the main issues. Knowing what the Bible and the Church has to say can have an impact on one's point of view too.
- ❖ If stewardship is one of our **values** this means we will reject any option which could harm the environment. Values become clearer the more we think about issues and try to explain to others our reasons for wanting to respond in certain ways.
- ❖ A person of faith will place their concerns before God in **prayer**. Then being mindful of the environment, he/she will follow their **conscience** and **decide** to do the right thing on a daily basis.

Caring for the environment.

Things we can do....

- ❒ Recycle paper, glass, cans and plastic.
- ❒ Use recycled paper in copies and notebooks.
- ❒ Don't waste electricity; turn off lights and heating when not needed.
- ❒ Avoid using aerosols with CFC's; use other products instead.
- ❒ Drop litter in the bin, not on the ground.
- ❒ Don't leave water running while brushing our teeth.
- ❒ Turn off the TV, consoles or the computer when not in use.
- ❒ Buy environmentally-friendly products.
- ❒ If possible walk or cycle instead of going in the car.
- ❒ Feed birds in winter.
- ❒ Help out on local clean-up days.
- ❒ Encourage the family to build a compost heap in the garden.
- ❒ Report any cruelty to animals to the ISPCA.
- ❒ Know why it is important to insulate the house.
- ❒ Support local groups that help the environment.
- ❒ Write to your local council about environmental issues.
- ❒ Contact your TD about local, national or international environmental issues.
- ❒ Help to plant a tree.
- ❒ Pray for creation.

Research

- Find out about St. Francis of Assisi, the patron saint of ecology.
  - Who was St. Francis and what did he do?
  - Why is he regarded as one of the best examples of how Christians should love and respect the natural world?
  - Build up a profile of information from different sources for a class discussion.

Questions

Knowledge

1. List some of the Earth's environmental problems caused by human beings.
2. a. Give examples from your local area of people not showing respect for the Earth.
   b. Give reasons why some people disrespect the Earth.
3. a. What is the role of a steward or a caretaker?
   b. What is the meaning of stewardship in relation to the environment?
4. 'Nowadays we act more as though we own the Earth than as caretakers of it.' Is this true? Why? Why not?
5. What did world religious leaders say to encourage people of faith to take environmental issues seriously?
6. What passage in scripture might influence both Christians and Jews to care for the environment?
7. a. What is the Christian attitude towards the environment?
   b. What did one Christian leader say about the environment?
8. a. What is the Jewish attitude toward the environment?
   b. How do Jewish people care for the environment in a practical way today?
9. List the steps involved in making a moral decision to care for the environment.
10. What can people do to show respect for, and be true stewards of, the environment?

Understanding

1. Explain what is meant by good stewardship of the environment.
2. How might a Christian or a Jew use the teaching of religious leaders and sacred texts to argue against either:
   - Rainforest destruction?
   - Pollution? *OR*
   - Intensive farming?
3. 'If Christians took their religion seriously there would be less damage done to the environment.' Do you agree or disagree with this statement?
4. Explain how a person's decision to do something to care for their local environment will affect:
   - Themselves.
   - Others.
   - The rest of the world.

Moral Failure

Key Concepts

Sin: any deliberate thought, word or action that damages a person's relationship with God and other people.

Judgement: the belief that, in the end, God will judge each person on their moral behaviour.

Objective

Outline the Christian vision of moral failure and its consequences.

Activity: *"Censoring Activity"*

TASK: TO BE AWARE THAT CERTAIN TYPES OF HUMAN BEHAVIOUR CAUSE HURT AND SUFFERING.

You will need:
- 8 to 10 copies of daily newspapers (broadsheets).
- Thick black crayons or felt pens.

✦ Divide the class into small groups. Give each group a newspaper and a pen.

✦ Ask everyone to examine their newspaper and circle all the headlines reporting any kind of bad behaviour. After two to three minutes of this censoring activity, re-convene to discuss the exercise.

Discuss

- What did you discover about the news?
- What kind of human behaviour causes hurt and suffering?
- Select one article and state:
  - what happened.
  - who was at fault and what did the person(s) do wrong.
  - what were the consequences.

Sin

There is widespread evidence that people behave badly and fail to do what is right.

Moral failure means failing to act as a moral person. This happens when someone:

❖ Does something that he or she knows is wrong OR

❖ Doesn't bother to do what he or she knows to be right.

In the Christian tradition, the term for moral failure is 'sin'. Sin means ignoring one's conscience and acting in a selfish manner. Sin always causes harm.

At times we sin by deliberately doing something wrong, as in acts of stealing, cheating or telling lies for example. These are called sins of *commission*.

At other times we sin by failing to do what is right, as in failing to speak up when someone is wrongly accused of something for example. This is called a sin of *omission*. So sin is not always something we do, more often it is something we don't do. It can be something we should do, but fail to do, because of selfishness, laziness or pride.

The effects of sin spread out like ripples on a pond.

Sin affects relationships

Sin is any deliberate thought, word, or action that damages a person's relationship with God and other people. Relationships are very important within the Christian moral vision and sin damages relationships.

A Christian lives in relationship with God, with themselves and with other people. Sin is anything that damages this important set of relationships. It results in the person being separated or cut off from God, from themselves and from others.

- ❖ When people are self-centred and want to meet their own needs exclusively, they cut themselves off from God and God's way of doing things.
- ❖ When people are selfish they become careless, and cut themselves off from the needs and feelings of others.

Adam and Eve (Genesis 3:1-20)

In the Bible, the story of Adam and Eve shows the effect of sin on human relationships. In Genesis 'Adam' represents man and 'Eve' represents woman. What happened is not an historical account of an event that took place at the dawn of time, but a symbolic story that sets out to explain the origin of sin and its consequences.

The authors of Genesis present images of good and evil. Their idea of heaven or paradise was a beautiful garden. Their idea of evil was the back-breaking work of cultivating poor soil in the land where they lived. God the creator meanwhile, was present everywhere.

Man and woman lived happily in the garden for a time. Then they realized they wanted something more; what they had wasn't enough. So they did the one thing they were asked not to do, they ate from the 'tree of knowledge'. This sinful act had a number of consequences.

They ate from the 'tree of knowledge'.

The effect of sin on the self

"As soon as they had eaten it they were given understanding and realised they were naked." Genesis 3:7.

Nakedness was a symbol of defeat and disgrace in ancient times. After they had sinned, the man and woman were embarrassed and tried to cover themselves. Sin had changed something inside them. They now felt guilty and uncomfortable. Sin had destroyed their peace of mind. It separated them from themselves.

The effect of sin on their relationship with God

"That evening they heard the Lord God walking in the garden, and they hid from him among the trees." Genesis 3:8.

The man and woman were now afraid of God, and felt uncomfortable in his presence. They were no longer conscious of God's love. Sin had destroyed their relationship with their creator. It separated them from God.

The effect of sin on their relationship with others

"...The man answered, 'The woman you put here with me gave me the fruit, and I ate it.' The Lord God asked the woman 'Why did you do this?' She replied, 'The snake tricked me into eating it.'" Genesis 3:12-13.

The man and the woman were unwilling to take responsibility for their sin. They made excuses and tried to shift the blame from one to the other. *'It wasn't me.' 'She made me do it.' 'It was all his fault.'* Sin ruined their relationship. It separated them from one another.

The Catholic Church teaches that there is original sin and personal sin.

Original Sin

Although people know the difference between right and wrong, they frequently do what is wrong. If a person feels a strong desire to do something sinful, he/she will often give in to that desire and hurt themselves and others in the process. Human beings have a tendency to do what is wrong rather than what is right. They are more inclined to be jealous, selfish or rude than considerate, peaceful and kind. They know they should not be like this, but it happens anyway. It is a part of being human. This is the effect of original sin.

Human beings are born into a world where weakness and sin are already present. They become part of it and then they add to it. People need help in dealing with this basic inclination toward sinfulness. They can manage to be good occasionally, but find it difficult to act this way all the time. They need help to strengthen their determination to always do what is right. Christians believe this assistance comes from Jesus and the sacraments, especially the sacrament of Baptism.

People have a basic inclination toward sinfulness.

Personal Sin

Sin is any deliberate thought, word or action that damages a person's relationship with God and other people. The Catholic Church teaches that there are two kinds of sin: mortal sin and venial sin.

- Mortal sin is the most serious type of sin, it *breaks* one's relationship with God.
- Venial sin is the less serious type of sin, it *weakens* one's relationship with God.

Mortal Sin

Mortal sin is very serious. If someone knows that an action is seriously wrong, yet still decides to do it, that is a mortal sin. To do something to cause great harm destroys one's relationship with God and other people.

If someone sets out to deliberately hurt another, they are ending their relationship with God. Their action shows that they have completely turned away from God, and God's plan for the world.

Murder, sexual abuse, robbery with violence are examples of mortal sin.

Venial Sin

Venial sin is less serious. Although the action is wrong and is done on purpose, it is not seriously wrong. Yet venial sin is to be avoided because if left unchecked it can lead to more serious sin.

Small offences can cause hurt and put a strain on relationships. Not only does venial sin weaken one's relationships with others, it also weakens one's relationship with God. But it does not damage either relationship completely. It does suggest however that the person is gradually turning away from God.

Telling a lie, telling secrets, cheating and cursing are examples of venial sin.

For Christians, all sin is a failure to love God and love one's neighbour in the way that Jesus taught.

Judgement

The monotheistic religions, Judaism, Christianity and Islam, teach that people will be held responsible for the moral choices they make in life. Judgement is the religious belief that, in the end, God will judge each person on their moral behaviour. The good will go to heaven. The wicked will be sent to hell.

Catholics believe:

- ❖ Heaven - is a state of being with God. A state of perfect happiness in the presence of God.
- ❖ Hell - is a state of separation from God. A state of total unhappiness in the absence of God.
- ❖ Purgatory - is an in-between state of preparation for eventual union with God.

Heaven, hell and purgatory are not actual places that exist somewhere. Each is a state, or a condition, that a person has chosen as a consequence of the choices he/she made in life. God does not 'send' people to heaven or hell. People send themselves. They 'arrive' there as a result of how they have lived their lives.

'I was hungry, but you would not feed me, thirsty but you would not give me a drink.' Matthew 25:42-43.

Questions

Knowledge

1. What is the meaning of moral failure?
2. What is the Christian term for moral failure?
3. Give examples of the selfish choices that people frequently make today.
4. What is:
   a. A sin of commission?
   b. A sin of omission?
   Provide examples of each.
5. a. What do Christians mean by sin?
   b. What effect does sin have on a person's relationships?
6. Give examples from everyday life of how sin damages a person's relationships with:
   a. God. b. Self. c. Others.
7. In Genesis, after the sin of Adam and Eve, was there any change in their relationship with: a. God? b. self? c. each other?
8. The selfishness of Adam and Eve spoiled the good life they once had. How can selfishness spoil good things in life today? Give examples.
9. Has the selfishness of another person ever spoiled something good in your life. What effect did this sin have on you?
10. In Catholic teaching what is the meaning of:
    a. Original sin? b. Mortal sin? c. Venial sin?
11. Give examples of:
    a. Mortal sin.
    (Explain what makes this sin mortal.)
    b. Venial sin.
    (Explain what makes this sin venial.)
12. What is the meaning of the Judgement after death?

Understanding

1. How does sin affect human relationships?
2. How do the authors of Genesis teach the different effects of sin?
3. Explain the difference between original sin and personal sin in Catholic moral teaching.
4. What is the Catholic understanding of heaven, hell and purgatory at the final Judgement?

Restoring Relationships

Key Concepts

Forgiveness: to have pity and be willing to excuse someone's mistake or wrongdoing.

Reconciliation: making the effort to heal and restore a broken relationship.

Objective

Outline the meaning of forgiveness in two religious traditions.

Activity: *"Blotto!"*

TASK: TO THINK ABOUT WAYS OF PUTTING THINGS RIGHT.

- Use a pen or a pencil and make a blot in your copy.
  (A quarter the size of one page is sufficient!)
- Doodle with the shape for a while, try turning the blot into a design.

kB

Discuss

- How did your design turn out?
- When we make a mistake does it have to spoil everything?
- Is there a way to put things right?

Forgiveness

People can learn from their mistakes.
Forgiveness often leads to new beginnings.

One of the hardest things Jesus asked his followers to do was to be forgiving. It is not easy to forgive as it does not come naturally, especially when the hurt is deep. The more instinctive reaction is to be vindictive or to look for revenge.

Think back:

- What was your reaction the last time someone did something to hurt you?
- Did you want to get your own back?
- Did you want to make that person suffer too?
- Did you hold a grudge afterwards?

Some things can be harder to forgive than others. Make a list of those things which you would find it most difficult to forgive.

It's sometimes not easy to forgive.

The teaching of Jesus

Christians believe they must follow the teaching of Jesus and forgive those who hurt or offend them. Forgiveness means having pity on someone and being willing to excuse their mistake or wrongdoing.

Jesus taught forgiveness through his:

- ❖ Parables
  e.g. 'The Prodigal Son' (Luke 15:11-24)
  'The King and the Servant' (Matt 18:23-35)
- ❖ Miracles
  e.g. 'Healing the Paralysed Man' (Luke 5:17-26)
- ❖ Table Fellowship
  e.g. 'Sharing a meal with a tax collector' (Luke 19:1-10)

Why do Christians insist that it is important to forgive? They do so because Jesus told his followers that God is forgiving. Christians believe therefore, that since God forgives them, they must forgive others. This belief rules out revenge. It is natural to feel vengeful, but it is not a Christian response. There is no place for revenge or vindictiveness in the Christian moral vision.

What does it mean to forgive?

Imagine one of us has a quarrel with a friend because he/she has betrayed us in some way. If the friend realises their mistake and says sorry and means it, then we forgive him/her and we can start over again.

Forgiveness does not mean:

- We forget about the wrongdoing and pretend it didn't happen.

Forgiveness means:

- Giving up the desire to keep on blaming and hating.
- Letting go of the anger and the hurt.
- Moving on, leaving behind any vengeful feelings toward the person who has wronged us.

Christians try to forgive those who have hurt or offended them. The process begins when they place the situation before God in prayer. They ask God to take away the hatred and bitterness in their heart. The very act of turning to God in prayer can be the beginning of forgiveness. But it doesn't happen instantly; forgiveness takes time, it also takes effort and constant prayer.

Jesus told his followers to be generous with their forgiveness. When they asked him how often they were supposed to forgive, Jesus replied that there should be no limit to their forgiveness.

> "Peter asked. 'Lord, if my brother keeps on sinning against me how many times do I have to forgive him? Seven times?' 'No, not seven times,' answered Jesus, 'but seventy times seven.'" Matthew 18:21-22.

In Jesus' day "seventy times seven" meant an unlimited number of times.

Enniskillen War Memorial in the aftermath of the IRA bomb blast.

Gordon Wilson

At 11am on the 8th November 1987, an IRA bomb killed eleven people and injured sixty three others in Enniskillen, Co. Fermanagh. Marie Wilson, a twenty one year old nurse, was among the crowd at the cenotaph that morning for the Remembrance Day Service. Her father held her hand as she lay buried beneath the rubble. "Are you all right Marie," he kept asking her. She managed to whisper, "Daddy, I love you very much."

The next day Gordon Wilson spoke in a television interview, "I have lost my daughter… We shall miss her. But I bear no ill will. I bear no grudge…. Our Lord taught us to pray, 'Forgive us our sins as we forgive those who sin against us'."

With the help of prayer, and a sincere effort, Gordon Wilson was able to forgive his daughter's murderers.

Reconciliation

People sin when they deliberately hurt others by what they say and do. Sin damages the relationship that exists between them. It is not easy to repair a broken relationship. This is because people find it difficult to say sorry and may be reluctant to admit when they are wrong.

When Christians damage their relationship with each other it directly affects their relationship with God. Their behaviour and the choices they make show they have turned away from God. Relationships matter and are very important, so when a relationship breaks down it cannot be ignored. It needs to be mended. People need to work things out and be reconciled with each other and with God. When people make an effort to heal or restore a relationship, this effort is called reconciliation.

❖ Jesus' parable of the 'Prodigal Son' (Luke 15:11-24) shows the forgiveness of God and the need for reconciliation.

Coventry Cathedral

Coventry Cathedral, in England, was bombed and badly damaged during World War 2. After the war German and British youth volunteered to work together to repair part of the structure. A work of art representing reconciliation was placed among the ruins. The sculpture provides a focus for prayer and reflection. A new cathedral was built alongside the remains of the original, and today Coventry Cathedral is famous as an international Christian centre for peace and reconciliation.

Reconciliation sculpture, Coventry Cathedral.

sorry

Christianity: Restoring Relationships
The Sacrament of Reconciliation

The Catholic Church recognises that sinful behaviour hurts everyone, not just the other person, but the whole community. In the Roman Catholic tradition, the sacrament of Reconciliation heals and restores broken relationships, bringing people back to God and to one another.

Catholics confess their sins to a priest, believing that Jesus gives the priest power to forgive sins. When Catholics confess to a priest they are, in a symbolic way, expressing their sorrow to the community and to the person they have wronged. Through the words and actions of the sacrament, the priest offers forgiveness on behalf of God and the Christian community. The sacrament of Reconciliation gives Catholics the power to rebuild their relationship with God and with each other.

The Sacrament of Reconciliation

Catholics prepare for the sacrament of God's forgiveness (individual confession) by:

- Finding a quiet place to be alone with God.
- Making the sign of the cross.
- Taking time to carefully examine their conscience.
- Being sorry for any wrong doing, and being determined to make a fresh start.

The penitent (the person seeking forgiveness) can choose to speak to the priest in a confessional box separated by a partition where the priest cannot see the penitent, OR in a reconciliation room where the priest and the penitent meet face to face. The parts of the sacrament are:

1. Confession - the penitent tells his/her sins to the priest.
2. Penance - the priest gives a penance to fit the sin.
3. Sorrow - the penitent expresses sorrow for what he/she has done wrong.
4. Forgiveness - the priest offers the person God's forgiveness for their sins.

Celebrating the Sacrament

The priest welcomes the penitent. The penitent makes the sign of the cross with the priest and says how long it is since his/her last confession. Then the priest reads a short passage from the Gospel.

POLSKA
ITALIANO
ENGLISH

Individual confession.

1. Confession.
   The penitent tells his/her sins to the priest. The penitent admits that he/she has made wrong decisions and is sorry about it. The priest listens and may give some advice on making right decisions in the future.
2. Penance.
   The priest gives a penance. The penance is a prayer or an action to make up for what has been done. The penitent may have to say a prayer, deny himself/herself something, or perform a helpful service for a neighbour or a relative.
3. Sorrow.
   The penitent says a formal prayer called the Act of Sorrow. It expresses his/her genuine sorrow for doing wrong and a promise not to sin again.
4. Forgiveness.
   The priest raises one hand over the penitent and speaks the words of God's forgiveness.
   'I absolve you of your sins in the name of the Father, and of the Son, and of the Holy Spirit. Amen'. The sign of the cross is made over the penitent, then he/she is told to 'Go in peace'.

Judaism: Restoring Relationships
The Festival of Yom Kippur

Yom Kippur is the holiest day in the Jewish year. It is the day when Jews make amends to God for what they have done wrong. They tell God they are sorry and ask God to forgive them for their sins.

> "O Lord, you forgive the sins of your people... You do not stay angry forever, but you take pleasure in showing us your constant love. You will be merciful to us once again. You will trample our sins underfoot and send them to the bottom of the sea." Micah 7:18-19 The Tenakh

The holiest day of the Jewish year

Jews fast all day on Yom Kippur. They try not to eat or drink anything for twenty four hours. However, older people, sick people, pregnant women and children under thirteen years do not have to fast. Fasting is a symbolic act. It helps everyone to focus their mind on what is important in life.

Jews spend most of the day praying in the synagogue. They pray to God to forgive them for their sins and for the strength to live better lives in the future. Sorrow for wrongdoing and God's forgiveness is the focus of Yom Kippur.

In the Synagogue

Everything in the synagogue is covered in white on Yom Kippur. The curtain on the Ark is white, the Torah Scrolls are dressed in white, a white cloth covers the reading desk, the Rabbi who leads the service wears white too. The colour white is used as a symbol to show that, when people are sorry, God will forgive their sins. The darkness of sin is taken away and they become pure again - like angels.

The dead are remembered on this day too, especially Jews who suffered for their faith in the Holocaust during World War 2. The Holocaust is called the 'Shoah' in Hebrew. Special candles are lit in memory of those who lost their lives during those terrible times.

Blowing the shofar on Yom Kippur.

A reading from scripture tells what happened on Yom Kippur or the Day of Atonement long ago. Once a year the high priest went into the Holy of Holies, the most sacred part of the Temple in Jerusalem, to offer sacrifice to God. He made the sacrifice on behalf of all the people to atone, or make amends, for their sins.

A special prayer called the Shema is said. Then the Shofar (a ram's horn) is blown loudly at the end of the service. This is a symbolic act to remind everyone to keep their promises, and do God's will in the year ahead.

Research

- Find out about the painting entitled "The return of the Prodigal Son".
  - Answer the following questions and share your findings with the class.

Questions

1. Who painted this famous masterpiece?
2. What art gallery has this painting in its collection?
3. Describe what is seen in the painting.
4. What story might have influenced the artist to create this painting?
5. Write a summary of the parable in one paragraph. (Luke 15:11-24)
6. What qualities of a good parent are highlighted in the parable of the Prodigal Son?
7. Describe the image of God that is presented to Christians in Jesus' parable of the Prodigal Son.

Questions

Knowledge

1. What is forgiveness?
2. How did Jesus teach about forgiveness?
3. What is the Christian teaching on forgiveness?
4. How do we begin the process of trying to forgive others, according to Christian teaching.
5. Describe an example of Christian forgiveness in a difficult situation.
6. What is reconciliation?
7. Give an example of Christian reconciliation in action.
8. a. Read Jesus' parable of the 'Prodigal Son'. How does the parable show:
   i. Sorrow?
   ii. Forgiveness?
   iii. Reconciliation?

   b. To whom might Jesus tell this parable today? Give reasons for your answer.
9. a. By what method does the Catholic Church offer the possibility of the restoration of relationships?

   b. How do Catholics prepare for the Sacrament of Reconciliation?
10. What are the four parts of the Sacrament of Reconciliation in the Roman Catholic tradition?
11. By what method does the Jewish tradition offer the possibility of the restoration of relationships?
12. What happens in the synagogue on the Jewish festival of Yom Kippur?

Understanding

1. How important is forgiveness and reconciliation in the Christian moral vision?
2. Why do Catholics confess their sins publicly to a priest, instead of praying for God's forgiveness in private?
3. Explain the meaning of the Sacrament of Reconciliation in the Roman Catholic tradition.
4. Explain how the words and actions at the festival of Yom Kippur show the importance of forgiveness and reconciliation in the moral vision of Judaism.

Law and Morality

Key Concepts

Civil law: the laws of a state that regulate the behaviour of people within the state.

Constitution: a document outlining the fundamental political principles by which a state is governed.

Objective

Outline the relationship between state law and personal morality.

Activity: *"Rules and Laws"*

TASK: TO DISCUSS RIGHTS AND ENTITLEMENTS UNDER THE LAW IN IRELAND.

- At sixteen years of age you **CAN** legally...
  - get a full-time job.
  - leave school.
  - get a licence for a 125cc motorbike.
  - get a student flying license.
  - be forced to leave home. (Parents and guardians must maintain you until your sixteenth birthday).
  - change your name with parents' consent.
- At sixteen years of age you **CANNOT** legally...
  - buy alcohol or cigarettes.
  - open a current account in a bank without parents' or guardians' consent.
  - be sent to prison.
  - buy a lottery ticket.
  - get a provisional licence for a car.

Discuss

- Are any of these laws unfair, in your opinion?
- What is the reason for the law in relation to some of the issues listed here?
- Give examples of times:
  a. When people may be tempted to ignore certain laws.
  b. When people accept that certain laws are for the common good.

Civil Law

Law is there for the common good of society.

RULES

All communities have a system of rules.

Every community develops its own system of rules. We follow certain rules at home, at school, in the class and in the clubs and societies to which we belong. The rules are there to ensure that people behave in a certain way and co-operate with one another.

The overall political community of the country also has a system of rules or laws. These are known as state laws. A state is a country with its own system of government. The state has a duty to:

- Protect the rights of citizens.
- Maintain law and order.

This is achieved by the government passing laws to regulate the behaviour of people within the state. Laws are enforced by the police and courts of law.

State Laws

State laws influence our moral actions as everyone in the country must obey the law. In Ireland and the United Kingdom there are two main types of law: criminal law and civil law.

Criminal Law

Criminal law protects the rights of citizens. In criminal law the state takes legal action and deals with those who commit crimes against others, such as murder, robbery, dangerous driving or assault.

SPACE
GARDA
GARDA
A Garda officer on duty.

Civil Law

Civil law concerns people's relationships with each other. In civil law the citizen takes legal action to settle a dispute, or make arrangements about such matters as adoption, divorce, house buying or compensation.

It is expected that all the laws of the state must be good, must be moral and must be for the benefit of the whole community.

- ❖ If a person breaks the law, he or she may have to face trial in a court of law.
- ❖ If found guilty, the court will decide on a suitable punishment.

Constitution

Laws are made for the 'common good'. A government makes laws according to its vision of what is best for the country as a whole. A government's vision of what is best for the country is expressed in its constitution.

A constitution is a document outlining the fundamental political principles by which a state is governed. The Irish Constitution contains a set of guidelines the government must follow when introducing new laws.

A constitution is important because:

- ❖ It prevents the abuse of power.
- ❖ It protects the rights of citizens.

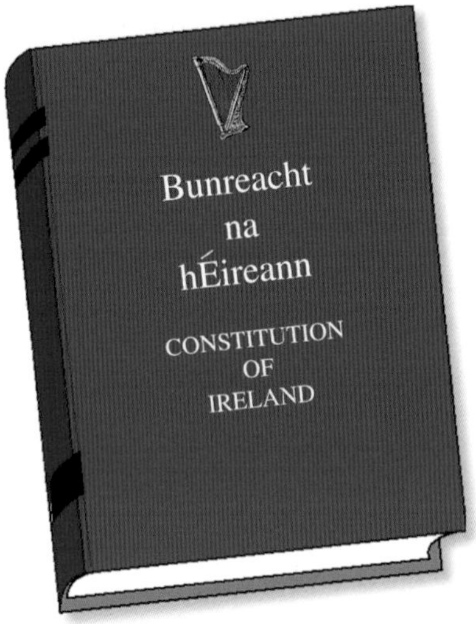
Bunreacht
na
hÉireann
CONSTITUTION
OF
IRELAND

Bunreacht na hEireann
(the Constitution of Ireland)

- ❖ Describes the position of the President, and how the President is elected.
- ❖ Describes the structure of the Dáil, and how Dáil members are elected.
- ❖ Describes the legal system.
- ❖ Outlines the basic rights of individuals living in the state.

For example the Irish Constitution guarantees:

- Freedom and equal treatment before the law.
- Protection of the family and the institution of marriage.
- The right to education.
- The right to own and inherit property.
- The right to practice religion.

The relationship between State Law and Personal Morality

My personal morality is my firm belief about what is right and wrong, good and bad. It is the sum total of everything I know about the way I should act. It is my moral vision, and it may or may not be rooted in a religious tradition.

Some people may think that law and morality are one and the same, that the law of the state should be the only guide for their moral behaviour. Others think that law and morality are not the same, but different.

A Christian perspective

Christians, for example, accept that people should respect and obey just laws that are clearly for the common good. However, they do not accept that the law of the land contains the final word on what is right and wrong. Christians say that there is a higher standard than the law of the state, and they believe this is the law of God. The Catholic Church for example teaches that:

> "God's law continues to bind no matter what the civil (state) law says."
>
> *Love is for Life* (Pastoral letter of the Irish Bishops)

Christian morality is about love and Jesus' message is 'Love God and love your neighbour as yourself'. His followers today try to do what is right out of love and respect for others, not out of fear of the law.

It is important to differentiate between law and morality. Personal morality is more than simply obeying state laws. A morally mature person is one whose behaviour is influenced more by their personal moral vision than by the laws of the state.

Conflict between law and morality

State law must be good, and it must be fair and just, and for the benefit of all. In other words, it must be moral. When the moral values of citizens are reflected in the laws of the state, the outcome can be one of unity and harmony. For example, if people believe that theft is wrong, and state laws reflect this, then citizens will freely support the law of the state. The state's duty to uphold law and order is made a whole lot easier when people can see that it is trying to do what is right and just.

In a democratic society, we can assume that the laws are just and are for the common good. However, it can happen that a particular law might not reflect the values of some people in that society. When the morality of such a law does not correspond with the personal morality of certain individuals, problems can arise.

Examples of conflict between law and personal morality

- In Ireland and Great Britain, state laws allowing Sunday trading have been introduced in the past few years. This created a problem for some Christians who believed that Sunday, or the Sabbath, should be kept a day of rest. Keeping shops open on Sundays, they believed, took time away from worship and family life. It affected both customers and staff who now had even less quality time to spend with their families. 'Keep Sunday Special' was a campaign to raise pubic awareness of this issue.

Sunday trading: a source of conflict between law and morality for some people.

- In some countries, state law demands that men and women be conscripted for a period of military service, even during peacetime. This creates a moral problem for some people, such as the Society of Friends (Quakers), who are committed pacifists. They are morally obliged to refuse military service because they are opposed to all forms of violence.
- Countries throughout Europe and elsewhere have introduced laws to legalise abortion. Many Christians, especially Roman Catholics, believe that human life is sacred and abortion is not acceptable for any reason. Yet most countries permit thousands of abortions to take place every month. Christians of all denominations and traditions protest against the extent of abortion provision in countries where it is now legalised.

In a society where a state law is immoral, most people, including many Christians would say that such laws do not have to be obeyed. If there is a conflict between the law of God and the law of the state, people follow their conscience and do what is right, even if it means breaking the law. Unjust laws have been broken by people of conscience in all parts of the world.

In a democratic country like ours, people are free to protest in a peaceful way. They can challenge the government about any law or issue that is a cause for concern. Christians, as well as people of no particular faith, can protest against unjust laws by joining peaceful demonstrations, signing petitions, distributing leaflets, contacting government representatives, and by attending public meetings and events. They can also use their voting power at local and national elections.

Questions

Knowledge

1. a. List three groups or organisations that make rules for the good of their members?
   b. What would happen if people did not follow the rules?
2. a. What is the State?
   b. What is state law?
3. What does it mean to say 'laws are for the common good'?
4. Give examples of laws that are for the common good.
5. a. What is the Constitution?
   b. Why do countries have a constitution?
6. What is personal morality?
7. What is the difference between state law and personal morality?
8. If a person believes that state law and personal morality are essentially different, how does he/she decide what is right or wrong?
9. How can one's personal morality support the law of the state?
10. How could one's personal morality be in conflict with state law? Explain using examples.
11. In Christian teaching, when is it morally right:
    a. To obey the law of the state?
    b. To disobey or challenge a law of the state?
12. In a just society, how can people object to a law that they consider morally wrong?

Understanding

1. Why are we expected to keep rules at home, at school, in clubs and organisations?
2. a. Explain why state law is necessary.
   b. What would happen if there was no rule of law in society?
3. Why is it important to distinguish between state law and personal morality?
4. What is the relationship between state law and morality?
   a. How are they connected?
   b. How might they clash or come into conflict?

Apartheid

Key Concept

Civil law: the laws of a State that regulate the behaviour of people within the State.

Objective

Outline the relationship between unjust law and personal morality.

Activity: *"Map work"*

TASK: IDENTIFY COUNTRIES WHERE UN-JUST LAWS WERE IMPOSED BY THE STATE.

In the United States, racial segregation in schools, public places and employment was permitted until the Civil Rights Bill was passed in 1964.

In the former Soviet Union and Eastern Europe, Communist governments imposed laws to forbid people practising their religion.

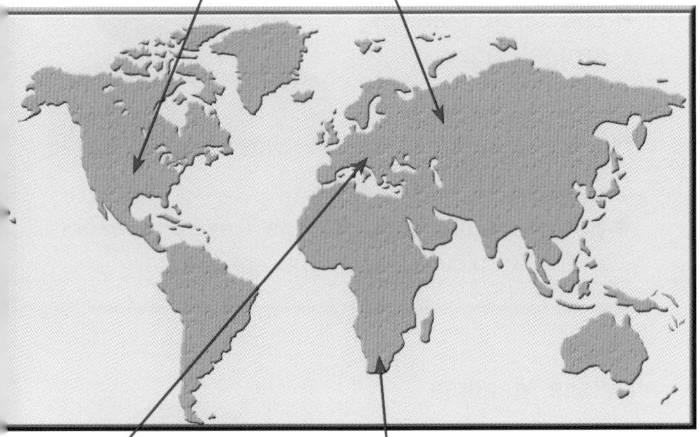

In Germany, the Nazi government imposed laws that discriminated against the Jewish population, and led to their genocide in occupied countries throughout Europe.

In South Africa, the government imposed laws that divided people along racial lines. It was known as the apartheid system.

Discuss

- Give an example of a state where legalized racism was part of state law.
- What is a just law?
- What makes a law un-just and immoral?

Civil Law

For a law to be moral, it must be just.

Some states are basically unjust, with the result that many of their laws are also unjust. In such countries, what is legal may not necessarily be good or even moral. This can lead to a conflict between personal morality and state law. During the last century, for example, the state passed unjust laws in the Soviet Union prohibiting the practice of religion. In Germany, the Nazi government passed laws that led to the persecution of the Jewish people.

In South Africa, racial laws led to the suppression of the majority black population. The system of pro-white, anti-black legislation in South Africa was called Apartheid.

Population distribution in South Africa

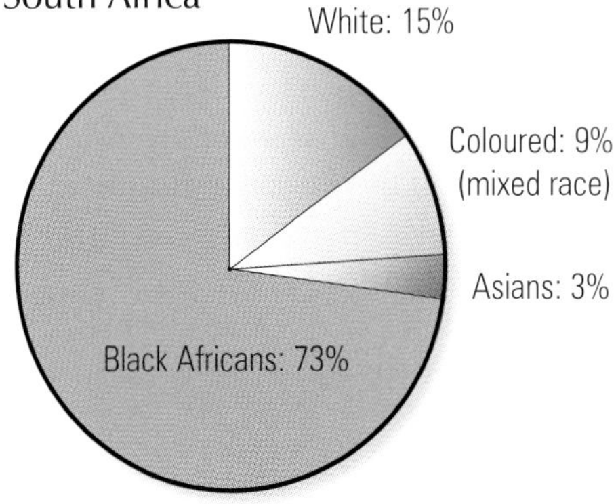
White: 15%
Coloured: 9% (mixed race)
Asians: 3%
Black Africans: 73%

Apartheid

The government of South Africa put a system in place called 'apartheid'. The word meant 'separate development' and was a form of legalised racism. The population of the country was separated according to the colour of their skin. The whites had all the political and economic power and ran the country for their own benefit. They had the best land, owned all the resources and lived a life of comparative luxury.

The blacks were in the majority but they came off worst. They were poor, had no vote, and no rights. They were forcibly moved to the poorest parts of the country. The black population was crowded into 13% of the land area in South Africa.

Blacks going outside their area had to carry a pass. Strict laws meant they were fined or imprisoned if they had no pass book or if they stayed away too long. Blacks were kept separate from whites in everything; they were not allowed to sit on the same park benches, use the same public toilets or walk the same beaches as whites.

GRENS TUSSEN
BLANKE EN ALLE RASSE
GEBIED
BOUNDARY BETWEEN
WHITE AND ALL RACES
AREA

A sign marking the boundary between the area for whites and other races.

The separation of blacks and whites in South Africa was supported by the full authority of the law. Black people who spoke out were put in prison; many were tortured and died in police custody. Others simply 'disappeared'. This situation lasted until 1994.

Conflict between law and morality

Christians campaigned for an end to apartheid, among them Nelson Mandela and Archbishop Desmond Tutu. They both believed apartheid was wrong and spoke out against it. In doing this they risked being branded as terrorists or communists, and risked torture, imprisonment or death at the hands of the police or the army.

Mandela struggled with his conscience, and decided that violence was necessary to bring about change. Tutu chose a different route, the way of non-violence.

Archbishop Desmond Tutu

- Born in South Africa.
- Trained as a teacher.
- Ordained as an Anglican priest.
- Led the non-violent struggle against apartheid.
- Won the Nobel Peace Prize in 1984.
- Became Archbishop of Cape Town and leader of the Anglican Church in South Africa.

Nelson Mandela

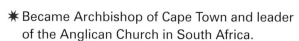

- Born in South Africa.
- Trained as a lawyer.
- Tried to overthrow the government.
- Imprisoned on Robben Island for 27 years.
- Worked to bring political change in South Africa on his release.
- Awarded the Nobel Peace Prize in 1993.
- Elected President of South Africa in 1994.
- President Mandela's government abolished apartheid in 1994.

Archbishop Desmond Tutu

Desmond Tutu preached against apartheid. He said it was against Christian teaching and was 'one of the most vicious systems since Nazism'. He made it clear that he was on the side of the oppressed and against the government on the issue of apartheid. He led peaceful demonstrations and marches. He organised boycotts and petitions. He invited the world's media to witness and record the injustice that was taking place in his native country.

In 1986 Desmond Tutu became the first black Anglican Archbishop of Cape Town. At a meeting in South Africa, the World Council of Churches agreed with him that apartheid had to go.

When President Mandela's government finally abolished apartheid in 1994, Archbishop Tutu was chosen to lead the Commission of Truth and Reconciliation. It was the beginning of the way forward for people on all sides in South Africa.

The way forward.

Questions

Knowledge

1. What countries had unjust laws?
2. What does the term 'apartheid' mean?
3. How did the system of apartheid affect black people in South Africa?
4. Who is Archbishop Desmond Tutu?
5. Who is Nelson Mandela?

Understanding

1. How was the personal morality of either
   a. Desmond Tutu, or
   b. Nelson Mandela,
   in conflict with state law in South Africa?
2. Explain why Desmond Tutu challenged the government about the system of apartheid.
3. Describe the methods Tutu used to bring about change in South Africa.
4. Why is it important to know about Nelson Mandela when discussing apartheid in South Africa?
5. How would you describe the role of the Anglican Church in South Africa during the apartheid era, and since apartheid was abolished?

Research

- Find out about the role of the Dunne's Stores strikers in Ireland during the apartheid era.
  - Who were the members of this group?
  - What was their protest about?
  - Where did their action take place?
  - How did people respond to their action?
  - Why did they undertake strike action?
  - What was the outcome for them at the time, and subsequently?
  - Discuss the issue of principled action and its consequences.

Religion and Law

Key Concepts

Pluralism: the view that all groups in society must have equal representation.

Religious Fundamentalism: the view that the laws of the state should be based on the moral laws of the dominant religion.

Libertarianism: the view that people should be free to behave as they choose, without undue interference from the state.

Objective

Outline the relationship between state law and religious morality.

Activity: *"Definitions"*

TASK: TO KNOW THE BASIC MEANING OF SOME COMMONLY USED WORDS.

✦ Match each word with its corresponding meaning.

✧Plural	- foundation. - more than one. - independent.
✧Fundamental	- going one's own way. - going to the root of the matter. - numerous.
✧Liberty	- original. - several. - free from control.

Discuss

- Provide a definition of each word.
- Give an example of the common usage of each word.
- Would you expect the meaning of the word to alter significantly if the suffix 'ism' was attached to the end of it.

Law and Religious Morality

Religion plays an important part in forming the moral vision of many people. How far should religious morality influence the law of the state? There are three different views.

- ❖ Pluralism.
- ❖ Religious Fundamentalism.
- ❖ Libertarianism.

Pluralism

Pluralism is the view that all groups in society must have equal representation, and that state laws cannot be based on the moral outlook of any one religious tradition.

A pluralist society is made up of people who come from various social, racial and religious backgrounds. People who belong to different religions, and those of no religion, can co-exist peacefully together. Each group retains its own beliefs, and its own unique outlook on life.

Having firm opinions, however, can lead people to disagree on some moral issues. The state must be able to accommodate all conflicting points of view. The laws of the state are made for all the people of the state. Pluralism means that the laws cannot be based on the moral vision of any one religion. All groups, no matter how small, are to be treated with respect. Minorities are part of society, and must be able to carry out their own religious and cultural practices. The state has the task of trying to balance the rights of all groups, including minorities, without favouring any group in particular.

Members of the Amish community, a minority religious group in the United States of America.

In a pluralist society, law and religious morality are ideally separate from one another. Does this mean that religion has no influence whatsoever on the law of the state? The Roman Catholic Church, for example, sees itself as independent of the state. It also believes it has the right to criticise a government if it makes unjust laws. When the state introduces laws concerning moral issues such as abortion, divorce and contraception, the bishops have a duty to teach Catholics about the implications of these laws for Christian living.

'We do not ask that Catholic teaching as such be enshrined in law. We recognise that morality and civil law do not necessarily coincide...but we do as pastors have a responsibility to offer moral guidance to Catholics to help them form their consciences in respect of their moral responsibilities as legislators or voters.'
(Love is for Life - Pastoral Letter of the Irish Bishops.)

The bishops believe that they have the right to campaign and make public statements about these issues. This is only fair, in their opinion, as other interest groups, with different views, have the right to campaign openly to influence public opinion.

When people vote in free elections in a democratic society, it is inevitable that the voting pattern will reflect religious moral values to some degree. To this extent, there is a connection between the laws of the state and religious morality.

Religious Fundamentalism

Religious Fundamentalism is the view that the laws of a state should be based on the moral laws of its dominant religion, and that no other viewpoint should be tolerated. Fundamentalist movements are found, for example, within the three monotheistic religions - Judaism, Christianity and Islam.

Religious fundamentalists believe that the religious teachings of their faith should be the only guiding force in society. Their inspiration comes from sacred texts, where every word is accepted as the literal truth.

Fundamentalists resist any attempt to update or modernise the interpretation of sacred texts in light of new evidence or learning. Instead they stick faithfully to the older, traditional interpretation of scripture. This results in an outlook that values the fixed and unchanging nature of religious teaching and practice. Religious fundamentalists want the moral laws of their religion to be made the law of the state.

Shari'a Law in Iran

Iran is an example of a country where religious fundamentalists have taken political action based on their religious beliefs. In the 1970's Muslim religious leaders called for the overthrow of the King, or 'Shah', of Iran. They stated that he had abandoned the principles of Islam and the values of his government had become foreign and corrupt. In 1979 there was a revolt in Iran. The Shah fled the country and Ayatollah Khomeini, a well known religious fundamentalist, came to power. He outlined his position clearly from the start: 'We want Islam, only Islam.'

An Islamic republic was established and the Shari'a, that is Islamic law, became the law of the state. The Shari'a is based on the teachings of the Qur'an, the Muslim sacred text. The dictatorship of the mullahs (religious leaders) has lasted ever since.

Libertarianism

Libertarianism is the view that people should be free to think and behave as they choose without undue interference from the state. The state must not interfere or try to limit the freedom of the individual. This outlook adopts the position that the individual's right to freedom takes priority over all other rights. It totally rejects any state law that tries to unduly restrict that liberty.

Libertarians see morality mainly as a private matter. Moral issues are best left to the conscience of the individual, they don't require the intervention of the state. The role of the state must be reduced as much as possible in all aspects of public life. While it can be argued that religious morality can be a support to state law in a pluralist society, this is of little relevance to those with a libertarian outlook. This is because religion, morality, and the state are all seen as forces that oppress individual liberty.

Different Systems of Thought

The three systems of thought, Pluralism, Religious Fundamentalism and Libertarianism, influence the law-making process of different countries.

In a pluralist society law and religious morality are ideally separate from one another. This is the case, for example, in Ireland.

In Iran religious fundamentalists believe so strongly in the fixed nature of their faith, that they have made its religious laws the laws of the state.

In Holland morality is seen mainly as a private matter. The way people choose to think and act is un-restricted by outside influences such as the Church or the state.

Questions

1. What is:
   - Pluralism?
   - Religious Fundamentalism?
   - Libertarianism?
2. Explain the difference between Pluralism, Fundamentalism and Libertarianism.
3. How might the opinions of the pluralist, the fundamentalist and the libertarian:
   a. Be taken into account by the state?
   b. Bring them into conflict with the state?
4. What would life be like in this country if the majority of the population had:
   a. A pluralist outlook?
   b. A fundamentalist outlook?
   c. A libertarian outlook?

Notes

Notes

Notes

Notes

Notes